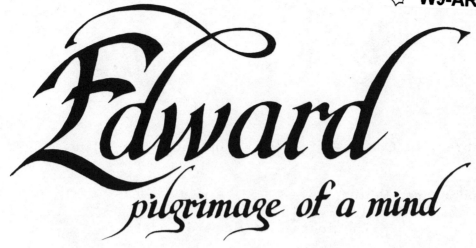

Edward
pilgrimage of a mind

The Journal of Edward Yoder

1931-1945

edited by Ida Yoder

PUBLISHERS

Ida Yoder
180 Hall Drive
Wadsworth, Ohio

Virgil E. Yoder
110 Northumberland Road
Irwin, Pennsylvania

Library of Congress Cataloging in Publication Data

Yoder, Ida, Editor
        Edward
                The Journal of Edward Yoder

        Includes index

Printed in the United States of America
        by Herald Press, Scottdale, Pennsylvania 15683

Library of Congress Catalog Number: 84-91402

International Standard Book Number: 0-96 14083-0-8

To Estie Miller Yoder,

Wife of Edward Yoder for twenty-five years,

this publication of his journal is

respectfully dedicated.

293

ACKNOWLEDGMENTS

We wish to acknowledge with deep appreciation the help of Lucille Kreider, whose assistance with the mechanics of editing, proofreading, and punctuation, as well as the preparation of the index, has brought this work to fruition.

Special appreciation is due to Guy F. Hershberger for the Introduction, Leonard Gross for the Foreword, and Sibyl Gerig for the art work.

We also thank the following who gave encouragement and assistance in many ways: Rachel Kreider, Estie Yoder, Virgil Yoder, Rita Yoder, Ruth Bender, Paul Bender, Dorothy Nyce, Loretta Andrews, Irma Blum, the staff at the Archives of the Historical Committee of the Mennonite Church at Goshen College, Goshen, Indiana, John S. Oyer, Director of Historical Library at Goshen, and Dona Maxon for typing the index.

A considerable number of others have been interviewed or have volunteered suggestions that have been valuable.

PREFACE

This book is a record of a man's thinking, of his reactions to life as it came by him, and of conditions in the Midwest in the first half of the twentieth century including the great depression of the 1930s.

Edward M. Yoder was born July 30, 1893, to parents of Swiss ancestry, namely Mahlon T. and Mary C. (Yoder) Yoder, in Johnson County, Iowa, seven miles northwest of Kalona. He grew up on the farm where he was born, in a rural Amish-Mennonite home where Pennsylvania-German was the spoken dialect.

There was, of course, no radio or television and magazines were few. Father and Mother both could and did read, in contrast to some contemporaries. Mother remarked how careful Edward was with books even as early as he could hold one. Available were the Bible in English and German, Martyrs' Mirror in German, a few religious books, a complete concordance of the Bible, an unabridged Webster's dictionary, among others. An older unabridged dictionary was later replaced by a new one on a mechanical stand. A set of Encyclopedia Brittanica was acquired for the home before Edward went away to Hesston, as was a Harris Visible Typewriter. Movies, shows or entertainment of any kind were prohibited. Edward was encouraged to do well at the one-room elementary school.

Work was the approved activity, of which young Edward did his share, but when the farm work was done and the other boys were tinkering around at some machinery or amusing themselves in their preferred manner, he would retire to his books in some quiet place in the house. My early recollection of him was his reclining on a lean-back chair with feet up on combination desk absorbed with a book. After he went away to school for some years, his mother was to have said of him, "They spoiled a good corn husker." He was the best corn husker (all manual) in the family until his youngest brother became his equal in speed and competence.

This Journal is as written by Edward for the most part. However, deletions were made in the interest of brevity or discretion. Anyone wishing to read the entire original Journal in the author's own handwriting will find it in the Archives of the Historical Committee of the Mennonite Church at Goshen College, Goshen, Indiana. On page X is a facsimile of his handwritten page. There are slightly over 1250 similar pages in the entire Journal written from January 1, 1931, to March 1945 when he died. While the writing covers only a period of fourteen years, with the use of "flash-back" his recollections extend over a period of forty years or more. He apparently had a number of purposes: first, to improve his writing skill; second, to clarify his thinking; and third, to record for himself and for future reference some interesting happenings. He laments his inability to converse easily with people face to face, and used this method of expressing his thoughts.

Edward was my big brother who went away to school. I remember writing to him childlike letters on the Harris Visible, reading what missives he sent home and listening eagerly and pop-eyed to adult conversations following receipt of these letters, especially when he was ill with typhoid fever. But I never really knew him. The summer I rode with him from the farm to the State University at Iowa City for five weeks, I learned more about him than ever before, but still comparatively little. He disclosed some things about his thoughts and feelings that took me a bit aback, but I was not inclined to draw him out, else something of my own thoughts or feelings might be exposed.

In recent years when I began to read his Journal, I immediately decided if there is any way possible, this must be published. Whereas during his lifetime I looked up to him in awe, each of us as silent as the other, through exposure to his Journal I have learned much about him: his ideology, his habit of critical thinking, his philosophy of life, and his love of truth. This, with our shared rebellion against some traditions such as fitting the mold, accepting as truth all that one hears or reads, foster a deep feeling of kinship. Perusing and publishing this Journal has firmed my own beliefs and removed a lifetime of shackles and dead weight.

I sometimes try to envision what Edward would have written in another forty years had he been permitted a more normal life span, what might he think and write about today's television and games culture, which requires and develops even less ability to think than his era did. Had he reached retirement with his faculties intact, what joy he would have had reading, reflecting, writing and observing humankind for another span.

However, there was also a more genial even though less obvious side to Edward. In other diaries which he kept in his teens and twenties we find some group activities which he enjoyed immensely. One was the Apollo Quartet in which he sang at Hesston over a period of two school years while a student. They sang at many and varied places. C. K. Lehman was named as substitute at various times for a member in bad voice. Edward's own words: "Memory will long love to linger around the scenes of the Apollo of 1917-18, especially over the fun, the jokes and social side of many of our meetings for practice. Some of the most pleasant and lasting memories of this entire school year will center around the dearly beloved 'Apollo' Quartet."

Some physical characteristics of his writing style:
> Incomplete sentences at times, especially opening of a
> new day.
> British spellings of many words as was his wont. Such
> were not changed as they seemed to be a part of him
> and of his style.
> Use of satire which he relished.
> When he uses the term "General Conference" as on page
> six and elsewhere, he is referring to the General Conference organized in 1897 in the Old Mennonite Church.
> In 1971 it was succeeded by Mennonite General Assembly.

From his Journal and from other sources we know of many activities and projects he had not finished to his satisfaction and some he had not even started. Here are listed only a few of them:

Investigate and record the origin and history of the garb (plain coat).

Research and record the history of the Iowa Amish and Amish-Mennonite community. Same for the Somerset County, Pennsylvania, and Garrett County, Maryland, community.

Spend summers in the West or Southwest.

Travel in Europe, especially Greece, Rome and Palestine; participate in archaeological explorations.

Continue constructing plats of farms of early Mennonite settlers largely from descriptions from deeds and from tramping over the terrain. He had done many farms in Westmoreland and Fayette Counties in Pennsylvania. These plats are in the Archives of the Historical Committee of the Mennonite Church at Goshen College, Goshen, Indiana. Facsimile of one is shown on pages 460 and 461. What more he had planned to do with them is not clear or what additional farms he still had in mind to do, except that he did mention wanting to spend time in several townships besides German Township of Fayette County and also in Butler and Mercer Counties and investigate Mennonite History in more distant areas in western Pennsylvania.

He had gathered considerable material on genealogies of many families. Here again there was endless research ahead of him.

He had hoped to do many things with Boy as he grew up.

As one ponders such a list it is easy to understand his first comment upon being told of his physical condition at the time of his terminal illness in March 1945 which was, "Oh, there was so much I still wanted to do." And then, "I guess I've had my share of miraculous deliverances. Jesus will take care of me." At this point he dropped all thought of himself and expressed concern for his family, his wife and son. He accepted the inevitable in the same manner he had always accepted life as it came by him.

Ida Yoder

April 27. For cultivating the imagination and at the same time making oneself realize the smallness and insignificance of man and his works—the reading of descriptive astronomy is most helpful. The mere feel of the mental largeness that attends the comprehension of astronomical concepts is a tonic for the soul, a rebuke to the pride of mortal man's spirit, and has a cleansing and chastening effect upon one's ideas, prejudices and obsessions. Several years ago, while doing school-work at Boulder, Colorado, I read through a fair-sized textbook on descriptive astronomy, solely as a few weeks' spare time and recreational reading. It was thrilling. Have ever since watched for opportunity to possess myself of some books along that line for my personal library. A brief article in Scientific Monthly tells of the Romance of Distance. Thus it takes light 8⅓ minutes to get to us from the sun; 5 hours and 33 minutes from Pluto, 4.3 years from the nearest star; ~~and light-year~~ 33,000 light years is the distance of the naked-eye globular cluster in Hercules and 850,000 light-years to the spiral nebula, Messier 33.

Facsimile of actual Journal page

FOREWORD

Edward Yoder comes out of that creative stock of Iowa Amish-Mennonites that defies ultimate categorization. A certain independence of judgment characterized a handful of church-wide leaders and educators emerging from the Iowa scene in the early twentieth century: Melvin Gingerich, Guy F. Hershberger, C. L. Graber, Esther Graber, J. D. Graber, Lena Graber, Glen Miller, Olive Wyse, Edward Yoder, S. C. Yoder, and many more.

Perhaps at the center of their way lay the conviction that each of them was part of the ecclesiastical process that determined the character of their Mennonite Church. For indeed, it was their church, and each of the above-named leaders from Iowa affirmed this principle that "the church is we" in his or her own way of responding to life. And only for those others in the church who did not accept this principle – and after 1898 there was such a handful of leaders at the very center of church life – was there an issue at stake that could and did turn problematic. "Such a handful of leaders" did indeed herald a new approach to authority within the church which reached its highest point of effectiveness in the late 1920s and '30s, and ultimately reached an impasse, not to be resolved until the year 1944, in large part through the efforts of an Iowa Mennonite leader, S. C. Yoder, who helped restore reconciliation within the Mennonite General Conference at its specially-called meeting at Goshen, Indiana, that year.

In the meantime, two full decades of authoritarian leadership had come into being, which entered center stage soon after the end of the First World War in 1918. The effects were a new approach to doctrine, seen in the 1921 "Confession," established at the Mennonite General Conference sessions in Garden City, Missouri. When Goshen College reopened its doors in 1924, these same doctrinal effects were felt there, educationally and theologically. Profound changes also took place within the semi-autonomous Mennonite Women's Missionary Society when in 1928 it was placed under the Mission Board and given a new name, the General Sewing Circle Committee of the Mennonite Board of Missions and Charities; a clearly authoritarian dynamic was at hand, overriding the concerns of the women leaders of MWMS. In those same years leading up to 1928, ecclesiastical change at the "center" also transformed Hesston College (see below).

It would be too long a story to recount how all of this came about. The larger framework, however, includes the terminus a quo of 1898, when the highly influential Bible Doctrines was published – the same year that the Mennonite Church became a formal denomination with the birth of Mennonite General Conference, only in its infancy in 1898, that would emerge by the 1920s as a new force on the Mennonite Church scene, challenging the traditional structures of autonomous Mennonite (regional) conferences, which had been the traditional church structures before 1898. During this same post-1898 era, Mennonite theology and piety also took on a profound doctrinal transformation.

It was during the height of this doctrinal era of authoritarian leadership that Edward Yoder created his Journal.

<u>The Nature and Significance of Edward Yoder's Journal.</u> Journals are lifelong companions, on whose pages may be entrusted all those thoughts and dreams that otherwise would escape at that given moment when they are most coveted and needed. All authors at certain points in their writing careers must have longed for more extensive journal entries from which to draw ideas and experiences – that unfortunately, meanwhile, had dissipated into thin air. A journal may well spell the difference between failure and success.

There is yet another reason to create a journal – rather, a reason that actually calls for the continuing of a diary well past the teenaged phase of "entrusting to its pages those secret areas of my life." What if my ideas and feelings, upon discovery, would lead to tragic conse-quences? Yet at the same time, my not dealing with my innermost thoughts and intuitions honestly, might truly also lead to emotional im-balance – we all know the need to deal honestly with ourselves in some manner or fashion if we do not want to go to pieces or find ourselves out of plumb with what we know to be true and honest and what we be-lieve to be in line with creation and its Creator.

Edward Yoder lived in a Mennonite era when it was dangerous to reveal those doubts which are part and parcel of one's faith, and when the genuine Mennonite forum of an earlier day seemed to be consciously curtailed. How to accommodate without compromise? Edward Yoder managed this delicate feat, in part through his extremely careful church diplomacy on the outside, and through an honest, reflective meditation between himself and his God, on the inside. The Edward Yoder, as known by those with whom he rubbed shoulders – including his closest friends – seemed very much in tune with the Mennonite political leadership which came into its own in the 1920s, and reigned until well into the Second World War.

A very different Edward Yoder is revealed to us, through the descrip-tive pages of his Journal that extend from 1931 to 1945 and include exten-sive flashbacks into the 1920s and earlier. Yoder must have certainly intended his Journal to serve as a source of specific ideas for future publications; he allowed it to serve as a catharsis as well, when there was perhaps no one else to whom he could entrust certain of his inner-most thoughts.

How should we view the classic, progressive, ever-questioning mind of Edward Yoder, and the myriad of ideas that cascaded from his prob-ing intellectualism – couched as they were within a Mennonite framework? Yoder had lived his first 15 years before the new Mennonite Church pub-lishing center in 1908 would begin what would indeed emerge as a more narrowly defined journal, the <u>Gospel Herald</u> (broadening its perspectives after 1943), than had been the case for its predecessor, the <u>Herald of Truth</u> (1864-1908 – see its last editorial in this regard). And Yoder him-self charts the path of influence of this new doctrinal movement, with the years just preceding 1928 as setting a sort of watershed, when waves of the new doctrinal approach finally reached Hesston College. Yoder mentions how a number of Hesston College faculty saw this transformation as "a narrow and shortsighted loyalty. . . [with] new ideas. . . [bringing about a] change in policy [which] became noticeable to thoughtful students, patrons and alumni and did much to destroy confidence in the management of the [Hesston] school." In 1928 and '29, three professors left or were discharged; "their places were taken by the new type, much inferior in personality and in teaching ability, but supposed to be more 'loyal' Mennonites" (September 3, 1931 entry).

One can only imagine Yoder to believe that the broader view he had known to be "Mennonite" up to 1928 at Hesston might again return. Indeed, it was this broader approach which Yoder himself embodied, and never gave up on. Some day, one can imagine, Yoder would have hoped that the earlier, broader vision of what it means to be Mennonite would again effect itself. The day would come when Yoder's ideas could finally find their rightful place, alongside of those of the doctrinal interlude, which had come into being within Yoder's own lifetime. The newer era would take its course, with a return to something broader, and more in tune with the traditional Mennonite approaches to life and faith before the turn of the century. And to be sure, there were positive signals of change in the air by the 1940s — during the last several years of Yoder's lifespan, cut short by cancer in 1945.

The Measure of a Man. Edward Yoder's interests ranged as broadly as the breadth and depth of his reading and reflecting. He read the Atlantic Monthly every month of every year, with relish, but also many other general as well as specialized journals in his established field of classical studies (Greek and Latin). His wide, wide world of ideas on the one hand were consciously honed with a Mennonite audience in mind, underscoring his churchwide interests and analysis thereof; yet he also could hold his own in the higher criticism of literature, and showed unusual interest in the history of the Jews, as well as in natural history — including a fascination for birds.

Yoder, however, gave himself lifelong to teaching potential disciples of Christ, at Hesston College, then Goshen College, and finally at the Mennonite Publishing House, Scottdale, Pennsylvania. He saw himself as a "confirmed individualist," which to him lay at the foundation of the very concept of discipleship and its outworking, tempered of course by the human interaction of the church. Thematically, if there was one area which Edward Yoder gave himself to, it was the reality of peace, and the biblical approach to ecclesiastical nonconformity which lies as a foundation to the way of love and the concomitant result of peace. Must Christians Fight, a 1943 publication of the Mennonite Central Committee, exemplifies Yoder's lifelong preoccupation with this theme, and his synthesis of this age-old problem of the Christian's involvement in society.

Yet as early as 1931 Edward Yoder separated himself from the posture of the modernist, although retaining many, but not all of the elements of the liberal, when he spoke about the worth of current ideologies, but also their limitations. And exactly here Yoder turns to his own tradition for clues to the answer of the question of the "isms" which were so hotly debated within Mennonite circles at that very time. We choose to close with this extended quotation which grants us the assurance that with this Mennonite bedrock, embedded as it is in the Jesus Christ of history and of faith, Edward Yoder the intellectual individualist had truly found those safeguards that allowed him to remain true to his Creator-God, revealed in human flesh:

" [There is a] definite delimitation of the human mind, and of the resulting corollary, that to make human reason and intelligence the final measure and tribunal of truth is unsafe. Amid the multiplied knowledge of our time, it requires the effort of a lifetime to master one field of knowledge or one particular viewpoint. It is practically impossible that there will be another Aristotle who will synthesize for us once more all knowledge into a dynamic system of thought. The field is too vast. Nevertheless each age has as its intellectual atmosphere a phase of a prevailing philosophy which colors and influences all thinking. Of the influence of the current philosophic mode or fashion no one can be entirely free; at the same time it seems clear that to keep an independent viewpoint, to develop a critical attitude toward modes of thought, would give one a truer perspective, a perception of truth that is nearer correct than is possible for those who are completely "sold" on the current mode. As Mennonites, with four and perhaps more centuries of nonconformist blood running in our veins, with traditions that are more or less radical and independent, we should be in a position to contribute something constructive to the stream of the world's thought – not to reform and direct this stream, but to do a small bit of good in that direction. To this end some few should dedicate themselves to the enormous and lifetime task of getting an understanding of world literature, history, and thought, of developing a style of expression, and of interpreting to the world at large the ideas and ideals that are our heritage. Too many in the past have cast off their heritage after the first or second draught of learning. Others, to arm themselves against such an issue, have adopted the closed-mind attitude." (November 29, 1931 entry).

The Process of Editing the Journal. It is fitting that the Edward Yoder Journal should be edited and published by his own sister, Ida Yoder, with interpretive reminiscences by Guy F. Hershberger, longtime friend and colleague of Yoder. Ida Yoder, an intellectual in her own right, has seen this project through every step of the way to publication. Hershberger, in the light of his lifelong friendship with Yoder, is the logical historian to attempt a more comprehensive survey of Edward Yoder's significance within his era than could be attempted in this Foreword by one who never knew Yoder personally.

Leonard Gross (November 27, 1984)

INTRODUCTION

Pilgrimage of a Mind is the life story of Edward Yoder (1893-1945) penned in his own hand during the last fourteen years and two months of his life as a continued series of "Occasional Notes," the total constituting a fourteen year Journal.

In The Mennonite Encyclopedia Paul Erb says Edward Yoder "was one of the more able scholars of the Mennonite Church." In the Gospel Herald (1945) Erb defines a scholar as a creator of learning, with a passion for the truth, who "recognizes the necessity for interpretation and evaluation. He is not a mere collector . . . of knowledge . . . . He is keenly aware that mere opinion and dogmatic assertion have little value."

As the reading of this Journal may well suggest, an alternative for its present subtitle might read as follows: "The Mennonite Church in the First Half of the Twentieth Century," as seen by one of her more able scholars.

As a youthful Bookworm (his own term) Edward read in the Wallace's Farmer that "there are three books in the English language which if read and mastered will make anyone in some measure" an educated person. "The three are the King James Version of the Bible, Bunyan's Pilgrim's Progress, and Shakespeare's plays. The Bible I had, Bunyan I easily procured at a drug store in Kalona." The works of Shakespeare he obtained by mail order from Montgomery Ward. This kind of reading, says the Bookworm, "cultivated my imagination and gave me inspiration for continued study and reading."

Fired by this inspiration and driven by firm resolution Edward Yoder, now 21, enrolled in the academy department of Hesston College in January 1915. By June 1920 he had earned both an academy diploma and the BA degree at Hesston College. Six years and four universities later he had completed the residential requirements for the doctorate. Then after two years of teaching Latin and Greek at Goshen College, while completing his dissertation on "The Position of Possessive and Demonstrative Adjectives in the Noctes Atticae of Aulus Gellius," he was awarded the Ph. D. by the University of Pennsylvania in 1928. In the summer of that year Edward Yoder, with his wife Estie, returned to Hesston to assume his new duties as professor of Latin and Greek, and dean of the college.

This outstanding academic achievement having occurred within the "golden era of prosperity and optimism" (1915-1928), it was only natural that Edward should begin the work of his new assignment with both optimism and zeal. Especially so since during his undergraduate years he had been deeply inspired by the idealism of the Hesston spirit and its vision for the future of the Mennonite Church which he was now serving in an official capacity.

Edward and Estie, living now in a refurbished "comfortable and cozy home nest," had no qualms as to the future. "We hope to spend for books, magazines and good pictures what money we can spare." Edward gloried in classical lore. "A monthly first . . . is the Classical Journal . . . . I usually read about all of it . . . , with genuine relish. It seems to be the terminology, the atmosphere, the feeling of classical things and ideas that I crave."

Greek and Roman history deepens one's understanding of the Bible. "Have been reading Sir William Ramsay's, St. Paul the Traveller and Roman Citizen. This writer on New Testament history in his scholarly and objective manner is a great favorite of mine. Especially are his discussions of the Book of Acts and the letter to the Galatian churches extremely suggestive and illuminating . . . . To me Biblical study based upon historical, linguistic, and archeological material is most fascinating."

"I find myself fired with the ambition to study more fully for myself the general social, economic and the religious life of the first two centuries from the original sources as much as possible . . . . It is very illuminating to read Epistles like Galatians and the Thessalonians in the light of the actual conditions under which they were written. Such a conception of these Epistles seems to me to be miles in advance of having to be limited to the quasi-oracular use of isolated verses and phrases for religious instruction and spiritual inspiration and as texts for hortatory discourse."

"My great desire is for leisure to steep myself in [this type of study] for a period of several years. Ah yes, I suspect, leisure has to be made to order, if it is to be had at all." Had Edward assumed that leisure was part of the order included in his appointment to the dean's office? Perhaps not. But then Hesston was a small college and the dean's burdens would not be heavy. And in 1928 the future seemed bright.

Suddenly, however, unforeseen changes came to pass. In 1929 came the stock market crash, beginning a decade of economic depression which wrought havoc upon many an educational institution, including Hesston. In 1927-1928 Hesston's enrollment had been 248. The next year it was 148. In 1930 the president resigned, leaving to Edward Yoder the painful administrative responsibilities which were not his forte. In 1931-1932 enrollment was down to 70. State accreditation was withdrawn and at one point the Mennonite Board of Education actually considered the closing of the school. Fortunately, however, in the fall of 1932 a new beginning was made, under the presidency of Milo Kauffman, with an enrollment of 55 academy students, but with no college department.

Edward Yoder then joined the Goshen College faculty in 1933. The family, which now included a son Virgil Edward nearly a year old, moved to Goshen that summer. Here they lived five years until they moved to Scottdale, Pennsylvania, after Edward had joined the staff of the Mennonite Publishing House, serving as general editor of Sunday School literature, and writer of the adult lesson quarterly. He served in this capacity until his lamented death in March 1945 at age 51.

Being unencumbered with administrative responsibilities, Edward was free at last to give major attention to the scholarly labors of his heart's desire. At Goshen he was involved in the work of the Mennonite Quarterly Review. He did much writing for the Gospel

Herald, especially for the peace section of its quarterly doctrinal supplement. His teaching of New Testament Greek involved continued study of the New Testament and the early Christian church in the light of its cultural environment and historical background.

Using the insights thus acquired as a measuring stick for an evaluation of the life, the teachings, the doctrinal and ethical standards, and the mission of the church as practiced by his own contemporary Mennonite brotherhood, Edward's Journal came to be generously sprinkled with constructive critiques for the education and admonition of the church and its leadership. Then with his "promotion" to Scottdale, and the leisure and prestige of the Christian education editor's chair, the Journalist enjoyed the advantage of an ever broader platform for the exposition and promotion of his spiritual and scholarly insights.

It needs to be remembered that the 1920s and thirties were a time of confusion and unrest within all of American Christendom, involving among other issues the fundamentalist-modernist controversy within the mainline Protestant denominations. When the Mennonite Church was confronted with this issue, demanding theological acumen, Scriptural discernment, and ecclesiastical statesmanship for its resolution, the church leadership, for the most part, was unequal to the task. And this for two reasons: 1. Its Biblical and theological education had been inadequate for the requirements of the time. 2. It had an inadequate understanding of even its own Anabaptist heritage.

The result of this situation, the roots of which reached back several generations, was a state of confusion and uncertainty. In many cases this led to distrust which could easily have culminated in disaster had it not been for an emerging generation of future leaders engaged in diligent search for a deeper understanding of the way of Jesus Christ as explicated by our Anabaptist heritage, working for peaceful change through loving reconciliation. Edward Yoder, in his uniquely quietistic manner, was an outstanding member of this group.

It is possible that some readers may regard certain of the Journal's critiques as going too far. But Edward was simply recording to the confidence of his Journal the truth as he understood it. This helped him to direct his own steps on the way to correction and reconciliation without broadcasting the faults of the church in a belligerent manner leading to further distrust or even disaster.

Regarding the quality of Biblical teaching within the Mennonite Church, the Journal simply does what the Epistle to the Hebrews does (5:11-14) when it pleads for a mature leadership whose nutrition consists of solid food rather than milk which is for infants. As to the proceedings of the Indiana-Michigan Conference, June 1934, this writer can testify, on the basis of personal experience and observation, that the description given on pages 219-221 of the Journal is not an exaggeration; that it is a fair description of the manner and spirit of its workings, for a brief period of years during the thirties, when the Indiana-Michigan Mennonite Conference was at its nadir.

The Occasional Notes being reflections of a growing mind ever on spiritual pilgrimage, it need not be surprising that here and there they record a smile, a disappointment, or a word of rebuke, as the case may require, upon encountering examples of church leadership manifesting too few indications of such pilgrimage beyond the stage of earliest beginnings.

One such example (p. 212) is that of "trepidaciously" shying away, on the part of the older generation, from "newer terms," such as "progressive revelation as applied to the Jewish and Christian Scriptures" (which Edward's generation was taking for granted), "and from any phraseology which chances to differ from that which they happened to acquire when they were in their formative years."

"Presumably I am too pessimistic" about these matters, says the Journal, but, "to my way of thought, it is this sort of slavish subservience to phrases [and antiquated interpretations] which render . . . [some of the older generation] incapable of leading and guiding the thought of young people who read and think more or less for themselves."

The Year 1944: A Mennonite Watershed

Reference was made above to Edward Yoder as an outstanding member of an emerging generation of future leaders laboring during the twenties and thirties to lay the foundation and to shape the program for the new day in the Mennonite Church which was sure to come.

Leonard Gross, in an article in the Gospel Herald (July 24, 1984), and in a longer supporting manuscript, speaks of the watershed year 1944 as the arrival of that day toward which the emerging generation had been moving. Gross cites certain events of this amazing year, after which the Mennonite Church could no longer be the same. Then he associates the names of seven persons connected with these events. The persons Gross names are: Harold S. Bender, Paul Erb, J. D. Graber, Guy F. Hershberger, Chester K. Lehman, Orie O. Miller, and S. C. Yoder. It is my feeling that three additional persons must be added to this list: Edward Yoder, Milo Kauffman, and A. J. Metzler, bringing to ten the number of persons contributing in a significant way to the watershed of 1944.

Of these ten it was Harold S. Bender, Bible teacher and Anabaptist scholar, whose two decades of Anabaptist studies were climaxed by the publication of The Anabaptist Vision in 1944. It was this work which laid the basis for a new Mennonite understanding of its own spiritual heritage. "He gave us back," says Gross, "our long standing vision of God's having worked among us over the centuries, and that our faith is rooted in his holy history."

It was in 1944 also that Guy F. Hershberger's War, Peace, and Nonresistance was published, giving the Mennonite Church its first comprehensive work on: the Biblical teaching on war, peace, and justice; the Anabaptist teaching and practice, 1525-1944; and the social implications of Biblical nonresistance, and its service to society.

Again it was in 1944 that Mennonite General Conference authorized the organization of a new church board, Mennonite Mutual Aid, upon recommendation of its Committee on Industrial Relations, initiated by Guy F. Hershberger, its secretary, and led by Orie O. Miller, member of the committee, who then served for two decades as the chairman of the MMA board. Miller was also secretary of the Peace Problems Committee from its beginnings in 1925, and later became executive secretary of the Mennonite Central Committee, in which capacity he was the responsible head of Mennonite Civilian Public Service during World War II.

Although no outstanding 1944 event has come to be associated specifically or uniquely with Chester K. Lehman, he was nevertheless identified with the emerging group of younger leaders, and in his own way, as dean and Bible teacher of Eastern Mennonite College, was a supporter of and contributor toward the goals which were being reached in 1944.

When offered the presidency of Hesston College in 1932 Lehman declined, giving way to the younger Milo Kauffman, thus enabling each of them to carry on his share of the new progressive work, the one working at Hesston, and the other at EMC.

A most significant event of 1944 was the special session of Mennonite General Conference, called as a last desperate effort to deal with the confusion, uncertainty, and distrust which had continued without resolution since the mid-thirties. The outcome of the carefully planned procedures of the 1944 sessions, under the leading of the Holy Spirit, was a dramatic climax of reconciliation which changed the character of Mennonite General Conference from that time on.

Although the conference was convened in the midst of doubts and questionings, the opening session on a Tuesday evening in August featured a keynote address on "Unity of the Spirit or Division" by John H. Mosemann. This was followed by discussion and a period of prayer. Three sessions on Wednesday and two on Thursday were given to the opening of topics and issues by respected leaders, followed by discussion and prayer. Before, after, and between official sessions there were volunteer prayer meetings where conference participants learned to pray together and to know and respect each other.

On Thursday evening a 1943 report of the General Problems Committee was removed from the table, opening the session to a free-for-all discussion of a score of issues under the general umbrella of Biblical interpretation, nonresistance, and nonconformity, around which the distrust of these many years had been centered. In God's mysterious way, however, the Holy Spirit, through two days of official and voluntary sessions had softened the hearts of many brethren so that the time was ripe for the proper person to speak words which would release the pent-up tension.

This person was 64-year-old Sanford C. Yoder, who in 1940 had retired as president of Goshen College. During the sixteen years of his presidency he had silently suffered much as liaison between the established, and sometimes reactionary, church leaders and the emerging younger progressives who were his proteges.

In response to questions and statements as to the reason for the current distrust, Sanford quietly rose to the full length of his 6 feet 3 and, in his soft-spoken voice, said words to this effect: You ask the reason for our situation? I'll tell you the reason. It is because fellowship has broken down. There was a time when we experienced the finest of Christian fellowship (in a certain community, which he mentioned by name), but for some time this has no longer been possible. Today the feeling experienced is one of ostracism. The fellowship is gone. This is the reason for distrust and tension within the church.

When the speaker sat down there was deathly silence. Had a pin been dropped one could have heard it — until a brother suggested a time of prayer. Then, after a long season of prayer the conference rose from its knees and discussion was resumed. As far as I can remember, however, it was confession more than discussion. One brother confessed that earlier during the conference he had spoken unkind words against Sanford Yoder, and now was asking forgiveness. Ever since that occasion this brother has been a different man.

As the meeting drew to a close it was announced that the Friday morning session would be receiving a report from the Resolutions Committee, followed by action on the 1943 report of the General Problems Committee. Following the benediction a brother said to me: Whatever is done tomorrow will have little meaning. The purpose of the special session of General Conference was achieved this evening. The brother was right. The dramatic evening session had given birth to a new Mennonite General Conference. The old had died. The new was born in 1944.

In addition to his part in the healing of the wounds of General Conference, a second gracious act of S. C. Yoder during the amazing year 1944 must be mentioned: his retirement as secretary of the Mennonite Board of Missions and his selection of J. D. Graber of the emerging generation of leaders, a brother with overseas experience, as his successor. Graber now became the first full-time secretary of the MBM, with time and opportunity for leading the Church into the broader understanding of its overseas work, and for launching that program on the way to its present world-wide dimensions.

We come now to A. J. Metzler, the youngest of the watershed ten, whose contribution was that of the young administrator, General Manager of the Mennonite Publishing House, who had the vision as early as 1937 to bring Edward Yoder, and then Paul Erb in 1944, away from academia to key editorial posts, giving each a direct line of communication with the rank and file of the Mennonite Church, bringing a fresh Biblical, ecclesiastical, and missionary perspective and understanding of the church and its work to the total brotherhood.

In the case of Edward Yoder there can be no doubt that the Scottdale years were the most satisfying of the family's years since the completion of the doctorate. "In a number of ways," says the Journal soon after the move, "we feel that for us life is really beginning, not even at forty, but at forty-five." "Somehow," says Edward, "I seem to catch occasional glimpses of an idea that this move will prove to be under the Lord's special guidance and leading, and that we may be due to experience His blessing in some particular ways in the time to come."

Before the year 1938 was over the editor was receiving "kind and appreciative words of commendation" for the quality of the new lesson quarterly. These came from throughout the church, Pennsylvania to Oregon. A most enthusiastic response came from Israel B. Good, influential Lancaster Conference minister and evangelist of the Weaverland district, diligent reader of philosophical and theological works, who at age 77 discontinued his weekly Sunday School teachers' meeting, telling the class that since they now have a superior lesson quarterly for their use they no longer were in need of his help.

Although Edward Yoder held no academic degree in Biblical studies, his teaching of both New Testament and classical Greek, and his continuous reading of classical sources and authorities in his study of the New Testament in the context of the social and religious life of the first two centuries — this in preparation for his writing of the Sunday School lessons — meant that he was better equipped for in-depth Biblical studies than anyone within the Mennonite Church at that time.

True enough, this was a far cry from making the Scottdale editor a world renowned authority in Biblical studies. But it does mean two things: 1. That it was he who set a pattern and pointed the way for a younger generation of thoroughly trained Mennonite Biblical scholars in the post-1944 era. 2. That his work represents an important first step in raising the editorial standards of the Mennonite Publishing House to the level of qualification for service in the new era. For these reasons Edward Yoder must be numbered with the watershed ten.

It was then the task of Paul Erb to take the next step in this same direction. He became editor of the Gospel Herald in January 1944 and, working alongside Edward Yoder during the last fourteen months of Edward's working days, he began the process of bringing "a new level of intellectual thought" to the official organ of the Mennonite Church.

"I carried a pretty strong feeling," said Erb, "that I'm speaking for the whole denomination, and I had my finger out all the time to get the pulse of the general body." Having begun his assignment in the very year of the dramatic 1944 special session of General Conference there was good reason why he should have this feeling. Therefore, by initiating the "Our Readers Say" column, both the older school and the younger had their say. By this and other new editorial policies and skills the Gospel Herald soon gained the respect of diverse elements within the Church, so that orderly change was now possible, as had not been the case during the previous decades.

Considering its available resources, the Herald of Truth during the 1870s and eighties had done reasonably well at keeping the Mennonite Church in tune with its Anabaptist heritage. It was the next generation of leaders, however, enamored by progressivism to the point of absorbing elements of an alien theology inherent within the work of the American Protestant Sunday School movement, which eventually was led to the acceptance and teaching of a doctrine of salvation which unwittingly excluded Christian discipleship and the peace teaching of the Sermon on the Mount as residing integrally at the heart of the gospel of Jesus Christ.

Not only did this step bring the Mennonite Church to a point on the theological scale farther out of tune with its Anabaptist heritage than had been the case in the 1870s and eighties. It was now also at the point where the door was opened to the errors of fundamentalism. While there was no wholesale entrance into this door, there was some such. And there was far too much appropriation of the spirit of fundamentalism, making for a doctrinaire type of authoritarian leadership.

In Anabaptism "the church against the world" is of the essence. But when the understanding of that essence is watered down, or even lost, the outward forms become its all-important substitute. And it was with the employment of this substitute, too much as its major theme, that the authoritarian leadership, though out of tune with its own heritage, continued to direct the ecclesiastical music, now so seriously lacking in harmony. It was this situation which had set the stage for the confusion, disharmony, and distrust against which the younger generation of the twenties and thirties had been laboring, bringing their effort to a climax in the watershed year of 1944. And it was for the prevention of such situations in the future that Paul Erb was striving to make the Gospel Herald an organ which would speak for the whole Mennonite Church.

Finally, in 1963, now retired, Erb gave an accounting to the Mennonite General Conference of his stewardship during his 18 years as editor. The accounting was in the form of an address, "A Christian Philosophy of Change." He was speaking of the philosophy by which he had operated during these 18 years; a philosophy which was the fruit of the church's growing understanding of its Anabaptist heritage; and a philosophy of change which he was offering as a guide for the Mennonite Church of the future.

Erb pleads for "open channels of communication bringing together various facets of conviction, leading through true dialog in finding the mind of the Spirit. . . . Coercion gives short answers, . . . seldom permanent ones. Collaboration is a necessary ingredient of the change process. We must do things with people, not to them. The time and situation wherein a church decides to part from a past pattern should be decided by a consensus within the congregation rather than by the arbitrary ruling of one or a few. . . . The process of change can be helpful or harmful to church life, depending on how it is conducted. Oneness in Christ rather than cultural uniformity must be seen as the basic requirement of the church. The achievement of New Testament standards for the church must be accepted as a fundamental goal."

Since change is inevitable, and in itself neither good nor bad, the church, says Erb, must play an active directional role at the creative edge of change for the good of the church and of the world: "Many changes have come about through the initiative of the church. The church must continue to be that kind of a stimulant to godliness and righteousness. It is the responsibility of the church to point the directions of change, to set up the targets of reform or action."

Assuming the possibility that these words, spoken by Editor Erb nineteen years after Watershed 1944, could remind us of the proclamations, admonitions, and prophecies of Joshua following his entrance into the Promised Land, we may venture the further assumption that the many words of observation, analysis, admonition and critique in Scholar-Editor Edward's Journal should remind us of the patient labors of Moses during the wilderness years, until from the summit of Mount Nebo he was able to look across the Sea for a faraway glimpse of the Promised Land — then to be summoned at once to that Better Land of Eternal Day.

Guy F. Hershberger

Occasional Notes - 1931

January 2, 1931 Yesterday began the new year, when the world presumably became a year older than it was on December 31. There is
still a widespread belief that the beloved goddess Prosperity is "just
around the corner." Many and frantic have been the cries and prayers
of her numerous devotees during the twelvemonth past. Like Baal of
old, the beloved deity has not answered by fire the desperate pleas
and antics of her priests and acolytes. Doubtless she too is taking a
nap or has gone on vacation.

The year 1930 has been a full one for Mrs. Yoder and myself. We
remodelled our house making it more modern and convenient. We like
the improvements very much, bathroom, city water, kitchen work table
and cabinets, General Electric refrigerator, Sunshine electric cleaner,
American Beauty washer, closets and a den for the man of the house;
partition, coal bin and fruit jar shelves in the basement. The total
cost of improvements on the house was about $ 1250. Besides we
spent about $ 475 for the new and labor-saving equipment. Having a
comfortable and cozy home nest, we feel but little of the present day
urge to "run to and fro in the earth." We hope to spend for books,
magazines and good pictures what money we can spare, rather than
for gasoline and rubber tires.

January 3, 1931 Have just finished reading the two-volume work by
Beard: "The Rise of American Civilization." A remarkable treatise.
Written in a clear style and a critical vein, it has afforded me a new
picture of American history. The basic motive from the beginning of
American civilization has been a grim economic struggle of acquisition,
only slightly illuminated by faint gleams of religious and social idealism. He (Beard) seems to give too little recognition to the influence of
religion and Puritan ideals. There is made a sincere effort to describe
men, classes, parties, eras, ages and all with impartiality. No halos
of glory are painted over the heads of leaders. It is all very refreshing and stimulating.

Yesterday afternoon I made a trip for the assigned purpose of solic-
iting funds for the college deficit. Results confirmed my personal conviction that I am not by any stretch of the imagination a public contact
man or solicitor. The upheaval of the past summer that has flung me
upward as the virtual head of the school for the time has been one of
the unfortunate casts of the fates. Give me rather the cloistered cell
with books for study and research, and I shall ask for no position of
honor or prestige.

January 5, 1931 Delightsome winter weather; dry under foot, moderate temperature. Mrs. Yoder and I agree on this: Kansas is one of
the best places in the U.S.A. to live. After having lived successively
in Iowa, Pennsylvania, and Indiana we vote for Kansas sunshine and
reasonable temperatures. Reasonable? Well, most of the time, anyway. Even with the mercury tube reaching to 108 F in the shade on
the first days of last August, it was not uncomfortable - unless one
thought so. The past two winters in Kansas have been marked by an
unusual amount of continued cold and snow. We think it is the turn

now again for a milder winter season.

January 6, 1931 Writers and thinkers are ever and anon pointing out the persistent downward revision of the general intelligence level in a democracy à la Américaine. Standardization is an accepted creed in education as well as in building motor cars. The high priests of standardization and mass production point with pride to small or negligible illiteracy ratios, to the universality of bathtubs, Ford cars, radios as the non plus ultra of human happiness. They can look upon the decapitation of the intellectual and moral giants among the citizenry incident to the levelling process without batting an eye. Perhaps they do not even see this detail of the marvellous operation, but only stare their eyes out at the beautiful sea of humanity stretching before them in endless expanse without a ripple on its surface. A writer in the Atlantic Monthly states that the broadcasting organizations of our country have it as their policy to adapt all their matter to the level of thirteen-year-olds. The ancient civilizations that produced intellectual and artistic giants were built upon a submerged estate of slaves and toilers, it is true. But it hardly augurs any good for the race when the toiling masses have been raised socially and economically a notch or two and then the intelligentsia lowered to a level with them. Advancement in any direction has ever been due to a minority, whether of one or a few. But the goal of American democracy apparently is one great majority with all minorities abolished. But perhaps the machine age will yet bring forth philosophy and art comparable to that of ancient Greece ! It is not easy to see just how a generation that masters no lessons or skills more taxing than turning dials, snapping switches, shifting gears and stepping on the gas can produce a Plato, an Aristotle, a Pheidias, a Sophocles or an Aristophanes. The age of mechanical devices so completely distracts the minds of its thirteen-year-olds that they will never even suspect that it is possible to learn to do one's own thinking and entertaining.

January 8, 1931 A question that frequently comes to one's thoughts is this: In order to be loyal and devoted to a given cause, what are the criteria and the standards by which to judge how much of one's time and effort must be poured into the cause ? Is it necessary to devote one's self utterly to the cause as it may stand at the present ? It is a question pertinent for young people, whether at any particular point in their progress towards man's estate, say at the end of high school, or the end of college, or after a master's or a doctor's degree is the time to stop learning and training and sink all their powers in a cause of some sort. It would seem that the person who at any time before the age of forty or fifty gives all he has and is in body, mind, and soul to a cause is like the man who in his zeal to sacrifice for the cause that is dear to his heart gives away all his capital at one stroke. Another man more foresightedly keeps his capital and gives of his earnings over a period of twenty, thirty or forty years and in the end has given more to the cause by several times over than the over-zealous man. Likewise that one whose zeal for a given cause leads him to sacrifice all his time, strength, health and effort to a work is more than likely to contribute less in the end to the good work, than he who reserves some time and strength for his own further growth and development. As rapidly as life and its conditions are changing, the man who today gives his all outright and directly will not likely be rendering service to the cause he loves in twenty years from now. By ceasing to grow himself and not adjusting himself constantly to changing conditions he is superannuated very shortly. All thinking on sacrificial service must take the long-time view rather than the short-sighted view.

January 13, 1931 We have just revised the schedule of our income and expenses for the first ten months of 1931. Never have had much success with a fixed budget, but are trying to learn. We find that we need to cut our expenditures to a minimum this year. The lady of the house thinks our item for periodicals is too high; it is to be $38 for the coming ten months. The total for the year is about $ 45. Seemingly a large sum, but what can we do without ? One's first impulse is to decrease expenditures by spending less for books and journals. In other words the demands of the stomach and the physical body seem in actual life to take precedence over the requirements of mind and soul. I have known people, who profess to do educational and religious work, to spend practically nothing from year to year for books and periodicals. Their own minds and souls were starved, weak and sickly, still they pretended to be able to minister to the growth and development of others. The spectacle of such a person for twenty years having as his staple mental pabulum the Farm Journal and the Pathfinder is one to make angels weep. Yet such a phenomenon has come under my observation.

We are prone to set greater store by bodily health and soundness than by mental and spiritual welfare. Many seemingly respectable people who would not think of neglecting their dress, going in rags, unkempt and careless, yet leave the soul naked and ungroomed. They feel no compunctions of conscience in wearing the mental and spiritual weeds which have scarcely ever been laundered and are long since become rags and tatters. The same ideas, notions, prejudices, viewpoints serve many from adolescence to the grave. What a tragic revelation it is to behold some religious leader berating a young female for not having the nether limbs of her physical body wrapped in the necessary inches of cloth, while his own soul and mind are almost stark naked, clad perhaps with the scanty fig-leaves of a few set phrases, stereotyped formulae and personal idiosyncrasies ! Why should the care and nurture of a hundred odd pounds of matter take precedence of the culture of the spirit in our plans ? Better to go hungry and be clad in rags at times, than to starve the eternal part of ourselves, even in administering such a worldly thing as a family budget !

January 15, 1931 Started last Sunday to read the much-talked-of book "Mother India" by Katherine Mayo, finishing it today. In a number of respects it was a revelation to me, bringing out certain fundamental features of Indian life that could never be discovered in reports of missionaries and the general run of magazine writers.

Some details of the insanitation of the land are disgusting in the extreme. The exaggeration of the sex instinct and its perversion, together with all the social and moral implications therewith involved, are almost past belief. The utter absence of the emotions of mercy and pity, the fatalism of their religious concepts, and the strange feats of logic in their thinking are brought out in a dispassionate and considerate description that has all the ear marks of sober, reasoned writing. One remark near the close is striking: that Britain is to blame for the state of degradation that exists in India today. Not because she has brought about the said conditions, but because she has interfered with the normal course of history by preventing stronger and more virile races out of the North from wiping out the Hindus as a race. It is an interesting subject for speculation whether the culture and Christianized civilization that spares and allows to propagate all and sundry degraded individuals and races is doing more or less for raising the general tone of the world's life than did the conception of world economy that functioned in the past and is portrayed in the Old Testament Scriptures. In those days when a given race, tribe or nation had sunk to hopeless depths of degradation and sin, when "their iniquity was full," they were ordered exterminated by the God of heaven. It was a sort of social and moral house-cleaning that was staged occasionally. The Augean stables of the earth were cleaned once in a while. It is no rhetorical question, to ask whether the disinfectants of a Christianized culture, of education, of democracy, can in the end counteract and remedy the sinful degradation and moral filth of peoples and races or whether the disuse of surgery and cautery will result in the lowered tonicity of the world's moral and social life culminating ultimately in the sinking of the whole world into the utter degradation of sin. According to St. Paul's philosophy of history, as hinted at in the first chapter of the Epistle to the Romans, the righteousness of God is the only antitoxin that will keep the races of the earth from sinking steadily and surely to such depths as those in which the people of India, a majority of them, are today. It would be hard to maintain the thesis that the current culture, education, democracy and Christian missions are exactly equivalent to "the righteousness of God."

January 17, 1931 In reflecting upon the claims made by varied groups of Christian people to the effect that the Bible is the rule for faith and practice, even the only and absolute rule, we are impressed with a number of interesting thoughts. As Mennonites we often make our boast that we give a literal obedience to the Bible, especially the New Testament, that we stand on a whole Gospel platform, for a full Gospel program. A critical scrutiny of this claim reveals several things or brings to the fore some questions. What is the correct method to use for interpreting the text of the sacred Scriptures? For the plebeian mind it suffices to say in answer to this question that we must accept the Bible for what it says and any child that can read can know what the text means. This formula, like many another, is a wet blanket useful mostly for smothering thought. No one, practically, today sets much store by the allegorical method of interpretation that once flourished among some

Greek church fathers. The traditionally accepted method among us seems to be the literal and textual method, which when applied zealously to reinforce traditions and personal biases, can produce some strange and wondrous results. When applied with discretion and common sense it fills a useful purpose. Its peculiar genius is probably its availability for bolstering up, buttressing, and anchoring doctrinal tenets, creeds, moral precepts, ecclesiastical policies, etc. Its technique is that of setting up the particular proposition desired and then by the aid of reference Bibles and concordances searching out proof texts all the way from Genesis to Revelation that will lend support to the proposition in hand. This method does its greatest mischief in the hands of partisans who pay no heed to the context and its import out of which they lift their proof texts in the form of isolated verses, phrases, or paragraphs. This is using the Bible as a book of oracles much in the same spirit that ancients used the Sibylline books at Rome or as the text of Vergil was used by some in the Middle Ages. Fortunately the method is rarely carried to a logical and consistent conclusion. The major objection to the method is its disregard, as a general principle, for the thought content of connected passages, and the ease with which undesired teachings can be overlooked in building up a body of religious dogmata. Sometimes it goes to seed in the counting of words and letters and working out number schemes and proportions which are supposed to teach spiritual truth.

Contrasted with this method, though not necessarily discrediting it entirely, is the historical method of interpretation. In this method the first concern of the student is to study all chapters and books in the Bible in the light of their historical setting. Before interpreting any passage, verse or word of the text, he learns all he can about the author, his age, his purpose in writing and the particular occasion, the circumstances and situation of the immediate readers to whom a book was addressed. An important question in using this method is: What was the evident thought in the writer's mind? The danger of this method is that in the hands of the unspiritual it may easily lead to a destructive higher criticism that regards the Bible merely as a religious source book or case book, on a level with the sacred books of other religions. Seemingly a judicious combination of the two would be a safe method.

The type of mind that a Bible student has seems to predispose him for one or the other of the common methods of study. One Bible teacher uses almost entirely the literalist method. From various sources, notably Scofield and the Companion Bible he has amassed a great, almost encyclopedic, array of curious and impressive literalist "facts". These he sets forth as divine truth, or at least as inspired expressions of such truth. He lays no stress on historical background, ignores textual variations, and pronounces the Revised American version inferior to the King James version. His discourse on the biblical teaching on dress, at least as he gave it in 1929 at Hesston, contained a number of illustrations of the fallacies of the literalist method. He ostensibly invited criticism of his discourse, but experience proved rather, to a few folks, that he deeply resents any criticism of his basic assumptions and of his general method and point of view. He seems not to live up to his repeated plea for "Christian contro-versy". His present agitation against some of the church leaders appears to be occasioned by several factors: He felt distinctly that he was blocked in his plans for setting on foot a church-wide cru-sade on the question of dress regulation. My personal opposition was not so much to his ideas as to his plan to use the school as a church institution to give prestige and impetus to a personal program of his own. Again he clashed unconsciously with the younger Bible teacher on the faculty, mostly in point of view and in method, in his classroom teaching. To his chagrin and disappointment seemingly he sensed that thinking students who sat at the feet of both teachers in turn felt more sympathy for the viewpoint and method of the younger man than for his own. Finally he took very seriously to heart some remarks a few of us made to him personally, more perhaps to elicit "Christian controversy" with him for the elucida-tion of our own ideas than to give our personal convictions on dis-puted subjects.

It is a bit amusing to recall now how he in the fall of 1928 for a time almost swept the field of Biblical knowledge around Hesston clean. The novelty of his viewpoint, the great show of knowledge and understanding that he staged, the seriousness with which he took him-self, all these made numbers fall at his feet in awe and wonderment. But after he had gone around his narrow circle of ideas about two or three times the spell was pretty well worn off. By the second year even the students in his classes began to sense the stifling small-ness of his horizon and to become encouragingly aware of his lim-itations. When, for instance, in a course in systematic theology he wasted hours on end in dictating pages of Scripture proof texts, even the most enthusiastic became fully disillusioned. It is my personal guess that what abilities and possibilities for usefulness he may once have possessed have been vitiated by his narrow literalism in Scrip-tural interpretation, his obsession with the notion of his own impor-tance and with the idea that the absolute truth on religion is coter-minous with his concept of the same.

January 26, 1931 Word has come lately that this year's session of our General Conference will not be held at Hesston but at Archbold, Ohio. There was long hesitation over a decision. Some expect that this next session will be an important one. The newly created Church Problems Committee expects to make a report and some are expect-ing action that will commit the conference to a specific and detailed program of discipline on various points. To date this conference body has been deliberative and advisory only. There are those who wish to see it vested with legislative and executive powers.

To me it would seem a sorry day when General Conference will step down from its position as a spiritually edifying body to that of a supreme court of church politicians, with pretended powers to di-rect and regulate the work of the Spirit of God. Our little denom-ination has so far in history been rather consistently known for the quiet, peaceable and pietistic living of its members. We have had little connection with the streams of the world's thought, activity and customs. But during the past decades we have been minded to get away from the simple unworldly way of living. One line of worldly conformity that is never mentioned in this time when many complain of the worldward drift of our group, is that of our aping after the spirit of our age and time in our feverish craving for organization, the multiplication of boards, committees, etc., etc. The question is inevitable: Is it still possible to hear the still small voice of the Holy Spirit and of conscience in this new era above the clanking of church machinery and the rumbling of its steam rollers made to flatten out differences and to crush the individual personality? The generation now growing up is being taught to think of Christian activity and of witnessing for Christ solely in terms of organized boards and authorized committees, a conception that is sure to be deadening to the idea and conviction of personal responsibility. Can it be a good sign for the perpetuation of our ideals of simple obedience to God and the simple guidance of His Spirit when even church leaders seemingly think of problems and their solution in terms of special committees and conference legislation rather than in terms of prayer and the leading of the Spirit? Some simple organization is doubtless necessary even in church work, but I am personally convinced that for our small group our multiplication of machinery has now become a genuine menace to our ideals that will smother and strangle the Spirit's efforts to use us as a witness to the world.

January 30, 1931 It is only gradually becoming evident how widespread and how acute is the present economic distress in the United States. President Hoover and Congress are at loggerheads about the method of bringing relief to the needy farm population. It seems that for all the bureaucracy at Washington, there is no means at hand for ascertaining exact information on unemployment and on the need for relief. The Republican politicians have been hard put to it to make good their promise for continued prosperity, and have apparently chosen to remain ignorant of the true facts as long as possible by hiding behind the conventional American optimism and doing lip-service to the beloved goddess, Prosperity. Doubtless it will become clear before long just how much damage the farm relief legislation and the increased tariff schedules of 1930 are going to do. Economists and theorists still proclaim the dogma that the general labor wage scale in America must not come down. While the average scale perhaps should not be lowered drastically at once, it is hard to see how industry can recover without some lowering of wages and of interest. There are signs that the temple of high wages may soon begin to totter. Numbers of state legislatures are working now to reduce state taxes, and are talking of lowering salaries of government workers. Railroads are reducing rail fares to two cents a mile. There is hope that, if the distress continues most or all of another year, people will come to more sane and simple views on prosperity, standards of living, true values in life, etc. Nothing could be more wholesome and salutary for the country as a whole than the chastening of a general reduction in some of our highly artificial standards of living. After a century and more of seemingly unlimited opportunity and of unbridled lust for acquisition, the people of America will need to settle down to a measure of sane and sensible living, to an active cultivation of the things of the spirit and of the mind. It may take a long while and much suffering to shake us out of the stupor of our prolonged spree of money-getting, pleasure-chasing, luxury-acquiring and prosperity-worshipping. It is devoutly to be hoped that some of the spell of our democratic mob-mindedness can be shaken off as we grow sober and sane again, giving us a chance to get acquainted with God and with ourselves.

February 2, 1931 Very mild, sunny weather for a few weeks past, more like the beginning of April than of February. Predictions for a mild winter seem to be coming true. Reports last fall were that corn husks were scant and loose, that tree squirrels did not build any nests for the winter in this section, and Mr. Martindale, forest ranger from Yellowstone National Park, told us in a public lecture that the beavers did not build their usual winter dams. Providence seems to be helping out the shortage of feed due to drought conditions of the past summer. There is also a great saving of fuel and the prevention of much suffering by the general mild temperatures.

The men of the faculty have been playing volley ball for exercise and recreation the past few months. I was prevailed upon to play with them just once, during the Christmas vacation. Personally I have no taste, or rather a distinct distaste for indoor exercise and so have begged to be excused. My conscience is not altogether at ease, because there are hardly enough men for two practice teams, especially since S. E. Miller and I refuse to help. I am pleased that they can have this sport and like to see it go, but have no further interest in it. Compared to exercising in the fresh open air by regular brisk walking, tearing around in a musty, dusty, ill-smelling gymnasium seems dirty and unhealthful. For my own exercise I am twice each week to go on a brisk hike, making usually from four to six miles in a little more than an hour's time, on Wednesday before daylight and on Saturday afternoon. The beautiful dry weather this winter has made these hikes a delicious form of exercise and recreation. I am aware that walking to many folks is too tame and uninteresting a form of exercise, especially walking by one's self. But this again is a matter of taste and personal preference.

February 8, 1931 An unusual thing has happened in that a committee of the Missouri-Kansas district conference appointed to study the matter of dress regulations has appealed to the membership at large for criticisms and suggestions made on the basis of the existing regulations. These regulations and decisions since the year 1923 have been distributed in the form of three mimeographed sheets closely typed, including a General Conference resolution of 1923. The effort and the burden that seems to lie behind these series of decisions is that of somehow preserving in some form that is effective for Christian character and growth the historical separateness from the general stream of the world's life and thought that has distinguished our Mennonite life in the past. In proportion as it is a heart-felt burden on the part of leaders, it is pathetic to observe their more or less blind gropings for a remedy. The tendency seems to be to conform to the world in certain respects to prevent conformity in other respects. The naive faith many seem to have in the panacea of legislation and machinery is part of the spirit of the age no less than to follow its fashions in dress.

Conditions are changing and some who are most dogmatic and cocksure in their ideas on dress regulation have such limited experience that either they are not aware of the real nature of the problem or else they willingly remain ignorant thereof. The day when all of our people lived in more or less compact rural communities and the vast majority of them lived with interests and experiences limited almost strictly to their communities is one of the past. Where the Old Order Amish people have escaped by disallowing telephones, automobiles, radios and other inventions from the first, we Mennonites have gotten us our problem by following the times and adopting the world's standards. If the correct aim of Christian living is that of semi-isolation, then the Amish have done much better than the Mennonites. If on the other hand the kingdom of God consists not in food and drink (and, may we say, in raiment also?), then there is comfort in knowing that the existence of problems and great struggles is a sign of life and vitality.

The issue in dress regulation seems to be this: Shall the church insist upon some form of regulation or uniform garb or shall the general teachings of modesty and simplicity be sufficient for separation from the world? As matters now stand, with the head-dress prescribed for the women, the cry is often raised that there is an unfair discrimination against the female sex. One group, to remedy this disparity, at once proposes that men be required to wear a mark of distinction as well as women. By this is meant the clerical (misnamed "plain") coat or the absence of a necktie or both. But this proposal discriminates again against an already large and steadily growing group of men in the so-called "white-collar" jobs. For farmers, laborers, artisans, mechanics can thus go about their work unembarrassed and unencumbered by a garb, while teachers, salesmen, clerks and others have only limited opportunities to exercise their callings. The contrary proposal that the required female head-dress be discontinued also has its problems. It seems that on any and all of these various questions it is impossible to make sweeping generalizations. In eastern Pennsylvania where there are large centers of Mennonites the opportunities for those with a garb are much greater than in other places. To me the whole matter seems impossible of solution by argument and partisan discussion. Perhaps the greatest single danger I see is that too many leaders will in devoting time and effort to legislative efforts, which cannot in the final end solve anything, lose the present opportunity to teach the basic principles of the Scriptures on this subject and on the spiritual life in particular. Nothing can be of more importance than spiritual teaching given in the faith that God's Spirit will direct so that in whatever adjustments and changes will come the essential principles will be preserved and continue to be a part of our testimony to the world.

February 20, 1931 It is interesting to observe and reflect on the divers opinions and experiences expressed on the matter of the regulation or so-called "plain" garb for men. Sometime I hope to investigate the history of this particular garb. Its most general signification today seems to be clerical. Is it a direct descendant of Roman catholic priestcraft? If so, how did it get into Mennonite circles, people who historically rejected all forms of Romanist tradition, e.g., statuary in churches, infant baptism, etc. Is it on the other hand a fossil remain of an earlier general style of coat for men? Or is it of independent Mennonite or Quaker origin?

This cut of coat, with military collar, has now become practically universal among the ministers, bishops and deacons of our group of conferences. There are still a few scattered ministers to be found who wear a regular business coat without necktie. A generation ago the latter costume was fairly common among the Amish Mennonite ministers of the Central and Western states. The garb among laymembers has been steadily gaining ground in certain sections of the West, having apparently started from settlers from older Mennonite sections in Virginia and Pennsylvania.

My personal experience with the garb has been varied and in many respects quite unsatisfactory. When I first came to Hesston in 1915 there was little agitation either officially or otherwise for the garb. When I was invited to prepare to join the teaching staff at Hesston, I cannot recall now that the matter was specifically mentioned, but I knew that it was the expected thing that all faculty members conform in this point of dress. I had no conviction that the garb was essential to Christian life and testimony, or even for church loyalty. On the contrary I had not, as some professed, any conscientious scruples against wearing the garb, since God was seemingly leading the way for me to be a teacher in a church school. As a matter of courtesy, and policy perhaps, I bought my first "regulation coat" in 1918. As I see it now, I never gave the matter any serious analytical thought at all up to that time. With the press of studies and activities, I confess that during my five and one-half years of school life I did very little hard critical thinking. And I never actually thought on the principles involved in wearing a garb until the pressure of stern experience forced me to do so. In a spurt of enthusiasm, of which I have repented many times since, I had publicly volunteered to put on the garb in a young men's conference at Pennsylvania Church in 1917. Not that I would not have adopted it in any case when the time came for me to take up my work as teacher in a church school, but the public pledge was entirely unnecessary and opposed to my usual principles.

February 28, 1931 After being graduated from college and starting into teaching, I began to do a modicum of reflecting on sundry things that had received little thought from me before. As for the garb, I continued to take it for granted, went to university in 1923 and spent

three years incidentally testing out the garb idea. Even during this
time wife and I were not isolated, but mingled with our own people
fairly regularly on Sundays. Looking back now over these university
years and trying to evaluate and interpret the experiences I had
with my irregular dress, I find a number of things that seem to
stand out clearly. In most practical respects I found the garb no
hindrance in my regular work as a student. In some general ways
I must say it was a detriment. In no way can I find it in myself
to affirm that it was a benefit to my life as a Christian or to my
testimony for Jesus Christ. This last statement may occasion surprise, in view of the fact that one function of the garb is claimed
to be that of directly witnessing for Christ. So far as my own experience goes, the garb is generally, but not always, an advertise-
ment of religion, but whether this type of testimony leads more persons nearer to Christ than what it drives farther away is doubtful.
I am personally convinced that no single general statement can be
made that is always and everywhere true regarding the garb as a
testimony for Christ. In academic circles this garb does not at all
stand for the same concept as it does in a community where the
Mennonites or some similar sect is known. It is everywhere in
learned circles taken as the mark of a clergyman, at least most of
the time, but sometimes stands for some connection with military
schools. As taken in these circles it is not a simple or even plain
manner of dress, but rather the opposite, a form of display, if not
of pride and class feeling. As a mere layman of the church, the
fact that my garb constantly, day in and day out, was misrepresent-
ing me to all those about me, steadily ground itself into my consciousness until I came to suffer from an insincerity complex. I
can see now in looking back, that this feeling, partly unconscious,
made me shrink still more into my own self, a thing I was naturally too much inclined to do. I shrank from and avoided making
friendly social and intellectual contacts which would have enabled
me to touch the lives of my associates in an uplifting and constructive manner, and thereby give my testimony for Christ in a way
that would have really done something to lead men to him.
As a result there is hardly anything I lament more than the cowardly way I failed to touch the lives of others in a helpful way. I feel
I sinned in not witnessing more definitely for Christ, and the garb,
as it reacted on myself, was one leading obstacle to what I have always cherished as my ideal, that of touching other lives in a positively uplifting manner. I feel that God has forgiven me this sin,
but what opportunities have been forever lost! Should I fortune to
spend any length of time again in academic circles, I should change
my manner of dress for that time being; would I have the courage
to do it?

March 3, 1931 Constantly writers are making bold to protest against
some of the unsavory features of popular thought, those ugly excres-
cences of current life and thought which will soon pass and doubtless
be a source of wonderment to sane people of a generation hence. A
pseudo-realism in literature and art, a studied striving for mediocrity of taste and ideals, an almost unbelievable credulity and even

gullibility towards the advertisers of goods, these are features of current life that are more and more drawing the critic's artillery. The principle of living one's life separated from the world has, to my mind, its basic and fullest significance in just this very matter, cultivating a genial aloofness from the transient modes in thought and in life, a smug indifference to what may temporarily be "the thing," a calm and unheralded devotion to the things that are true, honest, lovely, just, reputable, and so forth. To live a balanced life, a life characterized by poise, by quietness, faith and sobriety is of necessity to be separated from the world. Compared with this basic and fundamental separation from the current fads and passing foibles of life about us, the arbitrary method of making one's self separate by exterior marks and signs seems shallow and trivial. Yet this last method can be said to have some merits also, but only insofar as it leads to the transforming of the mind, giving a new perspective, a different outlook upon life about us.

March 8, 1931 Spent my spare time during the past two weeks in reading "The Metamorphoses of Lucius Apuleius." It is indeed a "right merrie tale", remarkable for its rather artistic presentation of foolishness and nonsense. I also noted the possessive and demonstrative adjectives used throughout the work intending during the next weeks to copy them out and classify them for study. Since finishing my doctoral dissertation, now near three years ago, I have, to my regret, not done anything in the way of research in my chosen field of Latin word-order. This is not a major field upon which one would wish to spend a lifetime. Nonetheless I have a great desire to carry it farther in Silver Latin and Late Latin literature, partly as a matter of curiosity and partly to cover a small field sufficiently so that I can enjoy a little of that comfortable feeling that comes with the knowledge that one is qualified as an authority in a particular field. At least, I should imagine it to be a comfortable feeling, not having so far been able to pose as an authority by my own right in any given subject.

My general ambition to carry forward my reading in Greek and Latin literature, followed by extensive reading in French, German, Italian and English literatures has also progressed but slowly. During the past six years I have given a deal of time and effort to the study and the translation of the Conrad Grebel letters. Have been very glad for this "sideline" of study and research, it having afforded me a good glimpse of Renaissance Latin, the learning and the writing of the time. I hope to go farther in the study of that very interesting period of history.

It was in November of 1924, as I can recall now, when the first call came for help in the study and translation of the Grebel correspondence, including in all seventy or more letters, almost all written in Latin. The call came from H. S. Bender and Ernst Correll at Goshen College. Their plan was very vague and uncertain, although the first idea was to publish a life of Grebel as a contribution to the quadricentenary of the inauguration of the Anabaptist movement celebrated in 1925. Being conscientious scholars these two men have continued their work and research in this line as there has been opportunity ever since that time. The proposed volume has been indefinitely postponed and promises to be an exhaustive work covering the life and the letters of Grebel, whenever it will finally be issued. My part in this work has been a great delight to me and has led to a happy fellowship with the two men who first conceived the idea.

I was living in Iowa City engaged in my second year of graduate study in the University there, when I was asked to assist in the work. I suspended some of my reading in the classical authors which I had outlined for myself for that winter outside of my work in courses, and for six weeks or so devoted all spare time to making a hurried translation of about sixty letters. I also prepared several hundred hasty notes on classical allusions in the letters. Mrs. Yoder typed the translations as they were ready and in the first week of January, 1925, I returned the volumes containing the Vadian letters and also the translations so hastily produced and so imperfect, as I realized later. A little later there were a few scattered items sent for translation.

The following winter, when we were living in Philadelphia, the Grebel scholars ordered sent to me from Zurich, Switzerland, photostatic copies of nine letters of Grebel addressed to Myconius. These I transcribed at my leisure and also translated. In July of 1927 I helped to edit one important letter for publication in the Mennonite Quarterly Review. Early in 1928 again considerable time was devoted to the study of all these letters. I went carefully over the Latin text and with the aid of my increased experience as a Latinist made many changes in the original translation. Also studied the language, the style and other details. Made an index of all important allusions, unusual words, expressions, and collected much detailed material for future use and reference.

Quite early in 1928 the suggestion came that I edit and prepare the nine Myconius Letters as a project for publication in the Review. During April and May also, after it was determined that I would remove to Hesston, Correll and I spent considerable time in going over the text and translation together, (that is, of all the Letters) in an endeavour to clear up dark places and further revising the translation. This task we never finished. I left Goshen for a month beginning near the end of May and when I returned Correll was gone for the summer. During June I had three weeks at the University of Pennsylvania between final examinations and convocation. [These were in completion of requirements for the Doctor of Philosophy degree. — Ed.] This was a unique opportunity for me to work on Grebeliana in the university library. I especially worked on the historical and literary background and further clearing up of many dark points, especially gathering materials for the editing of the Myconius Letters. Returned to Goshen, I spent most of my time for another month in preparing the final manuscript on the Myconius project, typing the translation and writing introduction and notes. The project was published in October, 1928.

Removing to the West in August, after spending five weeks in Iowa, I carried with me a box full of Grebel material, books, notes, etc., for my use in making a final and complete revision of all the translations. For further background I read very extensively in the Letters of Zwingli and of Erasmus. For the April issue of the Review (1929) I prepared an article on "Grebel as a Humanist." In March, 1929, began the process of a thoroughgoing revision of the translations, following the original text once more, but especially using rasp and file without stint, I tried to make a translation that was as faithful as possible to the Latin and at the same time somewhat literary and smooth. This task was completed about July 1, 1929. A copy with borrowed Grebeliana was returned to H. S. Bender in September following. The revision I typed carefully myself, numbering the lines, documenting the letters and inserting a few marginal notations in ink. No explanatory notes were prepared on the final typescript. That is a task for such a time as a decision will be made as to the type and sort of material that should go into the notes in the final published volume.

All in all the work I have been privileged to do so far on the Grebeliana has been a great delight. It has opened up a new field of study which I am hoping to have opportunity to enter into further some time. However, I am aware that for a complete background to literary studies in things medieval and Renaissance no knowledge of the Greek and Latin literatures can be too full and complete. My great desire is for leisure to steep and immerse myself in the latter for a period of several years. Ah yes, leisure, that's the rub. Like some other things, I suspect, leisure has to be made to order, if it is to be had at all.

March 9, 1931 Had our biggest snow storm of the season over the weekend past. Lots of wind, as usual in Kansas, blockaded the country roads, with even the few inches of snow that fell. The three winter months this season, according to government reports, were the mildest on record for Kansas, the average temperature being just a shade higher than for the winter of 1920-21. The six tons of coal I had put into our bin will hold out very well unless we should have a number of weeks of weather such as prevailed over yesterday and the day before. This morning Old Sol is smiling cheerily upon the earth. In Kansas almost without exception, no matter how fiercely a storm may rage for a few days with thick clouds, you can depend upon the sun to shine very presently with a brightness that sets your heart a-thrill with praises to the God of heaven. No long periods of cloudy weather, grey skies, are at all common in the Sunflower State. The present cold snap will hold back flowering bulbs that were coming out of the ground, fruit tree buds that were almost on the point of bursting into bloom last week. It seems hardly cold enough to have damaged them much as yet. Everyone is hoping for a copious crop of fruit this year again such as there was in 1929.

March 15, 1931 The Sunday School lesson for this morning included the two incidents narrated at the ends of Chapters 10 and 11 respectively of Luke's Gospel: Jesus being entertained in Martha's home and in the home of a Pharisee. For the lesson review period I tried to draw from these incidents illustrations of the opposite of balance, equilibrium, or poise in one's personal life. The balance between giving out and taking in, between activity and quiet, between service and reflective contemplation needs to be established by each individual for himself. Likewise the proper perspective with regard to essentials and non-essentials, the correct evaluation of things as fundamental and details, the training of one's self to view as a whole a given body of truth or teaching, these are needful for an equilibrium of mind. It is the absence of such a balance that constitutes worry, anxiety, fretting and their ilk. On the contrary, peace of mind, rest and harmony of personality are a result of the proper balance in attitude of mind. There are, of course, other factors that enter into peace of mind and soul, such as faith in God and His providence, freedom from sin and a sense of guilt. To my mind the ancient Greek ideals as expressed in their literature, art and philosophy constitute a well balanced, correctly proportioned and a harmonious system of thought. Have for years felt irresistibly drawn to them, in large part because of this fact.

March 19, 1931 We planted the early garden this year March 13-16, about the same dates as last year. Planted three dwarf arborvitae, called Burkman, along the foundation walls today, also a second yucca and a Hansa rose bush. For lack of funds we must do our planting of shrubbery and flowering plants on the installment plan, each year adding a few items. There is only one cloud on the horizon as we plan to expend money and labor in beautifying our home nest; to wit, the bare possibility that the pressure of circumstances and developments do not give the fullest assurance for the permanence of the college work here. But at the same time the work here looks to me as about as safe a bet as anything in these times of deflation and depression. In some respects the interest and the college enrollment next fall will be decisive one way or the other. Following two slumps in the college enrollment, another one might be fatal. I am not pessimistic personally. It is the equivalent of a thrilling adventure to face a future that is uncertain and fraught with possibilities. Faith in God and the assurance of His overruling providence makes such a world situation as the present one not only not a terror but a welcome prospect. The generally drab and dull status quo, and the security given by science and invention would seemingly make human nature cry out for physical, mental, social thrills and adventures in a way that will explain much of the present day craze for the novel, the bizarre, the irregular and the forbidden. A fully standardized, mechanized, and subsidized world would be absolutely unbearable to sane men and women. It is matter for great regret that so few seem capable of experiencing the thrilling adventure, which is at the same time wholesome and deeply satisfying, of religious faith and experience and of intellectual effort and thought!

March 26, 1931 Newspapers have lately featured items about new laws passed in Nevada, one legalizing again all kinds of gambling and another reducing the residence requirement for obtaining divorce from three months to six weeks. The latter change was an effort to avoid loss of business through competition and the former was seemingly to increase state treasury income by gambling licenses. In such fashion does the world move in these days! Another interesting comment on the present depression is the report given in the Literary Digest of late that the industries showing no decrease in business but actually an increase during the past year are the sale of tobacco and the motion picture business. A probable explanation of this fact may be found in this that masses of people seek to forget their misery and disappointment by stupefying their feelings and nerves with tobacco or by paying money to have their minds diverted by shows. There were occasional reports during the winter of efforts made in some cities, in the East particularly, to open theatres and cinemas on Sunday for the benefit of the many unemployed. Also some suggestions that picture shows be provided free for those out of work. In this way also does history tend to repeat itself. Juvenal in an earlier day complained of the demand of the permanently unemployed rabble in the Eternal city for panem et circenses. Next to bread for the stomach, the most urgent necessity for men and women seems to be and always has been amusement, something to divert their minds from the realities of life. Feeding and amusing the idle is perhaps the easiest and readiest way to render them harmless; otherwise the wealthy would have good cause to fear for their holdings, and their smug complacent existence. Occupation in the form of useful work and spiritual ideals are the surest guarantee of happiness. In their absence, "bread and shows" seem logical necessities.

March 29, 1931 Was called to McPherson College this past week to be critic judge of an intercollegiate debate, between two McPherson College women and two from Bethany College, on Wednesday evening, March 25. My first attempt to play the role of critic judge. I am usually enough of a sport to try anything once. But debating is not one of my hobbies. The question under discussion on this occasion was that of free trade and tariff, an old-time question for which there seems to be no final satisfactory answer under the present scheme of things. Apparently the system of high protective tariffs is necessary in an order of society that is actuated basically by selfishness, greed for getting financial power, and a narrow nationalism. Free trade would strike at these latter characteristics. The most hopeful outlook for economic peace in the world may be the growing system of international finance and credit; whenever tariffs begin to stand in the way of this development, then we may look for their gradual abolition.

It is now a month and more since a Mennonite minister created a sensation by sending out to every minister in the church a three-page closely printed letter addressed especially to the Mennonite Board of Education. It purported to be a "statement of facts" about conditions existing at Goshen College particularly concerning attitudes and practices on the matter of dress, the attitudes of some of the Hesston leaders (unnamed) on the same question and certain matters pertaining to the changes in the Board's constitution. There was no small stir at the Board's meeting in February over the matter. Close examination shows that some of the alleged "facts" are false, being based upon faulty observations and incomplete information. The whole broadside was an insinuation against the sincerity and the loyalty of the schools and the Board. Just what the total effect will be upon the schools it is hard to say. It will doubtless have some good effects and perhaps not as much bad effects as seemed likely at first. It has put another obstacle in the way of the unity and the peace of the church.

For myself, I find the thought of such strife and stress among professed brethren in the faith very disheartening at the first impact. But my consolation is in the thought and the assurance that church politics and the stress of externals bear no direct relation to my peace and my abiding in Christ. For this fact I have many times thanked and praised God. I seek to contend for the faith by giving my personal testimony to the teachings of the Word of God, but to engage in quarreling and strife, to argue and debate, for these the Lord has given me neither taste nor ability. I have faith in the vitality and the eternity of the principles taught in the Word of God and practiced by the minority sects through the centuries, even to the degree that their perpetuation does not ultimately depend upon human effort and human ingenuity. The ark of Jehovah does not require the steadying influence of unhallowed and presumptuous hands. Like Cicero, I wish for nothing so much as to take refuge in philosophy, in study and reflection, in cultivating my mind and soul to appreciate the fundamental realities and verities of life, as I become increasingly aware of the inane triviality of much of the talk and discussion, thought and contention, that is all about.

April 4, 1931 The blizzard and frost that swept the western plains a week ago froze some of the fruit. Apricot trees were in full bloom and are probably all frozen. The peach buds were not out yet and apparently have not all been destroyed. The storm was especially severe in Western Kansas and Eastern Colorado where many cattle were destroyed and a number of school children and others were frozen to death. Both its severity and the suddenness of its coming seemed to be responsible for the fatalities. Bermuda onion plants and cabbage that we set out in the garden three weeks ago look very sick; most will probably not survive.

Vacation is fine. More time for study and doing what one likes. Am gathering out of Apuleius' Metamorphoses the examples of possessive and demonstrative adjectives for future study as to position and use. Also spend some time occasionally in translating of Juvenal's Satires. Translation from a foreign language is recommended as among the best ways whereby to improve and develop one's style and skill in English. Cicero gives it as his method for improving his command of the native language and I have personally heard classical scholars bear witness to the idea. It seems to be especially helpful to myself in two respects: first, careful and conscientious practice in translation adds to one's active vocabulary, especially if diligent use is made of an unabridged English dictionary. Second, limiting one's expression to thoughts and ideas of one's own tends to stereotype the style of English, while transferring others' thoughts varies and vivifies the style of writing.

Yesterday for an hour of sheer recreation I leafed through numbers of the Hesston College Journal of the years 1919 - 1921 when I served as the supreme arbiter of the Journal's destiny and policy. Was powerfully impressed by the long-windedness of the editorials I wrote. Two pages of sixteen used to be devoted to editorial material, oracular pronouncements on a variety of subjects, which gave excellent opportunity for me to spread my wings in English rhetoric and also as an amateur, undergraduate philosopher. Was a little surprised at the clearness of ideas, which I scarce recalled as having possessed at that early date. In general, the basic ideas expounded so confidently in those early days I would not change today. They are still the background of my thinking and philosophy. I would however express these ideas in language a little less dogmatic, a bit more reserved and modest, with less of cocksureness and pugnaciousness. I have always enjoyed writing, not that I can write so well, but because it does help to clarify my thinking and I like to think that it's easy and natural enough for me to write at least readable English that I may with prolonged and painstaking effort be able to improve it to a point where it would be worth while to write for the sake of writing. Since it is to be my lot to serve in a small college on a nominal wage, I entertain a modicum of interest already in trying to fit myself to do some writing later on, perhaps as a means for adding a little to our income and also as a profitable vacation occupation. My conception at present of such preparation is to do wide and extensive reading for information, ideas, and experience and to translate much from Latin, Greek, German into English for the development of style and skill.

April 9, 1931 I usually spend a half hour or such a matter browsing through the Sword and Trumpet, a quarterly journal, the organ of the conservative element of the Mennonite Church in its most noisy and rampant aspect, a curious and unique journalistic effort, to say the least. It is practically a private project, having no official sanction to my knowledge, excepting permissive sanction from one local conference. The editor and leading contributor aims his heavy artillery mostly against certain monsters which he has labelled as "Modernism" and "Calvinism". The method and spirit throughout is pugilistic and almost quixotic. With absolute and unqualified faith in his own authority, the editor places labels on all and sundry people and ideas, pronounces judgment with an air of finality upon everyone and everything within his range of vision, and attacks with the cudgels of bold faced type and large capital lettering anything that chances to cross the path of his ideas. Somehow the impression goes out from his pages that in order to know the absolute, final, incontrovertible and infallible truth about any matter whatsoever, one need only send his messenger to consult the oracle at Denbigh. Particularly offensive is the ubiquitous and preponderant ego of the man that faces the poor reader in almost every column and paragraph. The reader is unmistakably informed that it is this editor who has saved the Mennonite Church from apostasy, that it is he that brought about the closing and reorganization (partial, as he constantly reiterates) of Goshen College in 1923, that he almost alone is defending the truth while most church leaders are weakly and timidly making their fruitless efforts, and that it is he who has authority to pronounce judgment on the ideas, opinions, motives of every man under heaven. The temerity of this man is truly appalling and his regard for honest and considerate statement is conspicuous by its absence. My first reaction to his diatribes and wholesale broadsides is usually a feeling of depression and disgust, but I thank God for a sense of humour, for when my sense of humour comes to the rescue, I feel that perhaps some good may come from his effort and not too much evil.

April 12, 1931 We planted more garden the past week, putting in beans, peanuts, tomato seeds and plants, sunberry seeds (something new that Mrs. saw advertised in a seed house catalog) parsnips, pepper seeds. The things that were planted four weeks ago are all coming up already excepting potatoes. Some of the Bermuda onions and cabbage planted then were killed by the hard freezing weather.

Mr. and Mrs. Paul Bender were so kind as to invite us to accompany them last Sunday afternoon to Lindsborg to hear the 149th rendition of Handel's Messiah by the famous Oratorio Society. It was the closing program of their Jubilee anniversary celebration of the annual rendition of the Messiah and also of the dedication of the new auditorium known as Presser Hall. It is a splendid auditorium for their purpose. This made the fourth time I heard the Messiah at Lindsborg, the other years being 1917, 1920, 1922. In 1920 the Hesston Chorus gave the Messiah under the direction of A. W. Slagell; I helped sing it this once. Since 1922, Mrs. Yoder and I heard this oratorio rendered by the University Chorus at Iowa City and by the Philharmonic Society in Philadelphia. The latter rendition we did not enjoy very much because of the inferior soloists and especially were we annoyed by the constant applause of hand-clapping. The tradition at Lindsborg is one of no applause when the Messiah is rendered. This together with the stated aim of the whole rendition as that of devotion and worship makes the Lindsborg Messiah very effective and pleasing as well as a service of worship. The large chorus is remarkably well trained and directed. All parts, chorus, orchestra, soloists did wonderfully well in interpreting the great masterpiece this time.

A writer in the latest Atlantic Monthly discussing the rather unpromising subject of the exactitude of science makes some casual but very interesting observations on the different kinds of knowledge. According to this writer there are three kinds of knowledge; first the intuitive knowledge of the mystic in religion. This knowledge is based upon feeling alone and uses freely and constantly any number of postulates or axioms, cannot be verified by the use of logic or empiricism and is not supposed to be, satisfies many people and enables them to live successfully, gives a certitude that is beyond the possibility of scientific knowledge. The second kind of knowledge is mathematical. This knowledge uses as few as possible axioms and postulates, is strictly logical within the limits of the postulates it assumes, but is purely a convention that cannot be ultimately verified by experience, precisely because there are no instruments of sufficiently refined precision to demonstrate empirically the propositions involved. Lastly there is scientific knowledge which is also based upon the fewest possible postulates but which, unlike mathematics, can be constantly verified and tested by experience. Both logic and mathematics are used in building upon the postulates, but they are not paramount. Hence as discovery and invention of instruments constantly go on and scientific propositions are duly checked against the facts of reality, these propositions or principles of science must constantly fall and be rebuilt. Hence scientific knowledge is in reality the least certain and exact of all the kinds of knowledge. The writer further deplores the futile and mistaken attempt to verify intuitional knowledge by recourse to logic and experience.

It appeals to me that there are some very suggestive ideas in this article. It certainly seems likely that we have made such a fetish out of the terms "science" and "scientific method" that we have well-nigh offered up religious faith and the knowledge it brings as a sacrifice to this strange god. How hard, how painful, and how distasteful it is for the spirit of man to learn that the mind of man is very, very small and can never hope to comprehend even a minor fraction of the knowledge there is.

April 16, 1931 A monthly feast for me is the Classical Journal. I confess I usually read about all of it from beginning to end, excepting advertisements, and most of it with a genuine relish. The Classical Weekly from New York, Professor Knapp's journal, is just about as good. It is such an exquisite tonic to read periodically discussions on a wide range of subjects in a scholarly, classical style and manner. It seems to be the terminology, the atmosphere, the feeling of classical things and ideas that I crave. The journal edited by Shorey, Classical Philology, is considerably more technical and specialized, so that I do not usually read all the articles in an issue. The book reviews and brief notes in all these are especially illuminating and stimulating with almost rare exceptions. Somehow I cannot help feeling that trained classical scholars as a rule possess just about the correct combination of mental poise, critical insight, frankness, dispassionate interest, and jovial humor to make their critical writings stimulating and even exhilarating reading. How often have I wished that we could learn to discuss religious and ecclesiastical questions with even a measure of the same frankness and consideration and good feeling!

April 24, 1931 It was just one year ago the day before yesterday that our General Electric refrigerator was installed. During nearly ten years of housekeeping we never owned any kind of refrigerator, although we did have an icebox to use at two places where we lived during our years of wandering. Our G. E. is truly a saver of food and of steps and of worry over our previous manner of getting along without refrigeration. It has given no trouble so far. A few times it has failed to start automatically. This is the only article we have ever purchased on the installment plan. The payments were to run over eighteen months, but in February I had the money on hand to pay the balance, which I did, thereby saving more than ten dollars on the sum it was supposed to cost. The total sum paid was $312.81.

I have somehow an aversion to the principle of installment buying. It is an expensive way of buying since the interest charged on the deferred payments is usually quite high. The only kind of goods I would at all consider buying on this plan are such as produce some income or effect some real savings. Luxuries and pure and simple comforts must wait with us until the cash is saved up. Have rather made up my mind that a new car belongs in the last class for us. The old 1923 Model-T Ford touring car seems not nearly so comfortable for cold weather as it did before we had ridden much in closed cars. Its general appearance is quite ancient after eight years, but it can well serve us for short necessary trips, shopping at Newton and occasional drives on deserted side roads. The present tires are all about three years old, and so long as the only expense is for license tags, gasoline and oil, we can shift along after a fashion. Beyond this no plans are made, save perhaps to assert our individuality by going carless.

April 26, 1931 Dr. Niebuhr is quoted from the Christian Century as having certain words to say regarding the dogmatism of modern liberal religion. No words seem more truly spoken than that much liberal religious thinking is highly dogmatic, and all the more insidiously dogmatic in the particular that it professes to disclaim all dogma. The theory of development, progress, steady and unavoidable advancement toward a goal of perfection is a dogma, a postulate assumed as axiomatic by modern thought in many fields of knowledge and philosophy. In business and commerce it fathered the insane notion that business, manufacturing and selling goods, could be expanded indefinitely, that human beings could be trained by the persistent propaganda of the advertising agent to consume an infinite amount of material goods. A result has been a financial debacle that hosts of people still believe is only a momentary lull before we move on to still greater and unparalleled prosperity. All America is suffering from a superiority complex, a blind obsession built up during two centuries or more. In religion this dogma of progress has led able and incisive thinkers to almost unthinkable depths of puerility, not to say asininity. Bernard Iddings Bell in a recent issue of the Saturday Review of Literature has something to say apropos of the inanity that characterizes the great mass of writers who today pose as prophets and inflict their "burdens" upon readers of religious books.

April 27, 1931 For cultivating the imagination and at the same time making oneself realize the smallness and insignificance of man and his works the reading of descriptive astronomy is most helpful. The mere feel of the mental largeness that attends the comprehension of astronomical concepts is a tonic for the soul, a rebuke to the pride of mortal man's spirit, and has a cleansing and chastening effect upon one's ideas, prejudices and obsessions. Several years ago, while doing school work at Boulder, Colorado, I read through a fair-

sized textbook on descriptive astronomy, solely as a few weeks'
spare time and recreational reading. It was thrilling. Have ever
since watched for opportunity to possess myself of some books
along that line for my personal library. A brief article in Scientific Monthly tells of the Romance of Distance. Thus it takes light
over eight minutes to get to us from the sun, five hours and thirty-
three minutes from Pluto, 4.3 years from the nearest star; and
33,000 light years is the distance of the naked-eye globular cluster
in Hercules and 850,000 light years to the spiral nebula, messier 33.

April 28, 1931 Our garden hopes have suffered a setback. There
has been a week of cool, untoward weather; two mornings last week
the ground was frozen slightly, yesterday morning another frost.
Potatoes were not up much, happily. We had just finished setting
out our fifty or more tomato plants; with cans we saved scarcely
half of them alive. Beans were up some and may need to be re-
planted in part. There was snow in north and west, and while none
fell here, the air has been persistently cool when the wind blows
from the north. Have been rushed for a week and more getting college catalog to the printer with still some more to prepare. As
president of the Alumni Association, there is some necessary work
that needs to be attended to now. The Spring Term for school teachers has started and I will apparently have several students in Latin
reading.

April 30, 1931 Mr. Orlando Joliffe, banker and millionaire from Pea-
body, was principal speaker on a program in Character Education
at the college yesterday morning. He left a check for $500 at the
close. This is about the first time an effort has ever been made to
touch such a man for money for the school.
    I read lately the suggestion that, since the terms prosperity and
depression, normal and abnormal, as applied to the state of the times
are largely relative terms, we may soon have to come to the place
where we are willing to admit that we are now returning to normal
conditions after the abnormal boom period of the past twelve or
thirteen years. Personally I suspect there is more truth in the suggestion than we are willing to admit. Once we change our viewpoint
and brand the boom period of the recent past as abnormal, then we
may hope for adjustment to the present more nearly normal times.
It is a hard pill, to swallow our pride and superiority complex. As
touching our school here I have had to think in this direction. Our
program and plans have been largely geared to the abnormal boom
period, not in all respects, as for instance, in teachers' salaries.
But practically all the expansion made during the past fifteen years
has been made painfully even with the economic boom all about us.
We have built up the bare essentials of what our program calls for
while prosperity, so-called, was in power. My question would be,
can we reasonably hope to maintain such a program in the less af-
fluent but doubtless more normal times? The administration building on the campus was built very largely from the extreme profits
made by farmers during the war years, 1917-1918. Numerous men
who by local pressure were induced to buy Liberty Bonds were will-

ing to salve their conscience by giving these to the school's building fund. Thus this principal building was the result of a very abnormal economic situation. Right now there is not enough money about to even take the necessary steps to preserve this same building. Most of one side has been caulked recently but elsewhere the rain comes through freely washing the lime out of the brick wall mortar and destroying plaster and paint.

As regards the attendance during the boom period, much the same can be said. During some continued years of abnormal prosperity the enrollment was flush, faculty plans and other plans were expanded liberally, always up to the limit of the available income. Now for three years there have been needed drastic reductions in teaching staff, so that the staff for next year will be reduced by more than a third from what it was a few years ago. No one can be certain that we have caught up yet with normalcy in this respect. Whether attendance will be large enough in normal times to justify the effort and expense necessary to keep the present program going, and even to meet the minimum set for standard requirements, is matter for thought and reflection. Standardizing agencies suggest as minimum attendance for standard junior college the figure fifty in some cases, in others sixty. Our experience shows there ought to be just that many to make the junior college a unit for efficiency and for commanding respect and confidence. To suggest a change in program and plans, even to think of it may be heresy. The logic of passing time and of economic normalcy must have the deciding vote on some questions such as these.

May 3, 1931 Our today's, Sunday, program was a distinct variation from the usual one. From Paul Benders came the suggestion to take provisions after the morning service, drive out to some quiet spot and spend the afternoon in resting. Found a very fine place along Little River about three miles west from the Alta Mills. There is scarcely any form of outing more acceptable to me than going to some lone spot among trees beside a stream of water and resting. There are the numerous sounds from birds and others of Nature's children that are of the truest music there is. There is the delightsome solitude and quietness that is as wine to the soul. It is inconceivable that folks should seek for rest and recreation by going to resorts and places frequented by the gregarious, noisy crowds.

Springtime is particularly delightsome in Kansas. Sometimes summer and autumn are drab and disappointing. But the spring is always beautiful. Widespread fields of rich green wheat and of alfalfa growing. Leaves and birds bursting out upon tree and bush. Flowers here and there. The large variety of birds and the great numbers of them that migrate here for the nesting season give almost unending opportunities for studying bird habits, observing species and learning of their beauty and value. Contrary to what one might expect, it is possible to find numbers of quiet spots along streams at comparatively easy distances from Hesston, places easy of access and not fortified with "Keep Out" signs. A little farther away to west and southwest are the sandhills which afford an interest and attraction of a kind. Shows and resorts devised to part quickly many fools and their money cannot compete with these little spots of quietness for refreshing one's spirit and nerves.

May 4, 1931 Professor R. G. Kent very kindly sent me an eleven-line clipping from Glotta, Volume XIX, being a notice of and a few comments on my dissertation. Glotta is a linguistic journal published in Germany. Through the courtesy of Dr. Kent and Dr. Rolfe I had previously received brief reviews published in "Revue des Études Latines" (Paris, 1929, No. 1, pages 113, 114) and in "Bulletin de la Société de Linguistique de Paris" (1930) of the same. One of these latter was by J. Marouzeau, a rather prominent Latin scholar of France. All the reviews so far that have come to my notice have been favorable and appreciative with only general constructive criticisms. My friend, Dr. Menk, now of Muncie, Indiana, with whom I studied during my second year at Iowa City in 1924 - 25, wrote a brief review, hardly more than an extended notice, of the dissertation in the Classical Journal last year. When in Lawrence for a number of hours on a day in March, in the general library I discovered a notice about it in Bursian's "Jahresbericht über die Fortschritte der klassischen Altertums-wissenschaft," issued January, 1931. It gave there a reference to "Bibliotheca Philologica Classica" which I did not have time to locate. Immediately upon its distribution I received personal letters of appreciation from two of my former university teachers, Professor Potter at Iowa and Dr. Ullman at Chicago. Received also letters from Dr. Laing of Chicago and Dr. Walter Miller, dean of the Graduate School at the University of Missouri. The latter two, I believe I recall, were written to Dr. Rolfe and kindly forwarded to me by him. The publication and distribution of the dissertation by the Linguistic Society of America has given it unusually wide publicity, in Europe as well as in America. The cost of this publication was very moderate to myself, amounting to something above $240. The printing was done in France owing to lower labor costs. The printed copies (200) that belonged to me came into the United States duty free. A hundred fifty of these went directly to the University of Pennsylvania library. Fifty came to me, of which I still have the greater number.

May 8, 1931 After a deal of hesitation I renewed my subscription to the Atlantic Monthly. I hesitated, not because I did not know whether I wished to read it longer, but solely because I might have borrowed the copy each month to read and saved the cost of subscription. As a rule I read most of it within a week after its arrival, not only with a relish but even with zest. This is the one magazine that is good enough throughout to deserve the active support of subscription, I feel, rather than the passive use of reading only. While being open and unbiased, its contents are usually the kind that tend toward comparatively conservative viewpoints and reasonably good sense. Nearly every month I get to look through other magazines as Harpers, Scribners, The Forum, North American Review, The Century, etc. While very good and thoughtful articles are occasionally found in all of these, there is so much of the radical, half-baked, jazzy thinking expressed also, such that I do not care to help to pay for its circulation . The few stories in the Atlantic I rarely read. Cannot interest myself in them as a rule.

May 10, 1931 For three weeks past all spare time seemingly has been taken up by extra and special tasks, preparing college catalog for the printer, attending to work and business pertaining to the Alumni Association, of which I have the misfortune to be president now. Have been figuring a little on a program of studies and work for the summer vacation. Want to do some really intensive work in my favorite studies. The last summer I spent scarce a week or two in intellectual effort, but instead dug our sewer ditch, harvested about ten days, and beginning July 15 or thereabouts worked on remodelling and improving the house, using all possible spare time even until Thanksgiving. The summer of 1929, the first one since returning to Kansas, I spent the month of June solidly in final work on the typescript of the Epistolae Grebelianae. The remainder of that summer was devoted to reading and study, but my eyes gave me some trouble and were a handicap. As for helping harvest, am convinced from last summer's experience that I should not indulge any more. Time was when eating dust and living in grime was my delight, but not any more. Some means of summer income would be welcome, but not threshing wheat.

May 14, 1931 Physical health is a prized possession most particularly when one does not have it. Mrs. Yoder has been struggling to get back her strength since the time of her goitre operation now three years ago. There have been slow, very slow gains in most respects.

With her trouble it is a serious question to know what should be done under our circumstances. It is quite possible that if one had means to try one thing after another, one sanitarium after another, one specialist after another, the remedy that will fit her case would eventually be discovered.

For us, on the other hand, it may be equally as costly in the end, not to spend money for "doctoring." It is a matter of serious moment. During the five years that we were away from Hesston, while I was in university and then teaching at Goshen while finishing my university work, my wife willingly sought employment to provide some income for our living expenses. She earned $1800 or more in cash during these years and did so under a great physical and nervous strain which seemingly aggravated her bodily trouble. For me to use the training and preparation to which she helped me so gladly and unselfishly in this place where it brings us only our barest living may not be right in the sight of God. To start out and find a place giving more income so we would have means for seeking health, appears to be such a great undertaking that the strain of it would perhaps offset again the benefits of a greater income. If the way should open to anything else that would bring us more income, I do feel that as a matter of duty to my wife and her health I would take it up. I wait for the Lord to lead the way.

May 17, 1931 Have had to think recently on some of the policies that are being used and have been used in carrying on the work of Christian missions. The question was raised by one in the class that is reading the New Testament in Greek just now. A thoughtful reading of Acts and especially of St. Paul's missionary labors is sure to suggest some questions, critical questions about modern missionary methods. Why was it possible in the first century for a missionary to make a leisurely tour through a section as a result of which churches were planted in which on a subsequent tour leaders and officials from their own number were appointed? Since this was possible then, why is it not being done today? Do the differences in culture, in language, in stage of civilization and in general philosophic and religious outlook in any measure necessitate such a complete change of method? Truly the comparatively meagre results that can be shown for the pouring out of millions of money and thousands of lives during the century past tends to emphasize and add point to the critical questions that arise.

In reflecting upon some phases of this matter, I have for myself had to wonder whether it is not possible that a partial answer to such questionings may lie in this fact: Paul and the early missionaries preached a simpler and therefore a more vital message as the heart of the Gospel truth than our present-day occidental conception of what constitutes Christianity calls for. Somehow I cannot help feeling a suspicion that our concept of Christian life and Christian service and activity includes a vast amount of material, mere lumber, that is not absolutely vital to the growth of Christian life and character. The simple truths that Jesus taught have gathered to themselves a mass of accretions, interpretations, creedal formulae, thought patterns, patterns for moral, social and ethical concepts even, which are distinctly western and should not be, perhaps can never be, placed upon orientals without modification. Too much of modern missionary effort is largely an attempt to civilize, i. e., to Westernize the East or Africa. We are obsessed with the notion that a Christian Church in India or China must be a precise replica of an ideal church in America. Should we not rather let each race to work out in the course of time its own distinctive forms, activities, institutions as the expression of the life of Christ? This is exactly what has been done in the west, perhaps far too often even to the misrepresentation of the true spirit of Christ. If the Gospel of Christ in its elemental form is a vital and living thing as we profess to believe, then surely it is our unbelief that insists upon making Christianity almost synonymous with Western culture and civilization and theology and that attempts to foist our particular concepts and ideas of Christianity upon other races.

The churches that St. Paul planted on his great missionary tours were not perfect and ideal. We especially think of the church at Corinth where Paul laboured for perhaps as long a season as he did at any one place. Think also of the seven representative churches in Asia Minor to whom John wrote in the Book of Revelation. Paul's conception of Christianity seems to have been that it is a vital seed to be planted far and wide which through the nurture of the Holy Spirit will in the course of time, perhaps centuries, bring forth its perfect fruit. When in our day we labour to plant the tree of the church and insist it must have fruit on it at once, even if it has to be tied on, are we not substituting for faith in the efficacy of God's power through His word and His Spirit our own feeble efforts?

Especially is our Mennonite concept of Christianity put to the test by a consideration of these matters. We make it our boast that we at least in our program teach the "all things" that Christ commanded His disciples to teach when they evangelize the world. The question then is whether we are not taking the liberty to include in these all things traditions, ideas, interpretations, thought patterns and what not which Jesus never taught. If we have faith that these same traditions, ideas, etc., are a part of true Christianity and are in themselves vital, why can we not also believe that the same Word of God and the same Holy Spirit that gave them to us, can and will give them to others, if we sow the seed diligently and give our testimony faithfully? On the contrary, our feverish anxiety to hand on in toto our particular body of interpretations and to inculcate them by law and discipline seems to be proof that we have at bottom but little faith that they are vital in themselves and will survive without our all-important thought and effort.

May 22, 1931 March weather still prevails periodically even though the calendar says it is May. Last week a few hot days when vegetation fairly shot upward. This week the roots can push downward again. A steady rain fell during most of yesterday. We were in too great haste in planting beans, peanuts, corn this year. Seemingly none of these should be planted before the middle of April. Wife canned some spinach last week.

Prosperity, that deity to which so many millions in our country do homage, still refuses to hear the pitiful pleas made for her return to reign and rule. The stock market has been tumbling for weeks with some of the most stable stocks selling at the lowest figure for years. Farmers in parts of Kansas are pledging themselves not to plant wheat this year unless they get one dollar a bushel for the crop that is growing now. This practice is prominently condemned as being a sure step toward the driving from their farms of these farmers to join the millions of unemployed in the cities. More bold and positive statements are constantly being made and printed in condemnation of the insane tariff rates. The American Federation of Labor is making loud official protests against the reduction of wage levels, perhaps another silly gesture to bid an ocean tide to stay back. A World's Wheat Conference is in session in London now. Seemingly the United States is bound to make itself still more the laughing stock and the fool of the world by doggedly insisting upon policies and plans that will keep sheltered our selfish and greedy standard of living which has become so sacrosanct and inviolable to most Americans. The U. S. representative at the Conference urges the world-wide reduction of wheat acreage, while certain European countries, and notably Russia, oppose the plan. And so the merry scene goes on. The spectacle of a world overfull of goods and foodstuffs in which many millions cannot get a chance to obtain their share is certainly a sorry one. The unequal distribution of wealth and of the control of the tools for creating wealth is undoubtedly just as great today as at any time in the world's history. The mass of the population of our country today has been beguiled by the boasts of liberty, freedom, equality that have been the credos of our national religion. As a matter of actual fact it is possible that, while the masses with us have a few more possessions with which to amuse themselves, ancient slaves in Greece and Rome had more economic and social security than the average citizen in this our land of the free and the home of the brave. It is rather clear that the United States, if not all the world, is on the eve of a gigantic readjustment period.

May 25, 1931 Within the next ten days the work of the school year will be over, which will mean a great relief for someone I know. The Spring Term class will continue for two weeks still, three days beyond commencement. There are about fifteen jobs, big and small, now waiting for my vacation time. There is considerable work to do on the premises, tasks that are still of the aftermath of the building program that was carried through last summer. Levelling off the ground in the back yard where the sewer ditch was made, disposing of the heap of old plaster that came from the walls demolished in remodelling, and a mass of soil and concrete rock that came out of the basement. These are major jobs that will provide physical exercise during much of the summer. My principal occupation is to be reading, study and research. The General Conference Peace Problems Committee asks me to do some writing for their propaganda program. But I have little interest in producing material to order and made-to-measure. May try to enlarge and rewrite the address given here on last Armistice Day, which was published as a January, 1931, College Bulletin, for their use. My earning power for the summer will doubtless be limited to two activities: first, caring for the garden plot and helping the good wife to put away abundance of vegetables and fruits for next winter's use; second, saving my clothes by staying at home and near home. Besides working hard about the house last summer, I hopefully sought to earn a little cash income by going through the tough experience of harvesting for about ten days. But alas, for all my pains, discomfort and vexation of spirit I have so far received not one-half of the amount that had been agreed upon as wages for my work.

The warm weather coming on brings well-nigh unbearable longings and despairing wishes to go off to the mountains for the summer months. Until such a luxury is possible we will content ourselves to be as comfortable as may be on the plains of Kansas. If the good Lord will bless our efforts to pay off our mortgage and other debts, we may confidently hope that in a number of years we can go to Colorado for the summer season — let's hope, annually.

May 30, 1931 Warm weather for a week. Rains on several days. Garden crops growing by leaps and bounds. Second planting of peanuts put in last Saturday are already out. Have had enough strawberries twice for our breakfast fruit, but not on successive days. The commencement week activities are on. I am supposed to have general oversight of public activities in an effort to coordinate all.

June 7, 1931 The activities for the school year came to a close with one final and grand rush during the past week. Crowds of visitors from near and far, good programs. A mighty exodus on Thursday and Friday taking with it many of our local folks.

The final address by M. C. Lehman was well given and well received. The subject was "Present World Conditions and the Mennonite Faith." There was considerable denominational emphasis, it being substantially the same address as given a few weeks previously at the meeting of the Board of Missions and Charities in Iowa. It was repeated here upon request. The principal idea of the address was to the effect that the historic principles of the Mennonite faith are almost exactly identical with the remedies that thinkers and critics are prescribing at this time for the troublous conditions in the world. The principles of the simple life, of separateness from the world's life, of peace, of spiritual devotion, all these are found to answer almost exactly to the maladjustments and evils that threaten our American life. It is a theme well worthwhile and one that suggests many points that are in need of further development and study. I firmly believe that these basic principles are vital, that there is no need for any apologetic attitude regarding them, but also that our interpretation and application of them requires intelligent and sympathetic criticism.

June 12, 1931 It is hard to start on a definitely outlined program following a regular schedule. The extra tasks accumulated over some weeks need first attention. Spent several days doing tonsorial work on the grounds. Also picked cherries, enough so that wife has canned fifteen quarts, some of them with mulberries added. Also helped pick and can the firstfruits of the pea crop a few days ago. Garden was getting a little dry, when yesterday and the day before several good showers of rain fell, so making garden crops look fresh and prosperous.

It has been suggested by a personal friend that it is my duty to consider attending the biennial General Conference session several months hence in Ohio. I had decided not to consider the matter of going. Aside from the fact that I have little personal taste for large gatherings and the generally platitudinous making of words that characterizes many of them, I feel that I want to practice the simple life among other ways by staying at home and not gadding about in the world, "running to and fro." One of the present crazes that is a mark of worldliness is the restless, nervous, almost insane lust for going places, going, going, going. Attending meetings and meetings where there is talking, talking, talking about problems, problems, problems is just another avenue of worldly conformity which Christians have taken up as an escape and distraction from their serious business of living a quiet and peaceable life in all godliness and honesty. It is urged also that as an official in a church institution, I should be in direct touch with the coming General Conference, which as some predict will be of more than ordinary importance, due to some issues which seem to be calling for definition. But again the prospect of an assembly where there is stress and friction, the opposite almost of Christian peace and unity, is one from which I recoil personally. I have almost come to the conclusion that I am not fitted to work into and become a part of a completely integrated and tightly articulated ecclesiastical system. The idea of such a system to me savors too much of man-made artificiality, too much of the clanking, the roaring and the rumbling of machinery that drowns out the still small voice of the Spirit. There is doubtless some place for systematic organization in Christian work, but for me the greatest phase of the religion of Jesus Christ is the quiet, inner, free and untrammelled working of the Spirit of God. This phase must always receive the major attention of everyone and even the whole attention of most of us.

June 15, 1931 A heavy rain last evening and also on Saturday night. There is plenty of moisture in the ground now for a while. In previous years the cellar of our house always became flooded with water in a season of heavy rains. The prospect of such a season holds no terror for us now that we have a sewer drain in the cellar. Some little water still gathers in low spots, but it cannot possibly become six inches deep as I have several times seen it.

It seems possible that there will be a wet season for the wheat harvest this summer. Since farmers have come to depend upon the use of heavy tractors and combines to do the harvesting of their wheat, they are more in dread of soft fields than in years past. Wages for harvesting help will probably be lowered considerably this year again due to the low price of wheat, which is now selling for between forty and fifty cents per bushel. Last year the wage rate for harvest hands and threshing was three dollars a day in this section of Kansas. Farther west the rate was higher. There is talk of $1.50 or $2 a day now. It is not possible today for young men to earn enough money during a summer of harvesting and threshing to pay their expenses in school for nine months after as was true ten and twelve years ago. I worked in the Kansas harvest fields in 1918, 1919, 1920, 1921, just a little in 1922, again a little in 1930. The summer of 1918 was a banner year for myself. Worked all summer for J. E. Yoder in Reno County, twelve miles southeast from Hutchinson, one mile north of Yoder, Kansas. Shocked wheat for about four dollars a day. But most of the summer I spent operating Mr. Yoder's Avery threshing machine during a long run of threshing from shocks and later from stacks. We operated about 42 days, as I can recall now, but due to much rain during the latter part of August, we lost time so that in September·I had to leave the job to enter school before the threshing was all done. During threshing, Mr. Yoder paid all his help at the rate of so much per hundred bushels of grain threshed. Pitchers received that year fifty cents a hundred bushels of wheat. The separator man always received double the rate of the pitchers, making my rate one cent a bushel. For the 42 days our machine averaged about 1250 bushels of wheat a day. The largest day's run was 1750 bushels. My total earnings for the summer were just a bit less than $750 and if the rains had not kept us from finishing the threshing run in time for the opening of school, it could easily have been a hundred more. In 1919 I again helped Yoder thresh from the end of June till August 15. My returns were about $360. I again quit the job early in order to take a trip to Iowa, Pennsylvania and General Conference at Harrisonburg, Virginia. In 1920 a number of fellows together, including Paul Bender, Jesse Martin, John Detwiler and myself, travelled in my Ford car on a harvesting tour. Went to Jet, Oklahoma soon after close of school and harvested there for Sam Troyer for several weeks. From there we went to Ford County, Kansas, to an Amish settlement south of Dodge City. Bender and I worked for an Amishman named Beachey. We got nine dollars a day for heading and stacking grain. From there we returned to Hesston about the middle of July. I went to Iowa, helped thresh there for a number of days, then travelled on to Pennsylvania for a wedding. [His own. — Ed.] In 1921 I shocked grain for E.T. Yoder east of Hesston and then operated Roy Smith's Minneapolis separator for about thirty days at six dollars a day. In 1922 my harvesting experience was limited to shocking grain and then pitching bundles for Ira Spangler near Hesston. 1930 found me for ten days helping Elmer Hershberger heading grain on windrows and then also threshing with a combine.

June 16, 1931 Thinking back over it now, my experience in getting my formal education of high school and college was rather remarkable in some aspects. It was on the high tide of war inflation that I was carried through college easily, not only without indebtedness, but with several hundred dollars to my credit. I did a little teaching as an assistant every year I was in college, in the days when no regard was given to the certification of teachers for the academy. So in a sense, I owe my college education to a combination of abnormal circumstances. Still another factor that figured in the situation was the fact that I escaped the military draft on grounds of doubtful or at least questionable ethics. While other young men had to leave college to go to training camps, I and a few others who were connected with Hesston College managed to be classified as theological students, candidates for the ministry, and so were never called to camp. It was argued that since we were members of the Student Volunteer Band, which was the equivalent of theological students in our denomination, we were entitled to such exemption. It is not only the point of the questionable ethics that was involved that makes me in part regret that I ever applied for such classification, but I have since had occasion to envy some of the young men who went to camps, my friends and chums, for their experiences in camp and then in relief work in the Near East. However, not all the conscientious objectors got to go to the Near East; some ended up at Leavenworth Federal Prison. So I have no way of knowing what I missed in escaping the call to military camp.

Another interesting feature of this experience in retrospect is that as a member of the Student Volunteer Band, and because of my own Amish background and experience, I was picked to be sent over to the Yoder, Kansas community for the summer of 1918, stationed there as the sole resident worker for the mission or extension Sunday School which had been started in March, 1918. Of course, I was to work and support myself. By the blessing of the good Lord, I secured the position with J. E. Yoder, and while sent out officially to do missionary work, I earned the largest sum of money in three months that I ever did in my life. All this, too, while my friends were spending their time in military camps. Looking it all over, it seems that God's hand led the way, overruled the mistakes perhaps made, and that I was able to do some good work and to have numbers of rich experiences that in some measure compensated for such as I missed in not taking my place in the military draft. What may be the ultimate meaning of the seemingly providential manner in which I was enabled to get so easily through my college years, and further through university by the sacrifice and help of my dear wife, all this must be for the future to disclose.

The following data was obtained through conversations with local people in the Yoder, Kansas, Reno County area in 1982, especially from Mrs. Noah Miller who attended the first meeting of the Sunday School organized in March, 1918. The young people in this Amish community were restless to the point where some were leaving the church, some young families joined the Mennonite church at West Liberty, and so on.

There was agitation to organize a S. S., have Young People's Meeting on Sunday evening and provide activities to keep the young people occupied. Word of this came to leaders at Hesston who decided a mission field was practically at their door. Thus Edward Yoder was asked to undertake this outreach. Others from Hesston helped in various ways, including ministers who preached occasionally for the fledgling S. S.

These services were held at Harmony school, soon too small to accommodate the group, then using Laurel school, in a district where the school board consisted of Amish who strongly opposed the S. S. endeavor and succeeded in closing the school building to the group with the aid of the Court. They then found a vacant store building in the town of Yoder, where services were held until they built a church building in 1919. Services in the school houses and store building were held on Sunday afternoon so these people could continue attending the Amish church service on Sunday morning.

Following is a summary from a diary recorded by Edward Yoder in 1918 and 1919:
Beginning March 10, 1918 trips were made week by week from Hesston to Yoder, Kansas. If a car went out he rode along; if no car was going, he rode the trolley from Newton to Yoder or Hutton, catching rides or walking at each end of trolley line, returning to Hesston for the next day's classes anytime from 8:00 p.m. Sunday evening to 3:30 a.m. Monday morning. Sometimes even though a group went from Hesston by car for S.S., he would go Saturday afternoon in order to conduct singing school on Saturday evening. Also while the car of helpers returned home after S.S., he would often stay to help with Y.P.M. Sunday evening, go home by trolley and walk the ten miles to Hesston from Newton. Except for two Sundays, he went to Reno County each weekend until he moved

out to J. E. Yoders' on May 30, 1918 to operate his threshing rig. He missed no S.S. all summer until September 8. When school opened at Hesston he continued these trips to Reno County nearly every weekend during the 1918-19 school year.

I was reading a review of a new book in the Saturday Review of Literature where apparently the new and dignified term "polarity" is used to denote the age-old idea of balance and sanity as descriptive of a philosophy and of conduct. The statement is quoted from this book under review to the effect that wherever there are two hotly contested sides in a controversy, either one alone is wrong and that the two together are necessary for a balanced and complete view of the matter under discussion. This statement, while not true of basic principles, is very true of all controversies regarding interpretations and applications and policy. At the same time it is necessary to note that in times of upheaval it has often been the radical, dogmatic type of men who provided the most effective leadership of the moment. So it was Luther who led the way to religious reform rather than the great Erasmus with all his balance and peaceable moderation. Seemingly Luther precipitated a movement that was a short cut to what the influence of Erasmus would have brought Europe in the course of time. No doubt the world needs both the radical and the balanced types of individual. The rank and file of the populace can rarely be aroused to action except by some spectacular and more or less radical leader. But the thrill of radical action wears off and then the leader with balance and poise is in demand.

June 23, 1931 A trained nurse and obstetrician from the mountains of Kentucky writes in Harper's Magazine on the question of whether it would be possible to better the economic and social conditions of the poor whites of the South by teaching them birth control. Her answer is in the negative. The leading point of her thesis is that there is a balance in the nature of things which regulates the birth rate among social groups. It is not the birth rate that determines the social and economic standing of a group, but rather the reverse. One factor especially was emphasized as contributing to lower birth rates, to wit, education. First of all, education postpones the average age of marriage to a time when the most fertile period of life is past, for the woman from the age of perhaps fifteen to twenty-five years. The young woman in school expends much of the vitality and nerve force in sports and intellectual effort which her cousin who marries in her teens puts into child bearing. The point was also brought out that history generally proves that persons of great intellectual or great spiritual accomplishment do not generally have descendants in posterity. Their nervous energy seems to be used up in their work.

Nature appears to have her own plans and methods for keeping up the balance of things in the world. It seems that numbers of the problems which men and women discuss so seriously as depending upon themselves for solution and remedy are being taken care of by Nature in the course of things. I have a feeling myself that this entire extreme emphasis today placed upon group activity, efforts to control and formulate the whole of man's environment, almost frenzied zeal to search out, define, state and solve problems is a misdirection of energy. It is another escape mechanism whereby to get away from the nurture and the cultivation of the personal and inner life, the building of character and the control and direction of self independently of the group.

Especially does the discussion and heated argument over the question of birth control seem to be beside the point largely. From a racial standpoint it is ludicrous to note the seriousness with which some folks talk as though on themselves and their ideas depends the control of a matter which Nature has for long millenniums been controlling. From a personal standpoint it would seem that the matter is one of personal choice. The Christian should be able to control sexual appetite to serve reasonable ends. The rich and idle who want to live viciously and desire no children, are not fit to be parents and Nature probably desires their kind to die out with themselves anyway. People who desire children for what they will contribute to their own life and character, for the opportunity they afford to contribute to posterity possible personalities, characters, talents and possibilities which they do not themselves possess, these folks, and fortunately these always comprise the great and substantial mass of society, will go their ways with only an academic interest, if any at all, in the discussions over birth control. One point that goes to prove this is the reports which state that the demand for children to adopt in childless homes is far greater than the supply available.

June 24, 1931 Summer weather is upon us in good earnest. Temperatures up to ninety degrees F. Garden crops are doing very well. We have canned forty pints of peas with still a few more to pick. Beans are beginning to come now. Picked quite a few mulberries from the one tree on our lot. They are fairly good fruit when mixed with some strongly acid fruit as cherries or rhubarb. One earns mulberries in picking them by hand. Our tree had a brown thrasher's nest in its top and my repeated presence in the tree caused no little worry to the lady of the nest. Her scolding "clacks" were a constant accompaniment to my tedious picking of mulberries. A robin has raised a family of youngsters outside of our dining room window. A Baltimore oriole has a nest suspended in the top of this same tree. A wren family has its headquarters on our front porch. These have been here now for several years. Last year a mocking bird built a nest low down in the rosebush by the porch, perhaps six feet away from the wren's box. When the eggs had been laid in the mocker's nest, Mrs. Wren deliberately entered and rolled eggs out of it. She did not want any near neighbors about.

The study and observation of wild life is becoming more fascinating for me. When I was at home on the farm, I had no interest in birds, excepting negatively in such as were pests about the place. My interest in birds and nature began while I was a college student. About 1921 I was made president of the Hesston Audubon Society as it was first organized. Did some considerable study of bird life for a few years. Since 1924 our study of nature has been only casual, but even so interest and appreciation has been growing. We read hungrily the articles in American Magazine by Archibald Rutledge on wild life. There is a distinctly mystical and religious note in his presentation and interpretation of wild life. Many times I sense a feeling in myself that I can learn and experience more truth about God, the Creator and Preserver of all Nature, by observing and reading others' observations of this incomparable handiwork, than by studying the reflections and abstruse philosophical speculations of theologians on the nature and works of God. Spiritual truth seems real only as it is felt. Definitions and propositions are almost meaningless where there has been no experience of this truth.

June 26, 1931 When hot weather continues long enough and severe enough that the nights become hot, then there is nothing I miss more than the opportunity to sleep out of doors under the open sky. We did speak of making a flat roof on the little west porch of the house and have it for that use particularly. But for last summer's time and means we had all we could do without carrying through this added project. Somehow in a town I do not so much fancy the idea of sleeping on the lawn, although like some other things it is probably just an idea or notion, as we call it.

One of my keenest satisfactions in my threshing experiences in Reno County of this state during the summers of 1918 and 1919 was that of sleeping out of doors under the spacious canopy of heaven. In order to be present at the machine early in the morning to make the necessary preparations for the day's work, it was my regular practice to sleep by the machine, usually all by myself, since the other hands generally slept in a barn or some other building. I recall sometimes walking one or two miles on a dark night, finding my way across plowed fields and coming to rest by a grain stack or a straw pile near the outfit. I had a folding cot and two light quilts, but preferred to sleep on straw using only the quilts, especially on cool nights. It always proved a blessed experience for me to be out in the great open spaces and feel the protecting hand of God, the good hand of the Lord upon me. Some would consider it dangerous to spend the nights out in the open fields. But I relished it as a happy experience. In Iowa while I was still at home we used to sleep outdoors under the trees at night during the hottest summer weather. While touring to Colorado in 1923 we slept in the open, which is fine if it is clear weather and not too cold. In the mountains it is not easy to keep warm through the night sleeping on an army cot unless one has a mass of cover material both below and atop himself. A very comfortable and luxurious way to sleep out in the mountains is to make up a bed of pine needles and twigs. Just once Estie and I had the experience of reposing on such a royal forest couch. It was west of Denver, near a small town on the southern edge of Denver Mt. Parks, where we spent a Sunday night. We rested in the Parks all morning and drove only a short distance in the afternoon, making our camp site early, before sunset. I cut off the ends of pine branches and underneath the pine trees made a bed of needles three or four inches thick, spread above it a blanket and then had ample covers for keeping off the cold. We did sleep royally that night, comfortably warm, reasonably soft and in the midst of the rich fragrance of pine forest odors.

June 27, 1931 News has come that the Indiana-Michigan Mennonite Conference, at its latest session, saw the radically conservative element placed in the saddle and taking full control of the machinery of the conference. Men who have been lifelong leaders in church activities have been omitted from all positions in the conference organization. There are other signs also pointing to a possible period ahead of radically reactionary control of official church machinery. In the general thought patterns and modes of the western world at large, the inevitable reaction to the orgy of iconoclasm and revolutionary thinking of the past decade and a half seems to be setting in. In our small group, there is real danger that radical leadership control will bring separation and division. To those who see in outward forms and customs the very essence of the Mennonite faith, there are wide enough variations of opinions and practices to well warrant division. But division in our group is not so easily and readily effected today as it seems to have been fifty or seventy-five years ago. Then it was largely a matter of breaking fellowship and each party of the division going its own way with little reaction excepting an aftermath of hard and unloving feelings. Today the issues that some try to force to the front cut so far and so deeply that division in the group will almost surely affect the institutions that the church has built up during the past thirty and thirty-five years. The Board of Missions and Charities with its holdings of considerable sums of money, the Board of Education with its two schools and some endowments, the Publishing House, all these institutions will be involved in any major division that might take place, if for no other reason than that it requires the entire body to support them now. It happens that these institutions are manned by personnels that are more or less liberal in their policies, in the sense that they are supremely interested in maintaining a modus vivendi in the church, so that the institutions can continue to grow. If shortsighted radicals in different sections of the church succeed in getting control of the official machinery it is impossible to predict just what may be the course of events in the immediate future. The whole is a difficult situation without question. I have no wish or inclination to have any personal part in any fight or war, if there is to be one. I mean to hold aloof and give what energy I may have to other things which to me seem more fundamentally important. The only form of solution in which I have any active interest is that of repentance and confession on the part of the entire church body for our faithlessness and unspiritual living, for our carnal-mindedness and worldliness, a worldliness that manifests itself even less in manner of dress than in our methods of service and in the tendencies now at work in our church government and ecclesiastical policies. Like Daniel and Nehemiah of old, the church needs, more than shrewd ecclesiastical politicians, men and women who will intercede with God in contrition and confession for our sins.

June 30, 1931 The heat wave that is now on seems to be very severe over many states of the Middle West. A total of 200 or more deaths have been attributed to the heat of nearly two weeks now. It is unusual to have such extreme temperatures so early as June. Garden vegetables will not do much any more without moisture. Onions and potatoes are fairly well along. We are sprinkling tomatoes and strawberries as also a few flowers.

The first half of the year 1931 is past with today. It has been an enjoyable year at our house so far. The lower prices on commodities have been a real boon to us. The Lord has given us health and has kept disaster and misfortune away from us. We take much pleasure in our little place, despite the fact that the back yard is not fixed up yet as we plan to have it. There are some very beautiful hollyhocks growing along the south side of the house, over a part of the back yard, and along the rear edge of our lot. These last we transplanted in a row this spring. All the others are such as grew from seeds that have been distributed and planted in Nature's way. When we came here three years ago, there were just a few of these by the rear porch. Now there are dozens of them and of the widest varieties of colors and hues and also of forms. Some are not the single flowering sort, having a single circle of petals, but having numerous rows in concentric circles and forming a very beautiful flower almost as wonderful as a rose. Colors that are common are pure white, dark red or wine colored, and many shades of pink. Some of the older plants have stalks growing as much as seven or even eight feet in height, not only one stalk to a plant but even three and four or more. They have been a very beautiful and inspiring sight for several weeks now. They seem not to be at all finicky about matters of moisture, soil, or nurture, but grow vigorously and beautifully with an air of independence and triumph that is all their own. The persistent pushing of strong south winds is too much for the tall ones to keep an erect posture, but even while leaning somewhat, they keep bravely on growing and blossoming. Some fertilizer applied at times, every two or three years, is much appreciated by them. We must get some manure hauled in this fall with which to fertilize all our lawn and flower grounds. Estie plans to gradually build up a flower and rose garden in the back yard. We wish very much that we could acquire the fifty-foot lot just to the south of ours and there plant strawberries, various sorts of bush berries as well as the annual garden crops.

July 2, 1931 Pleasant showers of refreshing rain fell yesterday giving a measure of relief from the heat and drouth. Assisted C. Hertzler about two hours yesterday morning putting away second crop alfalfa hay. Rain stopped our work before it was all done.

Atlantic Monthly has been presenting a pair of articles each month for some time on the business situation, attempts to analyze and identify causes and propose remedies. These doctors of business present an interesting variety of diagnoses and nostrums for the ailing business world. Interesting largely because of the lack of agreement on either what the causes of economic depressions are or what measures of relief should be applied. On the side of analysis the articles bring out some good points. But some of the suggested remedies appear very crude and naive. So for instance a late article argues for the much-recommended cure-all, that of inducing, cajoling, persuading, tricking or compelling people to consume more goods so as to provide employment for both the dollars and the men that are out of employment and want to work. The standard of living that a country has is without a blush defined as the amount of material goods that the people consume per capita. So it turns out that the chief value human beings have in the present economic system is that of consuming material goods. And this with the prospect that the species of homo sapiens may ultimately have as its sole and only use that of using up, consuming, wasting or otherwise getting rid of the ever-increasing stream of goods that come from the machines, thanks to the triumphs of technology and of efficiency. This poor human is to be little better than another machine used to consume gasoline, rubber, cloth, paper, wheat, pork, radios, moving pictures, tobacco, and a thousand and one other things. In other times and places human beings have been exploited for their physical and intellectual strength by a system of enforced servitude. This is known as slavery. Today in the reputed "land of the free and the home of the brave" millions of humans are being exploited for their capacity to consume material goods. By the all but irresistible propaganda of advertisers and by the psychological pressure, a variant form of violence, of our democratic mediocrity we are being forced to consume goods, goods, goods. For anyone or any family to choose his own personal standard of living and to refuse to be reckoned as a mere incinerator of material goods, is becoming increasingly hard and unpopular. It was Henry Ford, I believe, who stated that while there is a limit to the amount of goods people can consume with comfort and convenience, especially in the form of food, clothing and housing, there is no limit at all, so he said, to the amount of goods people can be taught to waste systematically. A critic very sanely remarked that he will not believe a word of this until Ford practices his own doctrine by placing sand in the bearings of his motors instead of oil. This is a sound criticism. Human nature in its aspect of dignity and self-respect, in its hunger for spiritual realities, is tough and resilient enough not to suffer itself for long to be degraded into a mere machine to destroy goods or even into an animal to swinishly waste them.

July 4, 1931 Today is celebrated as the birthday anniversary of American independence. For us it promises to be as any other week day, excepting the cracking of firecrackers and other noise that reaches us from a distance. It will apparently be a pleasant day, not very hot, with some indications for precipitation.

The heat wave that for about ten days had settled down on a large part of the country seems to have been dispelled for the time being. The last figure I remember having seen on the death toll due to heat was above 700.

Finished translating Juvenal's sixth satire, the famous one on women. It is very long, the longest of all he wrote, seeming his most eloquent theme. His cynicism and bitterness become rather monotonous in this piece. A few parts of it are not clear to me yet as to his exact meaning.

July 6, 1931 Within the week past I have read the book, now two
years old, on "Henry the Eighth" by Francis Hackett. It is one of
the psychological biographies which have been so much the vogue for
a number of years. I find it rather interesting reading, somewhat
informational, not extreme in its method or viewpoint. There is an
air of realism about it that I find refreshing. There is no doubt
about the vast amount of labor and research which the book represents. Six years is stated to be the time spent in its preparation,
entirely from source material, evidently in large part personal correspondence, but also official and diplomatic. In the course of my
study on the Conrad Grebel material I had a few faint glimpses into
the political and dynastic tangle wherein the Europe of the time found
itself. This same situation is pictured as the background for the
reign of Henry the Eighth, painted in striking colors and delineated
with a stark realism. Such an understanding of the selfish struggles
to build up national and imperial dynasts, of the canons of ethics and
morals that were the accepted mode in the political machinations of
the time, of the brutal and almost incessant wars that were waged,
often solely for personal interests and the avenging of personal wrongs,
of all this glorified selfishness, help much toward an appreciation of
the pacifistic tendencies and ideals expressed by some of the leading
humanists and protagonists of The New Learning.

July 10, 1931 Yesterday morning Estie and I witnessed the spectacle
of five young wrens emerging from the reed box on our front porch
and faring forth into the great world. Each youngster had to look
about for some time before finding enough courage to set out upon
his initial flight of even only one or two feet. All the while they
were greatly excited, giving vent to their thrilled feelings by loud
and constant clucking, both those already out and the ones still left
behind in the nest.
     We had for several weeks past often watched the parent birds as
they labored in carrying worms and bugs to their large hungry family
of children. The first sure evidence of young ones in the nest was
the chorus of thin squeaking voices that greeted the mother's entrance,
squeaking that sounded like that of mice. Thereafter almost every day
could tell a difference in the tone and quality of their vocal accomplishments.

July 13, 1931 Still dry weather here, threatenings for rain yesterday,
thunder showers to the eastward, a little cooler this morning, still
cloudy and the wind blowing from the east.
     Wheat is selling just now at local elevators in Kansas for 27-29
cents a bushel, said to be the lowest figure for any time since Kansas
has been admitted into the Union of States. At the same time Kansas
is reported to be harvesting one of the largest wheat crops in its
history, yields are high, thirty and even forty bushels per acre being
not unusual.
     Much space has lately been given to eulogizing President Hoover
for his proposal that Germany be given a year's moratorium from
reparations. The inveterate and deadly hatred of French politicians
for Germany has again been emphasized in their refusal to agree to

the plan, although after several weeks of negotiation the reports are that agreement has been reached. Indications are that Germany was or is rather, on the verge of financial bankruptcy, and perhaps other countries of Europe also. Such catastrophes would doubtless give the red communists of Russia just the opportunity they are looking for, to create revolution and confusion and extend Soviet principles and practices.

It is pitiful to behold the agony and the suffering of American editors and writers over their failures to conjure back the prosperity wave. Whatever the specific causes for the depression, as it is called, it seems to me plainly to be the inevitable collapse after the wartime inflation. We in the United States have been living in a fool's paradise ever since 1918. When the abnormal bubble of prosperity bursts and normal conditions seem about to return, we are utterly disconsolate.

July 20, 1931 Dry weather continues. High temperatures, but mostly such as are normal in Kansas. For bodily exercise last week I built a pavement beneath the wash line in our back yard out of old plaster and broken fragment of concrete flooring. Still have left some large blocks of concrete removed from the cellar last summer, which are to be planted in the form of a stepping stone walk from the back porch to the wash line. Finally there is considerable soil to move and level off before the back yard will be in order. Last Thursday, upon C. Hertzler's invitation, I accompanied him in his truck on a trip to Eldorado, Kansas. He wanted someone along as company on the long trip. Incidentally I picked out of a scrap pile owned by a Jew some materials to use in constructing a bird-bath on our lot.

Have been reading in one of Sir William Ramsay's books, entitled "St. Paul, The Traveller and Roman Citizen." This writer on New Testament history in his scholarly and objective manner is a great favorite with me. Especially are his discussions of the Book of Acts and the Letter to the Galatic churches extremely suggestive and illuminating. His statements are generally moderate and restrained, his viewpoint is conservative, yet highly scholarly and critical. To me Biblical study based upon historical, linguistic and archeological material is most fascinating. I do not have so much interest in speculative theology, although such preferences are largely matters of personal taste.

July 25, 1931 The summer vacation is more than one-half spent and I already anticipate that it will be all too short for me. Still have not finished my work on the grounds. Too many interruptions have been in the way. Made two trips to Newton this week in behalf of the July Bulletin for the college. Worked most of a half day yesterday digging out our potato crop, about three and one-half bushels of good quality potatoes. Wheat price is still around thirty cents a bushel, while the bread we buy costs ten cents a loaf, three pounds of bread for the price of a bushel of wheat. Breakfast food – wheat flakes — is still twelve and one-half cents for an eight ounce package. It seems a shame to pay twenty-five cents a pound for such foods when wheat sells for less than a half cent per pound. We hope to

bake most of our own bread, using whole wheat flour which Mr. Diller
grinds for us, and with it some white flour. This is the only way we
have yet found of obtaining real genuine one-hundred per cent whole
wheat flour. Graham flour and whole wheat flour sold on the market
invariably has something taken from it. With all the science and
manufacturing skill of our time, it appears that no way has been found
to market the flour of wheat ground just as it grows from the fields
without taking from it sufficient of the real nutriment so that the bugs
and worms will leave it alone. Still human beings are supposed to
be healthy by eating what worms will mostly leave alone! We use
whole wheat flour ground locally for breakfast cereal, thereby avoiding the payment of tribute to bakeries and breakfast food makers.
In former periods of history kings, princes, and emperors were often
in the habit of exacting tribute from peoples. Today the same process
goes on, only it is to the money-kings and the financial-barons that
we pay our tribute. The unique fact is that we do so willingly —
more or less so – under the delusion that we are free men and
women. How often do we waste sympathy upon subject peoples in
history, whiles we ourselves are involved in a gigantic and all but
universal system of economic and industrial feudalism with its bar-
ons, knights, and serfs just as surely as were our forefathers in
Europe centuries ago? Who can with any certainty maintain that we
have more happiness, more social and economic security than they?

July 27, 1931 Have finished reading the book, "St. Paul, Traveller
and Roman Citizen." Am more than delighted with it and wish to
acquire a copy for my own library, as a regular reference book.
Especially just now that the Sunday School lessons are taken from
the book of The Acts on the subject of the Spread of Christianity,
the book has been helpful and stimulating. The appreciation of Luke's
method and his purpose as a historian adds greatly to the significance
of the lessons we are studying. Luke's narrative is very brief and he
is content to state the bare facts which he has chosen as essential
for his purpose, without explicitly stating causes, reasons and results,
leaving the facts to speak for themselves. Hence in order to get a
complete picture of the history Luke is writing, the reader must seek
out background material from archaeology and other literary sources,
and also from a study of geography and of Roman political history,
as well as from the social, commercial, and economic conditions
and the philosophical thought as they prevailed at the time and varied from one part of the world to another. From my reading and
study of the Acts in the Greek I had learned to love the style and
the viewpoint of the writer. Now that I have gotten a further glimpse
into the actual life of the early church against the fuller background
of the general life of the times, many points have been illuminated
for me and I find myself fired with the ambition to study more fully
for myself the general social, economic and religious life of the first
two Christian centuries from the original sources as much as possible.
Especially helpful would be the reading of the papyri that have been
discovered in recent decades. As yet these are not readily accessible.
Then I want to read in Lucian and Plutarch for fuller information and
atmosphere of this general period.

This study of the Acts affords also glimpses into the possibility for me to get a better understanding of some of Paul's Epistles than I have been able to attain so far. It is very illuminating to read Epistles like Galatians and the Thessalonians in the light of the actual conditions under which they were written. Such a conception of these Epistles seems to me to be miles in advance of having to be limited to the quasi-oracular use of isolated verses and phrases for religious instruction and spiritual inspiration and as texts for hortatory discourse. The latter use is not wholly excluded by the fuller appreciation.

While waiting for the time to come when I will be able to study the Old Testament in Hebrew, I am studying parts of it from the literary viewpoint as presented in Moulton's Modern Reader's Bible. I find this very interesting and helpful.

August 2, 1931 Relief from the prolonged drought has at last come in the form of a three or four inch rain which fell last night and this morning. Many plants are today lifting up their heads in a gesture of pleased surprise at the long-deferred and all but unhoped-for drenching they received. Newspapers contain accounts of the devastation wrought by clouds of grasshoppers in states north of Kansas, also some damage by army worms.

Yesterday morning (Saturday) Estie and I started early for a cool and pleasant drive, leaving at 6:30. Drove west to Buhler, gathering some colored pebbles on the highway to use in decorating the birdbath we are planning to make. From Buhler we went on to Hutchinson through the sand hills, looking for some summer apples among the orchards along the way. But we were just a little too late for such apples. Want to go again when grapes and watermelons are in season. Striking on No. 505 a few miles east of Hutchinson we drove to Newton to do our shopping. Among other items we bought a bushel of peaches for $1.50, good quality Elbertas shipped from Arkansas. Also paid one dollar for a thirty-pound box of small white California grapes, cheap enough if they had not been beginning to rot already. We canned eight and one-half quarts at once and have enough left to fill two or three more quart jars.

Brother Herman arrived this morning from Iowa. He and Joe Weaver were here for dinner.

An article in the Literary Digest quotes words from some educator on the peril to the United States of having no religious and moral instruction in the public schools. Since public education has become as broad as life itself, being the sum total of education for the large mass of youth, it is a distinct injustice to deprive children of positive religious instruction. The rivalry and mutual suspicions of the sects which has been responsible for the exclusion of this instruction from the public schools, has as actual result fostered the sectarianism of irreligion and atheism in the schools. What this will mean, in conjunction with the decay of home life and its influence on morals and religion, it is not hard to predict, at least as to its general tendency. In this connection, it appeals to me, there is one opportunity for our church as a social and religious group to set forth an ideal and to outline a challenging program that will mark us as separated from the world and will attract and motivate the loyalty of young people in large numbers. Personally, I have a feeling that what is needed for our young people is some bold and courageous attempts by Spirit-filled men and women to define in new and intelligible terms our historic doctrine of nonconformity to the world, in terms and concepts that will have a meaning and a challenge for young people from high school and college.

August 9, 1931 Last Tuesday evening at eight o'clock we were invited to the S. B. King home to witness the marriage ceremony in which my brother, Herman, was a principal. It was a pleasant wedding on a pleasant evening. It was the occasion for a two-fold celebration on the part of Estie and myself, due to the fact that it marked the eleventh anniversary of our own wedding at Springs, Pennsylvania. An automobile load came from Iowa for the wedding, brother Dan, sister Barbara, her husband and two boys, and sister Ida. These started on the return drive very early on Friday morning, excepting Ida who is staying for a brief while. Herman and his bride left on Thursday for a prolonged tour in the western part of the United States including the Pacific coast states. They will locate on Father's farm in Iowa in October.

Some more rain fell last night. This afternoon the air is cooler with a strong wind coming from the north — Boreas spending his strength on the Kansas plains. This added moisture will cause to germinate the vegetable seeds which I sowed in the garden the past week. Should there be two months of growing weather with not too much of blistering heat, we might yet have a season of fresh garden vegetables for table use.

August 16, 1931 It failed to rain last night as it did on the last two Saturday nights preceding. Growing things need moisture again. I laboured hard the past week to get the article on "Peace Principles" completed and typed. It has a length of about 7250 words. I sent it by mail to G. F. Hershberger who will read the manuscript as the evening platform address at the Young People's Institute on next Friday evening, August 21. Then the manuscript is to go to E. L. Frey, chairman of the Peace Problems Committee of Mennonite General Conference. Also prepared copy for the College Journal and saw it to the printer. Only three short weeks remain until school begins again. All are looking forward to find out what the opening will bring forth.

Had my measurements taken yesterday at Newton for a new suit of clothes. This is the first time since May, 1928, that I have bought a suit. I exercise myself to make my clothes wear as long as possible. It is one way to eke out a meagre income. I recall that I paid in the vicinity of eighty dollars for my wedding suit in 1920. Bought another in 1921 or 1922, one in March, 1923, the next one in August, 1926, and none again until 1928. Shoes I require about one pair a year, although they run ahead some so that once in a while I pass over one year without getting a new pair.

James Truslow Adams in the August issue of Harper's has an article on "Wanted: Perspective". In this he sets up a little background against which to view the present financial panic. He does so by giving some facts about previous depressions in the United States, as in 1837, 1857, 1873, 1893, and shows that all the wild talk about the present panic being the worst in the history of the country or of the world is bosh — at least so far as it has gone in these twenty months. He cites evidence showing that in major panics of the past it took from three to five years to reach the worst point. Incidentally Mr. Adams scores a hit against what he calls "close-up" in the present system and procedure in education. The phrase is taken from the technique of motion pictures, concentrating attention on one particular set of actions, in disregard of all perspective and relative meaning. He pleads for educational foundations that include history, literature, and even the classics, to give balance and perspective to the detailed specialties that will engage the interests of folks in later life. True liberal education seems to be still on the retreat; Yale University has removed the requirement for Latin and Greek for the B. A. degree only lately.

August 20, 1931 Have been impressed by the eagerness with which people seek to learn the religious views and beliefs of eminent men. If a man has become an authority in some special field, especially in science, invention, or in finance, some reporter is sure to draw out from him some childish pronouncement about religion or morals. It shows on one hand the general interest there is among folks in the subject of religion. But the worst part is the evidence it gives as to whom the rabble regards as the oracles and the gods of the day. The American public is utterly given up to the cultus of worshipping the twin deities, science and success. The utterances of the priests of these cults are received with awe and reverence as were the responses of the ancient oracles at Delphi or of the Sibyl in Italy.

From a common sense standpoint it is very unfortunate that such persons should be led to express views on religion and morals for publication. It is very unfair to themselves. They have specialized in one field of thought and have become authorities in their fields. In religion and its current problems they are no wiser than schoolboys and make statements that are absurd and silly in comparison with their wisdom in their specialty. An interesting illustration of this practice happened several years ago. Luther Burbank, having long specialized in plant breeding and having acquired much success and fame (he was popularly called the plant wizard), was interviewed for his religious views which were broadcast in the public press. His pronouncements looked like awkward and garbled versions of what were the so-called scientific and scholarly views of the moment held by certain religionists who were more adept in the art of publicity than in spirituality. He did not live long after this. One report gave it that he received so many letters of protest and remonstrance that the embarrassment constituted a nervous shock from which he took sick and died.

Every eminent man in other fields is expected to be an oracle on religion. It were no less reasonable to seek out and broadcast every eminent man's views on scientific and technical problems, regardless of his field of special study and interest. It is not much the practice to interview the experts in religion and spirituality, even on religion, not to say on scientific, industrial, and economic issues. The religious expert has not enough standing in the popular mind to be an oracle.

August 24, 1931 I have for years read Ernest Gordon's monthly double-page in the Sunday School Times, being news notes and comments on religious events and happenings that reveal significant trends of the times. He notes particularly events of evangelical missionary progress and the trend toward religious liberalism in schools and missions. His comments are in most instances incisive and pointed. On only one subject do I find myself out of sympathy with his viewpoint; it is that of pacifism. It is true that there are pacifists and pacifists, with some of whose efforts I have little sympathy. I do not now recall that Gordon has ever committed himself on the matter of personal nonresistance. He evidently believes that pacifism and disarmament propaganda are unscriptural. He writes in a recent issue unfavorably of the 19,000 ministers in the U.S. who committed themselves against bearing arms in the case of another war. Kirby Page in "The World Tomorrow" published this item in a report of an extensive questionnaire submitted to the ministers of the country. Mr. Gordon quotes with evident approval the published criticism of this report from a military official, who regards those who make such a pledge as traitors to their citizenship duties and advocates that citizenship rights and privileges be taken away from such. The military man even assays to quote a text from the New Testament, a part of a sentence from Luke 11:21, taking the statement entirely apart from its context and setting. In the context Jesus is correcting the opinion of His enemies that He casts out demons by the power of the prince of demons. Jesus points out the absurdity of this theory, by showing that a particular system never works against itself in such a manner, or if it does it is in process of dissolution. He next teaches the truth about His own work by using a simple illustration taken from everyday life, how that when a strong man fully armed guards his goods they are safe, but when a stronger than he appears he is conquered, disarmed and despoiled. To argue that Jesus was here teaching self-defense is faulty exegesis and contradicts other teachings which are direct and pointed.

In the same number Mr. Gordon cites the experience of a missionary in Ecuador who preached to the soldiers. When these raised the conscientious question about their profession, the missionary quoted Luke 22:36 to prove that Jesus' program of peace and nonresistance was postponed till a later time when the Jewish nation rejected His claims. The passage in question is where Jesus speaks of those having no sword should buy one. The teaching here is figurative. Jesus is about to leave His disciples and the attacks of evil forces so far directed against Himself will now be directed against His followers and they need to arm themselves for this struggle. When a little later Peter used the sword he had, Jesus rebuked him outright telling him to put up once for all (aorist tense) the sword, enunciating the principle that they who use violence shall perish by violence.

The only question that might be raised in connection with this incident is why Jesus suffered even the two swords in the company to remain. Perhaps the incident that followed was necessary for teaching His followers the principle of no use of violence.

August 26, 1931 Peaches on our trees are ripening now, seemingly later in the season than two years ago. The dry weather in July apparently kept them back somewhat. They present a beautiful sight on the trees, growing large because of their not being so very thick on the trees and getting a pleasing pink reddish color on the upper side that faces the sun.

Yesterday a week ago (August 18) I went with Maurice Yoder on a drive to see a number of folks in Reno County. Coming home we came through Hutchinson. At a market there I paid a dollar for a bushel of small size Maiden Blush apples. They make very good apple sauce and we will get perhaps nearly twenty quarts canned from the basket by the time we are through. Grapes are soon ripe to can as juice or sauce — the only forms in which we care for canned grapes.

September 1, 1931 Have finished harvesting our fruit crop and feel that we have had a very good return from the ten trees on our fifty-foot-wide lot. The three peach trees bore in all seven or more bushels of fruit. Took off one and a half pails full of grapes from the vines yesterday. We had tied these up in cheese cloth to keep the birds from them.

September 3, 1931 One week hence registration for the first semester will be in progress. I have stopped attempting any prediction as to numbers but have prepared my mind for any possible event. The depression, that ever-convenient scapegoat, is to take much of the blame for lack of attendance. However, our enrollment began decreasing already in 1928. While undoubtedly financial considerations have figured in the continued decrease in recent years, it is possible to speculate as to other factors that have helped in the same direction. Some of these have been providential and some otherwise. Among my personal speculations are the following things. Seemingly the inner policy of the administration of the school had for a few years previous to 1928 been quite definitely in a particular direction, toward what a few individuals conceived of as a policy for more loyalty to distinctively Mennonite ideals and traditions, but a policy which, in the estimation of a number of others of the members of the faculty, was definitely aimed at a narrow and short-sighted loyalty. By 1928 this policy had been pushed to the extent of re-instructing the personnel of the faculty to fit the new ideas, getting more teachers of the so-called "Hesston type", whatever that was supposed to mean. Gradually the various reactions set in among teachers on the staff; some became greatly concerned for a change of policy and emphasis, centering their efforts on a change in the office of the dean; others developed a rebellious attitude with its varied defense machinery. On the part of several of the latter who were not so strongly attached, it took the form of voluntary withdrawal. Hence it came about that two left in

1928, one was discharged in 1929. Their places were taken by the new type, much inferior in personality and in teaching ability, but supposed to be more loyal Mennonites. This change in policy became noticeable to thoughtful students, patrons and alumni and did much to destroy confidence in the management of the school. It seems clear to me that two of these, among the best teachers Hesston ever had from the standpoint of personality and ability, could still be here, but for their being unnecessarily antagonized and crushed down. It is true they changed their attitude on some points, but it is my contention that they were driven to it.

The providential factors that have further shaken confidence and morale, were specially the death of T. M. Erb, the removal of D. H. Bender, and now the general depression. So much for speculation on contributing factors. One more is that my return has been a curse to Hesston, causing a steady and continuous decrease since the first year I came back!

September 5, 1931 Am at present reading in H. G. Wells' "Outline of History", more out of a sense of curiosity than for the sake of information and knowledge. The first 130 pages were particularly boring. They read like folk and fairy tales that are spoiled for the reader precisely because they are written as sober and serious history. There are scattered throughout this pre-history part qualifying expressions in regard to the details stated, but the general outline of evolution and development is stated and assumed as undeniable fact and sober truth. Such dogmatism would not be tolerated by modern writers in any field outside of the sacrosanct one of speculative science. Such is the arrogance of scientists, that they regard themselves alone as being qualified to speak, not only in their own special field of thought, but in every other about which they may condescend to express an opinion.

Mr. Wells tries to be a cautious writer apparently. But one trick of his logic repeatedly used is especially suspicious. Thus for example, in tracing the supposed development and appearance of species ever higher and higher, he almost invariably, after describing some particular advanced species, declares that it became extinct and the next higher race developed from another source about which nothing at all is known. This kind of reasoning, together with his insistence upon many millions and hundreds of millions of years (but always with some specified leeway) of time shows so starkly the deductive reasoning from an assumed evolutionary premise, that one can only be amazed that such a work should at all pass as authoritative truth.

September 14, 1931 The past five or six days have been busy, almost hectic ones for me. School has opened. The enrollment is a bit more than fifty per cent of what we should have had in order to make our budget come out satisfactorily. This fact makes a serious and very acute problem which has not yet been solved. There is also the question of what the State Board of Education will do about the accreditment of our Junior College, now that there are only sixteen enrolled in this department.

Midsummer weather has prevailed during the past week. Very dry

47

and much wind. Our garden which gave so much promise a month ago is again at a standstill. The few rains in August did start a large number of small tomatoes on the vines, so that we can take off quite a few now, although they do not grow at all to the size they should.

September 23, 1931 A decided change in the weather has come upon us — not an unwelcome change after two full weeks of very dry blistering hot and often windy weather. Relief came on Sunday. Rain began falling in the afternoon and continued much of the time until Monday noon, totalling nearly three inches.

One afternoon last week Paul Benders took us with them to a farm south of Buhler to look for tomatoes. We found some very fine ones, took all that were picked and paid a dollar a bushel for them. We had one bushel for ourselves. Also bought a bushel of apples for a dollar. Our tomato vines have been furnishing us about all we could eat since in July and with this rain now will continue to do so until frost comes. Estie has even canned some from our patch. From the seeds I sowed early in August we will apparently not get anything for our pains, unless it be a few turnips. We took off nearly two baskets full of squash — some large and some small — a few weeks ago. Peanut vines look lusty and green after rain.

September 24, 1931 There are many phases of the work in the school that tend to make one discouraged and that rob one of the mood to attempt anything in the way of building up or planning. The feeling is at present general among the officials of the school that the Junior College cannot be continued -- unless some sudden and unforeseen changes in tendencies come about — after this year. We have not yet disposed of the deficit problem for this year. Wage cuts of twenty-five per cent average have been made, taking over three thousand dollars away from the teachers. It is a most gloomy prospect for many of us, if we stop to dwell on that side alone. If the Junior College closes, a number of us will need to move on to something else.

Today at noon we enjoyed a visit from a family group of Maryland yellowthroats, the father with his coat of delicate yellow and gray set off strikingly by the black patches on the sides of his head and face, a female of more subdued coloring and at least three young ones who were also fully grown. They tarried for a little while in the cherry tree outside our library window, preening their feathers, hopping about for a bit of lunch, but apparently mostly resting before continuing their migration to a milder climate for the winter season.

September 29, 1931 The rush incident to the opening of school has about spent itself and I am ready to outline for myself a program of work and study for the coming months. Since I am receiving only half a salary for my work at the college, I shall regard myself as entitled to some appreciable fraction of my time as my own. Hope I can organize my time and effort so as to prepare myself specifically for possible changes and readjustments that are before me. For carrying on linguistic studies I have projected I need some texts and books. How to get these with only a modicum of income presents a delightful little problem. If nothing intervenes, I contemplate to be able to spend most of my afternoons at home in study and research.

About a year ago after remodelling the house we slew, chased out, and trapped what we supposed would be the last mice in this house. The remodelling evidently interfered greatly with the living quarters and habits of those then living here. A doorpost beside the cellar door had been raised from the floor and left an opening for the mice to get on the first floor, evidently the only place of its kind. I closed this place up and at once there were signs of something trying to chew a hole under through the cellar door, showing that some mice were penned onto the first floor. For a while before this Estie had on several occasions caught a mouse feeding on the seeds placed in a canary's cage in our dining room. The cage was supported on a stand of its own, the post of the stand making a semi-circular curve around the cage. The stand with cage stood near a window with long curtains. Presumably the mouse used the curtain as its right-of-way to reach the pan of the cage. But its manner of exit several times when suddenly caught and surprised in that rather exposed position was singularly interesting — almost ingenious. Leaving the pan and embracing the tubing of the stand she (it later developed that this was the mother mouse) slid gracefully down, around the curved part and down the straight part of the stand below the cage. Mrs. Yoder saw this performance several times. I set a trap for a week or more with all possible art and skill near the cage, but the wise old mouse steadfastly refused to indulge her taste for either bacon or cheese from a trap. We were also unable for a time to discover where this acrobatic mouse betook herself whenever she hastily had to abandon her lunch counter. At last Estie hearing the unusual noise about the cage one evening, quietly went to the dining room, snapped on the light and watched particularly to see where the mouse went following her usual quick descent. Sure enough, she saw her jump into the sewing machine that stood close by. It was a drop head machine and had on the lower side the usual narrow openings where the drive belt passed in and out. Through one of these Mrs. Mouse entered her hiding place. Informed of this, the man of the house at once laid plans against the life and welfare of Mouse. I closed the two openings into the cavity of the sewing machine with rags, hauled the machine out on the front porch, and armed with a stick of wood and with mind prepared to give battle, I opened up the top of the sewing machine partly. The old mouse was cowering in a corner, a little surprised at being thus outwitted. A few vicious passes at her with the stick as she darted from one corner to another finally stunned her. After properly beating up the poor creature I pitched the remains out into the dark.

So much for Mrs. Mouse. It was on the same day, I think, that I heard in the evening a commotion on the back porch. It was localized in a bushel fruit-basket sitting on the floor that had a little trash, papers etc. in the bottom. I quickly and as quietly as possible picked up the basket and made a dash for the outside door which was a few feet away. I had barely gotten my hand on the door and opened it to the extent of two inches when a large and vigorous mouse with a dash of fright had reached the edge of the basket and jumped for his life. Happily the path of his leap coincided with the narrow opening in the door at that instant and old Daddy Mouse landed some six feet below in the back yard out in the cold dark world. Within a few weeks after this I caught the five or six young ones of this mouse family in the cellar. They were still very small, but deprived of parents, hunger forced them to fare forth from the coal pile where they had their nest. Not having learned the shrewdness of their elders nor been instructed about the danger of traps, these innocent little mice knew no better than to try to eat the cheese from the traps set for them and so they were quickly caught and disposed of.

October 4, 1931 This is one of those perfectly delicious days of early fall that Kansas occasionally puts on. The atmosphere is in fact more like late summer than autumn. There is no air moving at all; the temperature is up, I should guess about ninety degrees Fahrenheit. It is two weeks ago today that the drought was fairly broken and the weather has been very fine since. We still gather enough tomatoes from the garden for table use every day. Carrots, beets, sweet potatoes are still growing. A number of eggplant are well started. The turnip seed I sowed about the middle of August has come up since the last rain. If growing weather continues until Thanksgiving time we may get some small ones to eat. The five rows of peanut vines make a pleasant green spot in the garden. The foliage on the soft maple trees about town has already begun twice to drop off as dead leaves, at the end of July and again the middle of September. Each time it was checked by a heavy rain, and even new leaves seemed to grow out after the rains came, so that the foliage is still beautifully thick. We are wishing for a short and a mild winter so that our fuel bill may be small, in proportion to our income.

Am still reading in Wells' "Outline" and find myself able to become enthusiastic over some parts of it. It is very illuminating to reread the history of our Western civilization, not as the only history there is that is worthy of record, but as it actually is, a mere segment of the great drama of world history. Our Western civilization takes on more of a meaning and a possible purpose when one views it alongside of other cultures and civilizations. Wells occasionally turns philosopher, and not always a foolish one either, in spite of the almost continuous shining through of his favorite pattern over which he tries to write.

October 9, 1931 After a few cool days there is balmy weather again. We have reset some strawberry plants this week, in spite of the lateness of the season. Brother Herman and his bride left yesterday for Iowa where they plan to make their home on a farm. They and also S. B. Kings and their hired girl were here for supper last Wednesday evening. Word came from Iowa on that day that Mother has been sick, but we have no word written since last Monday afternoon. Officials of the Mennonite Board of Education will be in this community next week according to plans laid recently. They have called for a meeting with conference officials, Local Board, and some others to discuss the Hesston problem.

Today I reached the end of the "Outline of History", a rather lengthy outline that reached through about eleven hundred pages. Mr. Wells writes a clear and vigorous style of English. He also writes with a moral earnestness, almost passion at times, which is stimulating. His insight into the significant movements of history is remarkable. He is not antagonistic to religion, even speaking in high terms of Christianity, at least in its primitive forms — as he chooses to speak of it. It is hard to follow him in his estimate of the Roman Empire with its rather insignificant tone. His chapters on the Middle Ages and the modern times are quite striking and arresting. Mr. Wells is, of course, sold completely on the idea of progress in human history, a grand movement toward a goal of perfection, the race ultimately working out its own salvation and solving its last problem by its own developing intelligence. The chief means for accomplishing this grand result are to be education and religion. He ends up his "Outline" with a very emphatic interrogation point as to what will be next. At the same time there is no shadow of doubt in his mind about the final goal and outcome. It seems such a naive faith on the part of some master minds, this notion that we can be dead sure of about where and how man originated and came to his present state as a race, and that we can be equally sure of the final goal of perfection, when at the same time confessedly we know nothing as to the definite manner in which either of these supposed facts came about and will come about.

October 11, 1931 For comfort I built a small fire in the furnace after dinner. Paul Bender took me with him yesterday on a trip to Wichita, mostly for the purpose of nosing around a bit in the hope of possibly finding some part time work for himself for this year in order to eke out his income. Incidentally we also used the opportunity to spy out the land a little in regard to any possibilities for openings for ourselves for next year, in the case that we should need to look for something elsewhere than here. Paul had made a similar trip to McPherson on the previous day, but on neither trip did he discover anything promising for this year. However, it seems fairly clear that he will have small difficulty in finding an opening for another year in case he should seek one. With his broad training, which fits him well to teach any or all of three subjects in college, physics, chemistry, mathematics, he can readily find opportunities. His address before the Kansas Academy of Sciences last spring has given him some little standing in this state. Opportunity in my field of teaching is more limited. Friends University has no Ancient Language department at all. Wichita University has a lady teaching Latin and Greek who has only a bachelor's degree from old Fairmount College.

The possible prospect of seeking a position in the educational world at large may soon enough be facing some of us here. Wife and I do not wish to locate at any place where we are out of reach of a community of our people. Furthermore for reasons of climate we would much prefer to stay in the West or Southwest. For myself I feel rather happy at the prospect of some kind of a change, although the process of changing is not in itself a pleasant prospect. The constant strain and uncertainty that is connected with the working of our school is not to my taste at all and I have now learned enough to steer clear of any more administrative positions. Teaching is clearly my line and the spending of leisure time in reading, study and research, and ultimately, I hope, in some writing. Work that requires appearance in public or the making of public contacts for the winning of public confidence through powers of personal magnetism, is absolutely not for me. It is unnatural for me, am always self-conscious when I attempt it, and suffer much misery from my failure in it.

October 16, 1931 Since the rain which fell last Sunday and Monday we have had a series of perfect autumn days, rather cool in the morning, bright warm sunshine during the day, no wind blowing, just such days as make one glad to be alive and to be living in Kansas. All vegetation is still growing lustily; seemingly it has redoubled vigor after its dormant season during the drought and heat of the summer. Time is here to clip the lawn again right now. Dandelions are blossoming and seeding with gusto.

October 19, 1931 Upon the invitation of the college students, Estie and I accompanied them on their annual outing last Saturday. The trip took us to the Twin Mounds, an informal recreation park about twelve miles northwest of the town of Canton. Chris Hertzler had taken us there once on a Sunday afternoon several years ago. This time our crowd were the only folks present and everyone found it an enjoyable place to spend a holiday. On the way going there we stopped in the Ritz oil field a little south and west of Canton and saw the process of drilling wells and pumping also. We enjoyed the outing very much. It was a complete change for one day and a strenuous one for me. My notion of an outing is to go out to a quiet place and in a restful and receptive attitude absorb sunshine, pure air, and drink in the spirit of Nature in her varied moods. The spirit and attitude of "doing things", everlastingly being active, aggressive, romping, yelling, etc., etc., is in my experience dissipative and quite enervating. This spirit seems to be natural for the young in whom animal spirits predominate. But to my mind it does little to foster the inner life, and is quite an obstacle to the fullest appreciation of Nature. For this latter one must place himself in the humble receptive attitude that is forever essential for the learner. For discovering many secrets of Nature especially must there be quietness, solitude, patient observation, the sort of thing that "bores to death" the modern person with the spirit of a go-getter. I often wonder to myself how many hundreds and thousands of individuals are diverted and guided away from their possibilities for full development of character and talents by the habitual dissipation that is incident to the speed and the scientific wonders of the day. Are there enough young people today growing up to cultivate mental reflection, depth of character, and strength of soul to supply the coming generations with leadership? The leveling process of modern democracy is gradually destroying both the opportunities and the sanctions for the contemplative side of life.

October 25, 1931 Summer-like temperatures continue to prevail. Skies partly cloudy today. Paul Bender and I dug out our joint crop of sweet potatoes during the past week; twelve and one-half bushels was the total crop. 300 plants of Nancy Hall variety gave five and one-half bushels; 200 of a red variety gave seven bushels in return.

The past week has been one of momentous doing in and about the school. On Tuesday a group of representatives of the Missouri-Kansas Conference met with three representatives of the executive committee of the Board of Education and some from the faculty. There was full discussion of the problem of raising the excess deficit for this year and also of the future of the school. The conference group has made itself responsible for the excess deficit and there seems to be no sentiment at all favorable to the closing of the school. But there are recommendations that next year's program be strictly limited to the actual prospects of demand and means. The matter of organization for the future involves two major points, first, the material reduction of administrative expense and, second, a change in the office of business manager. The last point is in response to widespread opinion and conviction in the constituent territory, especially in the immediate and nearby localities. For us on the inside, it means that within the next three, or four at most, months plans and a program for the next year must be pretty fully laid out and developed. It will be a task requiring a large amount of thinking and of talking.

November 1, 1931 Freezing temperatures were with us both this and yesterday morning, not severe frosts but sufficient to nip some vegetation. Peanuts, carrots are still to be harvested, the former soon, the latter in a month or so. Have had five tons of semi-anthracite coal stored in the cellar, which is to cost $7.50 a ton plus delivery costs. This price is fifty cents a ton less than a year ago.

B. B. King has been preaching at the Pennsylvania Church every evening for two weeks now. We were able to attend twice, a week ago this evening and on the Friday evening before that, once upon invitation of Burkharts and of Benders. Our old Model T has not been on the road for a month and has prospects of enjoying a complete rest, for the winter at least. In the eight years and a half since we bought it new it has had no general overhauling; the motor has never been taken out or repaired. Repairs have been made as they were needed, some of them on occasions of slight accidents and otherwise. I do not use a car as hard as some do, am very considerate of its feelings and wants, try to treat it somewhat as a living thing that will respond to humane and kindly treatment. Perhaps these reasons will explain why it has served us so long and so well. If we should continue to live here, being close enough to my place of work and to our place of Sunday worship to reach them as pedestrians, we would do without a motor car, at least for several years. While to be totally carless is an inconvenience, yet when a car is not absolutely necessary for existence, I should be pleased to make required adjustments and live carless as a part of our program for the simple life. Especially so if our income is not increased over what it has been so far. I am convinced that people are gadding around over the highways of the country entirely too much. I shall make my own protest against this nervous, eternally restless going, going, going, by staying more and more at home. I do want to travel, pay this modicum of respect to the wonders and the beauties of God's creation, if at all the good Lord gives me the means and the opportunity. My ideal is to tour the western United States and Canada, Europe and North Africa, and parts of Asia, not in a high-powered motor car at sixty miles per hour or as a member of a professional tourist party, but leisurely a small part at a time, preferably in the company of a friend or two, and some of it on foot. But it all seems an empty daydream to one who is practically a slave to his food and shelter.

November 4, 1931 Market prices on oil and wheat are moving upward during the past weeks. Some are already hailing the prosperity that is supposed to be returning. Writers in magazines have as a more general rule taken on a restrained and sober attitude toward the conditions of the times. They succeed in writing entertainingly of the "uses of adversity", critically of the predicted increase of leisure time for all laboring men, optimistically of the special reasons and grounds we have this year for thanksgiving when the big chief of the nation by proclamation summons the citizens to render thanks for blessings received.

Have finished gathering out of Suetonius the examples of possessive and demonstrative adjectives. They are now ready to be further studied and digested. Am reading in the writings of Tacitus at present for the instances of the same. The study of this particular phase of word order in Latin will yield also some interesting sidelight on questions of style and rhetoric. It will require considerable study over a period of some time to get data from widely scattered enough sources to give much in the way of final results that will be of permanent value. Have now translated all of the first six Satires of Juvenal. He is a hard author to comprehend in all details and also difficult to translate. Many details are coarse and unchaste. His pessimism overreaches itself at times. I do naturally love satire as a literary method. Horace is so mild as to be almost ineffective at times. Lucian is my favorite. Juvenal is good as an occasional relish.

November 8, 1931 A new book by T. R. Glover is entitled "The World of the New Testament." The author aims at drawing a brief outline picture of the outstanding elements in the life of the first Christian century as a background for an appreciation of the progress and development of the early church. The book is a good one, so far as its main aim and purpose are concerned. The chapter on "The Jew" I do not especially care for. His chapter wherein he discusses the character and work of Alexander the Great presents quite a different picture of that Macedonian than is drawn by H. G. Wells in his "Outline of History." Perhaps a combination of the two viewpoints would give one the truest idea. To me it is a very interesting study to note how the Mediterranean World was prepared politically, socially, religiously and even linguistically for the evangel of the Christ. As a demonstration that God works in history and overrules its developments, that particular fact is outstanding to my mind. It seems to be impossible for any single group of mankind or any one system of culture to maintain a just balance of the various phases of the truth and of life. Each phase of civilization is emphasized and developed by a particular group and its unique concoction is later poured into the general stream of the world's life and culture. The Jews specialized in the monotheistic idea and in the culture of the individual conscience. The Greeks specialized in beauty and in philosophy, the untrammeled progress of ideas and of thought. The Romans developed in particular the material side of life, government, organization, travel facilities and so forth. Some would lament the fact that the Jews were liberalized and Hellenized, especially those of the Diaspora. But it was precisely among those folks who were on the borderline of Hellenism and Judaism that the Christian church secured its first substantial foothold in the world. The study of Paul's missionary activities makes that point clear. It was the strictly orthodox Jews who rejected Christ and His claims to Messiahship.

A question worth studying is that of what influence, if any, did Jewish ideas and thought have upon Greek philosophy. It is well known that the early Church Fathers bluntly claim that the Greek philosophers stole from the Jews all their noble ideas on morals and monotheism. Someone well-equipped to do so should seriously investigate their claims on this point. The early Christian writers were of course pressing the claims of Christianity against the Greeks and might easily seize upon the familiar post hoc, propter hoc argument. Even so it seems hard to think that the claim would be so confidently made without any other objective evidence. The common critical viewpoint about the Old Testament that has been current and, we hope, has about run its course, would date the Old Testament records too late to allow of any influence upon Plato and Aristotle. Some day the question may easily become a live one and of no little importance.

November 16, 1931 There has been rain of late. Four inches in a single stretch fell on last Friday night and Saturday morning. Turnips and endive in the garden are still growing. Leaves on the trees are now falling rapidly. During the week or two past there has been a genuine spectacle of rich and gorgeous coloring on the trees hereabouts. Especially beautiful have been the many rich tints of yellow and gold on the apricot trees. Pear trees about town and the college campus were rich with rose hues and brown. The cherry trees outside our windows have been a Gargantuan feast for the eyes for a week or more. It is not always that the foliage of trees in Kansas is so wonderfully colored as we have seen it this autumn. Even the elm trees have had richly colored leaves the past while. Soon all the trees will stand with naked limbs about us, and the winter season will be upon us.

President S. C. Yoder of Goshen College has already extended invitation to Paul Bender and myself to consider joining the teaching staff at Goshen next year. To accept the invitation will mean replacing other teachers who are presumably entitled to their present positions. It is not pleasant to anticipate such a situation, especially for myself who did not choose to stay there when I was on the staff before. Besides wife and I will be very reluctant in deciding to move back to Indiana. The climate is too damp, too cloudy, not enough sunshine, too much coal smoke and soot in the air at all times, country too thickly settled and cluttered up in general with human specimens and their inventions. Winters are too long and too cold. We do not like Indiana.

November 22, 1931 Damp and murky weather prevail these few days. Unusual for Kansas. No freezing temperatures have visited this section recently. Heavy snow is reported in western Kansas and many western states.

Further thinking upon the contribution of the Jews to the general stream of history suggests the question as to what might be the historical function and purpose of minority groups, often despised and ridiculed, always more or less misunderstood. The Jews were a small nation fenced in by multitudinous religious, social and political restrictions, schooled by bitter experiences to the concept of themselves as a separate and distinctive people with a mission and a destiny of their own. Before their particular contribution was usable in history it had to be mixed with other ingredients. But it is hard to see, knowing that human nature is what it is, how the distinctive ideas and concepts of Judaism could have been preserved and developed into usable form without some such history as theirs was.

So with all minority groups, especially religious groups; in the larger scheme of history their aims are usually irrelevant as ends in themselves, but in order that the essential ideas for which they stand can be fostered and developed at all, their immediate aims and purposes must be promoted as being all-important and final in themselves. This is a paradox that appeals to me as being worthy of thought and further study.

November 27, 1931 (the day after Thanksgiving). Gray days continue with us, snow was falling yesterday and the night before, ground is very wet with snow lying in spots. There has been perhaps as much as six inches of precipitation in November so far, which is said to be four times as much as the normal average rainfall for November. Paul Benders invited us to ride with them to Pennsylvania Church where the Thanksgiving service was held yesterday. We enjoyed Thanksgiving dinner with ourselves this year, unusual because we have for the past several years been having students as guests for dinner on this day.

I have taken up Theocritus for casual reading these days. "The Bucolics," so far as I have read, are interesting. Atlantic Monthly for December has some fine stimulating articles. Ernest Elmo Calkins writes truthful words on the subject "My Country — Right or Wrong?" It is an urgent plea for a broader and a more common-sense attitude toward other nations and races than is fostered by the professional patriots of our country. Another writer expounds in a mock-serious vein on the decline of conversation, pointing out how the spectre of mechanization, mass production, and standardization has all but destroyed the need for an art of conversation. It is all too true. It is a sore grief to myself that I have developed no gift for conversation in social circles. At the same time, many times after observing the general level of such conversation as seems in demand on such occasions, I cannot feel that I have missed very much in being unable to take part. More or less conventionalized small talk, gossip, entertaining talk of doubtful wit and humor, casual bits of information, these seem to be the regular stock-in-trade for conversationalists. The discussion type of conversation, whether serious or trivial, the kind where there is the thrilling clash of wits with dispassionate give and take, the sharpening of ideas and thoughts for the sake of themselves, this style is especially unpopular. Even educated people — so-called — nowadays are too superficial in their general thinking and too greatly specialized in their own line to possess an adequate body of general culture and ideas in common with a group to engage in stimulating discussion with interest and profit. I also suspect that there is another reason why in our own circles we do not develop the free and intimate discussion of ideas. We are afraid to do so. On all fundamental and basic questions we have been schooled into the belief that such questions are not open for thoroughgoing discussion pro and con. We are afraid to look at carefully and actually handle ideas that we hold to be erroneous or unorthodox. We are on this point more solicitous for our reputation among our fellows than we are for maintaining the integrity and the intellectual honesty of our own souls. I feel in my own soul frequently the sharp pangs of a hunger for radical and fundamental discussion of sundry ideas. I surmise that merely to ruminate these ideas with myself is a very inadequate test and does not go very far in clarifying and refining my own thoughts. But so few and far between are the individuals who are interested in ideas for their own sake alone that it seems hopeless to expect ever to have opportunity to develop the art of basic and frank discussion.

November 29, 1931 Continued gray skies, humidity and mild temperature. Reminds us of Indiana days.

In the North American Review of last July Mr. Frank E. Gaebelein published a common-sense article "An Evangelical's Defence." To this Dr. Harry Elmer Barnes replied in the October issue under the title "Throwing Dust." Dr. Barnes intended that his chosen title should apply to the efforts of Mr. Gaebelein in his article, but to me it seemed much more truthfully to describe the efforts of the article at the head of which it stood. It contained the usual mixture of flippancy, half-truths, false assumptions, exaggerated and extreme generalizations, ridicule and, in this case, mild contempt and pity. A rejoinder to this effort is printed in the same Review for December from Mr. Gaebelein. It is an unapologetic, quite restrained and eminently fair reply, pointing out false assumptions and unsound reasoning in the article by Dr. Barnes. In reading such discussion it becomes very evident that the differences at issue are more deep-seated and basic than can readily be settled by logic and argument. There are basic assumptions and fundamental prejudices, if one may call them such, at the bottom of the widely divergent philosophies of such men as Barnes and Gaebelein. To me it is a forceful reminder of the definite delimitation of the human mind, and of the resulting corollary, that to make human reason and intelligence the final measure and tribunal of truth is unsafe. Amid the multiplied knowledge of our time, it requires the effort of a lifetime to master one field of knowledge or one particular viewpoint. It is practically impossible that there will be another Aristotle who will synthesize for us once more all knowledge into a dynamic system of thought. The field is too vast. Nevertheless each age has as its intellectual atmosphere a phase of a prevailing philosophy which colors and influences all thinking. Of the influence of the current philosophic mode or fashion no one can be entirely free; at the same time it seems clear that to keep an independent viewpoint, to develop a critical attitude toward modes of thought, would give one a truer perspective, a perception of truth that is nearer correct than is possible for those who are completely "sold" on the current mode. As Mennonites with four and perhaps more centuries of nonconformist blood running in our veins, with traditions that are more or less radical and independent, we should be in a position to contribute something constructive to the stream of the world's thought. Not to reform and direct this stream, but to do a small bit of good in that direction. To this end some few should dedicate themselves to the enormous and lifetime task of getting an understanding of world literature, history, and thought, of developing a style of expression, and of interpreting to the world at large the ideas and ideals that are our heritage. Too many in the past have cast off their heritage after the first or second draught of learning. Others, to arm themselves against such an issue, have adopted the closed-mind attitude.

December 2, 1931 An old bit of weather lore that I frequently heard at home was to the effect that the weather conditions of the first three days of December are prophetic of the general weather for the three winter months. Assuming that this bit of lore is truth, we may well look for a moderate and sunny average of weather during the coming months. The mornings have been chilly and very frosty, the rime lying thick on ground and limb and roof. The sunshine this week is so good. It seems glorious and golden after four continuous days last week in which no sun appeared. The present year of grace is swiftly drawing toward its close.

When a month ago the market price of wheat, oil, butter, and some other commodities were climbing upward, as were also stocks, there was much premature jubilation over the return of prosperity. The gains have in large part been lost again in recent weeks and respectful silence reigns again in the camp of the watchful waiters. If everyone would try with all might to forget at once all about prosperity, and would reconcile his mind to the present as a new status quo, there would be more happiness of mind, less senseless ballyhoo about depression, and a quicker and less painful adjustment to the conditions of the new day.

December 5, 1931 Some necessary fall work in garden and grounds is being much belated. Usually about the time of Thanksgiving, we gather in carrots, turnips, clean off the garden ground preparatory to plowing again. For two weeks the surface of the ground has been wet and sticky, slightly frozen on top some mornings, and impossible to work on. The frequent rain and snow of the past few weeks have given me some concern as to my opportunities for out-of-door exercise during the coming winter months. It seems easily possible that the surface of the ground may be wet much of the time this winter, in which case walking over the open fields and along out-of-the-way country roads will not be as pleasant a form of recreation as it has been some winters. Last winter especially was open and dry underfoot until in

March, making hiking a real pleasure nearly all the while. The men of the faculty are again playing volley ball for physical exercise, but I have not yet received the consent of my mind to join with them for mine. I have no clothing and shoes suitable for playing in the gymnasium, and do not feel disposed to spend money for any at this time. We have joined the money spenders' strike and are paying out only what cash is very necessary. So far we have been able since about July to make thirty dollars per month cover our regular cash supplies and necessary incidental expenses. We have had constantly much of our food supplies from the garden, which will be getting less from this time on. We pay cash in hand for all supplies we buy, having never gotten into the practice of buying on charge accounts. We buy in quantities as much as we can and also where we can get the most for our money. We have never reconciled ourselves to buying everything in the stores in Hesston. Somehow my home town loyalty has never been strong enough to induce me to pay anywhere from five to twenty-five per cent as tribute to local dealers just for the sake of exercising it. We even send to mail order houses for some things, items that are either not obtainable at all in the small stores or are unnecessarily high in price. Brown rice, for example, is kept in stock by hardly any stores. The drug store man in our town sells Russian mineral oil for one dollar a pint bottle and informs me that it is not possible to obtain the genuine article from dependable supply houses for less than this regular price. Nonetheless we bought from Ward's last July a gallon can of this oil, that fully suits our need, for about $2.90. I have stopped paying tribute to so many different makers of soaps by no longer paying twenty-five cents for a bar of shampoo soap and thirty-five cents for a tube of shaving cream. We buy good quality toilet soap at about eight cents a bar (still perhaps twice as much as should be necessary) and use it for all purposes, including shaving and shampooing hair, with results entirely satisfactory.

December 6, 1931 Six or more years ago the Sunday School at this place pledged itself to support Miss Ada Hartzler as a missionary in India. The annual amount required is $450 and has been raised by holding special offerings in each class on the first Sunday of every month. For two years past the S. S. has been steadily and persistently falling short in raising the required monthly amount. With today we are inaugurating a renewed determination and a more specialized plan for contributing the required sum every month. A suggested quota has been set for each class and department in the school. This provides the class with a definite goal and an incentive for doing its approximate share in this missionary support. The contributions today totalled more than forty-four dollars which seems to indicate that the new plan will work out very well. Most of the classes went "over the top"; only three of the young people's classes failed to make their respective quotas.
I am personally very much in favor of regularly giving something as a form of religious exercise and worship. It should be something, no matter whether the amount is small or large. It is a matter that needs to be put across to the young disciples of each successive

generation. I recall that from the time I was entitled to my own earnings I made it a regular habit to contribute to all regular and to most special offerings. At first I believe my offering was a quarter dollar, even when I was attending school and could not see where I would have enough funds for discharging all my accounts at the end of the year. A little later the regular amount of my gift was fifty cents or a dollar. After I began teaching, wife and I tried to follow the plan of giving away for all different purposes approximately a tenth of our gross income each year. This included all forms of bequests, missions, church support, charity, educational endowment, and so on. Without keeping a strict ledger account on the matter we aimed to make sure that our gifts totalled at least a tithe of our income. During the three years that I studied in universities, we did not follow that plan, because I was borrowing funds and paying interest. The past few years we have been helping what we feel we can, although we do not give one-tenth of our income. I have figured partly on the fact that our cash income is in reality counted as a living allowance only, and that from the standpoint of my assumed earning power, I have been regularly contributing from one to two thousand dollars a year to the schools in which I have served, particularly since I have been the holder of the doctor's degree.

We have not been able to make any advance in financial matters, considering the favorable circumstances under which we began our venture in making a home. Father advanced us five thousand dollars when we were married. He did not do all this immediately from the first, but had me sign a note for twenty-five hundred dollars of it at a low rate of interest, four per cent, I believe it was. Fifteen months later he sent me the note, marked paid, and also returned one hundred dollars which I had paid as interest. He stated he did not care to pay tax on the note as credit when I was paying tax on the property in which it was invested. With the five thousand we paid for the house and one lot, forty-four hundred, and for furnishings for the same. The two or three hundred dollars I had on hand at the time of our marriage we spent for our honeymoon trip, from Springs, Pennsylvania to Washington, D. C., Norfolk, Virginia, New York City, Lake Placid, New York, Niagara Falls, Kalona, Iowa, and finally Hesston, Kansas. Mrs. Yoder had several hundred in saving which was applied to house furnishings. During the first three years we fared well enough even on an income of nine hundred to one thousand dollars, having no rent or interest to pay. Every year we had some income from our upstairs rooms rented to student boys. Mrs. Yoder also did a little washing for students. Each summer I worked some at harvesting and threshing. When 1923 came and all our plans were set to spend some time away in study, we spent nearly four hundred dollars for a new Ford touring car to replace the old one which Father had given me four years before. Also sold our furniture to Mr. Driver who rented our house. I think the consideration was either four hundred or four hundred fifty dollars, payable in monthly payments during the following school year.

With my taking up residence successively at three universities, our finances began to go in the reverse direction. During the first summer, spent at Boulder, Colorado, we spent all the balance of our cash savings. The school year of 1923-24 we lived practically on the money received for our furniture and the rent from the house. Estie also earned considerable cash by doing house work, typing correspondence for S. C. Yoder, and other small typing jobs. For the second year I borrowed some money from Father, until Mrs. Yoder secured a position as dictaphone typist in an office in Iowa City. In 1925, when we set out on our pilgrimage to the City of Philadelphia, I obtained some more money from Father. In October Mrs. Yoder secured office work which supported us fairly well until in August, 1926. For three weeks she worked in an office down town, and thereafter for the Westinghouse Company in their office building at thirty and Walnut streets. During the two years at Goshen College we fared fairly well on an income of $1500 a year, where in addition I taught in summer school one summer and Estie addressed envelopes for Kunderd and Sons seven weeks. I paid back to Father $250 during this time, paid out near $250 for the publication of my thesis, and completed my graduation. Unlooked for expense during our second year there required approximately $500 for hospital, surgeon's and medical fees. To finance our move back to Kansas in 1928 and again refurnish our home, I borrowed $500 from D. H. Bender. I had three years earlier borrowed $250 from him also. With less income here than at Goshen, we have not been able to pay anything on our notes so far. Besides in 1930 we secured a further loan of $1000 by placing a mortgage on our house that was given to us ten years before.

December 7, 1931 As financiers we have no very attractive record to show up to this our twelfth year of homemaking. A mortgage is on our home that was essentially given to us at the first. The general deflation has decreased its assumed value to a degree, still with the addition of more than $1200 in improvements it is measureably more livable and also saleable, and should be reckoned as actually worth more than when we acquired it. We were unfortunate as to our choice of time for setting up housekeeping. Too much was paid for the house itself. Within sixty days after we had purchased our furniture of Mr. Sprinker in Newton, he announced an all round reduction of prices to the extent of twenty-five per cent. This year we had anticipated to liquidate at least one-half of our mortgage, when along came a drastic reduction in even our small allowance which mars our plans on that point. In September, 1933, it will all be due. Even so we could still have a slight hope of getting along by very rigid economy, if we were sure we could continue at all to live in our home which we have improved and made thus comfortable. Shall we be forced to move, the chances to sell the place or even rent it at any reasonable figure is sure to be small for some time to come. Thus we — that is my good wife and myself together — have contributed to the cause of higher education to the Mennonite Church twelve years of our active lives in return for our living, besides a good deal of invested cash. Still we can honestly say, I believe, it has been given gladly and we are willing to face the coming years trusting God who has been good to us.

December 12, 1931 This has been a hectic week again. A boy in school was caught stealing money from the library, walking into a trap especially laid for him. He is under suspicion for other thefts, but refuses to admit his guilt. Besides, he claims a special religious experience since being apprehended, in which he has made all things right with God, has been forgiven, etc. Many mysteries remain as yet; other boys have been questioned carefully, to the confirmation of their innocence.

Much cloudy weather still continues to prevail — much for Kansas, at any rate. The sun did shine yesterday all day long. The weather man predicts rain or snow for today again.

O. O. Miller of Pennsylvania will be about the College today for conferences on school matters. No light seems yet to be clearly dawning on the problem of plans and program for next year for this place. No one on the staff here wishes to assume such a prerogative as to pronounce the death sentence on any part of our institution, the school that has such a large place in the affections and interests of us all. Yet perhaps the most urgent need is for someone here with enough courage to advocate the things that the circumstances seem to call for. Eight and nine years ago it was Noah Oyer who, while a member of the faculty here and himself with no prospect of ever being anywhere else at the time, worked for the reduction of Hesston College from an unaccredited four-year school to an accredited junior college; but rather than a reduction, this move should properly be called an advancement. We of this time are all too timid and perhaps cowardly to promote a program that involves readjustments of a radical nature. So far we have only made such readjustments as were forced upon us by the absolute circumstances of the moment. Result has been that we have been just one year behind continuously in our planning. Now is the time to catch up with the times we are in and face squarely the situation we are in with our schools. For my part I still refuse to believe that we will swiftly swing back to economic inflation again. The great boom period of inflation that closed with 1929 was an entirely abnormal period and when all around adjustments have been once made, things will go along more smoothly, but will not be so ready to return to a state of inflation. Not unless President Hoover's program for numerous immense and increased credit projects will again induce an unnatural inflation. There is too much credit in the world today for soundness of life in general. Perhaps with the massing of wealth in the hands of a few it is inevitable that credit should be a major part of our economic life today. It is another and a slightly different phase of the age-old slavery question. Every form of credit extension is basically a form of enslavement over other individuals.

December 21, 1931   There are scores, if not hundreds of books I would like much to buy for my library, but low funds have forced us to put off buying books. Even so, as a matter of principle, I selected with almost painful care and deliberation and with a strange mixture of emotions a small number of books to get. Have in the past month ordered a number of Latin authors and others. I find it is an advantageous time to order books sent from England now. Bills come from there with the shilling rated at eighteen cents, making a saving of about one-fourth net due to differences in exchange. I like to order Latin and Greek texts from Blackwell at Oxford, as it is often possible to obtain second-hand copies of such authors there. Received several new books which I ordered from Stechert in New York. These were sent from their London office and bill came marked with London prices. Blackwell sent me a catalog of several thousand second-hand items on Greek and Roman antiquities; of several dozen that I wanted I ordered four or five. If what I ordered were not previously sold, they will be here in about two weeks more. I wish to get one or two of the one dollar books that are on sale, have been for a year or more, books that were first sold for three, five, or more dollars each. I have bought several of these, "Outline of History," "Mother India," "Story of Philosophy." During 1929 I was foolish enough to maintain membership in the Book-of-the-Month Club. Three of the books that I paid from $2.50 to $3.50 for (I only took five during the whole year) can now be gotten for one dollar each, namely, Ludwig's "Napoleon," Hackett's "Henry the Eighth," and Dimnet's "Art of Thinking." I have quit buying new books, no matter how highly commended, because almost certainly as surely as they are really good books it will be possible to purchase them for a fraction of the first publication price before many years after.

Christmas Day – This has been a quiet day at home for Estie and me. Our Christmas service was held at the college yesterday evening, a conjoint meeting with the folks of the neighboring Pennsylvania Church. A new feature of this year's service was that of each family taking along some gift of food or clothing for needy people in the community. There must have been near a thousand pounds of stuff brought in. Some young men distributed the baskets by motor truck after the service and another group of young people followed to sing Christmas Carols. A fine custom! The day has been beautiful, sky almost perfectly clear, genial sunshine, mild temperature. I seem to recall that on Christmas Day last year the weather was rather chilly and cloudy, for I spent some hours hiking, starting at sometime before dawn and getting home at nine o'clock, or barely in time to get ready for the morning service. Two years ago I can well remember, for I with four boys of a quartet ate a splendid dinner at the home of Art Herman's in Milford, Nebraska. We were on a tour among the Mennonite churches of Nebraska and Colorado, giving programs of music.

Fortunately or unfortunately we spent very little money as our share of the seasonal merrymaking this year. There appears to be so much nonsense and sacrilege in connection with the common ways of celebrating the season that we have little taste for it. We spent nothing for decorations for our home, gave away as gifts some few items from things we had on hand, and sent away a few greeting cards. "Aunt Ida" from Parnell, Iowa visited us for a short hour this afternoon. She is well and happy, has been a widow for about thirty years, and has been hard of hearing for longer than that.

James Truslow Adams in Atlantic Monthly writes a stimulating article on the apparent failure of democracy as it has been worked out in England and United States. Among other points made, he mentions the fact that universal ability to read, write and do sums is not at all a guarantee of the ability to think intelligently on the very complex and complicated political issues that confront governments in this day and generation. Another fact is that apparently the universal public schools that were intended to prepare an intelligent electorate in our democracy have very largely betrayed and prostituted their opportunities by inculcating and instilling a narrow and selfish nationalistic attitude of mind into the young, instead of a wholesome attitude of world-wide goodwill and fellowship, sympathy and cooperation. For myself, I have never had any decided conviction that I was at all qualified to exercise my right as a citizen to vote in state and national elections. I have not sufficient knowledge of political science to form an independent opinion on political issues on the merits of the questions themselves. To blindly vote a particular party ticket because someone else does or has done so, is not good citizenship in any sense. To vote for individual persons, because they happen to be able, honest, likable men, and ignore political principles and issues is equally as bad. As I have also never taken the time and the pains to try to understand political issues in all their implications, I have from that viewpoint alone never felt justified in taking part in blindly casting votes at election times. Religiously also our group of Mennonites have sometimes mildly and sometimes strongly urged against participation in "politics" even to the extent of voting. It seems to be a part of the "separation from the world," as this is interpreted by some.

December 26, 1931 A strong south wind has prevailed during this entire day. Luckily it is not very cold. Our little house lets the wind pass through it only somewhat less readily than a sieve. A house in this wind-swept country should be built with special pains and the use of specific insulating material to keep out wind and cold in winter and heat in summer.

Tomorrow we study in Sunday School the concluding lesson of a very highly interesting series taken mostly from the book of the Acts and having extended over about six months of time. The beauty and the compactness of Luke's writing have impressed me very much again in these studies. There has been kindled for me a strong desire to study as I may have opportunity the general life of society of the first century in order to enjoy a still fuller appreciation of the narrative of the Acts and of Paul's Epistles. Few things, too, would afford me more satisfaction than an opportunity at some time to assist in some kind of archaeological work in New Testament lands. It is too much to hope for, I realize full well, but still one needs his pet dreams and anticipations to use at times in relieving spells of monotony, though not many such come to one with plenty of work to do.

Am at present reading Quintilian for the possessive and demonstrative adjectives that he uses. I should in the course of the next six or eight months have carried this particular subject far enough forward to leave it rest in my extensive manuscripts of notes, lists, and comparisons, at least for some time. There are other projects that I wish to take up for intensive study in turn.

December 27, 1931 One blessing of this time of depression is that it forces numbers of people to do some serious reflecting, makes many scrutinize more than casually their plans, ideals, and purposes in life. As someone has lately expressed it: we have come to the place where we must challenge every assumption we have been in the habit of using in the past with such confidence. And not only our assumptions, but all the formulae and slogans that have served us heretofore need to be criticized anew.

A thought that comes to myself at times is on the matter of what I could do for a livelihood, in case I would be unable to obtain a teaching position. I cannot believe that I made a fundamental mistake in deciding to go to school and devote my life to intellectual work instead of staying on the farm, as had been the wish of my parents for me. The vision was too clear and the conviction in my mind too burning and positive to pronounce it all a delusion. My natural interest and aptitude was early in books and studies. I received my diploma from the eighth grade when fifteen years old. Had always read everything I could lay my hands on. Father used to buy some books for the home library occasionally. I started on a home study course once from Highland Park College of Des Moines, but did not get very far with it. As I would criticize it now, it was very badly put up for home study. I think it was a normal course to prepare one to pass county teachers' examinations. I had more success, in some subjects at least, by getting regular high school texts and studying these for myself. I worked my way about halfway through a high school algebra; also studied a text on rhetoric and composition. I did a good deal of free lance Bible study, and later, about 1914, finished a course of home study from Moody Bible Institute of Chicago. In 1912 I conceived the idea of trying to teach country school. In January of that year I took the examinations at Iowa City and secured a third class certificate. In June I spent a week in Iowa City attending teachers' institute and in the fall I tried a two-month's session of country school. It was a failure, mostly because I was not prepared in any special way for the work. Father refused to let me go to school, either at the Iowa City Academy or at Goshen College, and when I came of age, he again warned me against getting any notion of attending college into my head. Unfortunately the notion was already there and thoroughly ingrained besides. I reached my majority in July, 1914, and already then had all my plans laid to enter Hesston Academy the following January. Then in September I underwent an operation for hernia which took from me most of my earnings of the summer and fall which I had counted on to start my school course. But my determination was so strongly fixed that I refused to give up my plans, even though I had not enough money to see me through to the end of the school year.

[Edward's 1915 diary tells each day what tasks he performed living on the farm in Johnson County, Iowa. From it the following:]

January 27, 1915 Packed up and made preparations for leaving for Hesston, Kansas. Father took me to Kalona in the afternoon. Left Kalona at 5:20 p.m., arrived at Nichols at 6:30. Left Nichols at 9:00 and arrived at Columbus Junction at 9:30.
January 28, 1915 Waited at Columbus Junction until 4:00 a.m. Train was four hours late. Temperature was twenty degrees

below zero. Crossed the line into Missouri at about 10:00 a.m. Arrived at Kansas City at 3:30 p.m., being six hours late. Took a walk up to the business part of town and back. Took a Santa Fe for Newton, Kansas at 9:40 p.m. Slept some on train.

January 29, 1915 Arrived at Newton at 3:00 a.m. Went to bed and slept till eight. Got some breakfast. Hunted up the Missouri Pacific station. Left Newton at 10:30 and arrived at Hesston at about 11:00 a.m. Went to the Academy and registered in the academic department.

And so I came to start my academic career. I know almost positively that I would have been a failure as a farmer on my own responsibility, because I never took an interest in the work on the farm, used to sit in the house reading or studying books every chance opportunity that I had, even when there was work to do out-of-doors. But my father always took a kindly and Christian attitude toward my plans, after it came to the point where he saw I meant to carry them out. For several years he sent me some money each spring to come home with, paid me good wages during the summer months and helped me in very many ways. At the end of my Academy course he even offered to return to me all the money I had paid out during the two years and a half I had been in school, on the condition that I return to the farm and take my place as a Sunday school and church worker at the Lower Deer Creek Church, a place that was just then emerging from the status of an Old Order Amish congregation and was looking for aggressive workers. Again I had to turn my back on the offer and the opportunity and face the hard prospect of making my way through college and later through university. Looking over all these experiences and knowing my own aptitudes, I cannot believe that any other course, radically different, would have been of the leading of God. All this gives me faith and courage to believe that He will continue to lead us as we face the future.

January 2, 1932 The new year came to us yesterday with cold and cloudy skies. Today there was sunshine and higher temperature again. Hope springs eternal in the human breast. Papers reported that multitudes in the large cities joined in the ceremony of booing out the old year of 1931 with its gloom and depression. Everyone seems to be looking for better performance on the part of the new year, 1932. With the question still unanswered, whether the worst of the depression is over, and with a presidential election in the offing, the year before us promises well to be at least interesting. If only the actual want and suffering that exists in this country could be equally distributed among all the citizens, its effect would be entirely wholesome and might profitably last for a time longer. I am still of the opinion that nothing could be more beneficial for the people of the United States than a continuation and an intensification of the economic crisis to the point where the majority of the people are thoroughly cured of our chronic success-worshipping, egotistic, business-minded superiority complexes. One can only regret the suffering that is entailed in the readjustment process, and yet one feels a lurking suspicion that our self-pity for what we imagine is suffering is a very watery affair, being more a flimsy sentiment than a common-sense courageous attitude of soul.

I am reminded that Estie and I spent New Year's Day four years ago in the Elkhart, Indiana Hospital recovering from the removal of tonsils. It was a very cold, stormy and snowy day. The cherished vacation days are nearly spent again with increased work and toil ahead for several weeks to come. Am expected to teach a class in Special Bible Term three times a week for the six weeks. There will also be the work of getting courses, schedules, registration and other details mapped out for the second semester.

On last Wednesday (December 30) a number of the faculty here went to Hillsboro to attend the annual meeting of what is known as the Mennonite Teachers' Convention. Meeting was held in the Mennonite Brethren Church with a rather live program and interest. I presented a short discussion on the subject, "What the Old Mennonite Conference Is Doing to Prepare Its Youth to Meet the War Problem." Also gave my name to be elected as a member of the organization, which seems to be a rather loose and informal affair, largely to foster fellowship and understanding between the several groups of Mennonites in this immediate section of Kansas. The atmosphere of frank and open discussion was very congenial to myself; no one was afraid to express individual opinions, regardless of their effect.

January 4, 1932 It has been said that man is incurably religious by his nature. And when it happens that the current fashion is to discredit reasonable and historical religion, then men and women are found to turn in large numbers to superstition of various sorts. This fact goes to show that people cannot live without religious faith in their lives, or if not some religious faith, then its equivalent. With some, pretty sure to be always a minority, atheism and anti-religious sentiment seems to take the place of reasonable and normal religion, at least for a time. With others the pronouncements of fortune-tellers, astrologers, crystal-gazers and their like are a substitute for religious faith in their vacuous souls. A recent article in a popular magazine tells of the incredible popularity of these occult arts, especially astrology, numerology, and such like. The revival of these superstitions appears to have grown out of the spiritistic craze of a decade ago. Many millions of dollars are spent at present annually for such hocus-pocus by intelligent people of all ranks of society, from U. S. Senators, State Governors on down to the humblest artisan and toiler. It appears also that the revival of these superstitions coincides in part with the decay of vital evangelical Christianity, the religion that is a personal and a real affair, entering into the daily problems of life and experience. The doctrines of divine guidance and the Holy Spirit-led life are probably ridiculed as folly by the same persons who consult astrologers and necromancers. Yet to one who has experienced the life of Christ and the personal guidance of the Holy Spirit, these folks appear as poor dupes.

January 7, 1932 Matters regarding next year's plans for the school are getting into action of late, with good prospects that there will be some movement and action within the six weeks next to come. A general representative meeting is called for ten days hence. The executive committee of Missouri-Kansas Conference is sponsoring the project. It is to be representative of all Mennonite constituency west of the Mississippi River, which is the theoretical, more than the actual eastward boundary of Hesston College territory. The Hesston alumni representatives of the Mennonite Board of Education are shaking things up by mailing to most of the alumni lengthy statements of the crisis the school is in and an appeal for opinions as to plans and policies for the future. The time of the year is here for things to begin moving in some direction.

Have reflected frequently of late on what it apparently costs one to attain standing and repute in our Mennonite Church circles. The price set for such desiderata is high enough, in fact, quite too high for some to be able to pay it. Among the things included in this price that is set for popularity, is that of saying about what people desire to hear, saying these things in the generally accepted words and phrases, and saying them with the precise relative emphasis that is conventional and orthodox at the moment. A certain modicum of adaptation of oneself to the psychosis of the group that one desires to lead is undeniably essential. But it may be questioned whether the mere aspiration to be a well-liked leader of people is a legitimate ambition. My ideal rather is to serve; first to serve God and be used to help others, second to serve others by helping them to what is God's will for them as being also the best thing for people, whether such service renders one popular or the reverse. I have made a rather interesting observation from my own experience. In 1928, at the time we were planning to move back to Hesston, some months before we actually came on the scene after an absence of five years, I received notice that I was to serve on the program of the Workers' Conference in connection with the Missouri-Kansas Church Conference. The topic was one of those rather stereotyped kinds that have been in great favor in this district for some time, something about one's individual responsibility in upholding the faith of our fathers. I gave an informal talk as I could, treating it as I sincerely thought of it myself. I was scarcely aware that what I said was not according to the usual pattern with the precise vocables and the niceties of emphasis that those desire who are especially interested in that line of thought. Three brethren took the pains and trouble later to speak to me in commendatory wise on what I had said. They were M. D. Landis, Allen Erb and E. A. Miller, men whose opinions I value much because they think for themselves. One of these also volunteered the information that some had expressed themselves as having been disappointed in what was said on the topic. At any rate the ideas I gave out on that occasion were evidently entirely and completely satisfying, so much so that I have not been called upon to speak on such a conference program since. I congratulate myself on my efficiency, so far as that goes, for I always find it more or less an ordeal to speak before a large audience.

One is made to wonder whether this psychosis that makes many good folks reduce orthodoxy and religious truth to certain set and fixed formulae is not an escape mechanism to conscientiously avoid the hard and exacting task of thinking for themselves. I recall reading a statement years ago to the effect that there is scarcely any length to which people will not go to avoid the hard labor of thinking. One could write a long satire, I imagine, on the complacent smugness of large numbers of church people in their churchgoing and religious performances. Apparently many go to church and to conferences, not to get new knowledge and truth and vision, but to have their ears tickled periodically by the very familiar music of time-worn words, phrases, and ideas given out with that soothing and comfortable emphasis which they somehow feel is orthodoxy and good form religiously. Any slight shift of emphasis, all new and unusual terms or suggestive ideas strike upon their ears as terrible discords. It frightens them seemingly to be even slightly jarred out of their comfortable and unthinking security, and faced with the prospect of thinking something out for themselves. While many doubtless are incapable of thinking things through in religion, yet it is unquestionably true that numbers could do so if their spiritual leaders would force them to it occasionally instead of merely patting them on the back for the sake of their own popularity.

January 10, 1932 Much cloudy weather continues to prevail, although not continuously. The chariot of Phoebus, whenever his genial rays are not intercepted by murky clouds, is greatly appreciated by Kansans on those days when his splendor brightens the earth and cheers the heart of man.

The six-weeks Bible Term is on with an enrollment of fifteen students, a few less than it has been in recent years. I teach a class three times a week during this term. I do not enjoy the teaching of Bible courses; it is the ancient languages that I want to teach, the only courses I am prepared to give with confidence and enjoyment. Administrative work of various kinds will be rather strenuous during the next three or four weeks, another species of effort that I cannot relish.

Books I had ordered from Blackwell at Oxford on December 4 reached me on January 7; they include the three-volume Teubner edition of Lucian's works by Jacobitz, and the book on "Six Greek Sculptors" by Gardner. These are all second-handed; the two or three other items I had ordered from the same list had been previously sold. That is one disadvantage for getting second-hand items from special lists where one is two weeks away from the store. I have ordered two books by Dill sent new because the prices quoted for them were reasonable and with the further gain due to difference in exchange, it seems about the best opportunity there would soon be to obtain these volumes which I have long wanted. This must about conclude the list of books for which I can spare the cash at this time, for about another year, perhaps.

January 23, 1932 The press of duties and business has been much during the past two weeks. Spent last Sunday and Monday on a flying trip to Milford, Nebraska. Four of us in a Ford motor car, C. A. Vogt, P. Erb, myself, and E. Buckwalter as driver left Hesston on Sunday at 11:15 and at 5:00 p.m. reached Milford. Roads were sloppy here and became worse farther northward. We began to see a little snow beside the road less than twenty miles northwest from here; in northern Kansas fields were covered but the highway was bare; upon entering Nebraska the road was itself covered with snow and ice with approximately a foot of snow covering the fields. Mr. Buckwalter is a highly skilled driver. In spite of water, snow and ice he made the entire trip without a chain on a wheel. The distance registered to Milford was 247 miles and the total time for the trip was five and three-quarters hours. The return trip was made on Monday night in the same time almost to the minute, leaving the Mennonite Church near Milford at 7:30 p.m. and arriving home at 1:15 a.m. It was a most delightful trip, a brief and pleasant excursion into the midst of winter. The drive at night was charming, as snow-covered fields sped by the car, lying as they did in the soft moonlight. I performed the task of reading a paper at the Sunday evening meeting at the Mennonite Church while in Nebraska. Spent Sunday night at the home of Henry Stauffers. On Monday was held a full day of conference and discussion about Hesston College matters.

January 24, 1932 Here we are in the midst of another delicious and perfectly "scrumptious" winter Sunday afternoon. Bright sunshine, mild temperature, no wind to speak of and the afternoon at home. My own personal "den" at the head of the longer part of the stairway is very comfortable and cheery on such afternoons with the sun coming in from the west. Last winter we kept the door of the den closed nearly all of the time, thinking it would save much heat. But so far this winter it has been open continuously, excepting on a few of the very coldest nights, and it seems to require but very little heat. The lady of the house has taken the liberty to keep a few house plants in "my den," which also adds its bit to the cheeriness of the place.

The principal upshot of the discussion and deliberation at Milford, Nebraska, on last Monday was on two points: naming two candidates for president of Hesston College and Bible School, and a recommendation that the Junior College be temporarily suspended, unless a sufficient demand is evident to warrant its operation. The last proviso leaves an essential point still undecided for several weeks to come, or until some sort of a survey can be made as to the college prospects for next September. Scarcely anyone who has faced and studied the present situation and the prospects for a time of three months or more has any real hope that the Junior College can operate for next year. Those who are just now for the first time facing the predicament, both among students and alumni, are experiencing the same reaction that some others of us felt a year and more ago when such a prospect first came before us, that is that we cannot possibly see any part of the school closed. But longer reflection and contemplation has made many willing to submit to what seems inevitable now. For my own part, it seems that there is one proposition still that we have refused to face, in spite of all our talk about facing squarely all the facts; it is the question whether there is a real bona fide need for a school, especially a college, in the west for our group of conferences; whether it is not possible that Hesston College has fulfilled its mission; whether conditions in the educational world and in our own church have not changed enough from ten and fifteen years ago to warrant a change of policy and program on the part of the Mennonite Board of Education. I have no answer, but I feel it is a question that bears study and thought. So far as the present stress of circumstances is concerned, especially as conditions in the educational world stand, Goshen College's future prospects are but little brighter than Hesston's. Things can happen rapidly and conditions change quickly in our time. But it seems evident that unless Goshen can rally a united support and meet requirements for accreditment by the North Central Association of Colleges within a comparatively short time, its years as a four-year college are practically numbered. If there were a united support on a program for an accredited college, it would be easily possible, but as sentiment is now divided, one needs the faith of a grain of mustard seed to see it done.

January 30, 1932 I must write out and deliver a lecture on the subject, "Biblical Archaeology," about ten days hence. I have adopted the policy of always writing out in full and reading from manuscript every formal presentation of any subject, if it is at all more than five or ten minutes long. With the steadily increasing amount of administrative work that has been coming upon me during the past fifteen or sixteen months, I find my distaste for it growing more decided. As a subordinate official I do not find a minimum amount of such work unpleasant, but this unfortunate situation which has shunted upon me chief responsibility, of leadership as well as of routine business, makes me so keenly conscious of my unfitness for such responsibility, of a sense of failure, of a growing and ever-present feeling of frustration, and of an uneasy conscience because of not giving more of my time and effort to work that I am definitely trained and gifted to do, which I love to do and know from experience that I can do with some measure of success. The unforeseen and disappointing trend of circumstances, doubtless providential as may appear at some time, is responsible for the situation in this respect. When four years ago, I was debating the question of staying on at Goshen College or returning to Hesston, the picture I spread before my mental eyes of the work and the opportunities at Hesston College was quite different from what I have found it during these years. My idea, as I can recall it now, was that D. H. Bender as president would have the responsibility of leadership in general and I would work under him, doing mostly routine office work and use the opportunity for developing myself in the direction of personal contact work with young people. Furthermore just at the moment the plan and program for the new Bible-College course was being put forth and painted in glowing colors. I felt that the opportunity to teach Greek, and perhaps eventually Hebrew in such a course was better than training young people to teach Latin in high schools. Other factors that figured in was a sort of an idealized memory of early days at Hesston, the fact that we still owned our house here, and liked the country and climate better than we did in Indiana, and besides the numerous personal requests, pleas, entreaties that I return and help with the administrative part of the work here. Such entreaties came personally from D. H. Bender, M. A. Yoder, Paul Erb, and indirectly Paul Bender.

But scarcely had I done with the painful process of tearing loose from the Goshen faculty and moving to Kansas under great difficulties, when my disillusionment began. And it has been going on to this day, with prospects that it will soon be complete. One thing that I had not made allowance for in my calculations was the manner and the extent to which I had changed myself, in viewpoint, experience, judgment, and perspective, and also in taste. Another sorry disillusionment was with reference to the much-lauded Bible-College course. Verbal and printed reports at the time trumpeted abroad a great demand for this course. For three years a number were registered in the course and six persons completed the course, but this year only one student is enrolled and he is taking mostly regular college subjects. The demand was partly an artificially-formed one and seems to have totally died away to date.

While there has been disappointment in many respects, still we have been happy and feel well repaid in other ways for our return to Kansas. We love our home, especially since we have improved it further, and the Kansas sunshine and the wide open plains. If we must leave our home here in the near future, we do very much hope that we may find it possible to stay in Kansas. Estie would much love to go still further south where winters are yet shorter and milder. For myself, I feel that with the almost certain retrenchment in program in the school here that is in prospect, it is undoubtedly the divinely appointed moment for me to wash my hands clean of all and sundry administrative positions, at least, of all positions involving responsibilities of general leadership and initiative. My turn of mind is for individual independence, and too close articulation with a system or a machine is too cramping and confining for my taste.

January 31, 1932 Our coldest weather of the winter to date has been upon us the past few days. Two degrees above zero Fahrenheit was given as yesterday's lowest by the evening daily from Newton.

Japan is evidently taking full advantage of the embarrassment and the handicaps which the economic depression has placed upon the Occidental nations to promote her own pet plans for empire and expansion. Yesterday's paper gave the news that China was on the point of declaring war on Japan, who has seized Manchuria and lately captured Shanghai. The League of Nations has seemingly been entirely powerless even to influence the situation.

Professor Holtz of the Teachers' College at Emporia has written asking me to present something on the program of the Classical Association of Kansas and Western Missouri, to be held at Lawrence at the end of April. I wish to accept this invitation, though as yet I have not been able to decide exactly on a subject.

February 6, 1932 Sudden and extreme changes in temperatures have followed each other in a merry-go-round chase the past several weeks. There have been two descents to the vicinity of zero lately with a mild day in between.

Many things are in the air regarding future plans for the school here and plans for individual faculty members. Certain things must be precipitated shortly, if some folks will not be sitting high and dry about next winter, stranded on the shores of unemployment. There is still much divided opinion as to the person to be appointed for president of the school. What I dread to anticipate is the possible eventuality that the appointment will not be made, but will be put off for some future time. The situation in official church circles is deplorable, when radical minorities on different extremes are ready to form blocs and invent schemes for pushing their particular ideas, while the great mass

of balanced and essentially conservative folks are so devoid of courageous leadership that they can scarcely be heard in the general fracas.
Is it the prevailing psychosis that renders most of us supine and ser-
vile, fearful to be sincere and honest regardless of the consequences?

February 7, 1932 Last Tuesday was the proverbial "groundhog day."
In this immediate section the sun was shining during the middle part
of the day and the supposed rodent supposedly was frightened by its
supposed shadow and hastily returned to its supposed winter hole for
another six weeks of hibernation. It did well to hide away again for
the next day was very cold and stormy.

February 13, 1932 Special Bible Term has closed and some of the
heavy pressure on nerves and time has been taken off, and I at least
can breathe a bit more freely. But there is a good deal of work
ahead of various and sundry sorts. There is request that I send out
a very special appeal to alumni who are teaching, and to some ex-
students for cash donations for running expenses. Board of Education
meets on the 22nd inst., and all indications are that it will be necessary for me to make the trip to Indiana for it.
    I have just finished reading through Quintilian, and plan to take
some spare time during the next six or eight weeks to copy out possessive and demonstrative adjectives.
    Have been made to reflect much in recent weeks on the existence
of such a maze of cross currents of opinion and feeling as one sees
in our small denominational group. The task of keeping one's emotional balance is not at all easy, especially if one happens to be anywhere near the midst of the puddle. My own ideals of a more or less
balanced and reasoned viewpoint, and a perspective that may have some
semblance to reality, are not at all easy to attain and to maintain in
such a situation. Perhaps no easier in any other situation. As I think
over the historic principles and attitudes of our Mennonite group, there
are some tendencies evident at the present time which are rather disturbing. Seventy-five years ago there was doubtless a danger of dis-
integration of the body, but during the last several decades there has
been a rapid rush toward complete centralization and standardization.
Machinery, consisting of committees and boards, has multiplied like a
plague in Egypt, until one cannot make a slightest move without bumping into a committee. The ideal behind all this vast system of organization is control, complete and detailed control of every phase of
church life and activity. Such ubiquitous control, effectively and courageously applied is the highest ideal among some people. I recall reading somewhere the statement that it is much better for people to do
some things badly themselves than to have all things done perfectly for
them. And there is no mean modicum of truth in this terse criticism
of over-government. Perhaps the time has come to work for a decen-
tralization of authority and of control.
    As an ideal program to work for, for the immediate future, there
has been in my mind the thought that we should return to the standard
of self-help and self-control, at least for the local congregations. What
I would like to see in that connection is a thoroughly efficient system
(local, not general) of giving religious training and religious instruc-

tion to children and young people; such a program that will without fail make children well versed in Biblical knowledge and in the historic ideals of our own faith. There should in connection with this be some definite form of parents' training work also. Then when these young people, that part of them which will not settle down in the home community, go to higher schools and into any and all legitimate walks of life they will be witnesses for Christ, adding moral and spiritual fiber to the circles and communities where they will labor. If not all these will maintain their active connection with our group, they can still make their contribution to the world at large, to the forces of righteousness and godliness, to the very pith and marrow of stable society and the kingdom of God. More important than conserving our numbers and looking to growth in numbers as the essence of success, our program should prepare people to scatter out and to witness far and wide to the principles and ideals we cherish. If some will happen to do so under banners other than Mennonite, we should still give them our benediction.

February 16, 1932 Have been having snow, rain, mist, fog, thick clouds, slush under foot, and other varieties in the weather menu since Saturday last. Fortunately it has not been very cold these days, but gives promise of getting colder right now.

Prospects for changes in store for us are looming up pretty definitely of late. To stay on here would mean for me to spend about all spare time this spring and summer in working up credit hours in professional educational subjects with a view to qualifying for the high school teachers' certificate. Spending the time, while a serious enough loss, is not so bad as spending money for it, perhaps even as much as a hundred dollars. Should I undertake to do all this, the question still is left, what would I teach when I have the high school certificate? To think of teaching anything other than languages appears impossible and to have enough courses in languages for a full schedule in a small high school is entirely impossible. On the other hand, to return to Goshen College, as I have been invited to do, will mean a difficult expensive move, the possibility of leaving the house here standing empty while paying rent elsewhere, and paying off a loan on this place, which would seem like paying for a dead horse. What I should best of all like for a few years to come would be a teaching position in a Kansas College or junior college, or in some state still farther south or west. We should very much dislike to locate, even for a year, out of reach of a church of our people. But, if the Lord should wish for us to bear witness for Him even in such a place, perhaps we could bring ourselves to do so. It is of course rather discouraging to have to leave our pleasant little home, just after we have fixed it to suit ourselves. But it is also a joy to trust God for our needs and to anticipate the adventure of what the coming years may have in store.

February 17, 1932 I have been reading no general reading books during the past several months. Reason: we do not have any on hand that are just the kind for casual, spare-time reading. Have not even visited the public library in Newton for over six weeks now, and will probably miss most of the February magazines and journals. One feels as though he were losing touch with the stream of modern thought, not to at least get a glance through such magazines as Harper's, Scribner's, Forum, North American Review, and a few others each month. I never read many articles in any one issue of these, but skim through each and read an occasional article through which attracts my eye, either by reason of its title, or because the author's name is familiar to me. Occasionally one finds an article that is stimulating and informing. But these are decidedly a minority amid the throng of articles that fill space in magazines and periodicals of the day.

February 26, 1932 The past week has brought forth many experiences for myself. Left here by auto a week ago this noon, travelled as far as Indiana, and reached home again on Wednesday evening. Spent the first night in Kansas City at Miningers', Saturday night and Sunday forenoon in Iowa City, Sunday night in Chicago at the Home Mission.

On Monday afternoon and all day Tuesday the Mennonite Board of Education was in session at the Forks Church near Middlebury, Indiana. Spent Monday night in Goshen. Started out for Kansas immediately after the close of the last session and drove almost continuously for twenty-four hours to reach home. Pleasant weather was with us all along the way, good roads, and many friends. It was a recreational trip for me, but plenty long for comfort, since I make little pretence at keeping up to my regular habits on such rush trips. The sessions of the Board's meetings were attended with a rather tense and lowering atmosphere, with some crackling of electricity, and with a little animus displayed. It is just this kind of meeting that I care little for, where the atmosphere is shot through with suspicion, mistrust, political maneuvering, almost hatred. It almost appeals to me as mockery for men to pray for and talk about the guidance of the Holy Spirit in such deliberations where there is a marked undercurrent of intolerance and suspicion. Have been developing a burden, almost a conviction, to pray that the Lord may open a door of opportunity for me to serve for a time and witness for Him outside of the immediate circle of our present horizon.

February 28, 1932 The weather has been very much like spring the past number of days. No furnace fire was built the past several mornings. An early spring with its saving of fuel costs would be a great boon to many folks this year, as well as an early garden with its saving of food costs. Our garden is just about ready to be plowed now.

We are now beginning to do all our planning for the spring and summer in terms of moving away towards the end of the summer. It appears that nothing less than a complete removal is before us, with the junior college prospects such as they are. Where to move to, this is the pressing question. I have decided to make applications at different places in the West, not with much hope of finding an opening, but as a bare possibility to avoid returning to the East again.

A writer in Atlantic Monthly lately discussed "The End of an Era," drawing an illuminating comparison between the present deflation and that which followed upon the close of the Napoleonic Wars a little more than one hundred years ago. The crisis in the United States at that time was met by three major lines of adjustment; first by the beginning of a protective tariff, second, by a wholesale exodus of farmers and others to the new lands west of the Allegheny Mountains, and third, by some extensive public improvements as means for relieving unemployment. The first and third of these has been tried in the present crisis, while the second is no longer possible. The concluding and summarizing paragraph of this excellent article is as follows: "Thus the richest country in the world, with debts, public and private, due from other nations approaching twenty-five billions, seems to be more helpless than Henry Clay's semi-bankrupt United States of 1820; with protective tariffs kicking backwards, free lands nonexistent and occupied lands a burden to their owners, immigrants inadmissible and internal improvements doubtful, if not dangerous. Thus vast cities, enormous gold reserves, and innumerable smokestacks are of no avail. Has the prophecy of Henry Adams, that we are all on a machine which cannot go forward without disaster and cannot be stopped without ruin, come true? It must be a new era — new thought unwelcome and old thought inapplicable."

Henry Ford has gotten into the headlines again with his declaration that he is ready to stake all he has on a supreme effort to help end the depression, by turning out his promised new car with full force, perhaps at the rate of one and a half million cars a year. Thus do the makers of goods conspire to force their products upon the public, which is showing rather a disposition to make its material wants correspond more nearly with its actual bona fide needs. It really looks as though the vast system of credit and finance and economic interdependence that has been built up is thought by many people to exist by its own inherent and inalienable rights; that people are made for the system rather than the system for the people. My philosophy is that the individual human being with his basic and elemental needs is more sacrosanct than any system that exists, in fact, this individual is the sole measure and criterion of the ultimate value of any system, organization or institution there is.

March 3, 1932 One reads much in magazines and papers these days in comment upon the strokes that President Hoover is putting forth to cure the financial depression. His monster Finance Corporation has been existing for a month now. Its chief task is to carry on propaganda against hoarded money and to expand the credit system in general. Some call it credit inflation, which is supposed to be somewhat less naughty than currency inflation. Some writers predict actual currency inflation before long, with the result, if not the actual purpose of forcing the United States away from the gold standard. This would render present tariff schedules more nearly effective in the measure they were supposed to be; it would ease the burdens of debtors, both individuals and nations; it is further claimed that such an event would raise the prices of commodities. Needless to say, the whole situation, national and international, is fraught with grim possibilities. A writer in a late magazine article has seriously discussed what changes might be looked for in case revolution should come in the United States.

More earthy affairs are: garden was plowed yesterday. Rain upon it followed by some frost would help to make a fine, mellow surface. Plan to work on the lawn this afternoon for a while, applying fertilizer and grass seed. Rain is threatening with wind from the east.

March 4, 1932 After several days of threatening skies, the prelude to spring came suddenly to an end today. Snow and stormy wind have been on hand today. Flowering bulbs and fruit tree blossoms need just this discouragement to keep them from pushing ahead too fast and perhaps getting nipped later on. We do wish for a good fruit crop from our trees again as last year, since it may be our last benefit from the trees we planted eleven years ago, on our lot which was then as innocent of tree or shrub as the virgin prairie.

Have just made a fair start in copying from Quintilian the instances of possessive and demonstrative adjectives he uses. I copy a short line of context with each one of these words and some symbol or word as to its usage. These adjectives are very numerous in this ancient schoolmaster's books of the Oratorical Institutes. I calculate to have nearly as many occurrences from him as I found in Aulus Gellius, my first thoroughgoing effort at this sort of study, which constituted my doctoral dissertation. Have this winter read through most of Tacitus' extant writings and made note of these same adjectives, purposing to copy these out also during this spring and summer. Pliny's Epistles are awaiting the same process, although already in 1925 I copied on small cards these adjectives from at least six books of the Epistles, so that it will not require so very long to finish up these.

March 6, 1932 Wintery breezes and flurries of snow prevail today. The mercury column took a great fall on night before last when the lowest official temperature reported at Newton was seven degrees above zero. It has scarcely been above freezing since, as I should judge. Today is colder again than yesterday.

Two weeks ago today I spent in Iowa City, that is, until two o'clock in the afternoon, when we started on our way to Chicago. This was just three and one-half years since I last stopped in the old home community, which was a half-year longer than I had been away from there at any one time before. My parents are living in Iowa City this winter, with Aunt Leah in her house on Oakland Avenue. Mother is in bed nearly all of the time, although she seems to be getting better the past while. During the winter of 1923-24 Estie and I lived in the house where the folks are now living. Uncle Noah and his wife went to California that winter. Uncle died out there about the end of April. About May 1 we moved to a house on the steep hillside west of the Iowa River that led up to Manville Heights. We lived in it until September 15, 1924, when we moved to a two-room apartment in Mrs. Salzman's house on South Dubuque Street, where we continued for just twelve months. We paid $35 a month for these rooms and had all incidentals furnished. Also paid another five dollars a month for the privilege of keeping the Ford car in an old barn on the rear part of the lot. However, I fired the two furnaces that were under the house during the winter and was allowed six dollars a month for this service. The Salzmans were orthodox Hebrews formerly having come from Russia. It was a fairly good place to do light house-keeping. We had an outside entrance of our own, the rooms were on the first floor and at the rear. We had to share the bathroom with the family, however.

From this place we trekked far off to Philadelphia. We were about as simple about big-city ways as though we had been the Innocents Abroad. We had to find a living place at some reasonable figure and we knew nothing as to how to judge of surroundings, but we finally established ourselves in a one-room apartment with kitchenette in a rather dingy apartment house, one that was small and rather old. Paid $34 a month for this with all incidentals included. It was on the second floor and at the back, having windows on the east and the north. It was the kind of place where the occupants are constantly coming and going. When we left at the end of ten and one-half months, we had been there twice as long as any of the other folks who were there at any time while we were. We were never molested and naturally we never bothered anyone else. Our milk was stolen once or twice between the time the milkman left it at the outside front door and when I went to look for it. The Ford car I stored away on the second story of a garage on North Howard Street, not very far from the Mennonite Mission. Paid six dollars a month for this. Did not look at the car from November or December till July and then found it much altered, good tires and battery exchanged for worse ones, one wheel and the radiator also changed, and about all loose things taken off. It was a dirty deal that man gave me.

March 11, 1932 There has now been one solid week of winter weather, the longest and coldest spell there has been here all this winter. Official temperature readings were around six and four degrees above zero Fahrenheit every morning this week until this morning. The wind has blown steadily from the north and northwest all this while and a strong wind at that until today when it has abated somewhat. During all this winter the wind has never blown from one direction steadily for more than one or two whole days at a time. This time it has persisted so long that it will require many days' sunshine to rewarm the atmosphere and bring about comfortable atmospheric conditions. The violent atmospheric disturbances that occasioned our severe and unseasonable cold snap were about country-wide, carrying severe cold and storms to the east coast and to the Gulf to the south. Many householders are being forced to replan their fuel proposition. Ours has been reduced very considerably, but will still hold out for a time.

Read a book this week entitled "Your Money's Worth." It is a very excellent book, written in 1927. It uncovers many interesting and profitable facts on how for certain highly advertised proprietary articles the ultimate consumer pays fabulous prices for very ordinary and commonplace goods. The authors spare no words or rhetoric in unmasking the conspiracies against the ultimate consumer's purchasing power that are worked out and set on foot in the offices of the advertising agencies. Trade names, slogans, silly catch words, phrases, and ideas are put over on a gullible public by the sheer force of repetition in advertising. The whole scheme of advertising methods, supersalesmanship, breaking down sales resistance, and so forth calls for a Lucian, a Swift, or someone who can satirize it in an immortal way. The subject is certainly a worthy one for some such effort. According to the authors of this book, there has been much done in the way of testing goods and advertised claims which has slowly and indirectly benefitted the ultimate consumer. The Bureau of Standards at Washington does perhaps the greatest work along this line. But unfortunately its general practice is not to give out the facts and findings it discovers, hence the ultimate small buyer cannot now benefit by the much excellent work that has been done through the support of the taxpayers' money. The book does contain some practical hints and suggestions which make it worth owning and using for reference purposes. It is a library copy that I read.

March 13, 1932 More moderate temperature is the order of the day recently, a very welcome change from the rigorous weather of the past ten days. Members of the faculty in the school here are beginning to contemplate the prospect of doing without all or at least some of their pay for the remainder of the year. The first five months' salaries have been paid up to all of them. The sixth month's check was due the past week, but no promise was made as to when it can be paid.

March 15, 1932 The Local Board for the College met last evening in regular session. The matter of cash income for the remainder of the year was discussed at some length. If it were possible to collect the more than four thousand dollars now standing on the books in open accounts and also the more than three thousand dollars in notes that are past due or soon to come due, it would be very simple to pay up all accounts against the college. Even if the major portion of the four thousand dollars which it was planned to raise by special donations were forthcoming, it would not be hard to see a way through. It appears that interest generally in the school and its work is at a very low ebb. People are critical and pessimistic in attitudes. Public meetings and programs are not attended largely from this and surrounding communities as they were some years ago. Some would explain this as due to the so-called "high-class" music and entertainment the school has been putting on. A lecturer on electricity, with lots of gimcracks, apparatus, and spectacular demonstration is the only type of lecturer that can fill up the hall nowadays. There seems in part to be a maladjustment between the school with its ideals and the community and its ideals. The faculty as almost a unit fosters ideals of a collegiate community, whiles the mass of the student group and of the general community around can appreciate nothing above the high school standard or level in taste, culture, and intellectuality.

March 17, 1932 Am suffering from an unpleasant and disagreeable cold the past two days. On Monday evening for two hours I sat in the business office at the college where the temperature was a little below the comfortable point. During the night I was awakened by a sensation as of something clutching at my throat, the first onslaught of the congestion.
The chronic catarrhal condition of my nasal membranes makes my colds always settle in my throat and head. I formerly had such severe colds more frequently than during the past several years. More specific dietary habits seem to render me less susceptible than previously. We use considerable citrus fruits regularly — a grapefruit every morning, and lemon juice in drinking water, on salads, and for other sea-

soning, using near a dozen of these last each week all the time. I eat considerable cereals for breakfast, which are reputed to enhance the acidity of the blood stream.

March 19, 1932 Fair and vernal weather has been with us for some days. I scratched some on the surface of the garden yesterday. Today I mean to plant peas and potatoes, and I know not what else. Early and successful gardens will be a boon to people in general as a means to lessen the cash requirements of living.

A Capella Chorus gave a good program at the college last evening. In view of the school prospects for the next year, one has to shut his mental eyes and not look too closely at what such a fact may mean for the community and for our people of this section of Kansas. It is hard to enjoy such programs now, for thinking that there may not be such programs next year. But then all things do change and shift, and with a vision of faith it is possible to believe that most changes are for the better. In a number of ways I am made to suspect that a new epoch in my own life may be soon to begin. The question of getting on professionally and financially raises the grim question of laying plans for getting a better-paying position at some time before many years. This involves a great number of considerations, and requires no small measure of courage in facing them.

March 20, 1932 Funeral services for Mrs. J. P. Hershberger were held at the college this afternoon.

The aspect of the out-of-doors is dull and discouraging. Everything looks grey. There is less greenness of grass and fields than there has been all winter. The four or five continuous days of near-zero weather of two weeks ago gave a setback decisive to all vegetation. Grass on the lawn appears deader than in January. Hollyhock clumps that grew out during the rainy weather of last November and December managed to stay partly green all during the winter months, but now they are frozen clear down. While I am very much of an amateur in matters horticultural, it is nontheless my opinion, arrived at by examination of the blossom buds, that the apricot and peach crop for this year was completely "nipped in the bud" by the frost. Buds on the cherry trees however seem to be still solid and unharmed. Further observation during the coming month must be counted on to verify or refute my present conclusion. If the fruit crop generally proves damaged to such an extent, it will be a great disappointment to people, because there will be less cheap food for this coming summer and the next winter. A warm rain followed by sunshine is needed now to cheer Nature and dress her in verdant robes. But the east wind is blowing today; while the atmosphere is chilly, the sun labors to shine through an indeterminate maze of clouds. Spring is scheduled to make her debut some time tomorrow. Easter is only one week away. There is still fuel in our basement for several weeks, perhaps for a month, depending upon the temperature maneuvers of the weather man.

March 21, 1932 Presto-change! A howling, raging snowstorm of virtually blizzard proportions is prevailing today. Wind from about directly north; snow drifting freely where it can. Temperature is some lower already, but is not so far below the freezing mark as yet. No monotony is possible where balmy spring days are chased off the scene by a roaring, snorting snow storm. Today being the time of the equinox, doubtless a storm is entirely fitting and appropriate to the occasion. Boreas sends down his chilly blasts from his northland home to give us the winter scenes that failed to come during the winter months. The thirsty surface of the soil will drink in with gratefulness the moisture from the snow. But what will the small birds be doing on a day as this? Robins redbreast were singing right cheerily about us during the recent days. One was casually inspecting the fork in the tree near the house where a family was reared last spring. The remains of the old nest still clings, all weatherbeaten and awry, on the limbs. During the past several months the royally clothed Redbird, called Cardinal, has sometimes come to the feeding shelf outside the dining room window, not regularly, but only on very cold days or when there was some snow on the ground. For a while both the lord and his more modestly arrayed lady appeared to feed on the grain placed out for their convenience. His lordship, however, was not always courteous and kind to his mate, even being so unchivalrous as to drive her away from his board sometimes. Lately she has not appeared with him, perhaps she has deserted him — as he doubtless deserved.

March 22, 1932 The scene has changed completely once more. Bright sunshine all day long, a gentle breeze at times from the west and at other times from the south. It is a grand and wonderful show — this Kansas weather. A great grief to us it will be if it should be necessary for us to leave this state. If leave we must, our first choice will be to go further south, southwest, or west. The effete and decadent East, as it is spoken of, cannot attract us with anything less than a desirable job.

March 24, 1932 Fair weather. Vacation begins. Life looks darker and darker to some of the teachers who have received no pay check for near two months and with uncertain prospects ahead of getting very much more of the allowance agreed upon for the year. We have so far received five hundred dollars since September 1 of last year for use at our house. I think it is possible by a system of semi-barter to get most of our things to eat without handling cash for them, such as milk, eggs, butter, groceries, for the next several months. This can be done by letting people who owe an account at the college or who want to make a donation to the college deficit supply whatever provisions they have to teachers at market price. Fred Grove will supply us with milk by such an arrangement, perhaps Chauncy Hostetlers will agree to furnish us butter and eggs on such an arrangement. They have furnished us one pound of butter a week from their farm for a year or more. Eggs are about the cheapest food one can get nowadays. We have been getting ours from Mrs. Hartzler across the street for some time at seven cents a dozen. J. R. Diller brings us finely ground whole wheat flour for two cents a pound. Our necessary garden supplies we have already; only tomato plants will require additional cash outlay. We have on hand one thousand Bermuda onion plants and fifty

cabbage plants to set out one of the next days. For these we paid
$1.35. The task of planting all these is a tedious one, at least for me.

March 27, 1932 A beautiful Easter day is today. Warm sunshine pervades the atmosphere and cheers the soil underfoot. Big fleecy clouds
sail across the sky and occasionally hide the face of the welcome sun
for several minutes. The face of Nature still shows very few signs of
recovery from the pinch of the frost a few weeks ago. We set out cabbage and onions yesterday, working hard and diligently at the task.

Word has come here from a semi-official source to the effect that
C. K. Lehman will not be released from his position in the East to become president of Hesston College, to which position he was elected by
the Board of Education in February. It is as many people expected
that it would be. The whole matter of naming a president for the
school here is really becoming a circus. More ado is made over a
presiding official for our little one-horse school than is probably occasioned in finding a president for some large university. The Board of
Education has now made two magnificent gestures to seat a man in the
office — perhaps in fairness they should be termed efforts.

Two favorite sons of the panicky old-guard conservatives have now
been eliminated. What move will next be made is not known here, although it is reported that the Executive Committee of the Board in-
tends to keep on moving until they land someone in the place. Throughout the western conferences it seems pretty clear that the leaders have
an innate suspicion toward school-trained men. They never feel quite
sure that they can be trusted, perhaps because school men speak a
slightly different language, think in somewhat different terms, have
other ideals in part, and are not as emphatic and dogmatic in their
statements apropos of church tenets as is the accepted rule among
the church circles generally. It is unfortunate that such is the case.
Perhaps the gap between untrained leaders and university graduates is
too large to bridge over in a single decade; the leap is too great for
so short a time. In the Spirit it certainly should not need to be so. If
both sides were able to make adjustments to some extent there ought
to be no difficulty. But to expect that university training, wide reading
and study, and varied contacts will not change a person's perspective,
his ideals of truth and righteousness, his tastes and appreciations, and
even his language and emphasis, is quite unreasonable. For the school-
trained to assume themselves superior and entitled to special consideration is just as unreasonable. The whole situation reminds me strongly of the maladjustment that is reported to have existed between Soc-
rates and the established order in ancient Athens. As for myself I
can see wherein my study and reading has unfitted me for taking a
strongly partisan attitude on controverted matters, especially such matters as appeal to me to be of less than paramount importance. Perhaps
it is the fault of my own disposition also. I am too much inclined to
deliberate, to give due weight to every consideration for and against a
particular proposition. This attitude, I confess, militates against dogmatism. Perhaps also specialized study in the so-called humanities
has tended to liberalize my thinking more than I have been aware.
Among my own highest intellectual ideals are balance and correct perspective in views and statements, free and untrammelled inquiry, fear-

lessly facing new ideas and facts, a critical habit of mind, modesty in
statement, and tolerance toward those who differ in views and attitudes.
No one of these can be carried to extreme limits regardless of other
considerations, and they all need to be tempered with a spiritual and
believing outlook on life. There is a danger of worshipping the mind
and the intellect; of carrying critical thinking to a point where it becomes a skeptical habit of mind. The proper balance is the eternal
goal to strive for. Sometimes it happens that fundamentalists are
guilty of a towering intellectual and spiritual pride as obnoxious as
rationalists. Modesty of statement and duly conditioned expression of
opinion seems to me to be always in order for a Christian. But possibly not for one who wishes to lead the mob mind and to make himself
a leader of the masses.

March 29, 1932 In 1920 some few months before the time when I
thought to lead into matrimony a most virtuous woman, I fared forth
and bought a house. Now buying a house in which the virtuous woman
of the Proverbs can make a home calls for skill and the exercise of
sundry other manly qualities. But I was quite innocent of such qualities and a stranger to the exercise thereof. Nonetheless I bought a
house. I mean, I bought what was reputed to be a house even by responsible persons in the community, at any rate the seller represented
it to be a house. We made a brave effort to live in this house which
was purchased at a price much too great. It was hopeless. We decided
it was only a partial house, a semblance to a house, almost a sham
house. The organization of walls and stairs in parts of it was horrible;
some of the upper part was still skeletonic, no flesh and skin concealed
the bare bones and sinews. This make-believe house we tolerated, or
endured, or as you please, for a number of years. Time came when the
virtuous woman would have a house, a real house in which it is possible to live. We had barely existed for a long enough time without our
real house. Presently the horrible parts were torn out and reorganized,
water pipes were introduced with outlets and fixtures at convenient points;
all parts of its skeleton were aesthetically concealed and decorated. In
short, the house I bought ten years before now grew into a house in
which to live.
    One part that before had been skeletonic and proportionately filthy
and worthy to be shunned became a neat little storeroom situated right
at the head of the stairway. But not long was it a mere storeroom, un-
dignified and slighted. Its appearance had become so much improved
that it was promoted at once to the rank of a den, a real man's den.
Now a den may be a retreat, a lurking or hiding place for lions, rob-
bers, and other wild animals. But this is a man's den with cot, rough
bookcase, walls thickly decorated with photographs, clipped pictures,
cards, scenic views, and what you have, all according to a man's taste.
A den may be a pleasant luxury. This one is. Sprawled on the cot or
seated in an awkward old-time rocker with feet propped high on the
door jamb, there is comfort for a man. An afternoon's sun lends cheer
and a welcome light for reading, writing, musing, or whatever occupation may possess a man.

March 30, 1932 Had a Kansas dust storm yesterday. The wife spent much of today "digging out" of the dust and sand that was carried into the house by the swift south wind. Cooler weather today, but clear and sunny. School takes up again today with a steady run until the close. Many things will doubtless develop and work themselves out during the course of the next weeks. We all want to see things happen rapidly now.

March 31, 1932 Delegations and visitors at the college have been numerous yesterday afternoon and today. Boards, committees and individuals are still wrestling with the stupendous epoch-making problem of naming a president for a small tottering infant of a school. It should augur exceedingly well for the school's future that so much energy, talk, conference, patience are being expended on this matter. Another of the present administration and I were conversing a little while ago and lamenting the seeming fact that a group of a half dozen or more of us, who with high ideals and our heads chock full of visions and dreams prepared ourselves, as we believed then, to promote educational work in our part of the church, have now gone down in complete and ignominious defeat. It is evident that some of us were ten years ago living in a fool's paradise and hatching visions and plans and ideas that are our present apparent downfall. It was a time of inflation, not only financially but also psychologically. No Joseph dreamed or had occasion to interpret for another that there would be lean and ill-favoured cows following on the heels of the fat and well-favoured ones. It is very clear to me now that a doctorate is an impossible encumbrance in our small school here, and it still remains to be proven to my mind that the same is not true for our church educational program as a whole. However I am, while disappointed, not greatly discouraged even by present circumstances. The whole is a trying and a chastening experience, but also educative in the truest possible sense. We who have tried to carry on here during the past few years when things have been crashing downward sometimes have been wondering if the school's present situation is our fault. Yet our own consciences affirm that we did the best we knew how with the disadvantages and untoward circumstances we had.

April 3, 1932 Another day of wind that amounts almost to a sand storm. Past few days have been pleasantly warm. Sowed two rows across the garden each of carrots and beets yesterday. Put out fifty cabbage plants a week ago; nearly all seem to be starting to grow. We are gambling twenty-five cents on tomato plants set out on April first. The odds are clearly against us because of the early date that they will escape damage from frost. I cleaned up the grounds yesterday and also cleaned out the garage. Alvin King has taken the 1923 model-T Ford car off my hands giving me credit for thirty-five dollars applicable only on another car, new or used, sometime during 1932 or 1933. Specifications and prices on the newest Ford cars are given out now. We do not contemplate to get a car soon, unless we can come by a larger income. If we happen to be located where we can get to church by walking, I shall be in favor of doing without a motor car for some years. Want to use surplus income, provided there is to be any such, in paying off notes so as to eliminate interest from my yearly budget, and furthermore in financing a summer's trip to Italy and Greece as soon as possible.

Word has come that Milo Kauffman has been appointed president for Hesston College. He will be here tomorrow for helping to make plans for the next year. The junior college idea is evidently going to die hard if it dies at all.

April 5, 1932 Another windy day, not of such great velocity as was the gale that swept across Kansas a week ago today. What is much needed now is a number of gentle, warm April showers, to prevent field crops from blowing out and to promote growth generally.

Some time in February came a special book list from Blackwell at Oxford containing a number of thousand items in theological and religious books second-hand. Several dozen items attracted my eye, but at the moment I decided I had spent all the cash I could spare for this winter in that direction. But about March first the Spirit moved upon me strongly, some spirit at any rate, to send an order for some of the books listed. Hoped they would not all come; so I would not need to part with as much cash and still my conscience would have no occasion to feel guilty for having let slip by a possible opportunity for securing cheaply some volumes I have long wanted. They did not all come; four books reached me about ten days ago. Three volumes by Sir William Ramsay, which constitute a real buy at a cost of about five dollars. There are still one or two more of Ramsay's books I should be pleased to own, if ever I can secure them at a reasonable figure. Another volume that came is Papini's "Storia di Cristo" in the original; the volume is disappointing because of its merely paper cover. I can read the Italian only poorly, but in familiar subject matter I can make it out with some effort and pains. I should constantly read a little in it to gradually master vocabulary and syntax. I note that a revised edition of Jean's book "The Mysterious Universe" is now offered for one dollar. I fear I must find a dollar yet for this, and perhaps also for Cellini's "Autobiography" another one.

April 8, 1932 Once again a pleasant day. After a day and a night of wind rushing toward the north it all rushed back south again yesterday at top speed. Today quiet with sunshine.

Milo Kauffman, newly appointed president for Hesston College, spent the past three days on the grounds at work of creating a new organization for the coming year of school work. Plans are not completed as yet, although a start has been made. Change and readjustment are in the atmosphere everywhere nowadays. It is quite wholesome for folks to be shaken out of their set ways of thinking and to have their minds deflated, the wind all let out of their ego. It is trying to most folks. Common sense and sane reasoning seem to be coming back to replace some of the usurpers in the form of theories and ideals often fanciful and impractical. One's belief in the guidance of the life by the Holy Spirit is practical at such a time. It is thrilling, after a fashion, to face the future not knowing just what it will bring forth, and yet confident that it will be better than the present and the past. It is a fine exercise in patience to wait cheerfully and hopefully for the future as it unfolds its treasures, all too slowly for our impatience. In order to give the Spirit an opportunity to open doors for myself as a college teacher, I wrote several dozens of letters to college and university presidents during March, suggesting that I am looking for a position for next year. Have received many replies, several interested inquiries among them.

April 11, 1932 Read a brief address in chapel this morning as my first contribution to the series of chapel addresses to be given during April and May. Propounded some ideas on the "Uses of Adversity." As I recall my class oration back in 1917, upon my graduation from Academy, was on the same theme and text, but treated in quite a different manner. The five or six lines in Shakespeare's play, "As You Like It," beginning with "Sweet are the uses of adversity," have been a favorite memory text with me ever since I first read Shakespeare. My first inspiration to read Shakespeare came from an article I read as a boy on the farm in our then favorite farm magazine, Wallace's Farmer. The editor then was a cultured man, somewhat of a practical philosopher ripened by years of experience. I copied a number of articles from his editorial pages which I felt were especially good. This particular article was on the subject of getting an education at home. One definite suggestion given was that there are three books in the English language which if read and mastered will make anyone in some measure a cultivated man. The three are the King James Version of the Bible, Bunyan's "Pilgrim's Progress," and Shakespeare's plays. The Bible I had, Bunyan I easily procured at a drug store in Kalona. I sent to Montgomery Ward & Company at Chicago for a one-volume copy of the works of Shakespeare; the bare text, no notes or frills of any sort. Conscientiously I started in to read at the beginning of the book. The first play was "The Tempest." I went on to read the rest as they came in the book. I read slowly, actually became interested in the reading, read favorite parts over and over again before leaving them, even memorized choice lines and passages. During several years I read thus through somewhat more than half of the volume. This effort was as enjoyable as any studying of literature I have engaged in since in academy and college English courses. It added much to my vocabulary I am sure, cultivated my imagination and gave me inspiration for continued study and reading.

April 17, 1932 People are engaged in one of the favorite spring and summer pastimes in Kansas, wishing for rain and talking about the need for it. So far there has been no spring rain. Topsoil is dry and garden things do not grow well.

Sunday school lesson this morning was on Abram's call to leave home and friends and go west on a faith venture. This study brings to mind a theme I have felt some inspiration at sundry times to study out and develop; the function and use of the separated religious minority group in the advancement of the kingdom of God. The mere separation of good from wicked as is mentioned in the early part of the Genesis narrative, family of Enos from family of Cain, families of Shem and others from family of Canaan, did nothing toward advancing the good and restraining the increase of the wicked. The calling out of a single family and nation to be schooled, nurtured and trained in faith, righteousness, spirituality, served to develop a source of supply of these ideals and principles from which source a constant stream, now larger now smaller, is injected into the life stream of the world at large. For the culture of spiritual ideals and values very special conditions and surroundings are necessary, conditions which are superior to those found in society at large. Would such a figure as this be permissible: God needs small separated groups, insignificant minorities, for use as cultures from which are constantly produced the antitoxin and the serum needed for injection into the mass of society to offset and check the ravages of the sin principle? It is true that the Jews failed to carry the purpose of Abram's call to its logical and final conclusion. They became self-centered and regarded themselves as privileged religionists. But the larger purpose of Abram's call is being realized in the development of Christianity out of Judaism. Seemingly Christianity, better said the Church, was such an effective minority in God's kingdom for a little more than two centuries at the beginning of her history. Since the mass of the Church has surrendered her idealism, it is the minority sects which have assumed this same relation to Christendom itself. How to maintain and carry out in actual practice the two phases of this responsibility, enough separateness for spiritual culture and connection close enough to contribute most to the world's life, this is the eternal problem which cannot be solved by formula or rule of thumb.

May 17, 1932 My fourth week of enforced vacationing ends today. Arose on Monday morning, April 18, with a pronounced feeling of distress in my abdomen which I supposed to be indigestion from something I had eaten the evening before. Kept going much of that day; ate practically nothing after breakfast. Went to bed; slept soundly until about three o'clock a.m. when I was awakened with an acute pain in the lower part of the abdomen. Rested fairly easy during Tuesday forenoon but pain continued. Dr. Wedel came about twelve o'clock and after scarcely two minutes of examination pronounced for an inflamed appendix if not worse. Advised going to hospital for tests and detailed examination. Reached hospital at 2:10 p.m. Tests were made. Dr. Haury made examination. Took my place on the operating table at 4:10 and left everything else to the surgeon, doctor and gentle nurses. Thereafter I held down without interruption a hospital bed for 17 days and for two days more with only very brief periods of respite while I sat in a chair. The 19 days I enjoyed as best I could. The nurses were kind and helpful. Surroundings were pleasant enough. Food tasted mostly indifferent. Internal distress caused some suffering. Because the appendix was found ruptured, there was profuse drainage from the wound for at least two weeks. Came home on May 8, scarcely strong enough to walk a dozen steps unassisted.
    Since then strength has been coming back slowly but steadily. Weather has been delicious with health-giving sunshine nearly every day. Have increased the radius of my perambulations about every day, and today walked up to the bank for the first time. Several weeks must needs pass by before I can hope to be back to normal strength. Hope I may be blessed with better general health because of this experience. Before this illness I can only recall a few very occasional times during the past number of months that I felt what seemed to be slight digestive disturbances upon arising in the morning, which always passed away after being up and around.

While I seem to possess a fairly strong constitution, I have had at least two serious illnesses previous to this recent one, besides some minor ones. In 1904, March, I was very seriously sick for several weeks with scarlet fever. Came out of this with no complications. In February and March, 1911, I was deathly ill with pneumonia, which set in a few weeks after I recovered from an attack of measles. During this siege they had a trained nurse in the home to take care of me for three weeks. When the fever broke my temperature dropped from about 105 to 93, the pulse rate hovered about 42 for a day or two; and my respiration rate was about eighteen. The physician in attendance asserted that he never saw but one case where the temperature dropped to a lower mark, and in that case the patient did not survive the shock. Came out of this also with no permanent ill effects. In 1914, end of September, I underwent a surgical operation for hernia. This came as almost a calamity to my hopes and plans at the time. For more than a year I had been planning to start my high school career in January of 1915. This expensive operation coming just two months after I began earning my own money, almost swept away all I could earn between the date of my coming of age and the time set for my entering Hesston Academy. Nevertheless I managed to go to school at the time I had planned, needless to say, greatly handicapped. After coming to Hesston and getting partly started in school work I had another illness which made me consider quite seriously the idea of dismissing all plans and ambitions of going on with an educational career and of returning to the farm. Had a mild attack of typhoid fever and lay in bed on third floor of the dormitory for two weeks. After I was out again and well life and the future looked different.

May 18, 1932 While convalescing at home the past eight days I have read through Will Durant's book entitled "The Mansions of Philosophy," a ponderous tome of more than 650 pages. Durant's style is always interesting and he succeeds admirably in writing philosophy in a popularized form. As a whole, I liked this volume. Some of the chapters are more to my taste than others. The author tries to be fair to the various ways in which people look upon the problems of thought. Durant himself appears to be a vitalist in philosophy, a viewpoint which makes it possible for one to be a thoroughgoing evolutionist and still fight materialism and mechanism with some earnestness. He is also an incurable optimist, although he appreciates the pessimist's viewpoint and even credits him with possessing half a truth. His repeatedly stated formula is "Perspective is Everything." One is almost a bit surprised to find no suggestion given that evolution is only a theory; everywhere he builds upon it as a solid and unshakable historical fact. With faith in evolution, one can from it create the "perspective" necessary for a genial and comfortable optimism. The chapters on religion are disappointing. I must feel as I read this book that the writer is often in error, but, to use his own word, his error is quite "forgivable", because he is not inclined to be dogmatic, harsh, or intolerant in his presentation. Certain chapters of the book one should read over periodically as a welcome tonic and stimulant for mind and soul.

May 19, 1932 Do not feel disposed to do much that is called work.

Everyone advises caution and lack of haste. My legs are very slow in getting back to their normal feeling and function. I read considerable every day with seemingly no ill consequences. Already in the hospital I read some. I devoured the May issue of the Atlantic Monthly while still confined to bed. Some very good articles are found in this number. Flexner writes some more truthful words about "Universities in American Life." Another writer in a forceful piece is not so sure that prosperity is just around the corner, or even that the depression is past its decisive crisis as yet. How foolish appear now the ballyhoo and the optimistic predictions made one and two years ago about the speedy return of prosperity. Price of wheat on local market has been hovering between thirty-five and forty cents a bushel for many months. Butterfat commands a lower price at present than any time yet, about thirteen cents a pound. Eggs which we bought for seven cents a dozen for some time have risen to the exorbitant price of ten cents recently. Large stores in Newton are resorting to auction sales and receiverships in order to move their merchandise. Taxes in many rural sections are not being paid. Reports have it that one-fourth of the farm land in Mississippi is being sold for taxes. In one section of Colorado rural school teachers have received no pay since January 1, 1932 and are promised none before January 1, 1933.

May 20, 1932 There is no monotony in sight for us in the pathway of life that is immediately ahead. The luxury of my own recent vacation will take not a great deal less than two hundred dollars — whenever it becomes possible to pay it at all. The surgeon generously makes a discount of one-third to teachers. Other special expenses are also in the offing. So far only six and one-fourth months' pay has come to the faculty members of Hesston College for the present school year. A little more is likely to come during the summer, but no one ventures to prophesy how much it will be. What is especially interesting is that I have no position in sight as certain yet. Perhaps in the end we will get to go to the southland, procure a little piece of ground, and start life over again. But it seems quite impossible to sell any property at this time or to raise capital in any other way. The mortgage on our property here comes due in another fifteen months. Interest on notes comes due with absolute regularity. But it is hard for me to worry about these matters. It is better to keep cheerful and sensible trusting God for one's future needs, casting away all one's pride as to standards of living and keeping up with the Joneses or anyone else. I cannot bring myself to feel fearful and in dread of what may come; I feel only an eagerness to observe as objectively as possible the unfolding drama of economic, moral, and social readjustment, be the changes as radical as they may. None of the conditions of the status quo need be regarded as sacrosanct. Human nature seems to be tough and resilient enough to survive its various dislocations and upheavals. The general atmosphere of society will be more wholesome for such experiences.

May 23, 1932 Attended chapel service this morning for first time in five weeks. I enjoy working for a few hours each forenoon. It grieves me greatly that I am unable to work on garden and lawn. The absence of rain keeps weeds from growing very much — but unfortunately the same is true of other things which should be growing. After the close of school I hope to be able to do the physical labor necessary about the house and grounds. Cherries are already ripening — several weeks earlier than I have ever known them to ripen on our trees. But the birds are making havoc with them — catbirds, two species of orioles, robins and others. The ladies are canning spinach and asparagus to-day. Peas are about ready to pick. Tomato plants set out on April 1 are blossoming profusely with many small tomatoes hanging on. Rain is needed to make things grow. Temperature is summer-like, well above eighty degrees. Potato bugs need some special feeding. It is pleasant to have such an early growing season. A cool wet June would be a boon to gardens, if not to the wheat farmers.

May 27, 1932 Cool weather prevails. Some rain fell recently. Have been reading with great satisfaction and profit in the two of William Ramsay's books entitled, "Luke the Physician" and "The Church in the Roman Empire". The former is a collection of miscellaneous articles and reviews the longest and first of which gives the title to the volume. The second is a series of college lectures elaborated with additions and introduction. Ramsay's style and method as a historian appeal to me as inimitable and very challenging. The historical approach to the study and understanding of the New Testament books is stimulating and gripping to myself and gives the suggestion to my mind that I should by all means sometime make a thorough study of the early centuries of the Christian era. It is illuminating to read anew the epistles of the New Testament as these are fitted into their correct historical setting. They acquire in some cases an entirely new meaning and significance, a vitality which I never could make myself feel as I read them for devotional and inspirational purposes only. This approach and viewpoint in N. T. study is quite different from the naive idea which I received from the popular and unthinking viewpoint on the Bible, which rather gives one the impression that the various books were sometime handed down ready-made, as so many oracles from some ancient tripod. The historical viewpoint appeals to me as so very much more real and vital. It still does not minimize the value of the books for instruction and teaching, but rather makes clear and pointed the real meaning and force.

June 5, 1932 Commencement is past since last Thursday. Was able to do a little "officiating" during the last days of school. A sense of satisfaction comes over me with the thought that my career as an officiator is at an end. The past two years have nearly developed a thing with me which they call a "complex." For some reason I always felt out of place, was never free from a shadow of embarrassment and an annoying self-consciousness, when attempting to lead out or to officiate in some public way. The more I felt that way, the more I felt sure I was failing in the work I was trying to do. Along with this went the general decline of the school in its outward and visible aspects. All in all I am convinced that the experience of wholesale debunking and deflation will prove a wholesome one. Confessedly I am becoming somewhat more realistic in my outlook; I hope I shall not become a pessimist, at least not of the cynical type. I am not quite so confident any more that I am called to remake the world, to reform its religion, its science, and its philosophy. I do not care any longer to assert with cocksure dogmatism, or even to believe it is a dogma, that I and my group are just about perfectly right and sensible and civilized in what we do and think. I venture to think that I have grown a little in modesty and honesty of mind, have become a bit more tolerant and kindly, and developed an enlarged modicum of gratitude and appreciation for the blessings and opportunities that come to me.

Welcome rains have fallen upon our garden during recent nights. Everything grows luxuriously. Have had on the table from our garden already to date peas, ten days ago, spinach, three weeks ago first, onions, beets, carrots; potatoes and green beans will soon be ready; tomatoes seem large enough to begin turning red soon. Cherries and mulberries are ripe and provide fresh fruit for table use and for canning.

The first physical labor, more strenuous than picking cherries and spraying potato vines against beetles, I have so far essayed was clipping the grass on the lawn yesterday. Other tasks are awaiting my further effort: mulching the tomato plot with straw, clearing away weeds about the grounds, stirring the topsoil in garden. Plan also to make an effort to obtain some rhubarb and mulberries from the college campus for canning. In a few weeks, after the immediate rush is past, I hope to devote some time to intellectual labor and study. In all probability the task of moving ourselves and our household goods will be upon us before the summer ends, an undertaking that will demand much time and energy. Where to move to? The coming week or two should bring the final decision on this point. We shudder alike at the idea of leaving our place here and at the toil and inconvenience of moving into a rented house somewhere. Perhaps to insure that this will be our final migration we should go to southern Texas, settle on a small truck and fruit farm, and spend our days in peace and quietness!

June 15, 1932 No rain has fallen upon us at this place for an entire week, although other parts of Kansas have had some showers more recently. Spent four days of last week on a journey to Indiana and return. Started on Wednesday morning, riding with B. E. Miller in his motor car as far as Indianapolis. Spent most of Friday at Taylor University, Upland, Indiana, interviewing officials of the school. Returned by trolley, motor coach, and steam train, reaching home early Sunday morning. Spent in cash a total of about $23 for the trip, which I consider not so bad from the standpoint of our economic condition. Had my first experience on this trip with riding in a large motor coach, generally called a bus. If lack of funds is a basic consideration in one's travel, then travel by bus is worth considering. The vibration however, is such that I find it very unwise to try to read while the coach is moving. Hence one's only occupation is that of sitting and viewing the passing landscape, and in one's mind helping the driver operate the large vehicle. I experienced also my cheapest train ride coming from Kansas City to Newton on Saturday night. Return tickets from K. C. to Wichita were sold Saturday evening for one dollar. At the suggestion of the ticket seller I purchased one of these and then favored the Santa Fe Lines by getting off at Newton, so using less than one-half of the mileage I had paid for.

June 19, 1932 Just got through with one of my regular occupations of Sunday afternoon: slept for about three hours and feel much refreshed as a result. Last evening and last night gave us a much needed rain in which about two and one-quarter inches of water fell upon the thirsty earth. Considerable strong wind of almost cyclonic characteristics preceded and accompanied the rain. Sweet corn in the garden appeared nearly flattened out this morning. During the past week I found myself physically strong enough to exterminate a good deal of the weeds and superfluous grass about our place, working at it on the instalment plan. I do not undertake any heavy straining exertion as yet, but am thankful to God for the generous measure of strength which I have been able to recover up to the present time. Taking all things into account, the remarks of physicians and of interested friends, I must have made almost better progress than is customary following an appendectomy of such a nature as mine was. I have felt no sensations of any sort in the vicinity of the former wound for a number of days past. The total cost in cash of my appendicitis experience will probably be $175 or thereabouts. I have made a start toward paying the bill at the hospital, but do not have any definite idea as to when I can find the cash to pay the rest of the several bills. Much will depend upon what income I will have during the next year. Surgeon Haury very generously cut his charge one-third, which is, I believe, his usual discount to members of the teaching profession, at least those who teach in church schools. Dr. Haury is a fine clean Christian physician and gentleman. Newton and Harvey County seem to be especially blessed with Christian hospitals and doctors. The moral tone and even the economic standing of this and some adjoining counties is no doubt very decidedly affected by the large percentage of Mennonites who settled in these parts nearly two generations ago. At any rate some of us find this to be a very desirable part of the country in which to live for more reasons than one.

June 22, 1932 Have just finished reading through Ramsay's "Historical Commentary on the Galatians." With a single reading I could not much more than imbibe the general spirit and purpose of the author, but I am greatly enthusiastic over the viewpoint and manner of approach in this study of Paul's brief Epistle to the Galatians. It is a stimulating discussion and the volume will be highly valuable as a book of reference. The central problem with which Paul is dealing in this Epistle seems to me to have some rather specific counterparts in our own Mennonite church life and practice in this day and era. It appears that the Galatian Christians sincerely and zealously sought for ways and means whereby to help themselves to growth, advancement and perfection in the Christian life. Due to a misunderstanding of the force of the decree passed by the Council at Jerusalem and also of Paul's well-intentioned efforts to conciliate the radical Judaistic party, these Gentile Christians felt they could reach a higher stage in the Christian experience by voluntarily taking upon themselves Jewish ritual and ceremony in addition to the minimum requirements laid down in the decree, which was in fact a compromise measure and only temporarily useful. Their attitude reveals a somewhat narrow legalistic outlook upon religion, probably a hold-over from their pagan past, since in most pagan religions the basic idea in salvation is doing, performing works, ceremonies, etc., so as to earn some merit for the devotee. Their natural inclination toward such legalism was inopportunely confirmed and directed by some Judaistic emissaries who were combating Paul's interpretation of the Gospel and were trying to undo his work and undermine his authority as an Apostle.

Such a legalistic viewpoint is still found among individuals and at the present time seems in places to be striving for official recognition and enforcement in our church. Some places special forms of dress are made to take almost the identical position of circumcision in the Galatian controversy. In the dearth of sound and Scriptural arguments for supporting some of the traditional forms and extending them further, certain enthusiasts have resorted to tactics very similar to those used by Paul's Judaistic adversaries. For example, not daring to assert that a certain form of dress is essential for salvation, the insinuation is plainly made and suggested that full consecration, the deepest spirituality, the victorious life, eligibility for position in Christian work, all are unquestionably dependent upon conformity to "the order of the church." This insinuation has in recent years, as I have heard it made more frequently, increasingly impressed me as basically false and unscriptural. One result has been that I find myself feeling less active sympathy for the forms in question during late years. To my mind these forms can serve a useful purpose in our ecclesiastical economy in the present age only if they are left on a purely voluntary basis, where those who are so inclined are left free to adopt the forms for themselves as one of the ways, and only one, never the only way, in which it is possible to witness for simplicity and for an independent unconformed mode of life. To set up these forms, either overtly or by way of suggestion, as standards for greater spirituality, for fuller obedience to God, for a qualification for Christian work, is to revive in essence the Judaistic legalism of the first century which Paul fought all his life long after his conversion on the Damascus road, when he says he died to the law, and the life which he afterwards lived was Christ in him as he lived by the faith of the Son of God who had died for him.

June 24, 1932 American Magazine has an article against alibis. Too often we dishonestly blame our failures and shortcomings on circumstances or on other folks. Confessing one's faults is not only a Scripture injunction but is good sound psychological and ethical sense. Some persons again glibly pass off a failure or a mistake with a self-shielding laugh or chuckle which distracts or side-tracks their minds from giving any actual thought to self-amendment and self-improvement. Still others react to their shortcomings and faults with the attitude that they are just that way, were made that way, or prefer to be that way. It is amazing how versatile the species is in avoiding the arduous task of self-discipline. We resort to dishonesty, evasion, or mere laziness in order to keep up, in our own minds only, our poor shabby dignity and our smug complacency. I have long cherished, and am more earnestly cherishing all the time, the ideal of intellectual and moral honesty in all respects. Nothing is so attractive and desirable in my eyes as an attitude and a manner that is thoroughly simple and direct. I am by nature not given to making many words over any matter, and yet in personal contacts I often labor wickedly hard trying to make a gentle and imperceptible approach. I have concluded that it is on the whole mere hypocrisy. I crave a frank and natural way of approaching people; I want to say what I think in few and unambiguous words.

I have at times in my life felt great regret for my lack of natural gift in the direction of social conversation. Yet I have not a few times had to marvel at the gross bulk of the plain inanities and ineptitudes and vacuities that appear in much of social conversation. Taciturnity does not appear as such a grave fault at the times when I make such observations. At the same time I confess that there has always been in my mind a lurking suspicion that by some determined and systematic effort it would be possible to improve myself in the conversational art. One obstacle I have at times felt is that my reading and thinking have been such that it affords common ground with scarcely anyone about me. My reading is not wide and general enough, as it seems. Again I am not a controversialist and what I read rarely rouses in me questions and problems to defend or to refute.

June 25, 1932 I spend some time these days working on the college catalog which is belated this year because of the many uncertainties about the whole school situation. With economic conditions as they now are, the present prospects for the next year at this place are slender enough. What can be done about it? Seemingly nothing.

The Peace Problems Committee of our General Conference has several times in the past suggested to me that I prepare a "tract," as they call it, for propaganda purposes on the theme "The Church and the State." The theme attracts me, at least the title does. My thoughts occasionally recur to the subject, but farther than that I have not gotten. I did borrow a number of books on political science last winter from Professor Byler, intending to read into some foundational material. Did not read far enough at that time to become absorbed in the subject. I have reflected enough on the theme to become aware that it involves a number of basic problems in theology and in the philosophy of history. I do not anticipate that I shall write anything on the subject for publication very soon. Perhaps some day I may; I hope so. Much has been written on different phases of the subject and there are found expressed a goodly variety of opinions on the subject.

Mrs. Yoder brought from the garden today the first ripe tomatoes of the season. The plants were set out on April 1, (as I remarked at the time) as an April Fool joke. But the joke is all on the weather man, who did not succeed in killing the plants by frost. The near one hundred and twenty-five plants we set out have grown lustily and many of them are hanging full and loaded down with small green tomatoes. Sweet corn and squash will be usable in a short time. It is about the earliest and growingest garden season we have ever experienced. New potatoes are of goodly size and very fine in the eating. Onions are growing large in size and of good quality. We regard ourselves as very fortunate and richly blessed in having such an early abundance of vegetables and fruits this year.

After a complete vacation from anything like study and research for about two months and a half, I contemplate to start such activities again soon. Next week I hope to proceed with my work in Quintilian where I left it before. Should also like to do some translating for practice and also hope to do some writing, starting to work on a number of articles and projects, something to have in reserve against a time of need. Sometimes wonder if I am silly in entertaining an idea that I might some time earn a part of my living by writing. Doubtless I am so!

June 27, 1932 Another rain of a two-thirds inch fell yesterday afternoon. Today, cool and mostly clear.

The Sunday School Times has long been my favorite religious periodical, mostly for reasons of its general emphasis and point of view. In recent years seemingly the Times has become a little more narrowly dogmatic in its editorial pronouncements, sometimes in a tone that reflects a shadow of intolerance for other views. Perhaps it is only my own tastes that have been changing and I imagine it is the Times which is different. But I do not think it is altogether in myself. Sometimes its contentions appear almost like a "striving about words to no profit," a sort of petty quibbling over words and phrases. The Times makes much of the principle that the victorious Christian must never feel irritated or annoyed as he contends for the faith he holds. For the most part this seems to be true in its discussion, yet the strongly adjectivized statements it makes seem to betray a very dogmatic, almost "wise in his own conceits" attitude. Doubtless for a large segment of readers such a policy of strong language, bordering on exaggeration and overstatement, is the surest guarantee that some modicum of the truth will carry over and become a part of the thinking of individuals.

Life begins to look a little blue to me. It seems that the fates are conspiring just now to bring upon us soon some of the greatest tests and problems we have yet had to meet since we are married. Of the three prospective positions for next year, which were on the horizon three months ago, at least one of which I had hoped would materialize, all have vanished now. Along with this falling away of prospects for income has come my own illness and surgical expense and also further family expenses in prospect for the near future. It is a particular conjunction of circumstances which is interesting in itself and will be still more interesting in its solution. The thought of changing my occupation and line of work seems impossible at a first glance; and yet I do not suppose it would be so very hard for me to revert back to the farm and the tillage of the soil. All in all it seems a dismal prospect. It is such a crushing blow to my ideals and plans for self-development. What of leisure time for much reading and study, what of cash for obtaining books, cash for some travel in Europe and study in Italy and Greece? It seems to be about time to throw away all such ambitions and dedicate myself body, soul, and spirit to the job of getting food, clothing and shelter. Yet I cannot bring myself to let go of all that has seemed worth while in life. It is simply a matter of hope and of faith, I presume, for the time being. Mine is becoming a rather realistic world; much of my idealism of earlier and youthful days is vanishing away as a rainbow in a morning cloud. Faith keeps on

95

believing that it will be a better day tomorrow, that the sun will shine brighter after the clouds have passed away again. God's purposes seem dark and mysterious while they are in process of being carried out. My past experiences of God's presence and power in my life hold my faith unshakably fixed in Him still in this time.

June 30, 1932 New federal revenue taxes went into effect about a week ago. Postage rates on letters will be three cents instead of two as now, beginning next week. These new taxes will not affect us very much, happily. The only points where we are touched are in the increased letter rate, for such letters as we need to write; in the two-cent tax on each check written, which will not be a big toll here. My last check book filler has lasted me more than five months, less than five checks per month, which can be still a little more reduced by close watching, although such money as I send away in the mail I prefer to send by personal check, since it is cheaper than a postal money order and less trouble than a bank draft. There is also to be a three per cent tax on electrical energy. Whether this will be added to the bill which the consumer pays, or will be paid by the producer, I do not know. Aside from these few items we escape taxation because of our poverty. Income taxes are increased, automobiles, gas, oil, all luxuries, amusements, etc., etc., are rightly and properly taxed. It will be a long and disagreeable process to reduce very perceptibly the cost of government, but it will need to be lowered somehow during the next years, if budgets are to be regularly balanced.

July 4, 1932 Rain fell again last night, enough to do us for another week. Temperature did not drop down any this time over the rain. Felt obliged to grace with my presence the quarterly Sunday School Conference meeting at Pennsylvania Church last evening, solely because I was named on the program of speakers. It was sweltering hot in the meeting house.

Milo Kauffman stopped here again on Friday and Saturday of the last week. He is struggling with a great load, planning the work of the school for next year. He has an abundance of zeal and enthusiasm, which should rekindle some interest and at least reveal whether anything can be done to rehabilitate the work of the school. In his inexperience at the work of organization he is not definite and specific enough in his plans and policies. Such is perhaps the best one can do with the unknown quantities that are to be dealt with. Deliberateness and cautious planning did not save the situation during the past two years, and I say, let instinct and impulse be given a free hand for once. Somehow I cannot help feeling that at bottom it is folly for our Board of Education to refuse to concentrate its college effort at one point making it as strong as our resources warrant, which will be weak at the best, instead of scattering efforts and perhaps failing all around at the last.

July 10, 1932 High temperatures have been on hand the past few days. Some few indications for rain are about and another weekly shower would be in order again. This has been a very pleasant summer so far. For us it would be a perfectly enjoyable summer if we had not to have in our minds the untoward prospects for next winter, with perhaps little or no income in sight. There seems always to be an unwelcome fly in the ointment. I presume it would not be a good thing to have every phase of a current experience a pleasant one. But still think that the good Lord will have some way out for us. I often recall my own experiences years ago when I was struggling to make my way through school. After struggling against odds for three years, I fell upon my high wage job in Reno County which put me out of the reach of want for a number of years — until I married! Perhaps God will again bring to us an equivalent experience — sometime. It is a great disturber of our peace of mind and conscience to have unpaid bills hanging over us and the need for incurring still more of such. It is a fine ideal not to care about money, not to seek positions for the money that is involved. But will it hold out in a practical world — this is the question that comes to one under present circumstances. I fear that I will need soon to make some desperate efforts to get a position and will choose the one that carries with it the most income, not regardless of all other considerations, but regardless of some that have been sometimes considered essential.

July 18, 1932 Am laboring during spare time at earning some credit in professional education courses for the possible purpose of securing a state high school certificate for teaching. I am taking correspondence study work from Kansas University. They have good courses, well worked out and thorough. The one course I enrolled for, History of Ancient and Medieval Education, is pleasant and agreeable enough to my taste. But Educational Psychology, a course required absolutely, is more or less of a bugbear. The assignments to write out are long and tiresome. I can easily see that in no possible way can I get my required eight hours completed by September 1 as I had once hoped. Courses in educational theory have been bêtes noires for me. The material set for mastery in such courses seems always to me so very vague, unsubstantial, and theoretical as to be scarcely worth my while to study it. I have an idea that all the voluminous libraries that are being written and published by educational theorists are a necessary part of the process for arriving ultimately at some kind of a science of education. But we may expect that some generations hence some brilliant scholars will digest the mountainous mass of educational literature, will separate the few grains of substantial truth from the infinite amount of chaff, and will have something to present that will be worth one's while to study and ponder. But for an amateur to try to make head or tail of the chaos that now passes for pedagogical science — bah! The medieval schoolmen and scholastic philosophers are often today held up as perfect models of perfectly silly makers of endless distinctions and definitions, of absurd reasonings and problem posings. Perhaps they deserve their present reputation — and again perhaps not. At any rate the modern educational sciolists are not a whit behind the most abstruse of the scholastic philosophers when it comes to multiplying phrases and terms, making endless distinctions and definitions that mean nothing, and nonplussing the poor reader.

Dry weather is upon us. Our tomatoes and strawberries are suffering. The exceedingly hot and blistering sunshine is scorching the tomatoes where they are exposed to the direct rays. Harvested onions and potatoes last week. About two bushels of onions and five and one-half bushels of fine potatoes. We will probably use up all of these items in the course of the next ten months. Onions are almost a staple vegetable in my own diet. Our supply of glass jars is about all filled up now. If we still get tomatoes to can, as we surely hope, we will need to buy some jars. Prospects for income for the winter remain uncertain and negative. Three others of the last year's faculty here are in the same predicament — Byler, Wall, Miller. M. A. Yoder who tried keeping store for about six months has quit and has nothing to do. A headline in the daily newspaper speaks of factories reopening in Eastern states. Wheat is quoted locally at twenty-five cents a bushel right now.

July 21, 1932 Several days of pleasantly warm weather have just passed by, not so extremely hot as last week. No rain, however. Canned eight quarts of rhubarb on Monday; I gathered the stems on the college campus free of cost. Grass on lawn and weeds in garden do not grow and make work during such weather as the present. Have been watering tomatoes this week. Strawberry plants that were strong and green, full of buds and green berries two weeks ago are now dying right and left. We hardly feel we can afford to water them for the small returns we receive from them. Caught a turtle eating the ripening tomatoes yesterday and took him prisoner at once. Want to "take him for a ride" soon. He has been staying somewhere near about here for several years.

Hesston is a popular residence town at present due probably to the ridiculously low rent costs that are charged. The cheapest houses are from seven and one-half to ten dollars a month, for houses that are not modern. About every house in town is occupied now. One property changed hands the other day for a consideration of fifteen hundred dollars. It is an eight-room house, has an acre of land with it, also barn and a chicken house. Three times such a sum would scarcely have bought the place three years ago. Such is the deflation that has come upon real estate.

Board of Directors of our Alumni Association has reelected myself as president of the Association for a two-year term. Another of the worry-no-pay-jobs that always seem to come my way.

July 23, 1932 One always finds some measure of satisfaction in reviewing certain phases of the past, or in building air castles for the time to come, particularly when the present is dark and uncertain. Was reviewing in my mind how we "got along" financially when we first started up keeping house twelve years ago. For the three years I taught at that time I received nine hundred dollars the first year and ten hundred each of the other years. The first winter we were stocking up some with equipment and had nothing left for the summer, so I up and earned about two hundred dollars in the summer. At the end of second year I had five hundred dollars on hand to loan out. At the end of the third year I had not very much on hand, but we did sink four hundred dollars in two bare lots south of the college and did get a new Ford car as a preliminary to taking up university residence. How we managed to get through so well, especially the second year is a bit of a mystery. But it is to be explained in part by the fact that we had roomers in our upstairs rooms, I think three during the second winter, two during the first winter and only one the third winter. I recall too that my good wife did some washing for students every winter, without any power washer at that. This brought in a little cash. Thereafter began my university career, when for three years and three months I earned very little income. Wife was the leading breadwinner for us during these three years. Since then we have not been getting along so well, it seems. For five years I did have income to the extent of thirteen to sixteen hundred, yet I came away from university with more expensive tastes and standards so that the larger sums have scarcely sufficed any better than did the smaller annual income earlier. Another factor in late years has been the health expenses we have had. I have about developed a conviction as follows for my future plans, if the Lord so directs: Since my wife, who is worth many times her weight in gold, and the more I see of other women, the more fortunate I reckon myself for having her, since she is not endowed with a great deal of physical strength and energy, since she appreciates to the full the moderate conveniences which bring leisure and comfort, since she possesses intelligence for the appreciation of spiritual and intellectual values, since she sacrificed and suffered much in order to cooperate with me in securing my university training, therefore I cannot much longer with a good conscience give my services for a mere pittance and less than a decent living, causing her to worry and suffer still more. If the Lord should give me an opening with a living wage, I have about decided in my own mind that it would be my duty to take it. I realize that some will regard me as a heretic and backslider, should I do such a thing. The answer that satisfies my own mind is that I have now given nine years of service to our church schools, I will get out of the way now so that other young idealists who wish to give "service" in the church may have their chance. Furthermore the plain fact of the matter is that, whatever some others are able to do, I cannot make an adequate living teaching in our schools. This entire matter is, of course, a theory. If I am unable to secure any other position anywhere, I shall need to keep on existing as best we can, sinking or swimming, as the case may be.

July 28, 1932 Mailed out the college catalogs yesterday, after working on them at sundry periods on several preceding days, eight hundred of them. It falls to my lot to do up a number of such jobs about the college this summer, as no one else seems to look after them. The stenographer, Miss Nitzsche, left today for a vacation of some weeks extent, so I am left as assistant registrar, librarian, and office attendant. A.N. Troyer is attending to matters in the business office generally. An issue of the Journal must be prepared, published and mailed next month. All this devolves upon myself, even though I have not even been engaged yet to serve in the school for the coming year. Erb has been in western Canada since in April. Burkhart and family are in eastern states visiting. Kauffman has not moved here as yet. Driver has inherited, rather his wife, money sufficient to pay for a home. Byler is turning his property back to his creditors after trying for four years to pay interest and taxes on it. Such are some faculty facts at present.

July 31, 1932 Yesterday evening between eight and nine o'clock the

Benders came to our house for what turned out to be a birthday celebration. The wife soon brought forth from the electric refrigerator ice cream, and also cake and coffee, which were enjoyed by all. The occasion was my own passing of the thirty-ninth milepost of life, which seems like approaching middle age. About the age one grows out of the fanciful and high-falutin' ideals of impetuous youth and settles down to a realistic living of life. I am ready to make the change. Even now I seem to have some misgivings as to whether some of my idealism of former years was not of the nature of will-of-the-wisps.

Today has been a sweltering day, but thick clouds came up from the northwest which have given a slight relief. Promises for rain have not been made good.

August 3, 1932 Will Durant's favorite formula in one of his books is "Perspective is everything." Whether it is everything or not, I do not know, but I am well aware that it is something. Often in order to evaluate and make an attempt at interpretation of present experiences it is good to review past experiences and also to employ the imagination on the future possibilities of one's case. For myself, in times of stress I am particularly inclined to such reverie, such efforts at securing perspective in my thought.

One stabilizing factor in my religious experience, since I have come to what Bernard Iddings Bell calls the fourth or rationalizing stage, has been the perspective afforded by a contemplation of my own earlier experiences. Few experiences of my life seem in reminiscence to be so vital, so sacred, and so satisfying as those that accompanied the awakening of religious consciousness in my soul and the early steps as I learned to "walk in the Spirit." There is an aura that surrounds the various phases of these experiences in the memory, which sheds a glory over the whole and makes it one of the most real of realities for myself. Whenever I find that from reading the reasonings and rationalizings of men about religion, or from the observation of the hocus-pocus that with many folks passes for religion, I am inclined to question in my mind the reality of religion, then a review of my own past experiences in religion is as a refreshing dew and a genial sun upon my religious aspirations. It is not that I try to live now on some experiences of the past, because those are very definitely in the past and I have long since outgrown most of them, but their timely recall does afford a helpful perspective at times when the stress of a present moment tends to warp one's vision. St. Paul admonished his converts to forget the things behind and press forward to the goal; at the same time it is easy to see that he must have often rehearsed in his mind the experience of his own conversion on the Damascus road and so derived much comfort and inspiration for his task. The great experiences of the past I look upon, not as a goal attained, but rather as a pledge of the growth that is possible in religious experience, as a method for the making of progress to new and higher levels. The glory and effulgence which in the memory surrounds the first consciousness of religious awakening is not unlike the glory that attaches to one's first experience of falling in love, or other awakenings in the life. The emotional reaction leaves a more outstanding impression than the more prosaic but often greater experiences in later life of the same kind.

August 7, 1932 A pleasant day after the refreshing breezes from the north that blew down upon us yesterday evening and during the past night.

Recent thoughts of mine have been: I am personally, no doubt, becoming less useful and more of no account every day. Proof: I am unable to get any kind of a job in my line of teaching. I am a flat failure as Sunday School superintendent, even after some years of experience, because the attendance at the weekly teachers' meeting set a new record this morning, it being just zero besides the leader. Furthermore, the result of the great effort I made last November to rally the support of the S. S. classes to meet the missionary support pledge seems to have lasted just about seven months and is now running out. The July offering was already down to a trifle above one-half of the amount needed, and today's offering was a bit below one-half of the necessary monthly amount. Quod est demonstratum!

To reduce expenses at our house just a little more, I paid up my telephone service dues to August 1, 1932 and then disconnected the phone. It is no particular inconvenience to ourselves to be without this service, but it rues us a little to cause neighbors the inconvenience of having to call personally for small errands. I almost prefer to do my own errands by the pedestrian method. Besides the lady of the house never has formed the habit of visiting other women over the telephone. I have never known her to call anyone, or either to be called for that specific purpose. So there is no disadvantage from that angle. During the three years we first lived in this house we had no phone at all. In 1929, because I was a school official, I was urged by some and also felt inclined to have a phone installed, which we have been able to keep up until recently. To have telephone service here, one must buy a share of stock (for $20) in the local mutual company, and also buy his own telephone. I chanced to be able to buy a secondhand desk phone for ten dollars. I expect to retain stock and phone for the time being; may have to sell it later.

Have been spending some time tying up the grape clusters, which are just beginning to turn ripe, in paper bags, one or two clusters in a bag. Have already tied on over two hundred bags and will need to put on about one hundred fifty more to finish the job. It is slow and tedious work but in one's contest with the birds some pains and effort seem necessary in order to have the advantage over the smalle fowles. Robins and orioles are the most persistent thieves. They have ravenous appetites and can ruin a lot of beautiful grape clusters in a very short time.

August 12, 1932 Have given some time this week to cleaning several rooms in the house, my study and the den with its adjoining closet. There is about once each year an urgent need to organize and stow away accumulated material of all kinds, make clippings from magazines previously marked, file away notes made on sundry articles, file away magazines and journals of various sorts. When the occasion for such a clearance comes along I usually dust books and bookshelves in the study, place new acquisitions in a regular place on the shelves, and tidy up desk drawers.

August 14, 1932 Have been meditating to set down some general notes on the beginning, course, and progress of my religious experiences. Naturally my own experiences, in some aspects, seem quite unique, but perhaps only because I have not happened to learn of other persons' experiences in the same line. I suspect that it may be another pet delusion to entertain an idea that one's own particular experiences are extraordinary, special, or unique in some way.

Our home on the small farm in Eastern Iowa was a quite typical farm home for that section of the Amish-Mennonite settlement. My father's parents lived in a small house in the same yard. They were fine old people. Grandfather could read very little, but Grandmother could read, and did read both English and German considerably. I often loved to visit in their little living room. I associated much with Grandfather out-of-doors from the age of about eight to thirteen, when he died at the age of eighty-two. I learned many things from him about farm and shop work. But religion was not often directly a topic of conversation about our home, which seems to be the common attitude in Amish homes. I was never taught to say prayers before going to bed in the evening. Family worship was not practiced in our home until about the time I was nineteen or twenty years of age, when Father without any warning or explanation started the custom of gathering the family in the living room immediately upon leaving the breakfast table each morning. He regularly read the assigned daily readings indicated in the Sunday-School lesson helps by the International Lesson Committee. The prayer that followed he read out of a prayer book. Since then he has begun the practice of improvising the prayer offered. From my childhood grace at the table before eating was always in silence with bowed heads and hands held beneath the family board. After eating, a brief thanksgiving was again in silence with the same ritual. Later at about the same time that family worship was established by Father, he began also to say grace at table audibly, using short formal prayers which were long ago memorized.

I was taken to church services regularly and to S. S. at the Lower Deer Creek Church where all services were in German. The main instruction for the youngest pupils was to learn the spelling of German words and the reading of the catechism and the German New Testament. This was my first effort at learning a foreign language, and I congratulate myself on mastering it fairly well, considering the amount and type of instruction received. I believe Mother used to help me some in learning German reading. S. S. met only every other Sunday, while church services were held on the alternate Sundays in between. The S. S. lasted only from about April first to nearly Christmas each year. I remember I always enjoyed the S. S. sessions, learned many things that were basic for Biblical knowledge and later Christian experience. I seemed to have a natural insight into and appreciation of religious and spiritual things even from childhood, more so than many boys of my age, as nearly as I can make the comparison now. I recall my interest in the discussions of Biblical questions in the general adult review period of the S. S. I remember I had a sort of natural fondness for reading in the N. T. and any religious books I could get hold of.

In 1904, while in the eleventh year of my age, there came a strange experience and a change in my life. Both the experience and the change were unconscious on my part, so nearly as I am able to recall since, and it was not until more than five years later that the reality and the significance of what happened dawned upon my consciousness. It is also an experience which, because it all seems so strange, I have never related to anyone, excepting the wife of my bosom.

During the previous summer (of 1903) we had helping us on the farm a young man who had a very profound influence upon me for the time being. Unfortunately he was not very conscientious about some of his moral habits. He was not in any sense a wicked character, but did have the habit of using some evil language and had a considerable stock of evil stories and imaginings in his mind. I fell into certain evil habits, including evil language and untruthfulness that I especially remember. I was also at times very unkind and "mean" in the way I treated my younger brother, especially in school. These were the chief sins into which I fell and which were in the way of becoming habits and leading me on, perhaps, to worse things. I do recall, however, that I sometimes had strange emotional reactions when I would reflect upon these things and even shed tears in a sort of penitence. But I cannot recall since that I ever felt a definite conviction for sin or was conscious of anything like being a lost soul or at enmity with God. Father overheard me indulging in profane language once, and rebuked me kindly but sternly. I think that partly cured me of that tendency.

In March of 1904, from seemingly no source I took down with scarlet fever. For several weeks I was deathly and desperately sick. The memory of those weeks has been a total blank for me ever since. To my recollection I had no thought or fear of death in my mind, no consciousness of guilt, no reflection on my condition, made no resolution or decision. If any of these things took place, they must have been in the subconscious part of my mind, or were blotted out of conscious memory at once. But I recovered. I have distinct recollection of the later phases of my illness. I was not conscious of any change on my part at all. But in reviewing the matter and reflecting upon it in after years I recalled that all desire, urge, or temptation to indulge my former evil tendencies was absent. There was a new glory in life and in living that added a new thrill to experience. I think I had a more serious attitude towards life. As nearly as I can estimate it now, it was during this illness that, unconsciously on my own part, I went through a spiritual and mental rebirth; God's Spirit changed my heart and I was walking in a new world and a new life. But the reality of this was hid from my own eyes as yet. I thought of myself as an unsaved soul, because I understood that confession of Christ and membership in a church were essential parts of being a Christian. This was merely intellectual. I had no guilt of conscience, no struggle of surrender, no uneasiness of any definite sort.

August 16, 1932 I do not think I ever was a youth. It was not my privilege to go through the normal and usual experiences of adolescence. After the crisis in 1904, I was mentally already an adult, at least so I would define my attitudes, outlook, interests, and ways of thinking, whatever the expert psychologists might decide of it. I matured early in body also. I recall that people often remarked about the home how tall I was for my age at the time my years numbered about nine to

twelve, and while no records of measurement were kept, I am pretty
sure that I had attained my present stature by the time I was thirteen
or fourteen. I began to shave my face at thirteen which seems to be
three or four years ahead of normal. My health was not of the best
during these years of rapid and almost premature growth. I attended
common school one-half mile from home during the winter months until I was fifteen, when I passed the eighth grade examinations. Excepting on the district school playground while in school, I never took part
in any boyish sports, never learned to swim, to skate, to play regular
baseball. Parents were not interested in any of these activities, and I
was well content to work on the farm and take my recreation by myself
reading and studying books. I never formed the habit of running around
at night during my teens, such as going to town on Saturday evenings
and loafing. From the age of fifteen or sixteen I went to community
singings on Sunday evenings, when they were close by. To the play parties that were somewhat regularly carried on in the community by the
young people I only went once or twice. I felt conscientious scruples
against taking part in such affairs. My close friends and associates
were rarely of my own age after I ceased to attend district school, always older than myself and of more mature tastes and activities.

As an evidence of my intellectual tastes and interests after my
"conversion," I recall distinctly with what relish and consuming interest I devoured the issues of the Gospel Herald (or Gospel Witness,
as it was then named) when it then first began to come to our home
in 1906. All its articles were the joy and delight of my soul. (Today
I rarely read an entire article; mostly glance over headings, news
notes, reports, etc.) In my own way I began to cultivate the life of the
Spirit. I recall many satisfying and even thrilling experiences in prayer.
The habit of praying silently just after getting into bed in the evening
became fixed and served me well for many years and I can still readily
revert to it. Because of my interest in books and reading Father on
one or two occasions purchased a small lot of books, mostly religious.
Among them were a few devotional books with devotional readings and
prayers printed. I read and reread these with seemingly endless joy
and inspiration. One time I remember Father mildly remonstrated for
my reading in the devotional books so much. It seemed so strange to
me then, and even now yet as I think back, as I never quite understood
what he meant by it. In memory stand out clearly a few occasions during these early years of my spiritual life when being left at home all
alone on a Sunday or so, I experienced very remarkable seasons of fellowship with God. I would kneel in prayer in my upstairs room, pray
to God with tears of joy and satisfaction, so that my soul was filled
with glory and with love to God and living was like walking on holy or
enchanted ground. Many and varied experiences have come in my devotional and prayer life since equally as satisfying, but around none
does the memory draw such a halo of glory as around those early
trysts of the soul with God. All these early experiences, which were
for the most part spontaneous, the natural hunger of my soul for God,
the direct intuitional living with God and feeding upon His truth, were
barely understood by myself, as all real religious experience perhaps
never is at the moment. Later thinking and reasoning have often suggested doubt or uncertainty to my mind, but the unshakable foundation

of my knowledge that God is and that I can enter into personal fellowship with Him is precisely the unquestionable reality of my own experiences in those early adventures in soul culture and spiritual exploration. Many phases of formal and organized Christianity have always
seemed to me a bit jejune and tasteless, a trifle deadening to spontaneous fellowship with God. Sometimes one wonders if organized religion in the aggregate helps or hinders communion with God. I assume
it is best not to decide on this question solely from my own experience.

But the time came that I felt I should unite with a church and become a Christian (as I thought in my own mind). Conditions at the
Lower Deer Creek Church, where my parents belonged were not very
inviting to a young person. It was nominally an Old Order Amish congregation, but was not as extremely static as Old Order congregations
in other places. There had been church trouble smouldering for several
years. Practically none of the young men who attended the Sunday School
there were uniting with this Church, but went to East Union or West Union when they joined a church. In 1909 a large group of young women
"followed the church" at Lower Deer Creek, as the expression was, but
not a single boy or young man. On July 4 a S. S. Conference program
was given at East Union Church and for some reason it happened that I
was there for the evening program. The bishop of East Union, by way
of announcement stated that a number of applicants would be baptized at
the regular morning service on the next day (Sunday) and extended invitation to anyone else who so desired to join the class of applicants at
that time. The call went home to my heart and I felt an impulse to
accept the invitation. The next morning before breakfast with much fear
and trembling, I asked my mother if I might do so. Her reaction was
what I had partly anticipated it would be. She was grieved and troubled
that I should wish to join any church other than the one where they belonged. She wanted me instead to go to their church service that morning and apply there for membership. Father's attitude on the matter,
when it was announced to him, he expressed by saying that he did not
feel like standing in the way for anyone who interested and exercised
himself as much in religious reading and study as I did. Out of deference to Mother's feelings I did not go to East Union to be baptized that
day. Went to our regular place of worship but took no steps to unite
there. In September of that year Rev. J. S. Hartzler of Indiana conducted special evangelistic meetings at East Union. With Aaron Hochstetler,
who was working some of the time at our place, I attended some of the
meetings. One evening I stood up to make confession of Christ when
the invitation was given. Without directly consulting my parents further,
I went on with my determination and on a Sunday morning, October 24,
according to a note on the fly leaf of my old Oxford Bible I used then,
I was baptized by the aged bishop, Christian Werey. There were about
three others baptized at the same time, although I am not certain anymore at this time who they all were. It seems to me that two of them
were Millers, Chris and Marie, the latter being now Mrs. Beachey of
Kalona, Iowa. From that time on I attended services at East Union regularly. In the spring of 1910 Father bought me a buggy for my own use.
The other ministers there at that time were Dan Fisher and Fred Gingerich, who is now in Oregon.

It was shortly after my baptism that in the course of my meditations the whole outline of my religious experiences during the six years previous rather suddenly dawned upon my mind. I was husking corn in the field, an operation that had become largely mechanical, leaving the mind free for any amount of thought and meditation. I remember something of the thrill I felt when the truth dawned upon me that I had been "saved" during all these years and was not conscious of it, that the Spirit of God had changed my heart some time in March of the year 1904, that I had been growing in grace, spiritual knowledge and perception rather steadily, and that God had somehow led me marvellously during all the intervening time.

Numerous milestones in experience from that time forward still stand out clearly in memory. Early in 1910, S. G. Shetler of Pennsylvania, assisted by some others conducted an eight-day Bible Conference at East Union Church with sessions in morning and evening. These were a rich feast to mind and soul for me. It started me on a program of personal Bible study that lasted for a long time. In October of the same year D. D. Miller of Indiana preached a series of evangelistic sermons which were immensely profitable to me. Other ministers who during the following years handed out soul food that was especially beneficial to me and inspirational as well were, S. E. Allgyer of Ohio, L. J. Miller of Missouri. I began teaching a Sunday-School class at least as early as January, 1913. Before then already I had given talks on assigned topics in Young People's Meeting. Preparing and giving such a talk was then always a cosmic event of the first magnitude in my life. I have still somewhere among my old papers a note book in which I faithfully recorded all such occasions with all details of interest.

August 17, 1932 Prevailing temperatures are high. Clouds hover in the sky, but do not precipitate any moisture.

For mental pabulum among my staple reading for a goodly number of years was the Youths' Companion of Boston. I relished it in its entirety. The stories were all of good, wholesome type. The general literary and intellectual standard of this weekly magazine was just exactly suited to my capacity and interest at that time. In 1909 or 1910 when the Christian Monitor was launched at Scottdale I agreed to discontinue the Youths' Companion and read in its stead the Monitor. The latter however, to my mind, has never been of the high and excellent standard of the Companion, at least on the intellectual and literary side. But I did not so greatly regret the change, because I was nearly at the point of outgrowing that sort of reading as my staple mental diet. Another weekly magazine that I read regularly and appreciatively for a number of years, a little later than the time I lived on the Youths' Companion, was the Christian Herald of New York City. For several years I read the weekly sermon page with keenest delight, sermons by such preachers as Dixon, Parkhurst, Hillis, and others. During several years, perhaps 1911 - 1913, as nearly as I can estimate it now, this magazine conducted a monthly Bible quiz consisting of about ten or twelve factual questions on matter taken at random from the entire Bible. Everyone was invited to send in the answers. The sole remuneration was to have one's name listed in the honor roll the month after if as many as eight or nine questions were correctly answered. I answered these regularly for a time and gained a place on the honor roll quite frequently, although, not every time I attempted the questions. I have preserved somewhere among my papers the clippings of the question lists which I answered and a record of my appearances on the honor roll.

The criticism I would make of our own church literature and periodicals, were I to essay such a criticism, is that their contents are too stereotyped, not diversified enough to adapt themselves to varied types of minds and intellects. They all smack strongly of elementary Sunday School stuff, the preaching and moralizing are too very evident all the time for best results with youth who are mentally alive.

August 18, 1932 My ways and means of Bible study have constantly changed along with Christian growth and experience. Never had much success with reading the Bible through continuously from start to finish. Started such a procedure once and came nearly all the way through the Old Testament. From Bible conference attendance I learned the topical method of study and especially interesting to me was the use of the marginal references in the small Oxford Bible I used. I memorized a good deal of Scripture for my own satisfaction, mostly isolated verses, but also some continuous passages, as Psalm 1, Psalm 23, I Corinthians 13, Philippians 2:5-11, and at one time I had learned nearly all of the Sermon on the Mount well enough so that I could repeat it. In 1913-1914 I went through a correspondence course called Synthetic Bible Studies from the Moody Bible Institute of Chicago. This course I bought from Mose Miller near home who had started it but could not go on with it. I got it at a bargain. I found it quite helpful, finished it in due time and received a diploma which must still be somewhere among my numerous collection of such instruments. I bought a Revised Version of the Bible as far back as 1912, at least, for use as a study Bible. I still use it although its imitation morocco covers are ragged and much worn. During my early years in school after leaving home, 1915-1917, I practiced marking my Bible as I read it for devotional purposes. The small India paper Oxford Bible which I had used first for its marginal references soon became much underlined and its scant margins in some parts filled with notes of one sort or another. It had to be recovered and rebound and is still usable. My next advance in New Testament study was made after I had learned to read it in Greek. I happened to get a new copy of a Wescott and Hort Testament in eight-vo size for one dollar. When I first taught N. T. Greek in 1920-21, I came upon the practice of making finely written pen and ink notes in all margins, notes taken from commentaries and various sources. The Gospel of Luke was first so treated. The method proved to be so fascinating that I continued it afterwards at intervals until the whole copy is "annotated" now excepting Matthew, Revelation, and the last one-half of Romans. Galatians I "did" only during the past year. The notes are varied and miscellaneous for the most part, but have some little value even now for reference, although the chief benefit was from the process of gathering and transcribing them. The fly leaves of this copy, back and front, have received numerous references, quotations, comments, etc., copied from many sources. There is still room here and there for more such material and from time to time they are entered. The copy has become almost priceless to me. The outside covers are very ragged also so that its exterior shall not tempt anyone to steal it from me. In 1920 I procured a small handy copy of Nestle's Greek Testament which I used continuously, much of the time as a pocket Testament, for casual reading, and for classroom teaching. Its binding finally became completely undone and this year a new copy has replaced it in use. In Old Testament study I have made little progress in the last twelve years. My ambition has been to acquire a reading knowledge of the Hebrew language and use it in studying the Hebrew text of the O. T. even as I did the Greek text of the new. But so far I have not succeeded in mastering the Hebrew. Hope still lingers that this ambition may sometime become an eventuality. Meanwhile I have become interested in studying the O. T. writings in their true literary forms. I use Moulton's Modern Reader's Bible. The notes and discussions at the end of the volume and especially the printing of the text according to the forms of the literature are very suggestive, and I have been trying to appreciate and master especially the Psalms and the Wisdom Literature generally from this viewpoint.

Practically all my Bible study has been independent, that is, outside of formal class work. In my academy course here at school I took only the required minimum of one unit of work in Bible classes. This was all under J. B. Smith, Bible Doctrines and Prophecy, the latter being a sort of a joke, as it seems to me. In my college course, a course in Biblical Introduction was instructive and helpful with Noah Oyer as teacher. I was also in his course in Systematic Theology, which was philosophy more than Bible. As to what particular directions my interest in Biblical study may take next one can hardly guess. The study of Biblical writings as historical documents appeals strongly to me of late, using archaeological, linguistic and historical aids in gaining a fuller appreciation of the messages of the Biblical writers.

August 19, 1932 Religion has been to me essentially a personal affair, the quiet inner fellowship with the personality of God, the contemplation of God's character and His work, the yearning and striving to conform more nearly to His will. The features of formal and militant Christianity which include any forms of display, noise, blatant ballyhoo and the like have always been more or less distasteful to me. I think it is necessary to witness for one's faith, to exercise the expressional side of one's religion. But for me living day by day in the strength that comes from intimate fellowship with God is as potent as any form of religious expression, to my mind. However, to be dogmatic in insisting on any specific pattern of experience or any set formula or slogan in such matters, even if it be a latitudinarian formula, is still one degree worse than a noisy expression of religion. My notion is that varieties of religious experience are as numerous and seemingly infinite as the forms and shapes of the leaves and flowers that the Creator has fashioned. The cloistered monk and hermit saint of past ages did undoubtedly honor and glorify his Maker as often as the Christian today who runs hither and thither to conventions, conferences, meetings, and what not. Even the contribution of the former type to the advancement of religion can easily have been as great and as significant as that of moderns who are so completely sold on the slogan of "service." A favorite motto of mine has long been St. Paul's admonition: "Make it your ambition to be quiet and to attend to your own business." At the same time God needs active propagandists and I rejoice that He can find them for His work.

A few months ago a young Harvard graduate had an article in the Atlantic Monthly on what college did to his religion. It was the usual sophisticated undergraduate stock of ideas and phrases, attitudes and reactions gathered from the atmosphere of classroom and campus. The article revealed a total ignorance of what religion basically is, yet presuming to pronounce with finality upon its worth, bowing it frankly out of respectable standing among the intelligentsia of the day. In the latest issue of the Atlantic, Bernard Iddings Bell writes in partial reply to the young Harvard graduate and comments pointedly on the religious indifference of students in universities, blaming the latter more than the students. For a number of years past I have been reading Mr. Bell's articles and one of his books with considerable enthusiasm and interest. For an intellectualist he has about the sanest outlook on matters of religion and morals of any modern writer I happen to know of. His main thesis is that religion is the intuitive search for and fellowship with the ultimate Reality in terms of personality. Without using hoary terms and words that happen to be per se under suspicion by the mob-minded sophisticates of the day he states in other terms the basic facts of mystical and, if we please, supernatural religion. He outlines as stages of religious development four stages; the ritual stage, the myth-story stage, the faith-belief stage and the rationalization-interpretation stage. To him these stages represent steps in the historical development of religion. Perhaps so. At any rate it appears to me that these stages occur in the development of religious experience in the individual's life. Some persons never get any distance beyond the ritual stage, and many more never get beyond the story stage in their religious experience. To one who has never gone farther than this second stage, when he finds himself suddenly plunged into an atmosphere of scepticism, sophisticated doubt, and modish indifference to religion, the shock is very great. His first draughts of knowledge go at once to his head and he gets queered. The higher stages of religious experience are harder to attain, but are quite normal and necessary. It is a great misfortune when at any one of these levels a particular group organizes itself to standardize that particular stage as orthodox religion and by insinuation, suggestion, legislation, politics, and what not, proceeds to enforce that particular stage as final. Religious experience is a phase of life that brings unlimited opportunities for development and growth, for spiritual adventure and exploration, for progress and achievement of soul. Its higher stages demand for their realization no mean measure of courage and faith, partly because the technique of procedure is less well known generally, partly because it is generally a rather lonely path, the masses being satisfied with lower levels of experience. And not only satisfied to live on such levels, they also regard it as their calling to conspire against those who would go forward. Their own level of spiritual achievement becomes the measure of perfection. They know they "have arrived." If they are dogmatic besides, they are hopeless.

August 20, 1932 James Norman Hall in the latest Atlantic has a brief piece in which he notes some of his reflections on the occasion of his forty-fifth birthday. His essays have appeared before. He is an apostle of the gospel of leisure and simple living, of dignified loafing, as he wrote of it on a former occasion. He confessed to a growing "love of ease of spirit" which he declines to believe is a sign of dry rot, insisting it is more likely a sign of growing common sense. He also glories in the loss, somewhere since his thirtieth year, of what he calls social and political mindedness, the craving to reform and remake the world and its inhabitants. He satisfies his conscience by averring that the poets, which have fallen into sore neglect, must also have someone to read and enjoy them if the universe is to go on smoothly in its course. These sentiments strike a responsive cord in my heart. At times it appears that the number of the problems of our mortal race increases in direct proportion to the amount of "service", "uplift", and "reform" it gets, and these problems all grow in baffling complexity as they are talked about, discussed, and analyzed. Surely the gospel of the simple life, of the ease of spirit, of minding and doing one's own business needs its exponents in our day. Youth is naturally a time of activity. The ideal of doing things, of battling for something or other, of sacrificing (when there is little to sacrifice), all are potent to give release to the restless energy of youth's feverish spirit. With years and with reflection, with experience and the deflation of the ego, comes the hunger for "ease of spirit."

August 21, 1932 No wren notes have been made this year as yet. As last summer, a family of young were reared in the box on our front porch this summer again. They left the box early in July. We failed to see them "come out" this time and there were evidences that instead of five young as last year, only two or three were reared this time. Another family was hatched and started in life at the rear of the house. They left the nest August 12. It is not clear if it was the same pair who raised the family at the front or not, but it is possible. At the corner of the house roof, the cornice had an opening of a very narrow slot. Inside the opening the nest was placed. When the young (only two were seen, which is probably the extent of the brood) were about to venture forth into the wide world, one of them by some means or other started upwards through the hollow cornice of the gable roof of the house and found his way up to the very peak of the roof in his passageway. There he called for his food and the mother with much loud calling tried desperately to find some possible opening around the peak of the gable whereby she could deliver food to his hungry mouth. She carried on her frantic efforts during most of Friday. Late Friday evening I was watching her activities and then first discovered the real situation. It happened that while I was standing and observing what was going on, that the other little fellow in the nest clambered out through the opening that served as the regular entrance to the home and dropped straight down to the ground ten or more feet below, landing with a slight thud. Seemingly he was able to fly scarcely at all. I went to where he had made his forced landing, picked him up as he crept along the house wall in search of a place of concealment. After holding him a bit, I placed him on the ground and he sought cover at once. The mother wren happened to fly away in search of more food just before this youngster dropped to the ground and luckily for me, perhaps, she did not see me catch and hold the little one. Upon her return she found him missing from her nest also, so she gave her renewed efforts to get food to the imprisoned member in the gable cornice. Her efforts were pathetic to watch. After I left the scene, and came back to look again, she had located the one I had caught and was ministering to its wants. Dusk and darkness came soon after this. With the return of daylight the next morning, Mrs. Wren was again trying to get to the small prisoner. Before I ate my breakfast that morning I took hammer and bar in hand, went out through the upstairs den window upon the porch roof and partly loosened a short piece of the facing strip on the cornice at the peak of the roof and retired. Immediately the lady came back and in a few seconds she found the opening I had made. In she darted and in a few seconds out again. She had failed to locate her child. In she went again and was out of sight longer this time. When she emerged again, there were signs that she had fed the worm in her mouth to the little fellow. All at once she was happy and contented as if nothing had happened. When a half hour later I went out again to look, a tiny wren was creeping along the ground in the strawberry patch. I easily caught it. It was the ex-prisoner. He was apparently weakened by his long confinement and forced fasting; he could fly but little. I put him down and after a bit the mother brought him more nourishment. The family has been about the back yard much of the time since. One morning last week they were all in the garage, where the door had been left open over night.

August 29, 1932 In the words of Cicero when writing to his friend Atticus on a like occasion, I may write today "filiolo me auctum scito." This new individual appeared on the scene first yesterday afternoon at 3:48. He appears to be a goodly child, so far as one can judge from appearances at this date. He possesses a large head, abundance of cranial capacity and we hope it is or will be well filled with grey matter. My fondness for the great Roman poet led me to insist he must bear the name Virgil. My wife for some reason unexplained equally insisted that his middle name must be Edward. It is an event of major importance for wife and me; after twelve years of married bliss together, to have this joy added, seems well nigh unbelievable.

August 30, 1932 This is now the third day that a strong gale from the south has been blowing continuously. Not even during the dark hours of the night has this wind ceased its going or rested from weariness. With a little effort of the imagination, one can hear the sweep and swirl of a gigantic symphony orchestra, a harmony of many chords which is not unpleasing to listen to, as the strong wind sweeps through tree tops and grasses. The temperature has been high, but not oppressive due to the moving air. Indications for rain are not very specific as yet, although early this morning the eastern sky was painted various shades of red and orange. I wish for a real rainy spell that will start growing the seeds I planted in the garden. Tomatoes are still ripening, although there was a lull recently in the number. Many green ones are started and starting, promise for a continued supply.

I sent out the summer number of the College Journal on Monday. Most of its twelve pages are filled with alumni material of sundry sorts.

In another week school will be on the point of opening. One can only wonder what it will bring forth.

Rode along to Newton yesterday to see the young son and his mother. Found them doing exceptionally well. I am made to think about possible new interests and responsibilities. There will be numerous new things to learn and new adjustments to make.

September 1, 1932 Relief from heat and strong wind has come and welcome it is. Yesterday it rained much of the day, today has been cool, just what we have been wishing for.

Paul Benders left here early this morning on their journey to Indiana with a heavily loaded car. A truck had taken most of their household goods several weeks ago. Dr. Bender will teach in Goshen College this year, perhaps to become a permanent fixture there.

I am playing the role of a bachelor these days; keeping house, getting my own meals and washing the dishes. It is not an impossible job, provided it does not last indefinitely. The electric refrigerator still has odds and ends of left-overs which need to be eaten up anyway, and I am the one to do it! Have visited Estie and the boy at the hospital every day this week until today when I did not get to go. Went with Benders three days. Today I made myself all ready to go, expecting that Ruth Bender's ancient Chevrolet coupe which she left on my hands, would take me down. Unfortunately the motor refused to start, the battery seeming to be weak. So I missed out today. Hereafter I will be forced to depend upon the favors and accommodations of friends for my trips to Newton. The past ten months we have depended upon Bender's car, either riding with them or driving it myself. We had most things in common, they using our electric refrigerator and borrowing freely whatever we happened to have. It was a handy arrangement for both sides, but is unfortunately at an end now, unless we soon move to Indiana also — which we hope not.

September 4-5, 1932, 12 o'clock, midnight: Have just blown in from a seven and one-half mile trek on foot. I thoughtlessly took the old Chevrolet wreck and drove to Newton this evening before it occurred to me that there might be no lights with which to drive back again. At nine o'clock I started out of town to drive without lights, came west on First Street for about three miles at great risk of life and limb. Then gradually its heart failed, or something, and presently it died in its tracks. I left the thing about where it expired and hiked home. Now the thing is still on my hands, unless someone steals it during the night, or before I get someone to take pity on me and pull it somewhere. I presume it will next go to the junk man. It has been a beautiful night for a pleasant walk. Scarcely any air moving, only a bit from the north, deliciously cool, bright stars overhead, rich and fragrant odors arising from corn and other crops, pleasant footing below with no dust or mud.

Upon invitation I ate Sunday dinner with Driver's family. On Friday last Burkharts invited me to eat the noon meal with them. It spares me some trouble of cooking when neighbors so kindly invite me to eat abroad. The tasks of arranging for school to start are beginning to come before me. Met on committee Saturday for a number of hours.

Wife and small son are doing well. The young man is so eager for

112

sleep that he hardly eats enough to begin growing. Some think he takes after his father in sleeping habits and even in countenance.

September 11, 1932 Have just made my Sunday dinner on a quart of whole milk with cocoa stirred in and four slices of bread spread with peanut butter. Cooking and washing dishes becomes slightly monotonous when prolonged to a regular routine activity. Breakfast at our house has been pretty well standardized this summer. There is soft-boiled egg and sliced fresh tomatoes; bread and dairy butter; cooked whole wheat meal with raisins and milk; garden tea. This meal I can get with small trouble. Dishes I usually wash up once each day, at least. On Friday evening of the past week I ate evening lunch upon invitation with Mr. and Mrs. Milo Kauffman.

School has opened again. Have been extra busy the past number of days. Registration is now practically done and schedule-making too. It remains for me still to organize study hall. There is no college department of any sort left. Four or five students appeared for college work, but these have returned home or gone elsewhere. It is a sore disappointment, but yet seemed an act of mercy to decapitate the college, rather than leave it to linger on still longer. The stroke should have been delivered a year ago, or at least three months ago.

And so I am left with no employment or income in sight at the moment. One student wishes to be tutored in New Testament Greek.

The blows of misfortune have been falling thick and fast upon us in the recent past. What these "slings and arrows of outrageous fortune" may have as their intent only time may reveal. It all seems a hard lot and experience. But it is a new experience, and for that sole reason is not entirely unwelcome. New adventure and strange experiences are the zest and thrill of life. But I must admit that to be penniless under present circumstances is to me just a shade more serious than when I was fifteen years ago or more trying to make my way through school and college against difficulties. Beginning with the present year our troubles also began. First came the failure to receive regular salary checks, although the very first blow may be considered the one received about a year ago when I agreed to a decrease in salary of over thirty per cent. Next blow was my own emergency illness with the consequent inability to work during the summer when farm work was available. Then there was the failure to secure a college teaching position out of three that were on the horizon. Now has come the last blow which sweeps away even the tiny income that I had hoped against hope might be mine for this winter. Whether this is the final darkness before the dawn, it is quite impossible to know. There is the sole compensation that we have a son in our home, and if only Mrs. Yoder can regain her usual health and physical strength soon, I can have good courage to face the rest. At this time I have every reason to believe she will come out of her ordeal alright. But incidentally it has been revealed that she has at least three fibrous tumors in various parts of her abdomen, some large and some smaller. The physician affirms that these are not malignant or immediately dangerous, but naturally they should be removed by some manner or means as soon as possible. Mrs. Yoder sat up in bed today for the first time to eat her meal. She has considerable gas pains and thinks she will have them so long as she must lie in bed, mostly on her back. The young son lost some weight during the first week of his age and gained during his second week, but not all that he lost before. He is being bottle-fed entirely, to the advantage of both himself and the mother.

Financial prospects are slender enough for several of us who were teachers here before, and even for those who are teachers now. It should be possible, if we felt so disposed, to have a live club here for unemployed teachers. Off hand I think of possible candidates for membership the following: M. A. Yoder, J. N. Byler, Mary Miller, Chancy King, Mary Hess, and myself. Four of these were on the Hesston faculty before. A month ago I appealed to Bethel College for a position as part time teacher. Nothing came of it. Bethel has had no Latin and Greek department for some years. I suggested they might start one now for my benefit, but they have not done so yet!

September 14, 1932 Borrowed J. N. Byler's car for the second time last evening to pay a visit to wife and son at the hospital. They are getting along very well, it seems. The little fellow is growing and favored us with just a ghost of a smile last evening when he was brought in and preparations were made to give him his bottle at eight o'clock. He looks bright and alert in his eyes, and the nurses report that he makes gestures and movements or responses that indicate he is intelligent. The nurses also report that they are agreed he is the comeliest and best looking baby they have at this time. Miss Boese told Mrs. Yoder that she had not dared to tell her this so long as the other mother was still in the room with her; she left yesterday.

Report comes that my mother is very weak and is failing fast the past days. She has been bedfast and suffering now for over a month. There are no hopes for her recovery. Presumably she has an internal cancer; vomiting has been common during the past while, so that she cannot retain food enough for her nourishment.

It is now time I leave off scribbling and do some canning of grapes. I want to make juice and pulp out of the grapes I took off the vines over a week ago. Tomatoes also are to be canned today or tomorrow. My success in this venture is for later record.

September 16, 1932 Very pleasant September weather is with us. Nights are fairly cool, days clear and warm. Rain is needed for making things grow. I have been carrying water with sprinkling can to small turnips and lettuce in the garden. I expressed and put up in bottles about seven quarts of grape juice on day before yesterday; also about five quarts of the remaining pulp. Yesterday afternoon I labored and canned six and one-half quarts of real red-ripe tomatoes. This canning is not so very difficult, but requires a measure of skill and even of art. Today I peeled and prepared some apples for cooking. They are cooking now.

As soon as work at the college gets still further lined up and routinized, I shall have more time to spend at home. I have not yet planned a program and organization of my own leisure time. If it were not for the uneasiness regarding cash income for a few essentials, I should anticipate an enjoyable winter with time to do many things for personal pleasure and profit. But leisure wears a slightly different hue when it is enforced and there are no funds in sight for physical sustenance. Now will be a good time to work out a practical philosophy on the uses of adversity, the blessings of penury, and kindred subjects. Armchair philosophizing on such themes is no longer necessary, since the reality of such facts is upon us. A little time to think, and presently a philosophy will emerge.

September 18, 1932 This has been one day of terrific wind, strong and steady from the south. It has been most disagreeable to be out of doors; even indoors dust and grime settling down on all things make for unpleasantness.

Son Virgil and his mother came home from the hospital yesterday afternoon. I thought I had considerable housekeeping to do for myself alone; now it has increased three or four-fold over. I expect that for three or four weeks to come I will have all I can do with the house work. Everyone seems to be doing alright. The baby has been crying sometimes, perhaps due to a change made in his hours of feeding; a mere change of schedule seems to discourage him. The whole situation is new and novel for us. The one and only discouraging feature is the darkness ahead on the income question. To let the mind dwell upon the matter tends to discouragement. Yet it is an ever-present spectre peering upon us from the darkness and gloom.

My sister Ida called up by telephone on Saturday evening to tell of Mother's passing on that day at three o'clock. Had greatly hoped I might raise the cash to make the trip for the funeral, but could not do so today. It is a sore grief that I cannot go the short distance of five or six hundred miles for this occasion. Besides it would not be easy to arrange for someone to help here in the house during my absence.

September 23, 1932 Such a press of duties has descended upon my otherwise unemployed hands that I have found scarcely time to do any writing, not even for writing notes. Dishes to wash, meals to cook, nursing bottles to wash and sterilize, diapers to dry and fold, house to dust and clean. Each day from eight-thirty till eleven o'clock I spend at the college in study hall and tutoring Greek. The rest of the day I spend at home as maid-of-all-work. The young son is doing very well, he will ere long become an interesting center of attraction about the home. He is beginning to notice things with his eyes. He has had to cry sometimes while in the course of making adjustment to his new environment. His feeding hours come at six, ten, and two o'clock day and night. He takes about three ounces of milk specially prepared for his use. It is first boiled briefly, after which one adds lactic acid and Karo white syrup according to prescribed formula. He sleeps much of the time, and has not yet learned to entertain himself very well when awake, his chief manner of doing so being to grunt, whimper, or cry. He seems to have a goodly portion of temper and rather pronounced likes and dislikes. We placed him in his basket on the back porch this afternoon where he received some direct sunlight and had opportunity to breathe in abundance of fresh air. He seems to enjoy himself royally, judging by the way he is sleeping.

September 28, 1932 There has been rain in recent days, enough to moisten the soil well so that vegetation is growing again. Turnips are growing rapidly, at least the tops. But lettuce I sowed and nursed with sprinkling can looks very unpromising at this writing.

Penniless days, perhaps months, are descending upon us, bringing new and impressive experiences. Time to think and duly reflect has been scarce with me in recent weeks. Too many practical and worldly concerns occupy my mind for cogitation on theoretical and supra-mundane ideas. Such is life. It is a temptation to dream of the living, real living, one could do if there were no financial problems to engross one's mind and devour one's time and patience. But I presume the better part is to grapple with the reality of the present and wring from its unpromising inwardness the romance and the thrill and the satisfaction that make life rich and meaningful. The problem is to discover some alchemy of the mind that can convert the grey stones of disappointment and hopelessness into the pure gold of joy, peace and contentment. Resignation, pure and simple, seems to be an unworthy solution for such a problem and situation. To struggle, to fight, to plan, to hope and to dream, these also must have a part in real living. Life for me must ever be dynamic, not static; changes and adaptations are the very essence of living. Milo Kauffman in a sermon last Sunday morning dwelt at length on the matter of how to meet crises in life — a good discourse.

Edgar J. Goodspeed in the latest Atlantic writes pleasantly on the common and almost universal prevalence of the martyr pose among Americans. Every class and group delights in believing itself the victim of persecution by another or other groups of society. It is a sort of an American pastime to complain loud and long about the oppression one is called upon to endure. Unfortunately, perhaps, not many of these know of the Beatitude which pronounces as blessed those who suffer persecution (for righteousness' sake?), or at any rate, they do not utilize the comfort that may be derived from the saying, preferring the pleasure of shouting their own persecution from the housetops. By chance or otherwise, an exquisite illustration of such self-proclaimed martyrdom is found in a leading article in a recent issue of School and Society. Herein a sociologist, an enthusiastic devotee of the "social sciences," with many an eloquent phrase and considerable warmth of feeling, laments the lack of intellectual and academic freedom that is the lot of himself and his co-sociologists. The article also illustrates the typical obsession of sociologists to the effect that they, and they alone, know just how society and states ought to be, in fact must be, reconstructed and reformed in order to save civilization and render society ideal. Such are the dangers of a little learning!

Immediate personal plans of my own include the cutting down and cutting up of some trees out in the country as a part of the winter's fuel supply at our house. It is a long time since I used to handle axe and cross-cut saw to fell and quarter trees for winter's fuel and "saw logs" in the little woodland tract which Father owns south of Joetown in Iowa.

September 30, 1932 Just a few more hours and three-fourths of the year of grace, 1932, will be over and past. The years seem to slip by so quickly. Time passes and passes, and still we seem to make no progress toward achieving and creating an ideal situation in which to live and labor without worry and distress. We will need to run for refuge, if not to the philosophical mansion of stoicism, at any rate to some small vestibule or chamber of this very mansion. The blows of fortune one can welcome and with a tough mind and heart defy to do their worst. I sometimes catch certain phrases of Henley's "Invictus" running through my mind. The basic philosophy of this little poem is perhaps faulty, but its spirit and feeling are very essential for weathering the storm of troubles that the lean years are bringing.

Fall weather appears to be setting in, in advance of the usual date. Have built fire of mornings in the furnace a number of times during the past week to remove the chill from the house. No frost has been reported, although the mercury column showed in the vicinity of forty degrees F. on one morning lately. Today was a cloudy day. Rain threatened. Nevertheless the sun set clear in the west this evening with indications for fair weather. A number of weeks of warm weather devoid of freezing temperature will be duly appreciated and utilized for finishing up fall work about the premises. One job that I must soon do is to close up cracks in foundation walls so as to keep out cold, mice, and other things.

October 2, 1932 Typical autumn weather has prevailed for a week, very cool nights, some cloudy days, but also pleasant sunshine that is greatly appreciated. No frost has yet spoiled vegetation. Yesterday for most of the day I was a wood-cutter, having resorted to this occupation in order to contribute something to the solution of our winter's fuel problem. On a farm a few miles northwest of Hesston I cut down two large cottonwood trees. The wood of these trees may be had for the labor of cutting it up, provided one grubs the stumps out in cutting down the trees. This grubbing is a hard and laborious task, but since time and strength are more abundant with me than cash for purchasing coal, I will save some cash outlay by taking advantage of this opportunity. Milo Kauffman, I. E. Burkhart, and C. Hertzler were also cutting down trees at the same place, all of us cooperating in some measure. After cutting away as many of the roots as one could readily get at, Mr. Sommerfeld, the owner of the trees, hitches a team of mules on the tree trunk with a cable and pulls it down. Woodcutting is good vigorous exercise for one not used to doing manual labor of any strenuous sort. I feel no serious after effects of yesterday's toil, excepting a general stiffness, especially in my back.

Baby Virgil is growing finely. He gained nearly another one-half pound during the past week, weighing now just nearly nine pounds. He still cries occasionally when he is awake before his feeding time and thinks he is hungry for his meal. He usually awakes from his night's sleep before six o'clock in the morning and fusses for a time. Most generally he exercises his voice and lungs from five to six o'clock in the evening. He enjoys his sun and air bath about three o'clock in the afternoon. Today he smiled and played charmingly, showing that he had pleasurable sensations from the sunshine. But it also seems to enhance his appetite for food and long before the hour of six he is already broadcasting the urgent calls from his stomach for replenishment. We have just started the plan of preparing his bottles once a day for six feedings, which will save some trouble. The sterilizing of bottles we now do in the pressure cooker under steam pressure, which effects a marked saving of fuel and water.

Orie O. Miller of the General Conference Peace Committee writes again to urge me to write some propaganda literature for their committee to publish and circulate. With more spare time in prospect, the idea appeals to me more than before. A suggested subject is "Church and State", which is a very large order indeed. In my mind I have been playing with the idea of developing such a subject at some time. Some phases of the general theme could be readily developed, provided I can formulate a positive conviction and conclusion on the matter. The history of the theory of the State and of the theory of citizenship would be an interesting study as a background for the larger study. There is a rather wide variety of opinion regarding both the theory and the practice of the relation of Church and State among our group of Mennonites and just how to present the subject so that these divergent elements would be led to consider without prejudice the principles involved strictly upon their own merits is no small problem. Being such a highly controversial subject, one would need to balance himself on some middle fence with consummate and even acrobatic skill in order to avoid giving offence to some. Personally I have no interest in governmental politics. To me the gestures and antics of party politics are mostly horseplay. I have voted only once in any more lofty election than a home town affair. In 1914, I voted at home in Iowa, the first opportunity I had after coming to voting age. There was considerable interest in the state election that year due to the liquor question. Voting was a fairly common practice among our people in Iowa, very little being said against it. My reasons for not voting since have not been for conscientious or religious reasons. My own theory is that in all elections of state and national officials only persons should exercise the franchise who are well informed on the issues and the party principles involved, preferably only experts in matters of economics, political science, and law. Voting a straight party ticket as a matter of habit, without understanding the principles of the party platforms is bad practice. Again voting solely on the basis of the personality of the candidate is foolish. So I vote not at all, until such a time as I may understand politics sufficiently to vote intelligently.

October 5, 1932 On Monday afternoon another strong gale from the northwest swept down upon us filling the atmosphere with clouds of dust and driving temperature levels ever lower. This morning the temperature was very near the freezing point. Weather report in evening paper gave thirty-one degrees as minimum temperature. Tomato vines were nipped just a bit in spots and the outer ends of the vines. Heavy frost is predicted for tonight.

The weight of housework is being steadily lifted as Mrs. Yoder is taking up the regular work more and more. She spends considerable time in attending to the baby, supplying his needs and providing his comforts.

This is the season of the year when a number of journals for which I have been subscribing call for renewal. Among the inconveniences of having no income is the inability to renew some of these journals. Classical Philology and Classical Weekly I cannot renew and so must forego the profit of reading them, unless the publishers continue to send them in the hope that I can pay later for the year's subscription. Scientific Monthly is an excellent periodical which it grieves me much to forego, especially as it accompanies my membership in the American Association for the Advancement of Science, which I began about five years ago. We have had to order the daily Newton Kansan-Republican to stop coming also. Am renewing subscription to Literary Digest as the principal means for keeping in touch with world events.

October 9, 1932 Perhaps I shall fall asleep before I get many jottings set down. For four or five weeks I have been so much occupied with sundry and multiplied activities that whenever for ten or fifteen minutes I relax and try to read, write, or think, I fall asleep. My nocturnal slumber time is broken up since the new member of the family has come to live with us. He gets his milk at ten in the evening at which time I generally have put myself into readiness to jump into bed and go off to sleep. The alarm clock, which I keep within arm's length all night long, is set for two o'clock. I scramble out and warm the milk bottle and its contents. Then Estie gives it to the baby as I dive back into bed again, remembering to set the alarm clock for six o'clock in the morning. This schedule shortens the length of my total sleeping time and lessens my general efficiency. Yesterday was a fair day with a genial sun that shone all day long. But it was apparently only one of the weather man's tantalizing tricks. For today wind blows cool from the north, clouds hide away the sun, and temperature indoors is scarcely comfortable.

The two cottonwood trees which I felled a week ago were transported to the rear of our garden lot and are now ready to be cut into furnace lengths and split into sizable pieces. The heavy lifting that is incident to transporting heavy pieces of wood is hardly suitable and safe for my physical and especially my abdominal strength. Certain faint sensations are evident in the vicinity of my late incision after an exertion of such sort. If the present range of temperature prevails tomorrow, I know of no other plan than to get some coal delivered, hoping that the Lord will provide the money with which to pay for the same.

October 12, 1932 My wish has been that it might be possible to push our schedule for the day one hour ahead, sort of a daylight-saving plan. As it has been we are a little behind with our meals to fit in most smoothly with other folk's plans. For instance, yesterday morning when I had barely started preparing breakfast, C. Hertzler came along and wished to take me out to view some more cottonwood trees and mark them as candidates for our saws and axes. I went with him and had time only to eat a bite after returning. So in other ways setting forward our daily schedule would be an aid to greater efficiency. Whether it can be done is a question. We are experimenting this morning on the matter.

During the present week there is a public meeting each evening at the college. An evangelist of Ontario is conducting special religious meetings. He is always a popular preacher, it seems. His personality is rather unique and impressive and his platform manner is quite arresting. He is largely a self-made minister, a wide reader, and very spiritual in his presentation and emphasis. As a thinker and logician he is not so much, but then he would undoubtedly be much less popular if he were more profound in his ideas and more severely logical in his thinking. He is eminently successful in his work because he can adapt himself so readily to popular thinking – or unthinking — as you will. Spellbinding and demogogic harangue is entirely essential for influencing hoi polloi. Far be it from me to criticise and condemn such methods or the folks who are able to use them to good and useful ends. Neither do I feel an impulse to attempt to ape after such in order to make myself popular and influential. Each person ought to exercise himself according to his own gifts.

October 14, 1932 The storm of the depression that has raged about us for several years past has finally struck us with all its force and fury. Sundry gusts and squalls beforehand had warned us of its sure approach. The bank account has two dollars and certain odd cents to its credit. This with the contents of the pocket book will not at the moment suffice to pay the recent bills that are outstanding, petty bills that heretofore we have always had the careless habit of paying with cash in hand. We are adjusting ourselves as best we may in order to weather the storm until we succeed in finding some adequate shelter or until the financial and economic elements shall have spent their rage and calm weather again prevails. In a letter my father writes that finances have given him more trouble and worry during the past year than ever before in his life, and he is sixty-seven years old, having farmed over forty years. His troubles have been increased recently by the passing away of Mother. Brother Dan had a rather serious fire loss a few weeks ago which will make it still harder all around. I cannot help feeling sorry for Father as his difficulties have multiplied so much. He has a thousand or two thousand bushels of old corn on hand which he is holding and still hopes to sell sometime at a better price than it commands now. Still no one knows what the future holds in store. Politicians, both Republican and Democrat, are making dire predictions in case their respective opponents get into office.

October 15, 1932 In setting oneself so as best to weather the economic storm, it behooves one also to keep an eye open to what changes may come or be on the alert to make a jump when an opportunity comes along to get under shelter. To sit down with the mind set that we will let the storm pass over and after it is past we will dry our clothes on a fence and presently go about our ordinary business as usual, may be very foolish in this case. The world, society, government, the church, at any rate their routine functioning, may all be quite different than what we choose to term regular and usual. Whether the present world age reaches its consummation and a completely new order of things will prevail, great changes, wide shifts, radical readjustments and reallocations may easily be the rule soon. My theory is that a person should cease looking back to the past mentally and expect things to be as before, leave off to imagine institutions, customs, methods and standards will be esentially as before, but should rather turn the eyes to the future, be prepared to make adjustments, changes, and alterations so far as these relate to methods, ideals, customs and habits. Now is a good time to scrutinize and impartially criticise all premises and assumptions it has been one's habit to build upon in the past, decide which are basic and vital, so requiring to be ever retained, and what ones are of such nature that they can be discarded in case the new day and era should require such an eventuality. Changes and adjustments are the concomitants of all life everywhere. Only inanimate things change not at all or with imperceptible slowness. It is an inspiring thought to know that whatever changes, small or great, slight or radical, may become necessary in the outward forms of things, as in society, in economic structure, in church procedure, the reality of God and of religious experience are eternal and unchanging. Faith is still the victory that survives the changing order of the cosmos. In fact, varying experiences and trying tests are perhaps the very factors that are needed to develop religious faith and one's perception of the personality of God. These experiences should instruct us that it is not good to pin one's faith too closely to any existing order of things, whether in church or society. "The things that are seen are temporary." Not that the true church — the living body of Christ — will cease to grow and go on to ultimate triumph, but that the external forms of ecclesiastical economy are not in themselves the sum total of religion. They are a mere shell or husk, which may serve well for a time, but must be superseded in turn by other forms that adjust the inner reality to the conditions of life. The things external are perhaps as a cocoon which the emerging life will leave behind as worn out and useless. To be conscious of being in vital touch with the eternal Spirit, the inner reality of things, gives a peace of soul and strength of heart that makes one welcome external changes.

October 21, 1932 Boy is now crying (for his daily bath?). His mother and nurse reports that he enjoys his bath regularly before nine o'clock in the morning. In connection with his period of ablution he is fed a daily dose of cod liver oil followed by tomato juice from a teaspoon. These he likes also. He is getting fat and plump. He sleeps about the whole of the night time. Just now he notices and observes things near him, watches with big, bright eyes the movements of anyone near him.

Due to the penniless circumstances of his parents, we have been borrowing here and there the equipment he requires for his care and comfort. First a basket bed was borrowed for him from J. N. Bylers. This he presently outgrew and it was replaced by a larger basket bed borrowed of D. H. Benders, which he will be able to use all during the winter. A few days ago I returned Bylers' basket and brought along home their baby buggy for use when he will be able to go out for out-of-door rides. Last Sunday Nelson Kauffmans brought a small stand with castors below upon which the basket bed can be set and wheeled about as desired. They were also so kind as to bring an infant swing which he can use after he is able to sit erect. For weighing him and determining his gain in weight, we have been borrowing a household scale from Mrs. Jesse Hartzler, our neighbor across the street. For bath table he has a small stand of Ruth Bender's, which we also use as kitchen table. Borrowing things and bartering things and services is the great game these days.

"Making wood" is the order of the day, cutting up trees for furnace fuel. Since last Saturday, C. Hertzler, M. A. Yoder, Milo Kauffman and

I have been working on trees four miles south of Hesston on Mr. Louis Prouty's farm.

October 23, 1932 On the day before today the gang of "woodmakers" worked and experimented with a power drag-saw for cutting into blocks the large "saw logs" from the trunks of the nine cottonwood trees which we felled during the week. Mr. Hertzler bought for a pittance a drag-saw and frame and with power from his tractor, we tried sawing the heavy logs. But for some reason progress was very slow and so the experiment is still in progress.

To toil with axe in hand or by applying muscular energy to one end of a cross-cut saw has been my lot and portion. Am getting somewhat used to the physical exertion involved, although I happen to have only a moderate amount of bodily strength available for such efforts. The change from professor's desk to woodsman's axe is rather far and abrupt. Naturally, too, it costs us sober reflection as we administer the sharp blows of the axe or the push-and-pull on the saw blade which in a few brief hours lays low in the dust a noble tree that Nature labored forty or more years to create. It almost pains one's heart and qualms the conscience to engage in such destructive assaults upon venerable trees, which only God can make, trees which had already shed numerous autumnal garments of leaves before the time that some of their present assaulters saw the light of day. How many generations of birds, squirrels and other animals have enjoyed the generous hospitality of their shade and shelter! Now they are called upon to give up their sturdy lives and bodies in order that a few weak specimens of Homo sapiens may have some hours of bodily warmth and comfort to enjoy, may fend off such cold and storms as these giants have endured for forty and more winters.

The depression years are responsible for the cutting down and burning of many trees and osage orange hedges throughout this country. Here's hoping that at least some land owners who now allow these trees to be sacrificed for man's comfort will be thoughtful enough to start new trees and hedges, to replace the luckless victims of the depression. A country without trees is always a depressing sight. I recall that in the high plains of Western Kansas and Eastern Colorado trees rarely grow, save in the vicinity of an occasional creek or gully. Trees add an unconscious charm to a landscape, give a touch of beauty and variety that rests the eye. At this season of the year even Kansas in certain spots, as along creeks and elsewhere, can stage a worth-while show of lavish luxurious coloring of foliage. Rich yellows and browns and oranges that feast the eyes of man are often common. Even the trees on the college campus can present a thrilling spectacle of color now and a little later.

Mild weather has prevailed for near two weeks, with occasional cool breezes from northwest for one day at a time. Light rains continue to fall about every week. Sunshine, rich and golden as only October sunshine can be, is with us almost every day.

October 27, 1932 Teachers' meeting for the Sunday School teachers is now being held each week at 8:00 p.m. on Thursday instead of Sunday morning at 9:00. The change was made in order to rekindle the last dying embers of interest under the previous arrangement. This hour is convenient for a number who cannot be present at the early hour on Sunday and also is preferred by teachers of the primary and the intermediate departments. So the experiment is made, involving the breaking away from an almost immemorial precedent of teachers' meetings on Sunday morning. Personally I much prefer the hour just preceding the time when S. S. meets on Sunday. For the first two times that we have met on Thursday there was good attendance by teachers from all three departments, but this evening only a solitary representative from each of the lower departments was on hand.

Life is quite various and strenuous during these days for myself. The new experiences and problems should stimulate some constructive thinking on a person's part, whet one's appetite for bigger and better experiences, and stiffen one's resolution to wring from even these untoward times and their circumstances some distilled drops of wisdom and philosophy for use in later life. It might inspire charming poetry, but probably not in me. I do covet an attitude and a mental set which will enable me to profit in very definite ways from these days when the times are so much out of joint. Should the tide in my affairs come in at any moment, I desire to take it at the flood and set forth from these shoals.

October 30, 1932 A pleasant Sunday is nearly past again. Air is cool and crisp, but no wind is blowing. It seems that of late every week, about, has been in the habit of bringing us a decided cold snap with a day or more of high wind from the north. In between times there is often a period of mighty wind from the south. Either Kansas has had an extra large portion of strong winds during the past two months, or I imagine it has. Each of our recent cold spells is reported to have manifested itself as a severe blizzard in states north and northwest, with much snow and cold.

Today Virgil had his first outing in the form of a half-hour ride in his baby coach. He enjoyed the change and slept most of the trip. He is nine weeks old today. Miss Frances Loucks kindly volunteered to stay with him this morning while his mother attended morning church service. Today he is very pleasant and happy; occasionally he has a day when he cries a great deal of the time and sleeps very little. But we praise him greatly for his nocturnal sleeping habits. Not a single night yet has he failed to sleep regularly. After his six o'clock feeding each evening, at about 6:30 we move him to the bedroom, make him ready to sleep, put off the light and leave him to go to sleep, which he does with scarcely a whimper. At ten o'clock we wake him for his milk bottle, which he empties often while only partially awake. Thereafter he is turned on his stomach, in which position he sleeps with scarcely any interruptions until about five o'clock in the morning. On last Friday he was two months old. In celebration of the occasion we weighed him and measured his length. He weighs now ten pounds and twelve ounces and measures twenty-two and three-quarter inches from head to heel. To judge from present indications he will doubtless be a man of much energy and strong temper. Often when he has a crying spell he manifests indignation and perhaps anger. Perhaps he will prove to be of artistic temperament. He appreciates bodily cleanliness and comfort even now.

It is now somewhat more than a month ago that my mother passed out from this life. It is a little difficult for me to realize that she is with us no more, that her glad and happy welcome will no more greet me when I happen to return to old home surroundings. She was the first to leave our family circle. I must accustom my mind now to think of her body as sleeping under the sod in the little cemetery in the woods a mile west of the church where she always went to worship ever since I knew her. Her faith was simple and her piety was unobtrusive. I recall with gratitude her instructions to me as a boy, as also her corrections. Often she would enter into conversation on religious matters with me, a thing which Father not often did when I was a young boy. She read considerable, although her busy life left but little time for much reading. She was ever willing to help and to do for others, constantly and thoughtfully anticipating the needs and wishes of others. Her hands were always busy with household work, and as is common on the farm, with much out-of-door work in garden, with chickens, and milking often also. She was kind and sympathetic always. She loved flowers very much, and one thing I could never quite forgive Father was his attitude toward her efforts to have a few potted plants in the house and flower beds out-of-doors. I recall I often felt sorry for Mother at the time. He felt that such things were superfluous and not worth the time and effort required for their care. Mother was very tenderhearted and there were a few times that I know of that I caused her grief which lasted for a brief time, but I rejoice that the Lord guided my ways so that to my knowledge I spared her any lasting sorrow and pain of heart. The time that I decided to unite with the East Union Church instead of with the church where my parents attended sadness was her first reaction, and again when I first left home to go to school instead of remaining on the farm as my parents had fondly planned she was grieved. As a boy and young man I confided in her much more than in my father; she understood how to enter into some of my problems. But it shall always be a deep regret of my life that on the whole I confided so little in either Father or Mother. I seemed to be naturally uncommunicative and almost entirely uncombative. When I disagreed with parents in my ideas I said nothing as a rule, but kept my own counsel and arrived at my own conclusions, made my own decisions and bided my time until I was free to act upon my own initiative. Viewing the matter in perspective now, I am almost astonished at how much I actually lived in a world quite apart from the remainder of the family at home, especially during the last six or seven years I was at home, before reaching my majority. I realize I should have counselled more with my parents, confided more in them by speaking of the ideals, aspirations, and the strange motions of my inner soul, motions which I little understood then, which formed and shaped ideas and decisions in the secrecy of my own mind. In the course of the last fifteen years Mother has always been sympathetically interested in my work and problems. When Estie and I married she gave us an almost endless amount of household things, especially in the line of bedding, quilts, comforters, blankets, pillows, and so forth, to a number that I have been unable to remember, at least enough to last us these twelve years and, barring accidents, easily as many more years. My greatest regret is that I did not do more during these last years to cheer her, did not tell her more of my own thoughts and write to her more frequently and regularly. I shall never forget the nobility of her life and character, the sweetness of her disposition, and the willingness with which she served and sacrificed herself for me. Without any sense of boasting, I do rejoice that her life was mostly happy, so far as I was aware. In the home there was always sufficient means available for comfort and some measure of convenience. She did not need to see any of her children become wayward and walk in sin. Father cared for her tenderly and lovingly during recent years when she has been ailing. As for myself, while I have regrets that I came so far short many times of showing her consideration and love which I often felt but did not express, I do wish to live a life worthy of her memory.

November 6, 1932 The week past has been a strenuous one again. Laundry work on Monday. Sawing wood on Tuesday and all day Wednesday. Hauling wood home on Thursday. Helping saw wood again on Friday, and Saturday helping C. Hertzler rebuild a circular saw frame which we wrecked while using it. Our lot of cottonwood is nearly all at home now. There is still a trailer load to bring and some small sticks for kindling.

John Horst of Scottdale, inferring that I have much leisure time, has asked me to write articles on Education for the Christian Monitor. More no-pay work. Plan to prepare about six of a series of articles on the purposes of education. Shall probably lean rather heavily upon Professor B. I. Bell's writings for some of the material I shall use. In treating subjects that are a little trite and timeworn, I feel they should be dealt with in ways that are different, in the hope that the discussions may be more stimulating and suggestive.

Virgil Edward was taken along for the first time today to sit in church for a half-hour or more. He enjoyed it, seemingly and showed almost perfect church manners. He was pleased with the singing and smiled over it. Out-of-door rides appear to agree with him, giving him an increased appetite. This week past he has been especially good. He entertains himself with smiles and coos for some length of time now when he is awake. He sometimes smiles broadly in response to a smile or a whistle. We find out that he earned himself a name already at the hospital among the nurses. Mrs. Yoder received a letter from her nurse while there who referred to him as the "sheik of Bethel Hospital nursery." Even at the time they spoke of his good-looking qualities. More important than "good looks" physically to me will be the question whether he has mentality of average or superior quality. If he has, then he will be a perfect child. Naturally, our hopes for him are that he will be strong and intelligent, able to make a better success in life than his parents are making.

November 18, 1932 A beautiful day and really comfortable after nearly a week of cold with at least four strong blasts of cold wind from the northwest country. Temperatures well below freezing mark on a number of successive mornings. Virgil was taken out for a short buggy ride each day in spite of the cold, excepting yesterday when our time was all occupied otherwise. He likes to ride in his buggy, although he does not much appreciate to be bundled up tightly in out-of-door togs. During the past several days he has discovered his hands and spends much waking time in scrutinizing and contemplating them. He will probably soon begin to coordinate eye and hand movements and will need rattles and playthings. He is getting fat and chubby now.

During the past six weeks we have been getting experience in how one gets along in living without spending money. We have spent scarcely any because we simply had scarcely any. Our supplies of things in pantry and kitchen began one by one to "get all." It is a singular experience for one who has never had to refrain from replenishing supplies as they became exhausted. Eggs disappeared from our breakfast menus very suddenly and then shortly from our cooking recipes also. Dairy butter and peanut butter were stretched to a bitter end. Cocoa, a favorite beverage with us when made with milk, came to an end. Lemons for seasoning were not. As for oranges, bananas, or other fresh fruit, they are almost unknown now at our house. Crackers are being stretched for all they will stand. Sorghum, which usually stretches a long way, will soon be at its end. Happily new sorghum can be obtained for forty-nine cents a ten-pound pail. We certainly must get some as soon as we have in hand the forty-nine cents. What do we eat? Some friends of the college who live in Harper County this state sent several loads of provisions for the college family, students and faculty; these supplies were mostly cereals in various forms, and some canned goods. Friends at Yoder, Kansas, sent us some meat, dressed chicken, cured ham and sausage. So we do have enough to eat and we convince ourselves that corn meal mush, cooked breakfast cereals, pancakes, etc. are not such bad staples on the table. But to do without some lard, eggs, butter, and such like accessories is very inconvenient, to say the least. But perhaps our financial distress will be moderated just a bit gradually again, so that we can have a little of the variety that is needed for a balanced diet. The big bugbears along that line are this year's taxes and interest charges due. Clothing too has a habit of wearing out eventually. Already Estie has begun digging through old heaps of discarded clothing in order to supply present needs. Last week she recovered a pair of cast off trousers, placed a neat patch over one knee and I find them still very good and serviceable for use. She is also facing the task of making most of our small son's clothing for some time to come out of her trunk and suitcases full of old clothes and cast-off garments.

O. O. Miller of Pennsylvania visited at our house for a little over an hour on last Friday afternoon. He made certain proposals and suggestions regarding a line of work for myself in case I take up residence at Goshen College, namely to spend some time and effort in writing and lecturing for peace propaganda purposes. I am willing to consider it, consider anything, in fact, that may promise an income. But there are questions and doubts that arise as I contemplate the proposal. There are also attractive features to think about. At best it would be a rather uncertain and makeshift arrangement. The present financial straits I am getting into deeper and deeper, suggest to me to consider very seriously the securing, if possible, of some position that carries a little better remuneration with it. One hesitates to take what may seem a sordid and worldly attitude on the matter of getting financial income, but the force of circumstances leads me to consider whether the Spirit of God desires to guide our paths in other ways than we have thought and planned. Patience to wait for the unfolding of His plan and will is what one needs in order to be contented in the meantime.

November 20, 1932 A very severe cold snap visited Kansas during the first part of the week past. Now weather is pleasant and comfortable again.

On Wednesday afternoon Loyd Garber, wife and two daughters from Jackson, Minnesota, came and, according to arrangements made previously by correspondence, took up their temporary residence in our upstairs rooms, doing light housekeeping while Mr. Garber spends several months attending school here. For their special accommodation and as a measure for completing the equipment of our house we have installed lavatory and water toilet in the small dormer space upstairs on the north side of the house. Pipes and all had been installed two years ago when the plumbing work on the house was installed and everything was then put in readiness for installing the fixtures. I secured a second-hand toilet and a very slightly used lavatory from the Lehman Hardware Plumbing Shop in Newton and was fortunate enough to be able to trade our old well pump in as part payment on the fixtures. The latter were priced at twenty-one dollars. Credit for the pump was figured at eleven dollars, leaving ten dollars to pay in cash, to be gotten from the income from the rooms during the next few months. We are pleased to have this equipment of the house completed. It is now practically ready to sell to the first buyer who wants it at a reasonable cash price. Wish he would come around some time this coming summer!

Boy is growing and developing steadily. His new experience of the past week was that of sitting partly erect while propped up in the corner of one of the overstuffed living room chairs. He enjoys it for a while several times a day. He counts his age at twelve weeks today and is a fine specimen of boyhood. He enjoyed a trip to Newton and Dr. Haury's office on Thursday. Doctor pronounced him a healthy child.

The November issue of the Atlantic Monthly is its Diamond Jubilee Issue to celebrate the seventy-fifth anniversary of the launching of this magazine. Its contents consist almost entirely of reprints of essays, stories, poems, etc. from issues throughout the years. Naturally it is a very excellent number, giving of the very cream of its contributions. Especially good are three essays by Woodrow Wilson, John Burroughs, and Cornelia Comer respectively. Wilson's essay is, "On Being Human." It is in about his best style, is really solid meat, and one I should like to pledge myself to read and reread frequently. The human qualities he stresses particularly are genuineness, serenity, and the selection of interests. Throughout its length the essay pleads eloquently for the basic human qualities of sanity, balance, poise, sympathy, tolerance, humour. The appeal is masterly. Burroughs' essay is entitled "Expression". It is philosophical, but withal very good. The third is a "Letter to the Rising Generation". This too is well worth repeated readings.

November 24, 1932, Thanksgiving Day. Public service appropriate to the day was held at the college this morning. A beautiful day outdoors, with sunshine, crisp air, and a gentle wind.

For the past weeks and months I have been unable to do any work for myself because of the multitudinous duties that have thronged upon me.

Gathering and preparing fuel for the winter (and it is clear to see that the amount on hand will not suffice for more than a few months at the most) took large sectors of time off my hands. Daily chores take away hours from each day's length. Feeding the boy about one-half the time, when his mother is preparing meals, preparing his milk according to prescribed formula, drying dishes, feeding the furnace, and so on, seemingly indefinitely, subtract greatly from the leisure time I had expected to have and use. As it has been going at our house, I cannot obtain sufficient sleep for my needs. Soon after five o'clock in the morning I arise from bed. Comes evening and Boy has gone to sleep for the night and supper dishes are done away, then I feel more like sleeping than reading or writing. And sleep is what I nearly always do for an hour or two hours before ten o'clock, when Boy has to be fed again, after which we formally retire for the night.

November 27, 1932 Have become a little interested in the subject of calendar reform and proposed plans for revision. A late article in Scientific Monthly gives a clear and considerate discussion of the problems involved in revision. At bottom I do not personally see any urgent necessity for having everything in life absolutely regularized and made boldly uniform. The demand for revision seems to come from business interests largely, so being a reflection of our present-day business civilization and its dominant position in modern thinking. Perhaps before revision is effected, the modern god, Business, will have been dethroned, so removing the present demand. Business seems to desire months of equal length, and all holidays anchored to fixed dates so as to be better able to completely commercialize such occasions, as for example, Easter.

The two leading plans proposed for revising the Gregorian calendar are: a thirteen-month plan, all of equal length, a twelve-month plan, with quarters of equal length. Either plan would insist on beginning each year on a Sunday. This would raise the problem of what to do with the one extra day each regular year and a second extra day each leap year. Suggestion is made that the annual extra day be added to the end of December and counted as the second half of a 48-hour Saturday. In leap year the same would be done with the added day at the end of June. It is this feature, disturbing the strict sequence of the Sundays, that arouses religionists and the prejudice of the masses of people. Some would pronounce off-hand that it is mortal sin to tamper with the sequence of the Sundays, suggesting it is blasphemy even to think of such a thing. Personally, I have not made up my mind either way on this point, but I do not find this dogmatic objection entirely convincing. The most thoughtful suggestion I have yet seen made in answer to this particular objection is as follows: The particular succession of days is a somewhat relative matter even under our present method of reckoning time. The illustration is cited of the International Date Line, where conceivably for one crossing it at certain times there might be a doubling of Sundays or the entire omission of a Sunday, depending on whether one travels east or west. This idea at least is suggestive on the question as a whole. A question in my mind is whether it can be proved that the succession of the days of the week have never been disturbed during past centuries when calendar changes and corrections were made. It is a rather interesting subject to study.

November 28, 1932 Boy Virgil celebrated the completion of the third month of his age today, by getting himself weighed and measured all around. The data on his anatomical conditions are these: weight, 13 and 1/2 lbs.; height, 24 and 1/4"; head, 16"; crown (ear to ear) 9 and 1/2"; neck, 9 and 1/4"; chest, 16 and 1/2"; waist, 15 and 1/2"; arm length to end of longest finger, 9"; wrist measure, 4"; ankle measure, 4 and 1/4"; shoulders, 18". The young fellow is getting too long for all his quarters, his sleeping basket and the baby buggy. The past three days he has shown an urge to bite on his gums, trying to chew on his fist inserted into his mouth, as though he were having some teeth pushing through already. He is very pleasant when he feels well, smiles broadly and charmingly in response to a smile, a whistle, or when one talks to him. Sometimes he makes a row of sounds much in a conversational tone, and again he crows lustily, gurgles, and intonates a considerable variety of sounds.

December 1, 1932 This has been a warm day for the first day of the first winter month. Sky has been cloudy much of the day. Before sunrise this morning the scattered clouds in the sky were tinted with a wonderful display of coloring, such as people are said to climb to the top of Pike's Peak to behold. This weather is a mercy for the fuel supply which is on hand. For once again after some months of other occupations I find a bit of leisure for some reading and writing. Seems almost strange.

December 4, 1932 A pleasant day. Clear with light wind blowing. Cool enough for seasonal comfort. The past three or four days have been really too warm for this time of the year. Without the refrigerator it has even been difficult to keep foodstuffs from spoiling during these few days. A bit cooler weather would be nearer ideal, I daresay.

Have computed the cost in cash outlay that we must pay out for bringing our son Virgil into the world and starting him safely in the way of life. For viavi preparations we paid out $32. For hospital service and care, $70, and for the services of the attending physician, $20 (evidently his usual charge for such services is $35). Unfortunately the most of the total amount is still unpaid.

Received word from President Yoder of Goshen College yesterday that the college there will give me employment during the second semester on a part-time basis, allowing me $500 in cash and the use of an apartment in East Hall for eight months including heat, light, and water paid. It sounds very good to one who has had no income to speak of for six months. However, I have no intention of "counting my chicks before they are hatched." First thing: To contract for five hundred dollars in cash is not the same thing as receiving that much money in hand, as my experience with college budgets tells me. Second thing: We have absolutely no cash in hand to transport our few belongings from here to Indiana (the distance is nearly one thousand miles), nor even to move ourselves. Third thing: We are not exactly ready to remove to the East yet, even had we the cash wherewith to do so, as we still hope against hope that the way will somehow be opened for us to remain in the West. Such is the situation as it appears now. Only one thing is certain in my own mind as yet: I must get to Goshen and take up the offer made to me, and gratefully accept whatever cash comes my way, even a little being better than none at all. If no other arrangement is possible, I shall even try to "hitch-hike" my way thither and leave wife and child behind until there are funds for carrying out other plans. Even for such a drastic step some special arrangements must be made at this end for the living accommodations of the family.

C. Hertzler and wife entertained us at dinner today at their home. The first time that Boy was away for Sunday dinner, and he seemed to enjoy it greatly, sleeping most of the time.

December 6, 1932 Notes of progress in the development of Boy are: Making his first efforts at locomotion by creeping. A regular part of his routine each evening just before his bedtime lunch is to lie on the dining room table mostly undressed to air his skin. First he lies on his back and kicks for a short while. Then he is turned on his stomach side, in which position he struggles and wriggles, twists and teeters himself, and just the past two evenings has succeeded in moving himself ahead slowly. He can partly draw up his knees under his body now, but he cannot raise his trunk with his arms yet. He enjoys this vigorous exercise all in good humour, grunting vigorously and smiling when he is turned back again. He also shows distinct signs of modesty or bashfulness the past few days. Upon being spoken to quite often he will smile broadly and turn his head far to one side at the same time bringing one hand up to cover his eye.

In a late issue of the Sunday School Times a Miss Pankhurst writes an interesting piece on "The Hopelessness of the Intellectuals." Expressions are quoted from prominent men in current literature to show the common note of despair and severe pessimism which is the dominant fashion at the present time. Names as Shaw, Kipling, Mencken, Wells, etc., are used. I have had to reflect a bit on the significance of this trend. If from the Christian and common sense point of view such sentiments and opinions are absurd and silly now, they are no more so than were the sentiments of extreme optimism, of faith in humanity, which the same intellectuals championed a few years back when the tide of prosperity was running high. One absurd extreme most naturally follows another. Some of us who refused to be charmed by the prevailing psychosis of a few years ago and to put our faith into a creed of human progress, do not find any particular occasion now to share the opposite extreme of feeling, when the ebb tide has come upon the world. Persons who kept some measure of balance when prosperity reigned were likely to be decried at the time as pessimists and stumbling blocks to progress. But today these same persons feel little need for despair. Thus do the modes of thought shift and change. It seems to me that one more argument for nonconformity to the ephemeral phases of thought and opinion is to be gotten from this phenomenon. A philosophic aloofness from whatever is popular at the moment may appear as an unsocial and uncooperative attitude, perhaps even a selfish attitude. But in the perspective of a little time such an aloofness, properly tempered with activity, seems the only sane and sensible attitude to take.

December 11, 1932 Sunny Kansas-land has come to grips with Old Man Winter and the Old Man has the complete mastery for the moment. No genial sun has smiled upon us since last Tuesday. On the contrary a cold storm from the north with near-zero temperatures and several inches of snow. Yesterday and last night there was enough mist or fog in the air so that it froze on trees in the form of sleet and hoarfrost. Result, a very thrilling and inspiring winter scene is presented to our eyes as the dawn comes this morning. Not for several years have we had here such a sample of solid winter weather. It is very possible that the cold and snow will hold on for some time, as it seems to be almost country-wide in its scope.

December 15, 1932 Winter is still here in good earnest, although for a few days more moderate temperatures prevailed. The coldest morning was on Monday when temperatures of ten and twelve degrees below zero Fahrenheit were generally reported hereabouts. The fuel supply has been diminishing very rapidly since the severe weather began. A few weeks more of continuous cold will send me scurrying about for more coal or wood or both. The problem of finances for securing coal was threatening to be a severe one. But on Monday a letter came from my brother Herman in Iowa enclosing check for our special relief. So with rent I received for the use of my garage for about three months, and with another month's salary (?) from the college about due, and with the promised income from our upstairs rooms, we can tide over for a few more weeks, including fuel. Rent from the rooms at two and one-half dollars a week does not mount up very rapidly.

Indications are now that I shall teach part time at Goshen College during the second semester, beginning at the end of January. There is still not much light on the question as to what arrangements for our living we can possibly make. Without solicitation on our part, we learned of a girl who wants a place to stay and work for part of her expenses during the second semester and also from beginning of Special Bible Term. Perhaps this is a providential leading for the solution of our problem.

December 18, 1932 Only one week before Christmas, and soon this year of our Lord will be past and merely a matter of history. At this season of the year usually a number of added distractions come along. Last evening my presence was required at a banquet given by the College Journal Staff for the Academy freshmen, who won the subscription sales contest. On Monday evening coming I am asked to serve on the program of the Mennonite Historical Society at the college. On the evening next following this a faculty social is to be held at the dormitory dining hall followed by an open-house party given by the dormitory dwellers. On next Saturday evening is the occasion for a Christmas program at the College Assembly Hall.

My routine employment during recent weeks has been such as splitting up the big blocks of cottonwood and reducing them to furnace-door dimensions, reading some in the history of ancient and mediaeval education, and the usual chores about the house. Started reading on several books, but with slow progress as yet. Another article is due to be sent to the Christian Monitor within two weeks. Its outline I have already in mind, but not a line has been written to date. Have not had opportunity for several months past to do any reading in current magazines at Newton Public Library, and it makes me feel rather out-of-date. I must spend a half day before long in doing this much to keep up with the recent thought and ideas that are abroad in the land.

December 23, 1932 Foggy atmosphere; slow, warm rain; snow about all melted away. Such is the weather program for the past twenty-four hours. Not an unwelcome variation from zero and near-zero temperatures. The almanac pronounces that winter begins day before yesterday. Not a bad beginning so far.

My reading in History of Education during recent days has been relating to monasticism, mysticism, scholasticism, and the like. Personally I have always felt a sort of sympathy with the monastic ideal of life and learning. I have often fancied to myself that had I been living a thousand years ago, I should likely have been a monk. Under the conditions that prevailed during the long centuries of the Middle Ages, it is not hard to understand that the monastic life was the chief outlet for those who desired a life of peace, of study and of meditation. Such a mode of life has its attractions for certain temperaments and its decided advantages. On the contrary there is no need to discount its disadvantages also. The ascetic ideal is an interesting phase of life for study in its varied forms through history. Dean Sperry of the Harvard Theological School writes an article in the Atlantic Monthly on "The New Asceticism." Herein he tries to show that, whereas the mediaeval ascetics caused themselves pain by abuse of their physical bodies, the newest form of the same ideal is to inflict pain and discomfort upon oneself by abusing the mind. This is done by afflicting oneself with as many mental doubts as possible, making peace and comfort of mind as impossible as can be. It is a mild protest against the typical tough-minded scientific attitude so fashionable today.

December 25, 1932 This Christmas Day has scarcely seemed like Christmas, probably owing to the fact that it coincides with Sunday. It has been a very pleasant day, clear, moderate, joyous. All snow has disappeared and the rain seems to have removed the frost from the ground. Our house is more still these days, due to the absence of the family who live upstairs. They have gone to Missouri for the vacation time. There is no depression on the crop of new babies, as our part of town has been increased by two new inhabitants within the past week, a Mr. Hartzler and a Miss Burkhart. We felt justified in our home in receiving a new member into the family even though a depression is on, since we had no children at all. The knowing ones, uncharitably called gossips, report that more babies are due to arrive in these parts before long.

Am reading through a book at present by R. H. Fisher which is entitled "Religious Experience." Most parts of it are of consuming interest to myself. It is not so much theoretical as practical. The author is a Scotsman of Calvinistic leanings. His general viewpoint is sane and reasonable; also Biblical and quite evangelical. Many of his observations are acute and his presentation is forceful. It is a book I should very much like to own and use for reading and reference. There is something virile and arresting in the thought processes of this writer. His discussions, brief and pointed, on the topics of "varieties of religious experience", "responsibility for belief", "mysticism", "reason", "the fall", "conversion", "luxury", "the sense of failure", "the help of prayer", "temperance", "love", appealed to me as being particularly good and worthy of repeated readings.

December 29, 1932 A cloudy, almost foggy day. Slightly colder, but still very seasonable weather. Borrowed Fred Grove's team and box wagon this morning and fetched a load of coal for the furnace. The amount was 2710 pounds. This with the wood still on hand should last for about six weeks, depending upon the kind of weather January will bring us. Spent most of the day yesterday in Newton, attending two sessions of the Mennonite Teachers' Convention held at the First Mennonite Church. A good program of papers and addresses was given. Some of the educational leaders of the German Mennonite groups are beginning to work definitely toward cooperation in the work of higher education. I feel sympathetic myself toward such efforts. It should not be impossible for the various groups to cooperate in operating a college in this part of the West, if only we could get used to the idea of such a thing. It would be possible to formulate a plan of cooperation, which would leave each conference group free to maintain its own identity.

January 1, 1933 The New Year is being ushered in with a stout gale blowing from the south and a red sky in the east. The year 1932 is all safely tucked away in history now, and even as on this day one year and two years ago men welcomed the first day of the New Year with fondest hopes for better things ahead, so now the New Year again arouses the hopes and the fears, perhaps a larger amount of the latter than formerly, of the multitudes who are weary in spirit of the depression. Perhaps the hopes and expectations of us all are more sanguine, less inflated than in previous New Years.

A retrospect over the year 1932 shows a year full of changes, of varied experiences, of momentous events for us. Some of these experiences seemed hard at the moment, but by the abundant grace of God we believe they will work together for good in the final end. The prospects in the world at large are uncertain and unpredictable, in my opinion. Granting that the worst of the panic is over, as seems the opinion of many, there is left still the staggering problem of making readjustments in social and economic matters. There is talk about the return of prosperity, and everyone hopes that a sound phase of prosperity will gradually come back. But if the concept of prosperity we hold is the same as the status of things as they were in 1929, then we should rightly be doomed to disappointment. Such prosperity as prevailed up till 1929 is little less than a fool's paradise. Little short of a revolution is necessary to effect the readjustments that must be made. Technology and machinery promise to make unemployment a perpetual problem. One almost despairs of ever again seeing anything like a stable and balanced order of life in the world, because of the rapid and radical changes that are constantly being made in the conditions of life through the advance of science and of technical skill. The mass of society no longer has time to adjust itself to one set of conditions until the stage is again completely transformed by some group of scientists pushing a button somewhere. I presume men and society will keep on muddling through and remuddling. It seems useless to me to talk and think of man trying to control and direct the great intangible forces that work in society, in finance, and in all the movements of life. The only points at which to work effectively to influence movements of contemporary history are in personal religion and in individual intellectual development. The motives, the habits, the thoughts and attitudes of individual men and women are in the last analysis the only things that really matter. Attempts to regulate, to direct, to change the collectivity, while effective in minor ways, yet seem only to complicate matters more, to render confusion worse confounded, and to raise up ten problems where only one existed before. But most folks can think of trying to solve problems and reform the conditions of life only by starting societies, organizing associations, committees, boards, and so on ad nauseam. I am still a confirmed individualist in my sympathies and ideals, although I can see the need for a practical balancing of the individualistic and collectivistic ideals in order to have a good working basis.

January 8, 1933 One week of the new year has already passed by. A rather malignant type of influenza has been in progress during the past two or three weeks. Some people have succumbed to its ravages, especially old people. Ex-President Coolidge was buried yesterday, his death being due to heart failure. He was only a little past sixty years old.

Since Tuesday of this past week, the day on which the Special Bible Term opened here, we have a boarder and helper in our home in the person of Miss Julia Kauffman of Oregon. She is a student and will continue until the end of the present school year. She is helping work in return for the major part of her board; the small difference, whatever it will be, she will pay in the form of table supplies brought in by her relative Menno Troyer of McPherson County. For the next several weeks yet she will continue to have her room at another place, but beginning at the time when I leave home, she will room here and will tend furnace for her room. All prospects are that I shall go to Goshen College for part time teaching during the second semester, leaving here at the end of the present month. Numerous jobs and tasks of general work about the place here I must finish up during the next several weeks. Weather has been very pleasantly mild for past two weeks, being easy on the fuel supply. Most of the block wood supply which I had hauled up in October and November will be consumed within two weeks. Thereafter coal will be the staple fuel.

January 14, 1933 Another week has sped past. Beautiful weather continues to be the order of the day. I wish for at least one more week of continued dry ground out-of-doors; for I can then get all the wood moved to the cellar, clean up the garden and lot, and plow the garden, all in readiness for the spring sowing.

The two months since the national election fracas have brought no relief from the weight of the depression. In fact a few weeks ago wheat price made a new low record mark, selling at the elevator in Hesston for twenty-four cents a sixty-pound bushel. Eggs have been for some time worth as much money per dozen as a bushel of wheat, but these products of the helpful hen are down now to below twenty cents a dozen. Wish they would come down to a cent apiece so we could again eat them regularly at our house. The lame-duck Congress in session since December 5 seems to be doing very little but mark time. It misses few opportunities for embarrassing and humiliating President Hoover. One is forced to feel sorry for the President. The mob of our American democracy picks on him to be the political goat on whom to lay all that is amiss, against whom people feel free to vent all their spleen they have accumulated during three years of trouble. Only time can evaluate Hoover as a president, but he has worked hard and someone else will receive the credit for whatever results follow from his efforts and activities.

January 15, 1933 I am now at home while Estie has gone to the evening service at the college alone. I am "minding the baby", who is fast asleep and will be very unlikely to wake up before his feeding time at ten o'clock. We ate Sunday dinner, a sumptuous one, at C. A. Vogts' today; only the second time we have been away for Sunday dinner since Boy has joined our family. Everyone comments on what a good and well-behaved boy he is. Hope he will live up to the reputation he has made for himself so far. If only he will have plenty of energy, we shall be very happy to have him grow up as a good-natured and sweet-tempered boy, as he already gives promise to do. He smiles and laughs very readily in response to smiles, and gentle words, and playful gestures. On some days he has been in the practice of loud yelling, apparently as just his way of expressing his exuberant joy and good spirits, shouting at the top of his voice sometimes. He does seem to have a voice of good quality, rather melodious and pleasant of tone. At times he "talks" very pleasantly and gently, merely emitting a succession of slightly modulated sounds in a conversational tone and pitch of voice. His tones and facial expressions often have traces of real sheik-like qualities, especially his smiles. He rarely has real crying spells or anything resembling temper tantrums, as he had sometimes earlier. When he happens to be uncomfortable, or hungry, or eager to sleep he squalls or wails in expressive tones. For the past month or more he has had a slight congestion in his nose, and a few times when he had a slight touch of cold his nose became partly closed, particularly at night, so that he found difficulty in breathing normally. Several nights his nose became bad toward morning so that he had to wake up an hour or two before the time.

In speaking of him as a good boy, I recall to mind that I used to hear some remarks and expressions when I was a small boy which indicated that I had established a sort of a reputation in my early days of being that sort of a boy. At least, that is about the nearest I can come now to figuring out what they meant. I do not think I ever was very boisterous and energetically active as a boy, rarely got into any trouble with other boys. A very few times in country school I was punished for something by having to "stand on the floor" or sitting at some special place. I recall the punishment still clearly enough, but not the offences.

January 20, 1933 A sprinkle of rain has stopped my out-of-door activities upon which I was engaged this afternoon. Just had all my wood and kindling stored in the furnace cellar when it started to drizzle. Had also meant to clear the garden and back yard of trash and get everything in readiness for plowing the garden before I go to Indiana for a four-month stay.

It is with but little pleasure that I anticipate this sojourn away from home, wife, and Boy. It is almost constantly a source of wonder and romance to me to reflect on how the presence of the Boy changes so much of our thinking and planning. Such reflection gradually makes familiar to me the fact that Boy is a real personality and as such is making a place for himself in life and in the world. He already has amply demonstrated that he has his own likes and dislikes, his own loves and hates. We anticipate much pleasure, with no little profit to ourselves, in watching him develop along the different lines, and in guiding his first steps in the varied activities which he will undertake. We hope to be able to give him every opportunity for development as a personality, and not seek to make him like ourselves. In fact, as all parents probably do, we hope he will be different from ourselves in all those respects where we come short of our ideals, that he will succeed in all the respects where we are conscious of failure in ourselves.

February 7, 1933 This writing finds me at Goshen, Indiana. Since I last jotted down notes there has come a considerable disruption and upheaval in the even tenor of my way. The dear wife and the smiling boy I have left behind in sunny Kansas. Here there is snow and winter weather.

A summary of my activities of the past two weeks is in order. Two weeks ago I cleared off the garden and spent most of a day at plowing it and also Annie Landis' two lots. On Sunday morning, January 29, I came down with a violent attack of "flu". Was in bed for two days most of the time, severe headache, some fever, and extreme discomfort. I am now approaching normalcy in my general disposition and feeling.

The trip by automobile from Hesston to this place I made as one of a party of six persons on last Friday and Saturday, in Paul Erb's car, with J. N. Byler as driver. The journey, which lasted for about twenty-six hours, including brief and necessary stops, seemed to have no ill effect upon me, even though I was just creeping out from under the "flu", excepting that I became very weary and developed a strong desire for sleep. This I got at Paul Benders' place over Saturday and Sunday, sleeping at any time of the day or the night that I felt like doing so. So here I am in a situation almost entirely strange, but not entirely so, and trying to get my bearings and make adjustments. I have four courses to teach, taking about ten hours a week of my time in class. One class, two hours a week, in New Testament history, is a new one for me and will demand that I give considerable time for its preparation. The others are familiar courses and require but little effort. They are Elementary New Testament Greek, with one student, Intermediate N. T. Greek, with four students, and a Latin class of three reading Horace's Satires and Epistles. It is a real satisfaction to do regular teaching again. This and the convenience of having again some really leisure time for reading, research, thought, etc., are the two partial compensations I have for such an unnatural living arrangement. The compensation cannot be more than partial, but even as such it is "something." I want to try to dismiss from my thoughts the inconveniences which I suffer, and rejoice thankfully over the fact that I have something to do for which I may get some money with which to support life.

February 9, 1933 Winter in dead, grim earnest has descended upon the land. Mercury dropped to sixteen to twenty degrees below zero Fahrenheit last night and at five o'clock this afternoon is still reported to be hovering around ten degrees below. A strong west wind all last night and today made it hard for one to keep comfortable. My room has four good-sized windows; two looking to the west and two to the north. The steam radiator refused to function early this morning, so that I was obliged to emerge from my bed of repose in what certainly must have been below freezing temperature. Without tarrying longer than what was necessary to dress, I went to the reading room in the Administration building in quest of warmer surroundings. Now the room is fairly comfortable in the vicinity of the radiator.

This cold wave seems to be general over this part of the world, with subzero temperatures in many places. Government weather report gave the temperature reading for Wichita, Kansas already on Tuesday morning as negative eight degrees. Have wondered numerous times during yesterday and today how the home folks are faring in the matter of keeping the house comfortable.

Recently I finished my reading of the book entitled "Marius the Epicurean", written by Walter Pater. A year ago I saw a reference to it in some connection, and while the card catalog in the Hesston College library gave the book as being there, it could not be located at the time. Glancing along the shelves one day this past fall my eye fell upon the book, which I read during spare moments. It is a narrative (fictitious) with its setting in Italy and Rome during the reign of Marcus Aurelius in the second century. The education and youth of this Marius are given in a general way and indirectly. The author describes in some detail the experiences and the philosophical development of the man as he grew to maturity. He is pictured as coming into contact with a soldier who was a Christian, and through him with a community of Christians. He felt a natural kinship of spirit with these folk and was irresistibly attracted to them and their way of life. Accidentally he was arrested with some others who were apprehended for their testimony, and he managed to have his Christian friend released, himself staying in his place. He died from the hardship and exposure that followed. It is a very novel story presented in a rather novel way. The language is often vague and greatly involved, becoming tedious and monotonous at times, and yet withal possessing a certain charm of its own. The following lines about the author and the book are from the Encyclopedia Brittanica: "Marius the Epicurean, published in 1885. In it Pater displays, with perfected fulness and loving elaboration, his ideal of the aesthetic life, his cult of beauty as opposed to bare asceticism, and his theory of the stimulating effect of the pursuit of beauty as an ideal of its own . . . He wrote with difficulty, correcting and recorrecting with imperturbable assiduity."

February 14, 1933, Valentine's Day. More than a week has passed since I left behind me my dear wife and baby son and migrated near a thousand miles to live the role of a bachelor, more or less lonely. I can find enough to occupy my thoughts so that I do not feel the unnatural separation so keenly. Nonetheless I cannot help feeling a void in my heart, with just a bit of an aching at times. The reports which come to the effect that he is well are a great comfort. However he has been troubled with a cold and cough, having begun slightly with it already when I left. While he has not been sick, he has not had a very good appetite of late. Fortunately the little fellow seems to have a sound and healthy constitution, which is able to withstand pretty well the attacks of colds and the like.

My own routine in this life of exile or expatriation is getting somewhat fixed and settled. The time will pass rapidly enough, I feel sure, as I get it filled up with activities. I am just getting my pace in my teaching work. Am trying to fit into my schedule my recreation, in the form of pedestrianism, my research and special studies, and some general and promiscuous reading. I have set myself to the task of reading into the subject of peace, nonresistance, relations of Church to State, etc., as one major project for the coming months. Have finished reading a volume entitled "The Fall of Christianity", translated from the Dutch, by Heering. This book I found of unusual interest and very stimulating. A part of it deals with the basic problems of political philosophy, and I value this part particularly because it is the first time I have had opportunity to read anything which defined and outlined these problems in an intelligent manner. This reading gives me a definite start toward the development of my own thinking on the subject of Church and State.

Another book I am now reading is by Wright: "Conscientious Objectors in the Civil War." O. O. Miller of our Peace Committee has requested that I write a review of this particular book for publication. It is not a difficult book to read, and I do not anticipate it will be hard to review in some fashion. However, for the sake of atmosphere and general background, I wish also to read the books written on conscientious objectors by Kellogg and by Norman Thomas. My goal is also to orient myself in peace literature in general and render myself familiar with current thinking on peace, so as to formulate some ideas and convictions of my own on the subject. Perhaps I shall be able to do some writing along different lines relating to the subject of peace and nonresistance in war.

February 17, 1933 My teaching program for the week is over. It is somewhat of a relief to have "leisure" in prospect until Monday noon. Excepting, as is seemingly always my fate, that I am engaged to teach a class in Sunday School on the coming Lord's Day and speak during the lesson review period on the same day.

Received a letter from home on Wednesday reporting everything as going well. The house has a quieter atmosphere again since the Garber family left, on Saturday, February 11, and Estie found it a bit lonesome, especially with the maid also away for the day on Saturday and again on Sunday. I frequently feel a real bit of loneliness for wife and son. So I take a look at the pictures I have with me of them and then busy myself with other matters.

Have been giving my spare time to the reading of books and literature on the general subjects of pacifism and war, relation of Church and State, etc. Next week I should do a little writing on subjects connected with such themes. Read the small book: "Mennonites in the World War" by Hartzler. It brought back a few memories of that time to my own mind. My slowly developing feeling of partial regret for not taking my place in the draft was again revived as I read this book. Instead of doing so, I made application for and received classification as a theological student, which really required a stretching of the truth, as I was only a freshman college student taking one Bible course or so in a school that had "Bible School" as a part of its official name. There were several others at Hesston who did the same thing. Those I can think of were Chester K. Lehman and Paul Erb, although the latter was not enrolled at Hesston during that year, but rather at Bethel College. However, he was at the time a missionary appointed for work in India, I believe, and may have gotten his classification on that ground. At any rate both these men have since been ordained as ministers, so that perhaps this rite as ex post facto justified their procedure. But in my own case it has not been exactly justified in my mind and conscience to this day. Noah Oyer spent some time at Camp Funston, but he was called to go to camp before the system of classification was effective. He received his discharge before the end of the war. In the autumn of 1918 there were a considerable number of my acquaintances at Camp Funston and Fort Riley. On a day in October I accepted an invitation from Kings, near Hesston, to go along on a visit to the fellows there. We spent a large part of the day there, which was all that I ever got to see of an army cantonment. At some time during 1918 or 1919 I should have volunteered my services for relief work in the Near East, but I cannot recall now that the idea ever seriously appealed to me at the time. Hence my conclusion is that I was not supposed to go on such an errand. The opportunity for a bit of travel on that part of the globe should have been a welcome one, could I have visualized it as such at the time. As matters have gone since, there seems to be small hope of my travelling any in the Near East.

February 21, 1933 Life goes along smoothly enough for me here in my present status of a widower, so to speak. I try not to let myself get lonesome, and bravely keep up my courage with the thought and the hope that matters will again go better with us sometime in the not too distant future. So far as concerns signs for any general economic recovery in the country, there just are no such "animals". One wonders what the new President will do after the fourth of next month.

I enjoy my surroundings here. The students are very courteous and considerate. The meals are plenty good — better than they would need to be in a time of depression and hardship, such as we are in now. It is mostly myself that I am dissatisfied with. I repeatedly have the feeling and conviction that I just must be able to shake myself free from the inhibitions that keep me from communicating more freely in conversation at table and in the many contacts which dormitory residence affords. But I fail so many times that I frequently feel quite disgusted with myself. Have somehow not hit upon the secret or the method that will help me to remedy the difficulty. I feel that if under such circumstances as I now am I cannot mend myself in some measure, then I can never hope to accomplish anything in that direction. Perhaps it is that my ideal is too high. I do not care so much for mere conventional small talk and the common conversational pleasantries, but prefer to keep to a standard of talk that is elevating and uplifting. Of course, ordinary table talk cannot always be of such a nature, I realize.

Last evening I attended as a guest the monthly meeting of what goes under the imposing name of the Faculty Research Club. The meeting was at President Yoder's home. The program of the evening was the reading by Miss Florence Bender of a thesis of an hour's length. This reading was followed by an interested discussion for another hour and a half. The topic was on the subject of "Plant and Equipment for a Nursery School at Purdue University." Much of the thesis, however, dealt with the matter of planning and equipping the home for the convenience and welfare of small children. Much of the after discussion had to do with the principle of promoting nursery schools in general. One side maintained that the establishment of such schools would further undermine the influence and potency of the home. Another side claimed that such ideal nursery schools are now and should be kept solely as laboratories in conjunction with home economics departments of schools and colleges. Here parents and parents-to-be can be trained in the principles and practices of child welfare and so the movement will rather make the home more potent and efficient. These same folks claim they hope the nursery school will not become a regular part of the general public school system, but they fear that the "educators" will forcibly adopt it and thrust it into the system. Should this be done before there are plenty of trained supervisors available then the fears of the other side may well prove true, that it will be just another move to take children away from home and parents still earlier, at two or three years of age, and put them into the clutches of an impersonal system and feeding them so much earlier into the maw of the modern educational machine. Not so long ago a parent protested stoutly against this very sort of thing in an article in the Atlantic Monthly, entitled "Conscripting the Children." And I cannot help feeling a good deal of sympathy with the protest myself.

February 25, 1933 Another week is almost gone. I have nearly a half hour left until lunch time at the dining hall. Five-thirty is the hour for the evening repast here on Saturday. On other days six o'clock is the time — only it is dinner on those days, while dinner comes at noon on Saturday. The meals are very good and I think I have about completed my adjustment to the new form of diet and living. Instead of consuming so much milk and whole wheat meal, in various forms, it is potatoes, gravy, bread, with always a vegetable and some canned fruit. With dinner there is regularly meat, but unfortunately this is often more tough than I can chew readily with my artificial molars. But I manage to get enough of sustenance for my needs and think I am getting along well enough. I still take two or three oranges a day.

February 28, 1933 Today our son Virgil celebrates his sixth monthly birthday, that is, I assume he is celebrating, as it is the day for it. He probably was weighed and measured. He is, according to reports, well and vigorous, beginning to move about some. He managed to roll himself off the davenport onto the living room floor. No teeth does he show as yet, although his mother has begun to feed him a few things of more solid consistency than milk, such as mush made from whole-wheat meal and some juices of vegetables.

On last Sunday I was kindly invited to take dinner at the Martin home, and evening luncheon at the apartment of Mr. and Mrs. Willard Smith. Both were good meals and I think I did full justice to them. No service was held at the college on Sunday evening, but a vesper service was held at three-thirty in the afternoon instead. A rather strenuous Sunday, since I do regularly write a letter to Mrs. Yoder on Sunday afternoon. Before I left home she suggested that two letters a week would not be too often for me to write home. I remember that I rather protested at the financial outlay for postage, if we were each to write two letters a week, amounting to the sum of twelve cents every week. Well, she has been writing to me that number of times weekly, and since I greatly appreciate receiving a letter every Wednesday and every Saturday, I have begun to write as often myself. So each of us sends a letter in the mail every Monday and Thursday.

My study and reading has taken an interesting turn of late. It is still on the same general line as before. I have hit upon the idea of looking up the articles that were written during the war years, 1915-1921, and immediately following on the subjects particularly of conscientious objectors, pacifists, nonresistance. It is possible to find a considerable number of essays in a dozen or more of the outstanding magazines, articles representing widely divergent views and many differing viewpoints. The spell of the wartime psychosis gives in some cases an odd and interesting color to the ideas that are set forth. I think it will prove to be an excellent way for me to get a full introduction to these topics, as well as a complete orientation in the literature on the subject. I find that the public library in the city of Goshen has bound files of about all the magazines and journals which are indexed in the Readers' Guide to Periodical Literature. This is a fine opportunity to gradually read into this interesting subject matter. By present plans I spend several hours at the public library every Saturday morning. The book I am now reading is Cadoux: "The Early Christian Attitude to War." This is a remarkable little book, very systematic and scholarly. The author has gathered up about every line of literary evidence that bears on the question that survives from the first four centuries of the Christian era. It is what seems to be a fair presentation, and is very illuminating.

March 3, 1933 History is still in the process of making. Last week the Governor of Michigan declared an eight or ten day moratorium for the banks of his state. Seemingly the moratorium idea is quite popular, so much so that the report today is that it has spread to include over one-half of the states. I had some interest due to the Loan Company at Newton, Kansas on March 1. As matters are now tied up, it is impossible to say how soon it will be possible to get any money here with which to pay this and other obligations.

Tomorrow is the time when the country will begin to get a taste of its New Deal, when the new President is inaugurated. Evidently the mood of large numbers of people is such as to support the new regime in any moves made, if they will be radical and sweeping enough to bring about some real changes, for better or for worse. It seems indeed an auspicious moment for a new man to take hold of the helm of the Ship of State.

Today I really did something that I have not done for ten years, and never did more than a very few times in all my days. I watched a basketball game, between girls' teams playing, from start to finish. It was a novel experience and therefore interesting, from the viewpoint of an objective observer. Only once since I started teaching did wife and I watch a basketball game, at Hesston it was, and a long time ago. I fully planned during my three years in university residence to see just one real big football game. But I never did. Somehow I never could find courage to spend the necessary money for admission to such an affair. Being dependent upon the earnings of my devoted wife for most of our income for living, the price for such an adventure seemed too high, and so I have missed the thrill of being numbered as an atom among a mass of thousands looking upon the performances of struggling of football teams. And I expect to live quite as happily without such an experience. There are very few things in which I feel as little personal interest as I do in athletics. People act a bit silly in their excitement over sports, to my way of thinking, and my reaction is to ignore the whole matter. This observation today will probably do me now for another ten years. What I have regretted is our inability to attend concerts by musical artists. During the years of university attendance we went to only one concert of paid admittance charge. This one was by the Minneapolis Symphony Orchestra at Iowa City. We did also hear a Choral or Harmonic Society in Philadelphia, but as nearly as I recall we received complimentary tickets from Philip Macks on those occasions. The Bechtel young people and Macks sang in this chorus. Their rendition of Handel's Messiah impressed us but poorly, having previously heard this oratorio rendered by the famous Chorus at Lindsborg, Kansas. The last concert of real importance that we went to hear was by Madame Schumann-Heink. It was in 1927 when she sang at Winona Lake, this state. Some time in 1921 or 1922, we heard the great Polish pianist, Paderewski in the Forum at Wichita, Kansas.

March 5, 1933 Completed my reading of the book by Cadoux on the "Early Christian Attitude to War" this past week. It impresses me as a really remarkable work. The method of treatment is mainly objective throughout. Among the important conclusions that this rather rapid reading has left in my memory are the following: until about 170 there is no clear evidence that Christians served in the armies of Rome, and then only under the circumstance that soldiers already in the army when converted to Christianity remained there. By the beginning of the third century, there is evidence that some Christians began to enlist in the army. But all this time the leaders and officials maintained some testimony against this practice. By the fourth century service in the army was seldom seriously challenged and within another hundred years the law was that non-Christians could not serve in the army. Among the varied lines of influence that seem to have led to the abandonment of the early unanimous testimony against war are these. The ethics and standards of Old Testament practice seemed to justify war and bloodshed on the part of God's children. The free use of military metaphors and allusions for describing the Christian life by both New Testament writers and the early church fathers helped perhaps to break down the natural repugnance to participating in war. Also the general lowering of moral and spiritual tone within the church which resulted in a gradual and unconsciously growing attitude of compromise.

Many questions come to mind as one reflects upon this early period of the church's history. Did the church fail shamefully in not maintaining its destined standing and testimony? Or was she justified in making the adaptations she did? The usual judgment on the matter is that she lost her real power in making these adaptations, and even fell from her true calling.

March 10, 1933 My active duties for another week are done. I find no difficulty in disposing of my leisure and free time. Possibly I do not at all times plan and organize its disposition to the fullest and best advantage. At times I love to simply browse around according to the mood in which I happen to find myself at the moment. There is ample opportunity for such free-lance vegetating, being, as I now am, approximate to several libraries of modest size. And not infrequently such browsing yields very commensurate returns, often a pleasant surprise, when I chance to stumble upon some article or essay that proves with the reading to be very agreeable and very stimulating.

Just this afternoon in the college library I drew from the shelf a dusty volume of the Atlantic Monthly files, dating from the year 1914. More or less idly I ran my eye down the columns of the index pages at the front of the volume, just to see if anything would meet my eye that looked interesting enough to turn to. Presently I saw a title followed by the name of Bernard Iddings Bell, a name which without fail arouses my interest at once. The article was good and it was short, as many of his essays are. In it he spoke convincingly of the need for intolerance in thought, especially in religious thought. A genial tolerance for all and sundry, it seems, signifies the absence of constructive and creative thinking, a mere flabby sentimentality.

While reflecting a bit upon the excellent ideas I had so unexpectedly discovered and turning the leaves at random, a title across the top of a page suddenly arrested my ruminative thoughts. I became immediately interested in the rubric: "A Plea For the Erasmian." Here, I thought, must be something worth reading. And it was. I have for some years past been an enthusiastic admirer of the prince of sixteenth century humanists, perhaps because I have, ever since I first read a little in his writings and what others have written about him, felt vaguely a sort of personal kinship to his spirit and outlook, and even to his weaknesses. The article proved to be a most excellent one. For all his weaknesses and the things he was accused of by extreme partisans in the violent religious conflict which was precipitated in 1519, I find in this reading that much can be said in defense of Erasmus and of those who are mentally constituted like him. I conclude that I can qualify pretty well as an Erasmian, and naturally I appreciate reading such a clear presentation and defense of certain qualities of character which in my moments of introspection sometimes tend to make me discouraged as to my possible usefulness in life. Not that I would want to make virtues out of my shortcomings, but, since I am inclined to be extremely critical of myself, I find this article an excellent stimulant, giving me both some needed comfort and presenting moreover a challenge to set about to make the very most of myself, taking myself as I am, and not such as I cannot hope to become. The venerable sage of Rotterdam, it appears, saw too clearly and too far, so much so that he seldom found it possible to join any partisan movement. Nothing did he love so much as peace and peaceful reform. He was conservatively inclined to value highly the past and its tradition. Naturally very deeply religious, he yet could not find it in him to renounce the authoritative church with all its sins and vices. An outstanding feature of Erasmus was his singular aptness in the use of satire and irony with a vehement moral earnestness of purpose. Herein I come far short of being an Erasmian.

March 13, 1933 After some weeks of desultory search I finally on last Saturday got into my hands the book by Major Kellogg on "The Conscientious Objector." The college library index has a record of the book, but no one could locate the book itself. Professor Enss said he has the book, but was also unable to find it when he looked for it. But through his courtesy in telephoning to C. T. Soldner, minister at the Eighth Street Mennonite Church, I was able to get hold of a copy at his home on Seventh Street. This man Kellogg was a member of the Board of Inquiry appointed by the Secretary of War in 1918 to interview personally the C. O.'s in the various army cantonments. He professes to give an unprejudiced account of his impressions and conclusions about these curious creatures, but he comes far short of being purely objective in his treatment. His impression of the Mennonites (the majority of C. O.'s were of these) is quite one-sided. He makes sweeping statements about them as being stupid, bovine, moronic, and unsocial.

This volume I perused on Saturday afternoon. Yesterday between times I went through the little book entitled: "Garrison, the Non-Resistant." It deals with William Lloyd Garrison of abolitionist fame eighty years ago and more. Seemingly he was a fairly consistent advocate of nonresistance, so far as physical violence was concerned, whereas some of his methods and tactics in writing seem pugnacious enough. I had not before been aware of this man's position on peace and war, in fact had known but little about him, having only chanced to read his name in general American history. Peace agitation is by no means a twentieth century distinctive phenomenon.

The Ides of March! Nationalism is sometimes spoken of as the modern man's religion. In most respects it functions precisely as a religion for the unthinking and the lazy conformists. But how inconsistent is this nationalistic cult! Those who write textbooks for use in public schools and those who teach the subject of American history from them, are among the leading promoters of nationalism. When the child reads about the American Revolution, he is impressed with the belief that the American colonies were the great protagonists for freedom, liberty, and happiness, against the unspeakable tyranny of England who refused to give them political independence which was theirs in their own right. But the same books describe the Civil War of about eighty-five years later with such clever verbal jugglery that the child cannot help believing that it was the highest virtue to preserve the Union of the States, not allowing the seceding states to claim the glorious freedom and liberty, which is our greatest national fetish, as their inalienable right. The idea of greatness, imperialism in other terms, of ever expanding and growing materially, never retrenching or meeting reverses, this is the taproot of the widespread nationalistic cultus.

Naturally such an exaggerated patriotism is hostile to true spiritual religion. It is especially inimical to an independent and nonconformist attitude of mind. Social conformity in this respect, while it appears harmless enough in times of peace and quiet, disarms the Christian and at the moment of a crisis the intense social pressure of public opinion and unscrupulous propaganda easily sweeps away the conformist before he can get his bearings and alter his habitual mental set of conformity to the modes of thought about him.

March 18, 1933 The rain this morning prevented me from keeping my regular Saturday morning appointment at the public library down town. I have pretty regularly combined my regular hikes for bodily exercise with these reading periods at the library. Saturday morning has been one of these periods, and also at least one, sometimes two, afternoons during the week, on Tuesday and on Thursday. The weeks are slipping by in rapid succession. Just four weeks are left before Easter. I feel strong wishes to spend several days at home in Kansas during the Easter vacation. But how I may hope to get back and forth is an unsolved problem.

Life runs along pleasantly enough for me, although I shall be well pleased to change back to home life so soon as that is possible. On Mondays, at noon, each boarder at the dining hall, unless he is a permanent host or she a permanent hostess, draws a ticket for the table at which he eats during the week. But this grouping does not hold tight during the entire week. After Friday noon it is the custom for the groups to break up and everyone to rush to the first place he can reach. This is also a time for less formality and some less reserve and a diminished refinement. Usually men and women are entirely separated over Saturday and Sunday at table. The boarding is good. On Thursday evening during the dinner hour, usually some group or organization presents a brief program of a literary or musical nature. About 90 people occupy the dining hall when they are all present, at fifteen tables.

March 19, 1933 Mist, gloom, grey skies, wet, ugly, depressing! Such is the weather today, March weather in Indiana, without question or controversy! So much for the exterior. Within matters are better, more cheering, inspiring, uplifting. It has been the Lord's Day of rest and gladness. Time for meditation, relaxation, friendship and fellowship with God, the Great Spirit who sustains the soul and nerves it for continued effort. Not as quiet a day as is common, because three meetings were held at the College Assembly Hall instead of the usual two. My routine today began with reading the Sunday School Times while others were at breakfast. I read the copy in the men's social room. Sat in on the Sunday School class which was led by Paul Bender. Subject of discussion was the effects of alcoholic drinks, not such a bad subject to discuss just at the present time when legislative bodies in our country are breaking all speed limits in passing bills to bring back beer and wine as legal beverages.

The morning worship following S. S. included an address by Rev. Jacob Peltz, General Secretary of the Hebrew Christian Alliance of America. He spoke on the evangelization of the Jews, using as a text, Romans 1: 14-16. It was a good sermon, spiritual, fervent, logical and very inspiring. This man is a converted Jew, born in Russia, now engaged in doing missionary work among his own racials. During the afternoon he spoke again on his own experiences in becoming a Christian. And this evening, before a crowd that overflowed the Assembly Hall in all directions, he gave an illustrated talk mainly on the history and the work of the Hebrew Christian Alliance.

Between times I did a little reading and praying, slept a delightful nap, and wrote my semi-weekly letter to my wife who is bravely carrying on the household activities in our home. And so has passed another Sabbath. It is now the time again to retire.

March 22, 1933 Spring came in with a cold wave. Everyone is eager for full spring weather to come.

Things in governmental circles have been moving at an unwonted speed during the past two weeks, since the new President has taken up his office. Practically the first move was to pass a substantial economy bill, including the absolutely unprecedented thing of curtailing the doles handed out by the Veterans' Bureau. Three and two-tenths per cent legal beer is also promised for a short time hence. This beverage is under promise to conjure up for the United States treasury many millions of extra dollars in income. Presumably the fifteen millions of unemployed will drink a lot of the beer and provide this little added income out of the two billions of federal money that is to be appropriated from the treasury for unemployment relief. So simple are the workings of federal finance!! Farm relief legislation is also promised soon.

History is being made steadily in Europe also at present. Hitler as the head of the present government in Germany is on the point of suspending the republican government by asking the Reichstag for a complete dictatorship of four years length. MacDonald of England and Mussolini of Italy are making very desperate efforts to make the Disarmament Conference a success, presumably, as one observer remarks, to prevent the armaments of the nations from being increased more than fifty per cent at once.

March 25, 1933 Am staying in today again due to the snow that has fallen during the night. Paid two visits to the public library during the week and have practically completed the reading on the particular subject I have been prosecuting of late. Have tried to concentrate my efforts upon writing during the past week. How I wish I could write more facilely and readily. Only at great intervals do I get an inspiration so that I can write without long thought and hesitation. I seem to suffer from an over-abundance of inhibitions in trying to express myself. What I read, though it may arouse a warm response at the moment, does not usually drive me to express myself, either in conference with others orally, or in putting down on paper my ideas about things. I feel keenly my inability to enter into argumentative and provocative discussion with others of fundamental subjects of thought. I believe such discussion, were it possible for myself, would do very much to clarify and illuminate my own thinking. As it is it requires such a long time for thoughts and ideas to ripen in my mind and come to fruition. An idea I entertained when I began the practice of writing these occasional notes, was that I might in some way facilitate my habit of expressing ideas and clarifying my thoughts a bit at the same time. At times I am inclined to feel that I have received a little help in this direction; at times again I feel quite as if I make little or no progress. It almost seems as though about five to eight years ago I could write more easily and readily than I do now. It is doubtless my imagination in part that makes me think so.

At present I am finding much pleasure and profit in reading in Cadoux's book entitled: "The Early Church and the World." It is an exhaustive and objective study of the subject. The author employs the same methods as in his earlier book on "The Early Christian Attitude to War"; in fact this later book includes much or all the matter used in the former, and much besides. The only point that gives me occasion to pause in my admiration of his method, is the way he interprets the Apocalypse of St. John. All the teaching I have heard in our own church has been to the effect that the Book of Revelation is purely and entirely predictive prophecy, presumably covering the entire time between the writer's day and the eventual closing up of the little act on this terrestrial scene. As a matter of fact the teaching in our church has been more characterized by a complete silence regarding the closing book of the Bible than any other attitude. But such teaching as has been given within the reach of my own observation has been of the type I have indicated. This type of teaching about the Apocalypse seems to come from Bible students of the strictly literalist type, as opposed to the historical type of studies by other scholars.

Now the historical method of study sees in the Apocalypse a description of the conditions under which the writer himself lived. To be sure, the writer uses symbolic language in large measure, but this form of expression is borrowed directly from a widely prevailing and popular literary form in use among the Jews at the time and during the several centuries immediately preceding it. William Ramsay, whose writings I admire very much, naturally uses this method. And I must admit that I feel a strong inclination to accept this same method as the correct one. I reflect, however, that to accept the proposition that St. John was primarily describing the conditions of his own time and indicating how the Roman Empire and its rulers looked to him, need not necessarily exclude the idea that the same writings might have an ultimate and remoter significance as being predictive of the course of church history. But the interpretation of the Revelation in the latter sense seems a hopeless and impossible task, as each interpreter is at almost perfect liberty to make it fit any particular pattern of history which he may have in mind. I recall to mind my very first contact with such an apocalyptic method of interpreting the Revelation. My father when I was still quite a young boy bought a book from an itinerant agent entitled: "Daniel and the Revelation." In later years I learn it was a piece of Seventh Day Adventist propaganda. But as a young bookworm I read rather carefully through most of the book, in which the writer took the text of these two books verse by verse and identified the supposed predictions with the detailed events of history as it has since transpired. The idea appealed to me then to some extent. But the other approach, the historical method seems now so much more simple and natural and logical. I realize that this method has been used extensively in an attempt to disprove the existence of all predictive prophecy, even to the extent of dating the Old Testament books at a time after the occurrence of the events which they predict. In the case of the apocalypse there is no attempt to do violence to the obvious facts of authorship and date in using the historical approach to its interpretation.

Mr. Cadoux in the book I am now reading uses the apocalypse, along with the other writings of the period of 70-110 A. D., to determine the attitude of the Christians of this period toward the state, toward war, and toward the world in general. Regarding their attitude toward the state, he finds evidence in the literature of the period of several, apparently conflicting, tendencies. Some, as in the Revelation, regarded the state as intrinsically evil and Satanic, picturing it as a Beast and a Harlot. This attitude was fostered by the blasphemous claims of the emperors to worship and divine honors, and further by the persecutions directed against the Christians. But there was also a feeling that regarded the beneficent side of the state and gave honor where honor was due. Thus, it is generally agreed that Luke wrote his two books during this period. And it is not impossible to conceive one of his purposes in writing to have been that of presenting an apology for Christianity, which was then officially under the ban of the Empire. It is interesting to note that he stresses the generally favorable attitude taken by Roman officials towards Paul and his fellow missionaries; also showing how Paul used his Roman citizenship and was inclined to cooperate with the beneficent phases of the imperial state. Seemingly Paul in his later years entertained the hope and vision that the Empire might be favorable to the new faith and might adopt it. This attitude seems to be behind the famous passage in Romans 13:1-7, which on the surface presents much difficulty of interpretation.

March 30, 1933 Instead of going out for my regular exercise this afternoon, I thought to work in my room and catch up with some work that has to be done. After a little while slumber came over me. I lay crosswise over the bed and would take a nap of not over an hour's length. When I awoke it was a quarter to five by my watch! Then I had to act as janitor for about a half hour in order to get my room cleaned and dusted. Thursday evening has been my regular time to visit and loaf at Bender's place, so there is not a great deal I can hope to get done, unless I stay up late to work, having had several hours of sleep in advance.

I read just lately of an idea on Church and State which is at least suggestive to my mind. A writer was giving his ideas on the Jews and Force. He referred to their old-time request for a King as the beginning of a worldly state among them. He went on to say that the prophets of Jehovah who ministered to the nation from time to time were constantly in conflict with the state as such. These teachers entertained and taught usually a true international outlook. They proclaimed the king's ordinary advisers as false prophets and lying prophets. They were thoroughly unpatriotic from the narrow nationalistic point of view.

I am reflecting on the propriety of using this point as a part of an introduction to the treatise, tract, or whatnot, which I contemplate to write at some time on the subject of Church and State, or on some phase of this large subject. There is a great deal to be considered in reflecting upon such a subject. It has been a live question with some groups of Christians during most of the time of the church's history. Even the Federal Council of Churches is making a special study of it in our day.

April 2, 1933 On several occasions I have found recreation recently in reading some "Letters of a Homesteader's Wife" published in the Atlantic Monthly away back in 1913 and 1914. Just spent an hour now reading with avid interest two installments from the bound volumes of the Atlantic which rest on the shelves lining the outside wall of the college reading room. The volumes are seldom molested, as is attested by the dust and grime recorded on one's fingers after handling them. The Letters mentioned are grippingly interesting, at least I find them so. Not having been written for publication, but only out of friendship, they have a spontaneity and an artlessness that is charming. Then the subject matter, the experiences which the writer tells, the scenes she describes, and the sincere and elemental kind of living she reflects catches my imagination right off, and I could at such moments be easily cozened into a vow that I shall take my Estie and our Virgil and seek out some spot among the high mountain valleys of Colorado or Wyoming where we may live and grow strong close to the nature of things. A faint wish at times arises in my mind that our son might be reared amid the rigors and the beauties of nature rather than among the more artificial phenomena of a complex and bewildering human society. Not that I should wish to eschew all social contacts in a hermit-like existence, but rather to cultivate such intercourse in a society that is more direct and elemental, more natural and spontaneous. But particularly the joy of living in the healthful and bracing air of the valleys lying high in our Western mountains, the grandeur and the awesome beauty that is immanent everywhere among them, these I might justly wish should be the atmosphere that may nurture the soul and the strength of our boy. His mother is not very strong physically, but is it not possible that the pure air, the sparkling mountain water, the bracing aroma of pines, and the wondrous beauty of such surroundings may be just the elixir which will make her grow strong and healthy again?

I frequently play and toy just a little with the idea of adopting some such program for ourselves, and particularly so when I contemplate the slender margin by which my employment and income as a college teacher seem to exist. In the small schools of our own denominational group, the demand for courses in Latin and Greek cannot be large enough to justify my drawing a livelihood from that source, and particularly in the depression years that are ahead of us. The chances for securing a teaching position in larger schools are very small and the corollary of adjusting myself to a new and radically different environment has in it also certain risks and uncertainties. Just now I call to mind the fact that an uncle of mine, who now lives in San Francisco, California, many years ago bought a part interest in a gold-mining claim not so far, perhaps forty miles away, from Rawlins, Wyoming. My idea is to inquire of him sometime whether it would be possible for any of his penniless kin to settle on this land by his permission in order to have a place to live. I am not certain that he still has it or if it is any good for raising things to eat. I know that he lived on it himself some twenty-five years ago for a period of time in an endeavor to find some of the gold which was supposed to be there. He never found very much, probably not enough to pay his living while he worked on it. However, we shall not move there until I have seen the place, which will not be very soon.

April 9, 1933 One more week has sped by and brought the day of rest to men. Seemingly I have been busy all the time with this or with that. Sat through two sessions of a special committee's meeting this past week, a committee that has been asked to define objectives and policies for the future of the college here. Much laborious thinking and often ingenious reasoning is required in formulating some such project as this. Since there is confusion and uncertainty on many details of church policies throughout the constituent territory of the college, it seems impossible, in view of the widespread suspicion against schools and schoolmen among our people generally, to set up any fixed program covering such points here at the college and then set about to execute the same. Opinion on the committee seems to favor taking steps to strengthen the inner life of the school and especially to build up an aggressive evangelistic program in the local congregation. Also a definite objective needs to be laid before ourselves looking toward the inculcation of the historic principles and attitudes of our forefathers, with a thoughtful and fearless interpretation of these principles for the age in which we are living. Personally I have held to the opinion that it should be possible to so interpret, for instance, the principles of nonresistance and nonconformity to the young people as to make it a challenge to them to consciously cast in their lot with a minority group, even a despised minority, perhaps, in living out and defending such unpopular principles.

April 11, 1933 The Easter recess begins tomorrow at noon and lasts for just one week. For a few weeks I have considered much the proposition of trying to get home for a few days over Easter. The only possible way to get back and forth was that of "Hitch-hiking", or "thumbing", and due to the shortness of the time, I decided it were better not to try the stunt at this time. Perhaps I shall use that method for getting home in June, partly for the adventure and partly for reasons of financial economy.

I shall proceed to bury myself for a week in reading books, writing this and that and doing whatever else may please my fancy. Am getting awfully eager to see Boy again. While it might be a slight comfort to be with him for a couple of days, to leave again so soon would probably be harder than to wait until I can go home to stay. His mother reports that he has been gaining in weight and in length, he wants to stand on his feet sometimes, enjoys looking out the window watching the rain fall and trees swaying in the wind. No teeth have been reported for him so far.

Walked downtown this afternoon for a regular stint of physical exercise. A very pleasant and comfortable day on which to be abroad.

Have been feeling well about ever since I am here, with the sole exception that my rheumatism is very much more noticeable than in Kansas. My leg joints, and sometimes my left hand, are painful. Dr. Fred Brenneman, a few Sundays ago while in conversation, advised the use of sodium salicylate. I must get some vicious teeth extracted from my jaws as soon as ever I can spare the cash for having "store teeth" made, at least for my lower jaw. Estie writes that she has been suffering from rheumatism in one of her hands during the recent past.

The financial outlook for us has not cleared up yet. Very little money has been forthcoming from the college since I am here. Twenty-five dollars was advanced to me before I came, in January, and in March again an equal sum came into my hands, which I sent to Estie. She returned me two dollars for pin money and after paying up current bills recently she had six dollars left in her purse. I have made urgent application to the college officials for financial assistance, suggesting that they pay me the amount of forty dollars a month from now on until September. This will make a total of three hundred dollars from the college for the semester's work. While in correspondence last winter they spoke of five hundred that I could count on as cash income, but now it appears that they guessed that the Peace Problems Committee would pay me two hundred dollars for services rendered to it. My work for this committee is just beginning and I have very little idea that they will pay me any perceptible fraction of the above sum in one year for what I do. So the final disposition of my obligations of this year and some still from last year is by no means clear as yet.

April 14, 1933 Slept late this morning. Rain is gently falling from the sky again. Paul Bender invited me to ride along on a trip to Purdue University, some 120 miles away, but not being very enthusiastic about such a sojourn just at this time, the rain makes my decision finally in the negative on that deal.

Many times have I greatly wished for time and opportunity to do a great deal more of reading than I normally get done in the course of my routine duties. The present four months of sojourning away from home has brought me such an opportunity along this line as I have not had for a long time. I appreciate it greatly too. But there is also a disappointing side to the experience. I discover that continuous reading is in some ways a hindrance to thinking. The net returns from the reading seem to be rather meagre. Not enough time and leisure is left for digesting the material which is ingested. The result is that I seem to suffer slightly from mental indigestion. Especially the reading and skimming through so many current magazines and news sheets seems like a dissipation at times. Sometimes I think I ought to adopt Thoreau's attitude towards newspapers, at least a part of it. One can certainly waste a good many hours in a week's time scanning these sheets. I believe I shall cut down my reading of current matter. Several scores of magazines, weekly, monthly, quarterly, all consume a heavy quota of time and energy, when one tries to follow them all.

The practice of purposely reading much material and doing it rapidly so as to cover much ground, definitely creates a condition of chaos and confusion in my mind; my store of thoughts and ideas are a deep tangled wildwood instead of an orderly and well kept garden. When I do try to think in an orderly way and set down my thoughts in writing it is harder to do than when I read less and reflect more. The little book by Ernest Dimnet on "The Art of Thinking" has a wealth of good suggestions along just this line. I have read his book through twice, and must read it again frequently.

Have just completed the reading of a rather heavy book in German, entitled "Gewalt und Gewaltlosigkeit." This is a collection of essays and articles from several dozens of writers. Much of the book was illuminating to me. All phases of thought dealing with peace, nonresistance, and opposition to war were presented and explained. The material is just of the sort which I need as a background for my own thinking upon the subject of peace and war. The socialistic viewpoint is largely exploited in the book, and even the anarchistic viewpoint also. The evangelical religious viewpoint is mentioned, but is inadequately stated and is not particularly defended. It seems that a prevailing phase of the program of the idealistic pacifists is the use of coercion to abolish the use of war, and indirectly in changing the social order. These two ideas they hold to be inseparably connected as effect and cause. The Christian viewpoint to my own mind cannot allow for the use of coercion, even nonviolent coercion. Its chief emphasis must be laid upon dealing with individuals, by conversion, by education, by persuasion. The nature of the social order and the forms in which it expresses its life are in the last analysis determined by the likes of individual people.

Good Friday evening: This day we regularly observed as a holiday at home during my boyhood. It was quite regularly kept as a "fast-day" by my parents when they were still of the Old Amish Church. The custom was to refrain from breakfast and spend the morning after chores were done in individual reading and meditation. Since leaving home I rarely think of it as a holiday anymore. And yet it would be a very appropriate practice to distinguish the day from others by some kind of religious observance. Walking past the Lutheran Church in town this afternoon I noted its announcement for a three-hour devotions service from twelve to three o'clock. Had I known of it, I should have thought of attending it.

I note that the Pope at Rome has formally opened a holy year recently, proclaiming it on the occasion of what he believes is the nineteen hundredth anniversary of the suffering and death of Christ. But as I understand, the most generally accepted date among Protestant scholars as marking the death of Christ is 30 instead of 33. My faltering effort to teach the class in New Testament History during this semester has impressed at least that upon my mind. We completed the period of the life of Christ just a few weeks ago. In this study I was particularly impressed by the fact that there is not a single year-date given in connection with the life of Christ that is not seriously in dispute by scholars and students. In this matter I have formed a tentative theory of my own for the moment. It is this: The Holy Spirit in guiding the composition of the N. T. writings undoubtedly of purpose left chronological details in obscurity in order to minimize the possibilities for people, being naturally inclined toward outward forms and toward superstitions, in following ages to attach great merit and efficacy to the observance of anniversaries and days and times and seasons. Plenty of such has developed even in spite of the uncertainties in the chronology.

As a few instances of the obscurities and the various "certain"
dates which students fix for events in Christ's life we may note that
the year of His birth has been variously fixed in the years from 8 B.C.
to 3 B.C. The latter half of 5 B.C. seems quite commonly to be now
held as most probable. The length of His active ministry is variously
held to have been from less than two years to four years in duration,
with a bit more than three years as the length most generally held. The
year of His death is assigned all the way from 24 to 33, I believe. Here
30 is regarded quite generally as most probable. The chronology of the
Last Week of His Life is very much in dispute. The Crucifixion, most
commonly and also traditionally placed on Friday, is by some put on
Wednesday or on Thursday.

Several weeks ago I more or less accidentally, in the course of
magazine browsing, came upon a long and scholarly article in the
"Evangelical Quarterly," a Scotch magazine, wherein the author presents
an elaborate argument to demonstrate that Christ was born in 8 B.C.
and died in 24 B.C. His evidence for these unusual dates he marshalled
from many sources besides the New Testament, especially from astronomy, archaeology, and Roman history. Among the very interesting points
presented is the claim that literary and archaeological evidence have been
discovered which indicate that the story of the death and resurrection of
Christ was known in China at least as early as the year 27 or 28 A.D.
If this evidence is positive and genuine, as it is reported to be, then the
arguments given in the article offer a possible solution. I read the article only once and not with a particularly critical eye. But I did notice
casually one point in the way of an objection. Amid all the data which
the writer considers in dating the death of Christ he omits all mention
of the second item in Luke 3:1, that Pontius Pilate was Governor of
Judaea at the time that John the Baptist took up his ministry in Judaea.
As nearly as I can find Pilate only became Governor in about 26. Hence
I have not yet adopted as final the new chronology which is here advanced!

In order to polish up my limited skill in reading French prose, I have
with me a fine little book drawn from the college library shelves. It is
entitled "Petite Histoire des Lettres Francaises." It is easily and simply
written and not difficult to read. To my great regret I cannot pronounce
French words. Could I pronounce the words, I believe I could read this
French as readily as I do German. As it is with me now I transverbal-
ize most of it mentally into English and get the thought in that way. My
knowledge of vocabulary is rusty. I find I can get the thought most surely and readily if I run my eye rather rapidly along the line and get the
thought by phrases and from the general drift of the ideas.

Easter Sunday: The most dismal and gloomy Easter Day that I can remember of ever having spent! The morning dawned grey and chill with
the sky weeping gently. Rain ceased during the forenoon. The afternoon
grew darker and ever darker; thunderings muttered in the heavens; rain
fell faster and faster; gloom and murk grew ever thicker and thicker.
It has been hard to keep cheerful, but I have succeeded fairly well,
though not without strong determination and resolution. The spirit of
the day has not been in vain for keeping the blues at a respectable
distance. No meeting of any kind is to be held at the college this even-

ing, which makes another hour and a half that must be otherwise disposed of. Were it a pleasant evening, I might be minded to stroll down the street in the hope of finding a service somewhere.

After a sumptuous dinner and a period of rest this noon I betook myself to the college reading room. It was, of course, deserted and though only three hours past noon, it was dark and uninviting. Sitting near a window I found enough light to read by as I browsed through an old volume of the Atlantic Monthly of fully twenty years ago. Concentrating on anything serious was difficult. Robins were happily chirping outside revelling in the abundant supply of worms which the rain was bringing to the surface of the ground for their convenience. In the room, which normally teems with life during school hours on week days, all was strangely still, save for the slow and monotonous click, clock, of the electric clock on the wall, as it steadily marked the passing minutes with a special signal after each sixty seconds.

In the course of my browsing I came upon some letters written by a Down and Out, a man who had once been successful, but while still in his thirties lost his standing and position. He went to the far Northwest in search of work and an opportunity to start over again. His was an interesting story of hunger, disappointment, and heroic struggle. This was in 1912, while railroads were still being built and before unemployment became chronic and severe. No particular comfort or counsel could I gather from the story which the letters tell.

Well, leaving the reading room, I came to my own domicile; wrote a letter to my dear wife, none too cheerful, I fear, and rested some more. There seemed to be an unusual amount of general noise on the first floor of the dormitory, especially for a Sunday. A few fellows, none too genteel in their manners, were loafing about the social room, located in the north wing, and in the halls generally. Someone seemed to be talking nonsense with some girl in Kulp Hall over the telephone in loud tones. Someone was pounding away on the piano most of the time or strumming on some other instruments as a means for passing away time.

Yet in spite of all the difficulties, this Easter Day has brought me some joy, even if of the conventional sort mostly. It is always a pleasure and an inspiration to review the simple Easter story again and to meditate upon its meaning and message. The new hope and the joy that always follow upon the dark and dismal days come to mind afresh and rekindle faith that joy and fulness of life will be sure to come back after the present darkness is past. I pray to be able to profit by the difficulties of these dark days so that as Vergil says, haec olim meminisse iuvabit.

April 21, 1933 This has been one ideal day. Sunshine clear and unhindered all the day long. A balmy breeze coming from the south bearing on its bosom the odors and the gentle fragrance of the springtime. So positively alluring was the sunshine that it drew me irresistibly into the out-of-doors. Not having any class after luncheon today I took a book to read and walked abroad in order to drink in the beauties and charm of nature, opportunities for which come so rarely in these parts of the country. Between the college campus and the dam on the Elkhart River, which lies perhaps three-fourths of a mile west by south, there is a pleasant tract of woodland. Along its western end flows what they call the "race," an artificial channel of water diverted from the river's course by the dam. Along the race I sat down on the sloping bank in the sun's full view and enjoyed an hour or more in reading and observing nature. Many birds were singing and chirping all about, robins, cardinals, kingfishers, varieties of sparrows. Green shoots in abundance appear from one to three inches tall over the woodland floor. Especially welcome was the sunshine, of which I have absorbed very little since leaving the sunny plains of Kansas. The air was mild and laden with the first odors of spring. Grass is everywhere a beautiful green, which is restful to the eyes and soft to the tread.

A very interesting letter from home tells of Boy's progress in development. He is learning rapidly to utilize his hands for various purposes.

April 22, 1933 Several times during recent days my memory has dwelt upon my personal circumstances during these days just one year ago. It was the time when I was very glad indeed for the comfort of a hospital bed and for the gentle ministrations of nurses. My room in Bethel Deaconess Hospital, Newton, was pleasant enough. Its walls were comfortably tinted with a shade of tan and a stencilled border next to the ceiling. The room was just nineteen figures one way and twenty-four the other. But these details mattered nothing at all to me on that first Tuesday evening. Consciousness was returning by slow degrees, voices registered on the brain as faint and far away, vile phlegm in throat and esophagus had to be disposed of. I swallowed it down. The nurse in attendance prophesied to my wife that it would all have to be delivered up again later, but barely a gulp or two was returned in succeeding days. Eyelids were heavy, and hardly able to lift themselves even a bit; voice inarticulate; sleep and more sleep was most pleasant and welcome.

Days and nights followed upon each other in order: grey days, which the memory cares little to recall; nights of slumber under difficulties. The only problem for my mind was how to render the wounded body as comfortable as might be, by means of periodic and painful shifts and alterations in position.

Following the skillful surgeon's ritual in my behalf, occasioned by an appendix which was ruptured some thirteen hours before, the hospital bed, hard and patient though it seemed, was yet a comforting place of repose for many continuous days and the nights that separated them. After seventeen days I was able to give the longsuffering bed brief moments of respite while I sat in a chair. I felt sure it appreciated the rest it got.

For four days at the very first I was required to subsist on liquids, plain water, diluted orange juice, malted milk, and weak tea. Really there was no desire felt on the part of my stomach for stronger meat. Gas pains, alas, their memory is still a sort of subdued nightmare in my mind. Food seldom tasted good after the first few bites of a meal. Changing my position in bed was a painful process, mitigated only by a sort of technique which I was able to develop by practice and experiment. After a little time I was able to pass the time more pleasantly with reading: Greek Testament, Atlantic Monthly, Scientific Monthly, Literary Digest, and others.

Meanwhile for three entire weeks the national Congress had to carry on its puerile gestures to balance the federal budget without my interested presence on the sidelines. And the search for the Lindbergh heir had to go on its fruitless way without me. In fact rather disconcertingly I discovered that all the wonderful processes of Nature as well as the foolishness of mankind had suffered no interruption at all due to my nonparticipation. Trees and grass turned richly green while I could not even watch them. Have since then entertained a modest suspicion that my participation may not be so vitally essential to the ordering of the universe as I had secretly supposed.

April 25, 1933 My present mental foraging is in several books and the usual journalistic offerings. A man named Lecky some sixty years ago wrote a two-volume work entitled "The History of Morals from Augustus to Charlemagne." I have come well on toward the end of the first volume and I find it to be an interesting and instructive book to read. His chapter on the "Conversion of Rome" contains many curious facts and data regarding conditions in the Roman Empire during the first two centuries of the Christian Era. This view of the conditions outside and inside the Christian Church is perhaps the complement of the usual view given by religious writers on early church history. The author presents at length the different phases of moral conditions in society at large, picturing the scepticism in some parts, the restless hunger for religious experience in others, the almost unbelievable credulity in all parts of the social body, and he indicates how conditions were ripe for the success of a religion such as Christianity. He quite minimizes the idea that the triumph of the new Way of Life was of the nature of a miracle. He also takes pains to point out the more sordid side of Christian credulity, of the dishonesty of Christian apologists who forged a vast body of literature which was scarcely ever criticized by Christian leaders. Whatever may be the real facts about the conditions and the activities of that early period, it is painfully clear that it is very hard with our modern background and modes of thinking to really understand what all was going on at that time.

April 28, 1933 Special six weeks Spring Term for school teachers began a day before yesterday. I have agreed to teach six extra hours a week during this time. I will present the same course and material I have been giving and am giving in the New Testament history during this semester. The size of the class is indeterminate, due to the tardiness with which a number of persons will enroll. Am also guiding a Miss Stauffer through a reading course in ancient Roman private life, which will also take some time, but not much. And so I have more and more work to do and inversely there is less and less prospect for receiving financial income of any moment for this semester. Collections from students are slow and uncertain because of the general banking collapse of several weeks ago. Income for the college from other sources is entirely cut off. What is yet worse, no one has been stirring a hand to determine whether any funds and donations could be collected from friends and supporters. The Mennonite Board of Education is "against the wall" also in a financial way. They have a total indebtedness of some $80,000. Some of this is borrowed from a now defunct bank, from which there is some threat of legal suit or receivership, so I am told. The Board has also invested endowment funds to the approximate amount of twice the total debt. But some of this has apparently evaporated in the general financial storm of the past three years, and the income from such funds as still survive after the deflation has shrunk considerably. The net result is that income from endowment is barely sufficient to cover interest charges on debt and other unavoidable expenses. Such is the story of the situation as it has come to me in a roundabout way. Sounds serious enough to me!

To one who has invested years of time and thousands of dollars of money, some borrowed, in preparation to work in the schools of the Mennonite Board of Education, the prospect is dark and dismal. It is an open question whether the schools can survive on the old-time basis of operation at all. Hesston College is in the midst of a radical adjustment now, which is not complete, and its success is and will be a problem as long as the depression continues. As for myself, I try not to worry as I know such an attitude does me more harm than good. I am willing to lose my property at Hesston if I must, but I shall leave few stones unturned in a desperate effort to hold on to it until conditions improve and it will be possible to sell at a better advantage. The mortgage which we placed upon it three years ago will be due in September, and I have made no inquiry of the Loan Company as to whether it is possible to receive a renewal on the loan or not. Meanwhile I strain my eyes for some opening of an opportunity to earn a living for next year and the years after. The opening in that direction which exists here in Goshen College for myself is not promising enough to hold me back from hoping and praying that something better may come before me. On the whole, Wife and I refuse to let ourselves be overcome of fear and worry in this trying time. Too many times in the past have we experienced answers to prayers for guidance and direction, for the provision of our needs, for comfort and faith, to now lose courage and give up in despair.

Perhaps I should think seriously of giving up teaching. But there is nothing else I can do for a living, unless it be farming. I have not by any means forgotten how to work in the soil and I have little doubt that I could revert to it and we could raise enough food to eat. The capital necessary for starting up would constitute a large problem. Might be possible to trade the house we have on a small farm or plot of ground and try it out in good earnest.

The sun, a huge round ball of fire, is just ready to drop behind the horizon. From my west window I can look upon it in its splendor and glory. It has been a warm day. I walked downtown this afternoon. The air was mild and the fragrance of blossoms and of the springtime earth was on the air. The depression is bad, but Spring is good.

The Kalends of May! The gentle rain beats against the outside of my window this evening. Thunder and lightning rumbled and flashed since darkness has covered the face of the earth. Green leaves on bushes and trees have been pushing out rapidly during the recent warm days and soon everything will be green and lovely.

Three puellae candidae are reading in the Satires of Horace at present under my guidance. Their names are Donna Belle Hepler, a plump lady of generous lateral dimensions, Valeria Barnard, with slightly auburn hair and quick wit, Gladys Johns, a freshman maid with black hair and bright eyes. They are all three very capable Latin students and read Horace with a relish, I feel.

We are becoming very familiar with the substance of the old Stoic philosophy as the somewhat Epicurean Horace loves to portray it. He is especially fond of expounding the Stoic paradox in its various forms. The Third Satire of his Second Book, the longest of his Sermones, I think, reports a Stoic sermon on the theme that all men are so to say insane, all excepting the sapiens the philosopher. Everyone has his pet hobby, his own particular way in which he strays from the path of wisdom and scrupulous sanity. I have a faint suspicion that there is more of truth in this theme than what appears on the surface. Of course the ideal wise man does not exist excepting as an ideal. I am made to think of how many fine illustrations of the universal aberration from sanity, sound sense, a shrewd observer of society like Horace could gather up today in these United States of America and even in the whole world. The ever recurrent greed for wealth, position, fame, and the like, finds slightly different forms of expression today than in that ancient day in Rome. But some genial satirist could readily find abundant matter today to prove that all men are insane even as of old.

May 6, 1933 I feel as though the pressure were rather suddenly taken off myself just now. There is no article, essay, paper, manuscript which I must have ready now for nearly two months. Sent to the Christian Monitor today the last of my promised articles, and I emphatically will not promise another series very soon. The copy for the Annual Hesston Alumni Letter I sent to Bertha Nitzsche a few days ago. She is corresponding secretary to the Association. About July 1, I need to send copy to Gospel Herald again; meanwhile I shall enjoy some small measure of leisure from obligatory writing, abandon myself partly to some spontaneous scribbling and partly to general reading.

Just now I have gotten a good start in the second volume of Lecky's "History of European Morals from Augustus to Charlemagne." This work is interesting in most of its parts, contains much curious information on comparative morals and manners, and much suggestive information that may be very useful. The author has a comprehensive grasp of the problems in moral development and the factors that have figured in moral revolutions in the past. His description of the moral types and standards in pagan Rome seems reasoned and fair. The factors and ideas which entered into the conversion of Rome are vividly portrayed and the revolution which Christianity wrought in morals is traced out in detail, with especial reference to such features of ancient life as slavery, the gladiatorial shows, and the moral aspects of the imperial system, suicide, and so forth. The development of charity and philanthropy are traced entirely to the influence of Christianity.

But unfortunately there are also shadows in this splendid picture which is drawn of the transformation wrought by Christianity. The exaltation of poverty into the position of a primary virtue led to much abuse. Closely connected with the ideal of poverty was the entire asceticism which grew up so rapidly beginning with the Decian persecution at the middle of the third century. The detailed description of this epidemic of asceticism, which drew away from the active life of society and the church such large numbers of its capable members, is almost appalling in its horribleness.

I recall now that I have often in the past entertained just a faint wish that I could have lived in the age when monks were more popular than they are today, as I felt very sure that had my natural disposition for seclusion and privacy been reinforced by a popular movement I would have doubtless taken very naturally to the life and habits of a monk. However my own conception of an ideal monk was not that of an anchorite spending his lifetime in a desert doing penance by privations and maceration. Rather I thought of the coenobitic monasticism which was the form that prevailed in the West, where monks lived together in a simple form of life, did their little necessary manual labor by means of a division of labor and spent much of their time in study and meditation. This latter type of monasticism did a really great service to the cause of learning, culture, civilization, and even to the church during the Dark Ages. At the same time there can also be some truth to the contention that the thickness and blackness and duration of the gloom of those ages was partly due to the fact that so many of the ablest intellects of the time withdrew within the cloistered seclusion of the monasteries instead of contributing directly of their service to society as a whole. Hence I am not so sure but that I am glad after all to be alive in the twentieth century instead of in the fourth or the tenth. At the same time, I do contend that we lose much today through a failure to cultivate more the contemplative side of life. The tendency is too much to interpret all phases of life, to think of every phase of life in terms of social concepts, and for those who are disposed to live a little more apart and think, meditate, and contemplate, there should be some opportunity and encouragement, as a means to offset in part the over-socialization of modern thought.

May 9, 1933 Lecky in his "History of Morals" draws a dark and hopeless picture of the incredible spirit of superstition and abject credulity that prevailed in Europe from perhaps the fifth to the eighth centuries. The Catholic Church, he finds, deliberately fostered just this kind of attitude and spirit — in fact it was universal, including priests and bishops and all. Myths and legends grew up on all hands, holy relics were multiplied, ignorance and superstitious fear prevailed. The definitions of orthodoxy which were laid down in the course of several centuries of savage struggle, from 300 to 500, were stifling and strangling the last lingering sparks of heresy and freedom of thought. Doubt and all opinion contrary to orthodox belief were made wicked and criminal. As a means for finally crushing out all impulses to criticism of the dogma of the church, the threat of eternal damnation to a burning sulphurous hell was held before all who might have been inclined or been able to think for themselves. The descriptions of the tortures, the agonies, and the miseries of the damned were elaborated, classified, and drawn with all the gruesome and revolting details which a diseased imagination was capable to muster. The church had with these means effectively closed up every possible avenue of attack upon her system and her superstition. It was due to the contact of Europe with Saracenic learning and schools, to the recovery of much of the ancient pagan classical literature, to the growing economic importance of the towns, and to a few other exterior influences that this pernicious system was finally reformed in some measure.

It is undoubtedly difficult, if not impossible, for us of the twentieth century to realize the exact nature of the prevailing modes of thought of those Dark Ages. The right to freedom of thought is a great blessing, although in theological and ecclesiastical quarters much of the old spirit of stigmatizing doubt, and a critical suspension of judgment, and a rational inquiry into all matters, as being sinful and wicked still flourishes. The ideal of being strictly honest intellectually and not letting oneself be swayed by sympathy and emotion is perhaps impossible for any man, or for very few. At the same time, to keep an open mind, to formulate and hold all conclusions as tentative and subject to revision at any moment, to muster courage enough to give up the peace of certainty for the anxiety of doubt, to be willing to investigate all facts fearlessly, this, while perhaps a high ideal, is not an impossible one. I am naturally and by disposition conservative, hesitant to change my ways and opinions, and try to avoid jumping from one idea precipitately to another. On the other hand I think I am comparatively free from any strong impulse to ape the opinions of others. I am decidedly not a strong conformist. But that may not be saying anything either. My fear is that I may never accomplish anything constructive.

May 10, 1933 Regular letters from my wife at home bring news of their continued health and welfare. The first real spring rain at home fell on last Thursday, May 4. Our small son is growing and developing steadily. At eight months he weighed eighteen and one-half pounds and measured twenty-eight inches. And the last report is that he is displaying now his first tooth. He grows more active all the time and tries to raise himself on his legs. It will be a whole month more before I can hope to see him again. That he and his mother have kept so well and gotten along so successfully during my months of exile from home is occasion for no little joy and gratitude to myself. The end of my sojourn is now not so far in the future, and I find all my thoughts about my work here and the four weeks of time that remain falling naturally into terms of finishing up and going home.

May 13, 1933 My random browsing this morning brought an enjoyable thirty minutes, more or less, of pleasant reading. I lifted from its shelf a 1922 volume of the Atlantic Monthly and was soon absorbed in a brief piece by Professor Goodspeed on the suggestive title: "The New Barbarism." This proved to be a perfectly jolly comparative study in satirical vein of modern barbarities such as Noise, Odor, Confusion, the Religion of Travel, the Ways of Trade, its insistence and competition. This style and manner of writing is always at once my delight and my despair. I love its delicious suggestiveness, its genial allusiveness, and its Horatian telling of the truth with a smile. But I despair of trying to achieve such an inimitable style myself.

Another essay in the same volume which caught my eye was under the enigmatical title: "Change Cars at Paoli." I was attracted not by the title in this case, but by the writer's name which was none other than

A. Edward Newton. It is interesting how the acquaintance I have formed with names like Newton, Bell, Goodspeed, and others during the past six years in the pages of the Atlantic Monthly (it is only six years that I have been reading this excellent journal regularly) leads me to discover their articles of years previous to these.

The substance of Newton's article in this case is a delightful description of the beautiful Memorial Chapel at Valley Forge, with an account of the origin and execution, incomplete, of the idea which it represents. This splendid but brief description is very artfully framed in a pleasant motor trip through the beautiful country between Paoli and Philadelphia, all interspersed with charming observations a la A. E. Newton.

The article as a whole I found doubly interesting because of the memory of the visit which Wife and I made to Valley Forge on a Saturday afternoon in the summer of 1926. I was that summer attending a course in Vergil at University of Pennsylvania summer school and Estie was doing office work for the Westinghouse Electrical Company. She did not work on Saturday afternoons, so that during July and August of that summer we took advantage of Saturday afternoons and Sundays to drive to various nearby places and visit friends and acquaintances. On this particular Saturday we went to Spring City, in Chester County, to spend Sunday with a family named Swartz, whom we had known some years before at Hesston, Kansas. On the way to Spring City it was convenient to go by way of Valley Forge, where we stopped and spent several hours. Of course the chief attraction was the Memorial Chapel, which is really a Gothic Cathedral in miniature, a very excellent bit of architectural beauty. The Chapel itself was mostly completed except for the tower. In the absence of a tower to house the chime bells, these were erected on a wooden framework at the rear of the Chapel and elevated only a little way above the ground and exposed to the elements, except for the shade of some large trees. During the time we were there the chimes were played for a short time. There are eventually to be other buildings clustered about the Chapel, as museum, library, etc. At the time of our visit, a temporary building to one side contained the beginnings of a museum. Driving over the grounds we saw many marked spots, the outline of the trenches used by Washington's soldiers, and the building used as his headquarters by the General.

May 20, 1933 Since one week ago many unexpected and sorrowful things have happened within the ken of my experience. Last Saturday evening about nine o'clock two students were accidentally drowned on the mill race along the west side of Goshen. They were Ellen Hertzler of Hesston, Kansas, and Harold Burkholder of Markham, Ontario. A party of four were out canoeing after dusk and when the boat was accidentally overturned the swiftness of the current made it difficult for even two of them to rescue themselves. The girl's body was recovered in about fifteen minutes, but all efforts at resuscitation were vain. The young man's body was also recovered after two hours.

The terrible news reached the campus at about ten o'clock. The shock had the effect of dazing students and faculty. A funeral service, largely attended, was held at the college chapel here at three o'clock on Sunday afternoon. The same evening the bodies were started by train toward the homes of the dead. Anna Hertzler accompanied her sister's remains to Kansas, Paul Bender going with her as far as Chicago and assisting with the transfer from one train to another.

Ellen's two other sisters who were working in Chicago, Carol and Ruth, came to Goshen for the Sunday service. They wished to go to Hesston for the funeral. The students' Christian Association was inclined to send a representative of their number and the faculty also felt it would be appreciated if someone of its number could make the trip to carry a message of sympathy and condolence. And so it rapidly developed that Earle Brilhart would drive his Ford roadster, taking the two sisters and myself and in less than two hours we were on our way to the westward.

I occupied the rumble seat of the car alongside of the baggage. For my protection against the wind and air exposure, Mr. Brilhart provided for me his aviator's helmet. This with my light overcoat and a borrowed slicker raincoat protected me very well, although exposed parts of my face were burnt a little by the wind. The air whipped and beat around my face and head with thunderous noise. The wind was too strong in my eyes for me to use these to view the landscape and the sights along the way, the opportunity for doing which was otherwise unparalleled. I discovered also that the rumble seat is a dry place to ride while rain is falling so long as the car moves along at a speed of fifty or sixty miles per hour. When however a drop or two does meet the skin of one's face, while travelling at such speed, the effect is a sharp sting as of small hailstones striking the skin.

We left Goshen at six-thirty fast time and by eleven-thirty or twelve midnight we found J. J. Smith's home in Eureka, Illinois, where we enjoyed good beds and an early breakfast the next morning. By six o'clock standard time we were moving again, made good progress all day, and in spite of a forty minute stop in Kansas City we were at Hesston by nine-thirty in the evening. Needless to say I appreciated the stay of nearly thirty-six hours length at home. There was time only for getting partially acquainted with son Virgil, as he took me for a total stranger after an absence of about fifteen weeks. I found he had changed considerably since I last saw him. He had acquired a thick head of hair and they are slightly curly and of light, almost sandy color. Just now he wants to stand on his feet all he can, pulling himself up wherever he can get a hold of something.

The funeral service at Hesston was held at the College on Tuesday afternoon. Before nine o'clock next morning we were started on our journey back to Indiana. Made good progress until in Southern Iowa, where as dusk began coming on the motor began to ail. Becoming worse we were forced to stop at Ottumwa, and spend the night, so giving up our plan to spend the night with friends at Kalona, Iowa. It was past ten o'clock the next morning when we were able to get away from the place. Reaching Washington, Iowa, I telephoned ahead to my brother Herman's place and ordered a lunch prepared for ourselves. The three miles of dirt roads were muddy and were hard to negotiate. After this brief stop we continued swiftly and smoothly to glide over the concrete, reaching Chicago at dusk. There were only three on the return journey, and we left Carol Hertzler off at her place in Chicago, and the two of us were back in Goshen by about one o'clock that night. These two days since I have been slowly getting caught up with my sleeping quota. It was withal a pleasant trip, although a sad and lugubrious mission on which we went.

May 23, 1933 I seem to have brought a "cold" along back from Kansas. My lower lip is full of "cold blisters" and I am today feeling the usual congestion in my head and nose. Took a long walk in the pleasant sunshine today, travelling along the west side of the mill race all the way from the dam to the powerhouse down town to view the scene of the tragic accident of ten days ago. Did a little business at store and postoffice and arrived home again by four o'clock.

Have just this evening finished reading the six hundred and more pages of Cadoux's book on "The Early Church and the World," a book which, according to a previous reference in these notes, I started over two months ago. It is the kind of book which I, at least, cannot read rapidly. It will also, I believe, prove valuable for reference use. An epilogue at the end sums up the principal findings of the book. I like the book immensely and expect to use it frequently in the future. But it also raises some fundamental questions, rather annoying questions, the kind one would like to be able to answer finally and conclusively by some cut-and-dried formula or definition. But seemingly such a devout wish is doomed to disappointment. Well, the questions are such as these: Is the human race by the grace and revelation of God advancing morally and spiritually, or is it en masse sinking steadily from bad to worse in spite of the grace of God? Is human nature basically and essentially evil or is it fundamentally good? How is one to interpret the unmistakably eschatological teachings in the New Testament, in the writings of Paul, Peter, John, and among the teachings of Jesus himself?

My own training and the general teaching of our denominational group inclines me to the literal eschatological interpretation of such predictions about the end of the world and the personal return of Christ. But after all, in looking at the past history of this school of interpretation as well as the course of history, I am made to pause and wonder a bit. Sometimes I experience a feeling that the more I read, study, and investigate the fewer opinions and convictions I have which are fixed and unquestionable. "He that increaseth knowledge, increases sorrow!!"

May 30, 1933 Decoration Day. Cool weather. Cloudy at the beginning, clear at end of the day. My influenza is clearing away slowly now, but slowly at that. Cannot secure enough sleep. Flopped down on the bed a little after four o'clock this afternoon and was "dead to the world" until six-thirty, too late for dinner at the dining hall. Lunched a little on salted peanuts and milk chocolate, which I happened to have on hand. Feel so much refreshed from my two-hour "nap," that I am sure it was worth the price it cost. Regular class work is over for the semester now. During examination days I have one class meeting and one test to administer. For another week I meet the spring term class every day and then it will all be over.

Recent letters from home tell of the rapid development of Virgil. Since I was at home, he has started creeping all over the house, mostly on all fours. He pulls himself up into a standing posture and is perhaps learning his first steps in walking. And he has two teeth, the last I heard.

The college faculty had an enjoyable evening yesterday on the occasion of its annual banquet. It was a "depression" banquet, plates costing twenty cents each. Every person was supposed to contribute some labor in the way of getting ready for the occasion.

The college quartet, who will give an entire program of music on the coming Friday evening, is now practicing, as it often does, in the room immediately above mine.

June 3, 1933 The commencement season with its public programs, stir and bustle on the campus, its measure of confusion and excitement, is now underway here at Goshen College. I had planned to find considerable time during these days for some special reading and writing, but time is taken up with this and that, with that and this, so that not so great an amount of time is left for myself.

"It won't be long now," as is the saying. I have hopes of being at home in a week from now, if I can make travel connections as I hope to do. I shall be able to travel by motor as far as Milford, Nebraska, as it now appears. Ezra Hershberger is here from that place and the car has room for one passenger more.

June 13, 1933 After ten days I have come around to a scribbling of notes again. During the last four days before the close of school there was too much distraction to get into a frame of mind and thought suitable for writing leisure time notes. What with last minute closing of class work, public programs, numerous visitors, and oppressively high temperatures, I could not isolate myself enough to feel I was at leisure. Heat! Everyone was sweltering the last few days and it was quite uncomfortable to be on dress parade during these days with stiff linen collar about one's neck and heavy coat over one's shirt. But everyone lived through it and on Wednesday evening the climax was reached with the commencement address by the President of Geneva College in Pennsylvania.

On Thursday morning, June 8, I was able to start on the three days' journey home. It was a Chevrolet coupe that brought me along west as far as Milford, Nebraska. It belonged to a young lady, or her parents, Nettie Stutzman. She remained at Goshen to attend the session of the summer school and Ezra Hershberger drove it home for her again. Miss Yeackley of the same place was also a passenger. We had a pleasant trip, driving steadily at a rate of speed between forty and fifty miles per hour. Over the first night we stopped with my brother Hermans in Iowa. Had evening lunch, sound sleep, and a good breakfast there before we continued upon our way. Because of several visits and short calls made in the morning it was ten o'clock before we started. At noon a tire was flat. Followed a beautiful highway through Iowa, much of the way U. S. No. 34. It passed by many beautiful fields of growing crops rich in their greenness and luxuriousness, and quite frequently by a field of red clover or of alsike clover in full bloom, the sight and fragrance of which were especially pleasing and delightful. At Milford I spent the night at Ezra's home.

Some investigation failed to disclose any possible opportunity of my riding south into Kansas as a stowaway on an oil truck or some other.

Mr. Hershberger then offered to bring me to Hesston for the price of a bus fare from Lincoln to Newton. By five o'clock on Saturday afternoon we were here. And I was glad indeed to find myself at home again after almost continuous absence for eighteen weeks. Wife and Son I found well. But gardens and fields appeared dry and unpromising, and especially so in contrast with the splendid vegetation and fine-looking crops we saw in the states north and east.

The extreme heat of the eight days before came to an end — and an end for which all were glad — on yesterday, so that it has been comfortable enough today and yesterday. Some work on garden and lawn needs to be done. Hope also to get some work to do on a farm this summer which will net me a little cash income. It is just about a necessity for me to have a little income this summer, in order to relieve a little more the stress of our impecunious circumstances. But of harvest there will not be very much in this section of Kansas. Much of the wheat that was planted has succumbed to drought, wind, army worms, and what other foes there may have been.

June 18, 1933 There has been no rain in these parts for weeks, and scarcely any signs indicative of such a blessing since I am here. I have stirred the top of the ground — mostly dust — in the garden the past week, cut down some weeds and grass about the place, and done a few general chores. Had hoped to get some work during harvest time somewhere near home. So far I have no particular work in sight. If I had the cash in hand for the purchase of materials, I should make some work at home by repainting the house and garage with several coats and recovering some of the screens on windows and back porch. A few other minor repairs are needed about the house. Besides this physical labor, there is some writing I could be doing during this time.

But cash in hand is still the urgent problem with us. Plenty of opportunity is at hand constantly for building up credit, work to do for nothing or nearly nothing. When last winter negotiations were underway regarding my teaching at Goshen for the second semester, the idea was held out to me that about five hundred dollars in cash, in addition to my board and room, would be my remuneration for the semester. But, as I discovered since, a part of the cash proposition was a mere guess. The college discovered in its budget only one hundred dollars toward my pay. In addition, since I took over two classes of H. S. Bender's, and he was thereby to be left free for a project of research and writing for the Mennonite Publishing House for which he was to receive the sum of two hundred dollars, this sum was to be transferred from his salary account to mine. So then it appeared that my cash allowance would be just three hundred dollars for my teaching which was about a two-thirds schedule. When the mid-spring term came on and it was decided that I should teach six extra hours a week, they agreed to allow me fifty dollars extra for that. Out of the total of three hundred fifty dollars, I have to date been able to collect just a hundred eighty. Perhaps another ten dollars or thereabouts I have been able to take out through charge accounts at various places. I expect to collect much of the rest during the next few months, but the experience of the past months has taught me not to count such chickens before they are fully hatched. It will not be possible for us to move away from here unless I can collect a good part of the remaining cash due. The remaining two hundred dollars of what was originally talked about was a mere guess as to the amount of money the Peace Problems Committee might pay me for some work I was to do for them. But I have not done much work for this committee as yet. The first quarterly installment of the Peace Bulletin appeared in the Gospel Herald in April; the next one, on which I am now working, will come out in July. But of remuneration for this I have received none as yet, although I am sure of getting something in due time, while I am equally sure that the amount can be only a very small fraction of the amount which the Goshen officials originally guessed it might be.

July 2, 1933 Two weeks since I last have written any notes here. There has been no rain even yet which could be reported here. Showers have fallen at sundry places around us, but drought and high temperatures continue to be the order of these summer days. Excepting two fairly good rains which fell here in May of this year there has been practically no moisture for twelve months past. We have a protracted drought even for Kansas. Garden produce is very scanty at present. Dug out a half bushel of potatoes yesterday. There are also onions, beets, but scarcely anything else. Tomato vines are standing still, some dry up and die away. Sweet corn stalks are about two feet tall and in full tassel already. No ears can possibly form with the present dryness of the ground.

I worked at threshing, pitching bundles in the field, on six different days, putting in four and a half days of time, for which I received pay at the rate of one and a half dollars per day. Chris Vogt generously gave me a little extra money for the time that I worked for him, so that I realized the magnificent sum of seven dollars fifty cents from my efforts. Wheat was poor, scattered over much ground. The weather was very hot on most of the days I worked. Really I was able to endure the heat and the work better than I had imagined I could. Fortunately on several days when the heat gave promise of becoming unendurable in the course of an afternoon, scattered clouds appeared in the sky and intercepted the rays of the sun for a time, which proved a great boon to me. With longing, expectant eyes I watched on numerous afternoons the tantalizing forms and shapes of really good rain clouds which were either soon dissipated or moved off in another direction leaving us as dry as before. Besides the small amount of cash which I received for my threshing efforts I partook of nine good threshers' meals, to which I did a fair degree of justice. Also had some good wholesome exercise which seems to have dispelled some of my rheumatic pains which had accompanied me home as souvenirs of my stay in Indiana. Perhaps the greatest benefit of all was the generous quota of ultra-violet and other rays of reputed benefits to living organisms which I was able to absorb. Abundant exposure to direct sunlight always makes me feel better and seems to have a good effect upon my physical constitution.

During these extremely hot and dry days my mind has a number of times recalled the pleasant climate and surroundings we enjoyed for about twelve weeks at Boulder, Colorado, just ten years ago this summer. Estie and I, accompanied by Paul Bender, spent that summer very happily in that university town lying close up against the beautiful foothills of the great Rocky Mountains, about thirty miles northwest of Denver. Miss Margaret Horst was also with us during half of the summer. Often in the early evening we took a few cooking utensils and some things to cook in them, climbed up along some small canyon back of the city, cooked or fried something to eat and enjoyed a pleasant evening, walking back at dusk or by moonlight. Saturdays often found us on longer drives up Boulder Canyon and points beyond. We never joined any of the regularly organized and directed parties that went on hikes and outings, preferring rather to explore for ourselves and enjoy all the thrill of adventure and discovery. Not being particularly expert in following the faint mountain trails, we often wandered about, and even perhaps failed to reach our original destination, but enjoying the whole experience very greatly. On a Saturday about the middle of July or after we decided to try to get to the top of Arapahoe Peak by ourselves. Left Boulder very early in the morning; at sunrise or before. Drove our Ford car as far to the westward and skyward as we possibly could, over some very bad mountain road toward the last. When we finally had to stop our progress by this means, we ate our noonday lunch at an early hour, left the car standing in the wide open spaces and started out on our trek to the top. There were small showers of rain at the start. We got off the trail several times, wandered about on some snow fields, spent much time watching mountain scenery, especially after we had passed timber line, as is called that natural boundary between the altitudes where trees grow and where they do not. We succeeded in getting fairly well up toward the coveted peak. We were able to look down upon the famous Arapahoe Glacier from above, but we could not get upon it from the place where we were. Neither did we reach the summit of our Peak, and to my regret it seemed to be entirely my own fault. It was the highest elevation above sea level that I had ever reached in my life, and I found that my heart was not quite equal to the combined requirements of the rare atmosphere and the exertion necessary for climbing upward. Climbing only a few yards brought upon me a feeling of seemingly utter exhaustion, from which I could recover again quickly, but it made progress very slow and at last almost impossible. The others of the party did not experience such severe exhaustion. I urged them to go ahead and leave me behind, but they refused to do this. I still believe that had we not wandered around so much and wasted our strength before reaching the higher elevation, I could have possibly "made the grade" myself. Our lunch before starting was perhaps not the best selection of food for such an undertaking, and too we should have rested well while our digestive apparatus was in operation, instead of starting out almost at once.

When we were warned by the hour that we must start on the way back in order to reach our car before dark, else we would surely get lost, we started back. The automobile drive was possible after night and we were safely home a few hours later.

July 4, 1933 Today the citizens celebrate the birthday anniversary of American independence. For me the only respect in which it differs from the day before and the day after, as I anticipate, is in the village postoffice being closed so that we cannot get any mail. Probably it is open at certain times today, but I do not know when these are.

This day ten years ago we spent in Sunshine Canyon, I think that was its name, several miles to the north and west of Boulder, Colorado. Equipped with a few books, bird glasses, some lunch, and a full holiday from university classes, we walked out in the morning to spend the day at leisure. Sunshine Canyon is not a place of any particular attraction. A quiet place of retreat, rather barren compared with many other places near and around Boulder. Plenty of rocks, grasses, some birds, a scattering of bushes and thickets and some scrub trees of a kind I do not remember now. We enjoyed a pleasant and quiet outing, did some reading and meditating and some talking.

One memorable outing that Estie and I had was on a Saturday in August. Three or four miles to the south of Boulder is located a rather striking peak. Its top comes to a sharp point and its eastern side slopes almost continuously and gradually into the floor of the great plain that stretches to the eastward. The slope is wooded all the way up, but not heavily so. The peak is called Bear Mountain and it stands out a bit lonely, just a little in front of the numerous peaks and ridges of the foothills of the Rockies that lie close behind it. Many a time from Boulder I had looked and even stared at that peak. Something about the top of this Bear Mountain fascinated my imagination. As the weeks passed the resolution to climb to its top took shape in my mind. It was often mentioned about the university campus as the goal of a sizable hike or outing. Estie agreed to accompany me on a Saturday to climb this mountain.

We left home early in the morning carrying with us some things to eat, bird glasses, umbrella, etc. With no difficulty we reached the foot of the big hill, but we lost the trail that was generally used in climbing it. We clambered directly up the east side and it was well worth the somewhat difficult climbing which its trackless slope offered. For as we slowly made our way upward it was thrilling to look back at frequent intervals and find ourselves rewarded with an ever wider and wider horizon to the eastward as we looked out through the scattered trees toward the plains. We rested when we felt so disposed. At length a little while after noon we clambered upon the very topmost rocks of the peak. These dropped off sheer on three sides and there was a very narrow place at the top on which to stand, or rather sit. We sat. And for some little time we looked now in one direction, now in another. It required some time to drink in all the scenes that lay within reach of the eye here; it took quite a while until the eyes seemed to be filled with the sights. Eastward for many, many miles the plain stretched ahead. Motor cars appeared as tiny ants creeping along their diminutive ribbon-like paths. To the westward a vast uneven sea of successive peaks and mountain ridges rising ever higher and higher stretched away. All was vast, inspiring, thrilling. Man and all his proud accomplishments seemed after all to be very small and insignificant in comparison with the things God had made. The thought was impressed deeply upon my mind: "O why should the spirit of mortal be proud!"

Coming down from this wonderful spot, we descended over the northwest side of the mountain, a part of the time along some trail and again without a trail. Stopped to pluck a few mountain berries which tasted very good to mountain climbers who had no water to drink all day.

Near the bottom of the slope we came upon a good trail. We halted to eat the last of our lunch, but a sudden and vigorous shower of rain came upon us. We sat under the combined protection, such as it was, of some young trees and our umbrella while we ate. But the rain was not done yet by the time we were done eating. Waited a little while. Rain showed no sign of stopping. It would soon be getting dark and we knew we had to move on and find a more familiar trail before darkness fell, else we might have to spend a whole night in the rain. Folded up the umbrella, made a compact bundle of the few things we had along, and bravely set forth to defy rain and cold. I led the way and Estie followed behind. In a half hour or so we came upon our familiar trail where we had come in the morning. Soon it was dark and we plodded on steadily, wet to the bone, but not suffering any special discomfort. Reached home tired, bedraggled, hungry, but withal happy, and satisfied from our experience with Bear Mountain.

July 6, 1933 Our son Virgil is now a little past ten months of age. He is an interesting child, seems healthy and strong, and affords us a great deal of entertainment. Folks remark about his pleasant appearance. He weighs now about nineteen pounds and is twenty-nine and one quarter inches long. He is by nature friendly and sociable. He smiles and laughs readily. Has developed a number of ways of expressing himself. He can yell many times louder now already than even his daddy. To attract attention he gives out a clear grunt, "hough"!, or "ough"! His commonest way of carrying on conversation is to pronounce a vigorous "aech" with great expression and much force and at a high pitch.

July 16, 1933 The great heat wave and protracted drought has been relieved at least temporarily in these parts. There have been two rains within a week when about two inches of water fell. The moisture was most welcome and so have been the more moderate temperatures of the days since it fell. Unfortunately much of the corn in Kansas was past the stage of development where the moisture will benefit the crop. People are planting feverishly and hopefully more seeds in their gardens, with prayers, presumably, that they may get a few things more to eat from that source. Prices in general are shifting upward. Wheat is moving towards a dollar a bushel locally even. Bread prices are higher. The surcharge or processor's tax has been added to the price of flour. The first large-scale taxation for the benefit of a special class of people is now being tried out in the United States. It looks like a possible opening wedge for an unlimited movement toward the socialization of industry and agriculture in this country. Perhaps it is inevitable, but whatever it will lead to, economic life is pretty sure to be something quite radically different in the future in our country than it has ever been before. To me it appears that the root trouble is man's greed and his pride. This depression, instead of humbling people and driving them to rebuild the basic moral and spiritual foundations of life, has only confirmed the proud notion that man must and will plan his economic and industrial order and he will control its working and results. I partly fear it's a task too great for puny man with his secular and materialistic equipment.

July 23, 1933 Another week of pleasant weather has passed. Rain fell again to the extent of over two inches. Received six gallons of zincite paint by freight shipment from Montgomery Ward & Company, Kansas City, early in the week. On the past three days I have been applying the first coat to the outside of the house as a priming coat, having already covered three sides. Several weeks of pretty steady work will be before me to get all the painting and repairing done up. The house needed paint quite badly. Its surface was last treated to such decoration in 1926, which is seven years ago. It is not especially easy work, but since I am working for myself, I am free to work as fast or as leisurely as my taste and ability dictate.

After the refinishing job is out of the way, there will be packing of our goods and belongings for shipment to Indiana. Have already in a small way begun preparations in that direction. Made a capacious tool chest in which I expect to ship and to store all my tools of every sort, garden tools, a few carpenter tools, odds and ends of this and of that. Since we anticipate to camp in an apartment of limited size for the next few years, with not much room for storing things, I calculated that the best method for protecting and taking care of what few tools I have is the method I have adopted. When ten years ago we left Kansas for an indefinite sojourn in other parts, we disposed of about all our furniture, tools, and general equipment. Owing to the difficulty in again stocking up with such things, and also the expense, we decided not to do such a thing again. Hence we plan to carry with us our few earthly belongings, in fact, perhaps move away from this place for good and all (?).

July 30, 1933 The writing of this date reminds me that I have this day completed forty years of earthly life, and it seems as though I have scarcely started living as yet. This is Sunday, and it seems I can recall of looking up the matter at some time and ascertaining the fact that I was born on a Sunday. Today we were entertained at Sunday dinner by Joe Yosts at their farm home a mile north of Hesston. Chris Vogts were there too and Miss Lois Kauffman.

My time has been taken up during the past week with work of various sorts. Some painting on house and garage, cutting weeds and grass, a trip to Newton on shopping business, etc., etc. One day's time I gave to working on the college campus for the Grounds Committee which is making preparations for the holding of the conference on the campus in a few weeks from now. This coming week I hope to put the second and last coat of paint on the house, and the first coat of white paint on the trim. Then there will be various odds and ends of repairing and painting, and then packing of things and making preparations to migrate.

Of reading and study I have not done much this summer. I read through Petronius' "Satyricon" and the "Apolocyntosis", reputed to be of Seneca. Have also written out rough translation of Satires seven to ten in Juvenal. It appeals to me that Juvenal's "Satires" would be a fairly interesting field for a little intensive study for me, in the field of Latin literature. Satire is a form of literature and a method of moral reform which has a sort of a special appeal for me. Juvenal often preaches morals with all the zeal and desperate earnestness of an Old Testament prophet.

August 6, 1933 It has been an unusually warm day and it is pleasant to have the evening at home. No service is held at the college, because the Hesston Young People's Meeting program is being given at the Pennsylvania Church instead of here. Several weeks ago the Pennsylvania folks gave their program here and this is a return of the favor this evening.

As to what is going on in the world at large, I find out very little this summer. Have not been reading any daily newssheet since I left Goshen early in June. One feels a bit out of touch with life under such circumstances, but it is no really serious handicap and is perhaps an advantage; not so much distraction. The Literary Digest brings us a summary of world events in better perspective than a daily sheet and with less waste of the reader's time. The Digest changed its form and style of make-up somewhat about July first, and we feel it is an improvement in many respects. There seems to be more material presented and in more convenient form with no increase in the size and number of pages. The leading articles each week, instead of consisting entirely of the quotation of editorial opinions of various shades, are now well-written summaries or "digests" by recognized writers of ability, with only a limited amount of editorial opinion. Some new and added features are present items which appeal because of their human and dramatic interest. The publishers even announce that they will soon begin a department consisting of letters of opinion from readers.

One feature of the change which we do not appreciate much is the discontinuance of the Art Front Covers. For nearly ten years the Digest each week presented on its front outside cover a reproduction of some painting of merit, occasionally the work of some classical painters, but more often of that of the better class of modern painters. And always there was given somewhere inside the magazine a few brief notes about the picture and its author. But now the front cover is just another "magazine cover", reproducing some drawing or painting especially made for the particular issue of the Digest, usually reflecting some current theme.

For about eight years we regularly and systematically saved up the Art Covers and also the descriptions that accompanied each one, so that we must now have nearly four hundred of these covers. "Saved up" is the right term here, for the problem of arranging and mounting them in some way for use, study, and reference has not yet been solved. Whenever that is done we think we shall have a very valuable collection of reproductions of high grade paintings.

August 8, 1933 A splash of rain forced me to stop my work of outside painting early this afternoon, with the result that I am not as tired as commonly.

Virgil is beginning to walk without aid or assistance now. He easily raises himself to standing posture anywhere, and today we saw him several times take from three to five steps. He still lacks twenty days of being one year old. His bones and muscles seem to be well developed and he has no superfluous fat to hinder his efforts at moving about.

No words does he speak as yet. Some syllables and sound-phrases he uses constantly, but evidently the instinct for imitation has not yet made its appearance in his case. He makes no attempt to imitate anything that is said to him. Possibly he is made for doing things only from original individualistic impulse, and will do nothing by imitation. Who knows? On the matter of his learning to talk, I recall to mind a facetious remark our old friend, Ray Bender, is said to have made to someone years ago. It was only a few years after we had married and Ray asked of one of our neighbors who visited him in the East whether we had any children, and added that he does not see how they would ever learn to talk! Of course, he meant to hand us a back-handed compliment on our own inclination to be garrulous.

But in spite of Virgil's failure to talk so far, he does not fail to understand a great many things that are said to him. Mention the ball and he will be all interest and utter in a very inquiring tone his "Hough," meaning "Where is it?" When it is time to go to the dining room table, he understands when you mention "chair" to him. "Bath," "bed," "porch," are some other words he knows very well when he hears them spoken to him. He loves to hear someone imitate for him the sounds made by things he hears. He notices birds flying and hears their songs. He is all eyes and ears when a motor car passes the house as he is on the front porch and he follows it with his eyes as long as he can. For a month and more he has had four teeth to show, two above and two below, the middle incisors. His gums hurt him much of the time, and just now he is having another tooth coming through.

September 24, 1933 Nearly seven whole weeks have actually passed by since I last had leisure time for scribbling any occasional notes. They have been rather strenuous weeks. I shall need to record the train of events which has thus fully occupied my time and attention during this time. Some of the time I worked hard and needed all leisure time for rest and recuperation.

The middle part of the month of August was spent in painting the outside of the house and the garage. This work required more time and pains than I had anticipated. I consulted with an experienced builder and painter as to how much paint might be necessary for doing the job I contemplated. I was told to figure so many square feet for a gallon of paint, and then figure one gallon for trimming to every five gallons of surface paint. I went twice around the house with the grey paint and a third time over the south side, which had been weathered the most, and had used not quite five gallons of paint, not counting turpentine and linseed oil that was added for thinning. Therefore I contemplated that one gallon of white paint for trimming window and door frames, screen frames, face strip and eaves, would likely be sufficient. As it finally developed, I kept on buying more and more white paint, until the total amount purchased was three gallons. And then at the last I passed by the white surface under the eaves of the garage, not putting anything fresh on that part, both for lack of paint and lack of time.

The trimming took a great deal of time, especially the screen frames, which had been painted black before. So it happened that I was greatly rushed at the very last. I also helped C. Hertzler two half days with his well making outfit, mostly in order to diminish the amount of my indebtedness to him from last October, when he sawed wood for me along with the others who pooled our efforts in securing fuel wood.

Then in the fourth week of August came General Conference to

Hesston. I still had some painting to finish up even then, and nearly all of the packing and preparations to move away. Consequently I did not attend the sessions very regularly, but kept on doing some bits of work in between times. Fortunately I was not appointed to help on any of the committees, so that I was left much more free than most of the folks around home. Our preparations for conference consisted almost solely in filling two bed ticks with oats straw from Chris Vogt's barn, arranging them on the floor of our east bedroom upstairs for folks to sleep on.

As our guests during the time of the Young People's Institute and of the conference we had Paul Bender and Harold Bender of Goshen, Sarah Bender of Canton, Ohio, Jake Birky and wife of Lancaster, New York, my father, and for a single night, three Detwiler sisters of Thomas, Oklahoma, also a young man from Harper, Kansas. The conference was largely attended by people from far and near. It afforded an opportunity for meeting many old-time friends and acquaintances who had gathered in for the grand pow-wow. It was perhaps the largest assemblage that the town of Hesston ever entertained.

September 25, 1933 Class work and teaching have been in progress now for about ten days here. Gradually routine procedure is being established and soon most of my work will be a continuous and steady pull. Textbooks are still in part a problem, due to the shortage of the supply on hand. My courses number six, each meeting three times a week or the equivalent thereof. Elementary New Testament Greek is my largest class, and at the same time the largest class of its kind I have ever had. It numbers twelve aspirants, who seek instruction in Greek. The second-year Greek is being read by two students, John C. Wenger and Angelina McPhail. In Latin one class is reading Cicero's Essays. Quattuor puellae candidae perlegunt quod Cicero de senectute scripsit. Two maidens are reading in Pliny's Letters at present, Miss Donna Belle Hepler and Miss Marian Messner. Eleven students at the Elkhart YMCA are under my tuition in the rudiments of German. An evening class in Intermediate German has not started work yet, but will meet tomorrow evening. This is a full schedule of teaching hours. Only once before did I teach the equal number of hours, four years ago at Hesston, when I had three five-hour courses in as many beginning languages, and taught Vergil's Aeneid besides.

October 6, 1933 There has been pleasant weather during the past few weeks here, very good for Indiana. I recall that in 1926, when we moved to Goshen, there were weeks and weeks of gloomy, dismal and disagreeable weather right at first. This time our welcome to the state seems to be better. I am still struggling to become organized and routinized for my regular work and some additional work along the side. It seems to require a long time to get ourselves contracted sufficiently so as to be comfortable in our new quarters.

Estie has in addition to the process of getting settled, worked hard to take advantage of the fruit that is available to can and store away as much as she can for the winter's supply. So far we have bought three bushels of tomatoes at fifty cents each, two bushels of grapes at fifty cents and seventy-five cents respectively. Also secured a bushel of hand-picked pears for fifty cents yesterday. Apples are of reasonable price now, eighty cents to a dollar a bushel, and potatoes are coming down in price, being about a dollar a bushel now. If I can find a place to store several baskets of each in someone's fruit cellar, I may get us our winter's supply soon.

On our migratory journey from Kansas to this place we stopped for several days with our relatives at my old home near Kalona, Iowa. While there we were invited to exchange of our empty fruit jars for others that were full, which we were glad enough to do because ours were just about all empty. The result was that we came away with about seventy-five quarts of fruit and vegetables of various kinds. With some canning now and using fresh fruit as long as such is available, we may have most of our fruit supply at hand until the next season comes around. But of vegetables we will be forced to buy a good many, either fresh or canned, during the winter and spring.

From Kansas we also brought along a supply of wheat and of wheat meal. About a bushel of wheat we have, which my wife processes whole so that it is very good as a breakfast cereal served cold with sugar and milk. The wheat meal was ground for us by Mr. Diller of near Hesston on his stone burr mill. There are about one hundred pounds of this meal, which we will use for baking bread. These will easily last us all winter, perhaps an entire year. Very interestingly, Mr. Diller was not free to charge us for the wheat meal even though he ground wheat which he raised on his own farm. The reason was that he has no permit for processing wheat and selling it with the special federal tax that is now levied on such products. However, I presented him with enough cash to pay for the wheat and something besides. And so it happens that we shall not be helping much toward paying the socialistic bonus to the wheat farmers who are signing contracts to reduce their wheat acreage for the coming year.

So far I have made no memoranda of our moving trip. In its entirety this migration of ours was such an adventure that it seems worthy of a record for refreshing my mind in time to come. In view of the fact that one person who made a bid on the job of transporting our goods over the eight hundred seventy-five miles of distance from Hesston to Goshen, made a special offer to do this for one hundred dollars, I decided it would be worth while to try a piece of adventure in getting Father's truck from home and loading on it not only ourselves but also all our moveable worldly goods. Father drove the truck to Hesston on Tuesday, August 22, in time so he could attend the General Conference. It is a one and one-half ton Model A Ford truck. The bed measures about six feet by eight feet inside measure. There was no little misgiving about getting all the things on this bed, although I reflected that the dimension upward was quite elastic, and could doubtless be stretched to adapt it to the needs of the load. I was told beforehand that in hauling household goods one need give himself no worry about the weight, that only the bulk need give one concern. This dictum proved to be a fallacy in my case, as experience showed, for I had little furniture that was bulky, and did have many books and some very heavy pieces.

For several days during conference Paul Bender, since he thought he could stay over, help me load and then also drive through, made a real effort to find some way for Estie and Virgil to ride in a car as far as Kalona, Iowa. But no opportunity that seemed suitable was found, and so the others left and we stayed to get ready and leave at our leisure.

Saturday and Monday, August 26 and 28, I spent in packing books, dishes, utensils, knocking down furniture, such as tables and the like. I even took down my built-in book shelves and brought the lumber along. There were still bits of odd jobs about the house to do, in the line of repairs, which I interspersed with the other preparations. On Monday it was raining. On Tuesday we had planned to load, but there was still some rain and everything out-of-doors was soft and wet. So loading was postponed until Wednesday morning. It was impossible to guess beforehand how many scores of little things there are to be done in pulling oneself up by the roots and getting ready to move root and branch. And each item demands its quota of time.

Wednesday, the thirtieth, dawned bright and clear. I engaged I. E. Burkhart and Dan Driver to help with the loading. The first piece to be put on the truck was the G E Refrigerator. We loaded it at the rear porch, having called upon Chris Hertzler and Ben King to give us special assistance on this one piece. The remainder we loaded at the front porch, having backed the truck upon the lawn, now quite soft from the rains. The sequel to this feature will appear later.

Noon passed and so did the afternoon, yet the load was not finished. Every nook and corner was made to receive its box or bag or what-have-we. Bedsteads and bed springs were tied along the outside of the rack. Matresses were loaded on top of the cab in front of the rack. Legs of chairs reached a height of nearly twelve feet above ground level. And there were still some things to be put on: floor rugs, suitcases, last-minute packages, etc. Just at dusk, we decided it were best to pull the load out upon solid ground for over night. But the motor could not move it, and even Hertzler's truck hitched on in front failed to move the mass. The only movement which resulted was a downward movement of the rear wheels. The next task was to raise the rear end enough to enable planks to be inserted beneath the wheels. We worked several hours after supper by the aid of the porch light. Hertzler brought some lifting jacks and all sorts of blocking. Early next morning this parenthesis was finished, the load was rolled out into the street and stopped.

It looked precariously high and was known to be very heavy. I felt then that a trailer would in all probability be a necessity before starting on the trip. Earl Buckwalter was asked to examine the truck and its load and give an opinion on what to do. He advised a trailer. Kindly Burkhart drove around with me in search of a trailer. Got one soon from John Zook nearby, an old rather rickety-looking affair, with one tire that appeared about all worn out. Driver and I spent the rest of the forenoon of Thursday in reloading, placing considerable weight on the trailer, thereby reducing both the height and the weight of the load on the truck.

We had been entertained by Burkharts over the night before and for our meals on Thursday. After lunch Driver helped again. We roped and wired the loads so they would be likely to keep their place while travelling. At the very last I had a half dozen or so of errands to run, to Bylers I returned the baby carriage, to Rissers the borrowed baby crib, to Erbs a book, to the bank, to the garage, etc. It was a warm day and already nearing four o'clock in the afternoon. In spite of the lateness of the hour, we were all eager to be on our way; even Virgil appeared to be ready.

Our chosen route was to start out on motor route U.S. 50S, which we boarded at Newton. I drove rather leisurely for the remainder of that day, at least until I should be acquainted with the truck and the motor and their behaviour. We were soon going eastward and all seemed to go very well. The height and weight of the load made it necessary to go very slowly around sharp curves and turns. On straight road, especially on concrete, the outfit rolled along nicely at twenty-five to thirty miles per hour. At about six o'clock we came to the town of Florence, and because we saw a line of cabins beside a filling station we decided to stop for the night. But the cabins within were not as pleasant as their exterior promised. Everything was dusty. We had things along, enough to eat for our suppers. Estie and Virgil used the bed while I reposed on a folding cot which we were carrying with us. Everyone slept well on this our first night enroute.

With the break of day we were up. Made ready to travel at once. A pleasant morning was with us, although some threatening rain clouds were hanging off to the north and west. In fact there was threat of rain during all this day, but fortunately we kept away from it. Our load was poorly protected against rain; there was a light duck canvas over the top that might keep off a light rain, while the trailer had no protection at all. We prayed that no heavy rain might come upon us, and we can report that none did. At St. Joseph, Missouri on Saturday morning there was a light rain but not to any damage to our goods.

October 7, 1933 The travelogue goes on. On Friday morning of September 1, as the preceding narrative states, we left Florence, and after an hour and a half or so of driving we were at Strong City. We halted here for breakfast, which we got in a cafe. A while later we came to the well-known Elmdale Hill, a very steep and winding grade up which one starts immediately after coming off a bridge and turning almost at right angles. I suppose I was a bit scared and must have fumbled in manipulating my gears. Anyway we stuck dead still on the very first part of this bad grade. To our great good fortune or better said, providentially, as it seemed to us, two farmers with a team and wagon were just then stopping at the foot of the hill. They hitched on in front with a chain, we succeeded in getting the load started again and the motor practically pulled it all the rest of the way up. Estie came along behind carrying the boy and toiling up the steep hill. So we surmounted that obstacle without mishap of any kind.

At Emporia we were advised to go north by way of Topeka, because there had been rains eastward that morning. Driving was pleasant; some hills were on our way, but they were of moderate grade and on straight road. By gaining what extra speed one could in going down grade the ascent up the next grade was made easier because of the momentum of the heavy load.

Just at noon we rolled into Topeka, and when getting near the business section of the city a sharp whistle of air lasting for a few seconds told the news of our first blowout, the rear truck tire on the right-hand

side. Pulling alongside of the curb at once saved the casing in pretty good shape, but the tube was ruined. A tire service man was called
to mend the tire. While this work was being done we ate lunch of
things we had along, excepting that I bought milk for Virgil and had it
prepared for his consumption. So perhaps an hour and a half passed
before we were on our way again.

Instead of going east through Kansas City now, we went east and
north toward Atchison. It looked very rainy to the westward, sky was
all overcast, much of the road was winding and some hilly, so that our
progress was not very fast. Between four and five o'clock found us
about ten miles away from Atchison with the left rear tire down. This
time I knew nothing of it until the wheel was bumping along on the
hard concrete pavement. At the top of the hill I stopped and proceeded
to remove the wheel in order to replace it with the spare wheel and
tire. More time was thus lost.

In Atchison I stopped to have the tire repaired, but this time both
tube and casing were ruined seemingly beyond repair.

There appeared to be no choice aside from buying a new tire and
tube then and there. To roll along indefinitely with no spare tire was
out of all question. So I purchased a new Firestone tire complete and
had it installed on the wheel for the sum of $20.50, which was a se-
vere blow on my supply of cash and on my courage for continuing on
our way. It was nearly dusk when we crossed the Missouri River
bridge into Missouri and still nearly twenty miles from St. Joseph. We
kept on going, however, and after dark began to enter that city. Although stopping repeatedly to make inquiry about tourist cabins, we
found it was impossible to secure any on the south side of the city,
and we should have to go through town to the east side or skirt around
the southeast side and try to find a cabin camp that was well recommended in that part of the city. The latter course we followed and
without a great deal of difficulty found the place. Now St. Joseph is a
city of hills. This cabin camp is on a steep hillside and it looked
about impossible to pull in at the regular entrance, but an alley from
a cross street led part way into the place. The place was long enough
to get the train I had well off the street and sidewalk, but I would
have to back out the next morning.

Here we parked, but with numerous misgivings. The night was dark;
there was lightning and thunder in the distance. The load was poorly
protected against thieves as well as against rain. We took all our suitcases inside, and a few things that might be damaged by rain, only such
as were easily reached. Bought milk and a few items to eat for our
supper at a grocery store, cleaned up as best we could, ate a rather
cheerless supper, and prepared to take our rest, hoping for the best
during the night. The cabin was clean this time and better arranged
than that of the night before. But it must be confessed that I was blue
and much discouraged after this first day of tire trouble and difficulty,
when we were only about 250 miles on our way of 900 miles, and still
had 300 miles to go in order to reach our friends in Iowa, where we
were planning to spend Sunday. But we lifted our hearts to Heaven with
a prayer for divine leading and protection, and also not without thanksgiving for the dangers of that day which we had escaped so well. I was
very tired and my discouragement did not prevent me from falling

asleep promptly and sleeping soundly.

When we awoke the next morning the sky was still very threatening of rain and although no rain had fallen during the night, it began to drizzle slowly before we could start on our way. We started soon after daylight. I backed truck and trailer out without much difficulty and we were on our way. After getting on Route 36 we travelled eastward. This part of our route, from Lawrence to St. Joe and east as far as Cameron, I had not before traversed. At Cameron we paused for breakfast at a restaurant. After our morning repast, as I examined our outfit and equipment for anything that might be ailing, a thing I aimed to do every time we halted, I noted that the piece which we had appropriated as our trailer hitch was nearly loose where it was fastened to the frame of the truck. As a result we waited another hour on a blacksmith who remedied the broken part.

Skies were clearing as we continued our progress, now about due north into Iowa. Driving was pleasant; all the way was smooth concrete now. We stopped to get milk for Virgil's lunch at a small town in Iowa, the name of which I cannot now recall. It was perhaps between two and three o'clock on this Saturday afternoon that our first tire for the day went down. It was the one which had gone down at Topeka about twenty-seven hours before. This time there was no sudden blowout, but luckily I sensed from the behaviour of the truck that something might be wrong again. Stopped at once and found the tire almost flat. Removed this wheel and replaced it with the spare one. This occurred about sixteen miles south of the town of Osceola. At this place we accordingly stopped to have the tire repaired. The casing was found to have a rather bad break which I guessed it perhaps acquired on the previous day rather than this time. The repair man put a patch on the tube and inserted a boot over the break in the casing. But because of the condition of this tire, I decided to continue rolling along on the older "spare" and carry the newly-repaired one for emergency use.

It grew dark again before we came to a place which we found suitable as a halting place for the night. This place was Indianola, not very far south of Des Moines where we would turn eastward. At the southern edge of this town we found a splendid tourist camp with well-kept cabins and very kind and friendly host and hostess. The lady was very helpful in preparing Virgil's supper and also provided warm soup for ourselves. We were all tired and rather travel-worn now. But although it was Saturday night and we were one hundred thirty or more miles away from friends, I at least did not feel nearly so badly discouraged as the evening before. Anyway we had only one flat tire on this day, the weather was clear, and we had a pleasant cabin for our lodging and night's comfort. Everyone slept well.

On Sunday morning we were not in any haste to get up early and we rested as long as we could. We were still debating on whether we should travel on Sunday, or should stay where we were until the Sabbath was past. My supply of cash was now quite limited. It was no attractive proposition to loaf in our improvised quarters all day long. On the other hand since we by this time figured tire trouble as a regular feature of our travelling, and it being Sunday, I imagined that it would not be so easy to secure tire service along the way. Considering all things, however, we swallowed our scruples, and decided to move on leisurely, at least until we could go no further for some good reason. I called my brother, Herman, by telephone, told him of our whereabouts and also of our plans. Then after a good breakfast at a restaurant we were on our way again. On this day Virgil was somewhat indisposed and for a few days after he was not normal. After driving for an hour or more I discovered one of the trailer tires was sinking. I had stopped in front of a wayside filling station to examine it. Found it would not hold air, so we removed the tire, the attendant kindly helping me, patched the tube and put a boot into the casing. I was carrying no spare tire for the trailer wheels. And by the way, it was not the worst-looking tire which was ailing, not the one about which I was all along worrying. This halt of an hour or more occurred about five miles west of Knoxville, I believe. As we drove through Knoxville folks were just coming out of the churches. We felt rather heathenish, rumbling along in our worldly manner. I decided I should never in the future pass judgment on anyone I happen to see doing such a thing on Sunday.

When we reached Oskaloosa, it was somewhat past noon already. We stopped to get milk for Virgil and to eat a bit of lunch ourselves which we had with us.

October 14, 1933 This rambling travelogue still goes on its way. As stated, we were making a brief halt at Oskaloosa and upon passing a curious eye over the tires again, I found that the aged extra tire, upon which we had rolled since the last flat tire plagued us, was becoming soft. As fortune would have it, we were stopping immediately in front of a tire service station, and besides it was open and doing business just then. I called upon one of the men to remove the tire and repair it. This was soon done and we continued moving eastward. Within six or seven miles of Sigourney as we were surmounting a hill, a touring car coming in the opposite direction drew aside and off the pavement. The occupants hailed us earnestly, and to our great relief, they were Father, sister Ida, and brother-in-law Howard. We stopped. Estie and Virgil now changed to the touring car and Howard relieved me at the wheel of the truck. This was nearly four o'clock in the afternoon.

I had imagined all along that to drive at a lower rate of speed would be to spare the tires from an excessive amount of heat and friction. But the way the truck was now made to travel almost made me hold my breath. Actually I expected tires to be blowing out right and left at any moment. But nothing happened, excepting that the distance disappeared faster than before. A speed of about twenty-five miles an hour was my aim on level road, whereas now we travelled from thirty-five to forty miles an hour.

Reached Herman's place before six o'clock. The chance to relax, to clean up, and to rest among friends was indeed welcome. Spent Monday and Tuesday visiting with near relatives and in making preparations to continue on our way. Father bought another new tire for the truck. We contemplated getting another and larger trailer and by partly reloading to relieve the truck of some more weight, but nothing came of this.

Plans were made that Herman accompany me on the truck and that Father bring Wife and Son a few days later in the touring car. We started out between two and three o'clock on Tuesday afternoon, September 5. At Iowa City we paused for a few minutes of business. But the pause proved to be for the greater part of an hour. As I was examining the tires all around, I noted that the trailer tire which had been patched on Sunday forenoon showed a very bad condition at the same spot where a boot had been inserted then. And even as I sat for a few moments watching the spot and trying to contemplate the possibilities it had in store, it blew out almost into my face! As we had now prepared and equipped ourselves fully to do our own tire repairing, we soon had things mended and were off. The remainder of our trip of three hundred fifty or more miles was quite uneventful, for no more tire trouble came to be our lot. It was just at dusk when we crossed the Father of Waters into the State of Illinois, and because the driving was good, we drove across the state line into Indiana just at dawn the next morning. We changed off in driving and so both of us secured a little sleep. After dark we became conscious of the fact that our trailer had no tail light of any kind. We succeeded in improvising one by means of a pocket flashlight with a red rag tied across its head and fastened to the rear corner of the trailer. Before ten o'clock in the forenoon we were in Goshen. By getting busy at once with unloading we succeeded in having everything off the truck by four o'clock. Herman started back almost at once and must have driven all night again, for he was at home before noon of the next day. But he had each of the front tires on the truck to blow out for him, one soon after he left Goshen and the other at Davenport, Iowa. The trailer he loaded on the truck and so could travel more commodiously.

Father brought my family on Thursday. He returned on Saturday, after spending Friday at Nappanee. On his return way, when near Iowa City he had an accident, which was not very serious.

October 15, 1933 Since coming to Goshen, Sunday morning always brings me a queer feeling to which I have not yet grown fully accustomed. It is that feeling of having nothing particular to do, a strange and for me unusual freedom from responsibility. Not for many years now has it been my lot to have no direct Sunday School responsibility of a regular nature. For four years at Hesston continuously, every Sunday morning as regularly as the weeks came and went, I had to work up ideas and inspiration for the teachers' meeting and the S.S. review in general assembly. The latter was occasionally delegated to someone else, but most of the time I regularly handled both. Now to have none of these tasks on hand, does seem a bit odd. The sole responsibility I now enjoy is that of assistant teacher of Gustav Enss' class of young people, not so very young in years in fact, but such folks above college age as still wish to count themselves as young; result: the ages range up to forty and forty-five years, if not more. There are both men and women.

For one thing we have been thankful since coming here; the weather conditions have been very pleasant about all the while, a great deal of sunshine, occasional rains, no really killing frost yet to this date. All this has been in very marked contrast with our previous introduction to Indiana climate when we first moved here in the fall of 1926. Weeks and weeks of continuous gloom, rain, cold prevailed at that time.

Virgil has been doing well since we came here, seemed to be getting heavier and plumper, although we did not weigh him last month. We shall probably not weigh him oftener now than bimonthly, and as yet we have not the facilities to weigh him at all. On his first birthday anniversary he weighed twenty and one-half pounds and measured thirty and one-quarter inches in height. He began to walk two or three steps at a trial about the tenth of August and made rapid progress in learning the art of bipedal locomotion, so that by the time of his first birthday he was able to walk about the house freely. It is only within the past week that he has shown his first constructive instinct. For months past when he and I played together, all he knew how to do was to throw down the blocks I had built up. But now he is beginning to lay blocks on top of each other, and whenever he succeeds in making one rest upon another he expresses his satisfaction and triumph by laughing or smiling. When once he will have acquired some skill in manipulating blocks, he will be able to amuse himself much better than now. At present a plaything gets old for him so quickly that it is impossible to keep him supplied with enough different things to last him through the day. Each day, of course, he several times makes the complete round of all our rooms on his investigation and exploration and experimentation tours. It is his way of learning things just now. Books on the shelves must be wedged tightly enough, else he will remove them all for his examination. Magazines on the shelves of the rack he pulled down regularly for several weeks, but is getting over that now, so that he seldom molests them anymore.

It is interesting to observe his development and to study his behaviour and reaction to our efforts to guide and control him. His mother has a few times tried to penalize him for naughty conduct, specifically for turning up and bending back the corner of a small congoleum rug lying on the kitchen floor. But aside from crying a little from the pain inflicted by spanking his hand, he seems not yet to grasp the idea of punishment. His curiosity and hunger for experience lead him to repeat it at once, accompanying his action with an enquiring look and an inquisitive "Hugh!" Whenever he sees something within his reach which he has learned from past experience he cannot have, he employs the same inquiring gestures before he proceeds to touch it. Or sometimes instead of the inquiry gesture, he will utter a happy surprised chuckle to himself as he contemplates some interesting experience, as for example when he comes around and to his happy surprise finds the lower cupboard doors in the kitchen left unlatched and the way open to get at some interesting things. In general he responds well to efforts at control, and I find it is best not to thwart him in an excited, hasty, and direct manner, but somewhat nonchalantly direct him to something else. He has a great delight in finding shoes or bedroom slippers handy on the floor. He proceeds to handle them and to bite them. The latter act is quite forbidden as he pretty well knows now. When I change shoes he picks up one that is loose and starts to run away with it, but for some time now he makes no remonstrance at all when I take shoes away from him, always telling him interestingly that "the shoes go on the shelf." He gets angry only when one forcibly grasps things from him, and I aim never to get things away from him by that method. I am wondering if it is possible to train a child altogether without corporeal punishment; probably not, but I mean to get along with as little of it as possible.

October 21, 1933 Another week is gone. The successive weeks seem to follow each other quite rapidly, and the time seems to be taken up pretty fully with routine tasks, not leaving very much time for extra undertakings such as reading and research. Last week I got new lenses fitted for my glasses; I can stand it now to read for some length of time better than I could before. So much of the time I felt tired, exhausted, and inclined to inertia, and it was due very much to eye strain. As yet I am not sure that my eyes have fully adjusted themselves to the new lenses. But I surely hope I can read more and with greater comfort than in recent years has been the case.

The evidence is steadily accumulating which indicates that my infected teeth are causing me trouble and damage. Even the optometrist while examining my eyes raised the question of possible focal infection, which might be affecting the working of the muscles of the eye. And too I have been for some time suspecting that some of my chronic tiredness and inertia must be due to some such cause. My present oral equipment is getting so poor that I cannot masticate food with ease and thoroughness. Hence it is that I have made up my mind that next summer's vacation must be reserved as the time for having most or all of my teeth extracted and getting complete "store teeth" in their place.

My classroom teaching requires a good deal of outside time of me for preparation and reading of papers. With thirteen people in beginner's Greek and eleven in beginner's German, some written work is regularly necessary to secure thorough drill. This makes extra work now, which will be less in the next semester. My advanced Latin class is reading material which I have not taught before, and the same is true of the Intermediate German course, hence both of these require some preparation. Just now one outside activity is the business of editing a thesis, previously published in the Mennonite Quarterly Review, for publication as a project of the Peace Problems Committee. The article is by Wilbur J. Bender.

October 29, 1933 Our United States government continues its experimentation in political and economic matters on an unprecedented scale, and with a daring which at some time is pretty sure to be looked back upon either as a course of high courage and wisdom or as one of monumental folly, the latter if the whole program fails, the former if it succeeds. The entire program of the National Recovery Administration seems to me to be contrary to the basic laws of economics and of good sense. There is a far-reaching program being executed now to limit production of such commodities as wheat, corn, hogs, cotton. At the same time there are millions of people who are undernourished and deprived of most of life's comforts. It all seems so illogical. Processing taxes are being gradually imposed upon the manufactured products of the commodities which are being curtailed in production, as cotton cloth, flour, pork, and so on. This tax in some cases will work both ways, to lower the market price of the raw products, so reducing the farmer's income, and secondly to raise the price of the finished product, so working a hardship upon the ultimate consumer, making it possible for him to buy less goods rather than more. The processing taxes will produce the revenue with which the farmers who agree to reduce their production will be paid cash bonuses for their self-imposed idleness and inefficiency. This amounts to a piece of special class legislation, taxing the general public in order to pay a bonus to the farmers. Here is incipient socialism.

Some features of the NRA program, such as reducing the general average of working hours per week and raising wages equivalently, are not bad, but are directly in line with the kind of readjustment which must come if unemployment is to be reduced. It is merely a matter of dividing up more evenly among the people who want to work the limited amount of work which machines and technological progress still leave for the worker to do. But the matter of raising prices generally by arbitrary stimulation — that is something else again! Frankly, I have but little faith in the whole idea of arbitrary control and planned recovery, and my greatest hope and prayer is that all this manipulation will not succeed in making matters still worse. The entire readjustment process requires a long time and entails much suffering. And it is a reasonable question whether then the rate of adjustment for workers and their wages can keep pace with technological progress.

Personally I hold to the notion that if the capitalistic pattern of society's economics is outworn and antiquated, and some new pattern is in order, we should be ready to welcome the same. There is nothing really sacrosanct about any particular status quo, and even the Old Testament, as well as the New Testament economy, puts life and individual happiness above the right of property. The latter must give way to the former if the two become incompatible.

November 18, 1933 Here almost three whole weeks have again passed by since I last wrote in these notes. They have been busy weeks. Just today at last the manuscript for the Peace Committee's booklet is ready to be sent to the press. I found the matter of editing this previously printed monograph no small task. At once when I began working on the matter, I had a distinct feeling that the references in the notes which accompany the article as also the quotations in the text should be rather carefully checked over for accuracy and exactness. I decided to check over those parts for which I had the books and sources at hand. There are about 175 footnotes in all and perhaps four hundred more or less individual reference citations. So I found it a real task. What is more, I had not gone very far with this business until I was convinced that, for the sake of editorial respectability, every single reference should be checked if at all possible. For I found so many errors, slips, oversights, or what you have, due to carelessness on the part of author, typesetters, proofreaders and editors previously. But the obstacles for carrying out this complete program were numerous and great. For one thing, the disorganization of what is supposed to be the Mennonite Historical Library of the college here is so great that I had to invoke H. S. Bender's help repeatedly in finding items which were at hand, and several of these not even he was able to find. The worst of all is that several dozen references are to works which are not in the library here. How to get these checked over is still a problem.

November 19, 1933 Very few times since coming here in September have I been privileged to engage in my favorite Sunday afternoon diversion, to wit, in two or three hours of sound and profound slumber. There is generally a committee's meeting, or some special public meeting which demands my time. Today it is the committee on programs for Sunday evening Young People's meeting. Last Sunday it was a special service as part of the evangelistic campaign. J. D. Mininger of Kansas City held a series of spiritual meetings on ten consecutive evenings at the college. These closed on last Sunday evening, and were very good in their entirety.

The past two weeks have constituted a prelude, and an early one at that, to our coming winter weather. Snow fell repeatedly and temperatures fell in the general direction of zero for brief moments. There was sleet and rain and ice, all thrown in for good measure. Today is mild, clear, and pleasant; snow is about all gone. Perhaps there will be some more pleasant fall weather for a while. Many are hoping that such will be the case, and I should not regret it myself, I daresay. I derive no small comfort and measure of satisfaction from the fact that I need not concern my head about the problem of securing fuel enough to keep our living quarters comfortable. What makes this satisfaction especially keen is the vivid recollection of our last winter's experiences along that line.

Son Virgil had another spell of baby's illness the past week. Today he is eating again nearly as usual, and we discover too that he has two new teeth suddenly showing through. They are numbers seven and eight in his list so far. These newcomers were probably the occasion for his sickness. He has not been weighed or measured since he was twelve months old. In a few weeks he will be fifteen months, then we must find a way to weigh him and take his measurements again. He still refuses to talk.

Classroom work has settled down to a definite routine for myself now and I contemplate some spare time for reading and self-advancement. On the three mornings that I go to Elkhart to teach, I have two hours of time on hand while Samuel Yoder teaches his classes. I have now started a schedule by which I can use these periods with some profit at least. The first hour each day, the one preceding my class, I use in my preparation for the class to follow. The period following my class, I use as follows: On Monday and Friday, I go in swimming in the YMCA pool and on Wednesday I read magazines or go shopping. The reading is at the Elkhart Public Library.

November 25, 1933 Since coming here I discover that the question of millennialism is quite a live one among interested Bible students and teachers. Professor Enss is very vehement in his belief and his teaching of premillennial matter, and while he tries to be tolerant and considerate of the contrary view, he succeeds but poorly in showing full respect for those who hold conflicting views. It is a matter of common observation that confirmed premillennialists as a rule tend to be much more dogmatic, intolerant and critical of their opponents than are these opponents themselves. It has made me wonder and speculate as to the reasons for such a difference in attitude. On the faculty the older men and the officials are generally nonmillennial in viewpoint.

Occasionally a serious-minded student holds to the latter viewpoint.
One young man comes from a Mennonite Conference district where
premillennialism is officially taboo. He is a good friend of mine and
has loaned me several books which exploit his viewpoint on the question.
Some interesting things are brought out in the books written on the
subject. I read just now, what appears a simple and logical idea, that
Paul in predicting the apostasy of believers referred to the union of
Church and State under Constantine and all the consequences that followed thereon. The author sees in Catholicism a predominant element
of ancient Judaism and paganism. The same author sees in second
Thessalonians, second chapter, much the same idea, Jewish legalism,
dogmatism and arrogance, later to be embodied in Roman Catholic religion. Interesting to note is that Catholics make Peter the head of the
church instead of Paul, reflecting Jewish influence.

November 30, 1933 Thanksgiving Day. This is a rarely beautiful and
pleasant day, greatly appreciated because of the many clouds which
lately covered Indiana skies. The air is just pleasantly cool, scarcely
any wind is stirring, all is still, nature being hushed in a sort of holiday stillness and solemnity. Voices of children playing out-of-doors
ring bright and cheerful through the air.
The controversy over millennialism, which I lately noted, has some
little interest to me personally, although I have made no particular
study of the subject and so far have had no pronounced opinions about
it. In an uncritical fashion I absorbed the viewpoint which was generally presented at Hesston while I was a student there. J. B. Smith professed then to be expert on this theme, and J. D. Charles taught it consistently, but without making a hobby out of it. No other idea or viewpoint on the subject was even seriously suggested to us as uncritical
undergraduates. Hence I adopted most of the basic philosophy which
goes with this doctrine. But I must confess that I never developed very
much conviction or enthusiasm over the idea of outlining detailed events
for the future of history. The features of the philosophical background
which I adopted, and still hold for the most part, are such as the deprav-
ity and relative impotence of man to solve the problems arising from
sin and therefore the predestined failure of human efforts as such. The
catastrophic interpretation of history, as opposed to the gradual evolu-
tionistic interpretation of the same; or perhaps it were better to say,
I believe in a kind of degeneration in human history, due to sin, which
only the grace of God can counteract.
The terms civilization, culture, progress, and their like are all
vague and quite relative terms. But it seems to me that evidence is
constantly accumulating which goes to demonstrate that in some particular respects and in certain periods there has been definite and
fundamental degeneration and retrogression. Especially am I convinced
that in the line of artistic achievement, some phases of engineering
skill, and some fields of knowledge there has been loss, that is, not
all that was known and practiced then has been handed down to our
modern time. Archaeological evidence supports this viewpoint; linguistic and literature evidence does the same. Only last week a scientific
lecturer, Dr. Gable, spoke here at the college on the subject of "Cosmic Rays;" and in the course of his discussion he gave some lines of

evidence to show that the ancients possessed some knowledge which is only being rediscovered today by scientists. Incidentally he also gave proof that it was scientifically possible for man to live to great ages before the flood, in the time when there were no clouds, storms, dust, moisture, etc. in the terrestrial atmosphere. For then the ultraviolet light rays in a greater percentage could reach the surface of the earth than now. An interesting commentary on the early chapters of Genesis, this!

Coming back to the notion that the ancients possessed some important knowledge and information which has not survived unto our time, I was made to think of some things which Dr. Harry Rimmer said here at the college several months ago. He was particularly discussing Science and the Bible in a more or less popularized fashion, especially for the benefit of undergraduates. As his most pointed proofs that the Bible is a supernaturally inspired book, he enumerated a considerable list of things, statements found in such writers as Job, Isaiah, Jeremiah, Moses, Paul, which disclose knowledge that science has only recently discovered and demonstrated to be true. The contention was that the only possible source for this information was direct divine revelation and that even the writers themselves did not comprehend the knowledge which they were recording. For my part, I would not deny this contention in toto. In particular cases it was doubtless true. But a parallel theory, which I thought of at the time, and which has been confirmed to my mind since, is this: That some of this information was common knowledge among the ancients, at least among thinkers. If one argues that they could not have known such facts as the existence of atoms, the differentiation in the bloods of animals of different species, etc. because they had not the instruments and equipment needed for their discovery, one can answer that this is partly to beg the question. To limit the possible sources of information to those which modern man has invented and created is again an assumption which perhaps credits us moderns with more than we deserve. Somehow or other the macrocephalism of modern homo sapiens will continually crop out and posit assumptions and presumptions which are not proven, and perhaps cannot be proven.

As to my philosophy of history, it is as yet very vague and shadowy. Only a few dim strokes of the broadest outlines are visible. What I think is that history has been a complex system of ups and downs, ins and outs, depressions and upward movements, advances and retrogressions. And I have not decided in what direction the general and major tendency is. The verdict of reason as well as of the Bible is that righteousness, truth, and God must and surely will triumph over their opposites in the final end. And as a key to the vicissitudes observed in the visible part of the stream of history, I have a decided "hunch" that the Biblical doctrine of Sin, with all its consequences, is the correct one.

December 2, 1933 This is the Homecoming Season at Goshen College and since Thursday many visitors have been present on the campus, special activities are in progress, and a general holiday atmosphere pervades the place. Classes are not meeting this morning as usual, although they met about as usual yesterday. Personally I had not realized what a big event and important affair this Homecoming is. It is an event that has grown up since I was here before. For the promotion of school spirit and loyalty, cementing emotional ties with the college, it seems to be eminently successful, perhaps quite as much so as if its main show were a football game. On Thanksgiving Day a public religious service was held in the morning. A big "feed" with program attached took up the time from 12:30 till 4:00. Since the charge for a plate was fifty cents, I was not present for the occasion. Yesterday afternoon a basketball game largely attended was staged in the gymnasium. I missed this too, even though so far as I am aware, no charge was made for admittance. Last evening the second number of the year's Lecture Course was given in the chapel. Both Mrs. Yoder and I heard this. Mrs. Paul Bender generously loaned to us her admission ticket, since she could not be out. I invested in only one season ticket for ourselves. A company of eight Negro singers, called the Eureka Jubilee Singers, gave a very good program, singing and interpreting typical Negro songs and their music. Still other features of Homecoming today are a tea this afternoon and a social this evening.

Have just gotten my hands on a new book which came to the College Library a few days ago, entitled "Preachers Present Arms," by Abrams, a professor in the University of Pennsylvania. It gives an account of the utterances and the activities of the preachers and the churches in the United States during the time of the War, 1914-1918. The book has received high praise from reviewers and I have started reading it through, as I believe it will be a suitable book to review in the January installment of the Peace Department of the Gospel Herald. It is the sort of information in systematic form which I have long been wishing for. There are other books appearing continually which I wish very much to see and read. But the dearth of funds with myself is so great that I feel it is impossible to pay out any cash for books this winter. At the same time, the College Library is also greatly handicapped by lack of funds, so that not even it seems able to procure new books whereby we impecunious teachers can keep ourselves informed as to what the world is thinking on the basic questions and problems of life. A book by Reinhold Niebuhr, which has been widely reviewed and recommended, entitled:"Moral Man and Immoral Society," is another one I am craving very much to see and read.

December 3, 1933   Not infrequently my mind reverts to the experiences through which we were passing one year ago this fall, when we had no income to speak of and our expenditures were just about nothing. We could not buy things to eat and lived on what we had stored up from the summer and on what was brought to us by friends and supporters of Hesston College. This winter we buy a good many more things for the table, as peanut butter, honey, oranges, etc. At the present time we are getting fifty dollars a month in cash. The only expense about our apartment which we are paying is the gas we use for cooking and washing, which amounts to less than a dollar and a half each month. We have our electric refrigerator running regularly, also do baking on the electric range, the cost of which goes as part of the apartment rental.

Milk prices have been cavorting up and down. When we came here in September, certified raw milk was being delivered for twelve cents a quart, the price having been advanced to that level only shortly before, ostensibly as a part of the NRA program. We felt that this was too high. A few folks were getting milk at a nearby farm for seven cents a quart, not delivered. I was trying to make arrangements for getting ours there too. Then one of the inhabitants of our apartment hall was able to arrange with our dairy to have pasteurized milk delivered at wholesale price to the apartmenters as a group for eight cents a quart, ten cents for raw milk. Thereupon we changed to pasteurized milk, taking three quarts a day instead of only two. That was in October. In November, early in the month, a milk price war was threatening in the city with the net result that prices were put down to the level of the good old days before the NRA blessed the land to the damage and hurt of the consumer. We now get raw milk delivered at seven cents a quart, which represents a block rate price to the apartment house as a whole. We hope it will stay at this price indefinitely.

December 14, 1933 I may as well add one further note here about the price of milk, giving the latest information which has come to my attention. The report is that our raw milk delivered is costing now just five cents a quart, which is I think the lowest price we have ever been allowed to pay for this form of food.

A genuine snap of cold weather was upon us the past week; now suddenly it is warm and spring-like. The sudden changes are worse to bear than the cold weather itself.

Before another week rolls past, the Christmas vacation will be under way. Am not decided just what I shall try to get done during that time. I might try doing a little more on my studies in Quintilian which for more than a year I have worked at occasionally. But if weather is cold it will be impossible to work in my office here in Science Hall, because it will almost certainly not be heated, and to do writing or desk work, or even sustained reading at home is equally out of the question. For Virgil gives me scarcely any rest or leisure when I am at home. I shall therefore adapt my vacation activities to the times and the conditions which happen to exist then.

On last Sunday President S. C. Yoder and wife invited us to their home for Sunday dinner. There we met and became acquainted with Jacob Peltz, a Jewish Christian who is a preacher and missionary among Jews in Chicago. Mr. Peltz spoke at the College Assembly Hall both in the morning and the afternoon. He is the same man who preached here last March. A pleasant man is he and appears to be a splendid Christian, whose Jewish background serves him very well in the interpretation and presentation of Christianity.

The revival of vital personal religion, which some looked for and predicted would be an outcome of the economic depression, is not much in evidence, if at all. In fact, institutionalized Christianity seems to be desperately hard hit; church programs and missionary projects are everywhere being curtailed. But the attention and minds of people are everywhere too intently fixed upon human and governmental efforts to bring about recovery, to give men and women any time to think upon true personal religion and individual righteousness. No special signs of repentance are in evidence among the general population. Yet one hopes that true religious values are imperceptibly coming to be more appreciated by countless individuals.

December 22, 1933 My fountain pen of 1925 vintage, a lifetime Parker, is on a strike. The ink descends much too fast causing large ugly blots. So I come back to old reliable steel pen in a long penholder as my means for writing, at least until I can have the Parker reconditioned. Once before this same pen refused to function; however that time I could not fill the barrel with ink at all and had to dip the point in the ink bottle when I desired to do writing with it. Repairs were free on that occasion. Hope they will be again.

Vacation is now in progress; I am going in heavily for reading so far. Have several volumes under way at present. One is a history of "Mennonite Immigration to Pennsylvania in the Eighteenth Century" published by C. Henry Smith about four years ago. It is detailed and is interesting to me. Another book is a seven hundred page affair by Devere Allen entitled "The Fight for Peace." In spite of the length I am greatly interested in this, partly because of its humane and attractive style and partly because it gives a readable account of the organized peace movements of this country since their beginning one hundred fifteen years ago. Some very revealing pieces of information and also some significant comparisons are contained in this volume. On the whole, the impression I get so far is expressed in some connection by this author when he speaks of the enormous mountain of peace activity that brought forth such an insignificant mouse. The prominent peace organizations have usually pigeonholed their principles when the government prosecuted any major war — so during the Civil War and the World War. Opposition to the Spanish War was quite consistent. In the Mexican War they trailed safely along behind a large segment of public opinion that condemned the war. Yet in spite of constant temporizing and opportunist tactics, the author credits the societies and the unions with some accomplishments. I am eager to read widely into the literature on peace and pacifism. It is very illuminating and gives a much needed perspective for my own amateur peace thinking.

Our son Virgil is well and very active. He is all eagerness to investigate and experiment. He quickly learns caution about objects that cause him pain, as the steam pipes and the radiators in our rooms. He is very fond of books. For some time it was quite impossible for me to read in his presence excepting in a standing posture with the book held well out of his reach. But one or two firm refusals to allow him to molest my book while reading has brought him to terms and his only gesture now is one of cooperation when he comes around, runs his finger over the surface of the page and utters a succession of grunts and sounds as though he were reading aloud. But we have not yet come to terms as regards the possession of the Atlantic Monthly. This magazine has a bright orange-colored exterior, just the shade that seems to take his eye irresistibly and he insists on having it in his complete possession at once. I have thought of writing to the editors and apprising them of the sixteen-month-old boy's enthusiasm for the "Atlantic" thinking they might feel complimented thereby. If his taste at this age already runs toward journals of this type and calibre, then his future interests and ideals will probably be all that his fond parents can wish for him.

December 27, 1933 Snow and cold weather are with us now. But we can keep comfortable in our quarters. There are only two families staying in the apartments during this vacation season, Millers at the east end and ourselves at the west end.

Have just looked at the opening pages of a book by William Ramsay which I have not read before. It is a collection of essays entitled "Pauline and Other Studies." Somehow very few writers on New Testament studies impress me so favorably as does Ramsay. His philosophy and view of history are especially good. Just in the few new paragraphs which I have read he touches upon it. For example, he regards heathen religions as degenerations from an originally purer and loftier religion and some knowledge of the true God. It is a fascinating idea and seems to have been held by the apostle Paul. This view is so much more reasonable and satisfying than certain other views one sees advocated at times. I am thinking particularly now of the dogmatic and rather narrow pronouncement made by the Sunday School Times. Their idea is that all heathen religions, root, stalk and branch, are diabolical and demoniacal in origin and nature. Even the suggestion that Christian missionaries might find good things in heathen religions which they could build upon in presenting the Christian faith the Times denounces as heresy.

January 12, 1934 Here I have long delayed to start my note writing for this new year of grace. Principally I did so because my fountain pen has been out of commission. Had it sent to the makers for repairs. It now writes seemingly better than ever before. As a result of having no pen for about two weeks, I have considerable writing of sundry kinds to do now.

The old year expired at the appointed time and the new one came on the scene immediately after. I was up and on the watch for its first appearance. Since the eve of New Year came on Sunday night, the committee on Y.P.M. topics worked out a plan for combining the regular evening service with a watch night service. It was a good service, in charge of M. C. Lehman. During the vacation of upwards of two weeks I managed to get considerable reading and some writing done. Sent copy to the Gospel Herald for the special Peace Department. Wrote a leading article for the College Record which will appear in the current issue. Did some few small jobs about the apartment where we live, made a medicine cabinet for the bathroom wall, put up more shelves in a closet, covered the shelf under the gas plate with sheet iron, etc., etc. Also met with James Brenneman for German recitation about every day. He entered college nearly two months late last fall and so was busy making up German lessons which he had missed. He completed this back work only a few days ago. Another new task which I entered upon during vacation was my active duties as treasurer of the Mennonite Historical Society of this place and also Circulation Manager for the Mennonite Quarterly Review. This last position, in fact both of these, as I now recall, I held when I was here before. At that time the M. Q. R. was just starting to build up its list of subscribers. Today it is rather a strenuous sideline job, as there are orders for back numbers and for complete sets, etc. Unfortunately the reserve stock of about two of the earliest numbers is exhausted entirely and it will be a part of my early efforts to try and find some of these copies and repurchase them for our demand.

January has been pleasant so far, some very mild days, but entirely too many cloudy days for my taste and satisfaction. Should I ever get the financial means for doing so, I certainly think I should act upon an idea which has at sundry times been present in my mind. That is to adopt a policy, as long as we live in Indiana, of spending two or three months of each summer's vacation in the West or Southwest, Colorado, New Mexico, or Arizona. The chief purpose would be to get extra sunshine and ultraviolet rays, sufficient to make up for the deficiency of these items in this climate. A summer cottage well up in the Rocky Mountains would suit us admirably, some place a bit removed and secluded from the haunts of men, suitable for even practicing nudism in a private way in accordance with whatever tastes or desires we might have in that direction. For our boy's health and education such a program would to my mind be very good.

January 13, 1934 Oh yes, and Nudism. No little stir has been on occasionally during this last fall and summer about this new, or revived, cult of human nakedness. It seems that, beginning in Germany and France some years ago, this cult has in recent years become popular in some parts of our United States. Its purpose is for health culture principally, exposing the epidermis to its last fraction of a square inch to the direct rays of the sunlight and to the gentle kisses of the breezes. It is of course most practiced by city dwellers who are cooped up during most of their life in large cities and appreciate the opportunity to get out-of-doors and absorb sunlight and pure air. The practitioners of this art of nakedness have their isolated and usually semi-private colonies where the devotees can go for a weekend or for a longer vacation. Many of these places are regulated in some sense so that only bona fide nudists and health seekers are admitted to the grounds. Once in a while the subject breaks into the headlines of newspapers and gets itself talked about. Even our own unworldly monthly magazine, the Christian Monitor, had in its columns which take note of contemporary world events, a notice of this movement. It seems quite too bad that the matter should be given as much publicity as that among folks who generally know little of such things. One secretly wonders how long it will be until grave and serious-minded committees will be writing resolutions against nudism for church conference bodies to vote upon. The writer in the Monitor undertook to set forth what he thought the Bible had to say against human nakedness. And as he was a minister of more than average intelligence and experience, it was interesting to me to note how very hard he was put to it to find quotable Scripture texts on the subject. One verse from the third chapter of Revelation clearly, according to the context, has only reference to spiritual nakedness, and to quote it against nudism is to apply real violence to the Scripture in question. The chief other verses were taken from the ceremonial book of Leviticus, passages in which the phrase, "uncover the nakedness of" someone is used. According to the best of my limited knowledge, this phrase is in every case an Old Testament euphemism for the act of sex intercourse, and can only by a deal of stretching and imagination be applied to the mere experience of looking upon the unclothed body of another person, whether man or woman. It is just such methods and practices in the use of Scriptures that make one lose confidence in the literalist interpretation of Scripture. Many thoughtful persons of intelligence thus lose respect both for the methods and for those who employ them. To my own mind about the only possible Scripture passage that can honorably be invoked on the subject of clothes or no clothes is the Genesis account of man's fall and its immediate consequences. Even that story as told there may have in it poetical elements which would require interpretation before deciding its application to modern nudism.

Perhaps the chief considerations involved in the semi-private practice of nudism are aesthetics and canons of good taste. There is not so very much danger that the practice will very soon become general, for the very good reason that the undraped bodies of a vast majority of men and women are ugly and unsightly and their exposure to public view is offensive to those who have a taste for beauty in form and proportion. Clothing adds to the beauty and sightliness of most folks, at least as modern habits of diet, living, and posture have made the modern civilized physique. It will be a long time before people could venture to expose at random their scrawny, crooked legs and their unsightly pot bellies to the public view. Naked bathing in promiscuous fashion at public or semi-public resorts I expect will soon become common enough, but will hardly become the general rule.

The charge now made that the practice of nudism leads to immorality is probably a mere diatribe. There is no objective proof that it does, and in theory it is just as possible that it will prevent immorality. The treatment of the naked body as a thing commonplace and morally indifferent will have the general effect of diminishing the amount of prurient and filthy imagination in people's minds, especially men's minds. It is the suggestive decoration of the female body that exercises the imaginations of men, and not its frank and pure exposure. The romance and the seductive charm of a female is all gone when she is undraped. While the frank exposure of the unclothed body is somewhat of a shock at first sight, at the same time it seems that those men who are most volubly affected are those whose minds are most filled with nasty and filthy thoughts and imaginations. Is it perhaps true that the sight of women's bodies wholly or largely uncovered robs such men of opportunities for exercising a depraved imagination, and they are unconsciously protesting against the possibility of the atrophy which may come upon their imaginative powers, from the exercise of which they have long derived such wicked satisfaction?

Personally I do not find the idea of the human figure unclothed either shocking or essentially immoral. The human figure when healthful, strong, athletic, well postured is a thing of beauty and grace. It is not sinful to look upon, but is to me a source of aesthetic satisfaction and of inspiration. The idealized representation of the undraped human figure in sculptural art is something I appreciate greatly, especially the ancient classical Greek sculpture. Perhaps I am prejudiced. I have always had just a mild liking for nakedness myself. As a boy at home I occasionally indulged in the luxury of it. In summertime I might go out into a field of tall corn, remove my clothes and run about nude for a time. Or perhaps on Sunday afternoons in my own room I would lounge and read in the natural state. We had no real bathing facilities in our farm home and I was hard put to it to get a bath. Often in summer and fall I made it a practice to stay up reading on Saturday evening until the rest of the family were all in bed and asleep. Then take a pail of water, soap, towel, and a stiff horse brush, go out in the back yard and scrub myself. Not seldom, since I attended Sunday services at a different place of worship than the others and did not leave as early as they, I would on Sunday morning before going to church take my bath in the great out-of-doors behind the house somewhere. Several years ago I undertook to sleep at night regularly in "the raw". And I can truthfully record that like a true Spartan I did so for more than an entire year, even though our bedroom was unheated in winter. When the second winter started I succumbed and have again worn night shirt since. My wife was always more or less mortified or abashed or amused, or whatever, by my practice. Before we had a modern bathroom in our house at Hesston, I commonly did my bathing in our back yard after dark, even on bright moonlight nights. Like something of a Spartan I did this as late as November sometimes and early as March, I think.

January 17, 1934 Reading today in a magazine at the Elkhart Public Library, I found an article entitled about as follows: "Sigrid Undset and the Critics." The substance of this article is a summary of the difficulties which modern literary critics have in understanding and explaining Fra Undset's books which have been published during the past half dozen years or more. She is a powerful novelist, an experienced archaeologist, and a Norwegian writer of recognized fame and honor. She won the Nobel prize in literature some years ago; I am of the impression it was for the trilogy entitled "Kristin Lavransdatter."
    Now it seems that what the critics cannot get over is that this writer is a Christian who seriously believes that human beings are free and responsible moral agents. They choose for themselves their lines of conduct and reap the penalty in due time for their sins, as also the reward for their goodness. She works out this thesis in her characters, not as a quaint archaeological relic, but as a serious and realistic philosophy of life. She does so not as a case study, but with a moral and didactic earnestness which is so terribly disconcerting to the inflated modern critics of literature. Her first novels were historical and archaeological, and the critics interpreted their underlying philosophy as a clever and successful objective presentation of the thought and ideals of mediaeval Norway. I understand that she has since written a novel, strictly modern in setting, partly in order to make perfectly clear to the critics that she can write a modern novel. But the critics are more perplexed than ever; this novel, they say, is not modern at all. The thought, the ideology, the basic philosophy is to them still completely mediaeval. At the same time they cannot gainsay her power, ability and success as a novelist. What baffles and chagrins them apparently is the idea that any first-rate writer can today believe in such things as sin, free will, God, and the like. Their absolute canons of modernity, that is, of intelligence and rationality, are in some danger of being displaced; the modern gods are in danger of being cast down in favor of older ideas. They are truly in a predicament.

During the year 1929, I permitted myself to be numbered among the members of the Book-of-the-Month Club. The very first book which I received from this Club was Sigrid Undset's "Kristin Lavransdatter," properly a trilogy of three novels, each with a plot of its own, yet having one basic plot underlying the entire work. It was printed in one volume and was sold for about three dollars, as I recall. The title is the name of the heroine. The plot includes all of the heroine's life from birth to death. It was purely an accident that I got this volume then, as I knew nothing of this writer or her books before. I did not read it through at once, but did so within a year or so. I really liked it very much. The style is vigorous and carries one along without much effort. It has a distinctly archaeological flavor, both in style and in the matter. This feature appealed to me particularly, as I remember. The descriptive scenes of nature and landscape are very well done and the characters are sharply and distinctly drawn.

My wife read the book through before I did. She had no serious objection to it as a book for adults to read, yet her verdict was that it was not really fit to have in public view in our home or library. She numbers of times since has remarked about it and suggested that we should dispose of it or at least hide it away out of sight. But so far it has rested on my book shelves along with the rest of my books, although I have tried not to display it unnecessarily. The sole reason my wife objects to the book, I believe, is because there are perhaps three or four brief scenes where sex love, sometimes illegitimate and sometimes legitimate, is rather realistically described, not morbidly or even suggestively, but in a plain matter-of-fact way which is not offensive to my way of thinking. I would not give it to a young child to read, but properly taught young people of college age could well read the book. I felt at the time I read it, and said so in defense of the book as a whole, that its morals and its philosophy are sound. People's sins and misdeeds must be paid for in the end. Sin is not glorified or even in any way condoned or made attractive. My reading of the article giving the modern critics' reaction to the book, comes as a delightful confirmation of my own original impression. It was reported to me that when an English professor received this same book from the Club, his wife examined it, reading a ways to determine if they should keep it, and at once ordered her husband to send it back.

January 19, 1934 Last evening the college lecture course gave a very special number in the form of a lecture by Lorado Taft of Chicago. The lecture was illustrated by lantern slides, on the wistful subject: "My Dream Museum." Mr. Taft is perhaps the foremost sculptor of America today, an elderly man, and not at all a bad speaker. The matter of his lecture was a very brief and hurried survey of sculptural history, touching only the highest points, from earliest Greece and Egypt down to the Renaissance in Europe. The lecture served for myself as a skeletonic and telescopic review of a semester course in the History of Sculpture which I had at University of Iowa under Prof. C. H. Weller just about nine years ago. Weller was a keen enthusiast for all things Greek, and I managed to catch just a little of his enthusiasm for classical Greek art. The first semester's course was on History of Architecture, and the second semester on sculpture. Professor Weller had a nervous breakdown about a month before the year closed and Miss Lawler carried the class through to the end. I am not sure he was ever active after that, as he died about two years later, as nearly as I can now call to mind. I enjoyed very much these brief courses in the history of art.

January 21, 1934 Sunshine and mild temperature.
On last Sunday evening, G. H. Enss preached the sermon following the Young People's Meeting, and it was such that no small stir resulted then and since. The theme of his discourse was that of the Second Coming of Christ. It was not the theme that was so singular, but the manner and the spirit in which it was delivered. It appears that he was using the occasion to thoroughly lecture certain individuals, maybe particularly one person with whom he differs very heatedly over the interpretation of prophecy in the Scriptures. There was a good deal of heat in the discourse, some far-off rumblings of thunder and lightning. The method was mostly combative, with a very sinister emphasis upon certain words and phrases which had been previously bandied about in an indirect controversy. In view of the insecure tenure of position which he enjoys here at present, it was an unfortunate explosion. His position in the college is strange and anomalous. The Bible school of the college is to be expanded and strengthened and there is a place for a teacher of his ability and orthodoxy. But it has become very clear that he cannot continue to hold a place in the Bible department here and not be a fully recognized member of our own denomination and its conference. Very early during this school year this issue seemed to be in the way of being settled, for he voluntarily decided to unite with the church here if he were to be invited by the Executive Committee of the Board of Education, by the local conference and the congregation. By way of preparation he voluntarily appeared, on Sundays at least, in his regulation clerical coat. The Executive Committee of the Board invited and urged him to come into our church. As the final formality, the Executive Committee of the Indiana-Michigan Conference examined him personally. Their recommendation was that he be invited into the church as a member, but that his office as minister should be dormant until such a time as the conference sees fit to take up that matter with him. Result is that he will not come in under such terms. Aside from this particular phase of the situation, there is strongly divided opinion among the members of the faculty on the question as to whether he should stay here at all as a permanent part of the College and Bible School program.

January 28, 1934 After a week of springlike weather and a night of rainfall, there is today cold, snow, and strong wind, so that to look out into it one has a blizzardly feeling, which is not a bad feeling when you need not be out in it. Estie has gone to Vesper services where M. C. Lehman is the speaker today. Virgil and I are staying in together.
Past week was time for semester examinations so that for me six courses meant six examinations to give, although the total number of papers to read was not so great, counting up to about thirty-four. Have not read all of them yet. One young lady in second year New Testa-

ment Greek has not even appeared yet for the examination. She happens to be a law unto herself so far as class attendance and regularity is concerned. Tomorrow there will be no classes, but the new semester begins on Tuesday.

My fourth installment of peace literature in the Doctrinal Supplement of Gospel Herald appeared last week. A leading feature was a review of Abrams' book recently published and entitled "Preachers Present Arms." This week the Christian Monitor for February appeared; it contains a lengthy review and discussion by John Horsch of Scottdale on the same book. Neither of us, at least I can speak for myself, was aware that the other was writing. At any rate it is a slight satisfaction to know that my own writing was circulated first, whether it was written first or not. This double treatment so near together in the periodicals which many of the same people will read should give this particular book rather special and unique publicity among our Mennonites. The January issue of our local College Record came out this week with its leading article entitled "Nonconformity." I am guilty of being its writer. The title is striking enough to attract attention among our circle of Mennonites. It is an effort at a slightly, or possible completely new approach to a threadbare and well-worn theme. Several individuals have volunteered the comment to me that the article is a good one. I hope they are competent to judge.

The Sunday School lesson this morning was on the fifth chapter of Matthew's Gospel, the opening chapter of the so-called Sermon on the Mount. As a matter of curiosity and in quest of possible new information on this familiar section of Scripture, I looked in Moulton's Modern Reader's Bible. I was not disappointed in my search. Among the interesting, and to me new, things I found was the idea that the Gospel of St. Matthew is a philosophical record of the life and ministry of Jesus, conceived and presented as the logical unfolding of the spiritual kingdom idea. This author calls attention to the literary form of the book especially. He notes how the number seven is worked into the arrangement and organization of the material. This feature of the arrangement is not necessarily artificial, nor is it of any mystical significance. It is borrowed from a commonplace convention of Hebrew literary form, originally signifying perfect order in literary and philosophical expression. So for example the Sermon on the Mount consists of seven divisions which are presented in the form of the Literary Maxim. This form consists regularly of an opening text or proverb-like saying and followed by comment and elaboration in prose. In this instance the seventh division, in common with similar units in the old Hebrew Wisdom Literature, consists of seven miscellaneous subjects. Furthermore the first division has after its opening text, verse three, a sevenfold elaboration or illustration of the same, all repeating the opening word.

Occasionally someone makes a great point out of the numerology of Scripture. Some features of the literary forms are patently arranged with number schemes. However to count words and letters and to compute the numerical values of the latter in the Greek text, and to assert that they too carry out certain number schemes, seems a little fanciful. Great claims along this line are made for the several opening chapters of Matthew. As a matter of curiosity, I should like to have time some day to do a little counting myself to see if there is anything to it. Especially should I like to see what such numerical "scholars" do with variations of the text as we have it today.

February 1, 1934 Second semester program is getting under way. I have myself no new courses or classes. Two classes are starting in to read new Latin authors, one in Livy and one in Tacitus. The personnel of my classes changes little, two additional students for the elementary German class at Elkhart, two new exchanged for two old in the evening class in Intermediate German, one less in the advanced Latin reading. Two folks in the beginning Greek class are on probation and will need to master the work more thoroughly before the end of the year if they are to deserve credit for the course. Such cases are the perplexing problems in teaching otherwise interesting classes.

Just one year ago I was busy recovering from an attack of influenza so as to be able to start on the trip to Indiana. A year seems to pass by quickly. While this twelve months period has not put me ahead much in any way, it has brought many pleasant and profitable experiences, has given us much hope and some joy and in general finds us happier and more contented than before. Nothing has come to my ears as to what cash will be distributed to faculty members now that the first semester has ended. Intimation was given earlier that there would be something.

February 3, 1934 This is an interesting age, as I occasionally reflect, in which to live, partly because it is an age in which things happen, when changes occur rapidly, and when world events are just one thing after another, as they say. There is overproduction, but people are hungry and live almost like barbarians in holes and caves of the earth. There is overproduction, too much goods and too many commodities, yet frantic efforts are made to get people back to work, to reduce unemployment, all of which will surely increase production instead of reducing it. Unless all the unemployed can be put to work on public works projects which will not increase the supply of marketable commodities, there will be more unemployment rather than less. Meanwhile scientists, inventors, technicians and others are bending every nerve and muscle to the project of throwing millions more men out of employment, creating factories that are self-operative and increasing the efficiency of all industry and machinery. While farmers and planters are plowing in and destroying a percentage of their crops, agricultural scientists and their co-laborers are laboring to their utmost to prevent land erosion, to find practical means for combating insect pests which destroy crops and limit production. While the Federal Government is paying cash bonuses to farmers for raising less corn, hogs, wheat, and cotton, for leaving their land lie idle in part, the farmers in some cases use their bonus income to make their remaining ground more productive and cultivate it more efficiently. Furthermore while there is such a great surplus of all kinds of consumable goods and men are not allowed to work with full initiative and enterprise lest the avalanche of goods becomes still greater and overwhelms us all in the end, at this same time a noisy crowd of agitators for birth control are clamoring in the halls of Congress that the population growth

197

must be limited and controlled as a part of the social and economic planning that is being talked about. And so it goes and goes and goes. I get weary of trying to follow even longo intervallo the trend of the discussions carried on. While the age is interesting and exciting, it is not conducive to spirituality. The speed and the excitement, the great hue and cry all about, make us all worldlings. The great fetish of the day seems to be activity, problem-solving, and such worldly enterprises. The reflective attitude, contemplation and laissez-faire are all taboo. But are they really — one wonders!

February 9, 1934 In the College Reading Room. I am writing here for the sufficiently good reason that it is not comfortably warm in very many other places about the buildings today. The coldest weather of the winter is upon us. Below zero temperatures yesterday and today, even ten or more degrees below this morning, according to reports.

These are days of special activity on the college campus; special lectures for ministers and preachers are given mornings and afternoons, and beginning tonight there will be six sessions of a Christian Life Conference. Of these activities I am largely a spectator, although not an uninterested one. I recall that several months ago I sat through several sessions of a committee's meetings when the programs for these several meetings were discussed and laid out. It is a pleasant feeling of relief that I have, that of being free from all special responsibility. Such programs mean a good deal to the prestige and the popularity of the college. They also have a good and salutary influence upon the young people of the church who are on the campus. It gives them a little vision of the work and the worth of the church. There are many visitors about, most of whom I do not myself know.

February 11, 1934 Virgil is fast asleep in his own little bed. Estie has gone to the afternoon meeting at the college. The boy is suffering from another of his occasional periods of illness, caused directly or indirectly by his teeth and gums. It is about six weeks since he last had such a siege, and we had about come to hope that he would not need to have any more.

The little article on Nonconformity which I published in the January College Record has brought to me more personal commendation than anything I have published for a long time. And the extremely interesting phase of this little episode is the diversity of type of folks who have spoken or written to me about this. Several faculty members, a student of conservative tastes and general good sense, and this past week brought to me a letter from a gentleman who was sent away from college here because he seemed to be of incompatible personality and disposition. He was eloquent and fulsome in his praise of the idea presented. Have been puzzling with myself just a bit, on whether I must regard this recognition as a compliment or perhaps the reverse. So far no one of standpat or reactionary sympathies has spoken to me about the article.

This man is quite a unique character, a nonconformist in ways which I had not intended that my article should make room for. He has the highly individualistic complex, in fact is eccentric and has the temperamental vagaries of an artist. And an artist is what he is. He has adopted the ideal for himself of a bohemian type of life, seeing and experiencing all kinds of life as men and women live it, high and low, good and bad, inside and outside. He claims, I believe, to have hobnobbed with the highest of high society, and to have looked in upon the lowest type as well. He has bummed his way around the world; constantly does a great deal of long-distant travelling for none of which he ever pays anything, being sort of a past master at hoboing his way from one end of the country to another and back again at will. Highly sophisticated, tough of mind and moral sensibility, yet keenly sensitive to all forms and phases of expression. He is probably not an immoral man, but with his ideals and extreme sophistication he is hardly the right person to associate intimately with young girls of sheltered training and naive understanding. It was this last point which largely made him incompatible on a Mennonite college campus. Besides when he is in any way thwarted or opposed he reacts in a manner very childish.

On last Tuesday afternoon I borrowed Paul Bender's ancient Chevrolet car and took my wife and son to visit a doctor's office, for the first time since we have come to Indiana. We went to Dr. Young's office in Goshen. We had him administer toxoid to Virgil against diphtheria. In a few months from now doctor will make a test to ascertain whether the toxoid was effective, and will also vaccinate the boy against smallpox. The total charge for all this service is five dollars. I paid it in advance. Mrs. Yoder was also examined at the time. To our surprise, this doctor could find no trace of the fibroid tumors in the abdomen about which Dr. Haury at Newton, Kansas had made so much ado. Several of these were plainly in evidence during and immediately after her pregnancy in 1932. Haury had solemnly warned against another pregnancy before these were removed by surgical attention. Now it seems that they have disappeared. It seems too good to be really true. Had been calculating in mind about having another surgical and hospital bill to finance, not particularly as a preliminary to a larger family, but as a matter of safety and health. A week ago today brother Herman and wife in Iowa had a son born to them.

February 13, 1934 The so-called Young People's Class of the local Sunday School here has Professor Enss for its teacher. Last fall I was chosen as the assistant teacher, being supposed to take the regular teacher's place in case of his absence. Enss always gives the class he teaches something to think upon. Sometimes he is very emphatic and dogmatic in his teaching, sometimes again he is more mild and reasonable. I recall that a few weeks ago he spent a good deal of time and some warm emphasis in criticising the lesson title which the original Lesson Committee placed at the head of that particular day's lesson. For the present quarter the lessons are a full study of Matthew's Gospel. This lesson was on the Beginning of Jesus' Ministry. Now of course every systematic student of the life of Christ knows that Matthew does not even mention the opening period of Jesus' ministry, which had its scene in Judaea. Well, Enss had to dwell at length upon the "stupidity" of placing such a misleading title at the head of a S.S. lesson text. My own feeling of the matter was that the title could be justified on the basis that the lessons were studying the book of Matthew primarily, not the life of Christ.

As I take it, there are sundry ways of studying the Bible, each of which may have particular merits of its own. For a mastery and first-hand familiarity with the text of the Bible itself, some method of book study is in my experience best adapted and most useful. I feel that for most folks the most useful form of Scripture knowledge, is to know the contents of the various books, enough so at least that they can think through each book by chapters or general divisions, and will know where to find a goodly number of the outstanding passages and texts. Along with this should go some knowledge of the date, purpose, author, and results of each book. I realize that such a knowledge of the Bible might be characterized as mechanical and superficial. It is evident that this type of Biblical knowledge lends itself most readily to the oracular and textual use, the literalistic and uncritical use of the Bible. But at the same time I maintain that for the rank and file of folks such information is highly useful. The more systematic types of Biblical study are of course more scholarly, more fundamental, and more fruitful of critical results. So its history, its ethics, its theology, its literary features, as well as other phases of it, can be taken up and studied with fruitful results. But not very many unschooled folks can profitably study the Bible thus.

As to what type of instruction and method of approach is the best for use in S. S. teaching, is to my mind not a settled question. Naturally in the earliest years the teaching of stories and incidents without reference to historical or literary sequence is basic. The basic aim is to impart moral instruction, in fact this aim persists throughout all ages of S. S. instruction, and even predominates unduly to the exclusion of other possible aims. With adolescent classes it would seem possible to teach the history of the Old Testament and the New Testament periods in some systematic way. As it proves out now S. S. pupils of adult years have a very vague and confused idea of, say for example, the life of Christ. I discovered this fact in the course of my attempt to teach N. T. history to a group of some twenty college students last year, and also to a second group of five during the Spring Term.

Since these remarks started with Professor Enss' teaching in S. S. class, I may as well add my reaction to another dogmatic idea which he set forth recently regarding the conversion of the Apostle Paul. Just what point led to this discussion, I cannot now recall. At any rate, the notion was advanced in illustration of what a genuine conversion experience will do for an individual. Paul was pictured as a typical narrow, hide-bound, bigoted Pharisee of the Jews, whiles after his experience at Damascus and immediately afterwards in Arabia he was completely free from Pharisaic prejudices and had a completely Christian outlook. I should want to be among the last to in any way minimize the greatness of the change that came to Paul through his Damascus experience. At the same time a careful consideration of all the facts does not seem to call for such a dogmatic assertion about Saul's conversion. First of all Saul was not a Palestinian Jew, from which group seem to have come the later Judaizing party. He was reared in a provincial city of size and culture. His father, and perhaps more remote ancestors, were Roman citizens, hence of some social standing and perhaps also political. William Ramsay, who has spent a lifetime in studying and investigating the complex ancient life of Asia Minor and its cities, the social, political, and religious background of an important sector of early Christian history — this man makes out quite a different mental and religious set for Saul of Tarsus than is implied in the dogmatic statement cited before. Perhaps Saul's basic philosophy was not so much changed through his conversion as was his means and methods for carrying on his life work. There is nothing substantial to be gained, excepting a mildly sensational and dramatic form of presentation, by overdrawing and even exaggerating the facts of N. T. history and record. The more nearly we can understand the early personalities of the N. T. times as men and women of flesh and blood like ourselves, the more significant will become their message and experiences for us.

February 19, 1934 Here at the YMCA in Elkhart I sit to write a few notes to keep them up to date, as it were. My class in German here is of the same size as last semester. I lost two who became discouraged because of the low grades they made in their courses during the first semester, and so dropped out altogether, but two others came into the class, folks who were in the beginning German class at Goshen during the first semester. One of these, a Miss Smith, is a very welcome trade for any of the fellows who dropped out; the young man is of the same general calibre as those who are no more.

My principal outside activity during the present days is preparing and getting into the mail something like one hundred and fifty statements to subscribers of the Mennonite Quarterly Review. Half of them are one or more years past due already and it is with a devout prayer that these statements are prepared and sent, that folks may be able and willing to remit. The treasury of the Mennonite Historical Society, of which I am the treasurer now, is badly in need of replenishment. Hence I am concerned that a high percentage of these delinquents may remit for the Review this year. I took the time and pains myself to type the statements, and perhaps Mrs. Yoder will take of her time to address the envelopes. They will probably get into the mail after the middle of this week.

February 22, 1934 On Washington's Birthday. Our small college does not observe holiday on the anniversary of the first American President's birth. It is just as well, as many holidays are just too many interruptions to the program of study and learning in school. Am at work preparing a brief review for the MQR on three recent books which set forth some of the realistic phases of the late wartime. On the one, "Preachers Present Arms," I delivered myself previously at a little length in the columns of the Gospel Herald, of which I shall make a brief notice only on this occasion. The others are two books of photographs taken of scenes mostly in the fighting area in Europe. And such awfully gruesome and gruesomely awful scenes as these were! They are disgusting and revolting, nauseating and sickening. The insane destruction of human life and of property, all for what? Yes, for what? That is the question which is making the minds of men uneasy today. It seems as though not a single constructive result was purchased by that prodigal expenditure of life, blood, and wealth, by the brutal and sub-bestial behaviour of so many millions of men. The grand total of known dead in the conflict is set down at a few hundred less than ten millions of men, the wounded, seriously and otherwise, include the neat sum total of another twenty millions, and the reported number of prisoners and missing add another paltry six millions. The money cost of the war is reckoned up to the staggering total of 337,946 millions of dollars, of which sum 186,333 millions are counted as the direct cost, net, and 151,613 millions of dollars as the indirect costs. Such figures are altogether incomprehensible. Unfortunately a new generation has almost grown up since the war, a generation which did not know the war. The world-shaking disturbances which are the aftermath of the great conflict are probably taken by this generation as a more or less normal condition of things. This psychological aspect has its advantages in that it will probably set the new generation to work at reconstruction unhindered by past complexes. The principal disadvantage will be that they will think of war only in its idealized aspects, so that they will probably object little to being used as cannon fodder when the burly Mars again calls with his trumpet. The war picture books, it is to be hoped, will do something toward preserving the memory of the more realistic side of modern warfare.

The National Geographic Magazine for January, 1934, has for its leading feature a lengthy and fully illustrated article by John J. Pershing on the American War Monuments which have been erected in Europe, mostly at important places in the theatre of the war. They are, of course, designed and placed to commemorate the part which the American Expeditionary Forces took in the war. There are eight military cemeteries for American soldiers in Europe. Illustrations show these as beautifully decorated, well arranged and well kept grounds. Usually a beautiful chapel in marble or granite is a part of the cemetery, exquisite architectural gems. There are also shown the beautiful monuments erected upon the important battlefields. All this is beautiful and impressive, and it has its use in mercifully helping the human mind to forget the horror and the barbarity of the struggle in which these men engaged. On the contrary, it is just this activity that does much to idealize the war and make impressive heroes of the men whose bodies were mangled, torn, disembowelled, and otherwise disgraced in the carnage. So, thanks to the impartial eye of the camera, perhaps the realism of this last war will not so soon be forgotten, and perhaps more of the postwar generations will resolve in mind and soul to personally renounce war forever.

Only lately I sent in to the National Geographic Society my application for membership in this organization. Because I enclosed my remittance for three dollars, I was readily admitted to this honor, if such it be. I care little for the membership certificate, but I have for a goodly number of years hoped and planned that I might some day find it possible to receive regularly the magazine which the Society publishes monthly. Since we now have a son with us to whose education and training we are looking forward, I decided that this magazine shall be one contributing factor to his future interest in and knowledge of geography. We shall very carefully preserve all the numbers, file them away and hope that by the time the boy is old enough to use them profitably we can afford to have them bound up into convenient volumes with indices and all. Meanwhile we shall appreciate them ourselves too. One gets into this particular Society only upon nomination by someone who is already a member. For a few years I have been receiving notice that my name was nominated for membership. I have a dim recollection of seeing T. J. Cooprider's name on one of my early invitation notices as the nominator.

March 3, 1934 Our son Virgil was eighteen months old on last Wednesday. He has continued in very good health, is steadily developing, and becomes constantly a more entertaining source of interest and wonder on the part of his parents. On March first we took tapeline before he was put to bed for the night and took down for purposes of record some of his external physical measurements. As for his weight, we have been unable to weigh him since we left Kansas six months ago. Apparently the boy will have to grow up without being weighed, although a record of his weight would be fine to keep and refer to in time to come.

There is an unusual amount of petty thieving and even burglary around the college this winter. A trap was laid a few weeks ago and one fellow was apprehended. A few nights ago someone who was fixed for it entered the registrar's office and from there the safety deposit vault, helped himself to some fourteen dollars in cash and carried away my personal tin lock box, thinking doubtless that it was a box full of cash or stocks and bonds or something valuable. To their disappointment, I imagine, the box contained nothing but a few legal papers, several certificates, etc., a few things which I wished to protect against fire. Very conscientiously and considerately, in spite of their disappointment they, or he or whoever it was, returned the box and its contents to the front porch of Registrar Hertzler's home, where he found it the next morning.

Last Sunday, because there was a vesper service in the afternoon, and no meeting in the evening, we took the opportunity to entertain a few folks for lunch and the evening. They were Ezra Hershberger, Orden Miller, Marie Bender, Marian Wisseman, and Viola Bittinger. We have been unable to have company so far, but plan to have some more often now.

March 10, 1934 The weeks slip past so smoothly and rapidly of late that I fear Father Time will presently dump us down in the midst of commencement week and its high pressure activities. But before that eventuality comes, we can be sure of a brief breathing spell of a week over the Easter vacation, which will be here in less than three weeks. Heard a lecturer from Indiana University at the college auditorium last evening, a professor of Modern University History. He spoke on Hitlerism, or Modern History in Germany. A very good presentation it was, analytical, informing, almost inspirational. Only scattered morsels of indirect humor were included. The man is evidently very thoroughly informed on European affairs, and his discussion was illuminating to me. I find myself seemingly unable to follow daily or weekly news reports closely enough to really understand events and their relation to one another, nor is my general background complete enough so I can interpret the events as they come along. For these reasons the analysis of the German situation, the logical presentation of factors and events proved highly helpful to me and was much appreciated. I received some glimpse of the really stupendous changes which have been made in the past year.

Yesterday noon when I reached home from my work at Elkhart, a lady was demonstrating to my wife the value and necessity for owning a particular set of books which she was canvassing. "My Book House" is the enigmatical title for the set of six volumes. They are six illustrated books of choice literary selections from many languages and countries arranged and prepared for the home education of a child, beginning with nursery rhymes and songs, nature stories, fairy tales, Bible stories, and advancing by stages through these to serious literature for early adolescent years. There are also three books of pictures from different foreign countries, the pictures in several colors illustrating child life in other lands and being accompanied by rhymes, etc. A very imposing set, well made, and apparently just what a mother needs in order to guide her child's development in vocabulary, ideals, taste, habits, etc., etc. The lady was a good salesman. We had even felt the need for some such aid in our task of guiding Virgil's development, and were therefore quite readily convinced that this was what we needed. But there is always the question of cost. The entire nine volumes were priced at $59.75. For cash a discount of fifteen percent is allowed. Figuring that my April 1 check would just cover this, I allowed the lady to leave the books with us.

March 17, 1934 Lately finished translating the text of Juvenal's Satires into English prose, a task which I started on perhaps as far back as two years ago. I have now the idea that I want to enter into a detailed study of Juvenal and other satire, both earlier and later, as and when and if I find time and opportunity to do so. My translation is written closely in ink on sheets the same as this one. I shall perhaps interleave these sheets with others like them, whereon I can note comments, corrections, references, etc. Then I will need to get hold of all the editions, annotated editions particularly, and commentaries, theses, books and what there is on Juvenal. Perhaps I will purchase some, others I hope to borrow from university libraries or where I can.

National politics, the New Deal, as it is popularly called is still going on its course of experimentation. In the opinion of serious writers, it is still all an experiment and the final outcome is in doubt. People still talk about recovery, but perhaps there will be no recovery, at any rate not recovery in terms of 1926 or 1929, which seem to be the terms in which men are still thinking. A new slant on the program of President Roosevelt is given by the recent enactment by Congress of bonus legislation for veterans against his wish and advice. This action will perhaps upset the plans made previously by the President for the balancing of the Federal budget. In that case genuine inflation with fiat money seems to be brought one step nearer. My own reflections have run thus lately. Since so many people are having a prolonged taste, or rather a long meal, from the Federal treasury, it will be a hard job to wean them away from such a handy and dependable lunch counter. It is estimated that today nearly one-half, perhaps more, of the total population of our nation is living from the government treasury. This includes all who draw salaries from tax funds, veterans, and unemployed receiving relief directly or indirectly through government funds. Now this looks serious to me. If half of the people are living from the government, then of course, half of the nation's voters are among them. And so it is only natural that in a crisis, in choosing between hunger and a balanced government budget, these voters will be pretty sure to vote to feed themselves. And so we will soon be back where the Roman Empire was: people voting, in effect, free bread and free shows for themselves. But Rome could draw upon outlying provinces for revenue, a convenience which the U. S. A. does not have, unless the Philippines and Hawaii could play this role.

March 20, 1934 While reading yesterday in preparation for New Testament Greek class I came upon an idea which appealed to me as being suggestive, and I want to set it down before I forget it. Mr. John Wenger is reading Acts, and I enjoy reading it deliberately and carefully again myself. Miss McPhail seems to have fallen by the way since the semester began. The new notes and comments I am reading are from the Cambridge Greek Testament, author, Lumby. In reading the chapters where the same incident is related a second or a third time we observed from the text variations that devout scholars at some time seemingly were disconcerted by verbal differences in the accounts and tried to make them as uniform as possible by adding words and phrases from one account to the other. Textual criticism has probably discovered and corrected most of these overzealous efforts at verbal uniformity.

The matter has impressed me not a little as I have reflected over it. I wondered whether we are not still given over much to the same obsession in our attitude toward the text of the Scriptures. It is common to hear Bible teachers insist upon the idea that the Bible is verbally inspired, and even statements of doctrine have at times insisted upon such a theory as a necessary article of orthodox faith and belief. Is it possible perhaps to be too abjectly enslaved to the text of the Scriptures, to have our view focussed too immediately upon the form of the words, even upon particular translations, so much so in fact that this very attitude bars our view of the true spirit and meaning of the sacred writings? Is it possible to have an almost idolatrous regard for the form of the Book and the text, which is a dishonor to the author of the Book and blinds us to the true message of its contents? These at least are some questions upon which it may be worth while to reflect. Of course, the idea of insisting that a particular version or even existing manuscripts in the original are literally inspired in every word and letter, and so are perfectly inerrant and infallible, is too brazen an assertion to be tolerated by common sense. So the face of the theory is saved by the device of pronouncing the high-sounding formula, that the original autograph manuscripts of the writers were so inspired. But this is practically to nullify the entire theory. On the point of the attempts made by past scholars to make the text of parallel passages uniform, the author in the Cambridge N. T. remarks: "There have been times when devout men thought much of this verbal accord. It is therefore worth notice that the writers of the N. T. disregarded it utterly. The words in such a solemn inscription as that above the Cross differ in all the four Gospels, and St. Peter when in the Second Epistle, 1:17, he speaks of the heavenly voice heard at the Transfiguration, varies verbally from each of the accounts of the Evangelists." (p. 223)

March 26, 1934 What a change from yesterday, I mean atmospherically! Yesterday for once a day passed with a clear and cloudless sky from morning till night. Today! Snow began coming down at daybreak, must have snowed several inches, then rain and now sleet is rattling against the window panes. Gloom and darkness prevail. How one does wish for spring to come in Indiana! Much more consciously and wistfully one longs for spring, for green grass, flowers, balmy air, sunshine here than in Kansas.

A vacation of just one week will begin Wednesday noon. I have begun to feel it coming on, for an entire class of mine left on Friday already on the annual Men's Chorus Tour, going east this year. Mr. Wenger in second year Greek is the only one of his kind anymore. My work is shaped up so that I can anticipate a considerable degree of freedom in disposing of my time during the brief respite. My copy for the peace section in the April issue of the doctrinal supplement is about ready to type into final form. The manuscript of the pacifism tract for the Peace Committee is just about ready to send away now. This manuscript was planned to go to the printer four months ago! It has been delayed by one cause after another until this late date.

To my very pleasant surprise and also great convenience, there came a check for fifty dollars from the business manager of Hesston College last week, though in fact I had been previously apprised of such a possibility, so that no unbearable shock was caused thereby. This is a payment on my salary account of the year 1931-32. That year I had agreed to cut my allowance from $1300 to $900 in a desperate effort to balance the budget. But I have not to date received all of this amount. In fact I have lost all trace of how the account now stands. The salary accounts of that year are being paid from collections of student accounts of that year and before. There are plenty of such accounts, so that if collections continue to be made, the full amount that is still due will undoubtedly be paid sometime. As it happens this check will be just enough, lacking a few cents, to pay off our standing account at Bethel Hospital in Newton from two years ago. So that is where it will go at once. The monthly payments here of fifty dollars cash will continue until the end of the school year, when the business manager promises to even up all the salary accounts by distributing whatever cash he will have on hand, and the cash coming in during the summer will be distributed pro rata. Present prospects are that I shall teach in summer school.

March 28, 1934 Vacation is here. Time for doing and not doing, as one pleases. This morning I borrowed a book from the Elkhart Public Library for vacation reading, "Moral Man and Immoral Society," by Reinhold Niebuhr, which for a year and more I have been wishing I could read. Read in the Introduction this morning. The author sets forth in brief what he attempts to do in the volume. He gives out as his main thesis the proposition that individual humans can be made moral, can be taught to act sympathetically and considerately, act sometimes in the interests of others for the sake of the larger social welfare. But society, the collectivity, cannot be moral, is basically selfish and predatory, and cannot be made otherwise by any means and measures now proposed to that end. He scores severely the educators who believe in the infinite pliability of human nature, that selfishness is synonymous with ignorance, and that time and effort will bring about the same measure of social and collective control as has been achieved already in the fields of physical science. The sociologists are handled here equally as roughly. Their high-sounding phrases about substituting new and ideal patterns of social behaviour for the present undesirable type of behaviour patterns is described as so much verbiage. And the religious idealists who believe that moral suasion, goodwill, and idealism are well able to remedy the predatory instincts of groups are seemingly equally deluded. I shall be interested in going through his argument for these ideas.

I shall read this discussion as far as possible against the background of our own Mennonite group thinking or at least our thought patterns. We of course flatter ourselves by believing that we know the solution to this problem. Get every man soundly converted to God and his mind, heart, and soul filled with the Spirit of God, and presto! all selfishness, injustice, oppression, violence, etc., etc., will be as dead as the dodo. Yes, yes, all very true, but unfortunately the sentence above is in a conditional mode. Christianity which has this message of salvation in trust has long been blessing and sanctifying these very things: war, strife, greed, laying up treasures on earth which must be protected by force, etc. But as Mennonites, our attitude has very often been about like this: The world is evil; human nature is diabolically depraved, at least in its collective aspects, and here Niebuhr agrees. Therefore we ask only to be left alone to save our own souls and those of a limited percentage of our offspring. If we do not like the social and political conditions prevailing in one land, we take a few belongings and move on to another country. No particular climate, country or nation is our homeland. We look to the world to come for our abiding city. This outlook is so pronounced that we conclude that it is really not worth while to exert ourselves to remedy existing evils and wrongs in this present world. Some might even say that such effort is wrong and a debasement of one's effort. This attitude of passivity, of accommodating ourselves to existing conditions as best possible, of moving from land to land in quest of more comfortable surroundings, of disregarding evil conditions in this world in the vague belief that the final judgment day will see every individual soul rewarded or punished in the exact equivalence of its deserts, this attitude has been ground, pummelled, grained into us so thoroughly that it is with us a matter of conscience, an attitude exactly in accord with Biblical standards and requirements. But one must wonder sometimes whether such an attitude is so final or consistent. We like to think at the same time that God's will, His Kingdom and its righteousness will and must ultimately prevail over all else. We hold it to be right and imperative that we combat depraved human nature by preaching the Bible and teaching morals, ethics, etc.

March 31, 1934 Today is Mrs. Yoder's birthday, it being the completion of her forty-third year. Paul Bender and wife invited us to take evening dinner with them not over twelve feet above our own dining table. We appreciated both the hospitality and the change of place, even though it was so close by. It turned out to be a birthday celebration, for the cake that was brought on with the dessert had outlined atop of its frosting the numerals 43. Virgil demonstrated his skill at using fork and spoon in feeding himself, considerably to his credit. He has now been practicing for just one week, and gets along very well with solid foods.

Am reading in Niebuhr's book these days, and with considerable enthusiasm. The analyses which he makes of the individual's rational and religious resources for living in society and as a member of a group are very good and highly suggestive. He outlines quite vividly the various limitations of these several resources and how it is hardly to be hoped that a really moral and ethical society can be achieved from these resources. Some of the ideas I gleaned yesterday were as follows: Man's concept of the Absolute, which he gives as being the essence of religion, results in contrition, in a view of personality as transcendent against an Absolute background, and in a perfectionism of moral ideals. This makes for sympathy towards fellowmen, for placing a transcendent worth upon human life and personality. But it also places a high value on self-realization, as one feels responsibility to make the most, usually in service, of one's personal endowments. Contrition results, when faced with the crudities of social morality, in asceticism of varying degrees of severity. Love is another resource, which operates within narrow and intimate circles, or even more widely with persons of lively imagination. But an unfortunate result of the keen perception of the difference between divine and human morality, is to obscure the lesser differences between human moralities, so much so that indifferentism toward injustice, etc., results. Again, when a dualism (God-world, Spirit-flesh) is followed too consistently, the result is a defeatist attitude, which does nothing about the present status quo and concentrates its hopes of social morality in a millennial expectation brought in by catastrophe. On the contrary a monistic outlook too consistently followed out leads to sentimentalism, a romantic faith in the certainty of natural evolution into a morally and ethically ideal society. Significantly comfortable and dominant groups incline to the latter of these while oppressed and suffering classes hold the former. On this basis of classification the Early Church was clearly defeatist. The dominant middle class philosophy of western nations since the ushering in of the Age of Reason in the eighteenth century has been sentimentalist.

April 2, 1934 Yesterday was Easter Sunday; not a very pleasant day on the whole; it rained a good part of the afternoon, a warm rain which made the snow on the ground disappear rapidly. Today there is warm sunshine, a pleasant spring day. Hope it will come on in real earnest now. Taught Sunday School class for Enss yesterday morning, in fact have been doing so over half of the Sundays for two months past or so. For evening program I was slated to go to Yellow Creek Church, about eight miles west of Goshen. The entire young people's program was rendered by folks from the college as an extension project by the YPCA.

Harper's Magazine occasionally contains some valuable articles and essays. On the whole its offerings are not of a good quality, mea quidem sententia. It does not come to the college reading room now. Spent more than an hour at the city library in Goshen on Saturday afternoon last, reading several pieces in the April number. The one that impressed me most was entitled "The New New Testament," by a professor of New York University named Spencer. He wrote in a combative, slightly pugnacious vein, a presentation of the so-called "translation hypothesis" of the origin of the present Greek form of the Four Gospels. In brief, this hypothesis, worked out most fully and I understand recently published by Professor Torrey of Yale, is that all of the Gospels were originally composed, not in Common Greek but in Aramaic, and as thus composed they were then translated into Greek. In their Aramaic form they were complete, all of them, before the destruction of Jerusalem in 70 A.D. This last fact as to date of composition has always been held by conservative scholars, but for the typical higher critic it is a great departure from long accepted results of assured scholarship. It therefore comes as a pleasant confirmation to me in my backward way of thinking. Spencer's viewpoint throughout the article is the typical higher critical one, that is, as to the person and work of Christ and His apocalyptic teachings.

I had previously understood that it was generally accepted that Matthew wrote his Gospel in the dialectic Aramaic. The notion that they all did is news to me. In fact, I cannot see how Luke, the fellow traveller of St. Paul could have so written, since he was a Greek and was not especially sympathetic toward Palestinian Jews. Perhaps he used Aramaic documents as his sources and often translated verbatim from them. With such superficial reservations, it appeals to me as a reasonable hypothesis, to judge on the basis of the evidence adduced by the writer in this article. Naturally it can hardly ever attain any higher status than that of an hypothesis, for no Aramaic originals are known to survive. The sole evidence consists of a hypothetically reconstructed original text and then searching for possible errors in translation. About 250 of these are claimed discovered in all the Gospels, and if the method is trustworthy, some very puzzling and even meaningless passages are delightfully cleared up thereby. In Aramaic, as in Hebrew, only consonants were written, the reader supplying the vowels. As in other languages, some words differ only in the vowels used in them, so in reading the Aramaic the translator occasionally mistook one word for another and the result is a senseless translation. It remains to be seen how the hypothesis will fare at the hands of scholars in the time to come.

April 5, 1934 A Bishop Fiske of New York State writes in Atlantic Monthly something of his own attitude, in elemental form, towards the teachings and principles of Christianity. His remarks are reverent, considerate, reasonable, practical. He is entangled with current critical conclusions about the Scriptures and other points, but does not negate dogmatically the points he is not settled on. I found the essay stimulating, and also condemnatory. The Bishop dwelt particularly on the personal and mystical element in his relation to God. My own conscience smote me because this reading brought home to me how negligent and dilatory I am myself in cultivating this phase of my religious experience. I have at irregular times in the past tasted of the rich possibilities in that direction, possibilities for achieving peace of soul and mind, for victorious and abundant living, and for solid enjoyment of fellowship and personal communion with God. I cannot say that I have any definite feeling of being out of touch with the personality of God, but my impression is rather that I merely fail to draw upon the resources which I have at hand, neglecting to exploit the possibilities which I know are right at hand for the taking. The press of many things to do, the shortsighted program of using all my time and energy in promoting various and numerous projects, plans, etc., of my own, leave no time for the more intensive cultivation of my own inner life. And yet I know, more certainly than I know aught else, that my own personal efficiency, even in these extraneous pursuits, would be multiplied, at any rate greatly increased, and my enjoyment and personal usefulness would be augmented, if I could more consciously cultivate and nurture my own soul. Excuses and plausible reasons I could perhaps find, were I to search for them. But I still feel that sometime, surely sometime, I shall manage to do this very thing better.

Our boy is beginning to say words; at least he tries. He can sound a good many vowel sounds, but hardly any distinct consonant sounds. A neat little Kiddy Kar came by mail for him from New York, a present. He cannot ride it yet, but will probably soon learn. He shows signs of good ability in manipulation, in motor activity and control. He learned to creep practically all at once, on all fours at that, which is reputed to be the correct way. Walking also he learned readily, within a few weeks after he first stood erect without holding fast with his hands. He can lay up some blocks according to patterns I have taught him. His skill in making common spools, emptied of thread, spin by bearing down on one end with the forefinger attracts a good deal of attention among folks. I had imagined that such a simple way of improvising a top is common practice, when I taught him how.

April 12, 1934 Here it is cold and uncomfortable again. There was a week or more of very pleasant weather, too pleasant in fact to be of lasting quality. I was able to spend any leisure hours in my office as I might plan. Cannot sit comfortably for any length of time there now. Folks were beginning to work the ground in gardens, and confessedly we caught a mild form of gardening fever too. As yet we have not found any piece of ground for our gardening this year, and what is unpleasant, we probably cannot get any piece very close by our apartment house. We have gotten the gardening habit during the last five years while we lived in Kansas. In that state garden making is a major project, requiring planning, strategy, and perseverance. One must fight against late frost, drought, and such other acts of God. We were at the job just about long enough to learn most of the technique for raising at least something. Now it seems we must start all over again learning how to raise some foodstuffs in a garden. To have no fresh vegetables for table use is both an inconvenience, having to fetch them from a store, and an extra drain upon the family budget, which is always loaded to capacity as it is. Our supply of canned goods, much of which was brought from Kansas, e.g., peas, beans, spinach, is pretty well exhausted. Some things were canned here last fall. These helped out materially on the budget.

April 21, 1934   On the past Thursday afternoon I spent the entire half day in planting garden seeds and potatoes. Benders and we together were able to get the use of one fullsized lot from Mr. Wambold. It lies fifty yards or so back of the apartment house and is therefore handy for us to use. For the use of it we need to pay no rental other than for the plowing of another lot of Wambold's which lies just beside it. In addition to this we secured a half-lot belonging to the college which lies farther north forty rods or so. We are now well equipped with ground for our gardening ambitions. We are also experimenting with the use of commercial fertilizer for the first time, putting some in the bottom of the drill rows and mixing it well with the loose soil before sowing seeds there.

Cool weather persists. A heavy frost lay on the ground this morning. Reading takes up my spare time. Having frequently heard "Moby Dick" by Melville spoken of, I have been reading at spare moments in this for several weeks. A strange and fascinating tale it is, of whaling and cetology in general. It relates the adventures of a whaling ship and its crew, sailing from Nantucket on a voyage lasting several years. Also have a book from Elkhart Public Library by Laski on "Democracy in Crisis." He is a British political scientist. He argues for socialism.

April 24, 1934   Just finished reading the wondrous tale of Moby Dick. I had not expected quite the end to which matters finally came. The White Whale is presumably mortally wounded when he last rushes off the scene, but not until he had stove the big whaler so that she finally sinks.

Last Sunday evening Bro. Graber invited me to give the after young people's meeting address, sermon, or what you choose to call it. The evening's topic of discussion was the Christian's Relationship to the State. It was my first attempt to express myself on this particular theme, and while I probably did not enlighten anyone else a great deal, I am aware that my own ideas on the subject have grown clearer as a result of my organizing the few matters and ideas which I had gathered upon it. It is a vast and a profound subject, involving a complete theoretical philosophy about the State, human government, and politics. In surveying the history of thought regarding Church and State, one is almost led to the conclusion that some sort of arbitrary dualism is unavoidable. Jesus taught a specific code of ethics and morals for his followers. But both reason and experience demonstrate that this code cannot be applied in political relationships, or in the relationship of larger groups with each other. Hence in political thinking Jesus' code is either ignored or rationalized away, or else society is divided into two classes each with its own standard of ethics, or finally the individual personality is thus bisected, one sphere following Christ and another serving the State. In our own Mennonite circles we act upon the principle that man's personality cannot be divided between two ethical loyalties, and we do not conceive of different groups of men serving God on different planes of morality. At the same time we insist upon the literal and practical interpretation of Jesus' teaching. As for a complete synthesis on the subject we have none, except that it is the custom among us to quote Paul's expression or theory of the State in Romans, 13th chapter, as a formula that is meant to cover the whole matter. It runs about thus: God instituted mundane rulers to keep order and punish evil doers, and incidentally protect good people. At the same time we advocate nonparticipation in affairs of government, the implication being that men who as officials employ force, coercion, and violence in performing their duties cannot be followers of Christ living in full obedience to Him. The smallness of our numbers has kept us from being forced to make a distinct and clear analysis of the problem. It is an interesting field for speculation.

April 26, 1934 Spring term is starting off now, the special midspring term for rural teachers, but the number is small. For the summer session, the director has advised me of the possibility that I may be called upon to teach a subject in Bible and for a year course in German. Hope something will develop from that source, as a bit of income during the summer will be very welcome in our family budget. S. M. King is here to give the Spring Term courses in Education and Psychology. He has been studying for the past two quarters in Chicago University and is still undecided about returning to the Philippine Islands to teach.

My fifth quarterly installment on Peace matters in our Gospel Herald came out last week. The leading article, entitled "Conscientious Objectors to War," has brought me a response of appreciation from E. L. Frey, who is chairman of the Peace Committee of the General Conference. His further suggestion is that I enlarge it to pamphlet size for their committee to issue as a tract for free distribution. Do not now feel much inclined to do this. I was interested and a little amused by an editorial reaction from the editor of the Herald. In a book review I had occasion to mention the idea of progressive revelation as applied to the Jewish and Christian Scriptures. The editor inserted a side remark in parentheses, giving a strong word of caution against confusing this term with some evolutionary idea of the origin of Christianity. The side remark was entirely in place, and I have no objection to its insertion. At the same time it illustrates nicely how trepidaciously our older church leaders shy away from newer terms and from any phraseology which chances to differ from that which they happened to acquire when they were in their formative years. To my way of thought, it is this sort of slavish subservience to words and phrases which renders them incapable of leading and guiding the thought of young people who read and think more or less for themselves.

April 27, 1934 Not so extremely busy with side issues these days it seems. Spare time is more like spare time when there is leisure to turn to what one likes. This hour in mid-afternoon happens to be clear because my work for the next period was prepared on last Wednesday during this period, and because it happened to be the annual Senior Sneak Day, and my last hour class consists of one senior student, I did not need my preparation on that day and will use it today. In Acts, Greek, we are reading about Paul's labors on the second missionary journey.

Received a book catalog from Blackwell at Oxford, England, some time ago. Since I have an urge to build up my library in Juvenalia, I decided to send for Friedländer's commentary on Juvenal, which I found listed in it. The price quoted was in German marks 18.90, and I made a rough mental calculation that perhaps five dollars American money would cover the cost. It came promptly and the enclosed invoice called for an amount above seven dollars in our money, which was a decided shock to me. The whole is due to the disparity in foreign exchange, which in turn is due to our President Roosevelt's maneuvers with the currency for price stabilization. He devaluated the dollar to fifty-nine cents of its former value, and it has not raised prices at all according to expectations. One thing it should succeed in doing, judging from my own reaction, is to diminish imports and foreign purchases by Americans. Two and three years ago I ordered quite a number of books from Blackwell, and since the British exchange then meant a gain of about one-third over American money, it was a very opportune time for such purchases. But no more foreign book purchases for me now for a time. Occurred to me also, that I should have had my summer's travel and study in Europe before the exchange rates teeter-tottered as they did.

And our Roosevelt! Well, as one writer stated, the time for confession and repentance by the New Deal administration is just about here. The NRA is to be generally reorganized, so one reads; most things have failed to produce any miracles. CWA has been demobilized, and wise ones hint that the PWA is evaporating into thin air. The opinion is abroad that F.D.R. is moving, or drifting toward the right politically, slowly making terms with old guard capitalism. The high tide of his popularity, which was probably little more than just another classical example of gullibilitis _Americana_, may soon be spent. The President's genial smile and his wife's much travelling about, both exploited by press agents, seem not to be producing any magical economic and political effects. My faith in democracy by a majority of near-morons is not strong.

April 29, 1934 Today all clocks and watches hereabouts were supposed to be advanced one hour, so giving us daylight saving time for the summer. Not such a bad idea in this area which lies at the eastern edge of the Central Standard time belt. In this way one has long summer evenings since it does not grow dark in June much before nine o'clock.

Last evening Walter Yoder gave another Orthophonic record program in Chapel Hall. Several times earlier in the year such programs were given. Usually a dime was collected as admission fee, the proceeds to be used for the purchase of more records for the Victrola. The records are the property of the Music Department of the college. They purchase records of the masterpieces of classical music, for example Bach's "St. Matthew's Passion of our Lord," Symphonies of Haydn and Beethoven, are some I have heard. It is a very excellent idea, to my mind, and I am glad it is being done. Personally I know very little about music and its appreciation, but I am eager to learn. If such a layout for music were not too expensive, I would much like to have something of it for our home sometime. With a child in our home we must have some music after a while when he gets a little older than he is now. Such musical masterpieces of the classical sort would seemingly be the ideal musical atmosphere in which a child can grow up. I really have a negative enthusiasm for getting a radio in our home. I presume if we find it impossible to have the best victrola music, we will probably possess a radio sometime. I thoroughly detest the advertising system which so greatly dominates the radio broadcasting as it is now carried on. It is fondly to be hoped that some other and better system for subsidizing radio broadcasting will be discovered and applied before long.

At Vespers this afternoon a Burmese student of Chicago will be the speaker. Virgil is on a sick spell again today, and so I expect to stay at home with him while Mrs. Yoder attends the program.

Am getting fed up on subjects relating to Church and State. Read a book the past week by Shillito on "Nationalism — Man's Other Religion." Regarding this theme it is almost literally true "quot homines, tot sententiae." This writer has a new and fresh slant on the matter of nationalism about which one hears so much these days. Emphasis is laid upon the point that internationalism does not imply the obliteration of nations as such, but the opposite. It is not denationalization nor unnationalism. This is a suggestive line of thought. The type of nationalism which threatens to become dominant today is that which makes the state or nation an end in itself, an ultimate entity, an object of reverence and worship above all else. This is set forth as the ancient pagan political theory. St. Augustine is cited at length by this author as the man who defined the Christian theory of the State. The recrudescence of the pagan ideal dates from the writings and influence of Machiavelli of the sixteenth century. The general conclusion seems to be that the principles of Christianity must permeate nationalism to such an extent that a higher sovereignty and unity must be recognized as legitimate. Reinhold Niebuhr would probably set this outlook down as just one more romantic dream of mankind at its best, and at its worst perhaps an illusion. The Church must never be subject to the State; it must be a spiritual commonwealth over and above the State, free to give an undimmed and unhesitant testimony to the truth of God, perhaps supporting such phases of nationalism as are in line with her message, but never being made the tool of the State for worldly and national purposes. The Sunday School Times is now running a series of articles in which nationalism (of all things!) is defended as Scriptural. But the term is not closely defined and so it is not clear what is meant.

May 6, 1934 Warm weather and shortage of moisture. I am in favor of the former but not of the latter, for our garden crops cannot get started well under present conditions. Our son, Virgil, went to kindergarten Sunday School class this morning for his first time. Judging from the eagerness with which he participated in sand table activities he will probably be going regularly henceforth. Slowly he is learning to say some words more distinctly, but he does not speak sentences as yet. He is interesting at all times, and usually manages to have the attention of his parents, particularly when I am at home. His mother can ignore him successfully when she is at work, but he generally succeeds in getting me to help him with ball, or blocks, or spools, or looking at pictures and identifying the things he sees. There is considerable room for him to play on the front porch of the apartment house, where we place a fence to keep him from straying away.

I am fairly holding my breath now, wondering what the close of the semester will bring forth financially, I mean in the distribution of cash surplus to faculty members. I find that I shall need about two hundred dollars with which decently to meet my obligations during June, and could easily allocate another two hundred in items past due before now. The cash received since September 1 last plus our rent for the twelve-month totals the amount of eight hundred dollars now.

Have been reading at spare moments the past week the "Autobiography of Benvenuto Cellini," a work I have long aimed to read but never happened to have available. Samuel Yoder loaned me his copy for reading. It is a remarkable piece of writing even in translation, having been composed in Italian at the close of the man's life. Cellini was evidently a typical personality of the Italian Renaissance. Born in 1500, his skill as an artist made room for him readily. In temperament the artists of that day, perhaps most folks, seem to have acted like children, impetuous, self-willed, impulsive, and at the same time overbearingly proud, hating and loving desperately, and living a wondrously full and turbulent life. Mentally and artistically this man was eminently a genius, egotistic and yet not offensively so, ready to kill an enemy in self-defence or in revenge, and making enemies constantly by his outspoken pride and straightforward manner of address. When through treachery placed into prison and suffering much discomfort, he seems to have had a genuine religious experience, realizing the presence of God and Christ with himself, and using prayer and devotional exercises to no little profit and advantage. To hear him tell of it he was probably as good a man, and likely a better man than many of his contemporaries, such as popes, cardinals, dukes, etc. Life appears to have been frank and realistic, at least in certain particulars in which it is today hedged about by many and various hypocrisies and conventions. I presume their make-believe was employed in other directions from ours.

Leaves are coming out on the trees rapidly the past few days. Spring fever tends to attack students and teachers on such days. Some go out on green fields and knock some little balls about, and call it sport to walk after them. Walking in woods and fields appeals much more to me, following my nose rather than some small white balls. But have not done any so far, because garden work has taken what I care to spare from other duties. My teaching takes up too much of my time as yet. Once I can get my Latin courses well enough in hand so that no special preparation is necessary for each successive recitation, then matters will be more to my taste.

May 12, 1934 This week I read Walter Pitkin's book, "Life Begins at Forty," a very popular book during the recent past months, not long or difficult, 175 pages of large type, and not hard to read. I cannot say that I am greatly impressed by the book or its theme. There is a good deal of ballyhoo about it, lots of imagination, yet at the same time some very good ideas and suggestions are dropped along the way which are worth while. It is a popular critique of numerous phases of modern barbaric life particularly as it is lived in America. The main contention is that a new day is just dawning in which intelligent people will spend forty years in learning, experimenting, activity, and the vegetative phases of life, and at forty will truly and really begin to live, doing what they wish, as they wish, growing in the contemplative and the advisory phases of life, continuing in the possession and enjoyment of such a life up till ripe old age. But before men and women can begin to live at forty, or at any other age, they must be educated previously for living, and in a way radically different from that process as it is now carried on. He would combine earning and learning in an integral way over the whole period up to the time when life is said to begin. The implication being, I believe, that at forty every person will be in possession of such a competence that he can thereafter earn or not, quite as he may choose. In its broad outline the scheme of the book is very like that of Plato in his "Republic." The outlook for the future is altogether optimistic; there can be no doubt as to the direction in which human life is moving. The only reasons we are not all there already are our own stupidity, the lack of intelligent organization and planning, and the obsessions which cling to our minds. No hint or suggestion is evident to the effect that man suffers from sin, or that spiritual factors enter into human endeavors. To read such an exaltation of human possibilities in the light of past history makes one wonder, is man merely stupid and barbaric, or is he also subject to positive evil influences, emanating from an evil and diabolical personality? The devil has perhaps in the past often been made the convenient scapegoat for the wickedness and vileness of man's own heart and life. But why should thinkers now rush to the opposite extreme and absolve the devil from all responsibility for man's backwardness and perverseness?

As for myself, I am delighted with the idea that life begins at forty. I hail this as good news, if it is true. My reflection convinces me that life for myself must begin at or after forty, if it begins at all, for I seem to myself to have done no real living as yet. In retrospect I presume there are few major experiences in my life which I would be willing to forego, now that they are behind me. But I am still cumbered with debt and handicapped in directing my energies into the lines which I would choose for myself. Few things bore me more than the handicaps laid upon me by lack of financial independence, or partial independence even. Theoretically money should be incidental in this business of living, and how gladly I should look upon it as such! But debt is too realistic for me to regard it as incidental. Seemingly there are persons to whom debt is quite incidental a matter, but I am not one of that fortunate number. To pay out from a meagre income good cash for interest charges and taxes seems an awful shame. I am almost ready to conclude that, if some more sure form of old age support or of support for wife and child in case of accident were in effect, I should dispose of my property, give it away, if need be, liquidate my obligations as quickly as possible and then stop worrying forever about financial matters. But evidently an essential part of this living business is to struggle against difficulties, so I must keep on pushing and tugging. I have become convinced that for me, I must apply my mind and such mental acumen as I have to the problem of wresting by main force or otherwise a life, one of satisfaction, of progress and personal growth, of some kind of achievement, from the circumstances in which I find myself. It must be possible to live a creative life without money or financial competence. It is to this achievement that I mean to devote continuously more energy and time. Ever since I was a small boy I have been a dreamer, living a good deal in the better days which were surely ahead of myself. The small distance I have come I attribute to the fact that some of my basic boyhood dreams were cherished as profound convictions, and by dint of tenacious adherence to them I overcame numerous discouraging obstacles. There is a sense of satisfaction in retrospect, but not the kind that lets me sink back and feel I have now at last "arrived." I cannot be altogether discouraged with the past, but neither can I be absolutely satisfied with my present accomplishments. I must grow and advance, mentally and spiritually, especially. To give up this ambition is for me to die.

May 22, 1934 An ideal day, this; a goodly shower of rain fell last evening soon after dusk. The north wind today is cool and refreshing with clear sky and beautiful sunshine. Mr. and Mrs. Samuel King ate supper and visited with us last evening. They have many interesting experiences and observations to relate from their three-years' teaching sojourn in the Philippine Islands. They were fortunate in getting the positions they did in 1930, else they would have been unemployed during some of the time since, even as some of the rest of us. Their appointment is still open for them, I understand, they being in America on leave of absence, and there is a slight possibility that they may return thither, in view of the unemployment situation in this land.

Sat for two hours yesterday afternoon in a meeting of the so-called "Faculty Pool," all of the regular faculty meeting time. Now faculty meeting is called for today at four bells. This "Pool" is an informal organization of all teachers of last year. They have taken over all the financial assets, which are in the form of notes and unpaid accounts, from the last year. Their aim is to collect as much as possible from these and make regular distribution of cash as rapidly as the assets can be liquidated. I have only a very small interest in this pool myself, because I had enough effective leverages to obtain most of my small share of last year's disbursements. In fact I may have received more than the average percentage of last year's salaries which will be ultimately realized from the assets of the pool; some of these assets will in all probability evaporate before they thaw out.

Am reading through a document which is the tentative report of a Commission on Institutions of Higher Learning of the North Central Association of Colleges and Secondary Schools. It outlines the new procedures for recognizing and accrediting schools of higher learning. Dean H. S. Bender, upon returning a few weeks ago from the annual meeting of this Association, spoke very enthusiastically and optimistically of the possibilities of Goshen College making successful application for admission to the Association, but not until several years hence, for as he insisted there needs to be a great deal of intensive work done toward making our college more effective educationally before it is worth the effort of making application. As I read the report, I agree heartily that much needs to be done, more perhaps than can be done

in two or three years' time. Financial resources are the weakest
point Goshen College now has, I believe.

Pridie Kal. Jun. 1934 Examination days are now on. Reading papers
is the dull uninteresting procedure, but fortunately I have not a large
number. Two small classes I have excused from formal examination.
Two persons, because they are Seniors and have a good year's record
so far, are excused from elementary New Testament Greek examination. The beginning German students whom I have been instructing at
the Elkhart YMCA all year present some problems. Two fellows
dropped out very soon after the second semester started. Two others
entered the class there with the opening of the second semester, both
residents of Elkhart who had been campus students during the first
semester. One of these is a young lady equal in achievement to anyone of the group, the other a young chap who is as poor in that respect as the poorest, perhaps even a little poorer. He and two other
fellows are borderline cases hovering between passing and failure.
Experience seems to indicate that such extension work at Elkhart
places more responsibility for self-control and self-application, more
of the burden of initiative for achievement upon the students than is
true of campus students who spend more time in an atmosphere of
study and mental effort. Unless a student can direct his effort, budget
his time, and drive himself to get his work done, he is not so likely
to succeed under such an extension plan of taking college courses.
Theoretically he should have more time for productive application
than campus students who give much of both time and energy to extra-
curricular activities; practically he probably dissipates in other and
in worse ways, so wasting time and effort.

    Received today a catalog from Blackwell at Oxford, listing second-
hand books on religion and theology. Reason and economies counsel
me not to pay any heed to such lists for a time longer. Nonetheless
I hurriedly scanned the authors and titles, sent my order for three
volumes, closing my eyes to our shortage of funds. At any rate they
are second-hand and not expensive, and furthermore, being so far away
from England, these may be sold before my own order reaches the
place.

June 4, 1934 A lull is on today in commencement activities on the
campus. It is Class Day, and all the groups are scattering out to various places for outings and recreation. It is also a day of comparative
leisure for myself. All my examination papers were read and grades
turned in Saturday noon. Two people are to take special examinations
tomorrow. My own mental set is now toward the teaching of courses
in the summer session, which begins on the day following commencement. The director, Dr. Hertzler, is optimistic that I may have a full
teaching schedule, with enrollments up to or nearly up to the minimum
required for full compensation also. Naturally I wish it may come true.
I may be selfish, but I would not wish for many more than the minimum
number, as that would make me more work than I care to do in connection with my summer's teaching, especially in German where written
work is necessary, and reading many papers is very exhaustive for me.
The inefficiency of my eyes more than anything else makes such work

tiresome and nervously exhausting.

June 5, 1934 There has been rain! A vigorous shower fell yesterday afternoon about four o'clock, accompanied by some strong wind and hail. We were involved in some plans for an outing-picnic excursion to Lake Wawasee, some fifteen miles southeast of Goshen. A boat had been engaged for four o'clock for a ride on the lake during which time supper was to be eaten on board. Grabers, H. S. Benders, Paul Benders, John Bender of Springs, Pennsylvania, and a few visitors with ourselves were to make up the party. All were just about ready for the drive to the lake when the rain came; we were sitting in Paul Bender's car in the road before Harold Bender's place during the whole downpour which lasted most of an hour. In spite of the lateness of the hour, we all started off. Three or four miles south of the city no drop of rain had fallen; farmers were cultivating corn fields with clouds of dust flying as they stirred the soil. Arriving at Wawasee, a dark cloud to eastward portended more rain and sure enough, within ten minutes it began to pour down. So there was nothing for the party to do but to return home and eat picnic supper in H. S. Bender's dining room. To add further romance to the trip, Paul Bender's car in which we were riding refused to function when all were ready to start back in the rain. In spite of Mr. Graber pushing the machine for several miles, it would not start, the motor being dead. It was finally left in a garage in Syracuse; loads were doubled up and so to home we came. In between there and here it was still dry but the shower followed us later.

The Senior Class exercises which were planned for the college campus had to be given indoors with the rest of the evening's program. As reported, it is the first time in many years that the campus exercises could not be carried out as planned because of rain. The rain has been a wonderful blessing. Drought of seriously damaging proportions had been reported for a week or more in many central western states. The hail did a little damage to garden crops, but probably not serious. It is still sultry today and more rain may be on the way and will be not unwelcome as subsoil is very dry.

June 10, 1934 We have had pleasant weather since the close of school last Tuesday, coolish, clear, acceptable. I have my two courses for the summer already going. Paul and his Epistles has five folks enrolled now, the minimum number for full pay for the instructor. Elementary German, a double course that meets two class periods every day, does not have the required minimum, hence the remuneration will be less than full pay. There are four registrants, all capable students, and I plan to give them a great deal of work to do.

Spent two afternoons this week at sessions of the Indiana-Michigan Conference, on Thursday and Friday. These were held at Wakarusa, about fifteen miles west by south of Goshen. Paul Bender invited me each time to ride with him. We were perhaps mostly interested in making personal observations of the spirit and method of working and deliberating on the part of this body. Had heard considerable about this conference organization in recent years and its high-handed, sometimes radical and reactionary ways of working. The machinery of conference is completely in the hands of the radical and near-radical element. Outstanding church-wide leaders of such age and experience as D. A. Yoder and D. D. Miller are given no place or recognition in the conference organization. It is somewhat of a rude shock to listen in on the naive and uncritical discussions which they have, uncritical I mean in the sense of a blind, literalistic, often ignorant, and always dogmatic approach to the Bible and to the consideration of religious subjects. It is of course the best they know, and does some practical good and perhaps not a great deal of harm. It does harm only when it is coupled with political ecclesiastical methods and procedures which serve to keep a certain group dominant and concurrently suppress the expression of minority or conflicting opinion. Occasionally someone speaks for a strictly legalistic interpretation and enforcement of conference decisions. There is much discussion and haranguing that serves effectively to becloud and befog specific issues, a good deal of cudgeling critical opinion and critical judgment into silence by means of pompous slogans and formulas of various types. Blanket phrases and statements take the place of analysis and straight thinking with many. The ideal, the goal to be reached, and the program for reaching it are apparently fixed and settled in the minds of many of these zealous brethren. Conference for them is simply a means of providing props from Scripture texts and high-sounding resolutions for the platform, the specific program they have in mind. In one discussion we heard, a resolution was under consideration specifying the qualifications for acceptable workers in subsidiary church activities. The list enumerated included nine points, eight of which were fair and logical and could be supported by Scriptural texts. Sandwiched among them, third from the end, was one which designated specifically Mennonite qualifications, albeit in general terms, but which, as came out in the discussion, in the minds of some meant the absence of neckties for men, and perhaps others not so defined. When there was some very reasonable criticism mildly offered, certain men sought to clinch the whole issue by loudly, dogmatically, and with an air of complete finality, asserting some blanket statement, to the effect that the standards in question are Bible standards and no one with a shred of loyalty to the Bible could vote for any standard lower than the Bible itself. Evidently these statements were meant, and proved successful too in this case, to frighten honest minds away from any attempted analysis of the resolution and a clarification of the issue. It is such exhibitions of asininity and unconscious dishonesty that tend to discourage me and to make me turn away in disgust from all active interest in the official ecclesiastical machinery of the church. If I believed that the program and platform of such zealots would ultimately have to prevail, I should be truly discouraged. But all history proves that there are forces at work in shaping the destiny of the church other than the plannings and the imaginings of men often shortsighted, ignorant, and self-willed. The Holy Spirit is still a guiding factor in the development and progress of the church, in spite of the fact that some leaders have no confidence in the Spirit's guidance and direction, but place all their hope and trust for the future welfare of the church in organization, in conference guidance, in manmade safeguards, restrictions, and so forth. Sometimes for a longer or shorter period such an outlook and such methods may prevail sufficiently to make for a complete group stagnation. Sooner or later conditions change and matters are again rectified. The Gospel message is a vital message, and if the Holy Spirit has any chance at all to guide individual Christians, groups as ours can escape alike the rocks of stagnation and of dissipation.

June 17, 1934 Ten days of summer school are now past and I am getting my pace and my wind, so to speak. It is a definite change from the schedule I had during the regular semester, but on the whole not any easier. It is the same thing every day for six days of the week. Elementary German, with four students so far, but now reduced to three, meets at 7:30 in the morning for one hour. For two hours after that I prepare my class lecture in Pauline Epistles. At 10:15 the German class meets again for an hour of recitation. Thereafter it is chapel every day excepting Saturday. Following this brief respite the class in Paul meets for an hour. By 12:30 I am thus quite tired and worn, most too weary to relish my dinner. After the meal I aim to take a siesta including a short or longer nap. Afternoons I read German papers handed in by students, do some personal study and reading and writing. Evenings it is working in the garden or reading. Am starting in on a large book just now, a real heavyweight, Deissmann's "Light from the Ancient East." It is a book translated from the original German, and deals with the new and supplementary knowledge that has come to scholars of New Testament history, language, and general background as a result of the discovery and the study of writings found on papyri, ostracea, and other materials in recent decades. It is a positively fascinating field of study and exploration for me and I want to investigate it as much as I can. Such study sheds a flood of light on the linguistic problems of the N. T., and for me it makes the writings really live. After a few glimpses of such possibilities for N. T. study, the previous general concept of N. T. Scriptures with which I grew up appears very cramped, limited and mechanical. To recreate in some measure the atmosphere of the first Christian century and then peruse the N. T. literature, makes the latter seem alive and throbbing with human as well as religious interest. Also plan to familiarize myself this summer a bit with N. T. textual criticism, its history, facts, and conclusions.

And so my summer will be full and even strenuous. I do not mind particularly, as the small income from teaching is a real necessity for us this summer. I should personally prefer to have my summer months free from the necessity for earning bread and butter, and be free for doing projects of my own, projects that might advance my own knowledge and preparation. For the present I am very well content as it is.

June 24, 1934 The week days are full and they slip by in steady procession. Sunday seems the only leisure time I have for scribbling notes of any sort. Our weather and atmospheric conditions have been quite decent and tolerable so far. Rain showers are coming a little closer together all along, and perhaps the drouth will soon be actually broken. Garden crops are growing now; so are insect pests to molest them. We have now lettuce and peas, in fact have had for a week or more. Other things will be coming on presently. Fruits of any sort at cheap prices are the hardest to get hold of at this season of the year. Strawberries were not plentiful hereabouts, partly frozen by last frosts and partly dried up. Cherries are coming on now, and are only fairly cheap.

Summer school routine is going smoothly. My lot it was this past week to conduct chapel exercises four times. I endeavored to hand out some ideas, at least remarks, on the problem of individualism versus collectivism, just in general, nothing exhaustive or profound. This responsibility made my task extra heavy. At the same time I tried to prepare manuscript copy which is due a week from now with Gospel Herald at Scottdale. A good share of spare time this coming week will have to be given to this same project.

Virgil had a few days of illness this week past again. On June 14 Dr. Young gave him the second vaccination for smallpox. The first one in February did not "take," and the second one did, quite decidedly. His teeth still bother him a great deal when his resistance is in any way lowered temporarily. He still has four back molars to cut through. The two days of high fever have cut him down perceptibly. His cheeks are pale and appear thin. He usually is very cross-tempered when he is recovering from such an illness; he seems nervous and generally irritable. He enjoys going to kindergarten class in Sunday school, has been going regularly since about May first. Speech comes slowly for him. He tries to say many words. Insistently does he demand every evening before bedtime that we read to him from his book, Book One of the set we purchased in March. He is quite decided in his likes and dislikes; rhymes and jingles of all kinds are his favorites now. It is hard to get his approval of a new piece usually, but when he has heard it a few times, if it is of the right type, he calls for it thereafter. Each evening we must go through the entire volume; he points at the ones he wants read, identifying them by the accompanying pictures. He is beginning to pass over some sometimes, of those he has heard many, many times. During the day he spends a deal of time looking through copies of magazines: Parents' Magazine, National Geographic, Literary Digest, Better Homes and Gardens, besides the several picture books he has, looking at the pictures and illustrations, talking, in his way, about them and asking about them, usually by naming them, also in his own way. His mother has a large china doll, over a foot tall, one she must have saved up from her own girlhood days. With this he plays some, making a good deal of fuss and ado over it. His playthings he does not use so very much at present, excepting empty thread spools. Thanks to the generously sloping floors in our apartment rooms, he spends much time rolling the spools up-grade and then watching them return to him. He has developed considerable skill in rolling them straight and far. On his Kiddie Kar he is just beginning to propel himself a little, but still prefers being pushed; he can guide it readily and surely now. He needs very badly a marble-roller of some sort, and also a sand box in which to play. Neither has he been getting out into the sunlight as much as is desirable. No one has the time to spend with him out-of-doors. He does go along into the garden plot where he runs about while someone works. He is ever ready to go out-of-doors, and quite some time is necessary before he is ready to come in willingly. He is an interesting addition to our home, no question about that.

I receive a goodly measure of inspiration and enjoyment from my amateurish efforts to teach a course in Paul and His Epistles. For the daily class lectures and discussions I am working carefully through and outlining David Smith's "The Life and Letters of St. Paul." For concise and vigorous statement, for perspicacious organization and presentation of material, for complete but definite documentation, I cannot recall having ever used any book the equal of this one. It is a perennial delight to work through its solid, meaty pages. He is plenty dogmatic in his assertions on disputed or on partly imaginative features of the study. But no serious harm is done.

Independence Day, 1934 No summer school classes met today. Paul Bender and I left early this morning, went out in the country to the farm of Sylvanus Yoder and picked about one and a half crates of dark-colored sweet cherries. This afternoon we went to take part in the tail end of the Sunday school picnic. This annual affair was held this year in Miller's park about ten miles west of Goshen. So the day has about passed. The work of the summer school classes is plenty strenuous for my taste and I will be glad when it comes to an end. I should have a complete change for the month's time between sessions for recuperation.

Rain is badly needed here now. The garden, which has been providing us with some food for several weeks, needs more moisture before it will give much more. It is a real help to be able to gather things to eat from the garden instead of paying cash at the store for vegetables, etc.

Last Sunday evening Amasa Kauffman, in accordance with previous arrangements, came in and took me out to the Forks Mennonite Church, in the direction of Middlebury, where I had the privilege of the entire young people's meeting hour for an address on the general topic of Peace. This was the universal topic of the evening in our church young people's meetings. I delivered myself of a somewhat rambling discussion on the historical attitudes of the Christian Church on nonresistance and peace, together with a similar kind of discussion on several phases of the practice of nonresistance. And what is more, I am invited to give the same discussion at the Clinton Frame Church, several miles east of Goshen on this coming Sunday evening. This happens because our close neighbor, Samuel Yoder, is the leader for the evening, and since he is expected to arrange his own program, he has solved his problem in that direction by inviting me to give my address again.

Have finished reading Deissmann's big volume, all excepting the appendices. It is a thrilling theme to me. It opens up a wide vista of possibilities in New Testament study. I am constantly more and more firmly convinced that such an approach to N. T. study is fundamental for any really intelligent understanding of the N. T. literature. Deissmann's chief contentions in conclusion are that the N. T. Epistles of Paul are not really literary epistles at all, but were purely personal letters, never meant by the writer as anything more, and they owe their status as literature entirely to the fact that they were preserved and finally included in the Canon of N. T. writings. Likewise the other books included in the N. T. now were popular writings, written in the popular medium of expression and the everyday concepts of the lowest class of society. I think he pretty well establishes his main contentions, by citing many parallels of expression, vocabulary, etc., from inscriptions and papyri. What we have in the N. T. then are not finished and artistic literary productions, but documents of intense human and personal interest. It is an important distinction, I feel. Even Paul's so-called doctrinal Epistles are not reasoned and logical dissertations written as authoritative documents for publication. Whatever theory of inspiration one formulates to explain the nature of the N. T. Scriptures must take account of these considerations, it seems to me. And it is inconceivable to me that a man with as vigorous an intellect and as warm and sensitive a soul as Paul had would not in the course of fifteen years of active pioneering for a new cause change his ideas and thinking on some matters. I surmise that such changes are to be found in Paul's Epistles. Not so many months ago I rather diffidently put to Professor Enss a question to this effect, whether there is any serious evidence that Paul changed his mind or way of thinking on any important matter during the course of the period while his Epistles were being written. His answer was dogmatic and unequivocal and unhesitating. He declared there was no shred of evidence that Paul changed his mind on any fundamental matter between the time of writing say First Thessalonians and Second Timothy, particularly not on the doctrine of the second coming of Christ. My question was for information and I was not in any position to argue the matter then, nor am I now, for that matter perhaps. After his dogmatic answer, he added some very significant words to the following general effect: He remarked in a confidential tone, that I should just consider what such an idea of progress in Paul's thought, if it were true, would do to the doctrine of the inspiration of the Bible. I was rather singularly struck by the statement at the moment he said it, and no little amazed as I reflected upon it afterwards. I had supposed that a professor of philosophy and logic would have rather argued that one must study the Scriptures for all the facts about them and then formulate a theory of inspiration, rather than the reverse, as his answer implied.

July 12, 1934 Today I have an almost unexpected holiday. To "keep up a regular custom" the summer school folks went on an all day outing; classes were all dismissed, and I am free to do as I choose. I have taken part in several outings recently; on the fifth of July, a week ago today, I had an afternoon outing all my own when I went out to the farm of Sylvanus Yoder and picked nearly a crate and a half of small dark sweet cherries. Half a crate were for Mrs. Siddie Oyer. Again on last Tuesday evening, upon the kind invitation of Mr. and Mrs. Glen Hershberger, a crowd of us went to Lake Wawasee, twenty miles or so southeast for a picnic supper and short outing. Others in the company were Mr. and Mrs. S. M. King, Mr. and Mrs. Paul Bender and Ruth Bender, Mr. and Mrs. Harry Brunk and two children of Harrisonburg, Virginia, and Orden Miller. We went at six o'clock or past and did not get back home until ten or past, the latter much to Virgil's discomfort and displeasure. Had a very brief boat ride at dusk.

Today the crowd hired a bus and went to the Sand Dunes northwest from here. I had no desire to go so soon again, and the expense of one dollar for transportation is too much for me. I begrudge somewhat the loss of two perfectly good German recitations from that course. These holidays make a severe indentation on a double course like the

German, and I had planned to teach these folks all the German reading skill and grammatical knowledge they can possibly absorb in the time of nine weeks. They are doing very well. Lois Winey and Orden Miller are regular full-fledged members of the class. S. M. King is also registered, but not being interested in credit for the course, he does what work he has time for. W. H. Smith generally comes in for the second period each day as an auditor. Both the latter wish to get a reading knowledge of the language for use as sometime candidates for Ph. D. degrees.

Also had an invitation from H. S. Bender to accompany him and Dr. Hertzler to Chicago University and attend sessions of a Conference of Administrative Officials held there yesterday and today. I was mildly interested, but not enough so to miss yesterday's classes and bear the expenses of perhaps five dollars. I have a sort of an aversion to this idea of gadding about so much. It is better for me to "stay put" and conserve strength and finances.

July 29, 1934 I see that more than two weeks have passed by since I wrote any notes here. The reasons for this prolonged silence are several. For one thing from the 20th to 25th it was extremely hot and altogether uncomfortable, with the result that I, at least, did not one extra thing during these days other than what had to be done in regular routine. All-time records for high temperatures were shattered in this section of the country, and also in many other places of the Central West. On three or four consecutive days the official mercury readings here ranged from 105 to 109 degrees Fahrenheit. Reports were that at places in Kansas the official readings were as high as 115 and 117 degrees and dry! No rain has fallen here for just about three weeks. Grass and small crops are badly dried up. Our garden is not producing much food just now. We have good service in the college apartments this summer. Reason is that Mr. Gerber, the head janitor for campus and grounds, who was married early in June, is himself domiciled in an apartment and he personally keeps hot water on tap all the time, sprinkles lawn and keeps the grounds trimmed. Besides the terrific heat, I have myself been somewhat indisposed this last week with one of my periodic afflictions, a head cold or congestion.

And yet another reason for not doing anything extra during the past week was the extra German recitations I had with my class. Lois Winey, who lives far off in Colorado, wished to leave one week before the close of the summer session. And so our course, which was already a double course was redoubled this past week. My work in the Pauline course will be about closed up by Tuesday of this week, there being left the making of reviews and summaries, receiving papers and giving examinations. So with the gradual easing up of routine work, I will be having more of leisure for personal tasks.

Boy Virgil has been feverish and indisposed this past week, seemingly suffering from getting more teeth. I truly hope that the difficulty and distress he experienced this past year in receiving his teeth are indicative of their good sound lasting qualities, and that he will not have the grief and woe with his second set which his daddy has had. He still has a few back molars to push through. His mother has good teeth and I hope he inherits from her at least a good foundation for his.

My sister Ida of Iowa City visited with us a few days at the end of week before last. She graduated from University of Iowa in June and is also looking for regular employment of some sort.

A Hebrew Christian, missionary-to-be to the Jews of the Argentine in South America, spoke here today, both at the regular preaching hour this morning and again this afternoon at vesper hour. These converted Jews are always an inspiration as speakers and their enthusiasm for Christianity seems more vital than that of the average ministers.

August 4, 1934 Writing this date reminds me that fourteen years ago this day was our wedding day at Springs, Pennsylvania. We were married about noon, as I can now recall, and towards evening of the same day we left Meyersdale by train for Washington, D.C., where we spent the first few days of our honeymoon.

The drouth here is chronic now, and to all appearances at present, it is permanent. A few drops of rain fell the other evening, but not enough to even arouse serious expectations that we would have a rain. On this past Wednesday, Paul Benders took us with them in the afternoon on a trip to the Sand Dunes along Lake Michigan. It is perhaps seventy-five or eighty miles to the nearest point on Lake Michigan from here. It was the first time we had seen the Dunes which folks speak of around here. I had seen dunes along railroad and highway between Michigan City and Gary. The place where we were is a rather popular beach where folks go bathing and sunning themselves. We had a pleasant bit of diversion from the trip. We had on our part made no preparation for going in the water, although Paul had bought a bathing suit for Virgil and so he had his first experience playing in the beach sand and water. We built a small fire of wood and ate supper near the beach. The evening sunset on the waters of the lake was a beautiful sight.

Personally I am not especially enthusiastic about recreation on beaches, especially so since I have had a little experience in the mountains. If I could have my spontaneous choice between the two, I should not hesitate to choose the mountains just about every time. The higher altitude, the more rugged and individualistic aspects of Nature, the more isolated nature of mountain fastnesses appeal infinitely more to me. The rocks, the smell of fir and other trees, the flowers and birds are ever so much more elevating and inspiring to look upon than a sandy beach littered with cigarette stubs and other odds and ends cast off by humans. Even the rank and file of bathers with their indiscriminate physical exposures are not any particular aesthetic inspiration. Even the partial undress of bathers, or rather the contemplation of them, with a little exercise of the imagination is enough to convince me that nudism, as it is talked of nowadays, is not a matter of morals at all, but is one of aesthetics.

One of the objectives of our trip on Wednesday on Benders' part was to get a quantity of the fine, clean sand from the dunes for a sand box for Virgil to play in at home. Probably because of our own tardiness they have proceeded to make him an out-of-doors playpen, having borrowed some wire fencing from someone. They also secured a flat sheetiron tank for water and cleaned up another one, which was around the place, for a sand box. The pen is located east of the apartment house pretty close to the road. Now with the sand he is well fixed to play outdoors in the sun and get a tan coat on his body. But he does not care to play alone it seems. He wants someone to help him, and I doubt if he will soon be content to stay in his pen by himself.

On Thursday of this week we had callers with us over dinner from Wellman, Iowa. They were my cousin, Mahlon S. Yoder, wife and son, and a brother of Mrs. Yoder's. They are on a visiting trip in Indiana and Michigan.

Canning applesauce is the work of these days for Mrs. Yoder. We have been able to get several batches of summer apples. Samuel Yoder brought in from his father's farm over a bushel the other week, for which we paid a dollar. One day this week, P. Bender and Oswin Gerber went to search for apples and invited me to go along. We accidentally found west of Goshen a place where we could pick up apples that had fallen from the trees for twenty cents a bushel. I got one bushel.

August 9, 1934 Hot and sultry weather is the program still, meteorologically speaking. A few dribblets of rain fell during the past days — very dry rains they were. Our tomato vines are looking fine and barring accidents we will have considerable tomatoes for some time to come. I soaked up the ground between and around the rows for the second time on last Saturday afternoon. The eggplant too is "hanging on" now, and we have taken off a few for use already. Time is here by the calendar for planting fall garden, and I expect to sow a few small patches with endive, lettuce, turnips etc. And if it continues dry I mean to water enough to start things growing; it will surely become cooler later, and there is always some possibility that it will also become moister again.

Summer School closed yesterday with a Convocation. The address was given by Dr. Samuel Zwemer, a professor from Princeton Theological Seminary. The pressure is now off and I feel a sense of relief, even though I have a string of small tasks outlined with which to occupy my leisure time. I must do some physical exercising, possibly by strolling and hiking. I have never tried hiking across country in this section, so do not know if it will be possible to find enough open spaces to really stretch one's legs in. In Kansas hiking across country or along creeks was abundantly possible, though I never did a great deal of it. Here people live everywhere so that it seems hardly possible to find a place to walk without bumping into someone's habitation or running head-on into a "No Trespassing" sign. I think that the land along all rivers for a mile back, at least on one side, should be turned into public parks and playgrounds. The land should be planted with forests and marked off by trails and roads with public cabins for overnight lodging for hikers. Instead of putting all the federal and state funds into roads for automobiles, of which there are more than are for the economic health of the country, some facilities should also be provided for those who prefer to take recreation on their own legs instead of riding forever on rubber and burning petrol.

August 12, 1934 Several showers of rain have fallen within the past several days here so that the top soil is a bit moist. I put in the ground some small seeds yesterday in the fond hope they will yield us some things to eat before frost comes.

It is becoming more and more evident that large sections of the country are stricken by a drouth of major and calamitous proportions. The corn crop will be the smallest of any in thirty years and more. Cattle on the western plains are succumbing to the want of water and feed now, and it is too late in the season to expect that rains could still produce forage for over the winter. Even in this section of the country, farmers are speaking of the problem of securing enough feed for livestock over the winter. Iowa in many parts will have a complete failure of its corn crop. The so-called surplus of farm products promises to give place to a shortage almost over night. The federal AAA is beginning to back down from its program at least for 1935, although Secretary Wallace insists it must be in swing again in the year after. Business in recent months seems to have been on the slump again, and according to a recent press notice, the latest issue of government bonds failed to sell at par value, all of them. This is claimed to be a new and ominous experience. And the opponents of Roosevelt's New Deal, whether political or otherwise, are predicting direful things to happen when once the U.S. Government's credit begins to fail. The lavish spending program of the federal government, further accentuated by the necessity for drouth relief, will be a severe test of the government's credit and will probably prove whether the theory that spending money produces prosperity, and vice versa, is true or false. Fairly sane opinion at present is that the U.S. Government is headed for further inflation of currency, and the fear of such a thing seems to act as a brake on capitalistic business. Once the government can no longer sell its bonds for funds to increase its mounting debts, it may be forced to the business of printing paper money in order to pay its debts, or to some less directly unethical procedure that will accomplish the same end and still be in substance the same process. As I am myself in the debtor class, I am not worried about inflation, although I realize that this is a selfish attitude. At any rate I can't do anything about matters by worrying, so what's the use?

There are constant reminders, it seems, coming to my mind that I am passing into middle age and do not any longer belong to the group of the young people. For the past ten years or more wife and I had no trouble in counting ourselves young folks, partly because we married late and partly because we had no children. Now this last has changed — and no regrets here! Most young people about me, college students, were born either during or since the Great War, an event which is beginning to belong to an earlier generation, and which was an experience of my own early manhood. So likewise numerous other reminders are constantly impressed upon me. I have no particular regrets, excepting perhaps that I have been so slow in getting myself established, and feel I am not as fully settled in some ways as a man of forty years should be. At the same time I want to remain young in spirit and outlook; I want to be a learner and a student all my days. I matured early physically, but late emotionally, spiritually, and in thought life, which last I hope is a token of the long delay of mental and spiritual petrifaction! Since financial stability is such an uncertain quantity in these days, perhaps I have missed less in that direction than I think.

Twenty years ago this summer I reached my legal majority and began to make and work out plans for myself. It was at about the same moment that the Great War started. The passing years have brought me many rich experiences and opportunities, as I well realize. I have made many blunders along the way, but am aware also that God has many times guided me, overruled mistakes for the better, saved me from serious difficulty, and given me many grounds for acknowledging Him and bespeaking His praises. The next ten years were wonderful years in the way of opportunity and experience for me. Making my way through academy and through college, earliest teaching experience and beginning of my university study – it all seems now in retrospect a blessed period. The unpleasant features of the moment tend to fade out of memory's outline, leaving the good and the happy features standing out the more conspicuously and permanently. In looking back now from the standpoint of a wider experience and broader knowledge, one sees clearly enough how one could have done better by the opportunities that came along, but it was a part of real living anyway, and as such it was on the whole a happy experience.

The ten years since 1924 have not been uneventful either. It is ten years this month that I received my Master of Arts degree from the State University of Iowa at Iowa City. It seems scarcely half that long as I now look back – just another reminder that I am getting older. These years have brought a number of reverses and disappointments, just how serious or how trivial they were, judgment on this point must wait until they shall have receded into memory's background farther. Health has been a problem with its difficulties. Finances have caused some concern and uneasiness. There has also been advance for me in study, in my thinking, and in opportunity for serving and working. Times and their conditions are strenuous to be sure, but it is worth while being alive just to have a small part in such experiences. I am impressed that the calamity howlers and the prophets of gloom constitute a reaction which reveals how thoroughly ingrained was the worship of the American deity, Success, already when the depression came. I fear that even much of the religious talk one hears reflects the same thing. If preachers would call men to repentance and to faith in God, just so that folks can again get more money and be more comfortable, then they too are hypocrites and false prophets. We need a faith and a mental set which accepts adversity as a boon and blessing from God.

August 15, 1934 This is a welcome day of rain. For a change from many cloudless days, the gloom and the overcast skies are a welcome variation. It began before daybreak this morning and is still raining some. But skies are clearing to the west and the north now.

Cleaning operations are now on about the college buildings. The women of the local church are today joining hands in cleaning the two dormitories. Some boys, who are laying up credit against their bills due the college during the coming winter, are mopping floors and cleaning furniture in the Science Hall now. The college is working on the wise policy of having all possible work on the campus done by students so as to pay out as little cash as possible, excepting for materials and to the teachers. And the latter surely need all the cash they can get, at least so they think. A printer is planning to establish his small printing plant in the basement of Science Hall and he will employ all student labor besides himself, so again lessening the cash outflow from the business office, for the student labor will be exchanged for the college's printing jobs of all kinds. These policies and also the money from federal funds for needy students should help the college budget somewhat for the next year.

August 24, 1934 How the days and the weeks do slip past! Less than three weeks from now we shall be entering upon the strenuous labors of another school year. Have spent some days now, not entire days, in clearing off my desk here in the office, organizing my books and other material. Made a simple bookcase with twenty feet of shelving as a place to store my growing stock of books, growing it seems in spite of hard times. Silas Hertzler has moved all his belongings from this office to another place, and the prospect is that I shall have I. E. Burkhart as a pedagogical bedfellow pretty soon. He and his family are due to arrive today, according to reports. Have also made myself a small cabinet with seven shelves for papers, folders, etc., a place to keep such things regularly instead of stacking them to right and to left on my desk. Some drawers of my desk still remain to be cleaned out and organized. Spent parts of the past two days in attendance at the Indiana-Michigan Mennonite Sunday School Conference held at the Forks Church northeast of here. Rode with Paul Bender each day. Read a thirty-minute speech on Wednesday afternoon.

Last Sunday the Sunday school class here which Mrs. Yoder attends went out to Goshen City Park for picnic dinner, they with their families, all of whom together made a rather large crowd of folks. The picnic craze is quite pronounced around here; every organization, formal and informal, seemingly must have its picnic outing every so often. I pass up such as I can. We did go for the afternoon on July 4th, when the entire Sunday school had its outing.

Temperatures have been pleasant lately, even a bit cool today. Some predict an early autumn and a hard winter, but who can tell? Erratic weather conditions come and go in waves, it seems, and a very hot summer could easily enough be followed by a cold winter. I have no fuel bill to worry about, personally. I fear that living in an apartment house will quite spoil me, for I do appreciate being free from furnace operating, snow shovelling, grass cutting, and so on. It's like living in a hotel for the man of the house, but not for the housekeeper.

August 31, 1934 This is the last of August, for tomorrow will be the first of September. With the above statement a witty public speaker, I once heard, ended an anecdote about a dog named August that had the misfortune to be kicked by a mule.

Cool weather, such as to make one think of autumn, has been here for several days. Almost uncomfortably cool in the mornings. But the sun shines brightly every day, so making the days pleasant and agreeable. Have been disposing of sundry odd jobs this week. In another ten days activities will have markedly increased about the college campus.

My leisure reading has been quite desultory for I determined to have a vacation, so instead of driving myself to cover any stipulated amount of reading I have made my program depend altogether on impulse, whim, fancy, or what you like. I did read a small book by A. Hornack on "Bible Reading in the Early Church," a volume which contains much useful information and gives some suggestive ideas. It is scholarly and convincing. One purpose of the writer is to combat the Roman Catholic idea that Bible reading was always controlled and regulated at a minimum by the official church organization. The fact is that the Scriptures, from the time the early Christian writings were first recognized as such, were freely circulated and their private reading and study were constantly encouraged by the Church Fathers. Incidentally the point is also developed that Christianity in this respect stood in marked contrast to the popular mystery religions of that period. Have nearly finished a book by Deissmann, "The New Testament in the Light of Modern Research," a series of lectures given about 1929 at Oberlin College. It is a popular presentation of the main conclusions of Deissmann's large book, "Light from the Ancient East," which I read a few weeks ago. I am impressed with this man's reverent method and attitude, almost spiritual I would say, and yet scholarly and objective in a remarkable way. He is not iconoclastic and destructive in his attitude, which gives me respect for and confidence in his conclusions. He seems to me to dispose effectively, both by special mention of it and by the general method of procedure, of every theory of divine inspiration for the New Testament that involves any trace of mechanical or involuntary activity on the writer's part. Mechanical inspiration seems to me to degrade the whole process of written revelation, God as the author, the writers and the result. Whatever theory of inspiration one formulates must be derived from a study of the N. T. itself and it is quite unscholarly and irrational to formulate a theory of inspiration first of all and then proceed to interpret the Book in accordance with the theory. Such a method is legitimate enough, provided the theory in question is held and applied as a theory and not as a dogma. The mechanically verbal inspirationists make the same blunder as the dogmatic advocates of biological evolution; they postulate a theory for an axiomatic assumption. The statement of Paul that "Every scripture is God-breathed" states a general principle, and is not in itself a warrant for any particular theory of detailed method and result of the inspiration. Perhaps I am unorthodox in thinking such things, but I do not believe I am.

An article in the Atlantic Monthly for September starts off with a sentence about to this effect: Strong convictions are generally based on ignorance. This is another of those paradoxical sayings that has in it an element of truth. The prevailing scientific attitude of our time does unsettle many of one's earlier convictions; more of one's ideas, notions, opinions, if not also of one's beliefs, become more tentative, more relative. I sometimes for a moment feel inclined to envy some simple-minded folk their strength of convictions, their dogmatic sureness and certainty in what they think. But when I reflect further that the particular ideas and convictions which they are so sure of are in fact based upon ignorance, then I no longer envy them. I have an experience analogous to that of the Psalmist who was tempted to envy the prosperity of the wicked, until he came to see their situation in true perspective, when he changed his mind. Certainty of belief and opinion on all points is a very comfortable feeling to have.

This writer in the Atlantic is very sensible in his discussion. His topic is "Science and the Layman." The scientific method so far has been only destructive, outside of the very strictly scientific fields. The layman has placed the authority of science and of whatever claims to be scientific in the room of older religious, moral and social author- ities. In general the layman's attitude toward his newer authority is that of the same uncritical credulity which he had toward the older authorities. One reason for the present chaos in religious and philo- sophic thought is because the limitations of science have so far never been adequately and emphatically defined. There are millions who at every mention of "science" or "scientific" promptly perform a mental genuflection, perhaps even bow to the earth in awesome obeisance.

A good illustration of what this writer speaks about is found in an article in Harpers for September, entitled if I recall correctly, "Dark Days," or "Dark Years," perhaps. Anyway, the writer here is appar- ently one of those credulous laymen who are charmed by the word science, who very confidently and in a doctrinaire fashion class them- selves among the educated people of intelligence who can no longer condescend to have anything to do with Christian theology and the older sort of religious authority. Yet the entire content of his essay is a loud and bitter wail that life for the writer and his kind is mean- ingless and purposeless. It is against this fact that he rebels and re- volts with all his might. It is a truly pitiful plight for a human being of thirty-five years to be in. Seems to me such folks should be wise enough not to throw away an old compass before they have a new and better one.

September 4, 1934 Cloudy days, some rain, cool air are upon us now. Opening of school is only one week in the future. Most of my vacation jobs are now out of the way. I did not get all my writing done, but still a good deal of it.

September 6, 1934 Teaching program and plans as affecting myself are just now "up in the air," so to speak, for the coming year. The pre- liminary prospects for the Elkhart branch are poor; no second year work will be given there and perhaps no beginning work, although all details will not be decided until on registration day next Wednesday.

The one-year extension on my loan of a thousand dollars on the property at Hesston is again expired and still I have no means at hand for either paying it off or reducing it. The loan company in Newton agrees to make a further three-year extension now on conditions that are not unreasonable. Not having anything else I can do now, I have written them that it is OK with me. They want a flat fee of $25 for their services in the matter. The net income from the house this past year in rent has been $56 according to the statement I have from the Loan Company. Mr. Jake Baer of Hesston who acted as agent for the property regularly kept 20% of the amount he took in as his own com- mission. It is too much. Now after writing to him a second time and rather rigorously at that, I expect I am rid of him. At almost the last moment before leaving Kansas a year ago I turned it over to Baer, not knowing just what else to do, since he was about the only one engaged in such a business there. He had in the house a succession of four or five families of oil workers, as a rule not a most desirable sort of tenants. In fact Baer reported to me hardly a scratch as to when the house was rented and to whom and for how much; all this I have had to find out from other sources. Joe N. Weaver last negotiated for the occupancy of the house, but have not heard whether he has been able to get the other folks who are in it to vacate or not. If oil development continues in the vicinity of Hesston, property values may again begin to look upward. By another three years it may be possible to sell the place, let's hope.

September 19, 1934 Busy days, sundry handicaps and discomforts, usual uncertainty about details of schedule, courses, etc. First about the handicaps, two that I had not anticipated as an accompaniment to the start of what promises to be a strenuous year's work: on September 7 Dr. Carpenter, dentist, extracted three front teeth from my lower jaw and made corresponding additions to the denture I have been wearing to eat with for now seven years. Result: my mouth has been sore, cannot very well appear in public without my denture in its place, and cannot very well eat anything solid as yet. As a second handicap I have entertained a very nasty head cold since last Friday night. On Saturday morning during one class I simply had to stop, dismiss the class and apologize for my unseemly indisposition. Spent the afternoon and much of Sunday in bed. Got out in time to be solo speaker at Young People's Meeting program that evening. Have met classes and attended to other duties since but with little enthusiasm and comfort.

The usual upheaval and floundering about that attends the opening of school is all about us again. One week ago this evening at the end of the second day of registration the enrollment stood at 227; it has since risen to about 245. Freshmen number 104, according to last reports I had, a record-breaking entering class, I believe. The class recitation schedule is by now showing signs of settling down and one can begin to plan a program of work and study. My courses are seven in number totaling 19 class hours every week, which will be plenty to keep me going, I am sure. Besides this work regularly, I am appointed as chief publicity promotor for the college in local periodicals, a new venture for me but one which I believe I shall like fairly well. Have also been shunted into the position of chairman of the committee that is responsible for the Sunday evening meetings at the college. Then the Extensive College Survey that has been planned and inaugurated recently gives me some work: secretary of the Survey Commission as a whole, Chairman of the Library Survey Committee, and member of only four other sub-committees – and that is all – for the Survey.

October 7, 1934 Days and weeks have been crowded so full that no notes have been written here for several weeks. My daily and weekly program is becoming routinized now, so that a measure of system and regularity is possible. But there are constantly extra matters which fill up the hours not preempted by routine work already. Last week and the early days of this past week I spent some time preparing the quarterly part of the Doctrinal Supplement to the Gospel Herald on Peace and Nonresistance. The manuscript went out on Wednesday evening. On Friday I received a postal card message from Editor Dan Kauffman acknowledging receipt of material and enthusiastically commenting to the effect that this is the best instalment I have sent in yet, an encouraging bit of information, although Kauffman's tastes on quality of such material do not always correspond with my own. He likes to hear such writings "ring true," as his phrase has it, evidently depending as much on his instinctive taste in the matter as on the thought and logic of the material itself.

The July issue of our Mennonite Quarterly Review is not published yet, even though it is the time when the October issue should be in press. The latter part of August Editor H. S. Bender spent in the hospital recovering from an appendectomy, that time which he had planned to spend in preparing the manuscript for the July issue. Then with the opening of school he found no time at all for attending to it. A few weeks ago he conferred with the associate editors; it was agreed that under the circumstances we would combine the July and October issues into one number. When inquiry was made as to the postal regulations on this point, we learned that if no issue is mailed during one quarter, the mailing permit for the periodical is lost and the cost for recovering such a permit is an even one hundred dollars. This fact made us reconsider immediately, and when the postmaster at Scottdale agreed to give us two weeks of grace on the July mailing, the editors at once got busy and prepared manuscript copy for the number which was to be mailed to Scottdale on Friday evening. The Publishing House there agreed to rush the printing and mailing through posthaste and have the issue in the mails by next Saturday. I spent a number of hours in recent days on that project. The editorial work on the Review is chiefly the burden of Bender, who is the editor-in-chief, and when he is accidentally incapacitated no progress can be made; Professor John Umble and I are associate editors, the only ones now on the premises. We are always consulted for suggestions and advice, but are not in a position to supply much initiative for the editorial work.

I find my regular class work quite heavy. The class in Intermediate German numbers 37 now, and I must have some written work daily to satisfy myself that they all keep working; that means thirty-seven papers to read three times a week. Then planning the recitations requires some time and ingenuity, since it is a large group to handle – the largest I have ever had in all my teaching experience. I feel I shall enjoy the work with the class, and have received some little encouragement for feeling so from an indirect source. Miss Shenk, the French instructor, who gets into intimate personal contact with a good many students, reported to me voluntarily that one young fellow from the last year's elementary German class remarked that "all the German he knew he is learning this year." Mrs. Enss, as about everyone felt, did not put very much pressure on students to make all the progress they could in learning. She aimed chiefly at being interesting in class and having everyone feel happy and comfortable. She succeeded in that direction, evidently, but her pupils did not make the progress which college students should in a beginning language course. This of course was hardly fair to the students.

The Sunday school class to which I count myself has for this year elected S. C. Yoder as their teacher and myself as assistant to him. This is the same position to which I was elected a year ago, but as it turned out I had to teach the class most of the year. Whether the same thing is to be true this coming year remains to be seen.

October 12, 1934 Gorgeous and perfectly ideal days have been here this week, warmish, sunny, Indian-summer like. And the trees simply glorious with their many-colored coats of brown, yellow, red, russet, all mingling together as one's eye scans over them from some upper story window. No killing frost has yet stopped vegetation from growing, and few leaves are falling so far. On Wednesday of this week I wanted to walk in the woods for recreation and rest. From the dam I followed the Elkhart River downstream to the Plymouth Road bridge and from there tramped along the race to the business section of town. It is a fine stroll along the river north, a fairly good path much of the way. At times there is none, but one can get over the fence and walk along in someone's pasture field at such places. One sees some beautiful quiet woodland scenes along the river, particularly just now when leaves and grasses are pleasing with their many hues and shades of coloring.

Preaching services at the college each evening this week, with A. J. Metzler of Pennsylvania as speaker. Very interesting and impressive meetings are held, which will have a wholesome effect upon campus and school life, I judge.

October 14, 1934 Our boy at home is growing out of baby-hood steadily and surely. He is becoming more and more interesting every day. Of late with the pleasant sunshiny weather he has been out-of-doors a good many hours every day. He has Professor Miller's boys to play with, and his companionship with them has helped him develop in several ways. He has lost much of the extreme shyness which he displayed during the summer, and his speech progress has been very marked. He readily imitates words he hears and promptly attempts a new word or expression when one uses it in speaking to him. Earlier he was very timid about attempting new words, and would do so only unconsciously when interested in something else. Our reading stories and rhymes to him has also helped his speech habits, as in his spontaneous play he will much of the time repeat to himself phrases and words suggested to him by what he may be doing at the moment.

October 15, 1934 Duties are not so pressing today, so I am setting down a few more notes about Virgil. He always sleeps several hours of afternoons, goes to bed promptly at 8:00 or 8:15 in the evening. In the morning he wakes up before seven and insists upon getting up at once. Whenever I am about the house he is ever thinking up and suggesting some form of activity in which I am to help him. He has a basket full of spools, empty thread spools, and he generally suggests "'pin 'pools now." Last Easter time his mother dyed them various colors, and so they are pleasing to play with. He can make them spin readily by giving one end an impulse with forefinger, bearing down upon it until it escapes and spins rapidly, partly upraised on one end. With balls, of which he has three of varied sizes, we often play. He can throw them readily. He is right-handed, readily using that hand, although he still throws some with left hand. We coached him somewhat, earlier, but tried not to be insistent that he use his right hand against his impulse and instinct. He appears to have ability to adapt himself to manipulative skills, for he is quite handy with hands and muscles generally.

October 20, 1934 Cloudy, rainy, coolish weather is here today. Brought from the garden on Thursday more than two bushels of green and semi-green tomatoes which I today spread out on the floor near the attic window of the apartment house. We hope these will keep until Thanksgiving for daily use.

I fill the position of Chief Substitutor around this place. I rarely succeed in getting myself chosen or elected to a side line position, but whenever a substitution is to be made, my services are in keen demand. Not seldom this circumstance is due to the fact that I always am at home. Having no car of my own, and also being without the desire to gad about from place to place, I get abundant opportunity to substitute for those who are afflicted with such desires. On Tuesday evening of this week I was asked to take charge of S. C. Yoder's Bible Study class, consisting of the college seniors and juniors. The discussion was on the investment of talents, being the first chapter of a textbook the study groups are using entitled: "Investments of Life." Made a poor hit on that substitution. Tomorrow being Sunday, and President Yoder still being away from the city, I shall substitute as teacher of his Sunday school class again, and this is the third time out of four possibilities that I am substituting for him since he has been elected as the regular teacher by the class. Furthermore, over tomorrow morning many other leaders will be found elsewhere than here and I have the happy and unappreciated privilege of substituting for H. S. Bender as leader of the regular meeting of S. S. teachers which meets for three-fourths of an hour just before the session itself. The lesson is on "The Christian and Prayer," fortunately not the hardest possible kind of lesson on which to say at least some words, useful or useless as they may happen to be. Lastly, for next Sunday, October 28, I shall have the rare and wondrous(?) opportunity of substituting for Paul Bender in making a total of three speeches at a church near Elida, Ohio, as joint main speaker with S. C. Yoder. It gives me a sort of thrill to constantly do a lot of work for which other folks get all the official honor of position, rank and publicity. So for instance, Bender's name appears on the printed program for the meeting next Sunday, and his name is duly and officially announced for the position in a "field note" in the Gospel Herald of this week. It is a privilege to work without the limelight of publicity.

October 30, 1934 Last week in spite of a bad head cold which made working and even living disagreeable, I succeeded in giving six-weeks tests in two classes and wrote out two speeches of some thirty-two or thirty-three hundred words length. These I duly delivered at a church in Elida, Ohio, on Sunday afternoon and evening. My head is not very well cleared up even as yet. My state of general health is becoming a problem to me and I must sometime make up my mind to attack the problem systematically and scientifically. Since I matured early and somewhat precociously, it is possible that I may also wear out physically at an early age.

More about the trip on Sunday. I went with S. C. Yoder in his Terraplane Six and we had the entire machine for ourselves both going and coming. These new cars certainly travel easily and smoothly. Think of riding in comfort and ease a distance of one hundred and twenty miles, attend three religious services and return the same day! We left at daybreak and were home again before midnight. At noon we shared in a meal served cafeteria style in a basement near the church. Between afternoon and evening sessions we drove to Lima and inspected briefly the Mennonite Mission Church there. Then came back to the home of Preacher Andrew Brenneman for evening lunch.

I got through my addresses well enough to suit me. The audience listened respectfully, but I cannot say how much they were impressed by what I said. I read from manuscript each time. I still have not quite mastered the technique of reading from manuscript to my own satisfaction, but I feel I am learning steadily. I can do this easier and more effectively than to attempt to speak from notes. To my great surprise, and to S. C.'s as well, we were each given three dollars cash for our efforts upon the program. Additional money was given for the expense of the car. The first time I was ever paid directly for making a speech, so far as I can recall. I enjoyed the day very much, even though I was not in the best of condition physically.

November 4, 1934 Four-thirty o'clock and deep dusk already with a driving rain from the east. Fall weather is here in good earnest now. Hard freeze and a little snow a few days ago underlined this fact for us effectively. Several small trees in the front part of our college campus had held all their leaves until yesterday when these dropped all day long like snowflakes to the ground. Today they stand bare and desolate as the rest that had shed theirs earlier.

Another strenuous week is past. My extra-routine work this time was the repainting of chairs and table in our dining room-kitchen. The decoration had held out well, for it was the spring of 1929 that I first painted them. This decorative work I did on three evenings after supper. There is a bit of trimming left for this evening. Tomorrow (following annual custom) all campus students are entertained for dinner in the homes of the local community. This fact suddenly precipitated what had been a resolution of a year's standing, to wit, to repaint our kitchen set. The chairs were badly rubbed and cracked, partly from moving last year, so much so that we cared not to entertain company for a meal. Last evening the first number of the college Lecture Course was given at the high school auditorium, under the joint sponsoring of the College Lecture Board and the high school. Mrs. Yoder went along with Paul Benders, while I stayed at home with Virgil and my work of painting. The program was rendered by a Russian Chorus; Stravianski's, I believe, was the name.

On Friday morning I conducted the exercises in college chapel. Remarked briefly and vaguely on the matter of leisure time and its use and abuse. Read a brief essay on Wisdom from Ecclesiasticus, from Moulton's "Modern Reader's Bible". C. L. Graber, business manager of the college, had a nervous collapse several weeks ago and seems to be slow in rallying from it again. The college administration is a rather weak set-up here. The President is more interested in teaching it seems than in prosecuting the executive duties of his office. Dean Bender has great energy and very considerable administrative ability, but is loaded up with too great and too wide a variety of duties of all kinds to be truly efficient in everything. His is a case, to my mind, of misplaced talent. He should be free to devote himself very largely to scholarship and research, for he has real ability along that line, as also in writing. Mr. Graber is live and active when he is normal, but he burns up his energy too rapidly while he is at it and then gives out. But he has done some very creditable things the past year, one must admit. Viewing the situation as a whole, I am impressed with the fact that the supply of truly seasoned and qualified leadership in our church group is after all very limited. Our denominational experience and traditions have not developed any reserve stock of institutional leadership, and a college as this is correspondingly handicapped.

November 5, 1934 Reflecting on the financial situation of the college tends to give me a depressed feeling usually. So I refuse to let my thoughts dwell very much upon the matter at all, at least not too seriously. As nearly as I know the situation it is this. The college has not much debt in its own name and right, and most of what there is consists of unpaid teachers' salaries, which are not considered as debt. But the Board of Education has an aggregate debt of eighty or ninety thousand dollars representing accumulated deficits from Goshen and Hesston over a period of years. The interest on this indebtedness is paid from income from invested endowment which the Board holds in trust for the two schools. This means that the schools have no effective endowment at present. Each year's budget must depend for income on fees paid by students and on donations from friends. That in itself would not be so very bad with a fairly good enrollment on hand. But for the Goshen teachers the situation is further complicated by the financing program for the two dormitories on the college campus. These are being paid for over a period of twenty years from the income derived from room rentals paid by the students. Normally the profit from dormitories would be additional income for the college operating budget. So in effect the teachers are, through cuts and unpaid allowances, financing both the indebtedness of the General Board and the two dormitories as well. All this is easy to think and talk about, but what can one do about it? No one cares to walk out right now, especially with no definite place to walk to. One thing Mr. Graber has done the past year is to make the first full payment on the dormitories since they were built three or four years ago. Theretofore the payments were simply not made for lack of cash. Another policy now in force is to pay in full all bills aside from salaries and let deficits fall on teachers, as well as the burden of waiting for the liquidation of student accounts and notes of each year. This situation makes a teacher's work here very definitely a faith venture, and as such it has its romantic and interesting phases. For the time being such a procedure is possible, but as a long time arrangement there are some features and details which have not been worked out, as for instance, assurance for support for possible widows and orphans and for retirement and old age.

Tomorrow is election day, and the political fireworks have been spectacular in some quarters of late. My own guess is that life will keep on going along in some fashion even after tomorrow. Whether Roosevelt will swing to right or to left will be interesting to watch. Current politics is a muddle of which I comprehend very little. An occasionally good diagnostic article in magazines is illuminating, but from the day by day grist dumped out by daily newspapers I get practically nothing at all of worth. Ballyhoo, rhetoric, and mud-slinging are not to my taste. For politics I have no taste either. I am so indifferent to the entire subject that I do not even appreciate my privileges as a citizen of casting just one more unintelligent vote into the hopper that already chokes with millions of stupid, ignorant, demagogic votes. What does the average citizen know about the intricate economic and political issues involved in even state elections, not to mention national elections where international affairs figure? The basic motive of the masses of voters is plainly selfish; they vote for what they believe, or imagine, or are persuaded will add to their own comfort, their own wealth, ease, convenience. How many even try to see what policies of government will be of greatest advantage to the country as a whole?

November 10, 1934 This afternoon I am loafing for there is nothing I must do at the moment, strange as that may seem. Very little time do I have at my disposal for free and unhindered browsing this semester. My personal advancement comes in line with my preparation for teaching certain classes. Especially the German course in Schiller is interesting and profitable. We have read "William Tell" very carefully and leisurely and are about to finish him. It has been a real pleasure to reread this masterly drama. We will read in class "Die Jungfrau von Orleans." The members of the class are required to read one other play outside of class; most of them will read "Maria Stuart," which will also be real outside reading for me due to the fact that I have not read it previously. I feel that I shall very much enjoy doing further study in German literature and philology. I regret the time it will take but even that will not be a serious disadvantage. I pray for one thing in this regard, to wit, that it may be possible for me to combine my German study with a trip and a brief sojourn in Europe. For it is my set purpose, if the way opens financially, to spend a winter at some university in Germany or Switzerland. Then further, if I can possibly make it, I shall be pleased to spend one summer in Italy and another in Greece, mostly travelling and visiting sites of classic interest, perhaps also studying a bit in the summer sessions of the American Schools in Rome and Athens. All this would make a very strenuous fifteen or sixteen months of living. The tentative suggestion from the college administration is that this period of absence for study should begin as soon as 1936. I would be pleased if it did, but I am very skeptical myself. It will have to be on sabbatical leave with half pay, for I must borrow no money for further study, for does not "life begin at forty," and I am now past the time for making debt and assuming unnecessary obligations. The nine hundred dollars income on that basis might keep my family in food and clothing and shelter for the fifteen months of my absence from them.

That suggests yet another difficulty, of being separated from Wife and Son for so long a time. The boy will be at an age when he will need a daddy rather badly perhaps. Besides to not see him and to enjoy his companionship will be very hard for me. Still another practical problem will be to have the cash on hand with which to support myself for such a length of time. I have little faith that salaries of last, this, and next year can be paid near enough in full so that I can have a surplus on hand for such uses. My own premonitory feelings are that it will not be as soon as 1936 that I can start on such an ambitious program of foreign adventure, much as I do wish I could.

The little reading I can do aside from necessary lesson preparation, and in addition to some magazine reading, is not very much. I skimmed through a very odd kind of book lately entitled "Christianity versus War." It is written, or better said, compiled by an elder in the Church of the Brethren. The last part of the book is what is of real value, for it gives the record of experiences of men of the Brethren Church in the military draft during the World War. The first two hundred pages is a very quaint and strange presentation of "testimony," or better, the forth-telling of a "prophecy," being an unorganized tirade against war, filled to choking with rhetorical bombast and exaggeration, yet entirely sincere and earnest withal.

November 11, 1934 Armistice Day, as it is known since 1918, when the truce in hostilities was signed. Significantly, the Sunday school lesson this morning was entitled "The Christian Citizen." I expounded in the class I taught the proposition that the Christian, the Spirit-led devoted Christian who obeys God in all things and above all else, is a nation's best citizen. I made this proposition with the understanding that such a super-citizen will not take part in his nation's wars, will not concern himself much with its politics. It still remains true, in my opinion, even with that understanding.

Our boy has now and for a month past had a pet aversion in the form of his bath. His dislike and dread of getting into the water is strange. Some time ago he became frightened while in the tub, and since he has a dreadful fear of getting into the tub at all. It seems that his mother once pulled up the stopper and let the water run out while he was still in the tub, and the gurgling noise that followed must have struck a fear spot in his emotional make-up somewhere. Ever since, the instant that "bath" is suggested for him he starts to scream and cry in a most distressed manner. It is really pitiful to see his reaction and how real his suffering is from this complex. He may be getting a little better in regard to it. He seems to know better, but cannot control his emotional reaction in spite of himself. Fear complexes of lesser seriousness he showed last summer in regard to water running from a rubber hose out-of-doors, and also in regard to putting on a new and unusual article of apparel, particularly an outdoor sun suit which the Benders made for him and first tried on him by a clever trick. But he overcame both these after some little coaxing.

These fear complexes of Virgil's bring back to my memory a few of my own which were very vividly impressed upon my childhood memory. One was the mortal fear I had of stepping over a crack of three inches or less width at the entrance of the threshing floor of our bank barn at home. In a bank barn such a floor is in the second story of the barn and large sliding doors close the opening. At the bottom these doors are kept in place by a groove, which in our barn was a crack of less than three inches width which was open below so that dirt in it would fall four or five feet down to the old ground level; that is, the artificial "bank" that formed the approach to the large driveway or threshing floor was not brought all the way up to the foundation wall of the barn, but stopped four feet or so farther back and the remainder of the approach was a sloping plank floor. The crack in question was between this plank approach and the main barn floor itself. Well, I was in mortal fear of stepping across this crack, and Father always had to lift me across. I can still remember how on Sunday mornings he would be in the barn greasing the axles of the family carriage preparatory to going to church, and I would come to the opening where he had pushed the sliding door back a few feet, and I would stop at the crack, cry and whimper until he would come and lift me across, so I could watch him at his work. I do not know how old I may have been, but would guess three or four years.

One other pet aversion of mine at this same early age was that of kneeling, or seeing my father kneel, when the congregation of worshippers knelt in church. I think I used to set up a howl, anyway I can still recall rather distinctly that he sat upright and did his praying in that posture out of deference to my own taste at the moment. One feels but little pride now in recalling such tastes and prejudices of early childhood. It is good that we can outgrow them, but possibly we have others equally silly and nonsensical at a later age; who can be sure?

November 25, 1934 I had a sleep of between two and three hours' length this afternoon. Estie attended the afternoon session of a local conjoint Sunday school meeting. I went to the evening session. Though it is ten o'lock, I do not feel sleepy at all. My general state of health is inefficient and unsatisfactory. I think frequently of the many more things I could get done, if it were not constantly necessary to hold back for extra rest, relaxation, and recuperation.

Thanksgiving Day. A mild day, clear this morning, but light clouds later. Homecoming festivities are in progress on the campus. Many visitors from near and far, from Iowa to Pennsylvania, at least. I attended morning worship led by President S. C. Yoder. We had our Thanksgiving dinner at home, in spite of the fact that members of faculty families were offered plates at the college dinner for one-half price. We could not very well both go, and neither one was disposed to go unattended by the other. The piece de résistance on our Thanksgiving board was wieners, of all things! We wanted something different and unusual, and I guess we had it. The traditional fowl for such occasions does not so much appeal to our tastes and imaginations.

Estie is going to the music program this evening, and I shall keep house with Virgil.

December 23, 1934 As we say, much water has passed under the bridge since last I wrote any notes. Extra work, affliction with sinus trouble, and such like reasons account for the long silence. No time to get into a frame of mind akin to leisure. First week in December I was away from home for a day and a half on an auto trip to Dayton, Ohio. Had an aggravated head affliction for several days after that, so that all told it took me during much of the second week to catch up with my work again.

Then there was a rush to get some of the committee work on the college survey completed before Christmas vacation. Two out of the eight committees, I believe, have about finished their preliminary work of fact-finding. The one for which I am responsible as chairman is one of these two, and I find some bit of satisfaction in having my part of this work so well out of the way and on the scheduled time. I have assignments on three other sub-committees, one of which is done, and the others are not so weighty.

My head affliction is still a major problem to me. Infected and diseased sinuses are very stubborn to deal with and to treat. Drops from Dr. Young in Goshen gave some help but no permanent relief. Two weeks it will be tomorrow, I went to the drug store and stocked up with heavy artillery for warring against my affliction. Received some welcome relief from drops, and after the passages were thus opened, I applied some jelly-like ointment which contains Eucalyptus in a petroleum base. This gave a real sensation of healing and relief. Whether it will give help in permanent recovery, is very doubtful. Also got a fifty-cent jar of mentholatum. What will yet be the upshot of my efforts I cannot guess. Dearly am I paying for my venturous desire to learn swimming last winter!

Second day after Christmas. One half of the vacation period is already past. Have made some progress on my program of activities as outlined in advance for my guidance in the use of vacation time. Read through Schiller's drama, "Maria Stuart." I love him as a poet and dramatist. He is human and interesting in his portrayal of character and plot. There is something charming in his writings. In class we read "Wilhelm Tell" first and are now going through "Die Jungfrau von Orleans." The class is interested in the plays. Tomorrow I shall read his poem entitled, "Das Lied von der Glocke."

Have written one book review on a book that was read before vacation began. Finished reading today Von Kirk's book on "Religion Renounces War." Plan also to make a review of this one. The first one was Coate's book, "The Conscription of Conscience." A third book I will begin at once is on "The Power of Non-Violence." These three books I received upon written request as review copies for the Mennonite Quarterly Review; the reviews are to appear in the January issue. The typescript copy for the January instalment on "Peace" in the Gospel Herald was prepared also before vacation. I worked especially hard to have the material ready for typing early, for the girl who does the typing for me would not be about again before January 3, the very time the copy must go forward to Scottdale. Unless I am badly interrupted from now on, I shall be fairly well up-to-date with my writing when school reopens one week from today.

Christmas Day we spent this year not in our own quarters entirely but in part in Paul Benders' apartment immediately above us. We ate our dinner there at about three o'clock in the afternoon. Other feasters were Ruth and Ralph Bender of Pennsylvania, cousin Orden Miller and

George Holderman, students. It was a white Christmas, not very cold. Has been colder since, even down to ten degrees below zero. We received again some eight or ten Christmas greeting cards in the mail, also received a few presents mostly from our nearest neighbors. We sent no greeting cards, following our regular custom of late years. Presents we gave none. I did get a red dump truck for Virgil to play with. He is very fond of it. He received a few other toys. Our protest against the senseless giving and giving of Christmas presents has lately been not to give any to speak of.

On Monday, the day before Christmas, we entertained at noonday dinner Melvin Gingerich and family from Iowa. They are visiting at Grabers' for a few days. Mr. Gingerich is actively interested in peace and pacifistic propaganda. He was a former student in some of my classes at Hesston in earlier years. They have two sons, one of nearly five years and a babe of five months.

I walked down to the business section today, partly on business and partly for physical exercise. It was pleasant to walk, wind from the south and not strong. Bought an electric clock, perhaps as a belated present for ourselves. It is not of the finish that my wife likes best and will exchange it for another one. We have been using since September 1933 Paul Benders' electric clock as our only timepiece. It is time we return it.

December 30, 1934 A clear day this has been, very pleasant after a succession of gloomy, murky days. We attended morning services. C. L. Graber preached. Orden Miller ate dinner with us and helped us sleep this afternoon. I went to the regular evening Young People's Meeting. The crowd was not large, as it hardly ever is at this place. Somehow it is a perennial problem to get general attendance at Sunday evening meetings, unless there is a special program. Students appear to feel they need to get away from the College Assembly Hall once in a while for a religious service; if there is anything else to go to within reasonable distance, numbers are usually sure to go. Early in the fall I aired a few ideas I was entertaining on the possibility of putting on programs on Sunday evenings attractive enough to hold more of the student folks regularly as attendants. As one result of my suggestions I was put on as chairman of the committee in charge, it being the same committee that worked on the matter last year, but then with Samuel Yoder as chairman. We have tried to work out a plan of having alternately a regular meeting with student talent and a special open forum meeting on a vital subject with a teacher from the Bible department of the college in charge. Due to various interferences during the past two months, so far only two of the latter type of program have been carried through, and perhaps three or four of the first type. There has been fair attendance at those which were held, although not what there could have been. During the time that school is in session, student talent is used almost exclusively with the result that the local people apparently come to feel that their sole duty is to take in what is handed out to them, at least many of them. When vacation comes along and the committee makes an effort to give everyone a chance to do something, the response is very disappointing. Of the younger married and middle-aged folks, few can be induced to appear on a public program.

Pridie Kalends January 1935   Only a few hours are left in the present year, according to the almanac makers. I shall not stay awake to see the old year expire. There are doubtless enough folks keeping watch, so that we can go to bed and sleep comfortably and not worry ourselves about the advent of 1935. Tomorrow is after all only a few hours later than today and the arbitrary division between the years at midnight tonight means nothing to me.

Am reading with interest the book by Richard Gregg on "The Power of Non-Violence." It is an area of thought that I have never explored systematically, and it is almost fascinating. The writer analyzes the psychological and philosophical aspects of such things as fear, hatred, anger, courage, violence, nonviolence. The subject has some practical implications for our doctrine of nonresistance, implications which to my knowledge have never been adequately explored and elucidated.

January 6, 1935 School has taken up its routine course again after the brief pause of vacation. As always the recess was all too short, but I did get a respectable amount of work out of the way during the time.

My mental set towards the second semester's work is taking form. The matter weighs upon my mind more particularly at this time because it will involve for me a considerable change. Professor W. H. Smith is taking leave of absence from his teaching for residence study at Indiana University, beginning with the second semester. His leaving will vacate the office of Dean of Men, and I have been asked to accept this position permanently at the time he leaves. At my own insistence my present teaching load of nineteen class hours will be reduced by one course of three hours, which is still too much for efficiency. However, for this one semester I agreed to undertake the work on these conditions. Thereafter it is understood that my teaching hours are to be something less than a full schedule, with a maximum of twelve to fourteen hours. My impression is that such a reduction will be caried out as a permanent policy if I very firmly insist upon it, which is what I shall do. At least so far in recent years, the business manager has pushed with all his might to make teachers load up heavier. That phase of the problem seems now to rest entirely with the individual instructors, the maximum amount of work each one will be asked to do depending exclusively upon his own consent to accept no more. This probably states the situation too pessimistically, but it is the way some feel about it.

As for this new work, I am in a sense happy to have the opportunity to get into such work, although I fully realize the responsibility which it involves. Have long felt that I would like to cultivate the art of personal contact and of personal work, so-called. Had a small bit of experience while last at Hesston, and I am aware that I shall need to devote much thought and study to the work that will devolve upon me. The work of the dean of men has never been definitely outlined at this place, and the first thing I am asked to do is to study the work of my position thoroughly with a view to defining it more specifically and then devoting myself to the work as I shall outline it. It is a fine opportunity if I can rise to its possibilities.

January 7, 1935 It is so seldom during recent months that I have had time enough to get into the mood or feeling of "leisure," sufficiently to get any inspiration for offhand writing of notes. There has been a continual press of duties, which together with my frequent bodily indisposition has not allowed me to let my thoughts rove in reflective or ruminative channels.

Yesterday we were entertained at Sunday dinner by Walter Yoder and family; Chris Gundens with a part of their family were likewise guests for dinner. Enjoyed a pleasant afternoon.

Virgil has developed rapidly in his speech habits since he first really began to say words for the purpose of expressing himself. A year ago at this time he was not saying any words beyond imitating a few sounds, such as "cuckoo." He hardly said any words at all before the summer months of last year. Beginning in September, when he associated a good deal with Millers' boys after their return from summer vacation, he made rapid progress in vocabulary and sentence use. At present he attempts to imitate any words he hears and uses quite long sentences, although he does not use all the smaller particles, such as articles, conjunctions, etc. Our practice of reading stories to him just about every evening at bedtime seems to be a great stimulant to his imagination and to his powers of expression as well. During the day and in fact all his waking moments when he is entertaining himself, he is constantly repeating phrases and lines from his favorite stories. Sometimes he goes through rather long passages, saying the important words and passing over the smaller ones. He has two red toy cars since Christmas. Last week I stopped at John Zook's home on Eighth Street and bought him a marble roller. Had planned to try and make one myself but upon close examination of a model I decided that it were easier under the circumstances to pay a dollar and seventy-five cents in cash for one already made.

The boy is an interesting subject for study and observation of his emotional development. It is plain to see, and has been for some time, that his is a very sensitive nature. Rebuke or reproof, or any form of correction arouses anger and resentment immediately. Several months ago his most consistent reaction to reproof was to throw things violently away, whatever he happened to have in hand. At present his favorite way of reacting is to quickly suggest some compromising or divertive idea when he is corrected or commanded to do something. He does so on impulse alone generally – quick as a flash. Yesterday when we were leaving Yoders' place to return home, he had taken a very special fancy to three small red toy cars and he was determined to carry them with him. After a time of coaxing and explanation, he compromised, set two down and was ready to go with the third in hand. After more insistence that he give the red car to the little boy he made up his mind to give it up, but not to the boy as I suggested. He said "give it to the little girl" who was standing by, and when I verbally approved his suggestion, he still insisted on doing differently from what he was told to do, so he handed it to Mr. Yoder himself, saying "give it to man."

January 14, 1935 We are reading at present at our home the book by Marston entitled "New Bible Evidence," which presents some of the more recent findings of archaeology in Palestine. Assuming that the emphasis and interpretation is approximately correct, the results here described are almost phenomenal. The extent and degree of civilization in those early times is almost breathtaking to one who has breathed the atmosphere of our Western thought which has ever prided itself as being the crown of the world's progressive striving toward civilization and culture. It has been our basic assumption that progress and cultural evolution have been continuous from zero to our exquisite flower of culture today (perhaps it is in fact a thorny scrub rose that we have in our civilization today). Truly marvelous are the remains of hoary cultures and civilizations that must still lie buried under the dust and sand of those eastern skies.

I have never been a convinced believer in the facile doctrine of progress, which seems to have originated two centuries or less ago in the so-called Enlightenment. Progress as understood in our time is certainly a relative term, and to say that we have progressed far culturally needs special qualification in a number of directions before it would approximate the real facts. No doubt the term "culture" would also require definition in any serious discussion of the matter. My feeling is that one cannot justly think of Abraham and his forebears and contemporaries as primitive ignorant savages or even barbarians. The antiquity of written records is a sorry commentary on the earlier pronouncements of would-be scholars to the effect that Moses could not have written the Biblical books bearing his name for alphabetical writing was of course unknown then! Will intellectualists and rationalists ever learn not to dogmatize!

The work of the present semester is drawing to a close and before two more weeks pass it will be all over. Examinations bother me almost as much as they do the students, for I must frame and devise questions for them to struggle over. I heartily dislike it in most of my courses. I shall pass it up entirely in the Terence class of one student. The others will need to go through some sort of formality as a climax for the semester's work.

January 22, 1935 The day before the semester examinations. Work and ever more work is piling up for me. Here I had rather complimented myself with the prospect that for about two months I should have no extra writing to do, no major outside activity of any sort. Now all at once the prospect has changed. The editor of the College Record wants a leading article written for the February Record, which is to be a Peace issue, I understand. This will tax my spare time thought for at least one week. And this morning came to my desk a program of the proposed Mennonite Conference on "War and Peace" to be held here in less than four weeks from now. On this I find I have two assignments, and of no slight consequence at that. One is a major discussion, in the form of a prepared paper of "not over forty-five minutes' length," according to the program. The other is an opening discussion of a round table period following a major presentation by another speaker.

Over this coming weekend I shall be moving myself bag and baggage from my present office in Science Hall to the office in the Administration Building which Willard Smith is vacating. I anticipate having somewhat more efficient working conditions there than in this building. I expect that heating conditions will be a little better, and also lighting conditions. There will be more privacy, but on account of the work of the dean of men's office, I must expect more interruptions and general distraction. There will be a little less running back and forth from one building to another, so saving some time and energy.

John Horsch at Scottdale writes me a few lines in criticism of certain points in my latest contributions to the peace supplement in Gospel Herald. He questions my assertion about the position of the Sunday School Times on pacifism, which I criticized, and strongly enough as I am ready to admit, but I still think my remarks were not unjust. The references to pacifism in the Times are very unsatisfactory. Occasionally reference is made editorially to the efforts to promote world peace, and invariably the matter is dismissed with the remark that there can be no peace on earth before Christ comes and until that event the Scriptures predict that wars will continue. All of which is true enough, but it by no means exhausts the question of war and peace for individual Christians and for the Church, as is the implication of the ready formula which the editor uses for dismissing the subject. Hence I think most of his readers gather from his implicit suggestion that war must be, and Christians need not inquire any further about it.

On the whole I feel that I had better avoid the speculative and theoretical phases of pacifism, for I am really not equipped to deal with them in an adequate way. There is something about Horsch's viewpoint on eschatology that appeals to me as being at fault. But I have not the equipment at present for discovering exactly what it is and for combating it. His system of thinking is integrated, more so than mine. He is very sure and positive that he is right, whereas I lack such a dogmatic temper. Horsch fills a rather unique but unofficial position at Scottdale, in that he seems to be the theological and philosophical watchdog about the Publishing House. The editors in general lean upon him for smelling out all the rats of modernism and near-modernism. Yet he has had no special training so far as I know, in theology, philosophy, excepting what he has gotten through reading. Perhaps I shall some day have an equivalent equipment.

February 10, 1935 Leisure for writing notes has been entirely lacking during the past three weeks. Two weeks ago I had my turn with the influenza, though as usual it was mostly a severe head cold again. Then before I was fully recovered from that affliction, I was moving my office headquarters and getting established in my new place of business and at once plunging headlong into the work of the office of the dean of men. And this week just past Wife and Son have been afflicted with the common plague that has been about ever since the Christmas season. I have not yet caught up with my work, and by the end, or rather before the end of this week I must have an address of five thousand more or less words written out and ready to deliver at the week-end conference on "Peace and War."

I feel very much the need for a definite program of integration for my own thinking and activity. Especially now that more of my regular work involves the making of personal contacts with individuals and groups, which sort of activity I have always found most tiring and exhausting, and a heavy drain on one's strength. I simply must plan and execute a more systematic method for having quiet time, meditation, prayer, and fellowship with a greater Source of strength than myself. My efforts along that line have been too hap-hazard and casual in the past for real effective results. My most regular and systematic efforts in cultivating quiet time were made when I was a student at Hesston. The ideal has ever been before me, of doing something more definite and systematic. Now that I am face to face with the work of a responsible position and also the opportunity that it affords, I must do something about it. Quarters at home are too small for best results. But now that I have this office in the Administration Building which is comfortably warm more of the time, I think I can carry out something.

February 27, 1935 Less and ever less of leisure time for doing anything ad libitum, at least, so it seems. Am also beginning to feel the weight of my new office resting upon my shoulders, and as I remarked at home the other day, I seem to have developed a feeling of perpetual tiredness, weariness, or something of the sort. Decisions must be made, and for me making decisions is very wearing and tiring at all times. Meetings of this and of that are a drain upon time and energy — faculty meetings, committee meetings, etc. The heavy peace conference programs were almost killing for me; I was just getting over a head cold at the time, so that it was especially hard on me. The "extra" tasks in the offing just now are two: preparing material for the April Gospel Herald, and preparing a paper for reading at a conference of Greek and Latin teachers at Muncie, Indiana, in April. I was invited last year to present a paper on their program and turned it down; this year I felt I had better accept, for the invitation might not be indefinitely repeated in the future. I expect to work out a paper I had partly worked out three years ago for presentation at a like meeting at Lawrence, Kansas. Besides these matters I am reading up on the problem of movies and movie attendance, with a view to doing some official work against it among our student body. There seems to be considerable of such activities practiced surreptitiously, and the administration has generously loaded it upon the disciplinary officials for the first thing after I am on this job. It presents no small problem, how to control the matter in any effective way.

Have done but very little reading this month, aside from routine reading. Not even in magazines have I kept up-to-date. When the summer vacation comes, I pledge myself much reading and leisure time activity.

Weather this month has been "miserable." Alternately cold and mild; slushy, snow, ice, mud in irregular procession. The buildings here have been uncomfortable so often this winter because of cold. This office, however, is much more habitable than the one where I was before. Only seldom is it impossible to work here, something for which I am very thankful. I wish for warm weather.

March 24, 1935 With fifteen minutes before vesper service begins, I shall write at least a few lines so as not to miss out for a whole month without writing something in these notes. Busy, busy, going, going is still the order of the day with me. And now I am carrying on Mrs. H. Bender's Elementary German class of fifty or more people for the remainder of the semester. I feel really weary of this teaching of late whenever I relax long enough to think upon it. I shall appreciate the lengthened Easter vacation this year particularly.

Spring weather is here, but it seems quite too early to stay with Easter still three weeks away. Even so it is a welcome relief from the rough weather of previous months and we are enjoying it while it lasts. There has been rain too of late. Dust fills the air at times, borne here from the Western plains where unprecedented dust storms have prevailed.

April 22, 1935 On this last half day of the Easter recess, I once more take time out to write an occasional note. When the vacation began I was planning mentally to write many pages in these notes; oh, at least three or four pages on every one of the ten days with no school. But alas! while a college teacher may propose, it is often the weather man who disposes, at least he did in this case for me. The first day of vacation I spent on a trip to Muncie by railway train. But already on the day before that I had come into possession of a perfectly jolly head cold. So I was under obligation to entertain this troublesome guest, and he stayed the whole length of the period; not until today do I feel like doing anything. Besides, on the second day of vacation, a pronounced cold wave came over the country; in fact it snowed some on Monday. In vacation time of course, the college buildings cannot be heated, so it was impossible to comfortably do any work in the office in this building before today. It is just barely comfortable this afternoon, although by opening windows, some warm air comes in from the outside. So for two good reasons, I lay around at home and took almost complete vacation. Almost, for I did manage to get a kind of a speech worked out which I gave on Thursday evening at the Young Married People's Literary Society meeting at Elkhart. The speech was a fizzle, I am sure. The subject, Christianity and the Family, was quite foreign to me, and I copied from a book most all that I read from my paper. On Friday we started gardening operations by first shopping in town for seeds and plants. On Saturday I spent nearly a full day in the garden. Planted lettuce, spinach, radishes, carrots, beets, onions and peas. We are not working garden on quite as big a scale as we did last year. The whole project is as much a recreational and aesthetic project as a utilitarian one, for we do feel that we must have some place to go to be out-of-doors, a place to get a little exercise in the open air and sunshine, and a chance to watch some things grow.

We are ready to start on the last lap of the scholastic race to the end of the school year. There are only six weeks left and they will pass very rapidly, no doubt. Besides regular classroom duties there are a series of small projects ahead of me during these weeks. This week it is that of editing copy for the April issue of the Quarterly Review. Another is to direct the mimeographing of the addresses given at the Peace Conference two months ago. I finally have all these addresses in my hands, H. S. Bender having carried along to Europe three of them when he went. Also at the suggestion of two persons I may rewrite in part my chapel address of a month ago on "The Motion Picture Theatre" and submit it to Editor Horst at Scottdale for publication in the Christian Monitor. Furthermore I feel inclined to revise and perhaps lengthen a bit my paper on Aulus Gellius that I read at Muncie and try and crash my way into the Classical Journal with it. I may be foolish for trying it, but cannot see that any harm can come of the attempt. I do cherish a secret ambition to get something into the C. J. sometime. And again I want to prepare most of the material for the July Peace Section in the Herald before close of school, so that I can get it typed by my typist and need not do that myself during the summer. Another vision! I want my slate cleared as far as possible by June 1, so that I can be at leisure for the summer! And write reams of these notes!

June 7, 1935 The high pressure rush has been past for a number of days. I find it such a blissful sensation to be free from the continuous, incessant drive of a fixed and full schedule, hounded by the clock, feeling myself a slave rather than the master of my own time and resources. For the few days since Monday I have simply relaxed and reveled in the feeling of freedom and independence once again. Am not even now entirely free from routine work, for I have four persons reading the Intermediate German course. We meet two periods daily at 10:15 and again immediately after the chapel period. These are good students and will not cause me any grief or worry. Three of them have come directly from the beginning German course and the fourth is a splendid and able senior who is sure to get along very well. The part of my work which I had not counted on is that of the dean of men's office. The dean of women has left the campus and I am asked to look after all the disciplinary and personnel matters for the entire student body of sixty some persons.

Rain, cold, cloudy skies have been the order of the days since school closed on Monday. This afternoon the sun is shining brightly and I am eager to get out into it and do some work in the garden. How great a contrast this is with the conditions of last year, when it was hot and sultry and dry besides. I refuse to complain, for it is possible that heat and drouth may come soon enough in this part of the country. We feel quite isolated this summer, for Paul Benders have left town for the summer vacation, and we have no one to take us out riding in a motor car, either for pleasure or on shopping errands. The latter privilege we will miss the most, especially when the time for fruit, strawberries, cherries, summer apples, etc., comes along. Have considered the advisability of getting a good-sized coaster wagon for Virgil and using it to go to the market and to town for shopping purposes. He is himself too small to handle a large hand wagon at present, but it would last him a long time, should he get it now.

June 9, 1935 Our garden plot begins to show up nicely, peas in thick rows, four of them, and beginning to come into bloom. Four rows of onions, mostly onion sets, are growing nicely, although they look slender and spindly as if they might not grow to be very large due to the thinness of the soil. Two rows of carrots and two of beets are beginning to look beautiful. Of radishes, spinach and lettuce we have what we can use for the present. Ten dozens of tomato plants is the number that I set out on two different occasions and of about four or five varieties. They are well started, one variety being in bloom already.

We were slow in getting our beans into the ground, and they are just now coming through the rather hard surface of the soil. The garden is on Mr. Wambold's lot again as last year, only we are using the east end this year instead of the west end. The reason: Paul Benders decided not to use the part they had before, and as the Wambolds wished to set out raspberry bushes on a part of the lot, they gave us the use of the east end. I paid Myron Yoder two dollars and seventy-five cents, as I recall, for bringing a load of stable manure for the lot. Also invited the college campus force to haul two small loads of leaves and rubbish raked from the campus onto the lot. All this was plowed under and will probably help out some this year, but probably more in the year after for whoever may plant the lot then. With the abundant moisture so far, the prospects are good for some worth-while returns from the plot this year. Especially so if the moisture keeps on falling regularly.

Our financial prospects for the present and immediate future continue to be about the same as a year ago. There seems to be a persistent shortage of cash for distribution to the teachers of the college. We received our fifty dollars a month cash again as last year, but also again with no prospect of its continuation during the summer months. Besides the cash distribution, all teachers were allowed to purchase in and through the college dining hall food supplies at wholesale prices. No limit was officially set as to the amount that was allowed to each one to get in this way. Result was that rather unequal amounts were taken out. The business manager reported that about two thousand dollars worth of provisions were thus confiscated. There are certainly not more than twenty families that took out goods there, and I know that we took out less than sixty-five dollars worth, hence some surely got a good deal more than we did. It is partly another racket, of which there are so many nowadays. Personally we appreciate the service, for we do not have a car or handy means for getting to the cash grocery stores in the city and saving money in that way. On some things it is an economy to purchase at the wholesale rate, even if a surtax of seven per cent is added by the college for all that they handle in this fashion. But I think I shall protest against the continuation of the same policy of letting anyone order unlimited supplies in addition to their full cash allowance, even to the extent as is reported, that someone ordered such supplies and used part of them for paying off bills owed to other people. The thing that will probably happen to me, which would be in accordance with my usual luck, of course, is that I and a few others who do not push and crowd and scheme to get my full salary now, will find ourselves in the end holding the sack for the uncollectable part of the assets of these years.

June 10, 1935 Last week I enjoyed reading through a small book by Albert Jay Nock, entitled "The Theory of Education in the United States," which was a series of lectures given at University of Virginia a few years ago. It was delightful reading; the style of writing was excellent, the subject matter was of immediate interest to myself as a college teacher, and the method of treatment was quite distinctly to my taste. It is a criticism of American education, both theory and practice, and I always enjoy intelligent and honest criticism. I regard this book as such criticism. Mr. Nock might to some appear somewhat cynical and pessimistic. But to me he is not that, but rather genuinely realistic both in his line of approach to the subject and in his treatment of it. Using Plato's phrase he pleads for an attitude that seeks to "see things as they are." He outlines the theory that underlies American education under three heads or points. First is the doctrine of equality, an idea that was very much abroad in our land in the early days when our country and its institutions were taking shape. As a philosophical doctrine, equality among men is one thing, but as the doctrine was popularly formulated it has turned out to be quite something else. In the latter form it has been "degraded into a kind of charter for rabid self-assertion on the part of ignorance and vulgarity," at least so in the social sphere. Politically it has given sanction to the unrestrained exercise of self-interest. In education the same popular doctrine has assumed that everybody is "educable," to use Mr. Nock's word. But as this writer contends, "the philosophical doctrine of equality gives no more warrant for the assumption that all men are educable than it does for the assumption that all men are six feet tall." It is this assumption that all men are educable that has wrought havoc with American educational practice. It is responsible for the earnest and pitiful attempt to do the impossible thing in our educational system.

The second principle in our educational theory is that of democracy. In its popular form this doctrine has rested on confused thinking all around. The terms "republican" and "democratic" have been regarded as synonymous. Eighteenth century political theory held the notion that those who voted were they who ruled, whereas history has proven that the owners of property are the country's rulers. Hence popular error has accepted as democratic whatever was merely indiscriminate. This idea of democracy is animated by a very strong resentment of superiority in any form. Democracy must aim therefore at no ideals above those of the average man. The average man is idolized and any line of effort for superior achievement is regarded as taboo.

The third principle of our theory is that good government can be assured by having a literate citizenry. But reading does not connote thinking, and may even hinder it. The perversions of otherwise good principles have been made especially operative by a common American sentiment to the effect that every parent wants his child to have a better education than he himself enjoyed. Then too the confusion and futility of our educational efforts have been intensified, as Mr. Nock says, by the complete failure to distinguish between instruction or training and education. Education is the induction of minds and spirits into the Great Tradition, the cultural heritage of the race. The studies and the disciplines that bring one into touch with the Great Tradition are formative studies, maturing studies, "because they powerfully inculcate the views of life and the demands on life that are appropriate to maturity and that are indeed the specific marks, the outward and visible signs of the inward and spiritual grace of maturity."

I appreciate very much this lucid and sane discussion, I hope not just because it emphasizes Greek and Latin and the ancient culture, but because I have long felt from my small and limited contact with the Great Tradition, the brief glimpses I have had of it, that in this lies something of the maturity which this writer speaks about. For

twelve years now I have felt an increasing thirst for this water of
life from the ancient classics.

June 16, 1935 Warm summer weather has really come at last. Clouds
and threatening rain are with us here today. Had a good sleep after
our dinner at home and feel a good deal refreshed now. Estie and
Boy went to call on Mrs. I. E. Burkhart and children after they had
completed their naps. Virgil is quite an active boy this summer.
Millers who had lived in the east end of the apartment house, moved
out to Mrs. Burkhart's house just back of the apartments last winter.
Virgil wants to play over at their house nearly all the time. He plays
fairly well with Jerold, the younger of the Miller boys, although both
of them are older than he is. He really is not at the age where he
can cooperate with them on play projects. Millers have a small house
pup with whom Virgil has endless delight and fun. He seems to romp
with this dog more than the Miller boys themselves.

Since the weather has been warm and he plays out-of-doors, our
boy has suddenly lost all interest in listening to stories read to him
from his books. Even upon invitation and request he frequently refuses to listen to a story. His interest in particular activities comes
and goes in cycles and he will become interested in stories again in
due time. He is familiar with practically all the contents of Book I
of the Book House. I have read a few from Book II but he is not
quite ready for most of those. Within the past month he has reached
the stage of asking questions, as to "what is for that?" "who belongs
to that?" "what did he do next?" and so forth. I have started the
practice of telling him orally a few of the familiar stories. This
seems to interest him at times. But storytelling is for me an amateurish business, although I want to practice and cultivate this art so
I can entertain him with it. I want to learn a great many amateur arts
and skills during the next fifteen years while Virgil is growing up. If
possible we want to be pals together, learning things and working on
projects together. Just what kinds of things we shall undertake I cannot guess. Much will depend upon his own tastes, interests and aptitudes along the way. Possibly certain manual skills in wood-working,
making collections of such things as moths, butterflies, minerals and
rocks, perhaps learning amateur taxidermy, amateur bookbinding, and
a dozen other things of the sort. I cherish the secret ambition to make
his education, at least large parts of it as informal as possible, trying
to guide his interests and activities along wholesome lines, filling his
life with such an abundance of interesting and absorbing activities, so
that he will seek a minimum of entertainment outside his home. It will
be a hard and exacting undertaking, I realize. I almost shudder at the
thought of letting school and formal education, the kind that prevails
largely today, become the major factor in his education and development. I hope I can do something to save him from becoming an autom-
aton and blithely goose-stepping along with the masses of people. Particularly so if he should show any special abilities along any lines,
which I am naturally fond and perhaps vain enough to hope that he may.
At any rate I hope I can be candid and open-minded enough to let him
develop into the man his Creator wants him to be, whether that may be
clerk, farmer, preacher, scholar, archaeologist, or whatever. Since I

have often regretted that I cannot become the latter, a digger after
and a student of ancient ruins and their representative civilizations,
I have occasionally cherished the wish that Virgil might become interested in that line of activity. But that will be up to him largely.
I do hope we can maintain a cultural environment at home that will
give him at least the opportunity of growing up with a taste in reading, in recreation, and in other respects which will be above the level
of the tastes, blatant, crude, garish, vulgar and insipid as they usually are nowadays, of the common herd of humans. I fear my own
views on such crowd conformity may be so pronounced that he may
take on a proud scorn of the interests and tastes of hoi polloi. I hope
I can prevent any such consequences, but even that may be preferable
to a lazy and craven conformity to the current mores.

June 23, 1935 There is continuous cool and cloudy weather, although
a week ago we thought hot weather had come upon us when it was
warm and sultry for several days. Our second planting of beans is
coming out very well now. The first planting just seemed to disappear
without coming up at all. We had the beans soaking for more than
forty-eight hours, because due to rain we were unable to plant them
at the time we had planned. After they were planted a hard dashing
rain fell and made the surface of the ground so hard that some could
not force their way through. Scarce a fifth of the bush beans came
out and none of the limas. Everything else in the garden is growing
splendidly now. Peas are hanging full of pods; we had our first mess
of fresh peas today at dinner. Strawberries are plentiful this year; a
year ago there were almost none, at least we never canned a berry.
We got a crate of beautiful berries from Sylvanus Yoders on last Thursday and canned them. The lady of the house is impatient to get more
to put away. We paid a dollar and thirty cents for those, and she
thinks she has an opportunity to go out to pick some tomorrow for
seventy-five cents a crate. She has also canned fourteen pints of dark
green spinach, and last year we did not get any raised even to eat.
So our prospects for foodstuffs this summer appear to be a good deal
better than what we had a year ago.
    Asked to conduct the daily chapel exercises this last week, I took
the liberty to use the time on three of the days to set forth the main
points and conclusions of Mr. Nock's book I read the other week, on
"The Theory of Education in the United States." I appreciate Mr. Nock's
excellent analysis and am in thorough sympathy with his point of view.
I each time wrote out in full my discussion, for that is the only way
in which I can present any material of importance and get it expressed
in a way that is satisfactory to myself.
    Read the past week Grant Showerman's interesting little volume on
Horace. It is an appreciative and enthusiastic presentation of the philosophy, life and character of this most humanistic of ancient Latin
poets. I can myself become enthusiastic over much of his poetry and
his philosophy. I appreciate especially his insistence on the golden
mean, on contentment, on the simple life, on the vanity of human ambitions and hopes. I realize too that such a philosophy if carried too
far would not leave one much dynamic for moral reform or religious
propaganda. Yet even into the religious life and activity of our time

has come too much of the worldly spirit of restlessness, feverish zeal for results, and the like. My feeling always is that the Horatian spirit and manner on its best and sanest side fits in very well with the Christian ideal of sanity, sobriety, peace, contentment, simplicity, and freedom from ambition. Since this is the year of the Bimillenary celebration of Horace's birth, I aspire to a better acquaintance with the poet and his works. I was glad for the privilege of reading him again the past year with a class in college. We read all of his works (that are readable) excepting the last book of the Epistles. I had expected to give some outward recognition to the celebration that is in progress. But because of the great press of other duties and my own general indisposition, the entire year passed without getting anything done at all. Perhaps next December we can still do a little something along that line. I did get book markers for each one in the class and for myself, made especially as a part of this year's celebration. Two of the girls of the class, Mary Esch and Caroline Smucker, prepared translations of Carmina I. 22 and submitted them in the state contest for translating Horace, but a recent notice of the adjudged winners did not include their names.

The manuscript for the July instalment of the Peace Section in the Gospel Herald is just about all made up now. Expect to send it in this week as soon as I can get it typewritten.

I wrote a lengthy review of the book "Character 'Bad'," which I read lately and esteem quite highly. Showed the book to C. L. Graber and he read it. He had some very casual contact with Gray, the writer of the letters in question, at Fort Riley, Kansas during the war.

June 25, 1935 How cool our summer weather has been so far as compared with a year ago. It is pleasant enough in general, although just a bit cooler than is most comfortable at times. Virgil has only gone barefoot a few days, and what's worse his shoes are worn through at the prow so that he ruins his socks quickly. We have been hoping for a month that he could now surely go barefooted soon and keep it up until fall comes.

I shall close up regular class work with my German students tomorrow. We have read about 200 pages of German prose. The remaining 400 to 425 pages they must read "on their own," and pass necessary tests and reports on the stories read.

Am reaching the age when I find some pleasure in reminiscing of bygone years, though I am not in the habit of dreaming of the past. Am more tempted to daydream of the future. Ten years ago this summer we were spending our second summer in the university town of Iowa City. Mrs. Yoder was doing office work in the city. I did not enroll for any courses in the university that summer, because there were no hour or course requirements that I had to fulfill just then, and furthermore it was cheaper to help myself to the classical library at the university and so advance my acquaintance with classical authors. I recall reading Lucretius, Plautus, Terence, Propertius, Ovid, Petronius, Herodotus, and no doubt others I do not remember now. It was a profitable summer. We were making our plans and preparations for the trek to Philadelphia in September, to spend a year in the City of Brotherly Love.

And twenty years ago — can it possibly be so long as that! I was working on the farm at home for my father. It was my first summer vacation after I started my academic career. For just twenty years it was this last January that I started my study in school as a freshman at Hesston Academy. That was a momentous year for me. I had been at Hesston only six weeks when I was taken down with a mild form of typhoid fever and spent about three weeks in bed. Was I blue and discouraged then! I rather seriously considered the idea that fate was against my plans to go through school, and I dallied with the thought of returning to the farm and staying there the rest of my days. But many of the young fellows showed themselves friendly, and especially do I recall with gratitude the interest of two friends, Noah Oyer and Philip Mack, who often cheered and encouraged me, counselling me not to make any hasty decisions under the circumstances. Oyer himself succumbed to typhoid fever four or five years ago. Mack I had the privilege of meeting numerous times nine years ago when we were in Philadelphia. And so time goes on. I seem to myself to have accomplished very little in these years. My thought is not in the past, but in the future and in the present. If we can get ourselves settled, perhaps I can hope to do a few things that are worthwhile, if my life and health are spared and the grace of God be not denied to me.

Have found some diversion and satisfaction in recent days during some spare time looking through old files of theological journals in the college library. I find some things that appeal to me as being of possible future use. Hence I make notes and excerpts occasionally. Have been examining thus The Review and Expositor, from the Southern Baptist Theological Seminary and The Biblical Review from New York City. They are both excellent journals.

Pridie Kalendas Julias, die Solis.   Regular Sunday school and worship services this morning. I. E. Burkhart preached where we were in attendance, at the college, of course. Since February I have been regular pundit for the Men's Bible Class in S. S., a group of a dozen middle-aged men of varied and diverse sort. Most of them have little to say in general discussion. A few talk readily but say little. I mostly lecture to them and expound my own notions and ideas.

Sundays are largely routine for us here. We never go away for we have no means at hand for running to and fro. I believe we appreciate the quiet and simple routine which we have here. Today our program was irregular to the extent that we went along on a Sunday picnic trip. The way we happened to go this time was that we invited S. C. Yoders to eat dinner with us, but as they had already made other arrangements for the day, they in turn invited us to accompany them. Taking along picnic baskets they went a few miles east of Goshen to a school ground where others also foregathered for the occasion. Frank Kyles, Marion Erbs, and some of their family folks, Ben Kauffmans, Glen Millers, and a few whose connections with the affair were unknown to me, were there, and a pleasant luncheon and visit was enjoyed. I have personally no difficulty in doing my share on the luncheon part of such occasions, but I am not so capable on the visitation part. I enjoy listening in on the discussions that others carry on.

The July issue of Atlantic Monthly came the past week and contains some good things. Among them are some thoughts on Utopia, thought out and passed on for others' benefit by Albert Jay Nock. He is a virile thinker and writer, and I appreciate his ideas and thoughts very much as a rule. In this article Mr. Nock criticises the various Utopias that have been talked about in history, and also such as have been more than talked about, like the regime instituted by Lycurgus in Ancient Sparta. The upshot of his ruminations on Utopia seems to be that none so far conceived are worth the price they cost, and that principle around which they are organized one and all is at fault. Incidentally he applies his conclusions to the New Deal, the latest utopian dream as he conceives it. His constructive suggestion is that Utopias should be planned on the principle of liberty for the individual, the largest possible measure of freedom that is compatible with general welfare. I like the idea. Such freedom would work contrary to the one hundred per cent American brand of dead-level egalitarian democracy. That would be a good thing. The more superficial our American culture becomes, the more pressure, psychological and otherwise, will be applied to make the mores, the habits, the ideas of every mother's son alike. We will probably increasingly and of course unconsciously compensate for our subconscious sense of inferiority by imposing our ideas and our practices, or trying to impose them, upon all our neighbors. We are so poverty-stricken in spirit, soul, and heart that we can find no better employment for our energies than trying to reform our countrymen through laws, ordinances, constitutional amendments, and what not. We have not the mental energy and the stamina of soul, not the patience and the faith to work on fundamental things in the formation of human character. Many times have I wondered to myself whether it might not be true that men are being rendered weaker and weaker through the benefit of all our solicitous and painstaking educational efforts. Is not everyone being tended and nurtured with such high-pressure hothouse methods that true stamina of character has no real chance to develop, that the innate spiritual and mental fibre of many is not actually being weakened and destroyed? More freedom for children, not freedom to follow their own devices, but a true freedom to get at the real values in life, a true freedom to experience the best in life; more freedom for parents to direct their children's development would surely be a good thing. But no! Every infant must be regimented early and made to goose-step with the multitudinous herd. Every parent must surrender to the public school system the growth of the child; just because some parents are stupid, unintelligent, basically unfit to guide their children's education, for that reason must parents of culture, intelligence, and good judgment also deliver their progeny to the processes of mass leveling! The reply of American democratic stupidity is, "yes," with great emphasis.

Why should we ever think of such a thing as uniformity among men, anyway? Is it not an obsession of small, petty, and feeble minds to even think that men should all be alike in their habits, ideas? I for one surely think so. Does not nature all about emphasize the infinite diversification and variation of all living forms? Only man plans to subvert the Creator's wisdom and design, by striving to bring about uniformity. In the sermon we heard this morning, the subject was referred to, as to why well-meaning and conscientious Christian brethren cannot see matters alike and agree more fully. The suggestion was offered, that in this life people are rarely or never fully sanctified and consecrated, surrendered to the Lord, and so differences must be expected. Personally, I think Christians should be trained and instructed to see the harmony, the beauty, the divine design there is in diversity. It can be only little minds that see in diversity of practice and thought anything evil, wrong or undesirable. I'm for variation and liberty.

July 3, 1935 A recent writer in Christian Century comments interestingly on "The Abundant Life," a shibboleth that I think came into American speech, not directly from the Gospel of John, but from President Roosevelt's inaugural address over two years ago. The general notion among many seems to be that the abundant life signifies an endless supply of mechanical gadgets and enough money at everybody's command to buy them and wear them out so they can speedily buy new ones or trade for a newer model gadget. The eminent scientist Millikan is quoted as saying that "the progress of civilization consists merely in the multiplication and refinement of human wants." It is of course just the same old doctrine that capitalists and industrialists have been preaching all along, that prosperity and civilization must be interpreted in material terms, that profit is the basic motive in civilization, and that in the last analysis the human beings on this terrestrial sphere exist for the purpose of consuming material goods and an endless procession of gadgets and concoctions. What is to become of human dignity and self-respect under such a Frankenstein profit-monster? The chief end of man is no longer to love God and glorify Him forever, but to consume material goods and provide profits forever. The old catechism needs to be revised and brought up-to-date!

This particular writer points to telephones and automobiles as examples of things, contrivances, which we should seriously consider whether we need at all or not. I was pleased with his frankness in raising the question, for surely it is not an unreasonable one. No law can be laid down as to what and how many mechanical gadgets any individual needs. But the point is that most folks never consider whether they need or really want a thing. If they have the money, or the faith that they will get it and can convince dealers that they can get it sometime, they must get this and that, radio, car, golf outfit, or what not, and why? Well, everybody else is getting such things or wants to get them as soon as they can. An abominable reason, I should say! It seems incredible, when one stops to think about the matter, that the common practice about us should be such a pressure upon us and our conduct. We talk about personal liberty and freedom, but how willingly we wear the shackles of social conformity! At our house we are more than glad to be without a telephone. In emergency instances we can telephone from the college, but that is hardly once or twice a year. And radio — it has always seemed to me that any person who values the privacy of home would have no radio about. Especially is the way radio broadcasting in this country is tied up with commercial advertising a veritable shame, and an insult to the listeners. It is only another phase of the doctrine of the abundant life, that millions of gullible folks must be dragooned into buying and consuming material goods so as to make more profit for stockholders. In one of his letters Sir Walter Raleigh remarked that it was the stupid people who make all the work and then do it. "To believe that machinery enriches life is foolishness."

American Independence Day. As is usual the quietness of this annual holiday is plentifully interjected with loud reports of firecrackers and torpedoes set off by those who are celebrating the Declaration of Independence. It is a crude and vulgar ritual, but then if folks can get satisfaction from it, let them go ahead, although it is rather hard on one's ears and nerves, I confess.

This is the day for the annual Sunday school picnic at this place. Early this morning some rain fell and there is still a chance that it will rain more before the day is over. We are not going out for the day, nor had we planned to go. One principal part of a picnic is of course to eat, and just now I am rather handicapped in the eating business, for day before yesterday Dentist Carpenter took out a second instalment of teeth from my mouth. A week ago today he took out four and on Tuesday three more. In about a month six more (front ones) will go the way of the others and make place for a full upper denture. Last Tuesday morning I picked twenty quart boxes of sour cherries, which Estie has canned for winter.

Finally last evening I finished Broadbent's book on "The Pilgrim Church," a book I have wanted to read for a matter of three years or more and have been trying to get read for about a year now. I drew it from the college library last year sometime on special privilege, such as they grant to members of the faculty (though I fear I have grossly abused this privilege in the present instance), and had it over in our apartment all this time thinking I should surely get at it and read it through, but not until in recent weeks did my purpose come to a realization. I liked the book. The writer undertakes to trace the rather invisible streams and rivulets of unorganized, unworldly Christianity through the centuries. They were always dissenting groups, usually designated and persecuted as heretics by the dominant churches. It is a thrilling story, the attempt to reproduce apostolic Christianity in various times and places through an immediate appeal to the New Testament Scriptures and reliance upon the immediate and personal headship of Christ. My knowledge of general church history is not complete enough to evaluate the effort of this writer. Nevertheless I was led to reflect upon a number of points. This type of spiritual, evangelical Christianity has a reality and a spontaneous vigor that makes it attractive. But lacking and generally avoiding set creeds, comprehensive organization, regularly trained leadership, it seems so often to dissipate its energies in a shorter or longer time after the initial enthusiasm and the personality of the instigators have ceased to function. At the same time as it burns itself out in one circle, a spark falling somewhere will cause new blazes to spring up in unexpected places at any time. Such groups seem actually to flourish best in an atmosphere of persecution and opposition. Historically our Mennonites have been reckoned among the representatives of the Pilgrim Church. But viewing our contemporary scene against the background of such a discussion as this makes one raise serious questions. To me it seems, that while we still hold to the pilgrim ideals, we have been departing quite widely from them in practice. Our elaborate ecclesiastical organization recently developed is quite contrary to these ideals. Our growing emphasis on formal doctrine, our stereotyped missionary effort, and the absence of emphasis upon the leading of the Holy Spirit, are all of the same stripe.

July 11, 1935   This is holiday again for the summer school. A motor coach load and more went to Indiana State Dunes Park. As last year I did not participate. We have had company for two days. Estie's brother Ira and family from Fentress, Virginia, stopped with us from Tuesday evening to this afternoon. They are on an extended trip aiming to go as far as Oregon and California, spending perhaps five or six months visiting and sightseeing. They travel in a Ford car accompanied by a trailer. They have tent and equipment along for outdoor camping. It is a splendid way to travel for such a purpose. Ira's is a wholesome family, three sons of husky physique, two already grown and one half-grown. They have that easy-going Southern manner, open-faced and wide-awake. While they have no interest in formal education, they are versatile and by using their wits and senses have gotten a vast store of information, knowledge, and experience. Seeing their information about nature and life about them makes me feel that I know but little about life itself. As Virgil grows up, I hope to learn with him some of this lore.

July 14, 1935   Chatting with a friend yesterday, I was told that I should go to our General Conference this year, to be held next month in Ontario. I agreed that perhaps I should, but had not planned to do so. I did not further express my reasons for being so indifferent about attending this biennial grand pow-wow of our Mennonites. Yet I cannot work up any spontaneous interest in running to and fro even to church gatherings of such size and importance as this one. Frankly stated, I feel they are too big and pretentious for our small body of folks. I am more bored than edified by attendance thereon. The speeches are good and for the masses of folk are doubtless profitable enough. But I can get very little nourishment or solid food from them. The discussions present mostly, so I feel, mere intellectual and spiritual pap, thin watery soup, good enough for spiritual infants, babes, and invalids, but not nourishing for those who relish some solid food and substantial aliment.

An experience of mine has been quite revealing to myself. I recall very vividly the time when General Conference met at East Union Church near Kalona in 1913. I was twenty then and at the age when I was just beginning to grow spiritually and intellectually. It was the first time that I had set eyes upon such an assemblage of dignitaries and great men, many of whose names I had often read and whose writings I had perused in church papers earlier. I recall with what open-mouthed wonder I listened to the discussions. It was as heavenly manna to my soul and to my hungry growing mind. Particularly there stuck to my mind and memory a point made by G. R. Brunk, when they were discussing the inspiration of the Bible. He spoke of how in the Bible every word and letter was inspired of God, and pointed out how that in Galatians somewhere Paul makes his whole argument turn upon the singular form of a noun as against the plural. Here, I felt, was profound wisdom and deep understanding such as I had never beheld. And what a master mind and ingenious intelligence must lie back of such a discussion. Well, twenty years passed by and I had kept on learning a little in the meantime and had been able to do a little thinking too. I still recalled Bishop Brunk's striking point but was not so much impressed by it anymore. Had read somewhere that such argumentation as Paul's in Galatians was probably a hold-over from his rabbinical training where such methods of reasoning were great favorites. Well, at any rate, I felt it was a legalistic and mechanical line of reasoning and not of such very special significance for the inspiration of the Bible, perhaps. But the surprise came when two years ago at Hesston, Kansas, I again sat in on some sessions of General Conference and heard Brunk, after twenty years of time, in a set speech make the same point in the same words before the same body. It was a stunner to me, I confess. The idea that in the course of twenty years a great church leader should have advanced in his thinking and in his stock of ideas just about nothing at all! Well, if there is nothing new to be heard at General Conference oftener than in more than twenty years, I'd rather stay at home, read a few extra books and try to harvest a few fresh ideas for myself, than to chase around to Conference every two years. Presumably I am too pessimistic about the matter. But personally I am convinced that there is already a disproportionately large amount of energy being expended on the outward and ecclesiastical aspects of our small group, and that the most urgent present need is for people who will dedicate themselves to cultivate the inner spiritual and thought life of our people.

July 20, 1935 Summer temperature reported for yesterday was one hundred two degrees, the highest so far for the season. Late yesterday afternoon some few rain-like clouds began to appear in scattered fashion in different parts of the sky; even at seven o'clock one hardly thought seriously of the possibility of getting a rain. Then to the south and southeast of us the clouds began to concentrate and thicken rapidly. Brisk wind began to blow driving clouds of dust upon us. There followed hard thunder and lightning and at eight o'clock a real rainstorm was beating down upon us. Some hail fell but not sufficient to do real damage here. For a full hour the storm raged and soaked the ground for a few inches at least. Grass had been turning brown rapidly in recent days. It is hot again today with something like storm clouds hanging in various parts of the sky. Our garden had been about at a standstill; this moisture will refresh it again. The light sandy soil has no resistance at all against drouth.

This week I have spent some hours every day, generally afternoons, at the task of cleaning house in my office. Especially the drawers of the two desks have been the objects of my organizing efforts. The desk that was here when I took charge last February I had never set in order until just now. I insisted with the Business Manager until I now have a three-drawer filing cabinet in which I am depositing a good deal of the material that was choking the various drawers. The congestion in drawers of my own private desk has also been pleasantly relieved as a result of the proximity of such a filing case.

Have been enjoying greatly my comparative freedom of this summer. One delightsome occupation has been to go through the files of some religious journals in the college library, read articles and notes that have become of special interest to me. The Review and Expositor and The Biblical Review have so far been my happy hunting ground. I make such notes and abstracts and references as I deem may be of value to me in my studies. Others that I anticipate searching through as I have time are the Harvard University and Crozier journals and some others. The late Professor A. T. Robertson, of Southern Baptist Seminary, wrote an enormous Historical Grammar of the Greek New Testament some years ago. It has over a thousand pages in octavo size. Though I had often heard about the book and had seen it too, yet I never did use it or examine it closely. The other week I began reading the introduction and found it so fascinating that I read all of that part through, and I want to read more in it, for Robertson has a pleasant and urbane style in his writing and his wide range of knowledge makes him a delight to read.

Am finding pleasure in reading Chaucer just now, the "Canterbury Tales." Cannot tell how long I may keep on with him, though I do love to read the Old English language and diction.

The past week brought me a sizable shipment of books from Blackwell at Oxford, England. The original source of these books was Germany, for there they were produced and published. I am greatly pleased with my purchase. There are four volumes I received: A Greek-Latin text of the New Testament, a splendid work with copious critical apparatus and well printed. Then there is a Hand-Concordance of the Greek New Testament, a new work that will certainly be very useful. And finally a two-volume edition of the Septuaginta, beautifully printed with critical apparatus. All this I get for about two pounds English sterling or a little less than ten dollars. Considering the size and workmanship of these volumes, they are certainly cheap enough as compared with the price of books made in our United States.

I have a copy of the Septuagint that I acquired some years ago. But it is an old imprint with type hard to read with comfort and no apparatus of any sort at all. Now of course, I am better equipped for studying the language of the Greek New Testament, which is getting to be one of my hobbies, but to my sorrow I cannot make anything out of Hebrew. To use the LXX, I must some time yet learn to read a little Hebrew.

Pridie Kalendas Augusti, die Mercurii. Leisure time has been a scarce article with me in recent days. The tranquility of my summer days has been rudely molested of late. The story is as follows: Something like two weeks ago M. C. Lehman came to me wishing to give me a little writing assignment for a number of the Goshen Alumni News Letter. His assignment presupposed another assignment of greater import which I had not received then yet. Seeing he had intruded a bit, he felt bound to illuminate me further about what was supposed to be in the air. He went on to report personally that in June my name had been placed to his knowledge on a program of a so-called Conference on Nonconformity to be held in connection with the coming General Church Conclave in Ontario. Since so long a time had elapsed without my being notified I assumed with some confidence that the plans had been changed and the program as finally drawn up did not have my name. So I practically dismissed the matter from my thoughts. Last week, however, Mr. Lehman again reported that he had by correspondence verified his original report. So it began to look rather more serious from my angle. I began half-heartedly to write out some of the ideas I have at times been playing with on this, to some persons, all-absorbing theme, working at it for a brief time every day. Then today the mail brought me a regular printed program of the meetings in Ontario. All doubts were dispelled from my mind and my worst fears were verified. So now the strain is on again, and for several weeks I shall have this burden on my mind. I am preparing my address in written form so it can go to the grand powwow, even if I do not myself join the procession into the dominion of King George V.

At this time too I am rewriting my paper on Aulus Gellius which I read at Muncie in April, trying my very best to put it into such shape that I can persuade myself to offer it to the Classical Journal as an article for publication in its pages. I presume one can revise, amend, polish, and file a long time on such an article and still feel poorly satisfied with the result.

Weather has been pleasant enough of late. But there is something wrong with me; I cannot gain anything in pep, in active energy, in enthusiasm for some reason. The teeth I have had extracted so far were disappointing in this respect, that none seemed to show infection such as might affect my general tone of health. I am always tired, weary, rather lie stretched out on my back than anything else. And my feet feel cold in the forenoon, as though my circulation were poor. Passed through a period of discomfort again last week, but instead of being annoyed in my head this time, my stomach seemed to be on a peculiar rampage. It must be my eyes or something that affects my nervous system. Unless I can get some relief I shall be in a bad way to get through next year.

August 4, 1935 Fifteenth anniversary of our wedding day. Summer school closed yesterday with special exercises featuring Dr. J. A. Huffman as speaker of the occasion.

My progress on the paper pertaining to nonconformity has not been much the last days. This week I must concentrate upon it with main force and vigor. My effort along this line will probably resolve itself into an attempt to formulate a philosophical theory of nonconformism. My proposition in brief will be that vital and dynamic ideas cannot originate from or successfully germinate in the mass level of mankind, and that individuals or minorities more or less unconformed to the mass level are needed for the origination and culture of ideas that make for any kind of progress at all and for the moral and spiritual stamina to carry them out. Putting the proposition in religious terms, God cannot or does not reveal Himself, His will and purpose, does not give His Spirit in its fullness to persons on the general mass level of humanity. It is only to those more or less unconformed to the mass level, whether isolated individuals or minority groups, that the deepest spiritual insight, the greatest spiritual vision, and the fullest spiritual power can come. It is precisely this insight, this vision and this power which make any kind of real progress possible.

The idea of this theory delights me considerably. So far I have flattered myself in thinking this is an original brain child of my own. I do not recall having read or heard it stated in such a form. I presume I shall in due time find out how much truth there is in it, when it gets itself criticised adequately. Our popular democracy of today has so long affirmed the superior wisdom of group thinking, the divine right of majorities, the discovery of truth by consensus, by averages, medians, percentiles, and what not, that the value of minorities, of nonconformed individuals and groups to society as a whole is overlooked and ignored all too often. So I am at no pains to conform myself to democratic averages, nor do I feel called upon to apologize for being a prophet for minorities and nonconformists in general. But then again, I may be making a complete fool of myself by such an attempt, though even that will not be so bad. I have no present reputation to sustain, and have no ambition to make one for myself.

August 18, 1935 Two weeks of real vacation has not even left me leisure for writing notes. I have been doing about as I please – about, but not quite. Beginning last Sunday and continuing every afternoon and evening for an hour or two at a stretch, I have just finished the full-length draft of my paper for presentation before the august assemblage of General Conference. It covers nearly thirty-eight pencil written pages and I estimate that it will count up to somewhere near six or seven thousand words. It needs tomorrow's efforts for revision of language, and then will go to a typist. After final proofreading and correction it should be ready to send away. My plan is to send it to M. C. Lehman and let him read it or arrange for its reading. I am not planning to be numbered among the visitors at the grand jamboree.

Last week, on the eighth to be exact, I parted with the last of my teeth from the upper jaw in my oral cavity. Six came out at that time, making a total of thirteen extractions for the season. I have one grand consolation – no dentist will ever extract more than three teeth again, for that is all I have left of my native stock. One of the front ones showed a diseased condition, and I hope it was responsible for some of the things that ail me.

We have rain in abundance now. A heavy shower fell on Friday evening and another on yesterday evening. This afternoon the wind is blowing briskly from the east with heavy batteries of rain clouds massed together in various parts of the horizon. It is a boon to us through our little garden patch, which promises now to supply us with many things to eat during the fall and some things to can for winter use. Prices of some foodstuffs are rising rapidly, especially meat, eggs, and such like. We buy but little meat comparatively, but yesterday I bought liver at the rate of twenty-five cents a pound and bacon at about thirty cents a pound. Eggs come now at twenty-seven cents a dozen, so that all prospects are for higher living costs for this winter. The price of milk is certainly low here compared to some other places. We are paying eight cents a quart for raw milk at present. The Millers from Fentress, Virginia, who visited us last month reported that standard price for milk in their section was sixteen cents a quart. I have knowledge too that in many other places the price is some higher than here. Butter is at present twenty-five cents, and we get ours at almost wholesale price from our neighbor Mr. Hartzler across the alley, who collects and hauls cream for the creamery at Middlebury.

Our business at Hesston, the renting of our property there, is gradually turning for the better. There is getting to be a lively demand for houses in Hesston, and rental rates are rising a little. Joe Weaver who occupied our house last winter had sub-leased it for the summer months to a Mr. Regier. In July the Regiers inquired of me as to renting it for the winter in case Weavers will not use it. They offered to pay ten dollars a month. I gave them a favorable answer. Then I presently had a letter from Weaver that he had promised the lease to Milo Kauffman in case he decided not to live in it this fall, and that Kauffman will pay eleven dollars a month. I quickly wrote to all parties concerned and tried to straighten out the misunderstanding and my own mistake. All I have heard since is in a letter from Kauffman saying that Regier had just told him they would vacate the place by September first. I had urged upon Kauffman strongly that he should buy it at once, but he does not wish to do so at the price I ask. We are not so desperately anxious to sell this year. But in a year from now the loan on the property will again come due and the insurance will run out again, and we shall by then, I feel, be glad to move out of the apartment house into a home of our own again if possible. So if general conditions do not change to the worse, we shall be all set to sell the place next summer. Also we have hopes that when Kauffmans get settled in the house they will like the place so well that they will make a little special effort to buy it. So all in all it looks as though these affairs were perhaps shaping themselves up for a favorable turn before long. With general improvement in conditions, we are secretly hoping under our breath that we can straighten out and stabilize some of our own financial problems in the next few years.

August 25, 1935   This is a delightfully pleasant day. After some real coolish days and nights it is warming up, sun is shining bright and comfortably, scarcely any wind is stirring, cicadas in the trees are rasping out their shrill tunes. It all feels like the end of September, but the calendar says August.

The Sunday school lesson was a study of Barnabas, one of my favorite characters from the New Testament history. After a two-weeks' leave from teaching the class, I was at it again today. Because of my interest in the subject of the lesson I was glad for the opportunity to present my notion of Barnabas, his character and his work. Also was not reluctant because I did not need to make special preparation for teaching this lesson, for sometime last month the spiritus inflatus seized me and I sat down to write a brief appreciative essay of eight or nine pages on "Barnabas, A Good Man." Possibly after it has seasoned for a time, a further inspiration will come to send it away for publication somewhere. I have also in rough manuscript form an essay on "The Language of the New Testament," of this summer's vintage. I

think the direct inspiration for this came from my pleasurable reading of the 139-page introduction to Professor Robertson's massive volume on "The Historical Grammar of the Greek New Testament." Of
this summer's harvest also is a manuscript of perhaps 6000 words on
the "Criticism of American Educational Theory," which I read in three
instalments as chapel talks during the summer session. This is in
part a review or resume of Nock's book on that subject.

The manuscript I prepared for the Nonconformity Conference at
Kitchener, Ontario, this week finally reached the length of about 7200
words. Lois Yoder, the president's secretary and the only regular
typist around the college at present, typed it for me on Thursday.
Yesterday afternoon I put it into the mail under special delivery arrangement, addressed to M. C. Lehman at General Conference. I feel
it is a hastily compiled paper on a few ideas I have been thinking upon
during the past several years. I hope it will at least stimulate some
others to think out and think through these ideas and their implications
to some more solid conclusion.

At the present time I am putting into final form and typing by my
own method the article on Aulus Gellius. I have finally made up my
mind to send it to the Classical Journal for publication and hope to put
it into the mails by the end of the week. If it will be rejected, that
will have to be that, and I am prepared to be satisfied with rejection,
and surprised by acceptance, and yet I secretly hope it will be published. As I read it over to myself I really feel it is a worthwhile
paper and would not bring discredit upon the Classical Journal by appearing in its pages, but then I'm not the editor. I feel a bit encouraged by the fact that the editor is Professor Walter Miller of the
University of Missouri, who sent me a fine little note of congratula-
tion when he received a copy of my doctoral dissertation six or seven
years ago. I think my writing activities will soon come to a standstill, for it is now time to begin making plans for the opening of the
school year. I expect to have two full weeks of comparative leisure,
working in the office only as many hours a day as my impulse suggests.

Dr. Carpenter on Friday put into my mouth what at least feels like
a monstrous upper denture. It does not feel bad at all, gives no special discomfort, excepting for a few little tender spots, and does not
show up from the outside. To my great surprise and relief, it stays
put, and I can eat some with it and also speak a little. I bought the
very cheapest teeth the dentist could make, partly because being made
so soon after removal of the others they will likely be only temporary,
and partly because my financial circumstances demand it.

Our apartment house neighbors are returning now and the surroundings are not so quiet as they had been for a few weeks. Prospects, so
they say, are for a large college enrollment this fall. The induction of
freshmen will be the greatest project that I shall have a share in. We
want to set ourselves to do intensive work with the freshmen during
the first several months, get them started off right, if we can.

Kalendae Septembris, dies Solis. Extremely cool weather continues to
be the rule; unless there is a turn toward higher temperatures soon,
we may as well look for frost at an early date this fall.

On the past Wednesday, Virgil had the third anniversary of his

birth. As a celebration the Benders planned a picnic outing for him
and us. They took us to Shipshewana Lake, perhaps twenty miles
northeast from here. But it had just turned cold then and we did
shiver a good deal over our picnic lunch which included the inevitable ice cream and cake. Fortunately the sun was shedding his beams
upon the earth generously, excepting when an occasional black cloud
intercepted them. By sitting in a sunny spot among trees where the
strong gale of wind did not strike we were by the aid of sweaters
able to keep fairly comfortable.

I had two days of almost total leisure the past week while the oculist was replacing one lens in my glasses. The left eye did not require
any fitting, but for the right eye a new fit was necessary. In these few
days since I have them to use I seem to have found considerable relief
from former discomfort. I do very greatly hope it will be permanent.
The right eye must have changed not long after the lenses were changed
in October 1933, or else Dr. Wellington did not get it fitted right at the
time. Anyway, I had discomfort from reading that same winter, and
noticed distinctly that the distance vision of the right eye was very inferior to the other. If I can again read longer and more without bringing on that weary, tired, worn-out feeling, which I had almost in despair come to think might be my permanent lot, I shall be many times
thankful and appreciative. My experience with the oculist had another
happy outcome. From what he had remarked two years ago, I was
fully expecting that he would have to fit me with bifocal lenses this
time, which would mean a bill of considerable size. But he says I do
not need bifocals yet, and that I am fortunate that my eyes have not
changed more in the two years than they have. So with a bill of four
dollars at the oculist's and only about $25 at the dentist's, I feel quite
happy just now. I had imagined the possibilities of a combined expense
for these items of fifty or even seventy-five dollars.

A week ago I made a sandbox for Virgil to play in. At the southeast
corner of the apartment house against the east end foundation wall I
made a frame from old planks salvaged from the debris of the old In-
terurban freight house near the campus. On Monday Mr. Gerber took
us along in the college truck to a sand pit west of Goshen, and we
brought home about a square yard of sand and nearly filled the frame
I had made. The fifteen cents for the sand is all the cash outlay I
made for the sandbox. Of course, the sand will belong to all the apartment house children and maybe to some neighbors too.

Newspapers in headlines and articles have been telling of the des-
perado threats and preparations of Mussolini to make war upon Ethiopia. He appears to me to be a big blusterer, for why should he herald and advertise so long in advance his proposed attack upon a backward country in the equatorial regions of Africa? There will probably
be some kind of war yet, unless it "peters out" in mere braggadocio
before it gets started.

I can get less and less out of newspapers, it seems, for I read them
less with every passing year. I used to read the daily paper, partly
from a sense of duty, because I had an idea that an intelligent person
should know about what is going on in the world from day to day. But
my interest was always something forced and not altogether spontaneous.
Up to 1932 we paid out from four to seven dollars a year for a local

daily newspaper. Since then we get on without and really do not miss it. A recent article in the Christian Century tells something of the effect of newspaper reading upon the American people. A good article.

September 15, 1935   After some days of very cool, sometimes cloudy weather which suggested the possibility of a gloomy, disagreeable autumn in store for us, recent days have been especially welcome. Sunshine, comfortable warmth, all have made for pleasant opening days of school for another year. Registration days netted a goodly number of students for the college year, though without the increase which was generally expected. Because of the improving economic conditions among the farmers, the ready inference was made that more folks would surely go to college this year. But too much was taken for granted, so far as their coming to Goshen College, at least. There is a slight increase over a year ago, but all of this increase and more too is due to the great number seeking training for elementary school teaching. Of freshmen starting a four-year college program, there are less than a year ago by quite a few. The men's dormitory has fewer occupants now than a year ago. The women's dormitory seems to have more occupants.

September 22, 1935   With only ten hours of classroom teaching a week, I find myself strangely affected by some actual leisure time during the week. Not being rushed all the time and tired out and indisposed constantly, it is a grand and happy feeling to feel oneself the master of one's work and not the slave thereof. The college administration earlier announced the need for teachers this year to carry heavy teaching loads again. In view of that announcement, my present schedule is an anomalous surprise to me. If it holds out I shall have time, at least, to do some things to magnify the work of my office, as dean of men. I have in mind some things that could be done, though all I can do is to feel my way along and gradually build up a program of policies and duties for this office.

A moment ago I was interrupted by my colleague, Miss Royer, the dean of women, who spoke of the disturbance by the men in Coffman Hall last night when the lights were turned out. The college is trying out the plan this year of turning off the lights in the two dormitories at a stated time every evening and on again in the morning at stated time. The women's dormitory, being used to stricter supervision, does not seem likely to give any trouble on the point. But the upper class fellows in Coffman Hall, who have not been used to any special regulation, are not reconciled to this particular procedure. They have been setting up a great howl evenings when the lights are thrown off, just like spoiled children, so much so as to disturb the whole neighborhood. I had hoped it would die out presently, but last night was the worst demonstration of any time yet. Just how the matter can be handled to the best advantage and what the outcome will be is a bit uncertain just now.

October 11, 1935   Have just put Virgil to bed for the night. Mrs. Yoder went to the annual function called Sisters All at the college. I am at leisure for the evening. The last two weeks of September I was especially rushed with writing assignments of various kinds. There was the quarterly instalment for the Gospel Herald, about three major news articles, one for the Goshen daily newspaper on the achievement of H. S. Bender in winning his doctor's degrees at Heidelberg on September 21, one a monthly article for the Mennonite Weekly Review at Newton, Kansas, and lastly my first monthly news article for the Gospel Herald. For the College Alumni News Letter I prepared a 1200-word abstract of my paper read at Kitchener in August. And for the first issue of the College Record I wrote a leading article of 1600 words. With this mountain of writing cleared away, I expect to be comparatively free from such assignments for some time to come. I enjoy such writing, but I find that reading is a necessary stimulus for my writing projects, that for every thousand words I attempt to write, I should read five or ten thousand. I think that some of these years I must swear off all teaching and work at the college in the summer months and give myself entirely to writing and more particularly to reading. My slight experience this summer, only in a small way, gave me a small vision of what possibilities might lie in that direction. As it is, however, I find myself already pledging to help out a few persons in getting some German work done up next summer. Apparently I must plan to get away from the college vicinity in order to carry out my purpose for reading and writing.

H. S. Bender reached Goshen from his European trip on last Sunday. This week his class work started. Since my own load is not so heavy this year the desire came over me to realize what has been an ambition of years' standing, that is to acquire some mastery of Hebrew grammar and reading skill. So I started in Hebrew class this week. Ivan Lind, post-graduate student in Bible, is the only other student in the class. Once before, in 1928, I started out with a Hebrew beginning class at Hesston, with the Reverend J. B. Epp as instructor. But chiefly because of the heavy press of other work I dropped out after a month, and while I tried during that winter to keep on working at it, I never mastered the subject. As I go over the beginning lessons now again, though withal in a different text book, some of the material has a familiar air about it as of an old acquaintance. Under more capable direction this time, I believe I shall go through with the course and get enough knowledge of the Hebrew language to enable me to read some in the Old Testament, enough at least so I can in case of need know what the Hebrew text is that lies behind any particular text in the Septuaginta. For I plan to do some special studying in the Greek of the New Testament and pre-New Testament period. Hebrew grammar is really quite interesting, once a body gets down to studying it systematically. I believe I shall enjoy it.

We have had a pleasant fall season so far. There has been killing frost now, about a week ago. But there has been an abundance of foodstuffs from gardens on hand so that there has not been much need for cash outlay of late along that line. The commissary for faculty families in connection with the college dining hall is functioning again as last year, so that one gets there everything possible. In general the financial situation shows signs of easing up for us at our house. It is getting easier to obtain extra cash from the business manager for special purposes. In September I received altogether $90 in cash; besides the check that came spontaneously, there was $10 on the last year's account, and $30 special to pay interest on loan at Newton. And the other week President Kauffman of Hesston wrote about my old account of 1932 still pending at Hesston College. He suggested a settlement for about two-thirds of the account which stood at nearly $102. I wrote appreciatively and explained about my own unpaid accounts in Kansas, and offered to settle in full for $75. Very promptly a check came for just that amount. The idea of asking for more than was offered came to me from C. L. Graber, whose advice I had asked about it. I had all along planned that my credit at Hesston would be exchanged for a note of $100 I gave to the Mennonite Board of Education in 1933, as a special favor for paying taxes and mortgage interest up-to-date. The endowment custodian of the Board had agreed to accept this arrangement. Since he had done nothing further about the matter, I decided that an opportunity to get $75 cash at once should be accepted, as the note to the Board can no doubt be traded out on part of my back salary here some time. So I have the $75 in the bank now. Before long I shall pay the rest of my note with Dr. Haury. The rest of the sum must remain in the bank at Hesston as a foundation for my checking account. For the bank there is catching on to the practices of banks elsewhere, of charging a service fee when the account does not average so much for a month, their minimum however being only $25, or one-fourth as high as at the bank here. So it is still an advantage to do my little banking at Hesston instead of here. For sending away money, checks are still the simplest and cheapest way to remit. This fall I have sent a number of money orders, but they come quite high, so that I shall try to do most of mine by check. The way I discovered the new policy at Hesston was when I received notice of overdraft after they had charged me two dollars or more in service fees!

October 20, 1935 Very pleasant autumn weather is still with us. Mild sunny days, leaves still on the trees are beautifully colored, though the coloration of foliage is not quite so gorgeous as it sometimes has been in other years that I have seen it here. The pleasant days have lured us out-of-doors, for yesterday afternoon we strolled out along the mill race and river, coming back through the woods, spending about three hours out-of-doors. Today again we strolled for an hour or more, going north along the west bank of the race to the first bridge that afforded a crossing. Virgil is always ready to go on such excursions, although when he walks it is not much of a hiking trip for me, rather just a leisurely stroll. Anyway, he is starting his hiking experience at an early age. Perhaps he will not get the habit, so prevalent today, that of sailing over the concrete roads on rubber for recreation and diversion. I am less and less minded to get a petrol buggy for the time being. When the boy is old enough to profit by intelligent travelling, I hope we can acquire such a contrivance and do some educational travelling. None of the modern unresting eternal moving about, going places for us.

Monsignor Mussolini is finally carrying on his long projected war in Ethiopia, according to reports in the papers. I do not follow the news of this war so very closely, even as I follow other world news very indifferently. There is little that I can do about the matter, and world politics is not one of my hobbies. The tangle of such politics and the crisscrossing of the various national interests is a story to make a mere layman's mind reel. Occasional articles of a diagnostic and analytical nature I read with avid interest and find some illumination on the subject and faint glimpses of what it may all be about.

I wish I had a keener interest in all the phases of life with which I make or could make contact. My mind is not versatile and I need to concentrate rather definitely in order to accomplish anything of worth. My physical set-up seems to be improving a little, and my special handicaps of last year are less in evidence. I read continuously with much more comfort than a year ago, less of the almost constant feeling of weariness and exhaustion, a little more "push" to do my work and some extra things. If my regimen will keep me free from so much sinus affliction and head colds, then I shall be happy indeed.

The problems connected with the work of the dean of men and dean of women are coming up in real form of late. The matter of weekend leaves from the campus for trips to distant places, home or otherwise, was rather acute the past few days. It is a thing hard or impossible to regulate by rule, and there are usually so many factors entering into it, that it presents quite a puzzle at times. My difficulty personally is that I cannot think fast and clearly enough when confronted by a particular case on which decision must be made, to make my personal interviews altogether satisfactory. Perhaps I can in the course of time develop a technique that will make them more so. I really never have developed or learned the art of genuine, intimate, and realistic personal conference with others. I feel it is a great weakness on my part. I have never sharpened my wits and thinking habits by practice in sustained argument or debate. I am in such a situation likely to be self-conscious, or something, that obstructs the logical flow of my thoughts. I can always at a later time, after some hours or days, think of the things that should have been said at the time and were not. Whether there is anything that can be done about it on my part now, this is what interests me. But I know of no formula or panacea for my defects along that line. One thing is fairly clear to me: I must develop some skill in argumentation by experience else I cannot guide the freshmen even who know what they want and are determined to get it. It is not, as I see it, a matter of argumentation, so much as guiding and directing their thinking, perhaps.

There has been a plethora of committee meetings, regular and special, the last few weeks, and still there is some work that needs attention, which is lagging for lack of committee attention. I wonder sometimes why there must be so much sitting and sitting and sitting in committees. Would it not be possible to have more individual execution, so as to save some of the time spent in sitting? This fall some things had to wait for the return of H. S. Bender to the campus, which accounts for the recent rush in part. Then too, some time was spent recently in getting ready for a powwow that begins tomorrow at Elkhart, when there are to be some "conversations" carried on by various folks interested in the policies and the activities of Goshen College. Some of the critics are to be there to express their grievances, but withal in some official capacity. The endeavor of the college administration is to make this a time for fullest and frankest expression of opinion and conviction on the part of everyone. Whether such an aim can be reached or not remains to be seen. As it has been, there are always some things that some folks did not feel free to say, for the reason that others would brand them as reprobates or worse. And too, the discussions and criticisms on some points have rarely dealt with what are the really basic issues and principles involved therein. If anything can be done to make all the parties concerned face the real issues, then one forward step will have been taken. There is so much cant and indirection in so much of our ecclesiastical bickering, that one gets quite disgusted sometimes in thinking upon it.

Day after All-Saints, five o'clock in the evening. A Catholic young man came to me yesterday for an excuse for missing first hour class, saying that in his church it was an especially holy day and everyone has to go to church. But as he did not get up in time to go at five-thirty in the morning, he went at seven-thirty, so missing a class in college. I gave him the desired permit. The same lad wished to be excused entirely from our chapel exercises because he is a Catholic and attends his own church regularly. I persuaded him to try it and find out for himself whether he would be getting too much religion by coming to chapel. He has been coming.

The three young women who are reading the Satires of Juvenal are not especially enthusiastic over this author and his subject matter. Naturally not all are alike in their tastes. But I do relish Juvenal's Satires a good deal, although his exaggeration, his digressions, and his lack of perspective do become monotonous, I must say. Surely the foibles and follies of homo insipiens have hardly changed at all in twenty centuries. Have just been reading now in the fourteenth Satire, and a few of his sententiae are interesting. He suggests that human affairs in actual life are the very best shows there are. The fellow who has eyes to see and observe the ambitions, the pursuits, the amusements of the masses, need not pay out money to see the shows, but can find an abundance of matter for diversion and laughter in detaching himself from the mob and observing it for a time. One is reminded of it much nowadays, when, as was predicted for today at Columbus, Ohio, 80,000 humans assemble to watch a football game; when a prize fight between two brutes can attract a host of spectators and an innumerable host of listeners; when a little town like Goshen, as this week, puts on a street carnival with a lot of fool, daredevil stunts; when in general folks are more interested in the froth and frills of life than in its real substance. Life still calls for the services of a Juvenal today, but probably no one would read his lines!

November 10, 1935 It is nine-thirty o'clock and the evening service has just closed. J. C. Clemens of Pennsylvania is preaching today and every evening this week at the college. This afternoon I enjoyed an hour's sleep and so feel quite refreshed. The press of work and study is settling down a little more heavily week by week. The Hebrew study will consume all of my spare time at least for the rest of this semester, as I can well see by this time. I enjoy it very much, but there is such a mass of material for memory to absorb, that it becomes a burden of late.

Virgil plays a good deal now, using his imagination, acting out scenes he observes about him. He has great interest in his stories. He is blessed with a playmate near at hand of about his own age and size in the person of Patricia Brenneman, four years of age. Judging from present indications he will not be a recluse by nature, like his father. Of course, it is possible that he may change as he gets older, but he certainly seeks play company at the present stage of his development. If such is his tendency I hope we can also train him to live with satisfaction in his own company, making a more fortunate combination than it is my own lot to enjoy.

Tomorrow is another anniversary of Armistice Day and it is in order to take a look over the seventeen years of peace that we have had since then. It is perhaps significant that we observe the anniversary of the Armistice rather than that of the final peace treaty drawn up at Versailles. For experience has proved that it is still an armistice under which we are living rather than under a condition of world peace. The selfishness, greed, and imperialism, which was so evident at Versailles, and which perhaps broke Woodrow Wilson's heart, have in no wise abated since that time, and are still the most potent forces in international relations.

November 17, 1935 After evening service I again jot down a few lines of notes. I have a new regimen for health and physical fitness which I started following early this fall in the fond hope that I could escape my head cold afflictions which hindered me so very much during all of last winter. So far this fall I do seem to have more energy, less of the sluggish worn-out feeling that always made me want to be lying down to rest. My suffering from cold feet, which was so annoying last winter, does not bother me so much thus far. Hope I can get a regimen worked out that will make me more efficient. My eyes too are so much better now than the last few years, so that I can read more with less discomfort. For exercise I have been walking once or twice a week.

December 8, 1935 Too busy with extra things to do for leisure time jottings. When I was beginning to feel a bit of confidence that I might not be afflicted with colds, I caught a vigorous influenza bug. I got over it more completely and quickly than I used to last winter, so I have some reason to think my previous hopes were not entirely vain. For a week I have been taking the juice of two oranges and half a lemon mixed together every evening before going to bed. It tastes delicious, at least. Estie and the boy are also taking the same amount, excepting Virgil does not get as much lemon juice. This health problem is a rather puzzling matter and we must keep on experimenting until we find some way to control colds and such like afflictions.

December 19, 1935 Vacation begins today at noon. It is a real relief to me and I purpose to enjoy it, not however in total idleness, for I have a list of about ten activities or projects which I plan to work on at my leisure. Most of these involve reading various books and periodicals on which I have fallen behind during recent months. I may essay a bit of writing; in fact, there is a little that I must do per program.

Indiana skies have given us very little sunshine during the past two months. The snow of Thanksgiving time had about all disappeared until this week when more flurries have fallen. Christmas will probably be white again this year. First time for awhile we sent a few gifts away by mail. At our home we have always exercised a conscience against elaborate Christmas preparations. Since the depression we have given very few gifts of any sort. This year, since we can secure books through the college bookstore without paying cash out of pocket for them, I took three to send to the families in Iowa. To brother Dan's family we sent a copy of Egermeier's Bible Stories for the children, and to sister Barbara's family another copy of the same. To Herman's family I sent a copy of the new book, "The Triumph of John and Betty Stam," which is the story of the missionaries to China who lost their lives at the hands of bandits not so long ago.

A few weeks ago when Dean H. S. Bender took his turn in conducting college chapel he took the opportunity to air a few new ideas he had picked up relative to the immortality of the soul, death, resurrection, and kindred themes. He undertook to combat the current conceptions of the soul as surviving the body and passing on to another existence as such. This way of thinking he claimed came from Greek rationalistic philosophy and is not Biblical. Naturally the discussion was highly philosophical, if not metaphysical, so much so that the average undergraduate could not possibly comprehend what the speaker meant to say. Result was that a few isolated statements were caught by some, statements emphatically made and that of themselves were contradictory to commonly accepted thought upon the subject. So it comes to pass that queries are coming from various places questioning the orthodoxy of the teaching given here. I personally enjoyed witnessing the philosophical somersaults and handsprings of the speaker, but frankly saw no point in putting on the intellectual stunt before such an audience. It is a stimulating idea, and I would enjoy playing with it myself, but some folks, in fact most, cannot even appreciate the point in such a discussion. I never have developed a taste for speculative thinking, although I relish a little smell of it once in a while. The past, the real substantial past, attracts me infinitely more. For in working upon matters of the past I feel one has his feet upon the solid earth. Understanding and interpreting the things of the past is as substantial intellectual exercise as speculative ratiocinations.

Started reading a novel just now, "The Curse in the Colophon," written by Edgar J. Goodspeed, professor of New Testament Language at Chicago University. It is a story of mystery and adventure in tracing out the history and travels of old mediaeval manuscripts of the N. T. I enjoy it, especially the "atmosphere," very much, so far as I have come.

Shortest Day of the Year! That's what the almanac makers say of today, or is it tomorrow? It can be either day so far as my own observation goes. I take the liberty to lengthen out this day at the latter end, because I indulged in a long siesta today after a late dinner. Estie is getting her eyes fitted with corrective glasses, which, according to the oculist, she has long been needing. He judges only from his present examinations, for she never had her eyes tested before. For several years she has experienced discomfort and difficulty in reading much, something she has always been in the habit of doing. Sewing too has been a great trial, and especially in more recent months. I anticipate she will be doing these things with a good deal more ease and comfort from now on.

Incidentally, on our trip down town, we also did some Christmas shopping, mostly if not entirely of things for ourselves. Virgil and his mother acquired some footwear. Today a coaster sled for Virgil came along. But there is no coasting place within easy distance from here. At present he does not even want to sit on it for me to pull him. Wants to pull it himself.

Called upon Dr. Young to pay up our account of last year and consult about Virgil's health, etc. He has been having a good deal of cold in his nose and head all along, since October, when he had a severe attack. Doctor gave a tonic for him to take and also advised favorably on "shots" for immunity against whooping cough, which he thinks has in some cases created resistance against colds and running nose. We had him give the boy the first round of "shots," with two more rounds to come at weekly intervals. Virgil has no special fondness for the doctor. He has not much courage in the face of physical pain, something like his daddy. He is getting some practice in submitting to the inevitable. His reactions are quite interesting. When his will and feeling has been subdued over any incident, he will not talk about the matter afterwards. In fact, while it is fresh on his mind he will "converse" diligently about something else, so as to cast the painful memory of the experience from his mind. He has a very sensitive nature, and I can imagine to some extent what he must suffer as he learns of the realities of a stern and hard world. He will likely be shy and bashful, which as I can know from experience, will be a source of pain and suffering and perhaps unhappiness to him as he develops. Probably one of our greatest problems will be to help him adjust himself to a grim and often heartless world. We try to avoid making him self-conscious, and I realize our efforts along this line should be positive as well as negative. I feel very helpless in facing this part of the problem. We must somehow provide objective interests for him, so he will not come to brood and worry as he grows older and becomes conscious of his own thoughts and feelings. At present he plays a good deal by himself, impersonating, carrying on conversation with an imaginary playmate or with his toy animals. It is very embarrassing to him to be made conscious of what he is doing, and we try to ignore him when he is talking to himself and carrying on in our presence. Rather join in occasionally and help him on.

December 23, 1935 Die Lunae, bora vespertina. This is the year and month when the classical world unites in commemorating the bimillenary anniversary of the birth of the Roman poet, Quintus Horatius Flaccus. During this vacation I am playing a little with the idea of preparing a brief paper for reading in chapel assembly some Friday morning on Horace and posing it as a gesture, at least, in the Bimillennium celebration. I could prepare the essay without such an ulterior motive as that of hoping to read it in public. On the other hand the interest in Latin and classics generally, is so low here that

I have a conviction that such an occasion as this wide celebration in honor of Horace should by all means be used as a convenient excuse for giving a bit of modest publicity to the pursuit of Latin and to classical culture generally. I am not a go-getting publicity man, but such an occasion would be an acceptable opportunity for at least modestly calling attention to my own teaching department. The prospects just at present are far from rosy for Latin. No one started in the department either last year or this year, and it may die a natural death in the course of a short time. At the same time I live in the hope that the tide of time may bring in some Latin students by another year, so that I may have something to teach in my favorite field. If the Latin should dwindle down, I may need to prepare myself to teach more in some other field. Several years ago when the Ensses left Goshen, H. S. Bender sounded me out on the matter of equipping myself for teaching German regularly in addition to Latin and Greek. But really I have no special desire in going on with preparation in that line. What would interest me more at this time is the thought of doing more work in Biblical languages, both N. T. Language and Literature and O. T. Language. In fact, since I am studying Hebrew this year, Dean Bender has been suggesting just this very thing. He hints at a year of seminary study, mostly for training in Greek and Hebrew exegesis. He thinks I should also indulge in some theology, which is perhaps correct, although I am not so keen for it. Just what the advanced Bible department of the college here will become is hard to say. However, as the demand for more trained church workers is almost sure to increase, it seems reasonable to assume that it will grow some, though probably not too phenomenally in my lifetime.

I think I shall hereafter consistently refuse to do teaching in the summertime, with a view to doing more free lance studying and some writing. Were I not studying Hebrew this year, I would have fine opportunity to carry on considerable independent reading and study. But as it is, I have been doing very little. The survey commission is still struggling to carry on its work as outlined, which intrudes heavily upon one's time and energy. The organization of the college Peace Society has taken some time, and all in all, it was a pretty heavy load during November and December. But I really am happy to get my Hebrew after wishing for it so many years, and if I can master it as I wish, I shall count it a great achievement.

Christmas Day, 1935 The annual day of cheer and festivity is soon at the close. It has been a stormy day, with snow falling and sinking temperature about all day long. We ate our dinner this afternoon with the folks upstairs, same as last year, excepting the fact that until about the last minute the women had planned to serve it downstairs instead of upstairs. The hasty change in plans was due to Paul being doomed to spend his Christmas day in bed because of an injury received the day before while skiing. Estie did much of the culinary preparations in her own kitchen and then conveyed the results to the table above.

Christmas time begins to assume a more objective significance at our house as the boy gets old enough to appreciate the occasion. From various sources he received quite an array of presents for a little fellow. Enough to make the day seem just a little cluttered up, compared to the simplicity we still prefer. But it will mean something to him and he ought not be deprived of it.

The traditional Santa Claus brought me an unexpected present this morning: four dollars and fifty cents from the men's Bible Class, of which I have served as teacher since last February due to the leaving of W. H. Smith for Bloomington and the consequent choice of Walter Yoder as superintendent for the Sunday school. Yoder had been teacher of the Bible Class for some time, and with his leaving them, I was chosen by the class to be regular teacher. It is not a large class, eight to ten average attendance at the most. Most of them are appreciative of the efforts I make. One fellow, Mr. Slabaugh, last summer complimented me personally very highly for my efforts, saying something about the very best approach to and presentation of the lessons he has ever observed. He is the kind of gentleman who is rather ready to speak and express himself, and I did not take his expression as an occasion for feeling flattered over it. The group likes best to be lectured at, as seemingly it is hard to get much discussion and active participation from them.

And what to do with the unexpected cash that thus has come into my hands? It would come in just fine for eking out this month's budget, which has suffered considerably from the purchases made last week. On the other hand, since I did not buy any Christmas present for myself, perhaps I should still get myself an unexpected gift of some kind. A watch would be a possible suggestion, since for a year and a half I have lacked such a luxury. Experience has shown that it is not impossible to get along without a timepiece. The last watch I had was a dollar and a half brand of some popular make, which brother Herman gave me about five years ago. It served well enough for over three years. Had had some thought of investing in a wrist watch, since I never have owned a watch chain. The only watch fob I ever owned has long been worn out. It was a souvenir I acquired about 1918 at the Cave of the Winds near Manitou, Colorado. The leather strap could, of course, be replaced, for that is the only part worn out. The souvenir part I must still have among my relics somewhere.

While I could get some use out of a watch, since doing so long without any such appurtenance, I find myself about half wishing that I would not need to take on such impedimenta any more. The depression has taught us of various things that one can get along without, and such getting along has in some cases become almost habitual routine, and so has enough sentiment attached to it, that I really dislike to go back to former ways of doing. I believe we can really be happier by having less things about us. Even such "things" as a daily newspaper, a telephone, or a car, seem after all more like impedimenta, at least for us, than necessities of life. The world is at all times "too much with us" as it is, so that if we can learn to live without so many contacts with its noise, its spirit, its maddening tempo, and its distracting ballyhoo, we will be better off.

What I wish for, and hope we can have some time in fuller abundance, is the means for cultivating the mind and spirit, in the way of music, pictures, books, concerts, and the like. But it seems that during most of the fifteen years since we married our chief preoccupation has been the problems of comfortable animal existence, and especially in the recent years past, but one learns to utilize even meagre opportunities for such satisfactions and lives in hope of better things to come.

December 26, 1935 Very cold weather prevails, deep snow, genuine winter. Half of our vacation span is gone now. Soon enough again the burden of routine will drop full weight upon my mind and shoulders. The January issue of the Atlantic Monthly came today and I turned almost at once to an article by Albert Jay Nock on "Freedom of Speech and Plain Language." Mr. Nock is always a forceful writer, suggesting the sort of ideas that are good to whet one's mind on. I usually agree with him, for he is good at analyzing, has real breadth of vision and a far-reaching background. Especially good in this latest article is what he has to say on plain speaking and plain language. He lays it soundly on euphemisms and indirection, which are so common in American speech habits. This idea has many applications in various fields, and I should like sometime to go through with a study of it.

Ever since about September this last fall I have been taking enough of my valuable time from useful work (or work that seems to be or is supposed to be useful) to do the apparently useless work of solving the Double Acrostic that is printed in the Saturday Review of Literature. I get hold of the copy weekly as soon as it appears on the library shelves and set about to solve it. The process takes an average of several hours of time, but I find it interesting and recreational. The acrostic consists of two parts. One is a rectangular space filled with black and white squares, mostly white. In the white squares is room for the words of a quotation from some book or poem, each black space serving for word division only. There are usually between 150 and 200 white spaces which are numbered consecutively. The second part is a scheme with room for about twenty-five words, on an average, each letter of every word being represented by a dash line beneath which is printed the number the letter will have when the quotation in part One is finally and correctly filled in. These spaces for words are in a column, to the left of which are brief definitions or synonyms, about in the style in which cross-word puzzle words are identified. Only these identifications are not so stereotyped and plebeian as they are for the cross-word puzzles, usually. They are often words that occur in literature, as titles, authors, classical or mythological terms. And finally when the words in the column have all been discovered and filled in, the initial letters of these words read downward will spell out the name of the author and the title of the work from which the quotation in the rectangular box is taken. By then transferring the letters from the discovered words into the numbered squares, one can read the quotation easy as pie. In actual practice I work both ways, from above downwards as well as from below upwards. It is seldom that I can guess offhand more than one-fourth of the words that need to be discovered. After I have all I can easily guess and be quite sure to be correct, I transfer the letters to the numbered squares as far as they will go. Then usually the skeletons of some words of the quotation will be full enough to make a correct guess of the words they are in. Then by transferring letters to the numbers below it becomes possible to guess others of the words in the column. Thus by working back and forth, usually after correcting a few errors and wrong guesses, I get it all filled out. The one today, from last Saturday's Review, was as hard as any I have struck for some time. It is from Thackeray's, "The Mahogany Tree," and is poetry, which is often harder to decipher, and while I have all the spaces filled in and it sounds readable, yet the first word in the column seems to be a mistake; at any rate I have stopped puzzling over it and shall wait until the next issue comes and see where I have missed the correct solution, if I did. For one thing, I do occasionally learn something new, either some totally new word, one I had never seen or heard before, or something new from literature. My acquaintance with English and American literature, especially recent and modern, is very limited and so I am much handicapped for solving the puzzles quickly.

This and volley ball for about an hour and a half every week, constitutes my outlay of time for recreation. Sometimes walking comes in too, though not so regularly of late, due probably to the volley ball games. Naturally here too should be counted the time I spend, some about every day, helping Virgil play at home. He usually proposes something while we wait for the evening meal to be ready, either building a house with blocks, or playing train on the floor with blocks, or something else. On most evenings it is my task to read stories to him, so I get a good deal of recreation.

December 28, 1935 Spent most of yesterday on errands in town. It was a cold day and a little unpleasant. But we almost had to go, for Virgil had an appointment with Dr. Young and Estie with Dr. Wellington. I managed to get Paul Bender's ancient Chevrolet persuaded to go into action, and so we spent from 10:30 to 1:30 on that mission. Estie finally got her glasses and she is asked to wear them regularly. We had hoped she would not need to wear them except for reading and sewing. Dr. Wellington is very considerate of college teachers, for he deducted two dollars from the regular charge in this case, making the bill come to $10.25, which is not as high as I had expected it might be. Virgil reported at Dr. Young's office for the second series of "shots" for protection against whooping cough. He does not like at all to have the doctor hurt him, but he does not fight or resist when the dreaded moment comes, just cries and whimpers piteously. The doctor gives him a stick of chewing gum each time when the ordeal is over. The first time he suffered a slight reaction that made him miserable for several hours in the evening. This time, as the doctor predicted, the reaction was more severe; he felt very bad in the afternoon and evening; the tears flowed from his eyes and he could not understand what makes the tears come. This morning he felt much better, though he seemed to have a little fever. The third and last series next week is not supposed to affect him so much, and then at the end of four months he will be immune against whooping cough, for at least seven years. That is the length of time since such treatments were first given, and no case has been known of where any child has taken the whooping cough after the treatment. Dr. Young thinks that further experience with the treatment may prove that it immunizes a person for life against attack.

In the afternoon of yesterday I walked to town again, principally to read current periodicals in the public library. It was pleasant walking and not uncomfortable, with the fur-lined ear protectors of my cap turned down. The idling time of vacation is about past for me, and to get my work ready and all lined up for resumption of class work, I need to settle down into the harness again on Monday.

December 29, 1935 Last Sunday of the year. This year seems destined to pass out with people generally in the world feeling as much gloom and pessimism as has been the case for some time, so far as my observation goes. The situation in Europe is the cause of a great part of this gloom. Practically all observers see little ground for optimism. A general European war, perhaps a world war is in near prospect. A general feeling of fear, despair, and disillusionment seems to be settling down upon people, especially those who read and think. The widespread decay of idealism, the almost universal threat against human liberty, freedom, and individual personality, the rising tide of fascism, selfish nationalism, and hysterical militarism, all these and other factors combine into a vital challenge to Christian faith and Christian idealism. There is, to be sure, no ground for pessimism for the Christian believer, that is, absolute pessimism as a world view. For the humanists and all who know of no superhuman resources in human history, who believe that all of man's resources for his salvation are inherent in man himself, or in human society, a form of desperate pessimism is about the only possible result of a realistic view of the contemporary world scene.

Mennonites have not generally taken an active interest in world problems as such. Most of them have probably felt towards the variable and changing tides of political fortune about like a character in "Wilhelm Tell" expresses the matter, comparing such matters to the violent or gentler manifestations of the forces of nature, storms, floods, pestilence, earthquakes, wars, and so on. The growing popularity of fascism, of the concept of the totalitarian state, and kindred ideas is really about the most significant phenomenon observable today. Our Mennonite thinking about the state and government is directly affected by this thing and, I suspect, a good deal more so than most folks realize. The glib, easy way in which we usually hear the relation of the state to the Christians expressed among us, more in a formulaic way than in an intelligent way, I believe, is that God ordains governments and rulers to do their work, even as He establishes and maintains the Church. And that we owe full obedience and cooperation to the government, except on such specific points as conflict with direct Scriptural commands. This is a handy formula. But I myself am for rethinking the formula, especially in view of the prevailing and growing concept of the totalitarian nationalistic state in the world today.

Mennonites suffered from governments in Europe so long that when they settled in America and found here a veritable haven of refuge from persecution and suffering, they, it seems to me, have almost fallen over backwards in their reaction of uncritical support of government. It is not hard to understand this attitude which grew out of a feeling of sincere and heartfelt appreciation for the liberties and privileges they enjoyed in America. It has occurred to me that these very liberties, of worship, of speech and assembly, as they are written into our Federal Constitution came there through the grace of 18th century political liberalism more than through the religious ideology of that time. How nearly this is correct, I am unable to say. If in any way correct, it seems we should appreciate, and our active sympathies should now be with liberalism in politics and thought, rather than with the tendencies now everywhere gaining the ascendency, the tendency to curtail individual freedom in the interests of a supreme and paternalistic state. And yet, Mennonites are by their very nature conservative, have always made a great virtue of obedience, submission, discipline, regulation, etc. So it comes to pass that we will probably, in the early stages of fascism at least, give our moral support to and do our thinking in favor of the very forces that will in the end deprive us of the very liberties we cherish and appreciate most. In view of this situation I feel that some rethinking and some careful analyzing needs to be done.

Take now the oath of support for the Constitution, laws that are being passed in growing numbers in different states. Mennonite teachers make these pledges as a routine procedure. But is this only a matter of routine? Someone should study and analyze the whole matter, so that we may know what is involved. If the argument that teachers can as justly be asked to pledge support to the Constitution as any government official is granted, then we admit at once that public school teachers are in effect government officials. If that should be granted, then for Mennonites at least, and we believe for all Christians, two unchristian propositions are involved. First, nonresistant Christians cannot with good conscience hold government positions, and second, it grants the fascist principle that the public schools are a direct arm of the government to be used by it for propaganda of whatever kind it may desire. Here again clear thinking is needed and definite study.

The Sunday school lessons of the quarter just closed have been on the Old Testament History from Isaiah to Malachi. I find such historical study interesting for my part. For the review of the quarter, I tried this morning to philosophize somewhat on the meaning of Israelitish history. My ideas are fascinating to me, but still very hazy, I must confess. The O. T. history is essentially the record of God's program for creating a nation, a people, to be the advance guards of higher morals, purer living, more spiritual worship and service, in short of the kingdom of God as formally announced by Jesus. This program had as an essential, unavoidable, and perfectly logical concomitant the development of a separateness from the rest of mankind. It required centuries of endeavor on God's part, discipline, revelation, prophetic guidance to accomplish it, but the program in essential aims succeeded. For the Jews developed a group consciousness, a cultural tissue, a religious background that made them separate if it made them anything.

An article in the Atlantic Monthly which has just come, written by a Jew, is an attempted explanation of why the Jews have suffered throughout all their history so sorely from persecution. He, very interestingly, stresses this note of separateness. As a minority mixed in with majorities in various countries, the Jews by their superiority in morals and ethics generally, in God-consciousness, and in other ways, are a constant rebuke and condemnation to the majorities, hence in unconscious self-defence the majorities hate them and persecute them. The writer has good information on the Zionist movement. I wondered further in thinking about the article: Because the Jews today are what they are, and have been supernaturally and divinely created to be such, do not other men who seek not to have God in all their thoughts, react against this historical testimony to the fact of God by persecuting the Jews?

Received recently three books ordered from Blackwells at Oxford. Several times a year I aim to send for something from there, partly to keep alive my connection with this British bookseller so he will continue to send me his book catalogs of new and second-hand books. He has been sending regularly his lists of Latin, Greek, and Classics, and also of theological books. This time I ordered two books on the Greek of the Septuagint, and Milligan's book on the New Testament Documents. While ordering I also included a copy of the Blodig's Alpine Calendar. Have long contemplated getting this calendar, which Blackwell has advertised as desirable for its splendid collection of photographs. Since receiving it, I like it very much. I find it contains about one hundred splendid photographs beautifully printed of mountain scenes from different parts of the world though principally from the Alps in Europe. The calendar is printed in Germany though prepared in English. It costs three shillings-six pence net, and I shall appreciate it every day next year on my desk. I have paid enough visits to our Rocky Mountains in the West to enjoy and appreciate beautiful mountain scenery and views.

December 30, 1935 M.C. Lehman is quite interested in the possibilities of some conferences on nonconformity which he is working on. It is sort of a hobby on his part, and he thinks he has a line of approach to the whole subject that will lead us all out of the woods. He harps on the idea that simplicity and nonconformity must be made to apply to the whole of our individual and group life, implying that we have come far short of making a consistent application so far. I too believe in discussing and exploring the principles and the basic philosophies underlying the practices we hold or profess to hold. But simplicity is more an attitude of mind and heart than a matter of particular practices. Just like humility and some other Christian graces, which cannot be defined in specific outward forms, so simplicity is a general attitude, for some can be proud in plain clothing, and others can be truly humble in stylish clothing. Again like humility, I suspect very much that if we set out with deliberate purpose to cultivate this grace of simplicity, we shall end up by losing its essence in the process. With a firm and consistent emphasis on piety, spirituality, godliness, purity, etc., simplicity will be one of the graceful flowers that will blossom forth as a result. It is true that tastes for what is beautiful and substantial can be cultivated, for nearly all attempts at artificial beautification are disgustingly bizarre, superficial, frothy. But I can hardly conceive of avoiding such unsightly results by prescribing by law what must be done in all the details. So I do not know just how enthusiastic I am for holding a series of special conferences for the pursuit of this simplicity. It is almost too much like a will-o-the-wisp for such tactics.

I wish every possible success to those who are interested in promoting such tactics. But for myself I shall hesitate to pour a great deal of my energy into such channels just at this time. As for running hither and yon to attend conferences, I am frankly not interested. I already anticipate that Lehman will be urging me to prepare a paper of some kind. I feel that I made my contribution to the problem last summer, and anyway, this business of compiling on the spur of the moment a number of thousands of words is not my idea of constructive thinking and working on the subject. If I were to undertake anything on the subject, I should like to spend some time studying the idea of a special kind of apparel that is worn for purposes of religious identification, what is its origin in antiquity and its purpose and use in modern times. Is the clerical and monastic garb a hold over from pagan religious ceremonialism? Is the clerical garb among Protestant ministers a direct descent from Catholic practice? And is the practice among Mennonites an imitation of Protestant clergymen, or is it a fossilized remainder of an earlier general style of coat collar worn by men? When and how did it come into the Mennonite Church for laymen, etc., etc.?

Kalends of January! 1936 First day of a brand new year! Not much different from last year as represented by yesterday or the day before. Tomorrow the pressure goes on again. The year of our Lord nineteen hundred thirty-six! What is it destined to bring forth? As ever, hope for better things, for health, happiness, financial improvements and so forth springs and flourishes eternally. I note that Babson, financial and economic seer, predicts another ten percent improvement in recovery this coming year and return to normal conditions in the year following. Another financial prognosticator says that our country is headed for the greatest period of inflation in its history. As for several months past, war threatens daily to break out in Europe. So there is plenty to make life interesting. I understand that specialists in the details of Biblical prophecy have been predicting the years 1935 or 1936 as fulfilling some time predictions they find in the Bible. Time must tell us whether their ideas are correct or not.

January 4, 1936 Started this new year's writing by blotting the second page, and my pen has a bad spell right now; so I guess I shall not write very much today. Have not a great deal of inspiration anyway. Abominable weather has been with us, slush, rain, mist, fog, sleet, snow and such like. The changes in weather and temperature are more rapid than in Iowa or Kansas. A body has not time to get used to any kind or style of weather, for when one's physical apparatus has fairly begun to adjust itself to a particular kind, the whole situation changes and you must start over again. We took Virgil to Dr. Young for his third and last round of "shots" this morning. When we talked about going he was very visibly troubled and worried. He tried to be brave, to get his mind away from the awful experience he knew was coming. In tones of desperate agony he asked the doctor, "You will not hurt me much!" just before he pierced his arm.

January 11, 1936 I checked up this morning on my cash income for

1935, doing so through the business office of the college. Adding up all I got by cash, barter, rent, and so forth, it appears that the sum is about $1035 in value received. The only items I can recall to have received from other sources are $75 cash for closing the old salary account at Hesston, I agreeing to settle for that sum for the hundred plus dollars still owed by them. Thus the $30 received from the Peace Problems Committee for work done for them, brings the amount up to around $1140 as gross income for the calendar year, amounting to something like $150 more than a year ago. For I recall that when a year ago I figured up income to see if I was eligible to pay income tax in the state, I was just at the edge and did not pay any. Most of the added $150 has gone for taxes in Kansas. It so happened that I put off paying my 1934 taxes until February and June of this last year, while the last year's tax I paid in full in December of the same year, so that two years' tax came out of last year's income. That accounts for more than a hundred dollars. My hope is that I may be able to collect enough extra income during this present year to get all my arrears in interest paid up, which will require at least two hundred dollars. After four years of depression thinking, I really wonder what and how I would think if I were actually paid up to date and surplus cash would begin to accumulate on my hands. It would require a readjustment but probably not one as difficult to make as the opposite one of several years ago.

January 16, 1936 It is just a few minutes until time for the lecture of the evening. A Dr. Rice from the Indiana University medical school is to be the speaker of the evening. He discourses on some subject connected with diseases and their prevention. The same lecturer spoke here two years ago, on the interesting subject of "Postponing Our Funerals." On that occasion Mrs. Yoder went to hear him. This time she is staying at home.

A week ago this evening we heard Mr. George Sokolsky give a lecture on Japan and her part in Far Eastern affairs. A well-informed man who lived in China for a good many years after he was expelled from Soviet Russia, he proved also to be an interesting lecturer. We learned a good many interesting facts that evening. The gentleman has a sort of droll humor, a dash of charming irony, and a keen mind. He seemed to appreciate the interested and generally attentive audience; most speakers do; sometimes one expresses himself at the close or afterwards to that effect. This one said nothing, at least in public, but the way he warmed up in his manner proved it.

Here it is now two hours later, and the lecturer has just left off. He talked about the triumphs of medical science over diseases, told about the diseases still unconquered, and the general status of the fight against diseases. Four are still unresponsive to medical efforts: the common cold, influenza, menengitis and infantile paralysis. Cancer and the degenerative diseases are the occasion for the most deaths at the present time. The man is well informed, and is something of a philosopher, a moralist and a preacher. His closing preachment was over an outline of four points, four factors to which men and women must adjust themselves for healthful, happy living. They are work, play, love, religion. It was good doctrine, especially for the young people. Coming from a man of his experience and standing it carried considerable weight.

I. W. Royer gave a rather unique little talk in the regular devotional meeting this morning, reading a good deal from a book that quoted some poems, one on living in Goshen, and two answering poems, combating the escape philosophy proclaimed by the first. The poems originally appeared in the Christian Century, but hardly refer to our Goshen.

January 18, 1936   Strangely enough, I am for once not under such extreme pressure of work that must be done. I could write on an essay on Quintus Horatius Flaccus for presentation in a chapel lecture in about six weeks hence; I could prepare examination questions for torturing the students in my courses next week, which is the set time for the semiannual academic inquisition; I could do other things, if I so chose. For instance I might try to write a paper on the perennially interesting topic of nonconformity, for M. C. Lehman has indirectly asked me if I would prepare something for presentation, but I shall not comply this time. Perhaps for another year I shall feel the motion of the spirit to enter the lists of those who wage wordy combat over this subject. It is not a very deep and elemental and basic subject, in my opinion, and to try to isolate it as a major issue is, I feel, to expose oneself to the danger of losing one's perspective on the entire subject. Only as a sideline, a subsidiary and secondary subject, as a phase of greater issues can I think of the subject of nonconformity to the world.

Miss Royer, dean of women, and myself are proposing some plans right now for doing propaganda and educational work among our student group, aiming at influencing their behaviour and conduct. There are two phases to this problem as I see it. First of all, we seek to have students conduct themselves while here in accordance with the ideals and standards of the college. But we cannot feel satisfied with mere conformity on their part while here; the young people must become informed about the facts and principles that lie at the base of the ideals of conduct we uphold, so that they will with conviction live and teach them, not only here but wherever else they may go in after years. Our efforts along these lines have been too haphazard and spasmodic for very effective results. A year ago we were "worked up" over the subject of theatre attendance, and we did some things that helped the matter, at least that has secured some measure of general conformity to required standards. Just now we are a little "worked up" again on the matter of sex education for the students, partly because of a certain sad tragedy that has befallen a graduate of several years ago. From incidental remarks, I understand, or rather infer, that it was partly because she was ignorant of the technique of the sex act itself. How any person of even mediocre intelligence can go through college, study science courses and others, and remain so ignorant as that is a puzzle to me. Parents are, of course, basically to blame in such matters. But even so, a mind with any native curiosity at all, one would think, must come into possession of such facts in high school and college.

Sometimes I try to recall to my mind my own experiences in gaining a knowledge of sex facts as a boy and young man. Somehow I cannot call back many specific experiences, or how I came by the knowledge I did obtain. My parents never gave any direct or indirect instruction on the subject. I think among country school boys in the community there was a good deal of general information passed down constantly from one generation of boys to the next. Fortunately in our community this was not vicious or perverted information, but mostly factual and normal, although I remember that sexy stories were often told among boys. I was also a voracious reader as a young boy, of everything I could lay my hands on, and so I gradually discovered for myself most of the technical and scientific knowledge about sex life and human reproduction. I recall that we had a large home medical book, and I surreptitiously devoured all the information in it on gestation, child-birth, etc. Later, but before I ever went away to school, I extracted a good deal of technical information from Webster's unabridged dictionary, a special small dictionary of medical terms, and the English Bible, which is among other things a source of much sexual information, especially the O. T. I remember how I lone-handed figured out from the Bible and dictionaries what unnatural sexual vice was. The story of Lot in Sodom, I remember, probably first put me on the trail of that particular subject. I found other references to it in the O. T. The word Sodomite then led me to the dictionaries, and so on and on from one point to another. Then with this knowledge as a background, I understood several passages in the N. T., notably several verses in Romans, chapter 1, and a phrase in I Cor. 6:9, "nor effeminate, nor abusers of themselves with mankind." And after getting this information I remember discussing the matter with a friend, older than myself, who could not contribute much to my knowledge, as I recall now. And so, because of my own curiosity and mental hunger, such information became commonplace in my stock of knowledge. Of course, when I came to read in Greek and Latin literature, contact with such ideas was frequent. It seems to me that mental hygiene calls for just such an attitude toward all bodily functions. It is certainly unhygienic for the individual to be cumbered with the attitude in his own mind that the thought or the knowledge, or under proper conditions the discussion of the normal functions of sex is in any way more wicked or sinful than that of any other bodily functions or activities. It would certainly be an all-round gain if all young people could be given an objective and unemotional knowledge of all sex functions, uses as well as abuses thereof.

I recall now a curious experience I had just a few years ago. I was translating Juvenal's second Satire, and in rummaging through the dictionaries, I came upon the word "bugger" as a term applied to one who practices the unnatural vice. It was the first time I had ever found the word in a dictionary. Interestingly enough I remembered that the word "bugger" often pronounced "booger" was frequently used in our community at home, as a fairly common epithet of reproach, not the worst one that could be used, but I should judge about half-way down the scale of reproachful epithets. I never knew or heard what the word meant or where it had come from, and I doubt very much if anyone else did. Interestingly enough I found the word comes from the French. The French took it from the Late Latin word Bulgarus, literally a Bulgarian. The use of the word in reproach goes back to the middle ages when

Bulgaria was a center of nonconformist Christianity, of somewhat the type that we Mennonites like to claim as our own spiritual prototype. But these nonconformists were persecuted as heretics by the Catholic Church. They were accused of many crimes and vices, among them the unnatural vice of sodomy, so that Bulgarian came to be a violent term of reproach applied first to heretics and then to any vile wretch. An interesting side-light on Mennonite history, is it?!!

January 26, 1936 First semester examinations were given last week, and though I had only a comparatively few papers to grade, I still have the largest batch of them to read. Devoted a good deal of time during examination days to the special projects in connection with the Mennonite Quarterly Review circulation campaign. My teaching program for the semester that opens tomorrow includes two more hours of classes a week than last semester. Teaching of Latin is to be offered to two students.

I am determined to keep on with Hebrew study also. Instructor Bender announced that we will begin reading in the Hebrew Bible at once, a little every week, meanwhile also finishing up the remaining lessons in the Grammar, a matter of a dozen lessons or more. I had studied the first chapter of Genesis once, the time I started Hebrew before, so that if he starts at the beginning of the Hebrew Bible I should not have much difficulty in that part for a while. I just have not found it possible to master the vocabulary set in the Grammar the past month, but I must keep on working on them constantly, even during next summer, if necessary, for a mastery of basic vocabulary will certainly be of immense help in reading the Hebrew text with satisfaction and pleasure; that much I can easily see already. For Hebrew syntax is almost negligible, and the grammar is comparatively simple once a person gets the "hang of it." But vocabulary is the crux, for me at least. Particularly in view of the way Hebrew forms the different parts of speech and related words from the typical three-radical roots, the learning of the root words is very essential. Learning Hebrew is for me a really vigorous mental exercise, very tiring, in fact exhausting. But I feel it is real achievement, and that is the way I have always felt about language study. Language has never been easy for me, in fact it has been study of the hardest kind, but either because of, or in spite of this fact, I have always felt a genuine affinity for it. I suspect it is mostly because of it. For there is a real mental and spiritual satisfaction in mastering what is difficult. It is to me infinitely more satisfying to chew on something tough, solid, substantial, like Latin or Greek grammar, beefsteak as it were, than to try to use one's mental molars on frothy cake-icing or something uncertain like gum-drops, or chocolate that melts in one's mouth, like psychology, sociology, or what you have.

March 1, 1936 I seem unable to budget any regular time to this matter of writing leisure notes. So I find that more than a month has elapsed since I last sat down to such a task, which should be not a task, but a pastime. February was again quite a busy month. Gave considerable time and energy to a subscription campaign for the Mennonite Quarterly Review. Was also retarded by an attack of the influenza. It was as bad as and worse than any I had since just about three years earlier. I spent two entire days in bed and for another week did very little excepting necessary routine. This last weekend I was absent from home for a day and a half, in order to attend the sessions of a conference on "Christian World Order" at Manchester College. Here I was an interested spectator, making some useful observations. H. S. Bender presented the Mennonite viewpoint on many points in connection with the subject and did it real well. C. L. Graber took us down in his car. We had a pleasant trip and very acceptable variation in program, for me at any rate. But I did not get rested up any. I still suffer much of the time from a sort of chronic exhaustion, weariness, general tough feeling. It just seems I must be able to find a type of physical regimen that will enable me to get more work out of my bodily machine. When I sometimes think back to fifteen years ago, ten years ago and reflect how much reading and study I managed to get done in addition to regular work, I feel as though my physical and nervous and mental efficiency must be deteriorating rapidly. I may be beginning to see how much I really missed by not having better opportunities for study and getting started in my educational work at an earlier age. I have generally been consoling myself with the idea that I did not miss so much because of my late start. But I am not so sure of that any more. At any rate I must be too ambitious in the range of learning and knowledge I would like to reach.

April 6, 1936 Monday of Passion Week. The spring vacation for teachers and students at Goshen College is here. By some vigorous resistance I have won for myself a real bit of leisure during this period of eight week-days with no classes. And resistance it did require to get this leisure, for I was invited to accompany a group of faculty members on a peace speaking tour in the state of Illinois for about five or six days' time.

A campaign for increasing the subscription list of the Mennonite Quarterly Review, of which I am designated the circulation manager, was carried on. First of all we wrote about twenty letters to individuals whom we knew to be actively interested in the Review, asking them for testimonials of the value of the Review. After we had received about half a dozen we proceeded to make up the list of prospects and get materials printed for circularizing prospective subscribers. A few of the other members of the editorial board assisted casually in part of this work. The materials we sent out consisted of a four-page folder with information, a form letter with subscription blank attached, and a business reply envelope, all this enclosed in a regular first class letter. The total expense for materials was above twenty-five dollars. To date we have gotten returns to the extent of just about the cash expense for materials. But this does not raise the enrollment of subscribers to the Review, for during the past two years I have removed about twice that many from the subscription list. Whatever the reason may be, I am again convinced that I am a very poor salesman and promoter for anything. Perhaps the most disappointing feature of our subscription list is the small interest that alumni of the college have in the publication. Responses from this group were very rare. It seems to be true that very few of our college graduates carry away from the college an active interest in Mennonite history and Mennonite things as such. Equally bad is the very small interest our students acquire in really intellectual things, in scholarship and the things of the mind as such. It is an indictment of our work, though some perhaps would reason that for most of the young folks to be useful in our church, they should not have intellectual interests too far in advance of the rank and file of the folks around them. This is one line of reflection aroused for me by the Review campaign.

June 15, 1936   At long last I sit down again to scribble a few leisure notes. Leisure has been very scarce during the closing weeks of school. Now after about a week of vacation and real resting I feel a bit more as if I were living again. By flat refusal I managed to keep clear of teaching activity during the summer session at the college. With no definite income for the summer I cannot predict how we shall get through financially, yet we hope and trust not to be forced to beg for daily bread. Our garden has some good things in it to eat: peas, lettuce, radishes, onions. But the ground is dry, no rain has fallen for more than a whole week, and not a great deal has fallen here for three months and more. I appreciate the sunny weather, for I mean to get out into the sun just as much as possible, get all the tan I can, during this summer. A week ago last Friday the Freshman class was so kind as to invite us to accompany them on their all-day outing. They took us along to Camp Mack, a place about 15 miles from this place, mostly south, but a little east. We found this a very delightful and quiet place, where we enjoyed the outing a very great deal. This is a camp owned and kept up by the Brethren people, named from Alexander Mack, the reputed founder of the Brethren Church organization. There is a small lake of clear water, called Wawbee, right out in the open country. We went out for a ride in a rowboat, Leland Bachman, wife and son and the three of us. It was Virgil's first ride on the water, and naturally, for he is very conservative, he did not want to go in the boat, but when we took him on in spite of his protests he soon seemed to enjoy the experience.

I anticipate a pleasantly active summer. It feels so wonderful to be free of all administrative responsibility for the summer. About all I have to do regularly is teach the Bible class in Sunday school. Everything else is at my entire discretion. With reading and writing and Bible study and such like self-imposed duties, I shall enjoy the summer to its full. Many of the teachers who are not teaching in summer school are away traveling, visiting, or studying, but I appreciate very much the opportunity of staying quietly at home with time to think and to refresh my own soul and mind by reading and study. Travel does broaden the mind and bring recreation if one can do that, and I really hope by the time Virgil is old enough to benefit from educational travel we can do some of that. But frankly, I feel that something like ninety per cent of the present day running to and fro must be of the touring type, just merely going places and doing things and is not essentially educational or recreative. Rather it appears to be just another expression of the restlessness and congenital nervousness of this generation. With some books and magazines, and especially a college library at hand, no one needs to grow cramped or dwarfed in his mental and spiritual outlook, or if it should become so, it must be clearly his own fault. I am finally really getting started a bit on my long cherished plan to read extensively into the literature and life of the earliest Christian centuries. Just now I am browsing in "The Discourses of Epictetus," Stoic Philosopher and professor, who was contemporary with Tacitus and Quintilian. I am quite interested in the contents and the atmosphere of the discourses. Have also been reading some in Tertullian, finished his "Apology" a short time ago, and have started in on the "de Spectaculis." I am reading these authors in the Loeb Classical series editions, and find it quite satisfactory to have a good translation beside the original. A few weeks ago I ordered through the college bookstore nine volumes of Greek texts for part of my reading program.

June 16, 1936   For the present my program of activities calls for my spending the forenoon hours, from about nine o'clock until noon, out-of-doors either walking, woodsing, gardening, or tinkering or loafing about the house, and spending the afternoon hours in the office at the college, trying to do some more or less useful work. Yesterday morning I walked to town to make a few small purchases, and then in idle fashion I moved on to the city park and for about two hours I "took the sun" there. Today I decided not to take the sun, thinking it better not to get too much sunburn at once. Instead I read Epictetus a while at home, and walked out for a bit, south on the railroad ties, stopping to look over an old burial plot located on an elevation that overlooks Highway No. 15. The oldest grave I found, at least the earliest date carved on a tombstone, was almost a century old, in 1838, and the latest one I noticed was in 1893. Little can be gathered from the names or the inscriptions as to the class of people who were interred there. A few names suggestive of Brethren or Mennonites are among them: Stutzman, Cripe, Hess, etc. I shall rove around some more on later days.

This is again the year when many folks become greatly excited over the question as to who shall be chosen to reside in the White House at Washington, D. C., for the next four years. Judging from the flood of ballyhoo that is let loose upon the country, it makes a lot of difference as to who lives in that particular house after next January 1. But my own guess is that it will make very little difference one way or another. Most of all I am glad that I am not afflicted with any ambitions to live in that place. Somehow history has a curious way of making the political emotions and the ballyhoo incident to political activities look very trivial and ridiculous, if not actually foolish and absurd. I note by the papers that the Republican party convention has nominated Governor Landon of Kansas as their candidate. Well, I have personally benefitted by what Landon has been widely credited with, the reduction of taxes in the state of Kansas. My property tax on the house and lot in Hesston was last year just a trifle more than one-half what it had been the year before. It was very nice, but I shall refuse to vote for Landon for president, or for that matter, for anyone else. I have no personal interest in political matters even to the extent of voting for candidates for office. It is only a matter of personal taste with me, and I feel no disposition to oppose anyone who regards it as his duty to participate in such matters. The question of voting and holding minor offices in its relation to the principle of nonresistance and also of nonconformity has to my mind never been adequately explored and elucidated. I am sometimes mildly amused at the attitudes taken by individuals about the college on the matter of voting in elections. Many vote and in an indirect way defend their doing so, generally by pointing to a family or community tradition on the matter in practice. At times I have thought I sensed that some persons are a bit embarrassed by the fact that I usually cast the weight of my thought against voting, that anyone at the college should take that position. But all that matters nothing to me at all. H. S. Bender once undertook to question me a bit on the matter, but I made no serious attempt to defend my idea. Two years ago the college officials secured state accreditment for the elementary teachers' training course, and I gathered indirectly that the desired plum carried with it some implicit obligation to vote for the retention of the officials who granted it to the college. For the president approached some faculty members with the suggestion on how they should vote in particular cases. But I was not approached at all on the matter, strangely(?).

June 19, 1936 Yesterday and the day before, clouds and clouds; no rain. Today, sun. Of real summer weather, hot enough to bring on comfortable perspiration, there has been none here yet this year. I fear I will not get all my annual perspiring done this year, unless the mercury tube succeeds in reaching higher levels than it has attained as yet.

Virgil is rapidly growing into a regular young boy. He is attending the weekday Bible school kindergarten class at present, and enjoys it very much. Seems to be able to keep up with most four and five-year-olds. He does well in listening to stories told to the class, probably because he has had so many stories read to him regularly ever since he began to talk, or maybe it was even before he talked. His regular routine every evening has for a long time been, right after the evening meal, stories, usually three, then oranges, then bed. He has not slept regularly in the afternoons since early in the spring. Hence to get him to take enough rest we put him to bed in the evening between seven-thirty and eight o'clock. The sun is usually shining brightly at that time, but he drops right off to sleep.

As for his stories, we are reading now regularly from Number Two of the Book House series. We have not read quite all of them in this volume yet. There are perhaps a half dozen or so in the book that we do not care to read to him at all so long as he is small. In actual practice I let him select or name the particular stories we read of an evening. New ones I have to suggest myself, and he is not always in favor of trying a new one at the first suggestion, but usually talking about the pictures leads him to agree to read it. When he has found a few new ones that he likes, then he will be likely to call for them every evening for a good while. It is more than a year ago that we first began reading from Book Two, and then for a long time we would change off between Book One and Book Two, sometimes for longer and sometimes for shorter periods. But for quite some time now he has not called for any stories from the first volume. If he completes a

volume a year, the six books will not last him nearly through childhood. But of course they will last longer than that for they become
too advanced for such progress. It is surely a valuable work to have,
and we have often been glad we got them. During the winter when he
could not go outdoors so much he almost daily nearly pestered the
life out of his mother to read and keep on reading stories to him out
of Foster's "Bible Pictures and What They Teach Us." She read about
everything in that book to him. Since he plays outdoors, he does not
ask for stories during the daytime. Of the stories I read to him I am
sure he does not comprehend nearly all the words he hears, but he
somehow gets enough that he follows the story and likes it. Not often
does he ask questions about what is read, and he never goes to sleep
over a story, no matter how thoroughly tired he is or how near bedtime it is.

I have in mind to expose him to some opportunity to learn to read
this winter when he gets out-of-doors less and does not know what to
do, as he often says. Perhaps blocks with the alphabet and the numerals on he should have, and I wish one could still get hold of some
boards with moveable letters on like we had one or two at home when
we were school children. Something of this sort, with simple primer
material, and let him learn it if he will.

June 21, 1936 Sunday post meridiem. I have for the past year or two
frequently thought upon the matter of how somehow I could set about
to make my own personal devotional life more vital and effective. It
is a field in which I feel that for myself there must be a good deal of
unexplored territory, ground that invites me to seek adventure and the
thrill of exploration. But, for the kind of work that I try to do, I
sense the great need of a more intensive, more spiritual, a warmer
and more effective personal power for making personal contacts more
efficient and wholesome. Yet with all my thinking about it and some
little efforts to do something about it, I have not gotten onto a real
program for cultivating and nurturing that side of my life. I have done
just a little experimenting along that line the past year, enough to convince me that it is very well worth while to ao something definite
about the matter. Somehow my outlook upon life and its duties has a
more cheerful and more heartening color when I pray and take time
to establish that vital connection with God and his resources of power
and strength. I have noted too that I make some fewer blunders and
faux pas in my regular work when I have definitely sought and gotten
guidance from above for my daily task. Anyway the added composure,
restfulness, poise, etc., make the way of life and work ever so much
more pleasant than when one just drifts along more or less the victim
of the round of circumstances. Yet I have not been just able to ana-
lyse the difficulty I experience in doing something like this regularly
and effectively. At home we have morning worship together, grace at
table, bedtime prayers. But I need something more, a sacred and silent time for uninterrupted waiting upon God for His infilling Spirit.
Often I find myself worn out and weary, spending extra hours in bed
resting and sleeping, then to get through with my work I do not take
the time off for the other. Is it possible that I would be more efficient even physically, if I would take the time for spiritual medita-

tion and prayer? Possibly so. I do feel the need for getting hold of
some suggestive books that might give help in devotional thinking. The
small book by Clark on "The Soul's Sincere Desire" I have found very
suggestive and practical. One needs to disregard much that the book
contains in the way of theological implications, yet it is one of the
best things I have found for an actual technique for one's prayer life.

With me, living in the apartment as we are and have been for
three years, the only really suitable place for such a time of prayer
and devotion is in my office at the college. It is quite suitable, and
if I could manage to reserve the first hour of each day's schedule for
such a period, it should be possible to carry it through. I did that
for a while this past year, but for various reasons not regularly enough.
On the college teaching staff a number of us have increasingly felt a
desperate need for spiritualizing more the entire atmosphere of the
college campus, and certainly no such result can come until the teachers and staff have less of a secular attitude about them and more of a
marked spiritual attitude. Most teachers are overloaded with work, or
think they are; the rush, the pressure, the busyness of our lives makes
us worldly and secular to an alarming degree. The officials of the
college are preoccupied with a flood of things, from inside the institution and from without, with the result that they show an attitude and
a spirit that is anything but restful, at ease, poised, devout, spiritual,
much of the time. A stream cannot rise above its source, and it is
absurd to expect the spiritual life of students to be any higher than
that of the leaders of the institution. Thinking upon these matters, one
may have an impulse to get worked up about it, to perhaps make a
wordy scene out of it. But nothing of the sort will help the situation.
A few of us are desperately concerned to do something about ourselves,
and perhaps through mutual encouragement and united efforts and consecration, we can do at least a mite toward increasing the spiritual
voltage in the faculty group and perhaps on the campus at large. It is
a large field waiting for exploration.

June 25, 1936 Rainless days and days! Monday morning I walked out
into the woods and at a spot near the canal, secluded by bushes round
about but open towards the sun, I took in the sun. It was very pleasant; time passed without my being aware of it for I had no watch and
was engrossed in reading Epictetus. Reaching home I found it was
twelve o'clock and time for dinner.

The Democratic Party Convention is in session in Philadelphia at
present, and to judge from reports one reads there is being displayed
a minimum of dignity and general decorum, even for such occasions.
The conduct and goings-on at such occasions, seem to me to demonstrate just about the reductio ad absurdum of American political
democracy, or any other phase of democracy. My faith in the political
wisdom and statesmanship of demos has never been very great and
while it may be necessary to make the best of it under the circumstances, I find the outlook very discouraging. I am in favor of more
civil service, more government by trained experts, instead of the hit-
and-miss efforts of common people who can know very little about the
complexities of economic and financial affairs. They say that about
twenty-four million of our country's inhabitants are dependent upon

public relief today in some form or other, one-sixth of the total population living from the government, and then many more millions working for the government in some way or other. I have to wonder why the capitalists who so sorely dislike the high taxes do not seriously suggest letting most of the unemployed starve or in some more merciful fashion putting them out of the way, since it seems that industry will never again have any use for most of them. Of course, if these twenty-four million were no more here to eat and wear out clothing, then another sixth of the remaining farms and mills would be thrown out of employment and after these had in turn starved, consumption would be still further decreased, with corresponding unemployment, and so it would have to go on, I suppose, until the capitalists would alone be left to enjoy their paradise! Really, it seems to me a most absurd and insane policy to try to plan an economy of scarcity so that there will be prosperity. Absolutely it seems to me that prices should be brought down and down to their lowest possible level so that people would have power to consume the goods that can be produced by our tools and machines. There would of course be many painful adjustments to make, but it must be the only rational economy in the long run. Certainly all international tariffs should be gradually lowered and finally abolished as a relic of a bygone feudal age, and likewise with all immigration restrictions. If so-called civilized nations were to spend half of the money now going for war purposes of all kinds for helping the peoples of other nations raise their standards of living, they could soon do away with all nationalistic restrictions and there would be no occasions for wars and all their destruction.

June 21, 1936 Have struggled all week trying to prepare copy for the July supplement pages in the Gospel Herald. But tomorrow will probably see it ready for the typist.

Our Sunday school lessons for six months now have been from Luke's Gospel. In my class this morning with the men I tried, instead of exactly reviewing the lessons of the past months, to give them some little appreciation of Luke as a character and writer, and of his Gospel. Am not sure that my efforts were very successful at that, yet some I think appreciated the study. My ideas of Bible study and understanding of Biblical material have certainly been evolving, as I become aware when I look back at times and contemplate the differences that I find. Am also impressed in the same way when I read the average sort of matter found in journals like Sunday School Times, Moody's Monthly, etc. Well can I recall the time when those ideas and those particular viewpoints were as heavenly manna to my hungry soul. But they no longer satisfy my heart and mind as they once did. I can still read them, but they taste like pap and such things, giving no solid meat to feed upon. The simple, literalistic, superficial, dogmatic, cut-and-dried ideas on premillennialism, dispensationalism do not seem to me to really get at the meat and marrow of the message of the Bible. Though I presume for masses of the common folk who have little experience in historical study, such a method and such a system of interpretation is about the extent of their capacity, and if they were not interested in the Bible in that way they would not be interested in it at all. For this reason, and further because I have myself gone through that phase of Bible study experience, I cannot have any ill feeling toward those who find such a line of study and interpretation satisfactory and to their taste. I feel tempted sometimes when I read very dogmatic emphasis expressed of such a viewpoint, to grow tense, to tighten up in antagonism and rebellion, but I know I should not feel that way.

I read occasional articles in the quarterly journal, Christian Faith and Life, which I appreciate very much. They are usually sane and scholarly, and always evangelical and Biblical. Just read one today on the "Seventy Weeks in Daniel's Prophecy." This is the first time I ever found this particular line of approach used for interpreting this period of time. The author says we must first of all determine how the Jews and Biblical writers counted periods of time. This was, of course, to count all the periods whether full or not. Then he proceeds to determine the dates of the Jewish Sabbatic years. I cannot at all vouch for the details of his study, but he figures out that the last or 70th week began in 27 A. D., coincident with the baptism of Jesus and that all the details of Daniel's prophecy connected with the 70th week were fulfilled in the death of Christ. Whether all details are correct or not, I believe his principle in procedure is entirely right. His conclusion looks so much more reasonable than the common premillennial teaching that God's clock stopped with the death of Christ and the Church is a parenthesis in God's program, and the clock will not start again until God starts dealing with the Jews as a people, when the last half of the 70th week will be fulfilled. Something like this last idea clings in my mind, though really I have not read much along the line in recent years. It does not seem to me that the Bible supports any idea that God will at some time again deal with Israel as a national entity, for the New Testament teaching to me is that in the sacrifice of Christ the historic distinction between Jews and non-Jews is wiped out, that Israel had then served its divine destiny, and that now all men alike stand on exactly the same basis in the sight of God, that Israel is not cast away in the sense that they cannot find salvation, but that Jews must repent, believe and come to God exactly as anyone else. If there will be any large-scale turning to God by Jews it will be through the conviction of the Holy Spirit, accepting Christ by faith even as any other mortals. Christ very emphatically put away from himself in his first recorded period of temptation the idea of a temporal worldly kingdom, and again to Pilate his words were clear and unambiguous, "My kingdom is not of this world." The entire New Testament idea of spiritual worship, spiritual conflict and spiritual conquest, of spiritual allegiance, all are certainly on a higher level than the material, worldly, and literal concepts of the Old Testament regime; that it is almost unthinkable that after a period of spiritual activity in the world, God should again plan to revert to worldly, temporal and material procedures for advancing His kingdom. It would seem in that case to be a reversion to second childhood, a return to the beggarly elements or A.B.C.s after having progressed to a more mature level. All this may be just my personal notion, yet I find it more satisfactory as an outlook upon Biblical teaching than what I have left behind in my own experience.

The same journal some time back had an article on the interpre-

tation of the Book of Revelation. I was pleasantly surprised to find
a writer in a fundamentalist and orthodox magazine who wrote frankly
and sanely in favor of an historical approach to this difficult book.
As I recall his remarks now, he claimed we should first of all see
in the Revelation mirrored in highly symbolical language the conditions under which the Christians lived in the time that John wrote.
And for its interpretation one must be familiar with the apocalyptic
style and the apocalyptic convention in Jewish literature. I say I
was quite a bit surprised to read this where I did, for I had rather
concluded that such an approach to the Revelation would not be approved in a fundamentalist magazine.

There are two other magazines that come here which are thoroughly Biblical and scholarly, yet combat the facile premillennialists
and dispensationalists of the Scofield type. The Calvin Forum from
Grand Rapids had a review of a book written for doctoral dissertation at Evangelical Theological College in Texas, on premillennialism.
The author was a converted Jew and the president of the college in
a foreword extolled the author's orthodox Jewish training as a special qualification for him to understand and interpret the Scriptures.
The reviewer scored this idea roundly, saying that orthodox Jewish
interpretation of the Old Testament is bound to be unorthodox Christian doctrine. It occurred to me that there is something to his statement. Another journal more militantly Calvinistic comes from Scot-
land, the Evangelical Quarterly. An article last winter by Professor
Allis of Philadelphia, gave the best and sanest denunciation of dispensationalism as sponsored by Scofield's Bible that I have ever read.
He proved such teaching unscriptural and God-dishonoring. It was
refreshing.

Pridie Julii. There has been a rain! Last evening and night some
rain fell, not extremely much, but still enough to wet the ground for
a depth of several inches in our garden. With great promptness I
put some small seeds in the ground – lettuce, endive, radish, kale,
spinach, in the fond hope that the cool damp weather of today may
continue for a time giving them a chance to start. Walked to town
this morning to bring home a week's supply of fruit – bananas, oranges,
apples, lemons. Carried a big load, for we seem to get away with considerable quantities of all these right along, and usually one can save
enough by shopping in town to recompense oneself for the extra trouble.

My summer's reading program is slowly getting under way. Have
just nearly finished Zwemer's fairly recent book on "The Origin of
Religion." It is interesting and informing. The author marshalls and
presents the evidence in anthropology, archaeology, etc., in favor of
the theory that religion was everywhere originally monotheistic and
more or less spiritual. All forms of polytheism, totemism, animism,
etc., are therefore degenerate forms of religion. This is of course
the teaching and viewpoint of Scripture, and has always appealed to
me as true and reasonable. I have never done any great amount of
reading in evolutionary anthropology, though I did some in 1923 at
Boulder, Colorado. Yet I have never done any reading that is more
tedious, repetitiously monotonous, and fancifully puerile in general
than the endless pages of theory, speculation, and imagination which

so-called evolutionary scientists can get off when they try. Especially boring is their twaddle when they talk about the origin of mind, worship, religion, prayer and the like. So it is doubly refreshing to find that there is really scientific evidence in favor of the Scriptural theory. It is interesting to observe in book reviews of Zwemer's book by writers who are sold on the evolutionary dogma, how they react to an opposing presentation as scholarly and scientific as this one is. They usually pass it off with a gesture to the effect that it explains nothing for folks who choose to see religion as a product of evolution.

Dies Solis, July 5, 1936 After a few days of loud noises, poppings, crackings, deafening sounds, such as are supposed to be the appropriate ritual performance for commemorating the birthday of American Independence, a more quiet and peaceful atmosphere prevails about us today. A shower of rain fell again last night, cleared the atmosphere and makes this a pleasant Lord's Day afternoon. In fact it rained a bit this forenoon during Sunday school hour, and a goodly wind is blowing from the east by south promising perhaps some more moisture before long. No one that I know of would complain if it would rain a sizeable shower every night for several weeks. Such a supply of moisture would help us to circumvent a small part of the rising cost of living. Eggs we are buying for about twenty-two cents a dozen, butter for a little above thirty cents a pound, and our last month's statement on milk showed nine cents a quart, a rise of one cent over previous price. Then when we are forced to pay out cash for all our vegetables besides, the food budget mounts pretty well upwards to the sky.

Our fourth of July was spent with the multitude at our annual Sunday school picnic held at Miller's park about eight or nine miles west of Goshen. Professor Witmer and family took us with them in their car; we trailed all the way around Waapa Trail, that is Virgil and I did, along with Mr. Witmer himself. It is a piece of natural woods with a rough terrain, several small fish ponds and a little brook. Ate an enormous dinner, and between four and five o'clock ice cream was dished out in abundance. An hour or more I helped play about one and one-half games of croquet. Four men were engaged in a game, when suddenly two of them took leave to play in a baseball game. I took the place of one of these, so that Mr. Harry Roth and I were matched against Mr. Graber and Mr. Hershberger. We "beat" them both times. Croquet is about as strenuous a kind of sport as I care to participate in; even volley ball, which I took part in quite regularly last winter, is most too strenuous, although one can generally play as hard or as easy as one personally likes even at that. The picnic yesterday reminded us vividly again of the pleasant outing we had on June 5, just a month before.

Quite a number of visitors were present this morning in our services, perhaps because of the holiday that came in connection with this weekend. A minister by name of Ben Springer from Hopedale, Illinois, was present and was asked to fill the pulpit in the morning service. In the Sunday school lessons for the six months now starting we shall have interesting material to study on the early history of Christianity and the Church, based upon the book of "The Acts" and the "Epistles." At least for me it is one of the most interesting phases of New Testament study. I grow to love the Greek N. T. text and its study more every year. My growing familiarity with its pages that comes from my teaching it year by year adds increasing interest in its language, concepts, thought and teachings. I hope I can now in earnest set about to attain my long-cherished hope of familiarizing myself with the life and thought of the world contemporary with the N. T. times, and as a further background to study extensively the entire Hellenistic-Roman age of ancient history. Some weeks ago I read through with keen relish and absorbing interest the fairly recent book by Glover, the English scholar, on the ancient world. It was in the Introduction to the fine volume by Moulton and Milligan, "The Vocabulary of the Greek New Testament," that the statement was made that the Hellenistic Age was the most important era in history for study. With my limited knowledge of history in general, I believe it can easily be true. But Glover's book is a splendid work, very readable, in a style that combines fine scholarship with an exquisite sense of humour, and that I relished above anything I had read for some time. In all the parts pertaining to Hellenistic and Roman things the author is especially well at home. He has a chapter on the Jews which I found very disappointing by contrast with the excellence of the other parts. One could tell immediately upon entering the chapter that the author was not at home with the material at all as he was with the other chapters. His materials and conclusions were second-hand, and not especially well up-to-date at that. His discussion of the N. T. and Christianity was decidedly superior to that on the Jews, though perhaps not all one could desire on the religious side. I must say that Glover has greatly whetted my own appetite for a complete knowledge and appreciation of that wonderful period of history. I received numerous suggestions from his pages on ways to proceed in this study, on authors I should read, etc. I think the Loeb Classical Library volumes I ordered in May, most of the titles at least, were selected on the basis of suggestions carried away from Glover's volume. They were Epictetus, Marcus Aurelius, Philostratus on the Life of Apollonius of Tyana, and on the Lives of the Sophists; two volumes of selected Papyri. I am reading Epictetus' Discourses now with a good deal of relish. His Stoic doctrine on morality in so many respects reminds me of parallels in the N. T. Other authors I should get as soon as possible are: Plutarch, Josephus, Fronto, Seneca's "Moral Essays," etc. The difficulty is that the Loeb Library does not yet include all of these, especially not all the volumes of Josephus and Plutarch's "Moralia." One can easily see the part the Stoic and Cynic moral philosophers (professors of morals and conduct is what they really were) had in the ancient world, knowing that, in contrast to Christianity, ancient religion was largely divorced from morals and conduct entirely.

July 9, 1936 The heat of summer is upon us in real earnest. This is the third day of great heat. A few clouds in the sky and a light wind from the north make today a bit more comfortable than yesterday. From reports, drought and heat have been rather general over the midwest in recent weeks so that the farmers are in distress again. At least the Secretary of Agriculture is busy with measures for relief. One wonders what the farmers of our land used to do to keep alive in years past before a paternalistic Uncle Sam rushed to their relief every time a dry season came along and threatened a crop shortage. Meanwhile food prices are rising steadily. This section of the country, if there is a growing season, generally abounds in cheap fruits and vegetables of all sorts. But there is very little cheap stuff to be obtained at present. We bought one crate of strawberries at $1.50, which we thought was reasonable enough.

Took an extended stroll, almost a small hike, this morning. A book I had was due at the public library today, so to avoid the hottest part of the day I left home at about nine o'clock, stopped at the barber's on my way, then proceeded on into north Goshen, for I knew the library during the summer months does not open its doors before eleven o'clock. Walked away to the northwest end of Goshen, strolling through the cemetery that takes up the northwestern part of the town. I had hoped sometime to go to the Hebrew cemetery to see if I could read the Hebrew inscription over the entrance arch, of course to see if I could use my knowledge of Hebrew for any practical purpose. But I found I only recognized one word out of the four or five used there. Many of the grave markers also have Hebrew lettering on them, but I could make nothing out of them, they being all written in the unpointed script, and it requires considerable familiarity with the language to decipher the unpointed text off hand.

July 10, 1936   The heat continues. Though today at noon some dark clouds filled the sky, several thunderclaps were heard, and a few drops of rain fell and that was all. Some scattered clouds are still hanging about, luring one to hope that a rain may still be coming to us before all vegetation is burned up.

I read not so long ago in some periodical an article or editorial reporting the perfection of methods for raising all kinds of table vegetables under strictly artificial conditions and doing so profitably. The process seems to be to have large vats into which are placed just the chemical materials needed by the plants. Above this liquid "soil" is a grating or netting through which the plants extend their roots down into the "soil." The conditions for growth, heat and light are supplied by electricity and so are maintained at exactly right levels for maximum growth and development. The vegetables growing under such ideal conditions are said to be superior in quality and flavor over those grown under the highly capricious conditions that Mother Nature supplies.

This subject invites one to indulge his imagination and try to picture something of what results might follow from such a revolutionary process for producing food. One might imagine the apartment houses of the future having say one floor devoted to such "gardening," giving the future cliff-dwellers of our cities access to an abundant supply of the most healthful vegetables without dependence upon market gardeners, without the trouble of marketing and shopping. Perhaps every small town will have its municipally owned and operated "garden," so making it unneccessary for householders to occupy themselves with family garden plots except for flowers and perhaps fruit trees. But one must also reflect on what will happen further to the already hard pressed cause of farming. Our government must seemingly do one of

three things, buy up this new gardening "process" and destroy it
along with other scientific knowledge, or prepare to support yet larger
numbers of the people from the Federal Treasury, or devise an economic set-up that will give everyone an equal chance at the abundance
of goods.

July 15, 1936   After a record-smashing heat wave, 111 degrees Fahrenheit was the highest reading, we can breathe a bit more comfortably again today, with a cooler breeze blowing from the northeast.
This morning some clouds were in sight, rumblings of thunder were
heard, and apparently there were showers to left and showers to
right of us, all of which encourages one to believe that it will at
some time rain on us again. I have been during the hot days keeping myself comfortable by doing as little as possible. The forenoons
have been bearable in our apartment, when we closed windows and
doors in the morning and kept them closed during the day. The basement seemed to keep our floor cooler and perhaps even some cooler
air came up into our rooms.

I have this day finished my first reading of the works of the Stoic
philosopher Epictetus, his "Discourses" as arranged by Arrian and his
"Enchiridion." I have really enjoyed going through these, because the
subject matter is of interest to me and the style is not difficult at
all. While it is, I understand, generally agreed that Epictetus was not
influenced by the New Testament, I am impressed by the numerous
thought and language parallels I noticed in reading through the books.
Certain ideas and modes of thought must have been "in the air," so to
speak, and this accounts in part for their presence in parallel, but
unrelated writings of that general period. This idea is impressed upon me more as I study the religious, moral, and philosophic background
of the first two centuries of our present era. It does bring the N. T.
writings down to earth in one sense, in that it definitely relates these
to human life and human thought. For some persons, such a view
might seem sacrilegious, as debasing the N. T. and dragging it down
from its unique position as a divine revelation. But I cannot feel that
way about it myself. There is still a uniqueness about the N. T., but
I find it much more understandable as a book than otherwise.

I was especially impressed in my reading of Epictetus, of how extremely anthropocentric the Stoic system of thinking really is. That
ancient crippled philosopher said a great many very good things, with
an earnestness and an utter devotion that is often inspiring and admi-
rable. Yet the viewpoint is always that of the individual self. The
whole aim is to get oneself into an attitude and frame of mind and
thinking so as to suffer no discomfort, pain, worry, etc., to be unhindered, unhampered, tranquil, serene, undisturbed in mind. It is mostly
good sane common sense and well worth pondering. But one does note
the absence of the Christian emphasis on service, doing good, helping
others, etc. Presumably the Stoic disciple who practiced the teaching
to make himself unresponsive to wrongs done to him, would also not
inflict any ill upon others, but nowhere is the emphasis upon the side
of duty toward others. In some ways the Stoic approach to forgiveness, nonretaliation, etc., is quite basic and good. So for instance,
where a fellowman has done you a wrong, he deserves only pity and

perhaps instruction, for he has not really done you any harm, but only has harmed himself. This is an approach to the viewpoint of Christian ethics, I believe, if the idea of a transcendent God were added to it, that the offense is primarily one against God.

Anyway my reading of Epictetus has given me appetite to do further reading in the same line. Think I shall read in the "Meditations" of Marcus Aurelius as I can and have leisure. I read somewhere that no one should attempt to read Marcus like another book, but only a little at a time to avoid suffering acute mental indigestion. So I am forewarned in that regard. Then there are also Seneca, Plutarch, Fronto, and Lucian, whom I must make myself acquainted with in due time.

July 20, 1936 Cooler atmosphere has come to us in recent days but nary a drop of our much needed rain. Grass on the campus looks dead and brown.

I do not feel so much like writing extensive notes these days, for I am spending a good deal of time writing out sundry speeches and articles. Am writing a long lecture for probably our second house-meeting with the men of Coffman Hall after the opening of school this coming fall. It is to be the opening bombardment of a major offensive against the growing spirit of disorder in Coffman Hall and the campus in general. Just what can be accomplished in the way of inculcating a little more civilized and cultured spirit into the fellows who are enrolled as students of the college remains to be seen. But I am convinced it will require something more than the mild, easy, jovial, gentle suggestions that have been the chief means used in the past. I shall not assume very much of anything as to the knowledge, experience, taste, self-control on the part of most of the fellows, and I shall undertake to instruct and teach the men with what patience and tact I can bring to bear upon the task. I want to have prepared when school opens a schedule of house-meetings about one a month throughout the year, at most of which I shall deliver a lecture myself, and I wish I could have most of my lectures written out in some form before we begin. There will be much for me to learn, and I hope I can learn readily and improve my technique constantly as I go along, but absolutely certain I am that some effort must be made to train the young fellows in the elements of self-control and self-discipline, unless we are to have the rough, coarse, worldly spirit on our campus which is more or less the rule in high schools and some other schools. In so far as possible I want to make my efforts constructive and directive rather than merely critical. Our students, most of them at any rate, have still a background of reserved and quiet demeanor, so that we have a fair basis on which to build with some hopes of success. The lectures must be followed up with personal interviews and personal conferences with individuals too.

July 23, 1936 At last a little rain has fallen, hardly enough to allay the dust in garden and field. Yesterday afternoon I irrigated with the hose the tomatoes and a few other things in our garden. If more showers follow soon, they will perhaps be able to keep the ground I watered from drying out as fast as it otherwise would.

Last Monday evening we went on our first little family outing this summer, something we have at different times talked about but never actually did before now. About five o'clock, equipped with ready-made lunch packed in a paper bag we started out toward the dam. We found that more water was flowing over this than I had anticipated, in fact, quite a little more than was going over a week before. For then I could walk across the river at the foot of the dam on the stones and boulders with scarcely so much as getting a shoe sole wet. But on Monday we had to remove shoes and stockings in order to cross at all. Virgil I carried, and crossed the first time without any mishap, but returning I did slip and all but spilled myself and the boy into the water. I got wet up to my middle and Virgil had a wet foot. We sat down in a meadow beside a ravine at the edge of a woods, ate our lunch, strolled about a little and started on our way home. Virgil always enjoys the idea of going on such outings, but unless there is something for him to do, he is soon ready to "go home" again.

Mr. Sokolsky in the new Atlantic has an article entitled, "A Conservative Speaks." It is very good and sensible, I think. He makes out a case for capitalism, but is frank in pointing out its weaknesses and the dangers that beset it in our country. Such critically constructive articles are the kind I like best of all. Some writers are very able at proclaiming the breakdown of capitalism, its destined disappearance, etc., but the question that always remains in my mind after reading them, sometimes with enthusiasm, is, just exactly what shall take its place. I am pretty well convinced that individual freedom and democracy are more nearly compatible with capitalism than with many of the fantastical utopias that are supposed to take its place. Sokolsky always writes soberly and convincingly, and since hearing him speak last winter I appreciate his articles the more.

July 24, 1936 I find real interest occasionally in translating from some Latin author into English, just for the practice of transmitting the ideas of a classical writer from one language into another. It is a fine intellectual exercise, it makes one more conscious of the detailed turns of thought and style than just the reading of the passages, and finally it is an excellent type of training in one's own English style of expression. After having discovered the exact shade and coloring of a writer's thought, to cast about then for just the rightly shaded word or phrase to express this idea in English is an experience I find especially interesting and satisfying. For the past weeks I have translated some Odes from the first book of Horace and some from the Letters of the Younger Pliny. The Odes I do not attempt to put into metrical form, being well satisfied to get into my version some poetical turns of phrase and word, something that will reflect a little of the spirit and feeling of the original. Pliny's prose style is quite simple, the thought is rarely involved or very deep, and the occasional flourishes of rhetoric are not hard to handle. In the past I have at sundry times done some similar translating. At odd moments during the years from perhaps 1931 to 1933 I thus went through all of Juvenal's sixteen "Satires," making a prose translation. Some years farther back I translated between twenty and thirty of Seneca's "Epistles" beginning at the front end of his first book. I did some of Catullus' poems last summer; two years ago I translated one comedy of Terence. Started on a few other items but never went very far.

I am beginning a new technique for collecting notes and memoranda and references in my study of the Greek New Testament. In 1921 I got my first copy of the pocket size Nestle's text copy and carried it a good deal in my pocket for eight or nine years until it was coming apart badly. My second copy I have not carried much, so that it is not wearing out so fast. My plan is to take the leaves from these two Testaments, paste them on typewriter-size notebook paper and keep them loose-leaf style in a folder, building up each book separately as I may work on them. On margins of the leaves, on their backs and on inter-leaves space for a life-time of note making!

Kalends of August. Coolish, quiet, dry weather is the regular schedule at present. This week has had a little activity, not wholly leisure, so no notes have been set down yet. On Monday my father surprised us by dropping in on us near noon. He only stayed one night, returning home on Tuesday. He just came to see us, I suppose, probably because I had not written home for a good long time. I'm a very poor hand at carrying on a correspondence anyway, which of course is no excuse for my not writing more frequently to my father. He told us about their financial affairs and conditions around home in general. He has a V8 Ford car nearly new and seems to be getting along real well for a man who has just passed his seventy-first birthday anniversary.

Last Sunday Mr. and Mrs. Joe E. Brunk invited us to ride with them in the afternoon to Winona Lake, principally to attend a much advertised memorial service in honor of Billy Sunday who died some time last year. I had never heard Mr. Sunday speak, though I had read of his sermons and many references to things he said. The service last Sunday was not such a great affair, particularly as to numbers; although there was a goodly crowd there, still inside of the enormous tabernacle they did not make so much of a showing. Rodeheaver, Sunday's singer, was leader of the meeting. Mrs. Sunday was there and spoke, and three or four other persons. The general atmosphere of such meetings, with plenty of noise, ballyhoo, and begging for popular response, was of course, little to our taste. Yet I should want to be the last person to throw a stone at that type of evangelistic work, for it cannot help doing some good for the cause.

Also on Sunday our dean H. S. Bender returned from his trip to Europe where he attended and served on the program of the Mennonite World Conference in Holland. So I had some business conferences with him and sat with the library committee for a while engaged in the work of revising the periodical list for the college library. There was also a meeting of the faculty one evening. Then Miss Royer has returned from her term of study at Chicago University and we conferred a little. So the week has gone by again, and I feel that the vacation is nearing its close.

August 2, 1936 The coming week will bring additional activity to our campus community when a Young People's Institute meets here, one of a goodly number of regional meetings of the kind among our churches, but the first one to be held in this section for some years. The institute this year is the first one ever held here with the expressed approval and support of the Indiana-Michigan Conference. Heretofore they were either projects put on by Goshen College or by some church-wide agency. The local conference has only recently and reluctantly shown itself disposed to cooperate with anything that is associated with Goshen College. There may be a change, but a slow one, coming over the attitude of the conference body, such a change as only time can work by the recruiting of younger men as ministers, men who have not inherited all the old prejudices and hostilities against every-thing that has any connection with Goshen College. There has been little or no change of heart on the part of the earlier pullers of eccle-siastical-political wires, who dearly love to seek the chief seats in conference organization and to exercise influence in "regulating" this and that. Conference time usually disgusts the local men here who participate in its activities, and one hears despairing remarks about the petty politics of certain persons who happen to sit in the seats of the mighty. It seems that this conference is little noted for the spirit-uality, piety, and warmness of its official activities. The leadership in its Sunday School Conference is of a routine and stereotyped kind. The district mission board seems to do some aggressive work.

August 9, 1936 Last Sunday I was interrupted at this point on the page by a caller in the person of Cornelius Wall, an old friend and associ-ate of Hesston days some five years ago. He is of the Brüder-gemeinde group of Mennonites, a plain common type of man, interested in Bible teaching, very pious and spiritually minded. He is newly located at Mountain Lake in Minnesota and just now spending a few weeks in Winona Lake School of Theology. His family is with him, wife and two daughters, and they took lunch with us before they returned to Winona Lake. They were refugees from Russia during the time of the revolution and fam-ine, about 1919.

Last Monday afternoon I went with J. E. Brunk and some others to Winona Lake to listen in on a session and program of the No-Tobacco League of America. We were not so greatly impressed by the type of their activities, though they are probably doing a good work in their own way. Some men of the Brethren Church are among their leaders. We have long been looking for some suitable speaker whom we could with confidence invite sometime to come and speak to our student group, but in general the type of propaganda these folks carry on is not so well adapted to our needs and purposes. What we feel we need here is not so much popularized propaganda against the use of tobacco as some sane and sensible thinking on the question, and the making avail-able of material suitable for educational purposes, especially material that school teachers can take out and use in their work. And for that work the two physical science professors on our staff can do about as much for our people as one of these propaganda men could.

The past week saw a good deal of activity around the college grounds. Nearly 120 young folks had enrolled for Institute, many of whom are living on the campus for the few days. They make a nice sight, see-ing such a number of young folks, clean looking, serious-minded, and well-behaved. It is not so often that I get to see groups of other young people together, but one can readily observe the differences, even and entirely apart from a distinctive garb or dress to mark them off.

Among the visitors in services this morning were Frank D. King and family of Chicago. He is always an interesting man to meet. I am a bit amused at the first subject he usually speaks about when I meet him. He always asks if we have been out to Iowa to visit my folks lately. Reason is probably because there is one home in Iowa where we both have near relatives. My brother Herman is married to his sister Bessie. Last summer when they were here for a Sunday, I replied to his inquiry that we had not been in Iowa since two years before when we stopped there enroute to Indiana, and he was quite surprised and perhaps shocked to hear that for so long a time we had not travelled to visit our kin, and what was more, we had no plans for any such trip in mind. He was frank to offer the advice that we ought by all means to take such a trip and see the home folks. I refrained from committing myself as to reasons, and probably was not as sincere in my response as he was in his advice. Today again Mr. King spoke of the subject, only his query was, if we are going out this summer to see the folks. I could give no answer that might settle his apparent worry about our apparent dereliction in duty toward our kinfolks, for I said we owned no car and did not see any way we could get to take the trip. He was quite perplexed, even saying he had suggested to Hermans that they ought to apply pressure to bring us on a visit to them. Evidently this is another case where our own tastes differ almost radically from some others'. For me I cannot understand why people want to every year go on trips and trips, here and there, back and forth. Few things in the world bore me as much as spending time visiting, and travelling about for the mere sake of going places and doing things. I suppose our perfect contentment to spend our time quietly at home for years in a stretch is quite as incomprehensible to some other people. It is not that we would not like to see our relatives occasionally, but we just do not care to travel. We have not the energy, it seems, to put forth the effort and suffer the inconvenience of a disturbed routine of life. I especially love routine procedure, though I think I am not a slave to it. Anyway as long as Virgil is small, I think regularity and routine are the best kind of life for him. Unless we lose all capacity for enjoying travelling and touring because of our long abstinence from it, we hope to do some touring in later years as a planned part of Virgil's education. For my part I enjoy most a leisurely kind of touring and camping in a car, the simpler and cruder the better. On this point my wife does not share my enthusiasm. So when we come to make our educational tours, we must compromise on some kind of comfortable camping. But travelling, rolling along over the concrete on rubber, just going and going, so as to get away from home for a while, such a complex I have none. Even though we do not live in a home of our own, yet we would rather stay where we belong than to rove about elsewhere. However unconventional and odd such a desire may seem to others, we are not inclined to feel sorry for ourselves, or to be particularly apologetic for our own ideals along this line.

August 13, 1936   Three of us on the faculty, H. S. Bender, G. F. Hershberger, and myself, have among ourselves a kind of reading circle.

Between us we receive and read more or less in two periodicals which are not considered orthodox and Biblical in viewpoint and content. I like to follow these in a general way, though I do not read them through by any means. The two are the Christian Century and Christendom, of both of which C. C. Morrison is the editor. The Century has some good critical articles, and I get considerable help in the interpretation of current events and trends in some cases from these articles. I read them for their analysis and criticism more than for their conclusions, which latter are often not to my taste at all. Christendom is a new quarterly journal, now going for about a year. It has articles on all kinds of religious subjects, often good for their definitive and analytical value. Personally I do not care for articles or books that discuss religious subjects from the rationalistic and humanistic viewpoint. The thought always strikes me as being very thin, watery, and sloppy, in no sense satisfying or sustaining to one's mind and soul. But the newer note in so-called modernistic writers on religion does interest me a great deal more. This note is a reversion to the belief in the transcendence of God, of goodness and of truth, as against the emphasis upon the complete immanence of God as seen in the so-called social Gospel program and the more recent New Humanism. There are favorable signs on the horizon that religious thinking will soon swing definitely away from its slavish obeisance to the dogmatism of science that has been in the ascendancy for some time.

The summer issue of Christendom has several very good articles, and also some I do not so much care for. A Quaker writer has an excellent definitive article on the problem of sex-life for Christian believers — I cannot now reproduce the exact title of it. But I appreciated especially the note running through it which emphasized the self-disciplinary idea, the thought of controlling and directing the immediate urges, desires, impulses of the self toward larger and more cosmic ends. His discussion was set in the framework and pattern of current phraseology and vocabulary. It was stimulating to my thought.

Another article in this same issue was on Paul Elmer More. This man's name I had read at different times, but I have never read anything he wrote. From the titles of his books and the connections in which I had read references to the man, I have for several years entertained a desire to read in his writings. But so far I have not come upon any of them, and the books are rather expensive as advertised. Well, the writer of the article mentioned undertakes to describe, defend, and justify Dr. More's philosophical and religious doctrines. If these are what he describes them to be, then I am very strongly confirmed in my purpose to read More's writings some time. More is a Platonist, evidently a scholar and thinker not unlike in temper from the late Paul Shorey of Chicago with whose name I have seen More's associated somewhere. More seems to contend against the humanists for a transcendental standard of truth, of goodness, of beauty, and of God. He is described as maintaining a "two-world" view, and to do so without apology. The writer of the article in question writes with some degree of feeling and apology. He makes out that the world, as it becomes more unified, must choose between the two diametrically opposed views, between a thoroughgoing humanism and a consistent transcendentalism. He traces the political developments in central and eastern Europe to the desertion of transcendentalism in philosophy and religion. According to his view, the renaissance and the old humanism were a necessary and inevitable reaction from the dogmatism of the Middle Ages, yet the reaction has been developed to an extreme form in the new humanism, which makes man the measure of all things, man the center and circumference of all values, and therefore makes all standards of truth, right, goodness, faith, purely relative to man's thinking, reasoning, tastes, and even to his impulses, desires and wishes. On the whole the article is very stimulating and thought-provoking, and for me at least, it is philosophically nourishing and satisfying. Whether it be because of personal taste, de quo non disputandum est, or because of mere prejudice, or finally because of a Spirit-born conviction in my own soul, whatever the reason, I find the thought of transcendentalism, coupled with a reasonable humanism that lends some dignity and worth to individual men and women, as the most satisfying world view that I have yet seen stated in words.

August 14, 1936 Yesterday and the day before I spent the afternoon hours attending the annual Indiana-Michigan Sunday School Conference six miles east of the college at Clinton Frame Church. It was hot both days and I was more rather than less miserable sitting under the "big top" which was set up for the purpose of the meetings. Sunday School Conference time seems to serve a good many of our Mennonite folks as a regular summer vacation outing for the entire family, for there were large numbers of children there, from infants in arms on up. Yet most of these people, well over a thousand in number, I should guess, were content and happy to sit under the big tent during sessions from two and one-half to three and one-half hours long three times a day, regardless of the temperature. Of course the tent was about the only place one could escape the beating rays of the sun, for only a very few trees are found in the vicinity of the church. One is impressed, upon reflection, by the contrast suggested between the attitude and behaviour of such a gathering of people and a similar gathering, if one could imagine any such, of average modern American citizens; whole families coming and sitting patiently through long sessions of speeches on religious subjects. It is not that the speeches are so powerful and outstanding at that. They are quite elementary and naive on the whole. My guess is that if the speeches and the ideas were more mature, more advanced in thought, these people would not care so much for them. At the same time the folks with a bit more maturity of mind and understanding and appreciation would probably not come near such a place on days of such high temperature. It is all a very interesting psychological study, and I find myself engaged with such observations and reflections more than with the actual content of the meetings themselves. My own chief reason for going out was because I was asked to represent our Sunday school as appointed delegate. So I went out enough to be present at the delegate meetings each day. If one wants to work and serve the general public of the church membership, the only way is to gear one's thinking down to the immature level of the populace. It is not easy, and if one does succeed in a measure, how far does one stultify one's own integrity thereby?

August 17, 1936   Yesterday afternoon I made a trip to Middlebury, riding with missionary Jay Hostetler. The occasion was a missionary day program at the Mennonite church at that place. I served on the program, and as is usual, I did so as a substitute for another person. Being a substitute I did not prepare anything new for the occasion, but read under a different title, a manuscript I prepared nearly two years ago, when I substituted for another person on a missionary day program at Elida, Ohio. And yesterday morning in Sunday school I served as substitute superintendent upon a bare hour's notice. A week ago, J. E. Brunk who has charge of Sunday evening meetings at the college informed me that he would be away for three Sundays, and would I not substitute for him in looking after the arrangement of programs while he is away? I presume it never even occurred to him to arrange the programs and turn them over to the respective leaders before he left. So with substituting for this one and that one and the other one, a body's life does not get absolutely monotonous.

Here it is a bare three weeks before the opening day of another school year. Am not sure if I will be rested and recuperated by that time or not. Have visited Dr. F. S. Martin twice already, and think I shall give him a chance to see if he can keep me efficient this winter. My first visit three weeks ago today gave me momentary hopes that he could do something for me. He gave me a packet of big, fat, yellow pills and a three-ounce bottle of brown medicine, a tonic, I presume. A week ago last Thursday he gave me more of the brown medicine, but instead of yellow pills, another bottle of pale yellowish green liquid. Well, last week was worse again for me than the two weeks before. The first time he examined me a bit in detail, found my blood pressure a trifle low and my pulse a bit too rapid. The last time both of these features were corrected in the right direction. My head has not troubled me much of late, and my eyes cause less discomfort than common, though I do not use them very hard just at present. However, the rhythmical flare-ups seem now to be affecting my stomach, causing gas, some discomfort, but not exactly like indigestion.

One evening of last week upon invitation I rode with M. C. Lehman down to Camp Mack and back. We talked of various things, among others of my old Iowa community, where Lehman occasionally visits for the solicitation of students and other reasons. I remarked about the fewness of the young people in those large congregations who are at present interested in higher education. The interest in such education seems to come and go in waves in that community. I know that when I was about twenty there was a good deal of interest in going to school. I have been made to reflect upon the things and persons who interested me in further education, although I suppose that my innate and unquenchable thirst for knowledge and learning was the chief factor in my case. Those were the days when every year saw a number of Goshen College students teaching rural school in our section of the country. Because my interests lay in that direction naturally, I generally got to associate more or less with these folks. Among my best friends and most congenial associates were some persons of the community who were attending or had attended Goshen, especially John

Fisher and his sisters, Milton and Henry Brenneman, and others.
Mr. Fisher is today professor in a teachers' college at Bloomsburg,
Pennsylvania. He probably influenced me as much for an educational
career as any one person, though I guess I disappointed him when I
went to Hesston instead of Goshen to begin my school work. At the
immediate time I went he was not at Goshen, but was doing graduate
study in Philadelphia. Milton Brenneman had quit Goshen and was
completing his work for college degree at Iowa City. So there was
no such immediate personal attraction at the moment for me to go
to Goshen. Before I actually went to Hesston I had met only one
graduate from there with whom I associated in any intimate way at
all. This was Walter Gingerich. He is now in Oregon somewhere.
Just exactly what led me to start at Hesston instead of Goshen is
not very clear to me now, if it ever was. It may have been the matter of a difference in expenses, which I have now forgotten. It may
have been an urge or unction from some secret source that directed
me that way, for which I have had no real regrets. I still feel an
urge for going west or southwest, and if I could do it as easily as
not, I would move in that direction again, temporarily at least if not
permanently.

Dies Lunae, Pridie Kalendie Septembris, 1936 Two weeks have gone by
again without any leisure especially for writing notes. And yet in retrospect I seem to have done very little. The past week I spent largely
in manual labor. The first two days I spent in brightening up my office
here at the college. Upon inquiry I was told that materials and tools
would be supplied if I wished to provide the labor myself for repainting the walls and ceiling. So I proceeded to do that. It was not regular oil paint that I put on, but a special kind of kalsomine, supposed
to be washable. The result of my effort is that the room is a good
deal lighter and brighter than it has been for some time past. Happily the cleaning and scrubbing force was working on the second floor
of the Administration Building at this same time, so that they cleaned
up my floor and the woodwork of the office after I was done with my
part. Ruth Bender has been staying with us since just a week ago.
She and Mrs. Yoder came over to inspect the job after it was done
and I had gone over the furniture with a rag and furniture polish. They
fell in with my suggestion that it would be fine to have curtains on
my single window in the office. All the offices of administration on
the first floor of this building are blessed with some window drapery.
So today Estie is making curtains for the window.
    Also last week we entertained over night and for breakfast my sis-
ter Barbara and her family, and Mrs. Anna Yoder, an aunt by marriage.
They were on their way home from a four weeks' trip to Pennsylvania
and Michigan visiting relatives and friends.
    On last Friday Virgil had a birthday anniversary to celebrate, so
we spent the day celebrating. In the morning it was raining. But by
ten o'clock it had ceased and Miss Bender, who drives a car of her
own now, took us for a trip. We went as far as South Bend where we
had intended to do some shopping, especially for Virgil. We had rather
poor success, probably because we were poorly acquainted with stores
and shops. But we found a few toys that the boy liked. For our lunch

which we had packed and carried along, we stopped in Potawatomie Park located between South Bend and Mishawaka. It was a pleasant place. There were a few caged wild animals for Virgil to look at and admire. Before we left there I took the boy for a ride on the trolley car, riding in to South Bend and back again. Stopped at Elkhart, where the ladies reported better shopping success than in the larger city.

Also last week I painted and varnished a few small articles of furniture and equipment about our apartment and thus the week passed.

The week before last the only outstanding experience was a trip to Ohio for one day. C. L. Graber who was to serve on the program invited me to ride along free of charge, which I gladly did. Leaving on Wednesday morning, we attended the three sessions of that day of the Ohio Mennonite Sunday School Conference held at the Lockport Church in Williams County. Besides attending the day's sessions, I ate two substantial "conference" meals, paying twenty cents a piece for them. Stayed over night at Phil Freys' and returned home the next morning. It was a pleasant trip. M. C. Lehman also rode along and back. S. C. Yoder went along in.

As my own contribution to Virgil's birthday celebration, I got a few little accessories for his tricycle. One of his rubber handle grips had been broken and loose for some time, so I managed to get a new one that I could fit on. Then I also got a small bell to put on his handle bar and a reflector tail light to clamp on the frame. I figured it would not hurt him to have a few small things that the other children with whom he plays do not have, since they also have some things that he has not, and which he frequently says he wishes he had. Even the two Miller boys who seem to have about everything obtainable in the way of toys and playthings have not these accessories on their cycles, and I reckoned it would be wholesome for Virgil to have a few things which they do not have, for his own sake and perhaps even for their sakes. He enjoys riding around and ringing his bell as he goes.

This week I need to begin getting things ready about the office for the opening of school next week. It appears that I will have a full schedule of work, with thirteen hours of teaching, though some classes will naturally be small. Even Latin seems not to be as nearly dead as it looked the past several years.

September 20, 1936   The school year is now getting under way. The experiences of registration week were pleasant and also disappointing. Pleasant because it involved starting in on a new year's work, and the people and the work of every year naturally differ from every other one. Disappointing to me because my mild anticipation that the interest and enrollment in Latin and Greek might show some increase was ill-founded and unwarranted. As it is I have three Latin students in as many different classes. Greek has six students in two classes. My administrative work is heavy, so it seems to me. I feel that I am ill adapted to administrative routine; it is more wearing and more of a drain on my nervous energy than the equivalent amount of teaching load or even more teaching load. Whether I can ever get in a way of doing it easier, with less thought and mental energy, is hard to say.

This is just a few minutes before the beginning of the evening service. A Reverend John Greenfield is announced to speak this evening. He is a Moravian and recommended as an excellent speaker.

September 26, 1936 This is utilizing a few minutes before the beginning of an evening service. A. J. Metzler is conducting a few weekend meetings at the college. I missed out on the meeting last evening, because one of the boys of the dormitory asked me to go with him to see a doctor in town. We are all busy these days. I am doing what I can to help the young fellows in Coffman Hall to get started right for the year's life on the campus. Interviewed a half dozen yesterday and today, for giving of some advice and counsel. Estie is busy with canning, putting up things for the winter. She got a good half bushel of green beans one day this week, and on another day she had two bushels of concord grapes to dispose of. She got twenty-nine quart jars full of rich dark purple juice out of the lot. Adequate rains in recent weeks have made gardens flourish, after they had stood quite stationary all summer. We have abundance of tomatoes, squash, peppers, radishes, beans not so abundant and a few watermelons. Turnips and some peas are coming on if frost holds off for some time longer. There will be some banana squash of fair size too. And eggplant too we have in abundance. I failed to get any lettuce or greens started, though I sowed several times.

October 6, 1936 It rains and it rains! How we did wish last summer for such rains as now fall about every day, or several times in a day. It was reported near the end of September that over eight inches of rain had already fallen during that month. Our garden things are still out, what there are, even though a touch of frost last week nipped some leaves on squash and sweet potato vines. One of these days a sudden call will be upon us to rescue the things we want to save from freezing.

School routine has gotten under way fairly well. My student load this year is very light, but the odds and ends of administrative routine are taking a good deal of thought and energy. Eighty or more men in Coffman Hall make a real-sized job for Proctor John Coffman and myself, what I can help along. One fellow, or some fellows have been stealing money a number of times right from the start. We think we know who he is, but have been unable to catch him up on it. So it is with some other slight irregularities that need to be followed up rather promptly to direct things in the right channel for the year.

As for my general health, I really feel better since school started than I did last summer and a large part of last year. My wife has adopted a different program in cooking, guarding against certain combinations, avoiding cereals and starches in greater measure than had been our practice in the past. If I can in any way maintain a more efficient physical machine this winter than I did the two winters past, I shall be very highly gratified. When there is so much one would like to do along the side, as reading, writing, research, and then finds oneself handicapped by having to lie around most spare hours trying to rest up, and sleeping nine or more hours in bed every night — well it is discouraging to say the very least. Mrs. Yoder claims she feels much better and stronger than she had before the change in diet. Virgil has had a hoarse sound in his throat for several days, but no

nasal congestion. The change in diet habits came partly from my
father's visit last summer and partly from Wife's contacts with
Mrs. Oswin Gerber, who has been following such a plan for some
time.

October 13, 1936 For the past month I have been feeling comparatively "fine" much of the time. I feel highly grateful to the Heavenly
Father for what I cannot help feeling is His special blessing vouch-
safed to me this fall in the way of physical and nervous efficiency to
an extent that I had not hoped for. Our improved system of diet is
in part responsible, but even this we came upon more by accident or
by fate than by real planning and thought. I have also experienced
real strengthening, definite guidance and divine direction during the
past weeks. My personal prayer activity and conscious fellowship
with God have brought a deep-moving, satisfying, and even joyous
reaction and power in my inmost soul and life. My improved state
of bodily efficiency seems to make possible more efficient and concentrated periods of quiet time, but again, I have wondered whether
or not there may be some influence in the other direction too. Anyway I can witness that a definite exercise in prayer, somewhat along
the line and manner suggested by Glenn Clark in his chapters on "The
Soul's Sincere Desire," does work out practically for me.

In the past from conversations with various persons of the college
faculty, I have learned that some were interested in exploring the possibilities of a regular prayer group or circle among the faculty. When
some weeks ago Rev. Greenfield spoke here on the topic of prayer,
the urge came to me to suggest some concrete proposal for the carrying out of the idea some of us had talked about. The net result is that
to this time three times a number have met on Sunday evenings at six
o'clock for prayer hour. The attendance has been six and seven persons,
always the same ones so far. I find it very helpful for myself, and we
are praying definitely for a true spiritual awakening among our campus
group of people this fall. The need is great and with the large number
of young people here the opportunity is stupendous.

During the present week Rev. Paul Brosy of the English Lutheran
Church in town is conducting the devotional exercises in our daily chapel
assembly. He is a man of extra fine spiritual perception and also a
fine and painstaking scholar. He speaks on some studies he has lately
made in the first Epistle of St. John. His remarks are very stimulating
and searching. I had at times complimented myself a bit for what I
imagined was some respectable knowledge of the New Testament books,
at least a few of them. But after hearing Mr. Brosy's exposition of
I John I must confess that "I know nothing yet as I ought to know,"
about the N. T. writings. One is surely challenged to do more for one's
own understanding and comprehension of the marvellous literature of this
small volume. If only our young people here can get a vision of the
possibilities for studying the Bible devotionally, our deepest prayers
would be answered for them. We have a very fine group, but spiritually
very immature and infantile, to be sure. But the possibilities for growth
are the most encouraging feature of the group we have.

December 13, 1936 For a whole two months no time has been given to

312

the writing of leisure notes. Leisure has been very limited during this time, although there has not been the extremely pressing rush that I have known sometimes in the past. During November I worked on a program of brief student conferences with all members of the freshman class, which was a part of the program of the course in College Life. There were more than one hundred and ten people whom I thus interviewed during the month. For December I was asked to prepare talks or addresses on two programs, one this past week as part of a nonconformity forum discussion, and one an extended paper for presentation at a meeting of the College Peace Society. I succeeded in getting the latter meeting put off until after the recess, but nonetheless I must make the preparation during this month, although I shall have the vacation time in which to complete the preparation. The work in the course in College Life is practically over now. Dean Bender will address the class this coming week, and the first week after vacation the members of the class will be asked to fill out a vocational interests inventory sheet. And that will be all except for following up a few stragglers on the taking of tests and on conferences.

Weather has been generally pleasant here this fall, a little snow just at Thanksgiving time, some continuously cold temperature, enough to make ice for skating. My wish is that the open weather may remain until after the recess period which starts on next Saturday and continues over three Sundays.

During the past month I have had two little one-day trips which I have appreciated, both without expense. Four weeks ago today C. L. Graber invited our whole family to ride along to Archbold, Ohio, to be present, among several thousand others at the dedication service for a large new Mennonite Church, the largest in our branch west of the Lancaster Conference district. It was a very pleasant experience and trip. Virgil enjoyed it too. A week ago yesterday I rode with M. C. Lehman as far south as Danville, where with three other faculty members I was present at the sixth annual meeting of the Indiana Student Health Association. I was mostly a spectator, though strangely enough, my name was put on the nominating committee for the day.

December 19, 1936 The annual Christmas vacation began this morning. For several years past the faculty of the college has been struggling with the problem of getting the vacations started right, or the school sessions closed, whichever way one prefers to look upon it. Annually when the catalog is printed a calendar of dates is officially adopted and printed. Up to last Christmas, and including it, I once counted up that the closing date for six consecutive sessions was changed at the last moment, or near the close. This includes closing dates at Christmas, Easter, and in June. It became such a routine that students began practically to count on it as normal.

When the last calendar was adopted, some were enough in earnest about stopping such a policy of saying one thing and eventually doing another, that a calendar was made that should be fool proof. So the vacation was lengthened a few days so as to include three weekends. And to lessen the possibility of a last hour change, we listed the Christmas music program by the chorus for Friday evening after the close of the last classes. And this was published in the calendar of events and vigorously supported in every way possible. And so it was carried through. The reason in past times for changing closing date at this time of the year was because of weather conditions, as nearly as I can recall.

My vacation is being robbed of leisure time by the fact that I must finish the preparation of a long paper or essay for presentation at the next meeting of our local peace society. I am writing on Christianity and the State, an extensive enough subject, I find. I am not widely acquainted with the literature on the subject and my own thinking on the matter is hazy and fragmentary. I do welcome the opportunity to think on and around this subject. It is interesting but very difficult. My sources and references are mostly such as I have happened to come upon in the course of my reading. The conclusion – what Christians should do today about political participation – that is the hard point.

December 22, 1936 Winter began officially yesterday, according to newspaper reports of the findings of the astronomers, when the sun reached the point farthest south in the zenith. It is a beautiful winter we have so far, for today the sky is clear, a genial sun is shining, very little wind from the west is moving. Everyone will welcome a good deal of this sort of winter weather. The blanket of snow that fell over the last weekend is disappearing. So beautiful and mild is the day that I want to go for a several hours' walk this afternoon, unless someone gets up a volley ball game in the gymnasium for that time. Even then I may just pass up the indoor exercise for the outdoor kind. Men of the faculty have played volley ball regularly on Wednesday evenings this fall. Some get quite excited over the game; I too enjoy the exercise, though my playing skill is very poor indeed.

Sent two orders for second hand books to Blackwell at Oxford, England, this fall, one in September, and another in October or November. The first time I had very good fortune and the second time almost none at all. The first time I had waited longer after receiving the catalog list before sending, than the second time. At that time five rather valuable titles came in response to my order. One is Ramsay, "Pictures of the Apostolic Church," which I find is a series of fifty-two brief, pointed essays originally written on a year's course of Sunday school lessons and printed in the Sunday School Times. The course covered material in Acts and the Epistles of the New Testament, and just the sort of essays and in a vein and style and approach that I like very much. My guess is that the present management of the Sunday School Times would hardly find such excellent discussions on the Sunday school lessons "useable," as these appeared before the editor's conversion to a radical type of premillennialism, which seems to have rather lowered the quality of the lesson material which he can use. I shall prize this book highly among my tool books.

Another title is Hobhouse: "The Church and the World in Idea and in History." This I read through with enthusiasm and keen interest. Its theme is one of natural interest to me, and the line of approach is very good; most of its conclusions are good too. The material of the book comprised the famous Bampton Lectures at Oxford University for the year 1909. The material is well documented, there are a large

number of critical discussions in the appendix, and the book is indexed.
I have developed a real liking for the English type of Biblical scholarship, and this book is in line with the tradition I have become familiar with through the writings of such men as Wm. Ramsay, C. J. Cadoux, David Smith.

A third title is the small volume by Glover: "Christ in the Ancient World." The author's name attracted me to this, for I have read with appreciation a number of this man's productions. He is not essentially a Biblical scholar, but an expert in Ancient History, hence his approach to New Testament material is from the side of the history of the ancient world. He is always stimulating in his viewpoint and his method. More than primer skill is necessary to comprehend what he writes.

Two other titles that came with the same order were: Hatch, "Essays in Biblical Greek," and Nestle, "Textual Criticism of the Greek Testament." Here it was the titles that attracted my notice; they are both good, excepting that the one by Nestle is quite an old book and is not up-to-date for a subject on which new investigations and studies are constantly being made. A. T. Robertson has a good book on the same subject which I want to acquire some time.

The second book list from which I ordered had such a feast of titles which I wanted that I hushed the voice of my better knowledge and ordered a large number, enough to amount to perhaps fifteen dollars, which I could hardly afford. When the returns came in, I had one title out of about ten that I hoped to get. Evidently they are all valuable books which other folks want too, folks who live closer to Oxford than I do. At any rate they were reported sold before my order arrived on the scene. The title that came is a French one, Martha: "Moralistes sous L'Empire Romain." It is a standard work, has chapters on Seneca, Persius, Epictetus, Marcus Aurelius, Dion Chrysostom, Juvenal, Lucian.

On this matter of buying books, I guess I am going daffy on it, for one who has as meagre an income as I have with unpaid notes and interest on my hands. Yet I do love to acquire good books, some as handy tools for thinking and working, others for their value in lending a little atmosphere, or better perhaps, in making it around myself. I do not feel this is a matter of pride or display but sort of a normal form of expression of one's interests and hobbies. As I look back now over the recent years, I must congratulate myself on the amount of stern self-denial I was able to practice, especially when book catalogs and lists came into my hands. So I do not feel that I am in any way a slave to my hobby for collecting a library of my own. Yet I should confess that I did not always report to my wife when I spent a few dollars, even during depression years, for some titles from Blackwell's or elsewhere that I wanted very badly.

Just now I am contemplating to order a half dozen books or so from Campbell and Lennig, New York. They sent me a list of titles of rather standard works bearing on general cultural subjects, some of which I have long hoped to read. The titles tentatively selected for ordering, perhaps after Christmas, depending on how I feel by that time about the matter, are: "The Book of Musical Knowledge" by Elson; "Tales of the Monks"; "The Lewis Carroll Book"; "The Works of Rabelais"; "The Arabian Nights"; "The Decameron of Boccaccio"; "Emerson's Works."

According to the "was" prices, which the seller is careful to state as part of the description of each item, these titles were once for sale for thirty-seven dollars, whiles if I can add correctly they will be sent to me for the small sum of ten dollars and sixty-three cents, cash with the order! When one considers the matter from the angle of how much money one is really saving by buying them, it goes some distance toward answering the question whether I can afford at all to spend money for books I do not really have to have, at least not just now. But I must not dwell on that side too much in my thoughts, else soon my conscience will be smiting me for not buying more from the same list, which was ninety-eight other titles at similar savings of money!

December 23, 1936 For four months or a little more we have now at our house been following a special type of eating system. I am not sure it should be called dieting or not. We eat anything and everything we care to eat, but the combinations of foods for any one meal are closely regulated. As it has been, we get one fruit meal, one starch meal, and one protein meal every day, not that only one type of food is eaten at a meal, but that the staple food at a meal is of one type with some suitable accessories. I have stopped using much milk at all. For a long time we used to get two quarts of milk a day, now we scarcely average one quart, most of which is for the boy. My nasal and sinus catarrh is very greatly diminished. I have more energy and a general sense of better feeling over last winter.

Some people think it is silly to fuss around over foods and eating habits. There is plenty of pure faddism about the matter, no doubt. At the same time bodily health must be largely a matter of eating, for the body has only one source of fuel and that is the food eaten. It is the custom for scientists and medical men to laugh and make merry over all ideas of special dieting and special attention to foods. But their pronouncements are never quite convincing to my mind. Perhaps on general principles and possibly even for a majority of folks that viewpoint is true enough. But in doctor's statements, at least those which get into the newspapers, there is never enough, if any, room made for individual differences among people. The amount of attention that is being given to allergic conditions in individuals should demonstrate that there are differences, that according to the old saying, one man's food is another's poison. It is clear that under conditions somewhat near normal, one can eat anything he wants and likes. But I think there is reason to the idea that putting a promiscuous variety of foods into the stomach at one time is bad chemistry, and some persons' systems can get away with it, while others cannot. The "noble savage" probably filled himself with one or two sorts of food at a time. Today in civilized eating and cooking the scheme is to tempt the stomach to accept several times as much food as it should by tantalizing variations of all kinds. It is a matter of common observation that one can eat all the meat, vegetables, and so on that one cares for, all that the stomach desires, which presumably should be a sufficient signal to stop further ingestion. But when rich pastries and tasty fruit is passed around, it is possible to consume considerable additional quantities of comestibles, thereby vetoing the stomach's earlier vote and beguiling it to load upon itself an additional task which it may be able to perform, and again it may not.

For breakfast I have been having citrous fruit, either a whole grapefruit or a glass of orange juice. Then further two raw apples, a dish of plain raisins, a half dozen dates, and a cup of Postum cereal brew. Sometimes a taste of some kind of nuts goes with it. Estie eats nuts regularly with her breakfast of fruit. Virgil usually has milk, sometimes also cooked cereal with his. Other children around have been sick of late. Yesterday Virgil had a fever and lay around "resting," but today it is gone, and he is only "tired," probably weak from the fever.

I have had one fairly serious affliction this season. The last half of November I had a chest and bronchial congestion that troubled me some, yet I kept going regularly without much discomfort. The bronchial cough has all cleared away again. Last week I had a bit of sore throat, localized as it often is, in the Eustachian tube on the right side. I surmise that this was my own share of what has been going around the community lately. This vacation is a boon to me for I just feel like relaxing, not exerting myself except physically, to get out and walk in the fresh air and sunshine. If it were not for the paper I am preparing for the Peace Society my relaxation could and would be complete. I have not been working on it as much these few days as I really should, for it is so much more congenial to my sense of relaxation just to scribble notes like this, to loaf and feel that there is not a thing under the sun to do.

Tomorrow morning at six o'clock we are leaving for Elkhart to take a train trip to Iowa City, Iowa, to spend Christmas with our relatives. It will be a treat for the boy, and I hope he will enjoy it.

December 31, 1936 Last day of this year of grace. For one week I had a real vacation of a kind that for me has been unusual. This morning a week ago we left Elkhart by train for a brief stay in Iowa to visit our folks and enjoy a change. Virgil got a free train ride out of the project, perhaps the only one of that kind he will ever have, for after he has passed his fifth birthday he will need to pay fare for riding the train. He enjoyed the trip quite as much as we imagined he would, at least he did after he became used to the novelty of it, drinking in the experience as he went. Going west we changed trains at Englewood and arrived at Iowa City at 4:00 in the afternoon. Howard Gnagey took us out to the country. At home we found Father bedfast, for he had suffered a paralytic stroke two weeks before and was quite helpless, though very slowly getting better control of himself again. His right side was paralyzed; also his mind and memory are affected. He is seventy years old now, yet his pulse and blood pressure are quite normal, perhaps a little low even. He had been more active during the fall months, neglecting some of his customary rest periods, for they built a new house on one of the places for brother Hermans to live in.

Aside from Father's condition, we found things around the old home grounds very similar to olden days. Virgil has eleven cousins there growing up like he does. He enjoyed playing or tearing around with them, most and best with boys older than himself. He cannot get along very well with those younger or the same age as himself, for he has not learned cooperative play well enough as yet. The roads, mud roads, in Iowa were very bad, and he did not enjoy riding in a car that slid around. On the way to Iowa City yesterday morning it was pouring down rain, and he had to cry out of fear and uneasiness.

Roads were fairly dry when we reached Iowa. But weather was mild all the while; the last days it rained, making dirt roads a sea of mud. We did get outdoors to see the farm and its life only once, on the evening of Christmas Day when we watched some of the choring operations. Virgil had to laugh and laugh, until he could hardly laugh any more, when he watched the pigs eat and saw them pushing and jostling and scrapping around as they were feeding.

I figured up that the difference in temperature between this Christmas and a year ago, at least for us, was just seventy-five Fahrenheit degrees. For here it was eighteen degrees below zero last year and the highest on Christmas Day in Iowa this year was fifty-seven degrees above. We ate when in Iowa what people in Iowa eat, although it was a regimen quite in contrast with what we have been used to having. Result is both Virgil and I have a touch of cold in our heads today.

Coming home yesterday we had three hours time to wait between trains in Chicago. We went out for a little time at the Zoo in Lincoln Park. We were there only part of an hour between four and five o'clock. It was long enough for one visit, for it is very tiresome to walk around long. Virgil laughed again when he watched some monkeys playing with each other, and two-months-old lion cubs playing with a keeper, and an elephant eating hay and carrots.

January 9, 1937 One week of the new year has already flown past. I spent the first day of the year mostly confined to bed with a touch of the flu which has been widely prevalent during recent weeks. On alternate days I felt in turn fine and dull, a sort of regular rhythm.

It has been a grief to me for some years that my supply of energy has been so low that I seemed unable to do half as much work as I used to be able to do. So much of the time, seemingly all the time, I felt listless, worn-out, tired, exhausted. Dr. Martin has been suggesting I drink coffee once or twice a day as a stimulant. I have not thrown away the idea for my part, although my wife scoffs at the idea of resorting to artificial stimulation in such a way. I have much of my life been troubled with physical feelings of laziness, tiredness, and it is possible that a mild stimulant would be what I need. Just what the long range effects would be I do not know, though many confirmed coffee drinkers are healthy and grow old in years.

On Wednesday evening of this week I served on the program of the Peace Society, when I inflicted upon a small audience a paper of more than ten thousand words in length. This was perhaps my most ambitious attempt yet to deal in a comprehensive way with a comprehensive subject, that of Christianity and the State. For some years I have played around with the subject at various times. In this latest effort I have succeeded in clarifying my own thinking, my own ideas on the matter just a little more, though it is doubtful whether the paper was very edifying to the listeners. There are some phases and some angles of the question that I have never been able to get clear in my mind. The problem, of course, is to try to set forth a systematic doctrine of the relation of Church and State that takes into account Scriptural teachings, historical and philosophical facts, and also our own peculiar Mennonite psychosis on the matter; and that is a large order, believe me. Yet I feel sure we need such a synthesis in our group.

January 10, 1937 Just about a month ago I was placed on a program of a nonconformity forum here at the college. The Church Relations Committee of the Y. P. C. A. here fell into line with the recent rage for conferences and discussions on this particular subject. Mine was the first topic put on for discussion, "The Need for Nonconformity Today." As is my practice, I wrote out a paper of three thousand or more words and read it. In part of this I summarized some ideas I wrote out over a year earlier in my "masterpiece" on the theme. Also in a part of the paper I paid my personal respects to the American type of popular democracy, of course, in a restrained manner. Following the program H. S. Bender asked me for the privilege of borrowing the manuscript for his more leisurely perusal, which I took to be a fair compliment of its possible merits.

The discussions and open forum part of this project was attended with much interest. It is not a bad sign I take it, that young folks are becoming "nonconformity conscious" to some extent. I was assigned several questions for answer in the open forum part.

Last October a year ago I sent a manuscript to Moody's Monthly at Chicago for publication. It was accepted for their use with the intimation that it might be some time before it could appear. It has not appeared yet, and I have been watching the issues rather closely. I read this manuscript as a chapel address also last year, and H. S. Bender later paid me the compliment of borrowing it for use in a certain part of a course he was teaching. He suggested strongly that it be published in the Christian Monitor, and I told him it had been accepted by Moody's. The title of the paper was, "The Language of the New Testament." I confess I liked it real well myself, found much pleasure in writing it and in reading it. Should imagine that any magazine would be glad to print it as soon as possible!!

January 18, 1937 Mild, almost balmy weather continues to be the order of the day. Yesterday was rainy and misty all day long. Today is clear and cooler. We were invited out to take Sunday dinner with H. S. Bender and family yesterday. A pleasant time was had by all.

This week, though it is examination week, I plan to have some leisure time. Examinations for me are a holiday, for I shall have only eight persons to examine. College Life students need no examination. Last week I had expected a bit of freedom from extra duties and tasks. I had finished sending away copy for the Gospel Herald Supplement the week before and also the several monthly news letters. Then when I was just ready to relax, here comes the editor of the College Record and asks, could I not supply the leading article for the coming issue of his periodical, copy due in a week? He made a suggestion: that I condense my Peace Society manuscript to usable size. But for several reasons I decided I would rather not publish anything on that subject at this time.

Since every year for three consecutive years they have called upon me to supply such an article, I improved some of my leisure last summer in making some notes and writing out parts of an article I could use, if necessary, sometime to save myself some worry and help out someone else. Thus under the circumstances I fell back on the product of my earlier aforethought. I handed in an article on Greek and Latin. I felt it would be in order to do so, since I have never before, on any of the three occasions, said anything about my own field of teaching and study interest. I wrote on nonconformity, peace, and learning, in turn, and felt justified for once in saying a few words in behalf of the lost cause of classical study. Not that it will do the cause any good, but to let men know that a great and good cause does not die without protest, and that its death may not be as imminent as some are in the habit of assuming.

January 20, 1937 In the early part of last month one day a letter came to me from the manager of the Mennonite Publishing House which almost stunned me. It offered me outright a position on their staff of editors and workers, chiefly as editor of the Advanced Sunday School Lesson Quarterly. This alone would be perhaps a half time job. The rest of my time was to be given to other assignments about the House. I was momentarily surprised and bewildered. Thought the matter over for a few days and then turned it down, excepting that with the advice of the college officers I did offer to accept the one specific assignment they suggested, if I could do it in absentia on a part time basis. It is a month now since I replied, but as yet I have no additional word except acknowledgment of my letter and a personal call by Metzler when he was in this section of the country two weeks ago. At that time he suggested I might expect to hear from them in the course of ten days or two weeks. So I am still waiting for their decision.

Somehow the matter did not very seriously appeal to me, perhaps not as seriously as it should have done. I do like to exercise myself along the line of writing, and from that side alone it attracted me. Yet to bury myself in routine writing and use up my energy in that way, with little time for creative reading, thinking, and writing, did not appeal so much. On the other hand, I thought of the work and study a man like John Horsch has done while employed there; had I gone there I would probably have set such a career as Horsch's as my goal in general. One would be greatly handicapped in my line of interest and study to be away from a college library, and would probably have to build up a tool library of his own, which would not be very adequate at any time because of limited resources. I thought too of the fact that the work there is yet more confining than here, fewer vacations for recuperation, and no sabbatical leaves, so far as I know. Also the salary consideration is not what it is supposed to be here ideally. Economic security would probably be a degree or two better there than here, for the House makes money at all times, depression or no depression, it seems.

More basically, I do love to teach and have some liking for work that involves contacts with other personalities. How efficient I may be in these lines it is for others to judge. When this matter was up for decision last month I tried to elicit from college officials, or at least invite from them if they had such ideas, some hint that I should get away from here, but no such suggestion was forthcoming. So I concluded they had no wish to be rid of me, else they would have surely embraced this opportunity to ship me. In general the intellectual atmosphere (such as it is), the academic environment of this place appeal to me as more congenial than that at the House. Although I would not make a great deal of this point.

Furthermore I am a western man, and even Indiana is farther east than I would voluntarily choose to live and work. Pennsylvania would be still farther removed from where my tastes and personal desires are. With more vacations and leaves here, there is at least the prospect that we can get away in years to come to indulge our love for western scenes and places. Also ecclesiastically, the Publishing House smacks much more of eastern Mennonitism than my tastes call for. The management there has been catering noticeably to eastern sentiment, perhaps with good reason from the viewpoint of church unity and harmony. I understand from reports that on dress and customs the Scottdale congregation is going stronger for formalistic attire than it used to do. This too sounds none too attractive to me.

Just why it is so is unclear, but some folks seem able to talk authoritatively about all the details of the Publishing House's activities in connection with this vacancy and their efforts to fill it. The story goes that the executive committee of the Publication Board met with the House officials and after discussing a wide range of possible candidates for this vacancy, they narrowed the choice down to a list of four persons. With this list the officials at the House were to proceed with negotiations. Evidently I was first in the list of four, and report has it that my name was the only one on whom the officials were agreed, and that they cannot agree among themselves to offer it to any other. Maybe so – maybe not!! It gives one a sort of queer feeling to hear such gossip. It looks as though one were a bit important!!

Some persons also speculate on the political, so to speak, phases of the matter of personnel at the Publishing House. They say it reflects a healthy spirit that a leading church institution for once is really looking to Goshen College for help in its work. It might really enhance the prestige and influence of the College to have someone from its staff assume a position that could become one of influence in the East in the course of time. And to think further that they should turn westward at all, should select a doctor of philosophy, who is a mere layman, over other candidates who are ministers, all this, viewed against the background of certain attitudes that prevail in certain quarters, may be considered significant. Some even speak with regret that I cannot take up the offer, as thereby they imagine some western influence might be injected into the system at Scottdale, some anti-formalistic sentiment. All this talk makes one stop and consider maybe I should have taken it. But my real taste and conviction is not to that effect. So I wait for further developments. Really, from the standpoint of opportunities here, I wish heartily they would not take up my offer to accept the one assignment.

January 24, 1937 Thinking recently upon the call that came to me from Scottdale, I recalled to mind an earlier offer I had to join the forces at Scottdale. It was in 1919 as nearly as I can remember that upon the occasion of my first visit to the Publishing House, Aaron Loucks, then general manager of the place, in an informal personal conversation opened the subject with me. Whether he was speaking officially or not I was not sure, yet as I recall I gave him scant consideration for his suggestion. I was then ready to start on my last year of college, and as I had already been asked by Hesston management to join the teaching staff there, I was not interested in the other proposition. That was just the time they were discussing the matter of starting a new periodical and were fishing around for a possible editor. I was told at the time upon inquiry that it was not decided whether the new publication would be a missionary paper or a teen-age young people's paper. Within a year or two of the time, C. F. Yake started his Youth's Christian Companion, which has been a signal success in its line, much more so than anything I could have promoted and developed myself.

Virgil is growing and developing about as I assume a boy ought to do. He has almost a houseful of toys to play with, at least his mother thinks so when she sets about to keep the rooms clean and tidy in appearance. Yet he much of the time plagues her with the request: "Tell me what I can do." For Christmas he received (among the larger articles) as toys, a livestock farm, including barn and barnyard fence and fifty or sixty animals and accessories to keep in them, a toy freight train that runs on a track, a small blackboard, and others.

I wish I could take more time to do things for him and help him to do things. As it is I try to give him some time every day; usually it is for reading stories in the evening. During church service on Sunday morning he has been prevailing on me to spend a good part of the sermon period in drawing things on paper for him, especially cars, trucks, trains, houses, garages, trees, etc. He is quick to imitate and has developed a knack in drawing freehand some things that appear to be good work for a four-year-old boy. If only he had a better model to follow for his imitation in drawing. For I am myself a very miserable hand at any kind of freehand drawing. I have been itching to teach him to read, but his mother discourages the idea saying it may be a hindrance to him when he starts attending grade school. Still I feel that if he once shows an interest in words and learning to read, then is the time to help him to learn. I am not sure he has shown any definite interest as yet. He has shown a little interest in the letters of the alphabet, especially those in his name. Think I shall teach him the alphabet this winter if he cares to learn them. He has not been outdoors a very great deal this winter. There has been much rain, and he had a cough for several weeks, which he has just gotten over.

January 30, 1937 This week one day I sent in my annual gross income tax return to the Indiana State office. Last year was the first time I ever did such a thing. This year by dint of hard figuring and trying to recall all my income I was able to total up a gross income of twelve hundred dollars in round numbers. Of this a bare one thousand dollars came from the college, some from payments on a student's notes I took over from the business office of the college some time before, a dribble from the Peace Committee for writing, and about one hundred fifty dollars as rent paid on the house in Kansas. The first one thousand dollars of one's income is exempt from taxation, while above that you must turn over to the state one per cent. It seems hard to have to part with even a pittance of one's meagre income in this form of income tax, and yet I would rather pay my tribute to modern government in this form than in the form of a general sales tax. It is a more just and reasonable form of tribute than to tax people for buying the necessities of life.

For my work in preparing material for the quarterly doctrinal supplement in the Gospel Herald, for which the general Peace Committee pays me a small honorarium, my collections are in arrears now. I had been in the habit of handing in a statement of account twice in a year. My semiannual collections have thus been fifteen dollars as to amount. Last October when I went to collect, I was informed that the treasury of the committee is empty. They have very recently issued another small propaganda booklet which is now being mailed out as bait to bring in some cash contributions to the committee for its work. So in the course of time I expect to get my pay again, such as it is.

The January peace instalment which came out last week was the sixteenth of its kind, marking four full years of effort on that project. I receive occasional encouraging compliments on the work I try to do in this quarterly department. And they come from the type of persons whose opinions I value and esteem. In recent months, I recall offhand two persons who expressed warm and sincere appreciation of the material given out. One was Melvin Gingerich of Iowa, a thoughtful and intelligent judge of such matters. Another is Allen Erb of Colorado. Bro. Erb, by the way, wrote me this week highly praising one feature and at the same time taking issue with another. I appreciate the criticism, for it reveals the fact that someone reads the material with care and discrimination, and that in itself is worth more than the great silence of the mass readers who cannot even read with a critical sense.

I have long wished and hoped I could develop a style and mode of writing that will be effective. Without many specific measures to such an end, only general efforts, I seem to have gotten something accomplished. It appears that my literary ability, such as it is, has attracted the Publishing House management as much as any one thing. My own feeling is that my extensive reading of good quality magazines and books has done most for me in developing style.

February 7, 1937 It appears that the prayer circle among faculty people which was started last October with some interest has now run its course. Since New Year practically no one has appeared at the set time. Personally I find this hour just preceding the evening meeting a very fine time for prayer and meditation and I like to spend it in that way. My idea of the prayer circle was that of an informal gathering of such persons as would spontaneously assemble for a united quiet hour, mostly devoted to prayer. But it seems that when people are in a meeting they expect someone to lead, to talk, to discuss something. What I love and feel the need of is something like the old style Quaker meeting, where those present do not look to a leader or to a subject or to a show of words for their profit, but where people meet with, not each other, but God; where they expect to meet God and to fellowship with Him in a personal way, not as a group but as individuals first. In such a meeting there would be no subject or topic necessarily, but each one would wait for the Spirit of God to move him to say something or to keep silent, as the case may be. The other sort of meeting I am not qualified to lead in an effective way, and that probably accounts for the demise of the project we had started.

I am interested in collecting and studying some books on the subject of prayer. In recent months I have secured Zwemer's new book entitled "Taking Hold Of God," which I like very well so far as I have read in it. Just lately I got a little booklet on "Ways of Praying" by Muriel Lester. It is not a deep or profound discussion of the subject, but suggests some practical things in the way of cultivating an attitude of continual prayer, praying without ceasing, of practicing the presence of God in a real positive way.

Some of my own prayer experiences along this line have been most rich and satisfying. I was made to recall to mind my experience when I used to operate a threshing machine twenty years ago, both in Iowa and later in Kansas. A sense of keen responsibility always rested upon me; I felt I was responsible for keeping the work of the day going, to keep men from losing their time, and the work from being hindered. So I generally, when the wheels would start turning at the beginning of a new half day, found a real joy and strength in prayer, silent and in my own heart, to God for His help and direction. This became a habit with me, that of instinctively reaching out with my thoughts and my soul to take a new and fresh hold upon God and His power. I am sorry that I have somewhat gotten out of this fine habit.

I do at the beginning of the day when I reach my desk feel the need for God's help and presence; but I believe I should every time there is a knock at my door, reach out for a second to get a real hold on the presence of God for every contact I make with other individuals. I am too negligent along this line. Too much I trust to my own strength; too much I tend to look upon every call at my door perhaps as a more or less undesirable disturbance, at best as just another bit of routine to attend to. What I want to do is to look upon every such call as a golden opportunity for meeting someone and in this contact seeing something or receiving something of the Spirit of God from the person, and of giving some help, hint, suggestion to the other person, perhaps have something of God's spirit and power flow through my feeble self into the other person's life and experience in some way that will help me to honor and glorify my Maker. This attitude I hope I can cultivate and develop. The possibilities are truly great along that line. My great weakness is that of not talking enough, not expressing myself freely enough to share my own experiences that I do have. Whether I can ever come to talk more is a question.

February 16, 1937 My thoughts are more or less in a state of distraction this afternoon. I can hardly concentrate on any serious matter. The reason is that the necessity for making a rather major decision is brought squarely before me at this time. In December to my considerable astonishment I was invited to take up work at the Publishing House at Scottdale. I declined the proposition as a whole but offered to help out on a part time basis as a nonresident assistant if such service would be of any use to the management there. For some time no further word was given me, except a promise to let me know before long some decision on their part. On last Sunday A. J. Metzler spoke to me for any hint that I might have reconsidered the matter upon further thought. I said I had not changed my mind, but also that I had not closed my mind on the question. Today at noon, very strangely, I was invited to eat at the college dining hall at a special table with the college administration, all four of them. To my surprise they announced the receipt of a night letter from Scottdale, making a further proposition to the effect that they would put off for a year the final appointment to the position, and would I consider taking it up for a year, half time from now to June 1, then full time in residence at Scottdale, and again half time for the first semester of next year. The administration's object was seemingly to report the matter to me as a body and make clear their attitude on it, that they will not interfere with my decision about it, but will and can make necessary adjustments as regards my work here. It is O. O. Miller's feeling about the matter that has given just a little different color to the expressed attitude of the administration here. He spoke to me last Sunday about his personal views on it. I was just a little surprised at the strong feeling he had about the matter. He expressed himself strongly about my qualifications for the place and their need at Scottdale for my services. Yet he also emphatically said that if I have personal conviction on it, that must be the deciding factor.

So I have been trying to go over the whole situation again in my mind and see honestly with myself the reasons for going there permanently or staying here. For I have about decided that I must make my decision final one way or another now, instead of leading them on another six months in uncertainty. As I size up my thoughts about the situation now I really feel less and less that the work at Scottdale is the place for me. The opportunity for doing a good service to the church is very great, but I am not convinced that the opportunity is precisely for me. The work is more close and confining yet than here, where we have at least eight weeks of freedom from routine. I have found how badly I need these vacation periods for recuperation and for a little creative thinking. My feeling is that if I were to spend all my writing energy on editorials and routine writing that what little creative writing I might do otherwise would be impossible. I cannot do anything like that. Leisure is a necessity for me to keep fresh and growing. It is quite obvious that one would be loaded heavier there than here. And because my store of energy is rather limited and needs conservation, it does not look very inviting. Perhaps I am narrow and selfish. But as best I can evaluate my abilities and powers, this place has more opportunities than the other.

February 18, 1937   Am having my turn with the "flu" that has been raging up and down the land since the beginning of the year. Slept several hours this afternoon, so refreshing myself considerably.

The Scottdale offer is resting on my mind much these few days.

Beginning yesterday my own feeling about it has undergone a partial turn in the tide, and I am really considering it as I have not done before. The reason probably is that I have sensed a real change in the sentiment of others around, who have rather changed their opinions recently. It all probably goes back to the opinion and advice of O. O. Miller and to further conversations with A. J. Metzler over the last weekend. I noticed it first in talking with C. L. Graber, and then H. S. Bender. Several others have expressed the same general sentiment. So I find myself leaning that way too. I think my attitude is that if a considerable number of people of a wide outlook upon the Church and her work are decided in their view and conviction that I should accept the opportunity, then I might well overlook my own inclinations in the matter and consider it a call from God.

February 27, 1937 On Tuesday of this week a specialist gave the Mantaux Tuberculin Test to everyone he got hold of at the college. This included all students and members of the faculty, almost without exception. My reaction was read as a plus four, and my wife's as plus two. So we are both to get X-ray pictures made of the chest as soon as possible and if necessary have further examinations made. In my case the question in my imagination has been forced upon me whether it is possible that in recent years my system has not perhaps been fighting these bacilli, and this accounts for my much lassitude, exhausted feeling, need for extra rest, and especially for my periodic "flare-ups" as I have chosen to call them. About every three weeks, I reckon, on an average I have to go through a mild or serious spell of something, maybe a cold, or sore throat, or a slight gastric disturbance, usually with some supernormal temperature and accelerated heart action lasting for a few days. Just now this test seems to have precipitated such a set of symptoms again.

Last Monday I wrote to Scottdale my tentative acceptance of their offer to join their editorial staff at that place. I have reserved the right to make the decision final at a little later date, when it will be made clearer to me just what work they expect me to do. Only one matter was specified, the Advanced S. S. Lesson Quarterlies, about a half time job, and the remainder was covered by the blanket phrase "other editorial jobs." Since official appointment to the position will be made only in August by the Publication Board at its biennial meeting, I figured I was entitled to a little more time myself. But their answer has not been immediate, since after five days I have no reply.

February 28, 1937 This date reminds one that two months of our brand new year has slipped through our hands already. Time is on the march. Yesterday evening at home I finished reading a very delightsome new book I acquired a few weeks ago, "In The Steps of St. Paul," by an English author, H. V. Morton. The man is an experienced traveller and a rather fascinating writer. This book is the account primarily of the writer's travels as he tried to follow out the routes Paul travelled on his missionary journeys. He gives very interesting descriptions of his travel difficulties and of the present status of the lands and cities where Paul once travelled and labored. Along with his travel narrative he has woven in the essential facts of the book of Acts and even in part of Paul's Epistles, so that the reader who is not familiar with the New Testament will get a rather clear picture of that part of the N. T. history. The book has aroused my own ambitions to travel and visit the scenes of Paul's labors sometime. The book has given new light to me on a good many points of the history. The author is very up-to-date in his information on N. T. study; he follows to a very great extent Ramsay's interpretations and conclusions, who happens also to be my favorite Pauline scholar. He holds a generally conservative position in regard to Acts, although on disputed points he is not dogmatic, but cites opposing views. He does seem to lean strongly toward the theory that Paul's Prison Epistles were written at Ephesus during an unknown imprisonment there.

I think I shall collect all the books on Paul and the early church that I can afford to get. It is a very interesting field of study and one that attracts me greatly.

Among the things that this book impressed upon my mind with special force is the profound change that has come over the world of the Eastern Mediterranean Basin since the day that Paul travelled about in it. Where Paul and his helper could once travel with some facility are today the remote, unfrequented places of the world. A majority of the great centers where he labored to preach the new faith are today complete ruins, often as desolate as the desert. Surely what men proudly call civilization, culture and the like, exists by a very small margin of life. If such great cultures and teeming cities could once disappear from the face of the earth, surely the same thing can happen again. Why should the spirit of mortal man be proud and become vain? After all, only the truth of God, the realm of God, endures through the ages, and it alone merits the devotion and the service that humans can give.

March 5, 1937 For several weeks past I have been thinking about appealing to our business manager for some extra monthly income, such as I in other years had been getting at this time of year upon special request, for paying some urgent interest payments. Due to my refinancing operations of last summer, I have no mortgage interest coming due right now as formerly, so I struggled with my conscience over the question whether I had any need urgent enough to justify me in asking for extra income at this time, particularly in face of the fact that our regular checks this year are fifty per cent larger in amount than they were a year ago. Well, as stated, for some weeks I now thought I would go in and try to get some extra for paying some unpaid depression interest, and again I thought I would do nothing about it. Finally yesterday morning the spirit moved me to step into Graber's office, seeing his door was standing open and no one else was occupying his time at the moment; I screwed up my courage to plead for some extra lucre. To my great relief and no small surprise, he opened the conversation and handed me an envelope he had just addressed to me, but not yet sent, the which when I had opened it , I was almost knocked over when I espied a check for even one hundred dollars. It was from back salary of previous years, but nonetheless welcome, I must say.

I lost no time in disposing of it. Mailed it for deposit to the Bank at Hesston where I still have my account. By the same mail I sent a check for ninety dollars to D. H. Bender, which will bring my interest payments up-to-date with this creditor. Besides I have enough accumulated in my account at Hesston so I can now, without draining it dry, send to Father a check for the five years' interest which I owe to him. So it has happened rather suddenly that I will be without unpaid bills of any sort, no arrears, for the first time in nearly five years, and it is almost a strange feeling. If now I can soon muster around twelve or thirteen hundred dollars of cash and pay off all my personal notes, then that will be a glorious feeling. What it would be like to be without debt of any kind is really a hard thing to picture in my mind.

If by some miracle I should receive in a lump sum all my arrearage in salary from the college, I would be something like two thousand dollars ahead of my present circumstances. The plan is by next year to pay the regular salary schedule in full as they go. That will be a really new experience for some of us poor college teachers. To have income above what is just needed for food and clothing and most urgent interest charges; what an experience! Really I hardly know how I would act under such circumstances. I presume the problem of allocating surplus funds will be equally as serious and problematic, possibly more so, than that of doing without funds and the things these might buy.

March 8, 1937   About a month ago I bargained with the college bookstore for the acquisition of a new fountain pen. After a long delay, this new writing instrument has just been handed to me, a lifetime Shaefer's, feather touch, fine, priced on the tag at $8.75. I get the full benefit of the dealer's discount, as do all the teachers here for all they purchase through the local store, making the pen cost me about six dollars, and they have besides charged it to my account to be taken from unpaid salary. My Parker pen acquired in 1926 is still in use, although it takes queer streaks now and then. Anyway, Mrs. Yoder has long complained of the fact that when she does want to write an occasional letter at home, she can do so only when I happen to be at home and the family pen with me. Now one pen or the other can be at home and the other abroad, so making living a little bit more efficient than heretofore. I do not especially fancy this blue ink; black is my preference. I have never owned a pen that gave perfect satisfaction, but here's hoping this new one will give such a quality of performance!

March 18, 1937   After nine o'clock in the evening and I have just come from a discussion contest, the women's annual discussion affair. Six young women ranging from freshmen to seniors gave discussions on a variety of topics from tea to ventriloquism. As so frequently is my luck I had to be one of the three judges to decide upon the winners. This is now the third time, I believe, this winter that I helped in this part. I do not mind judging most of such contests. Last winter (or spring) when three of us tried to pick winners in the freshman men's peace oratorical contest, I felt we faced the hardest decision I ever helped on. Public sentiment scarcely supported the decision, and the judges were poorly satisfied with the outcome. It really was a hard matter to decide for several reasons. But most of the time it is not so extremely difficult to make a decision.

Over last weekend, when I had for weeks planned to accept a special invitation to attend an unusual peace institute at Manchester College, at the last minute on Thursday evening I turned sick with "flu" or something that turned my inside works upside down. Friday and a good part of Saturday I spent in bed. Even Sunday I did not venture out of the house. The last several days I have been feeling quite well for a change.

It is time now to bear down on the job of writing copy for the Gospel Herald in April. This project always rests rather remotely on my mind for two months or more, as I try to set a few ideas incubating hoping they may in due time hatch into something that is useful and good. Then when the time comes it is always rather hard to get down to real business and actually write something. Somehow I imagine that I could write a great deal better if it were not for the manifold distractions, trying to concentrate in turn, if not simultaneously, on a considerable range of tasks and projects. If I should decide to take up an editorial position, I might have opportunity to learn from experience whether my imagination is correct or faulty. I plan to try it out this spring and summer; shall spend a week or ten days at Scottdale in preliminary survey during April.

March 25, 1937 This year for the first time our spring recess does not come over Easter time, but starts two weeks after Easter. This week, because it is called Holy Week, the college has a few tokens of special observances. The chapel exercises on the first three days were a bit special, M. C. Lehman conducting them with particular reference to the death and suffering of Christ. Today instead of regular student devotional meeting over the chapel hour, a public service is announced for the evening. Also tomorrow evening a public service is to be held, and on Sunday morning a Sunrise Service at six o'clock.

Very recently I have had made for myself a new suit of clothes, almost an event in the routine tenor of life for me. An elderly German tailor who lives several blocks down Eighth Street in Goshen made it for me. He seems to have considerable success in making coats with the so-called "plain" collar in a way that it looks respectable, and not like a collar on a military uniform. I paid forty-four dollars for the outfit. The last previous suit I got cost less than forty dollars, as far as I can now recall. That was in the fall of 1933. I do not know whether I am more or less extravagant than others in the frequency with which I buy new suits. I can think back quite clearly to the last five suits I have purchased. Going backwards, the years were 1933, 1931, 1928, 1926, 1923, five suits doing service for thirteen years, which would seem to be a fair performance. I happen to know that I do not require as many clothes as some do to get along. Part of the explanation, a goodly part in fact, is that my wife is both very skillful and very patient in the business of mending clothing. I have not yet worn the new suit which I brought home a week ago. I have quite a strong aversion to wearing new clothes; the old are better, as says the Bible.

March weather is here in reality. A much varied program it has been giving us, occasional bright sunny days, balmy and spring-like, again stormy, drear and chilly. Yesterday was one of the latter kind, with rain and sleet, which during the night turned into snow, so that this morning we were treated to a winter scene. Sun is shining brightly this morning, with a cold wind from the north, which keeps the snow from leaving all at once.

The time is here again to prepare copy for the Gospel Herald, April supplement. Somehow I have a lack of real inspiration this time. It seems that I have pretty well gone the round of my stock of ideas, and find myself wishing for some new ones. But for readers, repetition may be the solution of the problem.

April 3, 1937   The last three weeks have, from the health standpoint, been in general "tough." It is the time of the year when I generally suffer most. Since the attack of influenza I have been going about much as usual, although I have not had much comfort in doing so. For one thing my neuritis in right shoulder and upper arm has been a real discomfort. Last weekend I stayed in, not altogether, but almost so. Have considered letting Dr. Martin search for possible sources of infection somewhere internally.

April 9, 1937   Vacation atmosphere has struck the campus already, even though classes are supposed to continue until noon today. The college choruses left in two large motor buses at about 9:30 this morning, which in itself breaks up the forenoon classes badly, and other folks do not care greatly whether classes meet or not.

The sun is shining bright and clear for once today and the out-of-doors is beautiful and attractive. Nothing would suit me quite so well just now as to go out walking today for air and sunshine. Instead of such leisurely activity, I am busy with thoughts and preparations for a trip to Scottdale, Pennsylvania. Will leave tonight from Goshen, and as I cannot bring myself to spend the extra money for Pullman fare and berth, I want to go to bed this afternoon for a period of rest and sleep. If I were sure the Publishing House will pay me at once for the trip, I would sleep and travel in comfort tonight. But I have in my time spent too much money before I had it in hand, to get the consent of my mind to spend the extra five dollars for a night's comfort.

April 19, 1937   This afternoon class work begins again after the interval of spring recess. It has been an unusual recess. I was away from home for just a week. Left on Friday evening, the ninth, and returned within four hours of the same time on the sixteenth. Had a very pleasant stay at Scottdale amid the hills of Western Pennsylvania. My headquarters in general for the term of my stay were at Charles Shoemakers'. They showed me every kindness possible, even refused to accept any financial remuneration for the six nights' lodging I had with them nor for the ten meals I ate at their family table. The other meals I took upon invitation in other homes. Saturday evening at Yakes'; Sunday noon at Homer Kauffmans'; Monday evening at Henry Hernleys'; Tuesday evening at A. J. Metzlers'; Wednesday evening at D. Kauffmans'; Thursday evening at George Louckses'. On Sunday I was present at the services in

their church both morning and evening. At their prayer meeting time
on Wednesday evening, Paul Erb of Kansas preached. He gave a typical Erb sermon, abundance of personal allusion and subjective emphasis. I had not heard Paul in a sermon for a good many years.

My time while at Scottdale I spent at the Publishing House orient-
ing myself for the work of preparing the Advanced Sunday School Lesson Quarterly. Ellrose Zook showed me how he has been doing this
work recently and introduced me to the material used in this work.
He had arranged temporary working quarters at the rear of the small
Assembly Hall with desk, paper, typewriter, etc. Here I labored for
three days to bring forth the material for the first lesson of the fourth
quarter of 1937, October 3 to be exact. The mechanics of copy form,
exact length, and so on was not so hard to learn and understand. As
for material, or rather tools to work with, I did not find anything very
extensive at hand. It seems that there is no working library available
of Bible commentaries, books of illustrative material, etc. Of the kind
that I am planning to use, such as Greek and Hebrew commentaries
and more recent helps and aids, there is nothing. It will be necessary
for me to plan ways and means to acquire some of the more essential
works for my own use. While working here, of course, the college library will afford very excellent means for the work.

May 20, 1937 One busy month has slipped away since I last felt I had
a bit of leisure on my hands. There are many things of which I should
make note in these pages, if I could find time for leisurely scribbling.
I have been carrying my classroom teaching regularly. Miss Esch has
now finished the work in the two courses where she was the only pupil,
which releases about five hours a week of time for me. In second year
Greek, where we are reading Acts, we have been meeting only two hours
a week lately, so saving an hour. But I have not been doing much for
that class, I feel, rather letting it slide along so-so. All my office work,
except the issuing of excuses for absences from chapel and classes, has
been handed over to others. The remainder of the time has been given
to writing Sunday school comments and studying for the same. I am up
to the schedule as I had planned it. I get out the material for three
lessons in two weeks time. That is, I plan to spend four full afternoons
on one lesson. However, I also plan to get out for a walk to town for
sun and air on two afternoons a week, sometimes taking an entire afternoon and sometimes only a part, depending on weather and other circumstances. For a week or more I was one day behind schedule, but
now I am caught up and expect to gain just a bit on the remaining five
lessons of the fourth quarter for 1937. Thereafter I must spend a few
weeks at Scottdale finishing up details on the manuscript before I turn
it over as final copy. During the same several weeks I want to prepare material for one lesson of the new quarter and propose for consideration the changes that I may want to introduce in this quarterly,
as to format and contents for the next year. I am doing the typing of
manuscript all myself and in my own way. Some parts I write out
quite in full in pencil first, and for other parts I simply make notes
in advance. It requires as a rule seven full typewriter pages of copy
for a lesson, double spaced, but long lines, I judge about three thousand words for a lesson, some of which I merely copy from other

sources. I cannot very well compose copy in final form on the typewriter or with pencil, for I always correct and revise what I write
before it satisfies me. Whether I can ever develop the skill to do
otherwise is doubtful, though I must try to work in that direction. At
least I hope to speed up this routine writing in some way to save time.

June 18, 1937 Here I am at Scottdale, some four hundred miles away
from Estie and Boy. I left them, it will be a week ago tomorrow
afternoon. A week ago this afternoon the three of us took an outing of
our own kind. We took a bit of lunch and walked to Goshen's City Park,
a distance of about two miles or a little less. We took our time for
the trip, walking along the path on the west bank of the canal most of
the way. It is a pleasant way to walk to town, except when the tall
weeds grow up and make it less pleasant. The park was beautiful, what
there is of it, which is not a great deal. Boy had been begging for a
picnic and since it was a warm, sunny day, we felt like taking a half
day off before I should leave them for a time. In town, I went to Dr.
Weaver, osteopath, for a last treatment before leaving town. Twice a
week this doctor had manipulated in his own way my right arm and
shoulder for at least six weeks. His efforts usually made the shoulder
feel a bit more comfortable for the time being, but really I have not
been convinced that he has done me any real good. If I had to pay him
cash out of hand at the special rate of $1.50 a treatment, I would be-
grudge him the money. As it is, he charges his work against my
credit at the college business office. I have not made up my mind
whether I shall go back to his office again later or not.

Also in town that afternoon I spent $1.50 for a pocket watch, which
has only run a few hours since I have it. As I left Goshen the next
day, I was unable to return it at the time. Had hoped that I might be
able to spend perhaps twenty dollars for a good quality wrist watch by
this time. But since I did not feel I could do so just yet, I thought I
would get along a few more years by means of a cheap pocket watch.
But perhaps I shall need to get along without any at all for some longer time. Having thus gotten along for three years, I sometimes feel it
would not be impossible in our simple way of living to go without a
watch or timepiece indefinitely. I imagine however, that once I have
income and all the cash in hand that I wish for, I will probably be investing in a wrist watch.

Well, to go on with the picnic story. After a little shopping for myself, I bought a quart of ice cream and returned to the park, where
the others were waiting for me. We walked around a bit, ate our lunch
and soon started to walk home. We were all tired but glad we had
made the trip.

On last Saturday I travelled with G. F. Hershbergers in their car
to West Liberty, Ohio, leaving Goshen at near five o'clock and reaching that place at ten. We stayed in that vicinity from then until Tuesday morning. Reason was, the Board of Missions and Charities met in
its annual meeting then. The first night I spent at a farm home, Joe
Planks', also for meals on Sunday. That night I stayed at Nelson
Kenagys' in town. Monday night I spent at Yost Hartzlers', a primitive farm home located on the edge of town. Sunday and Monday I
spent sitting in sessions with hundreds of others, listening to words,

words, words which I hope meant more to the other folks than they did to me. One or two of the speeches compelled my interest and attention. The rest bored me as most such harangues do, which give me nothing new or constructive to think upon. The meals obtained on the grounds were altogether typical for such occasions. Though there was still another day of sessions, we had enough for our taste by Tuesday morning. So we left West Liberty and by evening had travelled to Scottdale. Hershbergers drove on eastward the next day, where they will spend the summer in Germantown, Pennsylvania. G. F. will do research work in Quaker History of early Pennsylvania. He has a grant-in-aid of three hundred dollars from the Social Science Foundation for financing his summer's work.

So I am here for the time being. Since my leisure time is a little more abundant than it is at home, I want to use some of it for writing notes, trying to get caught up somewhat. It seems a shame that for this year so far I have had so little real comfortable leisure for this scribbling. It is surprising to me how much time I spend with Virgil, and yet not so much in actual time. I help him gather in the toys he drags outdoors during the day. This we do before supper, or the evening meal. Then as a rule after this meal I read to him for a half hour or more. Then I put him to bed by 8:00 o'clock. But by that time I usually am worn out sufficiently to desire to relax entirely, slump down into a chair and read something, or rest on the davenport, and by nine o'clock or soon after retire to bed. The weeks since my other trip to Scottdale were really strenuous, for it took much more than half of my working time to get the lessons written out on schedule. But I got them out. Now after working these three days here, I have just about put all finishing touches to the manuscript and tomorrow I shall turn it over to the printer.

June 22, 1937 This is after supper with still more than an hour of time before dark. There has been sunshine in this part of Pennsylvania today, after a day of hard rain. Yesterday evening after supper, since the rain had stopped by then, Ralph Bender, who also boards at Shoemakers', and I went out for a walk over the town of Scottdale. We did not need to walk long to reach the northern end of the place, and I found that the city is not so large as I had imagined, about the size of Goshen, perhaps a little less in population. The change in topography from northern Indiana is of course the most striking thing about this country. In a way it seems good to see Mother Earth with a few wrinkles in her face. Walking up and down hills is like a new experience for me, since it is so long that I have negotiated any hills or mountains. But I like mountains; they give a landscape a touch of character, it seems to me. Open level country is all right, if it is really open, like out on the plains of Kansas or Colorado, where one can see the skyline horizon in all directions at all times for the looking. When a flat country is cluttered up with trees and woods, human habitations and so on, it seems to take on a nondescript character that I never have come to like.

One thing that prevents me from feeling at home around here is the absence of books. There is a library in the House, a specialized Mennonite Historical Library, but I have practically no books of my own here, and there is no library of any account in town, so I am told, that is, public library. This is too bad, not to have access to periodicals for keeping in touch with current thought. And for working at my job, I feel quite "lost" without my books around me. Just to feel the presence of shelves full of books is in itself an inspiration in some way.

I have by hook, if not by crook, gotten possession of quite a few new and used books during the past several months. When it really appeared that I was going to do writing on the Sunday school lessons, I decided to stock up with Biblical reference works as I might have opportunity. Well, I saw one good opportunity – getting books at discounted price paid for from my unpaid college salary account. I approached the Business Manager for special permission to have some ordered through the college bookstore under such an arrangement. I set no specific or maximum sum that I might use, neither did he suggest any. I hinted that, since faculty members with cars were getting gasoline all year on account through the college, it might be only fair that I get some extra books charged against my account. So I set about to draw up possible book lists, which I studied and revised for some time before ordering any. Among those ordered were: The set of small volume commentaries on the New Testament by Charles Erdman, complete in fifteen or seventeen volumes, I forget which; the cost around eleven dollars for the set to me. Then I was desirous of getting as many volumes of the "Cambridge Greek Testament" as possible. They ordered a number of used copies from Blessing's store in Chicago. But I discovered that some of these volumes are really quite old and so are of inferior value. They say that few commentaries published on the N. T. before 1905 are of value, because not till then were any studies on the papyri widely available. So I did pick out a limited list of new copies of the Cambridge volumes, such as I felt would be valuable, and had them ordered. I have all these excepting perhaps a half dozen. They also ordered a few volumes of the "International Critical Commentary." The volumes in this cover both Old and New Testaments, but they are by no means equally valuable. Some of those on the O. T. are by radical critics and are hardly desirable for my use. Others on the N. T. are among the best that are published, especially Burton on Galatians and Plummer on Luke, but neither of these do I have yet. Another used set that came from Blessing's store is the five-volume "Expositor's Greek Testament." Eight dollars or a bit more is all it cost, and the volumes are only shelf-worn, some leaves being still uncut. In May came a book list from Blackwell at Oxford, England, listing remainders of religious books at about two-fifths original price. As a sampler I sent an order, mostly for copies of the "Westminster Commentaries." They came through in a hurry; just twenty-one days from the time I ordered them they were delivered by mail to me. They are commentaries on the English text, but appear up-to-date and scholarly, and not a bad purchase at the price I paid. There were a scattering of other books that I ordered through the bookstore: Dummelow's "One-Volume Commentary"; James Moffat's newly revised and final (as he claims) edition of the complete Bible; James Kleist's "Gospel of Mark", a Catholic scholar's work, the first of such that I have ever gotten; a fine little book of lectures by John A. Scott of Northwestern University entitled "We Would Know Jesus"; and, oh yes, I ordered thirteen volumes from the Loeb Classical Library, "Letters of St. Basil", "Josephus", "Greek Anthology", "Hesiod", "Select Letters of St. Jerome". And last but not least, I gave to Leland Bachman, a college student, my order for the five-volume International Standard Bible Encyclopaedia, at the very special price of $23.70. This I paid in cash, but it had not yet come when I left home.

June 24, 1937   The evenings seem long when I am away from home, for I do not have the job of reading stories to Virgil and putting him to bed. Weather has been perfectly ideal, if there is such a thing, for the past several days. Sunshine, a coolish atmosphere with wind from the north, everything just right for comfortable working. Today I went out after dinner for a half hour to take the sun, and it was very pleasant. Walking five or six minutes in the direction of south and west brings one out in a rough open field adjacent to a woods of some size. I did not go as far as the woods, for I wanted sunshine today.

I am getting tired now of boarding and living away from home, after twelve days away from home comforts and Wife and Boy. One is unable to relax quite as completely and be as natural and unconventional among strangers, comparatively, as at home. I hope to get home about one week from today, or from tomorrow at the latest. The people hereabouts are very kind and hospitable, but it just is not like home. Estie writes that Virgil is eagerly inquiring when Daddy is coming home.

On last Tuesday was my first payday experience at this place. I received a check for thirty dollars, which was my allowance, on half time, for the first two weeks of June. Also was handed an envelope containing another thirty dollars in currency, which was full time pay for the third week of the month. I am supposed to be on full time pay during the entire summer, and what a lot of money will be dumped into my hands; it seems too good to be true, really! After five years and over of very meagre and often uncertain income, with the summer months bringing in little or nothing, receiving such money seems like being in fairyland. I try hard not to betray my inner feelings when they hand me such income. Besides, accepting checks from the college was for me always accompanied by a kind of apologetic feeling, as though it was a decided favour from the business office that I received anything at all. Here I try not to look apologetic about taking what they give me. Do not know how well I succeed. Really, in some respects this opening here looks to me more and more like a Godsend. They have not said anything since I am here this time about a final decision on the matter.

June 28, 1937   It is convenient to have longer evenings for a while, for in this way I can scribble a few notes. I am really getting tired of this round at Scottdale; shall be glad to travel home in a few days from now. It is wearisome work, with no proper place to relax and spend spare time in the midst of home comforts. My work today was on odds and ends, partly getting ready peace material for the Gospel Herald, partly breaking ground for work on the first two quarters of 1938. The six months' lessons are a unit of studies from Mark. I believe it will be an interesting series of lessons to write out. And I am, foolishly perhaps, playing with the idea of finishing up the two quarters in the next two months, or at least by school opening in September. That would put me very nicely ahead of schedule and would be a satisfaction in more ways than one. My ambition is to get the lessons prepared one whole year ahead of scheduled time, except for times when I would lay off for some reason. This program for the summer will run me pretty hard, I fear, and I am not making it a matter of life or death, if I should fail to reach my goal. Somehow, I have the habit of always loading myself to the limit with planned work. Making a slave out of myself is what it seems like sometimes. Practicing a sort of asceticism on myself is my way of living, never satisfied, always loading on myself things to do, setting before myself heights to climb, making my way hard and toilsome, seems to be my nature. Stopping sometimes to watch myself, I feel a touch of envy for folks who are not thus afflicted with ambition and discontent with themselves. If I could, so I imagine, just settle back pleased and contented with myself, not bothering myself with what I do not already have, what a lot of trouble I could save myself!

July 4, 1937   This writing finds me at home again, comfortable amid home surroundings. Last Wednesday I finished up the preliminary work on the first two quarters' lessons for 1938, and since I had announced my purpose of returning to Goshen, the treasurer handed me a third week's full pay practically all in advance. Well, I left early the next morning and have done no work since – not a very conscientious record for wages received in advance, I must admit. One day I spent on the train, and as I came back with an attack of my periodic illness, I did not do much since. On Friday we spent the afternoon picking cherries, one crate of large sweets on the Bristol Hills Fruit Farm and a half crate of small sweets on the Judson Fruit Farm, both north of Goshen. Even though we picked these ourselves, we paid what seemed a good price for them, $2.50 for the crate of large and $1 for the half crate of small. Some of my time also the last two days was to attend to a few matters of correspondence that had accumulated during the three weeks I was away. I had planned to start in tomorrow morning on my program of work as outlined, but as it happens, the annual Sunday school outing is scheduled for tomorrow, and so I may not get really started.

This morning before time for S.S. to begin a special delivery postal package was brought to my hands. It proves to be the galley proof of my article on Aulus Gellius submitted to the editor of Classical Journal nearly two years ago. I received acknowledgement notice at the time and a little later acceptance notice, though the acceptance carried a reluctant tone, so that I gathered that the article got past the gates of acceptance by the skin of its teeth, so to say. Well, anyway the fact that it was accepted and will appear in print during the coming winter, is the source of a bit of proud satisfaction for its writer. To have one's first article submitted to a journal of this rank makes me feel that I have "crashed the gates" in a small bit of real achievement, even though it did take me full ten years from the time the idea of this article came into my mind to get it into print. Some more of my productions will see the light of literary day during this year, as it now appears. A short paper on "The Need for Nonconformity Today," read last winter at our Forum on that subject, is coming out in a few days, that is in the Mennonite Quarterly Review for April, 1937, a periodical that always comes out in the third month after its date. And the July issue is supposed to carry my paper on "Christianity and the State" read before the Peace Society of the college last winter. Some work needs to be done on this article to make it presentable. The paper on nonconformity I was not so very enthusiastic about putting into print, since it was mostly prepared as a piece of local propaganda, but in the judgment of some it merited permanency of form, so I withdrew my hesitation. I have in mind to prepare a few essays for the Christian Monitor, by-products of my work on the Lesson Quarterly for Sunday schools, one for October on the "Christian Walk," another for January on "John, also called Mark." If now the Moody's Monthly would presently print the article they accepted from me in November, 1935, I would be pleased all around.

July 24, 1937 Work for the week is over and among the "extra things" today must be writing a few lines of notes. My working schedule at present, and probably for most of the summer, is this: I write out copy for three lessons in the S. S. Quarterly every week. I find I can usually do one lesson by working three successive half days, or about twelve hours. At that rate I can have every Tuesday, Thursday, and Saturday afternoon free for doing other things, one of which is usually getting out in the air and sunshine. This afternoon threatens to be cloudy, but unless it rains, I mean to get the air and exercise anyway. I have put into my daily schedule now, very definitely and securely a siesta of an hour's length, and it is a genuine luxury, nay more, a boon and a blessing for efficient and comfortable working in the afternoons. Hope I can regularly do this in the future.

Last Tuesday evening M. C. Lehman and wife took all of us for a ride, in the air, going just for a trip down to Winona Lake and back in several hours' time.

With my work I manage to read some things too. In the college library I found a book by T. R. Glover entitled "The Jesus of History." Attracted by the author mostly, I took the book and read it nearly all now with real interest and inspiration. The book is twenty years old but is very stimulating to me. Mr. Glover's profound background of ancient history and ancient thought and religion makes about everything he writes of unusual fascination to me. It fires me with the determination to read more extensively in those fields myself. His approach to the character and the teachings of Jesus is always so fresh and invigorating that I am forced to confess to myself that I know practically nothing as yet of the spirit and deep import of His teachings. The traditional "Sunday school" approach is probably the best for one in childhood, but it is no more than a basis for a mature understanding of the Gospels and their message. The common orthodox approach with the regular kit of theological words, phrases, and concepts, all neatly classified and arranged, does not seem to take one very far either toward a real understanding of the Christ. The approach from the historical and human side is a fresh one for me and very appealing. This seems to me to approximate the approach the early disciples had to Christ, and it may still be the best.

August 7, 1937 On last Tuesday I finished the work on first quarter's lessons for 1938. Thinking I should have a brief breathing spell before I go on to work on the second quarter's lessons, I did nothing further on S. S. lessons during this week. Tried to do a few other things, but spent most of my time "feeling badly"; for I had one of my periodic general congestions. By Monday I want to start in again on regular schedule, if at all possible.

Changes are being made, as is the custom in this world. I have given my decision to resign from the college faculty and to accept the invitation to work at our Publishing House, beginning next June permanently. Because I have been relieved of all administrative office work for the coming year, I have received another professor as roommate in my office, in the person of M. C. Lehman. The arrangement will allow me less privacy and comfort for doing my work, but I intend to make the very best of it, and like it too. I secretly rejoice that they have not put me out of this rather pleasant office and stuck me into some dismal corner.

One week ago yesterday I celebrated my forty-fourth birthday anniversary. Estie made some ice cream for the occasion, as a surprise for Daddy from herself and Boy. And so the years go slipping by one by one. Often I reminisce on what I was doing a certain number of years ago. Well, five years ago this summer I spent mostly in recuperating from the operation that relieved me of my appendix and in wondering what in the world we would live from during the ensuing winter, since the prospects for teaching income were just very meagre. But we lived through all that, and have our splendid boy besides. Ten years ago I was teaching a Latin course in Summer School here in the college. It was Cicero's Orations, and in the class were Robert Bender and several others; it must have been a high school course, since it seems the folks I can remember were high school students. Spare time that summer was all spent in final revision of manuscript for my doctoral dissertation and during about two awfully hot weeks in August typing it for submission to the Latin faculty of the University of Pennsylvania. I can with distinctness remember those singular August days, in Mrs. Gouker's house on Madison Street, Estie typing the material as I dictated, reading from a manuscript too badly marked up for anyone to interpret excepting myself, sticking fast to chairs with one's clothing and sweltering interminably. Twice a day we would work thus for a period of one or two hours, then I spent the intervening time marking and correcting copy. But we plowed right through the job and in due time I became a Doctor of Philosophy! — save the mark. In August before the typing I spent two days looking up references for some footnotes to my thesis in the Classical Library of Chicago University. A dissertation would not look very scholarly or learned if it had not at least some footnotes in small type. That same summer, too, I had my first dental plate made by Dr. Carpenter, and here I am just ten years later getting that job finished, for several weeks ago he took out the last two home-grown teeth I had, and is ready to make a complete outfit of "store teeth."

Fifteen years ago, that summer we were living in Hesston, I worked

some for Mr. Ira Spangler, one mile southeast of town, during harvest
and threshing. Most of my time was spent in studying and writing
out correspondence lesson assignments in German and French from
Kansas University. I think that was the summer when I had my first
glasses fitted by a doctor in Wichita. I did get along with his lenses
for seven years. Then twenty years ago, this was the time of the
World War, during the summer that the U. S. Army draft measures
were being worked through. They were rather anxious days, yet I
cannot recall that I worried over anything. I registered with others
in June, but never received a call, and after the system of classification put into effect during the following winter, I was so classified
that I was not subject to call. That was the last summer that I spent
working at home. I had graduated from the Academy at Hesston in
May, and went home as in previous summers to work for Father on
the farm and operate the grain thresher during the season. The next
summer found me working during vacation in Reno County, Kansas,
"profiteering" from the high wartime prices and wages.

August 17, 1937 This is one of my regular afternoons "off." I plan
to have three of them every week; some turn out to be more "off"
than others, of course. Today I took only a brief stroll out to the
dam and back. The sun is too dim today for a "sun-worshipping"
hike, so I put off that feature until some other day. I have hit upon
a place and a ritual for "sun-worship" that serves pretty well.

August 22, 1937 This has been what I would consider almost an ideal
summer here in Indiana, especially of any that we have experienced
here. Meteorologically speaking that has been true, for there has been
no prolonged oppressive heat wave, but mostly moderate temperatures
and enough moisture for all vegetation to grow profusely. It has been
comfortable for working, sleeping, and living in general. Occupation-
ally for me it has been ideal too, for my work is enjoyable to me,
and I am favorable to the opportunity of devoting myself to editorial
and literary work. I gave my decision to that effect two weeks ago
in a letter to A. J. Metzler, and proposed that my connection here at
the college be continued until the summer of 1938. They have not fully
acceded to my proposal. The recent days past have perhaps decided
the matter one way or another, when the Publication Board was in session at Turner, Oregon.
   On Friday afternoon of the past week I enjoyed a good "sunning" on
a walk and "loaf" down the Big Four railroad track. I am having regular appointments, on my afternoons that are free, with dentist Carpenter. So I managed to stretch a point in my working schedule on Friday.
And was I happy that I did so! There has been no sunshine since to
speak of, for it rained on Friday night and some more yesterday.
   Two weeks ago today we entertained Ira Millers and Ivan of Fentress,
Virginia. They stopped over two nights and a day on their way to Wellman, Iowa. They were out on a brief vacation trip. Hope the time is
not too distant when we can get into a car of our own and go off on a
vacation trip once in a while. But vacationing in any form is no pleasure or rest if one has no money to finance it with. If you merely
shift and try to do your own cooking and all that in order to save a

few dollars, then it becomes a burden, especially for the one who does the work under such circumstances. If the Lord blesses us with the means and opportunities, we must treat ourselves to a few luxuries (or necessities, as the case may be) in the years to come. Especially by the time Virgil can take care of his own personal needs and can begin to profit educationally by such experiences.

My leisure time activity – at least a fair portion of it – will during the coming months be absorbed by special study and work on the Epistle to the Galatians, for it is planned now that I shall teach the course in Greek exegesis this year. I have never actually gone through such a course myself, and I plan to use H. S. Bender's notes and materials, which he has been using himself and originally gathered in his seminary course under Dr. Machen, now of blessed memory.

September 5, 1937 Yesterday according to schedule I finished up the writing on the S. S. lessons for the second quarter of 1938. But I must still thoroughly proofread and recheck the typescript for the two quarters and do odds and ends to prepare them for the printer. Naturally I feel that my summer's effort has resulted in some real achievement. Expect to go to Scottdale on Tuesday night and return on next Saturday. This time will be spent in making some final arrangements along a number of lines, and doing some ground work on the lessons for the quarters next in line for treatment.

There has been a week or more of hot weather, but yesterday it rained and cooled off pleasantly; today an east wind is blowing strong and it seems cold in comparison with what we had a few days ago. However the sun shines clear and the day is beautiful. All in all this has been the most pleasant and beautiful summer we have spent in this state. There have been rains right along. In June there was a good deal of rain, during July and August we had rain, a good rain just about every two weeks regularly, and then temperatures have been congenial too, in July one week was hot and now another week recently. Otherwise it was only cool or warmish, and clear sunshine always between rains.

I mean to keep up my hiking this fall and winter, more diligently than in years past, and I think I can do so. For I shall not have any office work at all, so that there are no times that I must be here. My fond expectation is that the schedule for my classes will be such that I can be on duty for the college five half days of the week, for my writing another five half days, and have two half days altogether free. But one can never be sure what the class schedule arrangement will do to one's wishes and expectations.

October 11, 1937 Since the last jottings, made more than a month ago, various events and happenings have transpired. I made a trip to Scottdale from September 7 - 13. Then school opened at the college, and while I have had only eight hours regular teaching, with two hours of Latin tutoring for one person, there has been no time for leisure thoughts. I relaxed altogether for a week or more, making no attempt to do anything except what had to be done in a routine way. Then I spent a rather hectic two weeks or more writing an article on "The Early Christians and War." John Horsch is to blame for the fact that

I had this task on my hands. Last summer he called my attention to
some articles published in the German Mennonite papers in Canada.
The ones in question were by B. H. Unruh, now of Germany, in which
he attempted to show that the early Christians did not as a rule and
principle object to service in war. Horsch felt that the articles required a reply, and in fact promised such a reply to one of the leading German brethren in Canada. But he failed in his effort to find
anyone to write the required rebuttal. So in September when I saw
him again he asked me to do the job, saying it was H. S. Bender's
suggestion that I do it. I promised, not knowing it would be such a
long and difficult task. I would have had to prepare copy anyway for
the Peace pages in the October supplement of the Gospel Herald, and
at Horsch's suggestion I have made this article of 8000 or 9000 words
serve for this purpose too. Horsch purposes to translate the article,
I think, for the German papers.

Somehow the task of preparing this article was made the more
difficult because of the groggy and indisposed feeling I experienced
during much of the past two weeks. I wish so very much that I could
enjoy the efficiency, especially mentally, that I did fifteen and twenty
years ago. But it seems that my mind is not half as efficient as it
used to be. Maybe I am going to simply be worn out some of these
times, unable to produce anything useful. Perhaps I need a complete
change and rest for a period of some months, and if I had the cash
in hand by next April, I believe I should work hard to arrange myself
a trip in Mediterranean lands for three or four months, just to see
what such an excursion would do for me. But what hope is there that
such a possibility may come my way? Here I have not done a stroke
of work on the Sunday School Quarterly for four weeks, and I do not
feel particularly zestful about taking it up again. But must start just
the same and try to get a quarter's work done during the next seven
or eight weeks. This next quarter, third quarter, 1938, will be rather
more difficult because of the subject matter with which they deal. My
classes all meet in the afternoons, so that I shall have the mornings
clear for work on the lessons. In my imagination, it will be pleasant
to be free from college teaching, though time will tell whether I will
regret my change of occupation.

November 14, 1937 Lest too long a time should pass without any note
of activity on my part, I must take a little time this evening after service to note a few things of recent weeks. There has been a great deal
of pleasant weather, mild in temperature, dry underfoot and generally
agreeable. My present weekly routine calls for Monday forenoons to be
spent in the open, or at least away from the campus. It is a device
for prolonging the weekend and getting some necessary exercise. Coming four weeks tomorrow I walked only up to the business part of town
because it was pouring rain all the while. Spent some time at the
music store in trying to learn what I could about Orthophonic Victrolas,
for I have the fever for acquiring one such if possible this winter.
Three weeks tomorrow I walked southward, three miles on the railroad
where I explored a good-sized cemetery for a short time, then struck
out eastward on a road that was unknown to me. The road kept turning southward until it crossed a railroad going eastward. This I

followed for nearly a mile before I found a road going northward. It was by now time to turn my steps toward Goshen if I wanted to get home in time for dinner. I must have been five or five and one-half miles away from the college at the farthest point, perhaps even six. But I had a beautiful country road to follow coming home and enjoyed it very much, though I was really stiff for a day or so. Two weeks ago we borrowed a car and took Virgil down town for some necessary articles of clothing. Then we all stopped in at the music store and learned a few more things about orthophonics. Last Monday it was a bit rainy, but I walked south and west through Waterford and on the road a mile west of the college north to town. Today it has been raining much of the time, and what tomorrow will be like is very hard to say.

I am at this time writing Sunday school lessons on the Old Testament heroes and heroines. It is a hard task for me to get inspired over such worthies as Deborah, Samson, Eli. They have so little about them and their stories that resembles Christian ways, that it is difficult to get interested in them. Eight lessons of this quarter I have now finished, and the remaining five I want to complete in the next two weeks if possible, then after another week of work on details and incidentals the manuscript for the quarter will be complete.

The last three Sunday evenings previous to this one I went out to Yellow Creek Church upon invitation to conduct studies in the book of First John. I was reluctant to undertake such an assignment, but managed to get through with it just the same. Every time some young fellow came in a car and took me out. Two weeks ago Wife and Boy went along too. The drivers took no pay for their trouble and expense, so the proceeds from the effort was clear profit for me. They passed the collection baskets and received $6.70 which was placed in my hands. I had really expected no such boon at all, so the surprise was a pleasant one.

Today there was a Sunday school meeting at the Clinton Brick Church, ten or so miles east and north. Mr. and Mrs. Hershberger were so kind as to invite us to accompany them, and as we had never been at this particular church, we were rather glad for the opportunity to go. Heard some pretty good things, especially for purely local talent.

Buying more books still! Had the college bookstore order nine titles from a used book list from Grand Rapids. The buy was only fairly good for the price, after they gave me the benefit of the twenty-five per cent discount. Titles I especially appreciate are: Glover, "The Jesus of History," Ramsay, "Was Christ Born in Bethlehem?" D. Smith, "The Days of His Flesh." Also sent for a list of fifteen titles in seventeen volumes from a list of new books, special editions called the Modern Library, twelve giant volumes of 900-1400 pages each, and five smaller ones. For these I paid $19.75 and I am well pleased with the purchase. They represent titles I have long desired to own for my personal library: James Boswell, Robert Browning, Hawthorne, Walter Scott (three novels in one volume), Gibbon, Symonds, Montaigne, Charles Lamb, Prescott, Beery, "History of Greece," Whitman, Pater, Thackeray, Marco Polo, Dickens.

January 3, 1938   One New Year's resolution that I could profitably make this year would be to write notes more regularly during 1938 than I did during 1937. Trying to concentrate on two different tasks leaves very little of leisure time for mere reading or mere writing. An attack of bona fide "flu" has kept me from working on Sunday school lessons according to the intensive program which I had ambitiously laid out for myself for the vacation period. Instead of writing out the expected seven or nine lessons since school closed, I wrote just three and those during the first several days.

Have spent some of our increased income for other things rather unexpectedly. During the second week in December the local music store delivered to us an Orthophonic Victrola, of older vintage but never before unpacked or used. I had in mind to get something of this type of music for our home, but had no idea one could get anything respectable for less than several hundred dollars investment, and so had no idea of buying before several years hence. This older model, electrically operated, but with the electric tubes used in the newer models, was offered at one-third original cost of $50, and when a further reduction of five dollars for prompt delivery was offered, we acted and bought it. Then we selected about $30 worth of records of a varied type of music, on which we received twenty per cent discount because I am connected with a school. So we have that; and all of us will start together in our musical education, learning to appreciate and receive inspiration from the great masterpieces of classical music.

February 8, 1938   Beautiful day with sunshine and mild temperature. The former article has been rare during recent weeks, while the latter has been comparatively plentiful. Unusually warm for this season of the year. Frost is probably all out of the ground now, so that we are looking forward to an early spring, or a postponed winter.

Have just about finished all the work on the fourth quarter, 1938, lessons for the S. S. Quarterly. I worked diligently during the past five weeks to get the block of work done up. Now I am resolved to "take off" from S. S. lesson writing an entire month as a vacation for doing a lot of reading, writing, thinking, and the sort of things that one cannot well do while pushing the routine work so hard. I found the fourth quarter quite interesting, it being devoted almost altogether to a thorough study of the Ten Commandments. Besides a number of lesson commentaries, I used several new books which I secured especially for use in this work. One was by G. Campbell Morgan and the other by Henry Sloane Coffin. These I found very helpful and stimulating, each in a distinctly different way, so that in viewpoint of approach and in application they supplemented each other very nicely. Morgan is a popular, thoroughly evangelical writer, while Coffin is of the liberal school of thought and theology. The latter is however not rabidly rationalistic or destructive; he is rather moderate and altogether constructive in his viewpoint. I could not use all his suggestions and ideas, but many I found directly useful.

It will be very useful for me to be well ahead of the required schedule in preparing copy for the lesson quarterlies. I am now four or five months ahead, and should aim to gain still a little more, say about six months, and for two principal reasons. First of all, three other writers are now expecting to depend on having my copy before them in producing their work on other quarterlies. J. R. Shank wants to coordinate his part of the Teachers' Quarterly with what I have written for the Advanced Quarterly, which is reproduced in toto in the Teachers'. Also John Horsch uses it more or less in his preparation of the German Quarterly. Then only recently Miss Royer, who prepares the Primary Quarterly, has expressed the wish to use my copy, mostly to get the viewpoint of the lessons and to make references to the Advanced Quarterly for the benefit of the primary teachers. So, it looks as if, provided I can make my work creative and vital enough to merit the recognition, my own work may prove to be setting the pace somewhat in the Sunday school literature, or in a goodly part of it. Such a prospect makes me feel especially the great responsibility which devolves upon me, and I want to feel it as a challenge to constantly put very serious and conscientious effort into the production of my part.

Kind and appreciative words of commendation have been reaching me, especially on the improved form of the Advanced Quarterly, which came into circulation with the beginning of the present year. I. E. Burkhart brought from Ohio one person's favorable comments, with the additional remark that the change was fully ten years overdue. G. F. Hershberger brought from an aged minister in Lancaster County, Pennsylvania, a very enthusiastic commendation of the change, and besides expressing a wish to see me (for what particular purpose I know not); he even offered the suggestion that I had better stay at Goshen College, at least away from Scottdale, so that I could maintain the bold, fearless, and original attitude which my work expresses. Personally, I have not much fear that I will be forced into a mould when I take up residence at the Publishing House. I believe it will mostly depend on me, how well I keep my own thinking and Christian experience alive, growing and vital. If I let myself be loaded up with a vast lot of routine hack work and get into ruts of thinking and stagnation of experience, then most likely I will become a conformist and do nothing but repeat myself whenever discussing the same topics again and again.

A few people of the local Sunday school have expressed to me their appreciation of the improved Quarterly. I. W. Royer and his daughter, Miss Royer, have done the same. Paul Erb of Hesston College wrote a fine enthusiastic letter of appreciation, even remarking that he finds this quarterly about the most stimulating material he can read in preparing the S. S. lessons. Other incidental reports from a few places in Kansas have come to my ears. However, the problem that concerns me, much as I appreciate these sincere expressions of compliments, is not the reaction of certain educated and thoughtful people, so much as whether I am writing anything which the comparatively unthinking masses in our S. Ss. find useful and helpful. Do I get at least some of the material on a level and in a form which the majority can reach and profit by? This pedagogical concern is more troublesome to me than the theological and ecclesiastical concern. But even in this I have had my surprises, if not astonishment that I seem to be getting away with some ideas I was dubious about.

February 10, 1938   Busy season is on about the college this week, special lectures for ministers, special weekend conference, etc. It all does not affect my composure very much, for I keep on going about as usual. The Religious Life Committee of the faculty, which arranges for these and other activities, sought last month to persuade me to take an assignment on the program for the three days of Ministers' Institute, giving three exegetical studies or lectures on I Peter. But for better or for worse, I refused to accept the assignment, partly because of the extra work and strain there would have been involved. I realize I passed up an opportunity to make myself acquainted to some persons who do not know who I am, but the incentive from that source was not strong enough to overcome my inertia.

One major extra job I am working to get under way this week is the annual work on the subscription list of the Mennonite Quarterly Review, sending out statements of accounts, weeding out delinquents, collecting dues and subscriptions from the local people for the Historical Society. John Coffman has been appointed as assistant treasurer for this year, and I am to direct him mostly in doing the work himself. I hope someone can be placed in charge of the subscription end of the Review who will succeed in doing more constructive work in building up circulation. The total circulation has been declining slowly but steadily during the years I have tried to work at this task. It has been a grief to me that so very few students graduating from the college can be interested in becoming subscribers and regular supporters of the Quarterly Review. The dismal fact is simply that hardly any individuals, scarcely one a year on an average, get a glimpse of scholarship as such, become inoculated with the germ of scholarly interest. The charitable interpretation of such a situation, I suppose, is to say they are incapable of such an interest. Then too we have long been disappointed that so comparatively few ministers are interested in the Review and its contents. Evidently larger numbers of them can become interested in a sheet like the Defender, sensational scare-sheet, from Wichita, Kansas. Here again one's conclusion in his own mind must be seasoned with charity, I presume. The fact is that probably our people have so consistently been fed through our church literature with almost nothing but infant's pap (figuratively speaking) and predigested at that, so that many become and remain intellectual invalids for life, while others are ready to turn to any handy source for at least a few original ideas, even if they are half-baked. In all humility I want to dedicate my powers to the task of injecting a little of solid food into our literature.

We, Wife and I, have had what one would call an unexpectedly "prosperous" year during the calendar year, 1937, at least financially. When we looked back to the beginning of 1937, we saw ourselves with nothing ahead but the same and more of the same kind of financial "sledding" as had been our lot for five or six years previously. Our total income from all sources had been running along about 1000 to 1200 dollars a year, and for several years, especially 1932 and 1933 it had been very considerably below that level. And of course with such minimum income we could do nothing at all toward liquidating our indebtedness or even in paying quite all our current interest charges. But last year our tide turned and we found ourselves with an unusual amount of income, in fact, it must have been the largest income within the space of twelve months that we ever had since we are married. It is possible that during the year of 1927 we had a total gross income from all sources of about $2000, although I do not remember the exact figures. Well, last year I actually received the amount of $120 in cash from back salary account unasked for and almost unexpected. But the chief source of additional income, of course, was my work for the Publishing House beginning in April. Things really for once worked out in our favor. The college business office was generous enough not to curtail the amount of cash they paid to me even after I began to receive income from the House. They did deduct from my salary account for the year the amount of money I received from the other source, but since they were regularly paying only about three-fifths of the salary in cash last year, they went right on paying the same amount for the remainder of the year, after April. That was clear gain of over a hundred dollars in cash by June 1. Then during the summer I drew thirty dollars a week pay from Scottdale, instead of exactly nothing during previous summers, and what was a real boon besides, we paid our rent out of unpaid salary of the regular year, so that last summer from June to September was a Godsend financially for us. This year, that is, since September our half-salary from here gives us enough to live from, so that our half-salary from Scottdale is clear surplus. So that we are faring better at present than we probably will when we live at Scottdale by another year.

Our total income for 1937 was about $2100, itemized as follows as to sources: Goshen College current salary, cash $567, rent $237, bookstore and other transferred charges, approximately $125, back salary, $214. From Mennonite Publishing House $765, from Milo Kauffman rent on house $150, from Peace Committee $45, and from a few miscellaneous sources a few scattered dollars.

Out of this unusual income I paid off some considerable interest and principal of debt, at least enough to provide a fair start toward that end. To my father I paid altogether during the year the amount of $363, including five years of delinquent interest. To D. H. Bender I paid out $380, and besides I begged successfully that he reduce the interest rate on the remainder from six to five per cent annually. By this maneuver I have no interest charges higher than five per cent now, and have reduced my annual interest charges from about $128 to $75, a reduction which is well worth-while. It affords one a feeling of real relief to reduce the load of financial burden from one's shoulders even such a small amount as that. Perhaps the day will yet come when the whole debt can be cleared away. And I do hope and pray that the turned tide in our worldly affairs may bring us a few more "breaks" before it changes for the worse again. If the good Lord would see fit to overrule further my own poor financial management, my almost utter inability to "manage" finances to my own fair advantage, and would bring me a buyer for the property in Kansas, contrary to all seemingly reasonable expectations at this time, and would further throw into my path, so I would be forced to stumble upon it, an opportunity to buy or build a house for ourselves at Scottdale, then I should

certainly be eternally grateful for His blessing. Our "luck," if such
it is, has always been to pay the highest prices for what we buy, and
sell for the lowest prices. We bought our property in Kansas at the
very highest peak of prices. We remodelled the house before depression prices had come into effect. Result — we cannot hope to get one-
half of the cash we put into the place out of it again. But I hope and
I even venture to believe that the Lord whom we serve will yet see us
through our difficulties, in spite of my inability to manage and finance
well. The depression has taught us a few tricks about buying things.
More and more we dislike and, if possible, refuse to pay regular retail prices for major articles and goods. All books I have bought during the past ten years have been secured at dealers' discount prices,
and the same policy will be possible at Scottdale through the bookstore
there. At Christmas time I bought a few small electric appliances at
discount price from a local wholesale store in the management of which
C. L. Graber has an interest, so that he gives the college and its em-
ployees the advantage of his "pull" for discount prices. Our Orthophonic Victrola and the records we bought came to us at school discount rates, the Victrola even at a better discount still, because it is
an older unsalable style. Another good turn which I pray may come
to us is the collection during the next five years or so of all or the
greater part of the $2400 of unpaid salary from the college, which has
accumulated during the last five years. Just what form of settlement
if any, I should demand before leaving is unclear to me. Again I find
myself wishing for more real financial acumen to think of some way
to help myself.

February 14, 1938 The mild and generally murky weather seems to
be moving out, at least temporarily, for ever since early this morning
the northwest wind has been blowing stronger and colder. It is not
comfortable at many points in the college building, least of all in my
office on second floor. A change to some steady cold weather would
be most welcome. Colds and influenza have prevailed mightily in the
community. Virgil had a sick spell on Saturday and Sunday, but went
to his kindergarten again today. I have myself been hovering on the
verge of something for a week or so. This morning I went on my
weekly stroll in the open country after doing a bit of business in the
city.

February 17, 1938 Last Monday the weather turned cold after a
stretch of mild, murky weather, and we were hoping it would stay
steadily cold for some time, cold enough to hold in check the "flu"
germs and free people from some of the affliction incidental to mild,
damp winter weather. The colder temperature continued for two days,
and last night it started to rain again with warm atmosphere. Since
Monday too I have struggled against an attack of congestion in my
throat and head generally.

This week I am literally doing as I please, choring around in my
filing case, on my desk, and entertaining the plague as suits my convenience. I have started reading Boswell's "Life of Samuel Johnson"
recently, for the first time in my life, which fact I should be ashamed
even to record. But if I keep on studying and working hard enough I

may be able to complete my growing up and my necessary education by the time I become an old man. Among the books I have recently acquired by purchase from England is one by Malden: "Problems of the New Testament Today." Finished reading it through the other day and was quite pleased with it. The author has the seemingly quite typical British viewpoint which allows full scope to the historical criticism of the N. T. writings and yet preserves a reverent, evangelical, believing attitude toward the Scriptures. He holds personally to the inspiration, defined in his own way, and the uniqueness of the N. T. writings, without being encumbered by the typical Fundamentalist verbal-literalistic attitude toward the Bible. His views of the Early Church and its life are very refreshing and inspiring. It is possible that I am becoming heretical in my views about the Bible, but I must confess that such an attitude toward the Scriptures is attractive to me. I would not commit myself to such a position as yet but to me it sheds light on many points and really makes the Scriptures more wonderful as a record of God's grace and God's working in history. I realize very well that for popular consumption it is quite impossible to present such a viewpoint in writings. It seems to be a viewpoint to which one must come by way of a progressive development in Bible study and spiritual experience. I further believe that it is a relative viewpoint and not an absolute one, and that there is no absolutely final viewpoint of spiritual things possible for the human mind, regardless of how spiritually illumined it may be. Without wishing to pass judgment on those who hold any particular viewpoint, I am inclined to think that it is a mark of pride and self-conceit to hold that one is right and that others are altogether wrong. A proper sense of humility should make one cautious about asserting the absoluteness of any particular viewpoint. There is point to the idea that unless one holds his opinions as if they were absolute convictions he is not able to make any serious impression on others or on the thought of his time. However it may be questioned whether that statement of the case is quite correct. The kind of people who are susceptible to ideas and suggestions of truth do not need to be impressed by an authoritarian tone and attitude; but on the contrary, for the others, which seem to be the vast majority, it may be necessary to use authoritarian bluster and absolute conviction in order to produce any effects worth while. And for such it is necessary to reach them on the level of their own thinking or feeling or prejudice as the case may be. Nothing is to be gained for the furtherance of truth or of good by feeding spiritual infants with "strong meat" which they cannot appropriate, and if they feel better by thinking that their food is the best and only there is, even that delusion is not to be dispelled by any intellectual incantation or verbal powwowing.

February 25, 1938   The past two weeks of self-appropriated vacation from writing S. S. lessons have been very enjoyable. It is a rich satisfaction to potter around and be doing exactly what the impulse of the moment calls for. Yesterday I finished up a job which was started several years ago, that of preparing myself a Greek New Testament for study purposes. The preparation was a matter of pasting on typewriter-sized sheets the leaves extracted from small pocket Testaments. I had practically worn out two such, one that was acquired first about

1921 and the other in 1929 or 1930. The margins were clipped off and the leaf then pasted near the center of a large sheet. The chief function of this arrangement is to provide space for collecting all kinds of random notes and references pertaining to passages in question. The small Testaments I used for providing the Greek text contained 668 pages of text, and so this drudging, mechanical task consumed a vast deal of valuable time during the past several years at intervals.

For some reason my services are in persistent demand as a judge of speech and discussion contests on the campus. Already in previous years I had to help do a good deal of this. This year it seems to have become the regular procedure. The annual peace oratorical contest in November was the first. Last week on Friday following chapel service the freshman men, five contestants, held their discussion contest. On Tuesday evening of this week the regular men's discussion contest took place. And today after the chapel exercise the women will contest in discussion. They have asked me to be numbered among the judges, this time however associated with two women, so that in case I prove a poor judge of women's talk, the women on the judging committee will be able to outvote me. Personally I get a little bit of a "kick" out of judging such a contest. But I have come to the place where I positively refuse to judge a debate, unless it be as one of three. Only twice in my life have I attempted to serve as judge of a debate. The first was some years ago at McPherson College in Kansas, when women from McPherson debated with women from Bethany at Lindsborg. Well, I was never called upon to repeat the performance at that place, so satisfactory were my endeavors. Then a few years ago Mr. Umble prevailed on me much against my own good sense to judge a freshman-sophomore debate on the campus here. He tried once afterwards to get me to repeat the attempt, but I flatly refused and shall do so forever in the future, so far as my present resolution goes. I am no good at all in argument or controversy myself, do not like it and avoid it instinctively. Something of this complex must be back of my aversion to pass judgment upon the argumentation of others.

Kalends of March, 1938 The first month of spring is now starting, and to look forth upon the day it promises to be a beautiful one, perhaps a pledge of a beautiful month, although when this month comes in as a lamb it is supposed to go out like a lion. Anyway, we can enjoy the lamb-like features while they are here. There is still some snow and ice on the ground. Yesterday was my day for walking abroad. Left at 7:30 in the morning, traveled southward. There is a small cemetery two and one-fourth miles south from the college on the west side of the highway. Here I paused for ten or so minutes and examined some of the oldest-looking gravestones. Then my steps took me eastward and southeast, following as closely as possible the Elkhart River on its southern side down toward Benton, a town or village about seven miles southeast from here. A short distance west of that place I crossed the river and made my way north to seek out a cemetery which I had espied from some distance away when I was down that way last October. My walk along a rather difficult country road, which was by now softening up under the impress of the clear sun that was shining, was well rewarded. Something like a mile west of the town a large granite marker stood hard by the side of the road. On it was inscribed the information that on this exact spot was erected out of oak logs the first schoolhouse in Elkhart County in the year 1830. This was interesting. The cemetery at which I was aiming was a quarter of a mile farther on. It is located on an unusual spot, something like a miniature mesa, the ground falling abruptly off on three sides and part of the fourth, so that the small plot of perhaps eight or ten acres rises curiously about ten to fifteen feet above the surrounding ground. Here I found the oldest gravestones that I have yet found in the county, and the earliest one I saw was 1831, which corresponds with the date given for the first schoolhouse. The inhabitants of this cemetery appear to be of general American or Yankee stock, so far as I could judge from the names. For my return journey I saw to it that I got into Road 33 toward Goshen in time for the practice teachers who come home from Benton at noon to overtake me and give me a ride. I had arranged with Oswin Gerber to do this so they were on the lookout for me. So I reached home in good condition and in time for dinner.

The walk last week included a bus ride to Dunlap leaving Goshen at 7:20 in the morning. From Dunlap I walked north a mile or more, crossed the Elkhart River and followed as closely as possible the course of the river southward and eastward to Goshen. The river was beautiful, snow covered the ground, some ice was hanging on trees and bushes, making a very beautiful sight, whenever I was in view of the river. The walking was bad, for on ice and snow one uses different muscles in part, and my upper legs and thighs became very sore.

I still continue to spend an hour or two every week working out the double acrostic puzzle in the Saturday Review of Literature. Since I have come upon a sort of technique of procedure, I get a good deal of kick and some real diversion from unravelling the acrostic. I work on the library copy of the Review, and no one seems to be inclined to challenge my privilege to solve the puzzles. Fact is, I imagine very few people would be able to solve one of them very quickly at the first attack. But there is a kind of psychology back of the puzzle and the definitions, which, once one has become acquainted with it, make it not impossible to unravel every one that comes along. It usually takes me several hours, though occasionally there is one that for me happens to be easy, which I can do up in an hour. I find my general knowledge of classics and ancient things to be very valuable. The line of definitions that more often stumps me than any other is references to current fiction or drama, or even recently past. My information in that direction is about zero. But it is possible to force the very last space to deliver up its secret, once a half dozen words in the list have been correctly guessed. I seldom read much in the Review, but rather believe that I shall subscribe for the sheet when I leave the college environs, and use its pages for inspiration and atmosphere for some of my contemplated writing and thinking, and also as a means of keeping in touch with current literature and its trends.

March 5, 1938 On last Sunday morning I went through with a performance which was the first of its kind in my experience, and very probably the last too. At the invitation and urgent request of Pastor C. L.

Graber, and in the absence of every one of the half-dozen or so preachers around this place, I "filled the pulpit" so to speak. Attempts to speak in public are uniformly painful and exhaustive to me, and I try to avoid them as much as possible. In this case I violated my personal rule to read from manuscript every address of any substantial length, and spoke from outline and notes. Most of the audience listened respectfully enough, either out of curiosity or from interest in the remarks that were offered. I developed and enlarged upon a theme which I had occasion to treat in a Sunday school lesson not so long since, namely, the first commandment of the Decalog.

One thing I dread about changing location again is the probability that I shall need to run the whole gamut of requests to speak on this and that program, enough so to demonstrate that I am not a public speaker worth hearing. Wish I could pluck up the courage to refuse all such invitations and so save myself much worry and embarrassment.

Just came from listening for an hour to Orthophonic music from Schubert and Schumann. I listen in on this music every Saturday morning in Professor Yoder's class in music appreciation. Thereby I hope to increase my acquaintance with the musical masterpieces and so decide what records I want to buy for our library.

Son Virgil is spending this forenoon with me at the college, instead of accompanying his mother on the weekly family shopping trip. He has engaged in a variety of activities so far, writing on the typewriter, drawing on plain paper, exploring the surrounding halls and spaces. He brought with him two of his toy cars, but is not playing much with them this time. He is active and so many times at home does not know what to do and with whom to play. I imagine he would learn to read about this time if the opportunity were placed before him. He is becoming printed-word conscious, asks what the boldfaced titles in his story books "say" and can already recognize the word "the" whenever he sees it. His mother advises against teaching him to read before he goes to grade school, lest he fail to fit in with his age group in school. I am not so sure a child should be held back for the sole purpose of keeping him in goose-step. The Book House, six volumes of graded stories he hears, serves him very well. Only it will not last him until he reaches high-school age. He has already heard most of the stories in volume three and a number of volume four. He makes his own selections as a rule and insists at times on stories that are certainly quite beyond him in vocabulary and thought. I read him fairy stories and all as it comes and he calls for it.

We used to hold scruples on our part against fairy stories as such, but in becoming familiar with them directly, the ones in Book House, I at least have discarded considerable of my scruples. A child needs something to feed its imagination, and in the absence of enough strictly "true" material the fairy tales seem to serve a purpose. And (this may be rationalizing) in any case I find the better type of such tales less objectionable on intrinsic grounds than some of the Old Testament stories in the Bible Story Books, such as feature soldiers, killing, violence, punishment, etc.

What this boy likes in the advanced stories which he selects for me to read, seems to be the sound of new words, of familiar words in new settings, of musical and "sounding" language. He seems quite apt at sensing humorous situations in stories. Last evening I read "The Wise Men of Gotham," about the twelve wise men who spent a day fishing and at evening believed they had lost one of their number, and about the two who met on a bridge and got into a silly quarrel over leading sheep across when there were no sheep about. These struck him as being very funny, though I suspect that the dramatic and vigorous language and forms of expression aroused his mirth more than the contradictory situation back of the narratives. It is certainly interesting to observe his developing mind and comprehension.

Nonae Martiae, 1938 My weekly stroll abroad today took me eastward to Rock Run Church of the Brethren, where I surveyed briefly a cemetery, then in the direction of Clinton Frame Mennonite Church, a small distance west of which is a sizeable burial ground. The oldest tombstone here that I noted was dated 1840. The residents here were mostly of Mennonite names, but evidently some were of the community about. Next I saw the Silver Street Mennonite Church and came home by Fish Lake Road, glad to walk on the pavement, for the welcome sun made the soil everywhere soft by ten o'clock. A strong west wind made the home stretch a harder pull than going out. At a distance of four or five miles east of here the terrain suddenly becomes hilly, with a kind of hills which I cannot recall having seen the like anywhere else. They are small abrupt projections with evidence of abundance of boulders large and small all about. They are evidently glacial formations, but of an odd kind surely and the name for which I do not know. It looks really pretty, and in walking I find opportunity for observing and enjoying the lay of the land. I have many times travelled in rapidly moving motor car along the same road east from here but confess that I never even saw the land until this very morning. This is one of the delightful rewards of walking over these roads, in place of riding on rubber.

Daily newspapers, in order to fill up space in their columns, publish some items of events that happened some conveniently round number of years ago. Sometimes I feel the urge to reminisce over past occurrences and events in a like vein. Well, I have several times since January 1 of this year thought upon what our experiences were during 1928, just ten years ago. We started that year, both Wife and I, as patients in the Elkhart General Hospital, both having tonsils removed. The school year 1927-28 I enjoyed a great deal. My teaching load was not quite full, my thesis for Ph. D. was just finished up, and I was free to do a great deal of leisure reading and study on Grebeliana. The foolish thing – if foolish it really was, of which I cannot say as yet – we did that year was to pull up stakes from here and return to Kansas. I am not sure but it was providential, but some times I "hae me doots." Estie had her operation for thyroid trouble that year in April. The next two or three years in our home were not easy, but by the help of God we got through them. In May and June we spent some weeks in Pennsylvania, Estie at Springs with her brother's family, and I in Philadelphia, where I underwent my final oral examinations for the Ph. D., and then waited about for the graduating exercises. During July and August we spent five weeks in Iowa among friends and then moved on to Kansas. It was a hard year on Estie, what with travelling about and trying to keep on with housekeeping. That was our last visit in Pennsylvania at her old home, since which time her brother Noah has passed on and marked changes have taken place there.

Considering the state of Estie's health as it was when we moved to Kansas ten years ago, we have reasons for special gratitude in the recovery she has experienced. Though she is not robust and energetic, at the same time she seems to have a basically sound physical constitution that stands up real well, and for these ten years she has been waging a persistent and relentless battle for improvement of her general health. Her intelligent and determined effort to study health questions, dietary and other matters, arouses one's genuine admiration for her pluck and good sense.

March 12, 1938 Started this week on Sunday school lessons for January 1939. My allotted vacation from that work has come to an end. During the next thirteen weeks I should be doing two lessons regularly every week. At this rate I can do two quarters' work in the next three months. And by that time we shall probably be moving to our new location in Scottdale, Pennsylvania. As yet we have no specific place to locate, although the business manager, Charles Shoemaker, an old friend of ours, is authorized to be looking about for something that would afford us shelter when we move away from here. It is now nearly five years since we settled down in the apartment where we are. Really, we have come to enjoy the place. From the viewpoint of the man of the house, the freedom from the mechanical responsibilities of providing heat, repairs, outside appearances, becomes a pleasant and delicious habit, perhaps a bad one. Except for lack of freedom and privacy to enjoy a little outdoor space, I could be well content to live the rest of my days in an apartment, perhaps one a little larger and better than the present one we have. But we must have more space for our boy to spread out, giving him a privacy of his own and space for his activities as he grows older.

For one whole week now there has been no rain nor snow nor sleet. There has been mild weather with very pleasant sunshine every day for a time. The ground is drying off on top, and spring seems to be in the offing. Have in mind to walk abroad on my weekly hike this afternoon instead of waiting until Monday morning. The pleasant weather might not continue, and besides I want to experiment with the possibilities of Saturday afternoons as a time for walking. I anticipate it would be possible to catch rides away from the college around noon on Saturdays to points like New Paris, Middlebury, Elkhart, Wakarusa. If this should prove possible I would have a little longer time available for hiking, and would have Sunday for recuperation. It is necessary for me to get farther afield during the few months that are left for me to explore Elkhart County, for I have pretty well covered the nearby roads.

Dies Martis – May 3, 1938 Time passes; the days hurry on into weeks and the weeks into months. Nearly two months have slipped by since last I took the time to write a few lines of notes. Yet some progress is being made, for I wrote out and prepared copy for the substance of the S. S. lessons of the First Quarter, 1939, and am one-half through the second quarter. Want to get through by June 1, then take the month of June for vacation from editorial duties. Lessons for first quarter were on the life and letters of Peter. I like Peter better as a man and a character since I had occasion to study him carefully, quite carefully, but not exhaustively. He seems to be misunderstood by many who write about or preach about his life and experience. Especially his experience in denying Christ is misinterpreted (mea quidem sententia). All in all he is a fine man and an average disciple of Christ, a man whom Christ changed from a mediocre fellow into a thinker, worker, and leader in his time. This is the interesting part in studying the life of the man. His denial and alleged cowardice, of course, make rattling good homiletical grist for superficial preachers and writers and really one ought not explode the idea entirely. Some day I hope to write a correct (?) estimate of the chief of the apostles. The second quarter, now under way, is a study of Paul, the apostle's work and life. Here I find myself actually embarrassed by the wealth of material and the extensiveness (?) of my knowledge about this, one of my favorite characters in N. T. study. There is some advantage in limited knowledge after all. It spares one from the hard task of selecting, sifting, synthetizing, and organizing a mass of material and have something coherent and cogent to present in a couple of thousand words in a lesson quarterly.

Since March 12 I have taken several very interesting long distance hikes. Made a trip to Chicago one day, going by automobile with Edwin Yoder of Topeka, returning by train. Visited Blessings Bookstore in the city and picked up a few titles to add to my collection. Over Easter Sunday we had all plans made to go to Iowa City by train, but twelve hours before we were to start, Virgil broke out with measles. So that was off, though we still hope to get out there for a brief visit before we move farther east. As yet we have no word from Scottdale whether there will be any place for us to live when we do move. We live on hope and are preparing our minds for this major dislocation, uprooting out of an academic soil.

May 21, 1938   Rain and clouds have filled the sky this week past. The schedule of work is coming along on time, but nothing extra at all, excepting necessary interruptions. Annual faculty banquet and after-dinner program was suddenly announced two days before its occurrence on last Thursday. Spent just about a full day preparing for a ten or twelve minute toast. Did not regret the result. Next week will finish up the writing on the lessons for second quarter of 1939. Then it will be time to begin actual preparations for tearing ourselves up by the roots and transplanting ourselves to a new state, occupation, and environment, sifting and organizing my materials filed away, placing them in a new filing cabinet, the first I have ever owned personally. Planning and making arrangements for moving will consume much time, but will be recreation for a change. We are hoping and praying just now that the house we own in Kansas can be sold, as there is a slight possibility for making a deal now. C. A. Vogt in Hesston is kindly acting as agent, but cannot tell what will come of it. Would be glad to get it off my hands, for sundry reasons.

Everyone is wishing for warm weather, even perspiring weather would be welcome to some. A hard freeze on two successive nights last week destroyed much of the fruit in this area and farther east. Most kinds of fruits were especially plentiful last year. Mrs. Yoder has been buying good apples at the local farmers' market even until very recently for from thirty-five to sixty cents a bushel.

At the after dinner program on Thursday evening I spoke on the subject of "diplomas." It afforded a fine opportunity for a bit of academic satire, and I tried to make use of it. Taking some hints from the educational philosophy of my favorite essayist, Albert Jay Nock, I endeavored to show up the scramble of the people for diplomas for the silly business that it is, and also to satirize mildly college faculties who are so eager to bestow diplomas on the mass-minded, uneducable aspirants for the same. Have always enjoyed satire very much, and it is one of my favorite forms of literature. Would not be averse to cultivating this type of thinking, at least I still hope for time to feed upon Lucian, Aristophanes, Erasmus, and the other masters in this gentle art of telling the truth with a smile, as Horace puts it.

Dies Saturni, Pridie Non. Jun. 1938   Weather has been cloudy with a good deal of rain the past two or three weeks. Today the early morning clouds are getting thinner with promise of sunshine this afternoon. Taught my last classes yesterday as a college professor. Will soon be nothing but a plain citizen of the ranks. Hope I shall not sink mentally and spiritually anymore to the common level. Next week come final examinations and then the absolute end. There will be no occasion for tears over moving out of the halls of Academia and taking up residence in the highways and byways of real life. Change is the inevitable law of life and growth. I tend to feel as though I have outgrown college teaching. It was said of Samuel Johnson that he was unsuccessful, and in fact unqualified to be a teacher of others. His mind worked in a manner and at a tempo too far removed from that of the ordinary pupil for him to have the patience and the sympathy with those who had to learn in a way different from what he did. Even in my limited experience it seems that the students who begin the study of Greek become duller with every passing year, or their instructor becomes less efficient, at least, less satisfied with the results of his teaching. In writing one sets forth the truth, his ideas and prejudices in the clearest and most emphatic way he can, and then leaves the entire responsibility for learning the same to the initiative and intelligence and application of the reader. It is a pleasing prospect to look forward to being in a situation where one need not worry about getting his clients through a given course of study and safely past the lowest minimum set for passing an examination. How much less nerve-racking it will be to set out the various dishes of truth and reason and enlightenment before the public, with never a thought or concern whether anyone will partake thereof or not. It is possible, of course, that if one would serve up mental and spiritual diet entirely regardless of consumer demand that his own bread and butter would gradually be cut off. So it seems that one must dish out some soup and gravy, and some pastries, pies, sweetmeats, ice cream and the like, else the shekels will soon cease to come his way. Maybe it will be permissible at the same time to slip into the dishes substantial bits of solid meat, spinach, and other things that folks need for the good of their mental and spiritual health. My hope is that in writing for a livelihood, I may also keep in mind the "remnant" of which Albert Jay Nock has so ably written, and may cater to this inarticulate element among the larger public.

June 26, 1938 My last participation in academic pageantry was when the college closed its year on Monday evening June 13. Such pageantry doubtless has its value, but it is sometimes a little hard to see its connection with the essential function of a college, that of educating the youthful barbarians of the land. A little tinsel seems necessary to humor the more or less unwilling victims of the educative process. Now I am no longer connected with the Academe, except on the point of collecting financial rewards once promised for past services.

With Wife and Son I spent a nine-day vacation on a trip to Iowa. With a good friend and his family, now also neighbors, we rode by motor car to Kalona on June 16, returning in the same manner on June 24. While there we divided the time between visiting cousins and all closer kin, attending certain scattered sessions of conferences and Board Meeting at East Union and Wayland Churches, enjoying the country scene, reminiscing on scenes and events of from twenty to forty years ago. The weather was pleasant, warm and comfortable under foot. Found Father fairly well, considering his paralyzed state. He is troubled just now by glaucoma in one eye. He is manifestly aging and weakening over what he was several years ago. But he seems to be adjusting himself to the inevitable, becoming reconciled to his inability to work and engage in favorite activities. Since his eye trouble came upon him he cannot read at all to speak of, with the result that time becomes long and tedious.

Farm operations are in many respects so different from what they were when I engaged in them that I would have to learn them all over again. Even cultivating corn is by two-row tractor outfit, so that I had no chance to get out into the sunshine by riding a corn cultivator for several days as I had hoped might be possible when we went out. My last exposure to the sun's rays was on June 13, when I skipped the last chapel service and devotional meeting on the closing day of school for a six-mile walk and exposure in the far corner of a cemetery.

Now for several days we will be working diligently to pack up our earthly goods for removal to Scottdale, Pennsylvania, with the further prospect of working some more to settle down in our new place when we get ourselves moved. It is a vacation in a sense, but withal a rather burdensome one. But change and new experiences make life interesting.

There is a strange feeling of melancholy that I invariably experience when I return to the old familiar haunts of my boyhood and childhood days in Iowa. Especially so at the Timber, or Lower Deer Creek Church, where my earliest religious impressions were received. More than anywhere else, I am there impressed with the fact that time passes and that the generations of men keep marching along on each other's heels. We stopped for a few minutes at the cemetery about a mile from the church. I had not seen Mother's grave since she was laid to rest nearly six years ago. My thoughts went back thirty years and more, as I viewed the gravestones of the older men who in the time of my childhood used to sit in the front corners of the church. I was interested in reflecting upon the regular and more or less orderly progression of life in a community such as ours, noticing the current of life as it flows on through the years. In the church house, the small folks, once they no longer sit with their father or mother in church services, start in by occupying the front part of the center section of seats. As they grow older they recede toward the rear in this same section, until with maturity they reach the back row. With marriage they move outward to the rear seats in the side sections. From there they progress slowly forward to the front again, so that by the time they have become tottering and grey-headed they occupy the corner seats facing the pulpit platform. From there the next step is to the quiet cemetery on top of the hill about a mile away. Such is the progress of life in the community, and one is impressed with it as he returns thither after an absence of some years and notes the changes from what he knew as a boy and youth.

Father I found rather feeble and tottering. He has always been an active man, scarcely ever ailing in his life. In 1936 he suffered a paralytic stroke which has left him incapacitated for work of any kind. His adjustment to the new conditions has been difficult, but he is resigned to the situation and takes it all rather philosophically. He has some special trouble with his eye now, with result that he cannot see sufficiently well to read. Consequently time hangs very heavily on his hands. It would be well if as a man of his age and conditions he could free himself from all financial and economic affairs. As it is he still holds 450 acres of land in his own name, all of which is encumbered in some form or other. On parts he has government farm loans, and on some he has easy term loans from his brother Lewis who stays in San Francisco. Uncle Lewis does not want any of this principal paid back, but only desires to receive interest as on an investment. Thus none of his loans are a particular burden to him, nor does Father do any actual managing of his land.

In 1920, when Estie and I were married, Father gave us the money to buy our home in Kansas. He then intended that he would give each of the children as they start in life an advance on the inheritance of the same amount as he advanced to us. But with the depression coming on he has not followed this plan up with the others, except that some time in recent years Dan has taken over eighty acres of land, at what total figure I do not know, with a donation of $5000 included in it. Barbara and Herman could just as well at any time take over some land in the same way for their appropriate share. As it is, they have been operating the land on a rental basis and Father does the financing himself. This makes his burden heavier than it should be for a man of his age and circumstances. If they will have a succession of fairly good years for crops and prices they can improve their condition.

July 16, 1938   This date finds us residents of Scottdale, Pennsylvania, of two weeks standing, after a number of days spent in uprooting ourselves from nearly five years of living in East Hall on Goshen College campus. Such a process is always a melancholy and painful one. Ties and attachments to a particular place are unconsciously developed and the extrication is not so easy. On Friday, July 1, we were about all done with packing our earthly goods. About four o'clock Harry Miller and his son Samuel arrived with their Chevrolet truck, one-ton capacity. The process of loading started about 6:30 p.m. The remaining several hours of daylight did not suffice for completing the job, so it was finished after dark with the help of such artificial light as could be provided. It was 10:30 when the load was full and ready to go. Six wooden boxes were left behind in the basement of East Hall, which must make their way later to this place.

Virgil, Estie and I travelled by train that same night, leaving from Elkhart. Slept some sitting up and ate breakfast in Pittsburgh. At Connelsville Mr. Shoemaker met us and we were in Scottdale in time to eat dinner. The loaded truck arrived soon after two o'clock, and in a few hours' time everything was unloaded. Then began the long and uninspiring process of organizing our housekeeping on a new basis in a larger place. During the first week we shopped a number of times for furniture and equipment. We had some delivered last Saturday, a bedroom outfit and a living room suite, together with some floor coverings. Today we had a gas range and kitchen cabinet installed.

We are spending a lot of money, it seems, but happily we have it in hand and can pay for what we are getting. We are getting better values and for less money than we paid either in 1920 or in 1928. Both of those times we were buying just before a break in the prices of furniture, and though we bought at discount prices both times, still we paid more at that than we are now paying. We paid over one hundred dollars for a living room rug in 1920, and in 1928, $37.50 for another, but a cheap grade, for it is worn out after ten years. Now we are paying $36.50 for a Wilton rug larger than the last one and one that seems to be of excellent value. We paid some over one hundred dollars for a living room suite in common velour, and now we get a mohair suite for $95. So it seems that for once fortune is favoring us, and in a number of ways we feel that for us life is really beginning, not even at forty, but at forty-five. And if it should so prove out, we will not regret the years of roving about and gathering experience and information, even if we gathered very little of the proverbial moss in the form of financial and capital reserves. Somehow I seem to catch occasional glimpses of an idea that this move will prove to be under the Lord's special guidance and leading, and that we may be due to experience His blessing in some particular ways in the time to come. But only time will tell whether this premonition will prove to be a true vision or merely a mirage.

One of the problematic things here is to know how to organize my facilities for work and study. I have a large fine office in the House hardly more than a hundred steps from home. Yet I have been convinced that I want to have a private study at home too. Time and experience must teach me how best to distribute my working tools between here and the working office. Probably I shall reserve this place especially for leisure reading, study, meditation, creative thinking and writing, and do as much of my routine work as possible in the other office.

Dies Solis, July 17, 1938 Third Sunday in Scottdale for us. Attending church here is much the same as at Goshen. Sunday school is not as favorably administered, due to a lack of room. A class of middle-aged men has been assigned to my care. Attendance among these seems to be irregular. Last Sunday two pupils out of about eight or nine on the roll were present. Today two were present, none the same as last Sunday, and one of these a visitor. At this rate it will be a matter of some time before I can even become personally acquainted with all my charges. In an open audience room where a number of classes recite at the same time, I prefer a small class, since this is all my voice can reach.

In a reminiscent mood, I recall that it was twenty years ago this summer that I spent in the community around Yoder, Kansas, with headquarters at Jake Yoders'. I enjoyed my stay with them very much. I was selected by some at Hesston to work in the community as a sort of resident worker in the mission Sunday school which had been started in March of that same year. When this was suggested to me, I went over and got my job with Jake Yoder, of operating his threshing machine for the summer, and of helping him with harvest and its preliminaries. That was the time of the war. Wheat sold for $2.10 a bushel directly from the machine to the local elevator at Yoder. My wages for the summer's threshing, nearly forty-five working days, averaged about $12.50 a day with just about no expense at all. It was my first taste of "big money."

But I enjoyed the summer's experience immensely. It was my first summer away from home. It was a new community, learning to know many new people. There was a new manner and way of threshing grain. The people were kind and friendly. I was a kind of outstanding leader in the new religious work that was started in that place. I imagine I enjoyed the temporary taste of prestige! I conducted the Sunday evening meetings all by myself, and was the only one of my kind around during the week. On Sundays a motor load of folks always came from Harvey County in the afternoon to help in Sunday school. The meetings at the beginning of the summer were still held in the one-room schoolhouse located one mile south of Yoder. But about the middle of the summer we changed to the schoolhouse one mile north and one mile east of Yoder, a place which was somewhat larger and more convenient. At Jake's place things were quite informal. I and the older boys sat at table on a bench at the back side. I had a pleasant room of my own, located over the summer kitchen, which was an annex to the main house.

On the last Tuesday we were in Indiana, I took my last outing at that place. Went south along the Big Four tracks for three miles to a cemetery. This place has woods and marsh ground on two sides. Along the front is a public road. In the far corner of this burying plot, next to the woods is a concrete burial vault, only this one is underground save for about one foot of its top. It has a slightly gabled top on it and around the outside is a concrete walk about two feet wide. In this country I am again at a loss to know where to look to find a place for private walking.

July 28, dies Jovis, 1938   Slowly the routine of my new position and work is devolving upon me. Working hours here are from eight to twelve noon, and one to five in the afternoon, although editors do not observe particular hours in their work. Still my conscience requires that I keep somewhere near to that schedule as a minimum. During the summer months the House does not officially operate at all on Saturday. The great and important adjustment I must yet make is to find the time and manner for getting outdoor air and exercise in quantity sufficient to keep physically and mentally fit. Somehow my time for out-of-door activity and the time of sunshine have so far failed to synchronize, and I am getting hungry for some rays of direct sunlight on my epidermis.

There is still a deal of work to do about the house in the way of getting things arranged and duly appointed for our daily home living. Some things are still to be obtained in the way of equipment and trimmings. We never did have much in the way of well planned, artistic wall decorations. Our problem is to study the matter and decide on what we want, and then to find a place to get what we want. Our Orthophonic Victrola came through in good condition, and so far as we have looked, no records were broken. Rainy, sultry weather has been the rule for two weeks now.

August 3, 1938 Read an excellent book lately on the Book of Revelation bearing the curious title: "The Lamb, the Woman, and the Dragon," by a Reformer professor in Michigan, Albertus Pieters. It is a sensible book, for the most part, one of the few such that I have learned of. The author himself holds to the "Preterist" interpretation of Revelation, contending fairly for two basic principles of interpretation: That the Book was first of all written to bring a message to contemporary readers, and further, that it is a book of symbolic meanings, a drama in fact, and it is bad exegesis to arbitrarily pass back and forth from literal to symbolic interpretation in going through the book. He consistently adopts the symbolic viewpoint, excepting in the scene of the Last Judgment, which he takes literally, for reasons which he rather poorly establishes, as it appears to me. While the author is fairly convinced in favor of his own interpretation, his discussion is very valuable for the fair way in which he surveys other viewpoints and criticizes and evaluates them. This feature of his book gives one a necessary orientation in the field of interpretation of Revelation, a very valuable thing. In his Bibliography he cites the leading works on Revelation, that is, scholarly works, and gives with each one the particular viewpoint the book sets forth. The author of this book is "dead ag'in" the dispensational interpretation of the Bible, and he takes some crushing blows at Scofield and his teaching. Millennialism, while he does not himself accept it, he claims, has full right of citizenship in the Christian Church, for it can be shown that the dispute between millennialism and a-millennialism really goes back to Church Fathers of the second century. They represent two opposite viewpoints regarding Scripture prophecy. But dispensationalism! Ah, that is something else again. Pieters makes out that it is genuine heresy in the Christian Church, dating from one J. N. Darby in England not many centuries ago. I believe the author has made his case well on this point. I do wonder if the Sunday School Times will condescend to notice this book and with what outcome. As for the preterist interpretation of Revelation, I have been personally drawn to that position, and now to read this excellent presentation of the viewpoint from a conservative, evangelical angle is highly convincing to me. One need now no longer feel he is holding heretical or modernistic doctrine in believing in the preterist interpretation. Am ready to teach it now as Bible truth.

August 5, 1938 Spent about seven days in recent weeks editing copy prepared for the Primary, Primary Teachers', and Junior Lesson Quarterlies. This job was as that of a "pinch hitter," relieving C. F. Yake, who has for some months been recovering from a nervous collapse. This gave me occasion to become really acquainted with the contents of these respective publications. Mary Royer, I am impressed, is doing rather solid work in much of what she prepares. Mrs. Brackbill's work is not quite as weighty, I feel, as Miss Royer's, but is also fairly good. One wonders how much "good" is really accomplished by the tons of Sunday school "helps" that are distributed every quarter. Possibly it is necessary to sow broadcast many bushels so as to make sure that the occasional spot that is capable of producing something good will receive its one or two kernels of grain for seed. Surely, like Jesus observed, most of what is fed to the public in the way of ideas and provocative thought falls on hard, stony, thorny soil, and it is only rarely that an idea gets a good spot on which to lodge. But when it does so, the produce is large enough to justify the wastage of the rest. Many are called but few are chosen.
So far as concerns the improved form of the Advanced Quarterly, I stumbled upon a few complimentary remarks during my stay in Iowa in June. A few at least were worth remembering. One man from Oregon, whom I had always thought of as rather narrow and critical in church matters, spoke some personal words of praise and encouragement. He said he likes to read something that takes him farther than he's ever been before, implying that the quarterly does that. A former college friend, now a worker in East Union Sunday school in Iowa, spoke appreciatively of the work. She quoted some one of her friends as remarking that the material seems harder than it used to be. But she appreciated it for that very reason, because it made the reader think, and her parting wish was "more power to you." Evidently the material is read rather carefully by many. J. L. Stauffer in a late issue of the doctrinal supplement of Gospel Herald did me the honor of quoting one sentence from a lesson on the death of Christ, as a horrible sample of false or questionable theology. His point and whole discussion was laboured and befuddled, although in a general way I favor the point he was driving at. There is a good deal of legalistic, Augustinian theology in much of our common thinking on Christology, that is scarcely Scriptural.

Dies Solis, August 7, 1938 Warm weather, not uncomfortable unless one thinks so, has been the order of the days and weeks recently. Nights however are very tolerable, the air being coolish in the mornings. It suits me very well, for I figure that cold weather with furnace chores will come altogether soon enough.
The coming week is conference week in this section of the country. Some will be going for a good part of the week to sit in on the sessions at Holsopple in this state. I want to go for a few sessions on Wednesday only, and chiefly because my name appears on the Sunday School Conference program for that day. But to go and hang around such an assemblage for days together is not for me. I am preparing a paper to

read for the occasion on Wednesday. It will probably be dry and formal enough to satisfy all concerned, at least to the extent that I will not soon again be called upon to repeat the performance. At places in other districts where I have performed similar functions, such was the result. Meanwhile coming to a new section as a stranger, there is probably nothing to do but to run the gauntlet again. Sometimes I think how much better it might be if I could firmly say "no" when such projects are laid upon me. Presumably it gratifies a person's vanity just a bit to have one's name printed on a program and appear before a crowd of more or less curious spectators. In general, I am happy that I cannot put on a thrilling and attractive show for the conference-going public. For I care nothing, or very little, for such gatherings. It will probably always be my preference to go as little as possible to such assemblages. One must evidently cater in some slight measure to the notion some have, that you are not quite loyal, not very spiritual, not very churchy unless you run here and there to church gatherings. But such attendance as I can give will necessarily be in the form of gestures to keep up a bit of reputation. Not a very lofty motive! Perhaps it were better discarded. At Goshen College the faculty in general has been censured at times by the local brethren, because they do not attend district-church gatherings sufficiently. At this place, of course, probably no such criticism can arise, for most of the leading figures are diligent church leaders too. Amid the general conference going, perhaps I can slip through with a minimum of such activity. John Horsch, long a worker here, has only rarely spoken on programs in church gatherings, and I am taking him as my pattern, rather than anyone else. One can keep himself from dying at the top by extensive and wide reading, as well, and in my case, better than by plaguing oneself to run to and fro in the land to attend meetings.

Dies Saturni, August 13, 1938 Coolish atmosphere, with an absolutely unclouded sky was today's record. After weeks of sultry temperatures and not a day without some or all clouds, it was a welcome day. Such a glorious day of sunshine coming in conjunction with the day of no work in the House required special celebration. I took the occasion for a real workout, the first one I have really had since June in Indiana, a workout for sun, air, and exercise. Along the foot of a steep hill lies a double row of abandoned, dilapidated coke ovens with heaps and mounds of cinders lying about them. The hillside above them is rough and unused. The general aspect of the area is that of a No Man's Land. The whole area appears to be worth exploring further.

Walking up and down over the Pennsylvania hills is interesting and sometimes thrilling. Country roads are romantic things to explore; one never knows when starting in on one whether it is an honest-to-goodness road, or merely a lane leading into some farmer's barnyard.

Country roads, the unimproved kind, are interesting for pedestrianism, more so than for motoring, surely, being steep in places, rocky, crooked. Less than three miles southeast, to the west of the main arteries of travel, a primitive road runs along on top of a high ridge. From here one gets an extensive view both to west and to east across valleys of considerable distance, the east one being wider. It is an impressive scene. Beside the road on this ridge stands a solitary elm tree, perhaps thirty feet high, maybe forty, outlined against the sky in majestic beauty. Near a turn in this road, along the edge of a cornfield, is an old neglected cemetery of considerable size. No trees are growing there, but weeds and briers in abundance. Some of the stones are evidently very old, for they have turned almost coal-black. In winter or early spring, when weeds and grass are at their lowest, it would be interesting to explore the place to ascertain the age and character of the plot. The sight of this cemetery and its condition reminded me of the sad state in which I found the small burial plot on our old home farm in Iowa. About forty rods west of the house were buried the remains of my father's maternal grandparents, together with one or two infants. When I was still at home it was kept clean and in good condition by my grandfather. A new fence was built around it within my memory. Since grandfather's death in 1906, it has not been kept clean of weeds and briers. I examined the spot casually in June one evening. The briers and brambles are tall. This burial place was started in the early history of the community, when no central cemetery had been planned. To remove the remains at this date is impossible, and presently there will be nothing left even worth preserving the memory of. A granite marker could be put up close to the fence that delimits the field and the plot itself eliminated and worked over. Or a marker could be placed in the central cemetery, stating where the individuals were buried, and making no further effort to preserve the plot.

Dies Solis, August 14, 1938   Activities the past week on my part included one day spent in attendance at Sunday School Conference at the Blough Mennonite Church near Holsopple, Pennsylvania, in what is known as the Johnstown district. This was an entirely new area of the country for my presence. The distance from here is about fifty or sixty miles north and east. The route thither takes one across two ridges of the Allegheny Mountains. It is a pleasant drive over hills and mountain roads. The church where the conclave was held lies on a long hillside sloping down toward a small valley. The location and surroundings are beautiful. As I sat in the church and looked out what seemed toward the northeast a charming view met the eye. Next to the church was a large field of buckwheat in full blossom, white as snow. Above this, farther up the slope was a cornfield, green touched with the brownish tinge of the tassels. Still farther up the slope was an expanse of woods of color still darker green. This was very restful to the eyes and also, as I found it, inspiring to the soul, maybe more so than some of the things going on inside the building. In the afternoon I read a speech of 4,000-word length during a rain and thunderstorm. Also during the day I met a few friends of long ago, especially Dan Stoltzfus and J. B. Kanagy both of twenty and more years ago in Kansas, whom I had not seen since.

   James Boswell in writing the life of Samuel Johnson quotes occasionally some sentences from that writer's Prayers and Meditations. It seems that Johnson was in his way a religious man. He seems to have written out many of his devotional and religious meditations. It would seem to be a good idea. So much of people's spontaneous and extempore thinking and praying is very shallow and often insipid. Perhaps the exercise of clarifying and deepening one's devotional meditations by reducing them to written form would be a real help in making them more vital and worth while. The idea looks attractive and appears worth trying. One difficulty I encounter in all my writing efforts is to induce my thoughts to flow freely and readily from my pen. If any kind of practice and application will help develop proficiency and readiness in writing, I shall be eager to engage in it.

Two weeks ago this evening it was thrust upon me to serve as solo speaker on a Sunday evening program at the church. The result was a paper on the subject, "Prayer and Living." In it I tried to express a few advanced ideas regarding prayer and private devotion. Immediately the paper was desired by one of the House editors for publication in his periodical. The advanced ideas seem to have been acceptable, to that extent at least. The subject is an interesting one and in need of extensive exploration.

August 16, 1938   During this week and next an evangelistic series of meetings is being conducted in a tent in East Scottdale, "across the tracks." It is really at the edge of town almost in the country. It appears that this kind of effort has been an annual occurrence during the past sixteen years, although I had never been aware of it from reading notices of it. Naturally all the folks who at all can do so, go from this part of town. One is supposed to go as regularly as possible and faithfully fill a seat for the benefit of the preacher, who at present is Ernest Garber of Idaho. He is an old-time acquaintance, from Kansas days, at Hesston, in fact. However he had graduated from the Academy course and was teaching school nearby, when I first entered the halls of academic learning. In a small Mennonite community such as this, one does well to take active interest in what is going on, even though one would rather spend the evening at home than go away to a meeting. It does one no harm to suppress natural inclinations in the interest of what is a community cause. It is valuable experience, to get occasional glimpses of the more simple and elemental thinking of the people, especially when one happens himself to be trying to write material for consumption by folks on the unsophisticated level of thinking.

August 23, 1938   For over two weeks our house has been frequented by company, more company than we have normally entertained in that many months. At Goshen we were not situated so we could keep company with any convenience or satisfaction. But now that we have more room the visitors have descended upon us. On August 6 Miss Ruth Bender came for an indefinite stay. On the day following Aunt Hannah Miller and three children from Springs came for Sunday dinner and spent the most of the afternoon here. On the 12th Silas Hertzlers with two children and a friend from farther east came to spend the night in Scottdale. We managed to keep them all for sleeping after the evening meal. They were on their way home from a brief stay in Mifflin County of this state. On the 18th, late in the evening my sister Ida came for a brief visit. She had been on a vacation to the New England states and was travelling with her friend Lucille Kreider of Wadsworth, Ohio, in her Plymouth coupe. They stayed until Sunday afternoon when they moved on toward Ohio. Ruth remained all the time until this morning when she packed up and went off to Pittsburgh. We shall undoubtedly be privileged to entertain more people in our home here than anywhere we have lived. This is a favorite stopping place for folks travelling over the country on vacation, going to conferences, and so forth.

August 24, 1938 It is sometimes the practice of small town newspapers to conduct a small department in which they print certain selected items under such headings as "Twenty-five Years Ago Today," or "Ten Years Ago Today," or similar titles. Occasionally I find myself in a reminiscent mood and reflect upon events of some round number of years ago, provided anything outstanding took place in my experience so and so many years ago.

Fifteen years ago at this time Estie and I, accompanied by Paul Bender, were enjoying the delightful mountain air and scenery about the town of Boulder, Colorado, a small university city nestled at the foot of the Rocky Mountains about thirty miles northwest of Denver. We went there in June and passed eleven pleasant weeks there. Study at the university was the primary excuse for being in the place. That was agreeable too. During August we went out on a few trips for mountain climbing and sightseeing, using Saturdays for the purpose. Paul Bender usually went out with a Geology class for field trips. Estie and I took a few trips on our own initiative. One Saturday, with a little lunch, field glass, umbrella, and a book we started for Bear Mountain lying several miles south of Boulder. Losing the beaten trail, a common experience of ours, we clambered up over the east side of the mountain. The view from the top is one I shall never forget. Many miles eastward stretched the level countryside with its highways like tiny ribbons running over its surface and motor cars like small black ants crawling over them. To the westward lay an endless succession of peaks and ridges, each succeeding one a little higher than the others. Coming down we made a path down over the northwest side. Near the foot we came upon the beaten trail. Rain began to fall. We sat beneath an umbrella for two purposes – to wait for the rain to stop, and to eat the last of our lunch. After a time there were signs that darkness would come on before long and also that the rain had no intention of leaving off. So we got ourselves girded up for wet walking and started out Indian-fashion. Soaked to the skin from head to foot we tramped for miles to reach home, which we did by bedtime.

Another outing long to be remembered we took, again Estie and I, through Boulder Canyon west to Nederland, north to Estes Park, east through Big Thompson Canyon and across country home. It must have been just about this time of the month. On Friday evening we were loaded in the Ford car and moving up toward the mountains. We stopped beside the road, tried to sleep on folding cots, but nearly froze before morning. We had a fire, but could not get enough heat for comfort. The early morning drive along the mountain road that wound back and forth around the heads of many small canyons, skirting along at the foot of a high ridge of the Rockies, with the higher peaks farther west in full view much of the time, this was very impressive. In Estes Park we consumed our lunch. The drive down through Big Thompson was really wonderful; one certainly traveled every possible direction of the compass at some time in its course. How many times since have I wished and hoped that the time may come that we can revisit some of those pleasant scenes. When the time comes that we have a means of travel of our own and Virgil is old enough to share in the enjoyment of such and similar trips, we trust that the means and the leisure will be at hand to visit the Rocky Mountains again. There is a majestic grandeur, an impressive "bigness" about them that the eastern mountains do not have. I liked them, I think, because they accented the fact of human smallness and human insignificance. Man is generally obsessed aplenty with the notion of his importance. His ideas, thoughts, convictions seem after all quite petty and narrow when one sees the works of God at their greatest in nature. This is not to say that God's works in nature are greater than His works in grace. It is a fine mental tonic.

August 26, 1938   The Atlantic Monthly still is one of my main sources of monthly doses of mental and literary tonic as well as nourishment. The September issue came yesterday. Every issue has from three to a half dozen really pleasing articles, and numerous others that are valu-able. Last evening I read an epistle from Albert Jay Nock. He is now domiciled in Brussels where he finds still a modicum of culture and civilization, and from where he looks forth upon the tides and waves and tidal waves of barbarism that engulf most humans of the western world. Almost without fail I relish his articles, not so much for their content, although that is often nourishing, but for his language and style, for his uniformly and mildly cynical temper, and for his habits of thought. He lambastes "social security" by government and pours gal-lons of rich irony and satire on the economic stupidity with which mod-ern governments are obsessed, the idea that one can spend and consume more than is being produced and keep on doing so indefinitely with ever-increasing differential between them. Except for a few malodorous words and expressions that could well be spared without devitalizing his ideas, I always chuckle when I read Nock. His posing with a gentle glint of mock modesty is quite entrancing.

Another exquisite piece in this latest issue is one by Archibald Rut-ledge. I was delighted to see his name under the title "Vision." Years ago we used to read his articles about plantation life in the South, espe-cially the nature study and the black people he used to write about. It seems to me it was in the American Magazine that we used to look with anticipation for his pieces. In the present article he dwells upon the southern plantation Negro's spiritual sensitiveness, his almost uncanny intuitions, and his somewhat mystical attitude toward his surroundings. He illustrates throughout with instances which he has personally ob-served, and the writer's understanding of the black folks is shot through with such an artless and unprepossessing sympathy that it is a real de-light to read his discussion. He emphasizes among other matters the Negro's universal refusal to complain of the weather and dislike of those who complain about it. He always takes it as it comes and feels it is always just right — like God wants it to be. Also with real admira-tion Mr. Rutledge describes the black man's ability to speak to the soul of an animal and make it do as he wants it to, whether it be an unruly young setter dog, or frightened animals stranded by a flood, or an im-mobile mule upon which all efforts to set in motion have failed.

August 28, 1938   This is our son Virgil's birthday, his sixth anniversary. And it was on Sunday too that he was born, in the afternoon at just about this very hour, 2:50, making allowance for the hour's difference in time between here and Kansas. That was, of course, a day of unique experience for us. When the nurse dipped him in water to elicit his first cry, the doctors remarked about his strong, lusty cry. And ever since he has been able to make lots of noise upon all occasions when his emotions find expression. He has a rather distinctive quality of voice that carries well, and is in no way unpleasing. Maybe unlike his daddy, he will turn out to be a public speaker or a singer.

For birthday celebration, since it is Sunday, we are not going out for an outing as we did last year. On the contrary we roasted the wieners in the broiler of the gas stove. Virgil wants to have wieners as a regular feature of his birthday celebration. Last year we went out west from the college at Goshen to the mill race at the end of Gra-Roy drive, where we built a fire and roasted the wieners for the occasion. In the way of birthday presents he gets plenty every year without our buying him any that are expensive. His aunt Ida Yoder when she was here a week ago bought him a fine red scooter over which he was very well pleased. His cousin Ruth, who has provided him with fully one half of his toys and playthings ever since his beginning, sent him a fully equipped pencil box for school use; however, everything in school supplies is here furnished to the children. Last evening he begged me to make good my earlier promise of a toy for his birthday, and he insisted on selecting it himself. So in a local dime store he found a toy truck and a small rubber ball that pleased him. So he has a right royal birthday, including ice cream still to come this evening.

Kalends of September, 1938   For a month there was abundance of rainfall here, but since the twelfth or so of August there has been hardly any. Everything is dry and dusty. Weather has been coolish too since the rains ceased, whereas before there was much sultry heat.

At the present time my labor is given to writing the S. S. lessons' material for third quarter, 1939, the lessons being character studies of eminent men, kings and prophets, from Solomon to about Isaiah. The material and outlines are not so inspiring as some series I have worked on before. Many of these characters were men of too varied traits and activities for satisfactory treatment in the brief space of one short S. S. lesson. I work on a schedule of getting three lessons a week worked out and I am just past the middle of the quarter's lessons now. One and one-half days of steady application usually sees a lesson out, including the necessary reading, writing, and typing of nearly seven typewriter sheets of copy. Between lessons I have a half day off.

Today on an "off" afternoon, I stretched my muscles by walking from here to Connellsville, said to be a distance of seven miles; at any rate two and a third hours of time along a pleasant road saw me exploring the streets and shop windows of Connellsville. The return trip was made by trolley. Purchased a few pictures for hanging on walls. Thought that surely it would be possible to find a music store in that city, even though there is none here, but failed to find a place to purchase the kind of needles I use on the Orthophonic Victrola.

Recent reading has included a good-sized volume by Angus: "The Religious Quests of the Graeco-Roman World." It is a scholarly and definitive work in which the author surveys the religions and the religious aspirations of the centuries that just preceded and just followed the beginning of Christianity. Especial attention is given to the character and influence of the mystery religions and their effect upon Christianity, especially in the form of sacramentarianism, asceticism, gnosticism, etc. In general it is very informing to get such a bird's-eye view of religious conditions, the mental and spiritual outlook, the modes of thought that prevailed in those times. For one's understanding of the Christian Church Fathers and their early writings such a view is very helpful indeed. Some suggestive light is shed upon New Testament interpretation also thereby, but not such a great deal. The author's basic assumptions regarding N. T. Scriptures are not in every instance acceptable. Still the book is very valuable.

September 11, 1938   A cloudy Sunday afternoon gives one a kind of comfortable shut-in feeling. After a refreshing sleep of several hours' length, it is enjoyable to be able to have some quiet moments for restful meditation and reflection. Have just listened to a half dozen records played on the Orthophonic; only sacred music is heard here on Sundays. But since coming here we have not taken time during the week for listening to any other kind of music. Before leaving Goshen and severing entirely my connections with the college, I purchased over thirty dollars worth of new records through the local music store at a discount of one-fifth from list price. We have not even played through quite all of them, and it is three months since we have them. Virgil is not much interested in passively listening to the music, not enough activity for his age and temperament. At first we tried to make listening to records a regular twice-a-week ritual for all the family together, for an hour on Sunday afternoon and again on one weekday evening. At first he listened pretty well, due to the novelty of the affair. But toward the last he began to show signs of rebellion, so we have not been trying to force him to listen. The time will probably come when he will take a more spontaneous interest in music. He really ought to learn to play something before long. He has at times expressed the wish that we had a piano, quite in the same mood as he has wished we had a car, or a truck, or a dog.

   The problem of Sunday observance in a town community with neighbors close about providing children to play with is on our hands. It seems an impossible and undesirable ideal to keep a small active boy in the house all day long, not playing on the side walks much as on other days. My idea is to establish the precedent that Virgil does not play out-of-doors on Sunday morning, that attendance at Sunday school and church services be a regular ritual, and that on Sunday afternoon he can be free to play as usual, except that a little time be set aside definitely for reading Sunday-school papers, current numbers and back numbers. Especially since we have never formed the habit of taking him to services on Sunday evening, that hour before he retires at eight o'clock is given to reading or singing in the home. Some such program would seem to set the day off from secular weekdays and help make the child Sunday conscious. The folks here, some of them, diligently take all small children to evening services, even to nightly revival services. But for Virgil it seems better to put him to bed at his regular hour than to make him sit through a second service on Sunday evening.

Dies Lunae, September 1938 Among the periodicals for which we have entered subscriptions since setting up housekeeping in Pennsylvania is the Readers' Digest. I long held out against the Digest idea as a way to read magazines, but have now at last succumbed, not as a substitute for regular reading of Atlantic Monthly, and some others of good literary quality, but as a supplementary measure for garnering ideas.

Dies Solis, September 18, 1938 This season of the year makes one think of school openings. Somehow something in my bones, or is it in the neural paths, makes me feel that I am missing something in not being around a school, college or university in the month of September. For the first time since 1915, I am not present for some kind of school opening. Still changes do come and making changes and readjustments is one means of keeping young instead of becoming old and fossilized. My mind is always ready for new ideas and new experiences and new scenes and new activities, so there is no reason for complaining because life has been constantly bringing changes for us.

The task of settling down is still going on here. Order has been growing in the basement here the past week. Ninety-six feet of shelf space for fruit jars chiefly has been installed. A small tool cabinet is in process of taking shape, which will make possible a more economical organization of my large tool box with its varied and crowded contents. Four and one-half tons (112 bushels in Scottdale parlance) of coal found their way from curbstone to the coal bin, thanks to my muscles and a wheelbarrow, yesterday afternoon. The total cost was $12.30, a great relief for one from the western prairies and used to paying eight to ten dollars a ton.

Dies Veneris, a.d. IX Kalends October, 1938 One wonderfully pleasant and beautiful day has just come to a close. The sun shone generally from a cloudless sky all the afternoon; a pleasant breeze from the south blew softly. The day was doubly appreciated because it followed hard upon the heels of a series of days of wretched weather; clouds gray and lowering, at times even dark, angry and menacing in aspect; rain, damp and cold wind that chilled to the bone; for two days furnace fire was a necessity. Now that summer has been escorted from the premises with his ugly parting gesture, perhaps autumn will show itself more congenial than its predecessor. The conventional equinoctial storm seems to have had its turn and is gone. On the Atlantic seaboard from New Jersey north to Canada this seasonal storm was a hurricane of unprecedented dimensions, destroying lives and property on an extensive scale.

Upon this first day of sunshine for almost two weeks, the desire to go out and absorb a few of its rays came upon me with irresistible force. A walk of six or seven miles in a circuit east of town took until time for a hearty supper of fried potatoes and fresh green garden onions, together with cooked cabbage.

Last week a salesman persuaded us to purchase a Health-Mor Cleaning and Sanitizing System, that is, a new vacuum cleaner with a wide variety of attachments for doing just about all kinds of household cleaning operations excepting washing underwear and socks, at least so it seemed. This system is to be ours for the sum of $89.50. Twenty dollars discount was allowed for our Sunshine Cleaner of 1930 purchase, for $69.95, and according to a letter of yesterday from headquarters another five dollar discount is possible if I pay the balance all in cash before October 15, which I shall do. According to written guarantee, we have now acquired a lifetime cleaning system, for it will be rebuilt by the factory at anytime for a maximum cost of ten dollars. In case it should be destroyed by fire it is to be replaced for the same sum. The old machine was not a standard make, and it seemed good policy, though in eight years it caused no expense, to trade it in for some consideration, and acquire a new and more standard outfit.

Pridie Kalendae Octobris, 1938   This afternoon was a fine time for outdoor walking and stretching of leg and thigh muscles. No sun shone too warmly, no wind blew too coldly. The weekly jaunt took me to Mt. Pleasant, a town northeast from here. Its distance from Scottdale was unknown, though I had ridden in a motor car over the road thither already. Someone guessed it was ten miles away, but after an hour and one-half of normal walking I was walking along its main street; a distance of five miles is all it is. The return trip was made by a longer route, six miles in two hours' time. Sunshine has been scarce the past week.

Bertrand Russell, English philosopher of a sort, has an article in the latest Atlantic Monthly on how to conquer power. There is much good thought and analysis exhibited in this essay, ideas on how to achieve democratic control over political and economic power, or better, over the holders of such power. He makes a good deal of the psychological factors involved in the solution of the problem. So long as men give way readily to mob hysteria in emotions of hate, rage, and fear, they are not citizens who can be trusted to deal democratically with the holders of power. This writer does not commit himself on whether such a solution can ever be achieved, though from the several specific suggestions he makes it appears that he assumes it can. It requires a profound faith in the capacity of the mass of men to develop a liberal and reasoned attitude toward the problems involved, to feel that there is even any hope for such an eventuality. Education could do something; but who shall first educate the educators for such a regime? It seems to me that religion, which Philosopher Russell refers to rather incidentally, might play an important part in that direction if it were intelligently applied. Still how many minds in a thousand are innately capable of attaining to a truly liberal and objective attitude on such matters?

Bernard Iddings Bell, whose erstwhile more frequent essays in the Atlantic I used to relish keenly, has also a brief piece in this issue, entitled, "More Dogma, Please." It is in his old familiar vein. He complains that people are urged to coordinate their religious thinking with the science they learn, when the sad fact is they have no religion worth the name to start with. So too the great hue and cry has been that folks should apply their Christianity to practical situations in social and economic life, when they have no real Christianity to apply. He appeals for more teaching of real religious truth, and most people can apply it once they have it to apply.

Dies Solis, October 2, 1938   This is a beautiful Lord's Day afternoon. Atmosphere is cool and fallish; sun is bright and comforting. After watching for a day of bright sunshine for nearly a week, and the chance to expose myself to its rays, then the first such day that comes along is Sunday when I do not care to walk abroad for such purposes. Still it is certainly best the way it is and like the colored folks of whom Archibald Rutledge writes so sympathetically, one should really not complain about the state of the weather, for God makes it.

Regular services at the church this morning were of ordinary interest. Naturally I am inclined to make comparisons between the church services here and at other places where I have regularly attended. They do not compare at all badly on the whole. So far as the content of the preaching is concerned, there is less spiritual meat than from our college pulpits. We are too recently arrived here to candidly judge, still it seems more stress is laid on practical and ethical and ecclesiastical matters and less on expositional and inspirational matters. There is not quite the depth to the worship services here which I learned to appreciate at the college at Goshen. In Sunday school and Young People's Meeting they use Derstine's song book, "Sheet Music of Heaven," which makes the singing inferior, more tinny and noisy. In the church services, I notice the same tendency that was evident at Hesston, that is, making the singing something of a filler to push into a few necessary interstices in the preacher's program. To a mere layman it always looked as though the preaching of one man was regarded as far more important than the worship activity of the numerous audience in singing. A little of the same tendency is evident here. One learns to appreciate the dignity and importance of hymn-singing in corporate worship when Walter Yoder conducts the singing. He selects uniformly good worship hymns, and he uses a hymn as a sacred ritual, never mutilating its message and its dignity by singing one or more scattered lines from it to fill up space or to use up time or for any other unworthy purpose. From observing Yoder's conduct of church music, one gets faint glimpses of the vast possibilities for improvement in our Mennonite congregational singing. He has given talks on the history of the hymns of the church which show that he has a highly appreciative interest in church music from a historical viewpoint. He has pointed out, and I believe he is correct, that the newer and lighter type of Gospel song music that came into our own church singing along with the great awakening of fifty years ago, has really been a degeneration from the earlier high quality of our hymnology. It is difficult now to push the multitudes back up to a higher standard again, for good, solid, and deep church music requires deeper thought and spirituality than the many have.

Dies Jovis, October 6, 1938   Beautiful October days, still no frost to kill foliage and vegetation, but cool enough for the promotion of fur-

371

nace fires. Too much cloudy skies for me coming from the western plains. Even during fair and rainless weather an entire day cloudless from end to end is rare, not as often as once in a week, and really two of them side by side I have not seen, I believe, since we came. For the past five winters our living quarters were heated by steam in radiators. Now to live again in proximity to a hot-air furnace is disagreeable. This is really a dirty, if not filthy way to heat a house, especially with the air unfiltered, unmoistened, and in no way conditioned. On the personal question of whether to rent indefinitely or to think of building new, a strong argument in favor of the latter will be the desirability of having a modern system of heating equipment.

October 11, 1938   Thick-lying white hoarfrost covered roofs of buildings on two mornings in succession lately, but now it is warm again; even the fire in the furnace is out, I presume, by this time.

Virgil had about his first experience with personal sorrow last week when "Perky," Resslers' pet dog, was run over by an automobile and killed. He took it pretty hard and insisted on a promise that he might have a dog some time, anyway by next summer. Perhaps a puppy would afford him some useful employment and diversion during the summer vacation about next summer. He certainly found the little white dog a congenial playmate. At present he plays most with Billy Kline, a boy from across the alley. He seems to take to school real well, though like his daddy, he does not talk about his experiences and activities, and he can hardly be blamed for that. Some exercises in coloring, which involved recognition of color names, and which he has been bringing home have had 100 marked on them. There is hope that he will show intellectual aptitude and interests that will take up some of his time and energy as he gets older and makes progress in his development.

Dies Solis, October 16, 1938   Warm days, cool nights, sunshine, brightly colored woods, everything pleasant and beautiful. On last Friday I went for a walk that was most enjoyable, but luck was against me, for the last hour I was out the sun's rays were ineffective; a damp, foggy air settled down especially in the valleys, and my bare pate being naturally soft and sensitive at the moment, became chilled enough to give me an unpleasant congestion in the sinal areas. I felt distinctly that my top area was getting too cold at the moment, but the situation being unexpected, I was helpless and unprepared to do anything about it. Holding or laying my flat hand on my hair did little good and laying a white pocket handkerchief on my top was rather too conspicuous for my pride, and so I went on hoping against hope that the exposure would not do anything too bad to me. So headache, dullness, discomfort are my lot today.

But the walking on last Friday was extra fine. A ten-mile circuit northwest and north took one through certain wooded, hilly sections where the scenery was delightful. And the heavy, rich odors that met one's nostrils! There had been a rain the previous night and with the lowering of the sun's rays odor laden dampness arose from roadside, leaf-strewn forest floor, as well as from cattle pastures and feeding lots, barnyards, etc. Some of the odors reminded me most pungently of farm days long ago. A few I identified as exactly like those that used to be familiar from commercial stock feed and Hog Remedy we used to feed on the farm. Whether they were actually the same odors, or whether they were psychologically connected, I cannot tell.

Yesterday afternoon the entire family of us took a leisurely stroll of one and one-half miles east and back, tramping over the high hill east of Everson and from Kingview back to Everson again over the road that runs along the side of the hill. One could see the woods to the southeast quite clearly, though a rather persistent haze did not let the eyes make much out of the woods four or five miles away to the east on the mountain sides.

Observed an editorial "thought" in a recent Gospel Herald issued here, a good curio. It is alright to crush in the top of a man's hat, if that is the shape of his skull. This however is very dangerous reasoning, for it might lead some to justify the wearing by the females of trousers and form fitting bodices, in this day usually considered altogether "immodest." But maybe the males and the females come under differing clothing codes, who knows!

Dies Mercurii, October 19, 1938 Strangely warm, balmy weather for this late in the season, reminding one of Kansas some years. Nearly ten days have passed since regular fire in the furnace was kept up. The nights are cool and chilly, but with the sun shining the house gets thoroughly warmed up by evening again much of which holds over the night. The afternoon sun is gracious to our side of the house. Perhaps we do have the coldest side of this double house, but it may also prove to be the warmest, getting the warmest exposure from the sun.

With all the new magazines, journals and periodicals which come to us upon subscription now, a heavy drain is made upon one's time for reading or even looking casually at them. All of them have started coming excepting the American Journal of Archeology, no copy of which has appeared yet. For daily news one can usually get a glance at the Pittsburgh daily morning paper that comes to the Publishing House in general. The local paper in Scottdale is a weekly, which we have gotten by purchase (three cents) fairly regularly the last while. It is useful for doing family marketing as a rule.

Marketing is easier here than at Goshen for us. Most of the fruits and vegetables and meat we buy comes to our front door, and what does not we can easily carry from the stores, which are close by and plentiful. It might be possible to save a little money on fruits and vegetables if we had an automobile and would seek out producers and buy in quantities. But hardly enough could be saved thereby to pay for the expense of operating a motor car. Frankly, I do not care to be troubled with either the care or expense of operating a car at this time. When son Virgil is big enough to help take care of one, then it may become necessary for us to have one.

October 25, 1938 Days are quite full with a writing project I have in hand now, and wish to finish up in another week – writing copy for a proposed "doctrinal quarterly," a kind of specialized substitute for the regular series of International Sunday School Lessons. It seems that certain agitators have been clamoring for years for a home-grown course of S. S. lessons to displace the International Uniform Lessons entirely. This little project has been devised by the powers that be as a compromise, or a "sop," by which to mitigate the excessive zeal of the reformers (would be). After the decision was made by others then they dumped the seed idea upon me with orders to gestate and parturate the desired infant. It is to be prepared with an eye especially for the high school age level. The theory of some is that if such material is placed where the thirteen-year-olds can get it, the older groups can surely get it too, a thoroughly pernicious theory to my mind. The practical application of this theory in our church literature has been responsible for fostering what I would charitably call religious and spiritual infantilism among people. Since the majority of people are of thirteen-year-old mentality much mental and religious soup and "pap" needs to be served up, but it is a fact that no particular effort has been made to supply mental and spiritual pabulum of a stronger type to those who have advanced or could advance beyond the milk stage of development. The result is that those who have grown to more maturity of thought have either had to starve or look to other sources for spiritual nutriment. And in general it has too much standardized and made acceptable a childish type of religious thinking among us. Folks with a more mature outlook are apt to be suspected and disliked. If there is any real opportunity and indication of demand for a more mature kind of religious thinking among us, I mean to use my efforts to minister to the needs of this "remnant."

Writing for thirteen-year-olds is not an easy task for me, and I have no way to know whether I am even measurably succeeding or not. One unit out of four proposed units of the course will be approximately finished next week. I do not anticipate that the result of this effort will make any special hit, but it may be a tentative, preliminary effort that may lead the way for better future plans and work.

November 7, 1938, Dies Lunae (the lady experienced a total eclipse early this evening as she began mounting the eastern sky). Warm, sultry, summer-like weather is here, mercury must have been going up toward 75 or 80 degrees. No fire is tolerable in the house today nor was it yesterday.

Last week saw me on a journey to Chicago and back. On Wednesday A. J. Metzler and his car traveled from here to Elkhart County, Indiana, between the hours of 9:30 a.m. and 7:00 p.m. The choo-choo train carried Mr. Yake and me on to Chicago in time to sleep at the Mennonite Home Mission for the night. On Thursday a curriculums committee was in session all day at that place, and even on Friday morning for a short while. As soon as the other sitters on this committee began to sit on a commission instead, I took advantage of the liberty to "beat it" for home. Again by choo-choo train and trolley finally reached home at 11:30 p.m. The little travel and diversion was pleasant, but the disturbance in routine diet and living was distressing. Lunching in haste on handy picnic "grub" for two days, one day going and one day coming. Home living is certainly fine living, for which no amount of committee sitting can even begin to be a compensation. Contacts are of some little interest, but they too are not indispensable. Still committees are supposed to be necessary and useful entities; maybe so, maybe so!!

Just about fourteen years ago this month, when I was in my second year of graduate study at State University of Iowa, two professors in Goshen College, Bender and Correll, sent me some Latin letters to translate into English, letters of one Conrad Grebel of Zurich who did some letter writing four hundred and some odd years previous to that time. The obliging professors asked would I consent to translate for them several hundred pages of Latin, a humanistic type at that? I would, for evidently they could not read Latin well enough to be able to get the data and information they wanted for composing a biography and complete life of this man Grebel. Rather poorly equipped myself for such a task, I yet enjoyed the opportunity to apply some knowledge of Latin and Greek. But the projected "Life and Works" of this man did not see the light of day, and have not to this day, in the form that was planned and advertised all these years. At intervals from 1924 to 1928, I devoted considerable time and effort to studying the Grebel Letters and their Latinity. In 1929 I made a completely revised, and what I please to feel is a fairly accurate and readable translation of these letters. At that point I left the matter. Now the matter about publishing these Grebel Letters is still a stirring issue. Bender, one of the co-editors, has produced a thesis on Grebel's theological ideas, including a substantial biography of the man. This he is about ready to publish. But the other part planned, the Letters and documents, with all the scholarly appendages pertaining thereto, are still not ready for publication, and if they were, there seems to be no money in sight for financing publication of such a work that will probably not sell sufficiently well to pay its cost.

The second co-editor, Correll, is on the warpath, objecting to the publication of Bender's part without the accompanying Letters being put out at the same time. He claims or imagines that Bender is planning to steal the show on this project, and get himself famous by publishing a work which incorporates many efforts of his co-editors and fails to give any credit for help received. Bender on his part charges that Correll is visionary about the possibilities of publishing a large scholarly work at all, that he has long promised to do work on the project, without actually doing any, and that he cannot be counted on for anything excepting grandiose planning and unfruitful talking.

In view of this decided clash between the two, I conclude I had better lie low and not get myself mixed up in their controversy, which is certainly in large part personal and temperamental. Dr. Correll was here some time ago, and by his talking took me in to a greater extent than I should have given way under the circumstances. I committed myself too far in writing – put my foot into it – so to say. Now it will be a matter of letting the dust subside and the atmosphere clear itself again, as I sit back and refuse to become involved in a personal dispute I was not aware of.

Dies Jovis, November 17, 1938 Mother went "out" this evening, leaving Boy and me at home. A number on a prominent lecture course at Pittsburgh was the attraction. A friend offered both transportation and admission ticket for the occasion. This may be our "trial balloon," to see what we think of the idea of more or less regularly going to a city nearly fifty miles away for such cultural features as lectures and concerts. When our family budget plan goes into effect, and experience shows the presence of funds for regular cultural items in our program, we may be interested in a number of trips of that kind every winter.

The budget is still in the formative stage. Beginning with 1939, we propose to regularly set aside a monthly amount from our income as savings, either for paying off obligations or for investments against future need. With income ranging from $120 to $150 a month, depending on how many Tuesdays in a month, my idea is to set aside regularly the sum of $50 a month not to be spent for living costs. An average of $75 a month should keep us in food, shelter and decent living surroundings. The income from the house in Kansas does a little more than balance the annual interest, taxes, and insurance costs of the property.

A year ago my personal interest in the so-called Teachers' Pool at Goshen College (which contains all the unpaid salaries covering the years from 1933 to 1937, and sufficient student notes and accounts uncollected to liquidate the salary claims) was to the extent of over $2400. Since then it has been reduced to less than $800. Unfortunately the difference between the two figures has not come to me in the form of cash, but mostly in credit. Two students, both now through college and earning money, Harold Miller, married and living in Illinois, and his brother, Clyde Miller, both of them some distant kin of my wife's, and perhaps mine too, have signed notes payable to me personally of the amount they left unpaid to the college. One note is for over $800 and the other is $300 or more. Cash received from the pool during the year was upward of $500, cash or its equivalent, though I saw checks for most of this sum.

Moving costs and household equipment have absorbed a goodly amount of capital for us during this year, and if this equipment proves a permanent investment, we will be pretty well settled financially, unless we decide to build us a house for ourselves soon. In view of all the work and bother of moving and settling down, I don't want to think about the process, not until the latest experience has more faded from memory's reach.

Dies Jovis, Kalendae Decembres, 1938   The days and weeks slip by, things and events happen in steady, unceasing procession. Outstanding big events in our otherwise comparatively quiet life have been as follows: On Sunday, November 13, Charles Shoemaker and family invited us to accompany them by automobile for a day's visit at Springs, Pennsylvania, sixty miles southeast from here. We greatly enjoyed the little outing and the visit at the home of Aunt Hannah Miller for dinner. For once in a strange Sunday school, and how it happened I do not know, I sat in class and assembly incognito. Was not called upon to teach class or speak in open review period. It is a rare treat for me to sit as an observer in someone's S. S. class. It is a wholesome experience to observe how others think and teach, especially for one who tries to prepare help for understanding the S. S. lesson.

Snow fell, six inches or more, on Thanksgiving Day, and cold prevailed with wind blowing strongly first from north, then for several days from south. Stoking the temperamental furnace in our basement was a major job and even then real comfort was absent in the house. Weather stripping outside windows and doors to keep out excess wind was a serious business for a while. Now it's warm again, snow mostly melted, and comfort in the house is a reality. Ten sessions of a Bible conference reached from Wednesday to Sunday last week, something to go to and sit through, although the effort to do so was not a total loss. Today Estie started working on a part time emergency job in the Publishing House, helping with the rush orders before the holidays. This evening she went to a lecture course number again in Pittsburgh. Virgil and I are keeping house by sleeping, presently.

December 11, 1938   A pleasant sunny afternoon. Weather has been gentle and kindly during these ten days of the first winter month, so far in accordance with the prophetic first days of the month, according to an old bit of weather lore. At home I remember hearing Father quote what was evidently a traditional saying to the effect that the weather on the first three days of December was a sample of the weather that would prevail during the three winter months. So far this season it has been true, for the first three days of this December in our area were mild and pleasant days. The stack of coal in the basement of our house makes better headway against the present level of temperatures than it did during the last week of November.

Started the last week writing S. S. lessons for October 1939, when begins a six months' stretch of lessons in Gospel of Matthew. This is a harder book to work in than was Mark, for it is more profound, more philosophical, and deeper in every way. My chief guides for my own study of this Gospel at this time are: Alfred Plummer in his "Exegetical Commentary on the Gospel according to St. Matthew," and the one volume commentary by Dummelow. Dr. Plummer is wonderfully good as an expositor, thoroughly evangelical, conservative, and scholarly, yet not bound down by a slavish adherence to a "wooden-headed literalism," to use Niebuhr's phrase. He is most stimulating and enlightening, leading one into the really deep things of this Gospel. I have used Plummer before, in Mark in the Cambridge Greek Testament. He has commentaries on some other New Testament books, which it is worth watching for in second-hand book lists, notably on Luke in the International Critical Commentary, and on Corinthians in the same commentary. The commentary by Dummelow is in general very good. Somehow the so-called most standard and orthodox commentaries, such as Matthew Henry, Jamieson-Foussett-Brown, and their like are not so helpful to my study as those of a little broader and more liberal viewpoint.

In November the Commission for Christian Education at its session in Chicago took it upon itself to appoint me to one of the secretariats of that organization, Secretary of Young People's Bible Meetings. For various reasons which amount to a positive conviction in my mind, I felt called upon to protest and, in fact, refuse the appointment. The issue is not regarded as finally settled by the general chairman, A. J. Metzler, but so far as I am concerned it may as well be considered settled. Some of the work of this office or position is routine, that of arranging topics for the Y. P. B. M. programs year by year. The other work is to study, analyze, and work out solutions for what ails this particular phase of the activities of the Mennonite Church. For the routine part I have no special aptitude or interest. For the developmental part, I not only have no desire, but a rather positive aversion and dislike. In the last six or eight years I have had at least two such projects placed before me for development, and my experience with these has absolutely convinced me that I have no business to even try to do that kind of job. One of these is the Education Committee, a standing committee on the Mennonite Board of Education. When the constitution of this organization was last revised and streamlined, the theory was that an education committee should be a permanent part of the set-up along with others. My name was placed on the list as chairman of this committee, and is still so carried in the current number of the Goshen College Catalogue. Except for a single time when others gave us a little routine job to bring before the Board, this committee has not done one thing on its hypothetical program. Several times I have sought to have my name removed from the committee, and without success, so I have ignored the matter year after year, not even submitting any kind of report to the Board at its annual meeting. So much for the first opportunity to develop a nonexistent program.

The second was the dean of men's office at Goshen College. This office existed as a name, with a small amount of routine work before it was given into my charge. It was intimated to me that the college administration desired to have a real personnel department, with means for regular counselling and guidance of students worked up and developed. The door before me was wide open and presented a grand opportunity for a much needed service. I undertook this task in all good faith and with the serious intention of making something out of it. In the course of two or three years I was able to do a few things in the desired direction. But compared with the nervous and mental energy expended, the results were meagre and disappointing. Not only so, but the effort brought me personally on the way toward nervous trouble and ill-health. So it was to me a providential and welcome opportunity to get away from the job entirely and enter upon another line of work. So my experience with executive and administrative work of a developmental nature has convinced me fully that it is folly and stupidity to let myself be loaded up with another job of that same general nature. Without any qualms of conscience, I have expressed my own viewpoint on the matter and unless my protest is heeded it will be necessary to let the place go by simple default. For my tastes and ability lie quite in other directions. The opportunities before me in those lines take away all excuse for trying to do work for which I am not fitted.

Pridie Kalendis Januariis, 1938 Here it is only a few hours any more before the year of grace 1938 is destined to expire to make room for the new year. Many folks are doubtless celebrating the passing of 1938 in the customary manner, with carousing and dissipation. My own way of celebrating the advent of a new year is to be soundly asleep in bed in accordance with regular schedule. There is little difference between today and tomorrow, just another day come along in its order.

1938 has been an epochal year in the world. The editor of the Christian Century in the closing issue of the year, as usual, took his retrospect, and sounded a rather pessimistic note as to the prospects for the year ahead. Evidently some real history has been made in the political world during the year that is closing. Only the perspective of time can reveal just what was accomplished and what forces were set going. Herr Hitler seems to be practically the master in European politics, and whether he is a shrewd and far-sighted statesman or another ambitious Napoleon, all remains to be seen.

In our own experience the year 1938 will remain as a landmark, the year we moved to Scottdale and undertook the major readjustment of changing myself from a college professor to an editor and writer. The professional adjustment may prove less difficult than the bodily adjustment to the difference in climate and atmosphere.

Two weeks ago I took out three days to sit with the so-called Curriculum Committee of the Commission for Christian Education. The meeting was here at Scottdale, which suited me fine, and those were the days that my latest siege of sinal congestion was budding. Following that I could work only with difficulty, until the last two or three days when working seemed about normal again.

Last Monday was observed as a holiday for Christmas celebration, since Sunday was the 25th. We celebrated at home, Ruth Bender being our guest then and for nearly a week altogether. We had a kind of special dinner on Sunday noon when Ralph Bender was also our guest. On Saturday evening at 6:30 we had Santa Claus time, when sitting about a small Christmas tree, gift packages were distributed. Virgil had a very exciting time and enjoyed the ceremony greatly. Among our Christmas presents from Miss Bender were tickets and a trip to Pittsburgh on December 13 to hear the Messiah rendered by the Mendelssohn Choir of the city. It was a very fine program and was excellent choral work. The only accompaniment was by pipe organ, and I missed the orchestra accompaniment which we have learned to associate with the rendition of the Messiah from hearing it three or four times at Lindsborg, Kansas, in years past. Mr. and Mrs. Ellrose Zook took us with them in their car to this program, which was held at Carnegie Music Hall.

Yesterday I had my second load of coal put in for the winter. The four tons and more of September was just about all gone. The furnace here takes too much coal, but happily coal is cheaper than in the west, two dollars seventy-five cents a ton dumped at the curb, and three dollars twelve and one-half cents wheeled into the bin. In the fall I wheeled the first load myself, but it was a severe strain, so I paid the extra amount this time and left the haulers do it. The furnace consumes so much coal because the house is not tightly built and because most of the heat seems to pass up the chimney, for the walls of the chimney are always very warm to the touch.

The Art Covers clipped years ago from the now defunct Literary Digest have in prospect to be pasted in scrap books. I had the book bindery department of the House make up for me ten scrap books, nine of fifty leaves each and one of sixty leaves. The latter was made to hold a special series of these Covers, those dealing with American history, most of them by Ferris. This book I have already made up and it is a pleasing job. The books were made for us at cost and amount to twenty cents each. The remaining Covers will fill at least seven more of the books eventually.

Compliments on the work done on the Advanced Sunday School Lesson Quarterly continue to appear occasionally. One young man of the Goshen College Gospel Team that stopped here on Wednesday, remarked about the help he is getting out of the quarterly, whereas he formerly used to pay no attention to it.

February 2, 1939 Ground Hog Day! Skies cloudy, rain beating against windows and no one able to see his shadow today hereabouts. More than a month of the new year has passed already. The last half month has been spent by myself in a very unusual manner, down with the mumps. Went to bed on January 18, and have now been up and about the house for about one week. Hope to get away from the house the next day the sun shines again and the air is moderate. Why both Wife and I should have waited forty or more years to entertain such a kid's disease as mumps is a mystery. And where we got them is not certain, for Estie started with a swelled face just twenty-four hours before I did.

Since getting up after a period of viewing the world from a horizontal plane for a week, there has been reading a good deal of the time. Read among other things C. K. Lehman's manuscript against millennialism. He makes up quite a weighty case for the nonmillennial position, one that ought to carry some weight with those not emotionally and finally committed to some kind of millennial doctrine. It is a fairly good discussion throughout. In spots there is special pleading of a sort. At points rather tenuous arguments are used. His major contentions and arguments seem to me to be well taken.

Other reading included accumulated periodicals. Christendom, latest issue, has several stimulating articles. The Christian Century editorials have given some searching criticism and analysis of President Roosevelt's messages to Congress. The chief executive had something to say about religion in his opening message. I did not read it closely enough to think carefully about it. But some of the syndicated writers in newspapers, Walter Lippmann, Dorothy Thompson, were enthusiastic in their interpretation of the unusual reference to religion. However, the Century saw it in another light altogether. It saw in it a kind of call to a Holy War against the totalitarian nations. Evidently there was no marked public response to the appeal, for in his call for armaments from Congress he asked for only a bare half-billion extra appropriations for that purpose.

World political events are indeed in a welter in these days. The most suggestive idea that I read recently has been to the effect that there is a possibility that Hitler in his Drang nach Osten may actually go into partnership with Soviet Russia in regard to the Ukraine. That would be a most interesting, but to me not surprising, development. For certainly the totalitarian states have more in common than either right or left type has in common with democracies. It would be interesting to see what then would be the reaction of people who sympathize with National Socialism in Germany and praise it for stopping communism in Europe.

One occupation during several days of partial incapacity recently was to pore and muse over the pages of the Hochstetler genealogies, the one that came off the press not long since, together with the early one of near thirty years ago. Occasionally I find myself in a mood to study into family records and try to clarify in my mind the family relationships of people I know or have met in various places. Only recently Harvey Hostetler sent me a copy, at my urgent request, of the earlier book, which is now practically out of print. Father has one of these, which I used to pore over when I was still at home. Now since I know people in other sections besides Iowa, as in Kansas and Indiana, I find renewed interest in looking over it. The new volume on the "Descendants of Barbara Hochstetler" who married Christian Stutzman, is also one of consuming interest. Seemingly all the Amish families in Iowa who were not mentioned in book number one, find a connection with the original Jacob Hochstetler through his daughter in this one. My own family was connected to this ancestor on both sides of the house in the first book. In the second book we are again connected with the same ancestor on Mother's side. So there are at least four lines of descent from this Hochstetler converging on our family at home, and now in our own home perhaps two more lines, for Estie's father's family appeared in the first volume and her mother's now in the second.

Another line of study that can be traced through these volumes, partly through footnotes given on related families, and that interests me, is the information on the Yoder families, especially those in my own line of descent. The Yoders on Father's side can be to a considerable extent traced out from these two books in this way. Some interesting knowledge about this line has recently become clear to me. Five generations back from myself there was a Henry Yoder, reputed to have been an immigrant, though just exactly what the evidence for the last point is aside from family tradition is not clear. He died either from the kick of a horse or from falling off a horse. He receives some notice in the Hochstetler annals because he was one of the twelve jurors who sat on the inquest over the murder of an infant child of a John Hochstetler in Somerset County Pennsylvania about 1810. This jury reported no clue as to the murderer of the child, and decided there were no such clues. Fifty years later in Holmes County, Ohio, another Henry Yoder, who however himself resided in Wayne County, confessed to his minister that he was the man who had smothered to death the Hochstetler child. This Henry was a son of the elder Henry, the juror. Interestingly enough, I never heard any mention of these incidents in our family tradition. In fact, there was little such traditional lore handed down in our family. This juror Henry was grandfather to my grandfather Tobias. My grandparents lived with us, in their own small house, but I associated much with Tobias as a boy. He died when I was nearly thirteen. He took special interest in me. We very often talked extendedly on various subjects, especially in his last few years, really more so than I talked with my father. Many times have I regretted that I did not question him about his past and his knowledge about family history. But he was not reminiscently inclined and I had no natural curiosity about such matters until some years after his death. Grandmother was better educated than her husband. She read a good deal, both English and German, but all grandfather could read, as I remember his wife's remarks about his reading, was about the first seven pages of a prayer book he had.

My mother's parents, who were Yoders too — Grandmother was Hochstedler by birth — also migrated to Iowa in Civil War days from Somerset County, Pennsylvania. In Grandfather Cornelius Yoder's family I can trace back the line of descent about the same distance — five generations – and there it seems to get lost. The grandfather of Cornelius married a Hochstetler and so from there the family is fully recorded. But all that is stated about this ancestor is that he was known to be closely related to a certain other Yoder, and was reported to have come from eastern Pennsylvania. If some day I have leisure time and some means for doing so, I would enjoy doing some research in Somerset County history, perhaps attempting to work up a history of the Amish communities of that County, and by the way trying to trace out the Yoder background more clearly. Meanwhile it would be well to write to a certain Lynn E. Yoder, somewhere in West Virginia, and see what knowledge of these Yoder families he has gathered. If Henry Yoder on Father's side was really an immigrant from Europe, it would be very fine if a genealogy of all his descendants could be published soon before the family gets as large as that of the Hochstetler ancestor now is. The only way to ever get Yoder genealogies published is to take one immigrant ancestor at a time, or even smaller branches, for publication in one work. C. Z. Yoder of Ohio has published some lists of his own family of Yoders.

February 3, 1939 Strange weather these days. One hour it rains steadily and the next it snows, then rain, then snow, etc. Happily there is no wind and no freezing temperature. Because of the dismal weather I have not yet ventured from the house, though I surely hope to work at the office again by next week. And Virgil is starting with the mumps just now, poor boy. He has been out of school for two and one-half weeks already and now for three weeks more he will not know what to do with himself.

One of the first days of last month I experienced a real surprise. Three years ago last October I submitted a manuscript article to Moody's Monthly. Almost forthwith they accepted it for publication. Two years passed and it had not appeared. I wrote a few lines of inquiry about whether it could soon see the light of day. They replied by some crabbing about a few points in the article and asked if I could not make certain alterations. I agreed and they sent the manuscript back. I promptly returned it and hoped to see the article in print. Another year passed and it was not printed. I had frankly given up hope, believing that I had not emasculated the article sufficiently to meet their approval. Then one day it occurred to me to take a look at Moody's Monthly in Editor Kauffman's office and to my astonishment, the January issue contained this article in a special Preachers' Number. The same day a postal card reached me in regard to it and three copies of the issue. They wanted me to suggest names of friends to whom they might send sample copies and solicit new subscriptions to their magazine. But unfortunately they sent me no check in remuneration for the manuscript.

February 12, 1939 Everyone at our house is practically recovered from the "mumps." Virgil has still seven days of school to miss before his isolation period is over. That will make for him five full weeks of absence from school and everything else outside of home. Hard to find occupation for him at home for such a long period of time. I invested in a Chinese Checker Board, which gives "something to do" for certain periods when someone else has time to help him play the game.

Visited the office every day last week and was able to get started on the next project of literary production on my slate, the second part or unit of what is commonly referred to as the "doctrinal quarterly." The first part is already in use in certain places during the present quarter. The work on regular Advanced Quarterly copy must therefore wait for more convenient time. The three weeks of mumps was like a vacation, and I feel as if I were somewhat recuperated in general. Will probably get no planned vacation this year, for my income was not interrupted by this one.

February 26, 1939 Spent the past two and a half weeks writing out in pencil the substance of part two of the so-called "doctrinal quarterly," working against time to get this number in print for use in second quarter of Sunday school year. With a little help on the typing end the manuscript should be ready for the typesetter by the week's end.

Read two books recently that were as meat for the mind and heart. An order to Blessings Store in Chicago a month ago brought a packet of religious books. Among them were two by T. R. Glover. The one read is "Jesus in the Experience of Men." This is a book published fifteen years ago, and is in the best vein of Glover, an author whom I have found very stimulating and suggestive. He is a very fine stylist and a widely read writer, a truly liberal thinker, none of the cocksure, dogmatic, iconoclastic, more or less shallow modernists. Not all details of his books are acceptable. The point of view is very fine and stimulates one's thoughts in a wholesome manner. Perhaps a half dozen of Glover's books have found their way into my collection since I "discovered" him. His viewpoint on Jesus, His life, teachings, work, and influence, at least deserves respect and thought.

The second book read is different. It is a newly published book, "Days of Our Years," by Pierre van Paassen, a newspaper correspondent of international dimensions. The book is partly biography, but very informing on events in Europe, Morocco, Ethiopia, Palestine, and Spain of recent years. The man is an idealist of deep Christian coloration. I found myself reading his book with more than usual interest and sympathy. As a personality he is deeply sensitive to the cruelty and brutality of man toward man. Wherever he saw men torturing each other or exploiting their fellows he was moved to the quick. As a result there is a good deal of gruesome and unsavory description at times throughout the book, though always told with some objectivity, so it is very impressive without being too revolting. The man's analysis of the fundamental trouble in Palestine today, and in Spain, are both very illuminating to me. They are partly this person's opinion, yet carry considerable semblance of truth to my mind. For Mussolini he has scant respect as statesman or personality. For Hitler more respect as a statesman, less as an ideologist. For Britain no very high regard, except as a pusher of imperialistic interests of her own in the Near and Far East.

Van Paassen's book came into my hands as by accident almost. During January I received at least three invitations identical each to each from the Book-of-the-Month Club to avail myself of their services by joining now. They offered as a gift the new edition of Bartlett's Familiar Quotations, a six-dollar book. That alone was enough to create interest. So they received another client. With the gift book they mailed the February book-of-the-month, the one mentioned above. It was happy accident that it came, for I had not seen announcement of this particular book, and from title and author's name alone might have decided I did not want it. The March choice is announced to be a new novel by Pearl Buck, scene laid in China. By accepting these two books-of-the-month, they announce that one will be entitled to a free book in April, as dividend, by John Gunther, "Inside Europe." And furthermore if one deposits in advance on account against books-of-the-month to be purchased at any time as wanted, one gets a gift book for that too. I chose Victor Hugo's book "Les Miserables" in the Modern Library Giants, of which I already acquired a number of volumes. So it may prove that by joining the Club now I shall be receiving three gift books, totaling $10.50 at list price, within a few months' time, and purchasing two books at about $5.55 in the same time. Not a bad inducement to bait new subscribers to the Book-of-the-Month Club.

During the year 1929 I had subscribed to this Club, but after a year's trial it was discontinued on my request. We did not care so much for their book selections. Only four books, the very minimum, were ordered that year and usually substitutions at that! From what can be gathered it appears that their selections may be a little better now. At that time there were no book dividends given out and no premiums for advance deposits on account. These added inducements and the worth-while gift to start with made the invitation irresistible to me and I ventured upon another year of membership in this Club. The chief problem is one of finding time, or taking it, for reading these books; the one just finished had above five hundred pages, and good-sized pages at that. If they are such as to seize upon and hold one's interest, it is easier to get them read than if one reads out of a sense of cultural duty or other obligation.

Everything going normally again at home. Virgil started to school on last Wednesday, after an absence of five full weeks.

March 5, 1939 The present month is coming in like the proverbial lamb, very mild yesterday and today. Ground is drying off on top, making walking possible with comfort. Virgil and his daddy took a stroll of nearly two hours' length yesterday afternoon. Estie went to evening church service, the closing session of a two weeks' revival campaign with S. J. Miller of Michigan preaching. Entertained a visitor at our house the past week, over two nights, Miss Alma Brenneman of Iowa, from the old home community. She has in recent years been working in Elkhart, Indiana and Akron, Pennsylvania and was now on her way home again.

The second installment of the so-called doctrinal quarterly came through in record time, the manuscript preparation part. Miss Esbenshade was assigned to help with the typing of the copy during the past week. The quality of this – good, bad, or indifferent as experiment may prove it to be– will go to show whether it is possible for me to produce by simply writing rapidly as I can draw upon my general stock of knowledge and ideas. Am not sure how successful it will be.

Since a year or more the Atlantic Monthly has been publishing the equivalent of three books in the form of four supplementary installments each. The last one, just ended, is by Nora Waln, entitled "Reaching for the Stars." It is her account of a four years' stay in Germany (1934 - 1938). It is a beautifully written work, breathing a fine spirit throughout. She tries to portray the life and culture of the German people; she describes her attempt to understand Nazism; she does not particularly seek to defend it or condemn it. Rather she reflects in very effective ways the impressions of what she saw upon her highly sensitive and artistic nature. The result is the reader, this one at least, is stimulated to love and admire the German people as such; and at the same time the sinister forces and movements now at work in Germany are felt to be darkly in the background. What the outcome will be is not indicated, but by casual intimations the author suggests that there is hope that the German people will themselves correct the errors of Nazism in time. Human dignity and the desire for personal liberty will gradually assert themselves again when the people's self-respect has been rehabilitated more fully. The writer is a Quaker by birth and training, from eastern Pennsylvania, and a genuine Quaker by conviction and intuition. Her writing is a delight to read. We read her book, "House of Exile," a few years ago at Goshen from the Public Library.

We had thought we had spent enough for living equipment, and would spend no more for the time being. But open book shelves in this country are just impossible. In the study I have two open cases, and they must be replaced as soon as can be done with closed cases. Dust and soot are terrible and books will soon be ruined.

April 8, 1939 This month seems to be colder and uglier than last. Snow was flying before dark this evening; air, damp and very penetrating, chilled one through winter clothes. This morning was cloudless with promise of a warmer day than had been the rule lately. Thick dark clouds began to sail across the sky at noon and they grew thicker and thicker during afternoon until rain started falling. Accompanied by our guest, Ruth Bender, we went for a hike of three miles going and coming. Air was too chilly for comfort, but the outing was enjoyable after all. A boy from the Deaf School near Pittsburgh, guest at Resslers', also walked with us.

Effort has been rather scattered here and there during recent weeks. Various essays and papers have been taking shape, outlines for parts three and four of the projected and partly executed course of lessons in Christian doctrine were prepared and submitted to the authorities that be, the theological censors. These eminent personages have not criticised seriously, until this time, one of their number feels that the distinctive doctrines of the Church are missing. Probably because in making up the outlines the old stereotyped words and terminology were more or less purposely avoided in an attempt to present these distinctive principles in a way and manner that is more fresh and purposely novel so as to induce a little thinking on the subjects themselves. Some persons are evidently so wedded to certain words and certain patterns of presentation in connection with the distinctive Mennonite teachings that when they do not see these words before their eyes they believe that the subject is not even under discussion. The fact is, that with too many, certain words are as charms and talismans that inhibit intelligent thinking on the subject itself rather than lead to any clear and rational thinking. This is certainly deplorable, for when words and symbols take the place of clear thinking then the life has gone out from the subject.

There are of course a variety of legitimate viewpoints on what exactly should be the method pursued in such a course of doctrinal studies. They might be definitely and purposely apologetic, or protagonistic for the so-called neglected teachings, overemphasized for the moment to make up for neglect otherwise. Or they might aim to give a systematic view of Bible teaching as a whole, in which the neglected teachings are given their place in somewhat their normal setting and perspective. To me the value of these teachings is enhanced when I can view them in something like their true perspective. And I am wondering whether young people in general would not feel more genuine respect for these teachings presented in this manner than in the usual apologetic, defensive manner, as a series of isolated "doctrines," disconnected except for the fact that they are unpopular.

Paul in First Corinthians, Chapter 11, for example, is dealing with the main subject of order and decorum in public worship in church assembly; he is not primarily teaching a doctrine about woman's head covering. And really the latter topic has no meaning when it is isolated from its setting and taught as a major doctrine of the Bible. The danger of its neglect may justify giving some special attention and emphasis to this, but to my way of thinking, it is dishonest then to ignore its context and setting. And the same can be said of other teachings that seem to need special emphasis in the view of some.

Two books I read recently were: "The Patriot" by Pearl Buck, my second Book-of-the-Month purchase. One reason I took it was to get the dividend book, "Inside Europe" by Gunther. The novel is like novels are; this one is fairly powerful in showing up the psychological conflict in the mind of a Chinese, who married a Japanese wife, when the war between the two countries broke out. There is an excellent portrayal of Chinese and Japanese life in the home and family. And one cannot help loving the Japanese for their refinement, culture, and heroic devotion to duty. At a few points just for brief moments in the story a western character is brought in to show up the more forcibly the great contrast in culture; the latter whether German or American come off as outrageous boors and barbarians.

The second book I have just finished was Glover's "Progress in Religion to the Christian Era." This was written in this author's usual genial, engaging and disarming style. He is one of the most stimulating of authors and thinkers I have ever read. When he writes about Israel and the Old Testament records he builds upon the results of the older criticism of the O. T. One senses that he is using second-hand conclusions and data and is not so sure of his ground as when he happens to be writing about matters Greek and Roman. Still his attitude is such that one is not offended by what he says that seems mistaken, for he is free from that facile and glib dogmatism which is crass and intolerant. One feels that he is perfectly agreed that a reader may differ from him in point of view. He is one of the best-educated and civilized men, in Albert J. Nock's sense of that term, that I have ever read. Nock is himself cynical, whiles Glover is always human, genial, optimistic, a true Greek in spirit and genius.

Dies Jovis, April 13, 1939   Weather of all kinds in rapid and unpredictable succession. Monday very warm, springlike, followed by several days of thick, dark, angry clouds sending down alternately rain or snow flurries. Last night cold and blowy from northwest. Today clearing and milder.

Easter started in with snow on the ground, ended dreary and dismal. We were guests at Shoemakers' for dinner on Easter Day, and ate plenty, enough to induce a bit of congestion in head and throat. On Monday evening an unusual event; a chorus of men, students from Hesston, Kansas, gave a program of song in the Evangelical Church in town. Two young fellows, Miller and Beyler, from Protection, Kansas, were our guests for over night and two meals. Paul Erb was the director. They were a well-trained group and did well for the comparative youthfulness of many in the group of twenty-nine men. The selections were of good quality and well interpreted. Professor Erb seems to be making better quality selections for chorus work than he did ten years ago. There was just enough Western atmosphere about the group to bring a touch of homesickness to one who will probably never help missing the beauties and blessings of the wide open spaces of the Middle West.

The Easter season brings special music to the fore in some places. The magazine TIME today gave a column or more to the annual Messiah festival at Lindsborg, Kansas, including a picture of Professor Brase, the director. The write-up reminded me of the times it was my happy fortune to hear the rendition of the Messiah at that place. I always did enjoy it greatly. At least four times I listened to the rendition. First time in 1917, just at the time, on the day in fact, when Congress declared war against Germany. In a light weight Ford car with its top neatly laid back, a Mr. Hartzell took two couples the forty miles and back. Again in 1920 a party of Sunday school workers who used to go with me to Yoder, Kansas, every Sunday morning for Sunday school, drove in a Ford Model-T, again with top laid down! from Yoder to Lindsborg for the evening rendition on Palm Sunday. In either 1922 or 1923 on Good Friday evening Estie and I drove our old Ford car to hear the Messiah once more, Mr. and Mrs. Dan Driver accompanying us. And lastly in 1931 Mr. and Mrs. Paul Bender took us with them on Sunday evening to hear the rendition. This was the only time I listened to the program in the beautiful new Music Hall. Before that it was always rendered in a gymnasium, a wooden one at that, with improvised seats. Sometime I would love to take a spring vacation and drive a car to Kansas, mostly to hear some of their music programs at Lindsborg during Passion Week, the Messiah and The Passion according to St. Matthew by Bach.

Dies Saturni, ante diem tertiam Kalends Maii, 1939   Ambled along country roads for several hours this afternoon, looking upon the rural scene and enjoying its sights and smells as the bursting springtime spreads these over the countryside. Fruit trees in bloom, wild shrubs just in the act of turning green, wild flowers in rich profusion in field and woods, the smell of the good earth freshly plowed, and the rich green of the hillsides, all was very enjoyable. About two miles west of town a stretch of dirt road winds along a steep hillside and not far from Jacob's Creek. The steep upward slope along one side is wooded and would make a pleasant place to go clambering around in search of flowers, plants and the like. It is one of the few patches of woods near about that is not either littered with dumped rubbish and tin cans, or cluttered up with "No Trespassing" signs and posters. There is also a meadow-like area between road and creek which is covered in part with thickets and trees, a veritable paradise for birds. Not having binoculars, I am unable to do much in observing birds, as my distance vision with artificial lenses is not as good as was my natural vision of fifteen years ago, the time when I was for a while really interested in observing birds in Kansas. A pair of good binoculars is on the waiting list of "must" purchases of the not too distant future. In this country of hills, if one gets on top of a high one it is possible to see the country with field glasses.

Spent just a full week, lacking several hours, away from home. Left on the 17th by auto to Pittsburgh, when Mr. Yake and I entrained for Goshen, Indiana. Sat in Curriculum Committee for two full days and a little more. Sat in meeting of the Commission for Christian Education for part of a third day, and then absented myself for other business. The most impressive memory I have of these sittings is the feeling of boredom which rested upon me much of the time. Am glad there are folks who enjoy such sittings, but this person is certainly not one of them. On Saturday, a week ago today, there was more sitting, of another kind. A special conference at the college on applied nonresistance took up the time and also on Sunday. That night in company with A. J. Metzler I was on the train from Warsaw to Pittsburgh, sleeping two in a lower berth, and by auto again reached home in time for a belated breakfast.

Taken as a whole the vacation was enjoyable and restful. Among the things that made it so were, a room to myself and breakfast at Paul Benders', familiar surroundings and congenial friends for brief visiting. It was quite different from going to a strange community for an ordinary conference or board meeting, the kind that regularly bore and exasperate me in a short time. Read a long and tedious paper before the filled assembly hall on Saturday evening. This week has been busy on third unit of so-called "doctrinal quarterly."

Dies Solis, May 6, 1939 First part of last week was cool, heat in the house was necessary, white frost on roofs three mornings in succession. Now it is mild, sunny days for most part, and really comfortable without benefit of furnace heat. Yesterday afternoon the sun beat down very invitingly. On the wooded hilltop a mile south of town I managed to absorb some of the pleasant rays.

Sunday afternoon sleeping consumed three hours of time today, and so on most Sunday afternoons. After a season of deep and profound slumber, I enjoy a really refreshed feeling, lightness of head, clearness of mind, and general sense of well-being. For best working efficiency with comfort and enjoyment the habit of an hour's siesta after the noon meal is found very helpful, and really involves no loss in amount of work done, rather the converse. Perhaps getting out into the sun's rays more during the summer months will make it possible to reduce my necessary sleeping hours somewhat. It used to be claimed by observers that in Kansas they required less sleep than in other areas where there was less sunshine than in the Sunflower State. The theory seems not impossible. One Saturday forenoon I worked in the sunshine on the church grounds, cleaning old bricks from the demolished church, and felt that I had gotten some "sun" on face and head. A week ago yesterday afternoon a walk of three hours in sunshine and a strong wind netted a feeling of slight sunburn on face and neck.

The woods along Jacob's Creek two or three miles west of town are a good place to go "woodsing" for birds and wild flowers. Picked up at random six specimens of flowers, only one of which I happened to know by name, the common violet. But the ground in spots was almost covered by flowers of various kinds. A flower guide is among our necessary purchases in the future, and then a determined effort to learn the names and habits of the wild flowers that seem to grow so abundantly here. Birds too are plentiful, but my distant vision with present glasses is not good enough to distinguish finer markings on the "smalle fowles," and so I put off studying birds too, until such a time as good binoculars come into my possession.

In general this will be an interesting country to explore and investigate, as to its flora and fauna, its geology and meteorology, etc. I anticipate the pleasure of doing some of my own "growing up" in cooperating with Virgil in the following up of boyhood hobbies along some of these lines during the years to come. Hope I shall find time to help him fill his time and interests with such constructive pursuits as will leave less room for the mob interests that usually attract boys.

May 17, 1939 Virgil is now suffering from swollen glands in his head and neck! He has been sick a great many times this winter, thus making it the eighth sick spell, including mumps and chicken pox. He will have missed between a fifth and a fourth of the school year. He seems to be run down, very nervous and irritable much of the time. Evidently needs some help in building up.

Read a notice in a periodical that William Ramsay, Scotch scholar and writer on Luke, Paul, etc., died recently at age of 88 years. The item interested me especially because his writings have been among the most helpful and stimulating I read in the field of New Testament study. His ideas, approach, and method in that field opened my own eyes wide to the possibilities and the richness in the study, especially of Acts and of N. T. times. I have acquired some eight or more of his major books and found them all rich feeding ground, though I do not read them so much any more. He has in some respects been superseded by other scholars who built on his work, especially David Smith, whom I constantly use for reference. Though the man never knew what he did for my religious thinking, I am made to reflect that perhaps one's labors will bear rich fruit in at least a few scattered places in minds just at the right stage of growth for such seed, and of which one will never hear. Thus the Spirit of God carries on and spreads ideas and thoughts in many ways better than men can plan and calculate.

May 27, 1939   After nearly a year on the grounds as a worker here, I begin to get adjusted and find myself getting into a more natural and spontaneous routine. The routine writing and manuscript preparation, the "producing," as they call it here, becomes gradually easier and expeditious.

Weather has been warm, and of all unexpected things for this area, the sun has shone every day for a week or more, not just fitfully, but about all day long, as though it meant business. Ground is dry and people wish for rain.

The boy is out again after nine days in bed suffering from glandular swelling. Still has a cough that interferes with his sleeping o'nights. I rub his back along the sides of his spinal column for a short time every evening now to help his nerves and build up his circulation.

June 5, 1939   Pennsylvania can put on comfortable, sunshiny weather too! For near three weeks there has been almost constant sunshine, so much so that there was complaint of a drought, which was relieved on Saturday by a downpour of rain.

It chanced also on Saturday that in the editor-in-chief's office I caught sight of a new book which I was eagerly waiting to see — "The Mennonites of Iowa," by Melvin Gingerich, who is an old neighbor and school friend from Iowa. The volume is of interest of course because it treats on matters, some of which I have first-hand knowledge and experience. It is an excellent piece of work, perhaps as good as or better quality than any regional history of Mennonites in the U. S. A. that has appeared. I admire especially the fine attitude, at once objective and sympathetic, which the author displays throughout in interpreting the events and facts he narrates. The attempts of outsiders, whether in fiction or in casual references, to depict Mennonite and Amish character and customs are never satisfactory. They fail to appreciate the inner spirit and the point of view of these people, and hardly achieve more than caricatures of them. Gingerich being an insider, and at the same time a widely read and well-informed historian, has achieved a happy result in this work. I laid my hands on the book at noon on Saturday, read over half of it on that afternoon, and the remainder on Sunday afternoon. It was the most exciting reading I have done for some time, because so much of it was familiar ground.

Have been playing with the novel idea of trying to create in my lifetime some sort of fictional or semi-fictional book in the setting of the Amish Community of Johnson County, Iowa, perhaps centering about my father and his active period of life. It is a bold idea, and for me would require long effort and labor in spare time as a side line. Whether anything ever comes out of this idea or not, I believe I shall indulge the pleasure of playing and working with it for some time to come. As faintly as I can now conceive of this book it should be a character study, with strong interest taken in the social, thought, and religious life of the Amish Community of that time. The literary reviews emphasize the importance of regional and sectional novels of the American scene. This might be one.

June 11, 1939   The days have been pleasant, occasional showers, warmish, somewhat clear and somewhat cloudy. Had planned a number of weeks of time interspersed with leisure for some other things besides pressing duties. When one has a brief breathing spell, then likely as not there will presently be a congestion of matters that need attention by some near date. Such is the case during the next three weeks here. First quarter, 1940, quarterly copy must be finished by July 1. Article for Gospel Herald, material for peace pages of doctrinal supplement by same date. Editing Shank's copy for 4th quarter teachers' quarterly, and office editing of Mennonite Quarterly Review, April issue by the same date. Slate must be cleared of these matters so that all of July may be devoted to producing fourth number of "Lessons in Christian Doctrine" for publication in August. August will be broken up by various interruptions. Yet hope to get started on second quarter lessons for 1940 during that month and then by steady application to produce in fairly complete form the manuscripts for second, third, and fourth quarters in the five months from August to December, so as to get back to regular schedule for Sunday school lesson writing, which is supposed to be one calendar year ahead of the date for using the lessons. The work on the reputed "doctrinal quarterlies" has thrown back my schedule on the regular lessons.

Rather suddenly our boy Virgil is discovering he can read, and he frequently passes some of his time scrooched down in a chair and silently reading to himself. He can do best in the Egermeier Bible story book. He has heard most of that read twice, and being familiar with the subject matter he can read fairly well, making out enough of it to hold his interest in the contents. That particular book is well adapted as to style and vocabulary for a child's reading. His reading for himself will help make him for part of his time independent of his parents' willingness and convenience for reading to him. That will be a decided gain for both him and them. On the other hand another problem may soon be fully on our hands: To keep him from sitting around and keeping his nose buried in a book the whole day long, to the detriment of his health and happiness and development in other ways. He had a good chance to inherit from both his father and mother a tendency to be a bookworm. If he can be helped to keep up somewhat of a balanced development, I am in favor of his reading widely and much as fast as he can develop in that skill. He will have more material to work on, if he does prove to be a bookworm, than I had when I was at home.

June 13, 1939 This month of this year reminds me that twenty years ago I enjoyed my first visit to the Rocky Mountains in Colorado. Following the close of the college year at Hesston in 1919, three men took a special course under J. D. Charles in General Geology, the first course of its kind ever given there. The course was interesting and instructive. The other two in the party were Noah Oyer, now deceased, and M. D. Landis. After about three weeks of intensive daily study on such phases as mineralogy, descriptive geology, and related matters, it was agreed that a field trip to the Colorado Rockies would be an excellent feature of such a course of study. Mr. Landis could not afford to make the trip, but the rest of the crowd made up a party, which included also Mrs. Oyer, who went along as cook, etc. Professor Charles provided the automobile, a Mitchell of considerable size and power for that early day.

We took a small amount of cooking and camping equipment along, including a tent to stretch across the top of the car, which made a commodious sleeping apartment on each side, where cots were used as beds. In those days Kansas highways were subject to ruts and waterholes in wet weather and we had some to deal with on our way going west. We stopped at La Junta, Colorado, on the way going, and at Limon, Colorado on the way coming back. My uncle Sam Yoder then lived on a prairie farm between the towns of Limon and Matheson.

At Colorado Springs, or rather Manitou, we rented a cabin, which we occupied at nights. The days were spent in trips to various places with the motor car, when it worked, for there was considerable difficulty in getting power out of it in the high altitude. Trips I remember with pleasure were: The Garden of the Gods, Seven Falls, Petrified Forest at Florissant. For the trip, to record geological observations, I invested in a Kodak camera of post card size, which was stolen from a checked suitcase a year later when we were on our wedding trip. I still have quite a collection of the pictures taken on that trip, in an album of goodly size. I have been in the Rockies of Colorado several times since, but that first visit was one well remembered. On the return home I came by train to my uncle's place for a stay of several days, while the rest of the party made a trip to La Junta, and then north to Limon again. The country around there was real primitive prairie at the time, though fairly settled. No trees to speak of, a mile high in altitude, slightly rolling surface, with the mountains dimly visible in the west.

The remainder of the summer of 1919 I spent at Yoder, Kansas, or rather only six weeks of it. Helped Jake Yoder do part of his wheat harvesting, and then tended his Yellow Fellow Thresher for the six weeks. Came the middle of August when I resigned my position and turned my steps eastward. For nearly two years I had then been away from home, so I was eager to see Iowa and the home folks again. But my travels took me farther than just to Iowa. Took my first trip to Pennsylvania, visiting for a week at Springs and then in company with Estie went to Harrisonburg, Virginia, for three or four days of General Conference. On the homeward journey I made my first stay in the town of Scottdale about a day and a night in length. Estie came to take up her work at the House after a vacation for entertaining me at Springs and going to General Conference. After spending one week or so at home I returned to Kansas in time for opening of the school year. The summer was accordingly my first experience in travelling for its own sake, sightseeing, visiting, and so on. It was a summer at once romantic and educational, long to be remembered. The zest for travelling was sharpened by the high rate of wages I received at Yoder the summers of 1918 and 1919.

July 11, 1939   Time passes so swiftly when filled with numerous and varied things to do. Third week in June found me at Goshen again for a day and a night sitting in committee, only during the day, however. Slept in Coffman Hall at night, sat at meat for meals in college dining hall. Trip was by train from Connellsville and return.

Last week in June Paul Benders stopped here on their return trip from Virginia. With them were two Weber children from Ft. Wayne, and Mrs. Brunk of Virginia. They were here less than twenty-four hours, but we were glad to see them and enjoyed their visit. July two to four sister Ida, now of Akron, Ohio, with her friend Lucille Kreider, visited us. Virgil was highly pleased to have company; especially was he interested in Ida's car, for he planned she could take us out to some places. On Monday afternoon, under the guidance of the Resslers, we all went to the top of Laurel Mountain, twelve or thirteen miles northeast from here, to private picnic grounds known as Bear Rocks. Some special rock formations, with deep chasms between and sometimes caves underneath in and through which one could walk were the main attraction. Not an especially wonderful place, but private, and on that day perfectly quiet, for we were the only ones there at the time. They charged us ten cents a person for admittance and five cents to park a car, high enough for not more than is there. There is an open clearing on top of the hill and they had evidently made some effort to cut the tall grass over most of it. Tables for eating were placed among the trees around the outside, a few rustic, crude swings and rough stone fireplaces was the extent of the furniture. The Resslers had a charcoal stove which they used for frying eggs and broiling ham. The food tasted good amid the out-of-doors, and we ate a lot of it.

On the Fourth of July the Yake family invited us to go out with them for a picnic in the afternoon. It rained on the way and cleared off again in time to allow us a pleasant picnic time. Mr. Yake took us out northwest to a place alongside the Smithton road, in a farmer's field near a little stream and along a wooded hillside. Roasted wieners were the pièce de résistance of this party and again the open air made keen appetites for a lot of food. These two trips enlarged my circle of acquaintance with the environs of Scottdale and suggested possible itineraries for a number of good cross-country hikes.

July 30, 1939 A few birthday notes before going to bed. Yesterday Virgil was whispering secrets to his mother telling me not to listen. This morning at breakfast they "surprised" me with a gift of a new penwiper rolled up and having a snapdragon flower stuck in its end placed beside my place at the table. This evening for lunch there was gingerbread cake and ice cream. The boy enjoys helping to plan for surprises and gifts of remembrance on the suitable occasions that come along. Otherwise the day passed as any other Sunday would.

Wrote my father a letter for his Birthday which precedes mine by four days in the calendar. He is seventy-four years old. Also sent him a bank draft to pay off the last of the notes that I gave him during the years of what Beard calls "the golden glow," the period just preceding 1929. Four or five times when I was attending university at Iowa City and Philadelphia he favored me with loans for living expenses, amounts ranging from one hundred to two hundred fifty dollars. Several of these I paid off in 1927. Then followed heavy health expenses, the depression, moving to Kansas and back to Goshen again, and no more was paid of these "golden glow" loans until in 1937 and 1938. And now the last one is wiped out. Looking back upon those years, I am greatly impressed by the readiness and thoughtlessness with which we borrowed money in those days. Either we were extremely foolish then, or have lost most of our courage today, for today I would abhor the idea of borrowing money with as little hesitancy as I did then. The difference in years makes some difference in one's willingness to mortgage his future earnings so recklessly. I am glad we could pay this off, for we have been favored a lot by the loans and the outright gifts when we started housekeeping nineteen years ago. Had we been forced to rent all these years or had we bought a property on borrowed money we could never have done even as well as we have in making a living and attending universities. A property purchased on borrowed money would have been like a millstone around one's neck; in fact, we could never have held it on the salary we have gotten during my productive years.

This business of economics is all very complicated. Father made money during his active life; of course, we children at home helped some toward earning it. Now we try to, or I do, give my service to the work of the Church, and have in effect had to live in part off Father's earnings. How to even and balance it all up is hard to see. Yet in all matters of money and wealth, it is much the same as this.

Dies Solis, August 13, 1939   The day of rest is always welcome, especially today, after a week of stir and commotion in the form of nearly five days of "Conference" of one sort or another. And last Sunday was no day of rest, because the occasion of the first use of the newly-erected church building had to be celebrated by elaborate, far from plain or simple, programs covering three sessions. We tried to lend our support to these activities, in a manner that at least should show no disrespect, by someone from the family being in attendance at all or part of every session. Beyond that we did not exert ourselves. Virgil can hardly endure more than one hour of public session at a time, and it seems to be to little purpose to force him at his age to sit quiet for two or three hours in church of some kind. Sunday school on Sunday morning he is eager and happy to attend without exception. The worship service of one hour following that he finds tolerable and knows of no exception. Beyond that regular routine we do not take him to services regularly. Most of the sermon period he spends busy with paper and pencil drawing something. Total inactivity for more than a few minutes seems to be entirely beyond his range of possibilities at this age.

And I do not incline to worry about our not taking him to all and every service in church, as some here practice very diligently, and others publicly advocate should be done. The reason I do not worry over it is because Virgil already regularly attends more than twice as many weekly services as I did when a child. Until I was sixteen I never went to Sunday evening services at all, and to Sunday school only on alternate Sundays for about eight months of the year, and to church services on the in-between Sundays, every two weeks throughout the year. Attendance at special meetings, conferences, programs, etc. was unknown. Somehow, by the grace of God I managed to get a start in faith and religion. It is only fair to recognize that today meetings and gatherings are abundant on all hands, and the fever to be going places is everywhere in the air, and that most folks would probably be going somewhere anyway, if the church would not be providing places to which the people can go. On the other hand the multiplication of meetings in the Mennonite Church is playing havoc with our traditional, simple, quiet type of piety and spirituality, and tends to become a burden to support and go through with. Remarks are heard of how influential and epoch-making were the first Sunday-school conferences, Bible conferences, mission meetings held at different places. Today it is hard to get and maintain a vigorous and interested attendance for all the sessions of "conference and associated meetings," so much so that bishops feel the need for urging faithful attendance, "from the first opening song to the last benediction." Because such conferences when first started served a wonderful purpose and filled a real need does not prove that five or ten times as many such meetings will do five or ten times as much good as those did. The law of diminishing returns applies in religious meetings the same as elsewhere. It is a complex situation. Many who need more religion and inspiration do not put in their appearance at these meetings. Some who have outgrown the gregarious stage of their religious experience find the multiplied meetings a burden, and the rest are not numerous enough to carry on.

There is opportunity right now for any conscientious "conference-goer" to spend ten days or so sitting in sessions somewhere in Pennsylvania, for the Board of Publication meets in Lancaster County toward the end of this week. And next week General Conference and associated meetings convene in Mifflin County. Because of Publishing House pressure it may be necessary for me to succumb and sit through some sessions of Board meeting. As a matter of duty I might go, especially since the House offers ten dollars toward travelling expenses. Had it not been for this, I had hoped to spend the week loafing and resting at home, so as to start work the next week on S. S. lessons for second quarter of 1940. The project of doctrinal lessons is finished now, except for reading the final proof. Work on this was begun just about one year ago, and am glad it is over. Only history can report on whether the year's effort was wholly or partly wasted.

August 25, 1939 Read a most interesting book last week, "Human Nature in the Bible," by William Lyon Phelps. This was the first book by Professor Phelps I ever read. Since quotations from his pen are frequently seen and he is often referred to in literary connections, it was because of his name and reputation that I picked out the above title in a second-hand book list as a reasonably safe buy. It is a kind of running narrative and commentary on the Old Testament history, centering around the outstanding characters. The book is most readable and enjoyable. It soars far above, or shall one say moves along at depths far beneath the critical and petty questions that spoil for many otherwise intelligent people the reading of the Bible as literature of absorbing human interest. Mr. Phelps makes the literature of the Bible such as appeals to one's deepest appreciation because of the very human qualities that mark its characters. His chapter on Daniel and Esther is really humorous. Some of this book I read during and between sessions of the meetings of the Publication Board at a church in Lancaster County where I spent a day and a half last week. Among others I went there on House time and expense, and enjoyed it as a novelty, and after a fashion.

August 30, 1939   There is a scribe who under the symbol "Quintus Quiz" writes a weekly column of simple clerical and Christian philosophy in the Christian Century. Once in a while he writes something on the art and virtue of walking as opposed to the almost universal practice of being "carried" on wheels. It is satisfying to see someone extol the spiritual and mental benefits of pedestrianism, for I too engage in this activity or ritual with something resembling religious diligence and seriousness. All other things being equal and given the choice between going with four, six, or eight cylinders, or with two cylinders of my own anatomy, I should certainly choose the lesser number. Walking is a healthful, mind-clearing occupation. And especially in this area in which I am a newcomer of only one year's experience, it is positively thrilling and romantic, as compared to Elkhart County, Indiana, where the roads nearly all run by the cardinal points of the compass, neither do they wander any in the vertical plane either. But Pennsylvania! Ah, that's different, for here roads run in every possible direction on the horizontal plane and change their course continually and without warning. And they go up and down too. East from here a distance of two miles or less is a little valley through which the Connellsville-Mt. Pleasant highway runs. Beyond that nothing is visible of special interest. Only a country road nonchalantly starts out across what looks to be a gradual slope up toward the first high ridge of mountains several miles farther on. One day out of curiosity and in a mood for a little adventure, I started out on that country road. It wound around a small hill, and in less than a mile gave the adventurer an unexpected surprise, for over the low ridge it led down into a beautiful valley where is located a spacious country club building or hotel with extensive golf links of close-clipped green grass, a small stream and golfers going about their pursuit. So that was a very rewarding little adventure. Going along the main highways it is not always possible to tell, when a road leads off at one side or another, whether it is a public road or a lane into some farmstead. And when one does start in on a strange piece of road, it is never possible to know in advance where it will take one in its course. So far I have secured no road map of the counties in which I walk. Do not know if such maps are in existence or not. At any rate I say "amen" to all who extol the wisdom and virtue of walking over God's solid earth to enjoy the sights, sounds, smells, and feels of country roadsides.

Kalendae Septembres, 1939   Started in reading Arthur E. Hertzler's book, "The Horse and Buggy Doctor." Received it recently as a substitute for the current September selection of the Book-of-the-Month club, it being a previous book of the month itself. I never paid a visit to Dr. Hertzler or his hospital at Halstead, Kansas, only fourteen miles from Hesston where we once lived, though some of our friends went to consult him for cases of special diagnosis. He had a considerable reputation in Kansas. The book is interesting to read, some points along the way being evidently overdrawn in the interest of making a rattling good narrative. Several things in it caught my interest so far. One is some descriptions of the ravages of diphtheria sixty and seventy years ago in this country, when sometimes whole families of small children were wiped out in a short time. In the time of the Civil War my grandfather Tobias Yoder, then living in Garrett County, Maryland, lost four out of the five they then had in a few days' time one August. For this reason descriptions of diphtheria ravages hold some interest for me. Another interesting point was Hertzler's incidental tribute to the value of Latin and Greek, especially the latter, for those preparing to study medicine. Hertzler grew up in Kansas, and he states his parents were Mennonites, who, as Melvin Gingerich in his book on Mennonites in Iowa notes, once lived in Lee County, Iowa, for a time.

Occasionally editor-in-chief of the Gospel Herald brings around a slip of paper some subscriber has sent in with a "query" on it, to be answered in the columns of the weekly paper. Today I handed him a 1500-word answer to the latest one handed to me. Some of the questions are intelligent ones, others are merely childish. I cannot always write answers that satisfy in every word the tastes and ideas of the editor. I usually try to give a rounded out, too comprehensive and too philosophical answer, but they seem to pass muster.

Over last weekend and even into this week Dr. Ernst Correll from American University, Washington, D. C., visited in Scottdale. Have known him since 1925 from days when he was almost a fresh émigré from Germany. He came for a personal conference with H. S. Bender and myself over plans for finishing the work of publishing a major opus on Conrad Grebel of Zurich, begun already in 1924. Correll is a pleasing sort of personality, sociable, genial, rather vague and inexpeditious in getting work done as projected and planned. He took Sunday evening lunch with us and he and I spent the evening chatting about this and that. He is interested in books and ideas, especially in much that pertains to Mennonites, though not himself a Mennonite.

Dies Lunae, September 4, Labor Day, 1939 Work and occupation with us as usual. With many, a day of motoring on crowded highways, getting killed or injured in motor accidents. In Europe they are getting themselves killed too, once more, on the grand scale of war. Newspaper headlines and booming radio voices yesterday and Saturday reported that Hitler's forces were invading Poland, that England and France are declaring war on Germany. So to all appearances the dogs of military warfare are being unleashed and the world, large parts of it, is on its way to another blood bath. It is all rather depressing as one contemplates prospects. Yet there is no need to be totally discouraged, for worry and uneasiness and distress of mind do not prepare one to view events and meet practical effects of this World War II with intelligence and sanity.

Naturally one is reminded of the time just a month more than twenty-five years ago when World War I broke out. There were no radios then to fill the air with the bellowing and booming of so-called news and dispatches. I was in the rural area of Iowa at the time. During those early days of August, 1914, I was helping Joe Gingerich, one of our neighbors, operate his clover hulling outfit in a community several miles north of Kalona. Newspapers from Chicago or Iowa City brought the news of what was happening, usually a full day after printing, to our part of the country. No one guessed then what the next four years would bring.

September 7, 1939   This is a beautiful, fresh morning, one that makes a person glad to be alive and inclines one to praise the Great Maker of all things. Cool nights remind one that fall and cold weather are on their way to bring discomfort to the inhabitants of the house in which we live. In the winter we suffer discomfort from the cold here. The heating is inadequate and the house is not built to keep out wind and cold and it is exposed to the blasts of the most persistent and prevailing winds that come roaring from the southwest along the front side of the mountain ridges just to the east of here.

Last week's Saturday Review of Literature has several unusually good articles. One is a preview of a book on "Henry Thoreau" to be published in a month by Henry Seidel Canby. Judging from this sample, I feel this volume is to be on my list of "must" purchases some time. I am a kind of secret admirer of Thoreau and his philosophy. The other important article is by Irwin Edman on "Man's Humanities to Man," a title in parody of the more common, "man's inhumanity to man" as a characteristic of modern economic and social practice. The article is a description of the present trend in some academic centers to turn students loose at reading the great classics of the humanistic tradition of Western culture.

September 11, 1939   Finished reading "The Horse and Buggy Doctor." A good book on the whole. The writer has a gruff and blunt exterior, reflected in his style of writing and in his habits of thought. One cannot help feeling or at least suspecting that some of his hard-boiledness is just an extra flourish added to his style for effect's sake. He takes his flings at preachers, churches, conventions, and so on, but they are not convincing, more or less conventional in themselves. But underneath the gruff exterior, and shining through it plainly in many places, is a genuine dyed-in-the-wool honesty, sincerity, idealism that gives the book its real merit. The old fellow has a deep and profound regard for children and child-life, an unmistakable passion for relieving suffering in human beings, a keen understanding of human nature and human problems that lie deeper than the physical body. He shows exquisite respect for human personality, but feels only disgust for sham and hypocrisy. He ends up with a strong plea for the medical practitioner as a human friend and counsellor. He is of course against modern ideas of group medical practice. If this comes, then the old type of family doctor with his possibilities for intimate sympathy and understanding will be a thing of the past. The psychiatrist will then be more of a necessity. My idea is that the trained religious advisor and counsellor would be able to best take over the psychological side of the old family doctor's work. It is true, of course, that serious and skilled psychiatrists come around more and more to the importance of personal religion in personality and emotional adjustments. The old style doctor, whom Dr. Hertzler represents so well, succeeded in doing much "healing" that skilled pastors should be able to do, if they could get as close to the suffering as the old doctor did.

Our friend M. C. Lehman of Goshen, Indiana, visited in town yesterday, being with us here for lunch in the evening. He is still searching for a position for the coming year. Hope he finds something, for he deserves some consideration at the hands of fate. He preached at the church both morning and evening, really the most uplifting and inspiring sermons perhaps that we have heard for some time here. That kind of homilies are not the rule here. One preacher does as a rule put real work, study and preparation into his discourses, and sometimes embodies real spiritual food. The other's discourses scarcely have any crumbs of fresh thought or ideas that do not smell of fifty years ago, and are worn so thin and ragged as to be of little spiritual potency. One of my friends once characterized him as an ethical preacher, and that term describes very well about his forte. All his sermons have the same age-old pattern. Whatever may be the starting point or the topic, he always gets around to matter of doing so-and-so, doing this way and not doing like the world, keeping away from such-and-such places and these-and-those practices. It is unkind to find fault or to blame him. He is too old to make any changes in his thinking or his mental patterns or to get any new ideas. The absence in his ministrations of what I consider reverent reserve and dignity of procedure is often fatal to one's desire for worship and devotion. More than likely I could do worse than either, if I had to carry on public ministrations, so why should I grumble.

The war in Europe goes on; we find out little about it. I would not subject myself to the nervous shock and tension of listening to news over the radio at present for anything. Five or ten minutes a day with a newspaper is plenty for me. The shock of the outbreak sets off afresh such folks as are emotionally unstable and makes some want to prove to all and sundry that Christ is going to be here right soon. A lady stopped in Sunday noon to ask me about it. I listened to her talk and mostly played "stupid," for I have no affinity for such excited and sensational talk, for it brings into disrepute the truth.

September 19, 1939 On Sunday we had guests at our house, Ruth and Ralph Bender all afternoon, Mr. and Mrs. Roy Umble for evening lunch. Virgil is fond of "company" at our house and he frequently asks when we will have company again. He goes to second grade in school now. Has a spelling book he brings home evenings and says he knows all the words as they come. During recent months he has become map and geography conscious. He has a small U. S. map of his own and while Ruth and Paul Benders were on their auto trip to the west coast and back, they sent him a picture folder every three or four days, till he has thirteen. He learned to locate the places on his map and followed their route as they went. He wanted to know last week how many maps I have, so we got out the fifteen large maps saved up from the National Geographic Magazine, which he spread out on the living room floor, all there was room for, and wanted me to look at them with him and talk about them. He also has a ten-inch globe which he often studies and uses.

Pridie Kalendis Octobris, Dies Saturni, 1939 September has come to its end – nearly. So far we have escaped building fire in the furnace, the heater, as men say around here. Last year artificial heat in the house was necessary for comfort already ten days before this time. Rain in the air this afternoon precludes the possibility of a ramble in the open country.

The last such ramble was on Thursday of last week, a most beautiful afternoon, and new unfamiliar stretches of country road north and west of here made that jaunt highly enjoyable. Happened upon Zion Lutheran and Reformed Church not far from Alverton, surveyed casually the adjoining cemetery, copied an interesting epitaph from 1827 as follows:

> Remember Man As You Pas by
> As You Are now so wonst was i
> And as i am so must You be
> Prepair for deth and follow me.

The oldest dated marker that I saw was 1814. Some of the oldest markers are inscribed in the German language. The names Licthi (Leighty, Lichte) and Hough occur very frequently, also Snider (Schneider), a few Weavers. I noted today that the oldest marker in the southeast corner of Scottdale cemetery is dated 1813. In the Zion burial ground many old graves are marked with rough, unhewn slabs, and to judge from the uneven, sunken ground in places, many others were not marked at all.

The present year and month reminds me that it was thirty years ago somewhere along the middle of this month that I took the step of standing up in evangelistic meeting at East Union Church near Kalona, Iowa, as a preliminary to becoming a Christian and uniting with the Church at that place. In July of that year I happened to attend an evening service, where Bishop Warye invited anyone to join the class of candidates and be received into the church at that time. The idea struck home with me. I remember with what trepidation and misgiving I ventured to ask mother the next morning whether I might go to East Union and receive baptism that day. Mother took it very hard that I should think of joining any church other than theirs where I had always attended. Three months later when I felt the time was right to start my application for church membership at East Union, I proceeded without asking anything further about it. I was baptized on a Sunday morning, October 24. Mother was reconciled, though she seemed to regret my step for some time.

October 8, 1939 Warm weather now, although a week ago heat from the furnace was necessary for comfort for several days. Last Wednesday afternoon was fine for an outing on foot. Mine took me to Pennsville, to Country Club, to Wooddale and Mt. Vernon Park and return to Scottdale, probably twelve miles. Stopped a few minutes at Wooddale Grange grounds where a community fair was in progress, called the Bullskin Township Fair, in Fayette County. Was having some little difficulty with my running gear, or feet.

October 20, 1939 Indian summer days are here again. Three heavy frosts fell last week and early this week. The woods are putting on their gaily colored fall robes and dresses. The outdoors is nearly every day beckoning and calling for its devotees to walk abroad and enjoy the beauties of the season. For farmers the lack of moisture is an unwelcome feature of this autumn season. No rain of any real consequence has fallen for several months here. The percentage of sunshiny days has been unusually large.

In reminiscing over past experiences whose anniversaries come along, I recall that twenty-five years ago this month I was convalescing from operation for abdominal hernia. The surgeons did their work on one of the last days of September. They came to our home in the country and did their job as a piece of what Dr. Arthur Hertzler in his book calls "kitchen surgery." Dr. Stutzman of Kalona was the attending physician and Dr. Whiteis of Iowa City, as I remember his name, was the surgeon. Alice Kempf of Kalona was the nurse in attendance on that day and for one or two weeks after that. That experience came at what was for me an inconvenient time. I had just two months before begun to earn income for myself, for July 30 had marked the beginning of my legal independence. Besides, for a year or two before that I had calculated and planned that I would enter school at Hesston, Kansas to continue my higher education. Then to have medical expenses sufficient to consume about all I could earn between July and January, when I had all plans set in my mind to leave home and begin making my way through high school and college, that was a serious disappointment. But by dint of determination and grim resolution the hopes and plans became a reality, though under handicaps greater than I had anticipated. With any lesser degree of determination, the unlooked for obstacle might have diverted me entirely from the course of getting an education. Father was not in sympathy with my purposes, and he even offered to pay the medical costs I had incurred in return for my winter's choring on the farm, if I would consent to remain at home and engage in farming on a partnership basis with him. But the offer made no impression on this obsessed young fellow. I paid the costs myself and went to Kansas in January too.

October 26, 1939 Virgil is in bed asleep. Mother went in the car with Miss Ruth Ressler to hear a lecturer in Pittsburgh. There has been rain last night and yesterday and the temperature is high for this time of year.

Came a short friendly letter the other day from a former student of mine, one of the Latin majors at Goshen College a few years ago, Mary Esch. She asked if I had seen a recently published book of poetry by Louis Untermeyer in which he translates some Odes from Horace. Have not seen the book, but noticed reviews of it I think. Miss Esch is one young student who entered into the spirit and got an appreciation of the Latin authors we read in college classes. She was apt in Latin, and Greek too, for that matter. Somehow she was able to grasp a Latin author's meaning and was not squeamish about translating frankly such passages as appear a bit delicate in English dress. Three young women read Horace most of a year, and they really appreciated his Odes. Horace, Vergil, and Cicero were authors I always loved to teach in college courses. For several years translating Horace has been an occasional hobby of mine. Began with Book One of the Odes and am now well along in Book III. There is a quality about his Odes that is delightful reading and translating. His sane and reasonable outlook upon life and its activities is very healthful and healing to one's spirit, and I enjoy going over his Odes repeatedly.

Sometimes I have a feeling that I try to do too much current reading and deprive myself of opportunity to do extensive reading and rereading of Latin and Greek authors, and English classical authors as well.

Which of the two kinds of reading is relatively more profitable is a question. It is a principle of mine to constantly do some translating from foreign languages into English; only not enough gets actually done to be really profitable for maintaining and improving my style of English writing. In the last ten years, little by little, some translating has been done. All of the Satires of Juvenal have been roughly turned into English prose, one book of Pliny's Letters, a few of Seneca's Epistles, a play of Terence, some poems of Catullus, a little in Lucian, and so on. It is enjoyable work as pastime occasionally, but should be made a serious and regular part of one's weekly schedule.

One job that has been waiting for seven or more years, which is at last practically done, is the pasting of over four hundred Literary Digest Art Covers, gathered from 1921 to 1932, into scrapbooks. A year ago Mr. Cutrell of the bindery department in the Publishing House made up ten scrapbooks of one hundred or more pages each. Eight of these are filled with the Digest Covers. The vast majority had a clipping with them giving some information about the artist or the picture reproduced. In a few cases I had carelessly missed making the clipping. For those cases I went to the Scottdale and Connellsville Libraries to copy from the bound volumes the overlooked clippings. In some other cases no information was given in the Digest about the picture. In such cases I searched for data on the artist in Who's Who in America, old and current volumes, in Readers' Guide and Encyclopedias. I finally found some data on all but perhaps a half dozen of the artists whose reproductions are pasted in the books. There is one book containing paintings on American history, mostly by Mr. Ferris. Another has reproductions mostly of classical foreign painters. The last six are all by modern or comparatively recent artists, mostly Americans. Each of the three groups are arranged alphabetically for the most part. The last ones have no table of contents in front. Some kind of lettering on outside will be needed to finish off the job. Then they will be ready to serve the boy's need if he becomes interested in studying paintings; anyway he will have some chance to educate himself in the enjoyment and appreciation of them.

Several other published collections of pictures have come into our possession in recent months. "A Treasury of Art Masterpieces" in full color, 144 of them, from early Italian to modern American, in an eight-pound book, came through subscription at the pre-publication price of $8.50, instead of ten dollars later. It is a fine "art gallery," though reviewers of the work have managed to find some faults in it. Thomas Craven is the author, writing a one-page discussion of every picture and its painter. Another portfolio by the same compiler, "One Hundred American Prints," came as a book dividend from the Book-of-the-Month Club in September. They are prints of etchings and lithographs, some good and others very modernistic and impressionistic, but worth having as a gift volume. Through the Pittsburgh Post-Gazette, I got a portfolio of about fifty reproductions of masterpieces with accompanying lectures on the artists. These cost only five or six dollars all told. Latest investment in art at our house is a signed, hand-colored lithograph print entitled "Wild Flowers," by Grant Wood. It came ready framed from the Associated American Artists of New York City, for a sum of $13.25. It is a fine piece, and we enjoy it much. Just a few more prints for hanging on walls will fit us out with pictures for the time being.

November 9, 1939   The war in Europe is mostly at a standstill, from a military standpoint, though diplomatically and other ways it seems to be going on as usual. Hitler claims that Germany cannot make peace because she was tricked and deceived into a false peace by England in 1918, when England gave out the lie that if Germany would stop fighting all Europe would disarm, just boundaries and colonial possessions would be fixed and a League of Nations would set up machinery for preserving peace. On the other side English leaders declare they will not consent to any appeal for peace from Hitler, because his word and promise are worth nothing, since he has officially lied about his intentions a half dozen times in recent years. So with the pot and the kettle calling each other black it is not very hopeful that a peace will be made soon. And the winter season will preclude any major military engagements on land for some months.

It is very depressing to read discussions on the supposed philosophy and faith of National Socialism as expounded by the Nazis. Some want to make out that it is a profoundly revolutionary philosophy, amounting to nihilism. Much of the discussion is based on reputed quotations from Hitler's "Mein Kampf" to show that lying and deceit is a professed part of his creed, that the German race must dominate and rule the world, that Christianity as well as Judaism must be destroyed. It appears that pure force and violence are supposed to prevail and hold sway over all that Christianity and liberal culture has built up and cherished through the centuries. A recent book by an ex-Nazi, named Rauschning, is being much discussed in reviews and digests at present in which this nihilistic aspect of Nazism is played up. It seems incredible that the whole western world would fall for such a suppression of spiritual, cultural, and personal values as is implied in these discussions. One would certainly think that people would in the end revolt against it, and if faith in God and His revealed Word is anywhere near the truth, it would seem impossible that naked force and brutality and oppression could for long triumph. On the contrary, I feel that no Christian should identify Western Christendom with the cause of God and His Kingdom. Maybe much that we cherish as civilization and culture is doomed to perish as dross. Doubtless many social and economic changes of a radical nature are already overdue. Certainly the materialistic and humanistic elements in modern liberalism are making the whole thing bankrupt and impotent. What will come out of the world revolution that is certainly already under way, no one can predict. All attempts to destroy religion are absurd gestures, often tried before and doomed again to fail. The forms and institutions connected with religion may well be changed, but they are not religion.

Dies Solis, November 19, 1939   Temperatures have been pleasantly and welcomely moderate during the past week; three days of uninterrupted sunshine in succession is almost like making a record for this season of the year. Failed to get out more than one-half day because of special extra work in the form of preparing essays or speeches, one for a program near Johnstown of a Peace Conference on this coming

Thursday, and the other near Lancaster in two weeks at an annual meeting of Sunday school officers and teachers.

This fall we invested five dollars in a season ticket to the lecture course put on by the Pittsburgh Academy of Art and Science. Nearly every Thursday evening from November to March they sponsor a lecture at the Carnegie Music Hall, and a season ticket admits two persons to them all. Many are very good and desirable lectures. So far this year Estie went once and we both went another time, each time going with Ruth Ressler in her car. It is too much travelling to go every time, but usually there are folks who will gladly use the ticket we own and help finance Miss Ressler's trip. On the evening we went a Mr. Brian lectured and showed pictures on Poland. He was in Poland when the war there began and showed scenes of the destruction in and about Warsaw. It was remarkable, for he just happened to be there and in some way which he failed to explain was able to take pictures and get them out of the country after the German occupation.

This coming Thursday there will again be some lecture on there, planned before President Roosevelt juggled the Thanksgiving Day date, which now also comes this week. I see by the local paper something about a Community Forum at Greensburg, which presents lecturers during the winter. For tomorrow evening they announce William Lyon Phelps of Yale to speak on "The Philosophy of Life." Would much like to hear Professor Phelps speak some time. His writings are very pleasing to read. Lately he has published some kind of autobiography, a work which has been widely and favorably reviewed in various periodicals. He seems to have a sane type of philosophy, and a very genial personality. I have one of his books, entitled "Human Nature in the Bible." It is mostly a presentation of some outstanding characters in the Bible as seen through the keen eyes of one who has observed and studied human nature for many years. His knowledge of the Bible is not inconsiderable.

This evening closes the two weeks of evening services at the church. E. M. Yost of Greensburg, Kansas, has been preaching during most of this time. He is an unusually fine type of evangelist for our church group, though he did grow up in the Holdeman sector of the Mennonite Church. He has the platform ability of a C. F. Derstine. We had him as our guest for supper on Thursday evening of this past week.

November 29, 1939 Weather continues pleasant, like fall, sunshiny, without strong insistent winds. Nearly all fall it has been reasonable weather, so much so that we can well use two Thanksgiving Days for giving all the thanks which we ought to give for the weather and for all other uncounted blessings. In my last notes I noted the lecture by Professor Phelps at Greensburg as coming, with the intimation that I would like to hear him speak. Next morning Mr. Alderfer called at my office to tell me about it and solicit my interest in going in a motor car to hear it. He would telephone and have Elam Hernley, who works as a typesetter in Greensburg, procure the necessary tickets for our admission. Gladly I embraced this opportunity to make this trip. Mr. Zook took us in his car, Floyd Shank being the fourth passenger. Yet more good fortune was in store for us. Mr. Hernley happened to secure the use of four complimentary and unused tickets for our party.

So we paid nothing to hear a seventy-five-cent lecture number. The lecture was good though nothing profound. Very sensibly Phelps defined "Living" as "Being in relations." He went on to illustrate at length some of the relations everyone should and can cultivate to make his living richer and fuller. He is an interesting personality, but no spell-binding speaker.

On last Thursday, Thanksgiving Day in this state and in several dozen others who took President Roosevelt's suggestion that the occasion be stepped up by one week over the traditional date, spent the day at Stahl Church near Johnstown, sitting through three sessions of a Peace Conference, not one to make peace, but one to keep people in a state of peace in spite of present and future states of war in the world. This was only my second visit in that section of the state. Most impressive were the mountain-like hills with steep slopes, which are nevertheless subjected to cultivation by more tenacious farmers than a son of Eastern Iowa would make. For some slopes are at such an angle to the horizon that it appears as though men and machines could literally roll off, if by some accident they might happen to get started. Following a habit of mine, I walked out to explore the surroundings between sessions. Behind and above the church is a small, neatly kept cemetery. Surveying the names inscribed on the markers, my attention was suddenly arrested by the name Christ Pfeil. I had often heard my father speak of a contract carpenter by that name with whom he had worked at the building trade before he married. I knew the man later went to Kansas and died there from a fall off a barn roof. Upon inquiry from Bishop Shetler, I found this was the very man. The little discovery added interest to my trip and to that place, a little more of Phelps' "being in relations."

December 13, 1939 December 1 - 4 had a pleasant outing trip to Lancaster County of this state. A. J. Metzler drove through by motor car and offered the opportunity to ride along. The driving distance is about 225 miles. Stopped with Menno Millers in Millersville over Friday night, and enjoyed their kind hospitality. They are both acquaintances from earlier days when they were students at Goshen College. Saturday I spent at the Mellinger's Mennonite Church five or six miles east of the city of Lancaster. Appeared on the platform three times for shorter and longer exhibits. Hope I satisfied the people there, for from various intimations I gathered that one reason my presence was called for at that time and place was because the Sunday school workers of Lancaster County district wanted to get a look at the latest editor of the Advanced S. S. Lesson Quarterly. They are probably satisfied by the exhibition, and hope they are satisfied with my speech making, so they need not call upon me to repeat the effort. The main tour de force on my part that day was the reading of an essay on "Profitable Bible Reading." When the matter was first broached to me, the hint came with it that they would appreciate some discussion on the various versions of the English Bible, including something that would shut the mouths of certain enthusiasts who in that part have been proclaiming the superiority of the so-called modern versions and translations. My first response was that I could not serve with good and honest conscience in such a project, for I used and believed in the use of different versions of the English Bible.

Well, their desire for their planned exhibition evidently overcame their desire to have the Authorized Version extolled above all others, and they told me to come and speak on whatever subject I might choose. I told them I liked their subject, and gave them some idea of what I would present in discussing it. The committee on arrangements made no further suggestions, printed their programs and I appeared at the appointed time. The effort and the personal response did not leave me disheartened, in fact, I felt I made rather a clever defense of the use of several English versions of the Bible side by side. Not so long ago Mennonite preachers used to read the English and the German versions side by side, compared them with each other, and gained in their insight into divine truth by this method. Today there is danger that Mennonites become shut up to the exclusive use of a single version of the Bible, a practice which would result in a decided loss. Moral: Use at least one or two other versions along with the A. V., for a better approach to the truth of God's Word. Some people got the force of that comparison, I feel sure.

A visit to Lancaster County is a treat from one point of view. Everywhere one goes the villages, farms, streets of towns present a bright, cheery, clean, spick-and-span appearance. Houses are all painted up nicely, shutter blinds are used on all wooden houses and sometimes on brick and stone houses, and these are always painted another color from the house walls. The style of architecture in houses is more consistent in general than here, where there is only a nondescript variation in house styles. Here too houses have been so long unpainted that they make town and countryside appear drab and dull and depressing in comparison. In this part of the state nothing is kept neat and clean and tidy, roadsides littered with papers and general refuse, banks of streams made unsightly with tin cans and all manner of discarded trash, vacant lots ragged and unkempt – the contrast is certainly most marked.

Besides the Millers in Millersville, I saw and visited other friends at Ephrata and Akron on Sunday. Spent Saturday night at Amos Horst's home in Akron. Abe Hallman took me along to the Ephrata church for morning service. Spent the afternoon at Hallman's. Visited briefly with Orie Miller in afternoon and for evening service Dwight Yoder took me to Stumptown Church. By previous arrangement I went with a minister to his home, David Landis by name, where I slept for five hours before the Metzler car came along to pick me up en route to Scottdale. Reached home before nine o'clock, none the worse for the trip and experience.

Last week went one evening to Pittsburgh with D. Alderfer to hear a man lecture and demonstrate on sound transmission and allied subjects. Walking has been limited more or less. One brief stroll took me around south to Owensdale and the old Pennsville Mennonite cemetery, where I examined more carefully the tombstone inscriptions for possible light on early history of the Mennonite settlement here. Another trip took me to West Overton where I looked at the Historical House which is kept as Henry Clay Frick's birthplace, whose mother's ancestors were Mennonites, by name Overholt.

Dies Solis, December 17, 1939   For a few weeks my schedule is taken up with miscellaneous items of varied nature, clearing decks for regular work on S. S. lessons. Will be starting on 26-lesson course in Gospel of Luke, a project which I anticipate with much satisfaction. Luke is a great favorite as a writer and personality, and the lessons from his Gospel will be several months of pleasant work.

Finished reading the book "In the Steps of the Master" by H. V. Morton. Liked it very much. Found many illuminating comments on incidents and sayings in the gospel Evangelists, which have been duly recorded as references in my folders on the study of the New Testament books. This writer has suggested indirectly both in the book on Paul and in this on Jesus the idea of myself sometime making a trip in Palestine, Syria, and Mediterranean lands generally as a kind of free lance traveller, going and coming by oneself, keeping out of the hands of professional guides, tourist groups, and the conventional travelling manner. From his descriptions of experiences in travelling in that way, one can see that for a person totally innocent of foreign travelling experience it would be rather difficult to travel in that way. Still for myself I should not care to travel in Palestine any other way. The distances in ancient Palestine are not so great but that walking would be possible. Expenses could perhaps be reduced by seeking out one's lodging in foreign hospices, YMCA headquarters, and so forth. Upon suggesting this idea once to H. S. Bender, he mentioned as one difficulty that of having to depend upon native food and cooking, which might require a pretty durable stomach. Only experience could prove whether mine could be equal to such an experience.

Am reading more intensively just now in Gibbon's "Decline and Fall of the Roman Empire." He is a fine stylist and one does not get tired of reading in his pages, also a vigorous thinker, independent and rather inclined to be dogmatic. I marvel at the breadth of the man's grasp and his skill in marshalling facts so as to make a readable narrative of such a vast, complicated subject. He is not particularly tender toward the sentiments of those who think conventional thoughts on religion and politics. He is refreshing and informing to read. I have his complete work in two thick volumes, each one running to 1300 pages or thereabouts. As I am not a rapid reader, particularly of material like that for I love to do some thinking as I read, it will take me quite a little time to get through the whole work.

December 22, 1939   Shortest day of the year; sun reached its farthest point south today. Twenty-four hours of ripping, roaring cold wind ended its blowing during the day, and winter is officially here for three months to stay. The sun barely peeped through the clouds during past three or four days. Today with its shortest course to run, it never showed its face until just about time to set, and then how ashamed and embarrassed it was for having hidden away so long, for was its face ever red! Then away to the southwest, what seemed more south even than west, it dipped behind the hills, not without promise of hoping to show its face more tomorrow than it has done lately.

Christmas shopping and activities fill the atmosphere with the holiday spirit and add a touch of cheer to the days now. Ruth Bender is here for a few days until after Christmas Day. Virgil has the habit of expecting and demanding a Christmas tree every year, and he and I together went down street yesterday and procured one, a small one for on a stand. Trees for Christmas were never a part of my experience of the day, and only in the most recent years have we been having one. It all started three or four years ago at Goshen through Ruth's planning and initiative together with the Boy's. It doubtless adds something to his joy and happiness on the Day and we indulge him for the occasion.

The House treasurer's assistant today brought around Christmas presents in the form of an envelope bearing a holiday greeting card and a currency note, for five dollars in my case and two dollars in Wife's case. It is a generous token from one's employer.

Sent a few gifts to Iowa. Our family has followed the plan of each one drawing the name of some one other person to whom he makes a gift, which is more sensible than each one buying something for everyone else. So we sent three gifts to Iowa, one from each of our family. At home such articles are given and received between ourselves as are needed articles for use. That is one way of getting some extra fun out of spending from the family income. Virgil once some time ago suggested making a "bed" for Ressler's little dog, Penny, to sleep in. So I am making a bedstead for him so the dear creature need not sleep on the floor any longer.

The Christmas season means somewhat more in our home since the boy is here growing up. The celebrative festivities mean more to a child than to sophisticated grown-ups, and even to us they mean more in seeing a child's joy and happiness on the occasion. Again "a little child shall lead them." But I note that Editor Trumbull of S. S. Times warns against misquoting this verse to apply to anything else but the future millennial age and the conditions to prevail there!!

Christmas Day, 1939 Cold and blustery out-of-doors. Dinner preparations on an unusual scale are in process in the kitchen with a large goose as the chief center of cooking for dinner consumption. As guests the three Ressler ladies are expected, and also Ralph Bender and Ruth, who is already here these several days. Yesterday afternoon Christmas packages were opened amid much glee and exclamation on the part of everyone concerned. Boy Virgil has plenty of things just now with which to amuse himself, mostly with a toy farm outfit, barn, fences, sheds, and some animals, though Sears Roebuck and Company failed to send the toy animals and implements which were advertised to come with the outfit which was ordered.

Among the gifts we gave to Ruth Bender was a copy of the newest edition of the Smith-Goodspeed Bible. Rather ambitiously it is called "The Whole Bible," a title which to some might invidiously suggest that the ordinary English Bibles are not the whole Bible. This one includes the so-called Apocrypha, representing literature that came between the Old and New Testaments. Fundamentalists are very positive that they are no part of the Bible at all. Main reasons for so thinking are that they are not part of the Hebrew Bible, because they were written in Greek and came into modern Bibles through the Septuagint and its Latin translation. The other alleged reason is that Jesus quoted from many books of the Old Testament, but never from any apocryphal book. Professor Goodspeed who has newly translated the Apocrypha for this edition of "The Whole Bible," credits the Puritans for expelling these extra books from the printed English Bibles, following a lead given by Luther, who arranged them in a group at the end of the Old Testament. It is interesting to note that Menno Simons seems in his writings to quote from the apocryphal books on the same basis and in the same spirit as he does from any other Old Testament book.

It would seem as if the extreme and dogmatic position on the difference between canonical and noncanonical books of the Bible, as also the extreme position on verbal and literal inspiration, are comparatively recent developments in biblicism, say, within the past two or three centuries. It is possible that due to pressure from the rationalistic and sceptical schools of philosophy, or at least as a defense maneuver against them, the Christian apologists and defenders of the faith took up an extreme position on these points, a position that is almost one of falling over backwards, and one that cannot in the long run be maintained, and is unnecessary once the philosophical climate changes again, as it certainly will. Meanwhile the overemphasis on Biblical inspiration may be keeping numbers of fair-minded persons from honestly and candidly examining the claims and merits of the Christian faith on its merits. Some would go so far as to say that all doctrinal discussion must begin with an article on inspiration of the Scriptures; but then the cart seems to be before the horse.

Pridie Kalendis Januariis, 1939 In a few more hours a new year is scheduled to appear. The year 1939 is supposed to expire as a gray-bearded old man with the last grain of sand trickling through his hourglass, or is it a year-glass, and newborn naked infant named 1940 is to take his place. It is a nice idea, and one that may comfort some people a good deal. Time does march on in ceaseless procession, and along with the tide is said to wait for no man. There is no virtue in designating the next few hours as 1939, and then suddenly marking their successors as 1940, excepting an accidental convention. Still it is an encouragement to feel that the past is past now and a new and unsoiled page lies before one. If the past could be made really past as easily as turning over the leaf in a book, then human problems would quickly find their easy solutions. It is nevertheless well for one to face the future at times with a new outlook and a new faith.

During the past week our entertainment of "company" included, on Monday which was Christmas Day, Ruth and Ralph Bender, Lina, Rhoda, and Ruth Ressler. Mrs. Yoder and Ruth B. "cooked the goose" and we enjoyed feasting on the product of their skill and effort. On Wednesday at noon a family of old time neighbors and friends from Kansas were our guests: Mrs. James Kauffman and three of her children, Melva, Daniel, and Bobby. The young people appreciated some records on the Victrola, especially numbers from the Messiah. In the evening of the same day, John C. Wenger from Goshen College sat at table with us. He was in Scottdale for the day on committee business.

Winter in good style descended upon us on last Wednesday when six or eight inches of snow fell. Only a slight wind from the east allowed it to fall and get packed without drifting. Not very cold and windless

days followed, until today the wind blew cold and ugly from the southwest, so that it was impossible to be comfortable in the house where
we live.

January 14, 1940 Sunday school lessons for fourth quarter of 1940 are
being prepared now. Inclement weather unsuitable for out-of-door tramping has kept the editor at home and by diligent application he hopes to
produce copy for three or four lessons weekly until first quarter for
1941 may be completed by March 10 or thereabouts, about the time it
may be possible to begin spring rambles.

The House management is waiting for me to get to work on reor-
ganizing and systematizing the House library collection, largely consisting of material on Mennonite history and literature. John Horsch
has collected the books and organized them in his own personal way,
and in general has managed the collection more or less as a personal
collection. Result: it is fairly serviceable to him, but not very useful
for anyone else in its present condition. In fact Horsch has several
hundred of the essential books at his own home, where he does his
work for the most part. Just how to make the necessary changes so
long as he is here and working is a serious problem in procedure.

A letter from Howard Gnagey, brother-in-law in Iowa, inquired
whether we wanted to buy Father's Ford V-8 of 1936 vintage at the
price of $250 or less. Unfortunately, or fortunately, we do not have
use for a car often enough to justify the trouble and expense of keeping one, so we are not buying this one or any other. Some people
waste pity on us for being carless, trying to make one feel as if being
carless were about as unconventional as going about pantless, or minus
some similar article of apparel. But such psychology has no effect at
our house at all. Why should one profess nonconformity as a special
article of faith and then encumber himself with things just because all
the Joneses and Smiths do?

At our house we have been making a number of capital investments
this fall and winter, so that cash savings have not been able to accumulate very fast. About December 1 we traded our washer of 1930 purchase at $99 for a new Easy Washer priced at $59.50. Aaron Brilhart
offered to allow the sum of $20.50 for the old one in exchange, which
offer we accepted. So Estie has a washer at least as good as the old
one ever was for $39 cash outlay. Some months ago she saw a set of
dinner dishes that just suited her exactly as to pattern, number of pieces,
quality, etc. For several years past she had been watching stores for a
suitable dinner set. Relatives in Iowa nineteen years ago gave us an
ordinary set for a wedding present, and aside from occasional pieces
and supplementary pieces we never did buy many dishes for table use.
Well, this set was just right, a set of service for twelve persons, of
ninety-four pieces, and marked down from $69 to $49. Happening to be
in Connellsville on January 5, I took a look at the set, and thought it
suitable too, and besides now marked down to $42.50. The news of this
new low figure set the pot a-boiling, and a few days later the lady of
the house travelled to the store, paid the price, and ordered the set delivered at 607 Walnut Avenue, in Scottdale. So a few days ago they came
and were installed in the cupboard in the kitchen. Now we can feed
guests in style and dignity, provided we can put on the dignity and re-

finement that must go with such a set of dishes. If guests were all like myself, the food would be the more important part of dinner entertainment.

Editor Trumbull of the Sunday School Times still indulges his penchant for making sly insinuations against those whom he chooses to pronounce blind as to their understanding of the Bible. Someone wrote in to inquire what kind of a ruler the Times talks about when it speaks of someone some day ruling the earth with a rod of iron; is it a Hitler or a Mussolini or a Stalin they have in mind; surely it cannot be the divine Son of God? The editor went on to explain with a tone of finality and superiority, unalleviated by any expression of modesty or humility that the Times in common with all who believe the Bible (sic!) holds that the Lord Jesus Christ will Himself rule the world with a literal rod of iron, bringing order out of chaos, etc., etc. Also recently a brief editorial paragraph gave some sentiments on "freedom," commenting on the puerility of all modern ideas of freedom of thought and assuring all like-minded people that during Christ's reign in the millennium there will be no freedom to think false and erroneous ideas and promulgate the same; everybody will be compelled to think right, which by implication, will be just like Mr. Trumbull and his kind now think and believe. Evidently he believes in fascism when it regiments people according to his pattern. One looks in vain in Trumbull's writings for any hint of humility or modesty of expression, making room for the possibility that he might himself at times be in error. A cartoon lately showed a man looking into a telescope (the Bible) pointed in the direction of certain prophetic fulfillments, and unable to see a millennium and related things, because he had hung his hat (of unbelief) over its outer end.

January 22, 1940 Old Man Winter has just delivered us his second and worst sock on the jaw. First week in January saw cold reaching within four or six degrees of zero, but this time the mercury dropped to six below and scarcely rose above zero at all for forty-eight hours. Today sunshine returned, if it will really stay now for a time. Atmosphere feels more comfortable than for about a week. Severe cold was general over the middle west with numerous deaths reported due to exposure and overheated houses burning down. Evidently we kept as warm in our leaky house as some other people who live in the modern apartments on the upper story of the Publishing House. On Saturday the complaint was widespread, even in the offices that there was not enough heat on hand for comfort.

February 4, 1940 A slight break in the backbone of winter seems to be evident at last. Temperature reported this morning at twenty-two degrees Fahrenheit, the highest morning temperature for some time. Our coal bin was completely exhausted on February 1, or rather on the day before already. Even at that it held out very well, considering the heavy assaults of Old Winter during the month of January.

Did a great deal of intensive work on S. S. Lessons during January, working ahead, so as to have leisure time later for extra walking and out-of-door exploring. Three and four lessons a week came through the mill the last while, finishing last quarter of 1940 and starting first quarter of 1941. Lessons for those two quarters are from Luke, which is a favorite Gospel in many respects. The human and humane side of Christ is specially stressed; this side as Luke presents it has always made Jesus seem more like a real person than perhaps any of the other Gospel accounts. Three more weeks should see this series of lessons from Luke pretty well completed.

Weekly teachers' meeting held at the church on Sunday morning from 8:30 to 9:05, which was started October 1, 1939, continues to be fairly well attended and with some manifest interest. It is hard to judge of the degree of success and to know just the type of thing that should be attempted in such meetings.

Excursions away from home have been limited to trips to Pittsburgh for evening lectures. Estie went early in January for one, and I went in on January 25. On this occasion Cleveland Grant gave a lecture on "Adventures in color with American Birds." He showed Kodachrome pictures, all of them taken since last May. These were uniformly very good, showing wonderful artistry and skill on the part of the man who captured them. In December I purchased from the National Geographic Society their two-volume Book of Birds. Virgil spends considerable time looking at its pictures and reading the legends printed beneath the pictures, enough of which he is able to grasp to learn some exciting facts about the birds. He is quite enthusiastic sometimes over them.

Extra reading has not been much during these weeks of intensive lesson writing. The end of the month always brings a concentrated shower of magazines, the reading of which fills up spare time for several weeks: Atlantic, Readers Digest, Religious Digest, National Geographic, Scientific Monthly, Classical Journal. Atlantic is still staple mental food. Two weeklies are perused regularly, Christian Century for Christian opinion on current world happenings, and Saturday Review for literary opinion and also some staple pabulum in up-to-date stylistic dress.

February 8, 1940 It is evening. Mother and Boy left for Pittsburgh to hear a lecture on Australia. After threatening us with another cold spell, Old Man Winter has had to retreat, for the air has suddenly warmed up again, perhaps in preparation for rain. The feel and look of approaching spring is in the air these days. Easter comes very early this year, being only about six weeks in the future. That may be a sign for an early season, or it may only give spring a false start, with an unpleasant set-back later. My feet and limbs are beginning to itch for the open roads, paths, and trails. When terra becomes firma again, snow has all disappeared, then the call of the out-of-doors will become irresistible.

Next weekend will take me on a trip by train to Goshen, Indiana, for several days. Committee sessions is the excuse for going. So long as no one discovers that I am not worth the expense of travelling to committee sessions, I am glad for the little excursion once or twice in a year. It is a bit of diversion and recreation, and there is a pleasure in exchanging greetings with some earlier associates and acquaintances again.

Today I wrestled with Luke, 16th chapter, in writing a Sunday School lesson on "Christian Attitudes toward Possessions." This involved an interpretation and exposition, at least in part, of the familiar story of the rich man and the beggar at his gate. All commentators, expositors, and writers I had at hand frankly spoke of this story as a parable, all excepting my predecessor in the office, who not only declared in his writing that it is the narrative of an actual occurrence, and factually described, but further made the invidious observation that persons who deny the eternal punishment of the wicked in hell like to define the story as a parable. All conservative and orthodox writers I examined, perhaps six or eight, spoke of it as a parable, and in one or two of them allusion was made to the other view, which it was stated had been held and taught by no less personages than Tertullian, Calvin, and James M. Gray! Inquiry of C. F. Yake as to House practice in interpretation of this passage revealed that the point had evidently been debated before with some heat, and that the uniform practice had been to teach that the passage is a narrative of fact. An appeal further to the supreme court of the House on doctrinal matters brought forth no hard and fast decision that it had to be emphatically taught that way. So we are referring to it indifferently as a parable or as a story, and placing the emphasis in its study where it appears to belong, on the direful results of selfish and self-centered living by those who have wealth, to the ignoring largely of detailed points of eschatological speculation. I am convinced that one definitely creates disrespect and disbelief in basic Bible teachings by stretching and twisting doubtful passages in trying to gain a little more textual support for a point that is assailed. The truth and certainty of the eternal punishment of the wicked does not stand or fall with Luke 16: 19-31, and an unreasonable appeal to this passage as a factual description of Hades weakens rather than strengthens the argument and proof for that truth.

February 24, 1940 Just a week ago I boarded the Pennsylvania Railroad train at Warsaw, Indiana, for the return trip home from Goshen, where two days were spent in committee sessions. The outward journey was made on Thursday before that. On the morning of that day, after a snowstorm that lasted more than twenty-four hours and left snow a foot or more deep all about us, I left Scottdale on the train for Pittsburgh. It was a beautiful sight, viewing the countryside from the train window. The snow perfectly white, fresh, and glistening. Trees and bushes loaded with thick snow, wires with either a load of snow riding on them, or thickly rimed with frost, and the sun just coming up over the eastern hills. It all made an unforgettable picture and was a wonderful feast for the eyes.

That evening I reached Goshen at about seven o'clock, where there was no snow at all. Stayed two nights at Paul Benders' house, and ate most of my meals with them at their table. On the return trip I slept on the coach cushions and soon after five in the morning was ready to get off at Greensburg. My thoughts were all set for a forty or fifty-minute wait for the first electric car to Scottdale. Then to my happy surprise, John Horst stepped up to me, having been in the Pullman from Chicago. He said he had his motor car stored in Greensburg and that I was welcome to ride home with him, reaching home at six o'clock.

Dies Lunae, March 11, 1940 Four weeks ago this afternoon there was sunshine, mild air, dry ground. Walked out for several hours. Saw a man plowing in the field. In spite of snow and slush in spots, it was a pleasant stroll. From that day until this one it has not been possible to get out. Today because the sun shone genially for a change, an outdoor tour from 3:15 to 5:45 was in order. The ground was solid enough to keep one on top most places. The wild and marshy woods along Jacob's Creek one and one-half miles west from here were interesting after an absence of so many weeks. Nothing green is showing up from its wintry bed, although there are signs that things are waiting and ready to grow as soon as they get a chance.

Casual interest in matters of local Mennonite history is growing on my part. Have started to go through the files of the Herald of Truth, from 1864 onward, and noting all references to Westmoreland and Fayette Counties. It is a very great pity that there was no such periodical in existence fifty or sixty years earlier. Original historical data on the development of the settlements in these counties are very hard to find or recover. There are county histories of some pretentious size and compass in existence, also biographical dictionaries for both counties. Considerable information on the early Mennonites of these counties is imbedded in these books, but is far from giving a complete picture of the history.

For some years it has been claimed for the Masontown community, that the first Sunday school in the Mennonite Church was held there by Bishop Nicholas Johnson. More recently evidence has been found and published to the effect that at Kitchener, Ontario, a S. S. was operated in 1840, the same year as was claimed for Masontown. The testimony for the Masontown date is conflicting. J. F. Funk in 1873, in writing a sketch of the bishop, Nicholas Johnson, then lately deceased, gave the date for the beginning of his S. S. as 1842. The testimony of J. N. Durr, now also deceased, and of J. B. Moyer, also deceased, from his mother's memory, both gave the date as 1840. All the testimony agrees in saying that Johnson's S. S. was entirely a private affair of his own for the first years of its existence.

The Historical Committee of Mennonite General Conference appointed John Horsch, Paul Roth, and myself as a special committee for ascertaining the facts, if possible, so that the proper bodies can engage in some kind of celebration of the completion of one century of S. S. work in the Mennonite Church. On this project I spent last Friday partly in Uniontown Public Library and partly at Masontown. There seems to be nothing specific to recover on the date of Johnson's S. S. at that place, and it would be the sheerest accident if any more direct evidence could be discovered at this late date. A. J. Metzler is also interested in the question as to which community was first entered by Mennonite settlers, around Masontown or in the area where Scottdale now is located. He suggested that while looking for historical data on the S. S. question, I might also gather historical information on the general early history of the communities in each section. He specially encouraged me when he learned that I was engaged in a little study of the Mennonite history of this area. It will be an interesting kind of hobby to follow at times partly as diversion, and partly as a contribution to the cause of historical knowledge in general. The sociological and religious phase of this community's history appear to me as being of considerable interest, although I do not know much about it as yet. Why the church here nearly died out at the end of one century of settlement? Another question might be: How much did the industrial development of this area affect the condition of the Mennonite Church here, the coal and coke industry in particular? Mennonites or their descendants seem to have figured prominently in the coal and coke industry, as also in the distillery business in these parts. All these matters will make interesting subjects of study, even if not specially profitable.

April 4, 1940   After three months of steady winter weather with much snow and cold, the weather man last week gave signs of changing to spring weather. Easter Sunday and Monday had been cold, only eight and ten above zero. Then by the end of that week the air was warm and balmy enough so as to leave the house warm with a cold furnace. This week the air is coolish again; a low fire in the heater keeps the chill away from the house. A very heavy rain fell last Saturday, beating down the frost-loosened topsoil and washing away debris of the winter's accumulation. A three-hours' tramp on Tuesday afternoon took me along a marshy place beside Jacob's Creek several miles west from here. Had almost to wade mud and slime left by the rain and high water of a few days before. Country roads were firm and dry; every gully and streamlet flowed with rippling, gurgling, musical water hurrying on its way to somewhere. The fields and farmyards smelled delicious to one whose memory recalls such odors from boyhood days on the farm. Farmers were plowing, and while nothing had really started growing, there were signs that vegetation was experiencing a ground swell and was only waiting for the first few warm days to burst out in all its green and luxuriant splendor.

On Good Friday (without the usual special respect one should perhaps show for the day) we spent afternoon and evening in Pittsburgh. Miss Ressler took the whole of our family along, as also two of the Cutrell young folks. First we went to see the Flower Show, which was well worth seeing, being held in a spacious municipal conservatory in Schenley Park. Next we spent some time in the Museum in Carnegie Hall. One could well visit this a number of times for a day at a time, to begin to see all there is there – classical art and architecture, natural history, Indian relics and antiquities, archaeological findings of numerous ancient peoples. There is also a collection of paintings to be seen. And a special feature at that moment was an exhibit of forty-four masterpieces of painting of the old masters from Europe. Last year these and perhaps other paintings were shipped from European art galleries to the U. S. A. specifically for exhibition at the World's Fair Expositions at New York and San Francisco. Before they could be sent back the war broke out in Europe, making the ocean unsafe for the transportation of such unique treasure. As a result these paintings are being kept in America, sent about and exhibited from place to place while marking time until they can be returned to their homelands again. So we were able to see real European art treasures in almost our next door house.

Finally in the evening of that day was the opening of the 27th annual Pittsburgh Salon of Photographic Art. This exhibition which began then is to be continued for a full month. There were three hundred twenty-four selected photographs on exhibition, all in large-sized prints. Some were in color, but most were in black and white. This we enjoyed greatly. Artistic photography seems to be growing steadily and some real good work is being done, according to what one can see at such an exhibition as this.

Miss Ressler has been very generous and accommodating in taking us into Pittsburgh for the lecture course this past winter. She refused to accept more than twenty-five cents per passenger trip from us for this favor, which made lecture attendance very reasonably priced culture and education for us. No record was kept as to how often we went, and the rumor is that the sponsoring Academy of these lectures has so much money on hand that next winter they will provide eighteen instead of fifteen lectures for the members.

April 16, 1940   Three days ago it was cold and snowing. Sunday morning we woke up to find about three inches of snow covering the ground.

Had company at our house on Sunday afternoon and evening. Miss Marion Charlton, of Williamsport, Maryland, an old school friend of twenty-five years ago at Hesston visited here. Her prospective husband, a widowed Mennonite deacon, was with her.

During this month my time is comparatively free for spontaneous and leisurely reading, thinking and writing. Sunday school quarterly copy is practically done for lessons up to April 1 of 1941. The work of rearranging the contents of the historical library is waiting temporarily for the coming of George Smoker, who will join the force at the House before long, upon the completion of his theological course of study in New York. He is supposed to be sort of handy man and second assistant in handling the library.

Read two pacifist books recently which were unusually good for their kind, in my opinion. One by Macgregor, entitled "The New Testament Basis of Pacifism." A very fine study and presentation, based quite largely on early books by C. J. Cadoux and by Heering, a Dutch pacifist writer. I recall with what joy and thrilling satisfaction I devoured and digested as best I could the books of these latter men about seven years ago. They are all "meaty" books which stimulate much hard thinking. This one by Macgregor is in the same vein and affected me very much. There are a few small points of theology which some may not agree with. Yet my feeling is that when a writer comes to such a fine, scriptural conclusion, that Christians on religious grounds should refuse all participation in war, then why should I object to the route he travelled in order to get there?

The second book is of a slightly different type, and yet is also good in its way: Muste on "Nonviolence in an Aggressive World." He gives much recognition to the religious basis of pacifism, although his handling of the Bible would by some be considered modernistic. His main thesis is that the world and its political affairs have today come to such an impasse that absolutely the only way out is the adoption of the nonviolent method for changing people and world condition which Jesus Himself used during His life. The author argues this point vigorously and even passionately. He discusses ways and means for making a beginning in that direction, one of which is absolute refusal to take part in war.

Another leisurely task that has long been waiting in my mind and which is receiving some time is a thorough study of the first epistle of Peter. For years I have wanted to practice more intensive and microscopic study of some books of the Bible. The chief impetus for this ambition came from hearing the delightful brief Bible studies which Rev. Paul Brosy, Lutheran pastor at Goshen, presented in the college chapel several different years a week at a time. His studies suggested to me the possibilities in such a method. One begins by reading and rereading as high as fifty times a single book in its original until its features and emphases and characteristics begin to stand out clearly in one's mind. Later comparative and exegetical studies can be made to whatever extent and degree one cares for. Now I am reading Peter, rather a simple book, yet very worthwhile for study. Have made a free running translation of my own in connection with the reading. The possibilities of the method are becoming apparent, for already certain ideas, words, phrases, points of view, are beginning to stand out from their repetition and rehearsal in different parts of the epistle. Peter's thought is not as deep and involved as Paul's, and his letter is a good training ground for practicing such a method of study.

Additional leisure time goes into the reading of a new book-of-the-month, "The Star Gazer," by a Hungarian writer, it being the biography, in fictional form, of the mathematician and astronomer Galileo.

Dies Lunae, Aprilis 22, 1940 Cool, damp, rain, rain, rain has been the weatherman's program for this month so far. Last Sunday again small snow flurries could be detected in the air early in the morning, and looking off eastward to the mountains ten miles away the open spaces showed up white all day, showing that snow had fallen. The coal supply in our basement has really been performing well, considering the persistent cold. Last week for several days we made no fire. The fuel will still last several weeks at present rate of using.

Very little chance to get out for walking the past weeks. Ground wet, one must stay on the solid road. One afternoon last week the clouds looked rather thin, thinner than for some time before. Hoping it would not rain for several hours at least, I set out at three o'clock for a little stretching of legs. In less than an hour precipitation started and continued and increased. A small coal shed at rear of a country church house afforded necessary shelter for good part of an hour. The heavy shower passed over and a lighter sky promised relief from soaking rainfall, sufficiently so to invite one to tramp for home by the shortest route. A kind-hearted farmer overtook me, and upon offering me a ride into town found himself hauling a hitch-hiker. Having several years ago experienced what it is to refuse a proffered ride when there is rain falling, I was glad to accept the man's kind offer.

Today the sky cleared — slowly, reluctantly, and perhaps surely — with a cool northwest breeze putting a chilly touch in the air. And tomorrow, if the clouds really stay away as they give promise to do, it will not be possible to keep my feet from seeking out some pleasant country roads and still unexplored parts, perhaps of Bullskin Township in Fayette County.

The reading of "The Star Gazer", life of Galileo, is completed. Very informing and interesting. It brings out the extreme difficulties under which a genius in seventeenth century Italy, as a Catholic country jealously watched over by the Inquisition, had to do his thinking, teaching, investigating, and writing. To our modern way of thinking it seems horrible that a man should be forced to swear solemn oath in the name of Jesus Christ and the Church to a lie in order to save himself from being burned at the stake. One's first impulse is to condemn the poor old man for saving his life for a few more years by such a price of integrity. Yet in the end one is not so sure whether it was the worst thing he could have done. It seems terrible that a Church should have taken such an attitude toward discovery and thought. Yet today that science which Galileo promoted has shattered the integrated mansion of thought and faith which sheltered men's souls; it has atomized society so that the individual souls are lonely, insecure, and often hopeless. Will the next phase of man's philosophy be a return to a religiously based social salvation?

Dies Solis, April 28, 1940 This has been a real, genuine, undoubted, dies Solis, for the sun did actually shine from its rising till its setting, bright, genial, warm, cheering, and welcome. Yesterday too was a sunny day. The two days were the first real sunshine we have had in weeks or perhaps month. So unusual and cheering has it been that it is something to talk and write about. Even the night sky is clear and bright for once, and the stars are clearly and brilliantly visible.

Yesterday afternoon Virgil and I spent three or more hours out-of-doors, borrowed a field glass, took along a bird guide, and walked in the country, resting a while in a bit of woods a mile or more north from town. Last Tuesday afternoon the sun shone with some brilliance most of the time, although accompanied by a stiff, cold breeze from the north. Made nine or ten miles on the open road east and north from Scottdale. The tramping season is now here, what with buds and leaves bursting open on every bush and tree. The wild flower season will be in full and brilliant sway in a week or two from now.

Semiannual communion service was observed today at the church here. The service brings out to meeting some persons who are rarely seen during the intervening months. The officials of the church are very conscious of their responsibility for keeping the church in Gospel "order," and also manage to impress on others their concern for such "order." Yet as a newcomer here, one is impressed by certain features of the congregational life which appear more nondescript in character than otherwise. There are, as it happens, more women than men members, at least judging from the average audience. And too there are a goodly sprinkling of men members whose wives are not members of the church, either belonging elsewhere or not belonging to any church. Only in rare cases does the wife of a home belong here and her husband elsewhere. Coming from a background of Amish church life, all this seems very odd to a person, and far from ideal, a condition that is hardly offset adequately by strong enforcement of so-called "order" of the church.

Among other projects for the present months at the office, when scheduled quarterly writing is not taking up the time, is that of reading in earlier Mennonite literature. Just recently I have been using in my personal devotion the little classic devotional book, entitled "Die Ernsthafte Christenpflicht," which was used among Mennonites and

Amish already in Europe and has been reprinted within the last twenty-five years. This exercise serves a double purpose just now, making me acquainted with the historic little booklet itself and giving real spiritual help in personal devotion, for the devotional prayers in the book are truly inspirational and deeply spiritual in tone and thought. It is a pity that the present generations have cut themselves off so completely, that is, the Mennonite group, from the rich treasures of their heritage, and believe, many of them, that improvised prayer is the only genuine kind.

May 11, 1940   Headlines in newspapers in tall type announce invasion of the Netherlands by Nazi forces, and the English and French forces going forth to meet in battle with them. One almost hopes that the blitzkrieg technique will be decisive one way or another in a short time and that whatever changes in the world must come may come soon, so as to have the horrors overwith. My own personal feeling leads me to believe that likely a major world crisis or revolution is in store for the making of history on this planet. It is another of those convulsions that changes the direction of history and brings in a new order of things, roughly comparable to Alexander's conquests, Hannibal's wars, Julius Caesar's exploits, the fall of the Roman Empire, the Protestant Revolt of the sixteenth century and so forth. Some unstable, unsophisticated folks like to believe it must be the approaching end of the world.

The sad tragedy of the matter is that the Christian Church has so miserably failed in living up to the ideal taught and practiced by the Master whom Christians worship and claim as Lord. Churches have so widely identified themselves with the social and political status quo, with nationalistic and militaristic states and their society, that they have lost all power of moral and spiritual leadership in a world order that is cracking and gaping at the joints and threatening to founder soon. If only Christian people could dedicate themselves to follow Christ in taking His way, the way of the cross and suffering, I verily believe it is true that thousands, perhaps millions, of people would flock to the churches. Men are everywhere puzzled, bewildered, afraid, disillusioned, cynical, and in despair. They grasp at this or that form of political and social ideology in the desperate hope of finding something to hold them up, not unlike a drowning man grasping at straws. If now the church, that form of the church which men know best, were standing for Christ, and against all that is contrary to Christ and His way of life, then men would know of something to which they could turn.

A little book, "Nonviolence in an Aggressive World," by A. J. Muste, lately read has in it much good food for thought. The author thinks and writes in terms of social and world revolution. Interestingly enough he argues and pleads passionately for the Christians and the Church officially to take the uncompromising stand for the way of Christ, by renouncing all participation directly or indirectly in warfare. Until the Church does this sincerely, and at whatever immediate cost of trial and suffering, there can be no hope for solving world social and economic problems. Or until some nation, some leading nation does so at the price of whatever it costs, there will be no moral leadership to help the war-torn world to find any better way to meet its problems.

A small pamphlet by Richard B. Gregg is devoted to a detailed study of how the pacifist or nonresistant person can prepare himself best to meet war, fascism or the threat of war. It is a very sensible and suggestive booklet, and carries much the same emphasis as Muste's book, although treated from a different point of view, largely from the individual's viewpoint.

May 25, 1940   Rain fell yesterday and this morning. Clouds fill the sky, air is cool and damp. Hence it is an afternoon to stay at home or indulge in only limited excursions away from a roof to keep one dry.

Within the last two weeks there have been several very fine days for holding tryst with sunshine, woods, green grass and spring flowers. Excellent use was made of these on four occasions. On Saturday afternoon, just two weeks ago, I walked down south to the abandoned farm along Jacob's Creek, though it is now no longer entirely abandoned for someone is working parts of it this spring. Started there determined to follow the south bank of the Creek as far up this way as possible, hoping it might be as far as to the bridge on Rd. 819. Scrambled through the bushes for some distance. Found some steep, shaded banks where trillium, both white and red, were growing, the first I had found these flowers in this area. Suddenly a wire fence shut off further progress along the Creek, and menacing placards on trees in numbers threatened direful things against all trespassers. Turning to right I climbed up over the steep side of a wooded hill. The exploration was interesting and worth-while. Brought home more specimens of wild flowers than I could identify with facilities at hand, which were limited to illustrations and descriptions in the National Geographic Magazine of August 1939. That was a very delicious afternoon to be outdoors for a ramble, and the adventure over new terrain was rewarding and profitable.

On the following Tuesday afternoon, May 14, the sky was without a cloud, a gentle breeze was blowing and everything was perfect for a fine hike. Without apology or compunction of conscience I dropped everything, started early after a substantial dinner and tramped westward. At a place called Chaintown, though I have several times looked for a town without success in that vicinity, I began to follow a railroad track on westward along Jacob's Creek. That was exploring! Jacob's Creek becomes a regular mountain stream flowing noisily along over rocks and boulders. The wooded hills rise steeply on both sides from its banks for three or four hundred feet. It is a wild forsaken country. The railroad follows along the creek most of the time in sight of it, crosses it four times in the course of six or eight miles, and makes an ideal place for a fine walk. No house or sign of human habitation appears for perhaps five miles. The silence, the wildness, and the beauty of it all was most unexpected and impressive to this walker. Over three hours I had walked when ahead was a tunnel through a high hill. Calculating the time it would require to reach home, I had to turn back from a point which must have been nine or ten miles away from home. The woods were most beautiful that afternoon. For miles the steep hillsides were almost covered with the showy white trillium, Snowy Wake-Robin, and other spring flowers. Birds were everywhere flitting, singing, and chirping. Badgers could be seen at some distance running for cover, frogs croaked in pools, and one beautiful shiny black snake, at least three feet long glided away, crawled up on the limb of a bush and looked to see what this strange pedestrian was. Fortunately along the embankment of the railroad it is possible to obtain water to drink, for evidently the builders at some places where they cut their way through a bank would drive an iron pipe into the fissures of the outcropping rock and secure a flow of clear spring water for drinking. At one of these springs I refreshed myself to my great comfort and convenience.

Last Saturday afternoon we made a party out of the beautiful day. The Ressler sisters in their car took us all, including our guest, Ruth Bender, to the woods near Cunningham's Bridge, the same place along Jacob's Creek several miles west where I so often go. Mary Royer of Goshen was also with the party, which was interesting to all. Some thirty kinds of birds were identified by the crowd. My eyes are not as good for seeing and identifying birds now as they were twenty years ago when I first became interested in that pursuit. The readiness with which others in our group saw and described the flitting creatures last Saturday served to remind me more especially of that fact. More time and patience, plus 8-power binoculars will be necessary for my birding expeditions now.

The fourth excursion into the sunshine was on last Tuesday morning from 9:30 to 11:30. The sky was again crystal clear after rain, and nothing could keep me from getting out. Twenty or twenty-five minutes from the house brought me to my favorite hilltop south of Jacob's Creek and sundry rows of old coke-ovens.

This outing into the sun was taken in the face of the special meetings of the Mennonite Board of Publication which were in session for a number of days. It was a considerable powwow, lots of talk, talk, talk. Must confess I did not attend the sessions very diligently, but enough to know some things that were going on. Including Sunday morning service there were in all ten public sessions. On Tuesday noon all the workers were invited to eat lunch with the guests who were fed by the Board in the basement of the Church, and on that afternoon the plant did not operate at all. Received for my work on S. S. Quarterlies numerous criticisms friendly and otherwise, including an official visit by a committee of two.

August 30, 1940 After an interlude of more than three months, I find myself with leisure and inclination again to scribble a few notes. Should really take off a day or two in order to catch up.

It has been a rather full and strenuous period. Many things have transpired which seem worth recording. One may as well start at the beginning and keep some semblance of chronological order and sequence, even though some of these events seem already like ancient history.

The official criticism which was engineered through the machinery of the committees of the Publication Board against my point of view in the S. S. lesson quarterly left me momentarily puzzled and a bit upset. With time and perspective I have since tried to evaluate and assess its meaning and significance. As I have assessed the whole squall, it does not appear so serious or important. Because I do not cater to the millennial and Scofieldian viewpoint in my exegetical comments, some are quite dissatisfied. In order to make a worth-while case, J. L.

Stauffer combed two or three issues of the quarterly for possible theological and doctrinal errors. He had quite a long list. Some of these I was ready to admit careless or unwise statement of what was written. Others were rather puerile and merely matters of opinion. Fortunately Simon Gingerich was present when Stauffer laid out his line of exhibits. When he ended up by pleading for me to adopt the premillennial viewpoint, for that of course was where the shoe was really pinching, Gingerich calmly stated his own experience with the common millennial teaching and in addition counselled me to avoid controversy by mentioning both viewpoints when explaining disputed passages of Scripture. This I felt was sane and sound advice. But as for adopting the millennial point of view, or in any way compromising the general point of view from which I have been writing the lesson quarterly, to satisfy the common run of millennialists – I first of all could not conscientiously do so, and secondly it would be against the advice and wish of many with whom I have spoken about it. Paul Erb, for example, a man of education and one who himself holds to the premillennial view, who is also a member of the very committee which was officially after my scalp, came to me personally and confidently encouraged me to maintain my general method and view in the quarterly. Others who have spoken encouragingly and with concern are H. S. Bender and J. C. Clemens. So I feel no reason for being alarmed or scared. It is a satisfaction and one of my aims to make my writings on the lesson stimulating and provocative of thought, instead of merely routine. It is very acceptable to me that people should take issue and criticise, if only they will meet me fairly and objectively, instead of setting in motion ecclesiastical machinery to accomplish their purposes. The line for me to work on is to keep my writings objective, positive and constructive, and avoid antagonizing others. H. S. Bender warned me however, that I shall find it impossible to satisfy the aroused radicals. So I am not expecting too much.

An important event for us in May was a trip to Hagerstown and Williamsport, Maryland. On Decoration Day we all went by train from Connellsville to Martinsburg, West Virginia, in time to be present at the wedding of Marion Charlton and Mr. Eshleman in the afternoon. In the evening they took us to the Marion Church near Chambersburg where a special meeting was going on. Met there a few acquaintances and shook hands with numbers of others whom we as promptly forgot. Stayed at the Charlton home over that night, and the next forenoon Fannie Kauffman brought us back to Scottdale, driving her fiance's car. She was herself getting ready then to get married about ten days later to Mr. Sarco, a young man who has been at home with the Charltons for some years. We all enjoyed the trip very much, especially Virgil. Weather was cool and rainy. We were almost total strangers among the wedding guests, less than a half dozen of whom we had ever known before. A few from Virginia, and Roger Charlton, at whose home the event occurred, and Marion's mother, comprised the list of our acquaintances. We enjoyed it anyway.

Letting my mind run back over the past several months, a number of experiences stand out very interestingly. During January and February of this year I worked very steadily on quarterly material and was well in advance of the required schedule. During April and May I did some desultory work in getting more fully acquainted with the historical library of the House. Mostly I did general vegetating and browsing much to my enjoyment and profit. About June 10 I had all plans in readiness for working out more quarterly lessons and was just on the point of starting on these. At that moment John Horsch told me he could not possibly produce the copy for the fourth quarter, 1940, lesson help and that he was sure I could do it very well. This task was a "stunner" to me at that moment. Conference with the House manager confirmed the assignment and so for about full time over five weeks, I labored at preparing German copy. It was strenuous, taxing work, but by close application I was able to get the copy out. Some parts of it I copied from previous quarterlies written by Horsch, some parts I paraphrased, adapted, and translated from my own Advanced Quarterly copy. Mrs. Horsch later revised the diction somewhat, and she also read the proof. So that was my first experience with preparing German manuscript. I would enjoy doing it some more, if there were more time and leisure to work at it. By leaning heavily on previous quarterlies and riding the dictionary hard, I could perhaps develop a German style that would be intelligible.

Following the German writing period, I plunged into the writing of second quarter, 1941, advanced copy. This was about mid-July, and the time for our vacation was set at August 12. With strong determination, I resolved to have that task completed before going away on vacation. Happily the lessons were on Acts and the early Church, my favorite field of Bible study. I set to work at top speed. One week I wrote copy for four lessons, the next week for six lessons. The next week was broken up with a three-day absence from home. But before August 12 the copy was finished, although it may need more editing than is usual because of the speed with which it was prepared.

Because of this rush schedule, I passed up all attendance at the annual district conference, held at Martinsburg, Pennsylvania. Much to the astonishment of some persons, I made no effort to make myself present there, although the idea that is fostered here is that one ought to serve the Lord by going to every conference gathering which one can at all reach. It was a regrettably embarrassing situation for me. On Friday before the sessions began on Tuesday, someone here happened to refer to the fact that my name appeared on the printed program. In my busyness I had entirely neglected to get a program and inform myself as to its contents. I was not a little mortified to find my name thereon and no time free for preparing anything and all my time filled with a must schedule of work. Besides I had been elected to be delegate from this Sunday school to the S. S. Conference. In spite of all this inducement to appear in public and get myself advertised, I stayed at home and carried through my schedule of work. Three days of that very week I had set aside especially for preparing two speeches which I had months earlier agreed to give in Lancaster County.

August 6-8 I had a trip which took me first to Wadsworth, Ohio, and from there to Lancaster, Pennsylvania. Leaving Monday evening from Connellsville, Mr. Yake and I arrived at Akron, Ohio, near midnight. Sister Ida met us at the train and took us sixteen miles out into the country to the home of Henry Kreiders where we slept till morning. The day was spent in committee sessions at the Bethel Church. Dinner at noon I had at some Grabers' home, and supper in the evening at

Kreiders'. Ida then took me to the train at Akron. This was my first visit in this part of Ohio. Upon leaving Akron, I was undecided whether I should get a berth and sleep or try to rest in the day coach. The latter I discovered would mean changing twice during the night, and riding some of the time in a coach where some uncivilized women incessantly sucked cigarettes. Before reaching Pittsburgh I went into the Pullman, paid some five dollars extra, and went to bed to stay until six o'clock next morning.

August 31, 1940 A day in Lancaster County, August 7. On Wednesday morning before breakfast I found myself getting off the train at Lancaster. Walking through the station I soon met a frock-coated Mennonite preacher who was there looking for me. His name was J. C. Habecker, with whom there had been some correspondence previously in regard to this trip. In his car we motored five or six miles southwest from the city to his country home. He is a retired farmer, still owning land which is rented out to someone else. A large brick house shelters himself and his wife. They never had any children at all. House furnishings and appointments suggested they have plenty of money. He is the senior preacher on the "bench" of the three churches on the southwestern edge of Lancaster County. An elderly man of rather quaint, old-fashioned manners and ideas. After a good breakfast we went to Masonville Church, where an annual Harvest and S. S. meeting was to be held that day. The day was pleasant, fields were beautiful, with corn and tobacco making the most splendid showing. At the church a large crowd gathered, a typical Lancaster County Mennonite audience. The day was quite warm but everyone, men and women, young and old, infants and greyheads, patiently sat through the three-hour sessions. My lot was to read one paper in the forenoon session: "Distinguishing Doctrines of the Mennonite Church," and in the afternoon: "The Book of Psalms." Lunch at noon was in the church basement. The evening meal we took at Habeckers' home. The evening session was endured by all in spite of the heat.

Met only a few people there I knew. It was an interesting glimpse of Mennonite life in "the county." Yet the trip and its experiences left a bad taste in my mouth, for the reason that I was out of pocket the sum of ten dollars or more on expenses. It was an assumption on my part that ethics and Christian courtesy would dictate that an invitation to appear on a program included a pledge to meet the necessary traveling expenses to get to the place of the program. An offering was lifted at the last session for expenses and for missionary work. So I had good hopes they would reimburse me at least for expenses. Spent the night at Habeckers' and next morning before the brother started out to take me into Lancaster, he with a gesture of generosity took out his billfold and handed over a five-dollar bill as a gift of appreciation and for expenses. I kindly refrained from telling him the truth that my expenses were at least three times that sum. In fact he did not ask what expenses I had. As I analyzed the situation it was about like this: This Habecker seems addicted to quaint ways and notions. He had been a Normal School classmate and good friend of J. A. Ressler. This sentimental interest in the editor of the S. S. Lesson Quarterly probably gave him the idea he would like to see this successor to Ressler. Seemingly it was his own influence that got me the invitation from the "bench" to appear on their program. And they likely supposed that I would be so pleased to appear that I would gladly stand the travelling expenses for the privilege of doing so. I do not hold anything against them on my account, for they meant well, knew no better, and intended no hardship on me. But the experience has equipped me with one more good reason for declining invitations to travel to distant points for making speeches on programs. It is this: I cannot travel as cheaply as a minister, and cannot afford to pay my own expenses to do so. Habecker then took me into Lancaster to Menno Miller at the Book Store, where I spent several hours. From there my steps and the trolley took me to the Pennsylvania Railroad station, and so home on train and trolley just in time for supper on Thursday.

By this time all thoughts and plans were directed toward vacationing. This was the first formal vacation we ever took, going away from home just for that for a specified length of time. Seemingly it was through Ruth Bender's suggestion to Mrs. Hannah Miller at Springs that we began to plan some months before to spend two weeks taking care of her house and place while she would be away as chief cook at Arbutus Park near Johnstown during Young People's Institute. But anyway, so it all came about that we had this splendid opportunity for a delightful vacation in the country at little expense, and at the same time helping someone else out while doing so. Ruth had spent a week or so in our home and she was returning to Springs herself for work at Fred Bender's. So on Monday afternoon we travelled to Springs (August 12). Had planned to use the trolley to Mt. Pleasant. However, Rhoda Ressler volunteered to take us all by auto, which we accepted with pleasure. By bus we travelled from Mt. Pleasant, via Somerset, Berlin, Meyersdale, to Springs, arriving there at 5:20 in the afternoon. That evening I received instructions and practice in doing the daily chores, which consisted solely of feeding and watering two flocks of chickens and gathering eggs. Hannah and Alvina left next morning, leaving us in charge of the place. We enjoyed about every minute of the time, although not everything was perfect. It rained for a number of days during the first week. Had planned and hoped to get a good bath of sunshine every day, but were disappointed in this. Even the second week when there was no rain, the sky was often filled with big masses of sailing clouds which shut away the sun. The elevation there is about 1300 feet higher than here and the air had a different "feel" to it, more cool and the sun when it did shine burned one more quickly. Besides choring daily, we managed to cut some grass and weeds, pull some weeds out in garden and flower beds, and a few other small items. Estie spent two days of the first week in bed with a bad sore throat. Spent quite a bit of time on our cooking, which had to be done on a coal-burning kitchen range. Virgil fed the cats and enjoyed himself playing with Millard Bender, a neighbor boy. He took three music lessons on the piano from Rhoda Bender. Ruth showed us the site and location of her proposed log cabin in the woods a mile east of Springs. And so the time passed quickly. Much of the rainy time I spent lazily vacationing, sleeping, and luxuriously doing nothing at all. The most profitable feature of the vacation for me personally was the tramping I did over the country in search of historical information. Had provided myself with geological contour maps in advance for getting around the country.

September 4, 1940   When in August we found ourselves resident in Somerset County, I conceived the idea of doing some local exploration and some historical investigation as a vacation pastime. That general area of the county had been the home of my ancestors for eighty or ninety years before 1863 or 1864, when my grandparents moved from there out into the wild western state of Iowa. Naturally many of the forefathers are buried in the rocky soil of Somerset County, in Elklick and Summit Townships. Historical curiosity prompted me to try finding some of the old places where they once lived and if possible to locate their final resting places.

As preliminary preparation for such exploration I had done several things in advance of our going over there. For one thing I had sent to the Geology Survey at Washington, D. C. for three of their contour maps, covering the Grantsville area, the Meyersdale area, and the Berlin area. These would supply information of roads, mountains, streams, etc. Then also I went through parts of Harvey Hostetler's two books of family history, and made notes on the old burial grounds which he mentions in those parts, and also of some of the locations of old farms once occupied by our Hochstetler and Yoder ancestors. In this way equipped, I felt I could spend some vacation time very profitably in tramping over the hills of Somerset County. Rainy weather held me back some. The first week I did not get out very much. Only two afternoons was it possible to get out on the road at all. Tuesday after equipping myself with a walking cane from the adjoining orchard, I set forth rather late, perhaps three o'clock or later, just for a ramble and having no special objective in view. Went east and south of Springs, finally reaching Grantsville, finally returning home by the cement highway to Springs.

On the Thursday following the day was cloudy, gloomy and threatening rain. Some mist was in the air which threatened to turn into rain. Nonetheless the wanderlust took me on the road. Went north and east from Springs. Soon reached Niverton and came upon the Amish Church house there. The neat little cemetery across the road from the church engaged my attention for a half hour or more. There I found the grave markers of many Yoders, among them those of two names which I recognized as uncles of my father, also an aunt of his and her husband. I copied most of the Yoder inscriptions, many of whom I found later were more distant cousins of ours. Moving on northward over a road which I knew not where it might lead, since I could not carry my maps along with me, I came upon another Amish Church house, which from the names on tombstones I guessed must be the Conservative Amish meetinghouse. We had once been there, just a few weeks over twenty years before, the Sunday before we were married. Father and Mother were along. But I had only the faintest recollection of the surroundings and could scarcely recognize it as that place.

This second meetinghouse was the one known as Oakdale, as was learned later. The cemetery there is very small as yet, the oldest markers being dated about 1900. Continuing still on northward and watching for a road turning right which might lead to Salisbury, I next came to a place known as St. Paul, a village with a scattering of houses and one imposing landmark in the form of St. Paul's Reformed Church. Took a hurried walk over the cemetery close by. Found no Amish names to speak of, but some which suggested Dunkard family names, like Engle, Kretchman, and others. Took next the road south-eastward which brought me to Salisbury. Without halting there, I continued southward along a concrete road, took the first road that led off to the right. This road leads one through a delightful woods, and soon across the Casselman River. After three miles or so of tramping and climbing of hills I reached Springs, and had to feed the chickens just at dusk; they had to get down from the roost for their suppers.

Did not stir about much the rest of the week. Saturday forenoon Virgil and I went to Upper Springs and spent a little time going through the Miller machine shop, watching the men work with their machines, etc. On Sunday, besides attending Sunday school and church services in the morning, we all took a walk over a part of Amos Yoder's farm, just south of us, particularly to see the old burial ground on that place. It is very old, nearly all the markers being rough stones without recognizable inscriptions.

This Sunday was the first day Estie was back to her normal self, after suffering from severe sore throat which had kept her in bed for several days during the middle of the week.

On Monday, August 19, I spent the forenoon cutting grass on the lawn. In the afternoon I took the road for Grantsville, expecting to visit with Jonas B. Miller. Talked with a young man on the Ezra Yoder place, learning from him where the Conservative Amish Mennonite meetinghouse near Grantsville is located and also where Jonas Miller lives. Visited the cemetery by this church, and then went on to Miller's place. He was away from home, having not yet returned from a trip to Iowa for the annual conference of their body. Went on out to Grantsville again. Walked east along the Old National Pike to the old arched stone bridge over the Casselman, which is no longer used, since the road has been straightened out and a regular level bridge built about thirty rods farther up the river.

On Tuesday we pulled weeds in the forenoon, getting some sunshine between the batches of clouds that sailed across the sky. In the afternoon we all took a walk, going a round about way to get to Dan Otto's place, and the Brick Works which he and his sons operate. While Mother visited in the house, Virgil and I went to watch the operations at the Works. Unfortunately they were not making brick or tile that day. However we saw the steam shovel digging out the clay, dump it on little cars, which hauled it on a little railroad track and up an incline into a building, where it was dumped into large bins. All this work was in preparation for making tile on the next day. But we did not go back the next day to see the rest of the operations. Virgil was not enough interested to bother. He by this time had found a very congenial playmate in Millard Bender, a neighbor's boy.

Wednesday, August 21, was one of the biggest days of our vacation experience, at least for me. The day was bright and dirt roads were dry. The vacation period was drawing on to a close and I had not yet gotten to all the places I wanted to see. About ten o'clock I fixed myself some cheese sandwiches, took them with some fruit and cookies in a paper poke, and at 10:30, with walking stick in hand I set out on a long trip. Set out for St. Paul, taking from Dan Otto's corner the dirt road north through woods. It was a beautiful walk amid very delightful scenes. The goal ahead was the Joel Hershberger farm, which I understood was between St. Paul and Summit Mills. Inquiry at the combination store and gasoline filling station at St. Paul resulted in no more exact information as to the location of this farm. Continued on in the direction of Summit Mills. About 12:30 I stopped to rest on a roadside terrace of sod while the lunch tasted very good and revived my strength and spirits. I decided it was now time to stop at the first opportunity and make inquiry. When I reached a farmer's lane where a number of mail boxes were, I stopped to examine the names. Fortunately the names were plainly lettered on these boxes, and one was J. E. Hershberger. This thrilled my heart and no time was lost in marching up the lane. Several grown boys at the barn informed me where the old burial plot was and after a few friendly words I hurried a quarter mile back into the field and found myself on the spot. It is a neat well-kept cemetery, where the oldest marked stone bears the date 1805. Numerous rough stones are there having no inscriptions at all. A few interments have been made there in recent years. The inscriptions on many of the stones I copied, especially of the Yoders buried there, some of whom I could in a general way identify from what vague knowledge I had of the family tree to which we belong. One rough but partly shaped stone had on it some crude marks which I could not decipher at first, as follows: H m jo 1829 M 18. After going over the plot, I came back and studied this one more carefully, and at length decided that they stand for Henry Yoder, and that he died on March or May 18, 1829. This discovery was a genuine thrill. For if this was the person whom I guessed it to be, he was grandfather to my grandfather, Tobias Yoder. Beside this stone was another having on it K J, perhaps his wife, Katie Yoder. Other stones had names of the son of this Henry, named Yost, and numerous of the latter's descendants. Harvey Hostetler in his first family history says that in this burial ground rest the remains of John Hochstetler, the first Hochstetler of ours who came to Somerset County, and some of his family, and that this Hershberger farm is part of the pioneer Hochstetler's own land. As I stood there reflecting on these matters and casting my eyes out over the nicely rolling fields in different directions, I felt that I was truly standing on historic ground. Without tarrying too long on the old burial plot, I went back to the house where Joel Hershberger lives, found him just coming from the house, introduced myself and began to speak of my interest in the local history and in our family history. Mr. Hershberger is not himself directly related to the Yoders buried on his farm, except that his first wife was a granddaughter of Yost Yoder buried there. He invited me into the house, where with the assistance of his present wife we talked of the Yoders who long ago had lived in that community. My special line of inquiry now had become that of the place of residence and place of burial of my great-grandfather, Jacob Yoder. I knew in a vague way that he had once lived in the vicinity of Summit Mills. The Hershbergers knew of the old farm where he lived. It was on the Saylor Hill, as they called it. As to the place of burial of Jacob Yoder and his wife, they knew nothing. Except that they recalled hearing it said that at one time there were some marked graves on the farm which he had owned. They were not certain whether the old markers were still in existence there or not. Very generously Mr. Hershberger offered to hitch up his horse to the buggy and take me around to see the old place and make some search for the old burial plot. The drive took us several miles over back roads. He pointed out to me along the way the old historic farms, especially the farm where Joseph J. Yoder now lives, which was the place which Yost Yoder, Jacob's brother, once occupied. When we got to the top of the "Saylor Hill," we stopped to look around where they had supposed the old gravestones had once been. But in the tall weeds and shrubs along the margin of a cornfield, we could not make out anything. Hershberger went on down to the buildings where the present owner of the place was at work. This owner, Mr. Clarence Bender, reported that during the three years he has worked this place he had seen no sign of old grave markers in the field where the old burial ground was supposed to have been, although he too knew of the tradition that there once was such a place there. We then drove on down past the old buildings toward Summit Mills. Have regretted I did not stop and look more closely at the old buildings, if they actually are the ones in which my grandfather grew up a century ago. The present owner is erecting new buildings a little farther down the slope. It is possible that the old buildings may soon be demolished.

This place was about a mile east of Summit Mills. Next Hershberger took me a mile or more north of that village, to another place where Adam Yoder and some of his family and descendants are buried. It is a very small plot on the farm of Galen Peck, right by the line fence of Elmer Brenneman's farm. All this land once belonged to the Adam Yoder, who got it from his father Yost Yoder, who got it from his father Henry Yoder, who got it from the pioneer Gnagi, according to a note in the Gnagi family history. The time was now growing late for one who had the prospect of walking seven miles after we reached Hershberger's place in order to get home.

It was five o'clock when I clambered out of the buggy and started tramping homeward. About two minutes before I got out a truck rumbled around us, and a glance told me it was one of Elam Miller's egg trucks, and it was an easy guess it was on its way to the barn where we ourselves were staying. Sure enough, upon reaching home it was there, stored for the night. Nevertheless the walk home was beautiful, and two hours found me at home doing the nightly chores. A car offered me a ride for the last half mile or more. That was an eventful day, and though the body was weary, the spirit was happy and satisfied with the day's experiences.

By this time my curiosity was really aroused over the question as to where the Jacob Yoder and his wife were buried. The curiosity was a challenge to find out or at least make a determined effort to do so. Next day in the afternoon I was on the road again, this time headed for Niverton again. Someone had suggested that Mrs. Milton Hershberger, who is first cousin to my father, might be able to give information on family history, since she was interested in such things herself. After a bit of wandering and asking directions, I found her place of residence. A lively little old woman, very sprightly and intelligent, welcomed me warmly and enthusiastically the moment she learned who I was. We talked for an hour or so. She gave a great deal of information, reminiscent and otherwise. Among other things she knew where her grandparents Yoder had lived last and were buried. According to her story,

Jacob Yoder had sold his farm to a coal company when he retired from active farming, and went to stay with his oldest son Henry, who lived just a short distance farther east from Springs than where Mrs. Hershberger lives. She told me further that Jacob's wife died while they were staying there and was buried not far from the house, where a few other bodies were interred before or after. But the graves had never been substantially marked and their exact location cannot probably be determined now. After his wife's death Jacob Yoder went to Holmes County to stay with his son Samuel, where he later died and was buried. This was real firsthand historical information and was like making a discovery. After exchanging further conversation, I asked directions for getting to the farm where this lady was buried. People by the name of Oester live on it, the lady of the house being a descendant of Henry Yoder who earlier lived there. A brief walk brought me to the place. The lady of the house was very gracious and kind. She had knowledge that her own grandmother was buried on their place, but had never heard that her great-grandmother was also interred there. She took me out east of the house to show me where she remembered once having seen some rough stones which she thought had marked the graves. The place is between a small chicken house and a public road which runs on out to the Casselman River and to Salisbury. The place was overgrown with tall grass amid which it was impossible to discern anything that indicated the possible site of the old graves. I was very glad to see this farm and know about where the spot of these graves was thought to be. The fact that Mrs. Oester had no knowledge of Jacob Yoder's wife being buried at that place, made me place a small question mark over Mrs. Hershberger's information. Later verification of her knowledge through Mrs. Simon Miller of near Springs and Mrs. Lydia Bender of Scottdale, both surviving grandchildren of the lady in question, have in my mind established the certainty of this recollection, and is one fact of family history which I hope to rescue from oblivion. A letter since received from another grandchild of Jacob Yoder, Mr. Jonas S. Yoder of Baltic, Ohio, gives some information about Jacob Yoder's birth, death, and place of burial. But he is ignorant of his grandmother's place of burial.

The rest of my journey that day took me to Salisbury, where I strolled hastily over the cemetery. On the way home Roy Otto in a truck took pity on me as a hitchhiker and gave me a "lift" most of the distance home. On Friday I stayed at home feeling slightly indisposed. Saturday noon Elam Miller offered me a ride to Grantsville, where I patronized a barber shop. After a lunch and some loitering about, I went near a mile north of the lower end of Grantsville to the home of Jonas B. Miller, a rather well-known church and community leader, who I supposed could provide me with some historical information about that area. Mostly I wished to get some idea of what and what kind of work he has done in the line of local Amish history in Somerset County, Pennsylvania, and Garrett County, Maryland. Spent a very profitable three hours in talking over various phases of local and family history. Received from him one very valuable clue pertaining to the more remote history of my own Yoder family. I had read and heard it said that the Henry Yoder, whose tombstone I believe I found in the Joel Hershberger cemetery, was an immigrant from the old country.

Mr. Miller had a note among his papers, to the effect that one J. J. Yoder, living on the original Yoder homestead near Summit Mills, the place I had passed on Wednesday before in Joel Hershberger's company, has in his possession certain old deeds of land transfers, showing that this Henry Yoder in question had bought that land from his father Yost Yoder, who received it originally in 1775 from a Mr. Büchli. This bit of information was another first-rate discovery, and the whole business was getting to be to me very exciting.

On the following Sunday afternoon, Elam took us in his car to Meyersdale to see their new house. Someone had suggested to him that I was interested in seeing Joseph J. Yoder, and so on the return trip he drove around by way of Summit Mills. In the brief half hour or so which we could stay at Yoder's place, and amid general visiting and becoming acquainted, I could not do more than glance casually at the two old documents and note that the Yost Yoder who had gotten that land in 1775 in the other instrument is still named as from Earl Township, Lancaster County, when he transferred it to his son Henry in 1791. This led me to suspect that Yost was probably never himself a resident of Somerset County, which explains the absence of his name from the assessment lists which I have seen printed from the early years. At some later time I must go back to J. J. Yoder's and study carefully the old documents, perhaps copy them for reference and possible reproduction somewhere. Yet my mind was very much set at ease through that brief visit, for I now know that the documents are in good condition and are being well cared for in a good-sized fireproof safe in a country home. Mr. Yoder is a large scale farmer, no longer young, and a bishop in the Old Order Amish Church of that area. A very friendly man, who invited me to return some other time for further study of family history. That ended the thrilling explorations for that period, for on the following Monday afternoon we returned to Scottdale, and in the few weeks since have been getting back to routine life and work again.

Excepting the fact that, just one week later on Labor Day, the occasion of the annual Miller reunion near Grantsville, we all went over again. Ben Cutrell drove us and Ralph Bender over in a car. We enjoyed the reunion gathering very greatly; brought back the eight quarts of canned huckleberries which Wife had put up while we were over there. Saw, met and talked with various people who were related and otherwise interested in us. The reunion was a real community gathering, affording at least one occasion in a year's time where the various grades of Amish and Mennonites and evidently Dunkards and others can get together in a neighborly and social way. Specifically this reunion is in commemoration of the memory of one Joel Miller, who was grandfather of my wife on her mother's side, and of a host of others now living in that region and even farther afield. That Miller and his children were evidently prolific progenitors and have a numerous progeny today.

September 11, 1940 It requires much time and scribbling to catch up with the busy activities of our past several months. Some visitors in our home during this time have been: Ruth Bender for a week, just previous to our vacation at Springs. Since coming back, John C. Wenger and family took the noonday meal with us last week one day. Ira Miller, Estie's brother of Fentress, Virginia, with his wife and son Ivan, stayed overnight last week.

August fourth, on a Sunday, was the twentieth anniversary of our wedding. It was Estie's idea to observe a celebration of the occasion and she made all the plans. She invited Charles Shoemaker and family to be present for dinner, and of course Ruth and Ralph Bender. When they were all assembling around the dinner table it came out what the occasion was and everyone entered into the spirit of the celebration. Mr. Shoemaker, then still unmarried, and his since-acquired wife were the attendants to the bride and groom just twenty years before at N. E. Millers' home near Springs.

Virgil has had a fairly successful summer. He has been able to occupy his time rather more easily this summer than in previous summers. He plays more readily and happily with other boys than he used to do. At Springs he specially enjoyed himself, playing with cats, romping around in the woods, in the barn, and over the place in general. He is developing more and more into a boy, though some childish habits tend to cling to him longer than his parents think they would need to. He has started in third grade at school and should get along well. His temptation will likely be to assume he can get his lessons without study, and so may learn to waste his time and application.

September 18, 1940   Taking time out for a few notes. A beautiful day made it impossible for me to let all the fine sunshine go to waste on the Fayette hills on the other side of the creek. Left the house at eleven o'clock, carrying a bag of lunch, and a Religious Digest to read. I used to go on the old railroad track which runs north side of Jacob's Creek towards Owensdale and Broadford. Following the track down to Owensdale, then climbing up on the track of the Pittsburgh and West Virginia Railroad, and walking westward on it for a mile or mile and a half, this was about the most private place for exercising one's right to walk shirtless and look like a hobo.

January 15, 1941   A major sideline during October and November just past has been that of carrying on some planned and detailed research in local Mennonite history. The occasion which called for this effort was the celebration in the local church of the sesquicentennial anniversary of the first coming of Mennonites into the region along Jacob's Creek. For about a year and as a hobby this study had been interesting diversion and pastime. When the decision was made to hold a public celebration for the occasion, it devolved on me to prepare a paper on the history of the first one hundred years of the settlement. It was without reluctance that I undertook this assignment, for it might be a useful proving ground to help me decide whether I can really do anything worthwhile in the field of historical research and writing. Among the things that were undertaken in making this study was a combing of the files of the Herald of Truth from the beginning of its publication to about 1890, about 26 years, for every reference or mention of Westmoreland and Fayette counties, particularly the death notices and reports from travelling ministers. The county histories and biographical dictionaries were also scanned rather carefully, though not combed thoroughly. Family histories and genealogies afforded some help, notably the Oberholzer, Fretz, Beidler, Funk histories. One day was spent in the archives of the recorder's office at Greensburg, one day likewise at Uniontown, as well as a later visit of several hours to the office of the Recorder of Wills at the latter place. Visits to a number of nearby cemeteries and study of inscriptions on the markers gave some further help. Informal conferences with Aaron Loucks were helpful too. Several partially compiled but unpublished family genealogies were consulted, particularly of Stauffer, Stoner, and Sherrick families. All this was very interesting to the compiler. A paper of some twenty-five or more pages was prepared, about two-thirds of which was read in the fifty minutes time which the program allowed.

Since the reading of that paper, H. S. Bender, editor of the Mennonite Quarterly Review, who happened to be present for that program, has requested the same for publication in the Review. Consulting locally with those interested, particularly John Horst, it was felt that for publication the record of the last fifty years of the local history should be written down on the same plan as the first one hundred years, so making a rather complete project. With the understanding that this be done, together with further revision of what has been written, we have agreed to supply the article for the Review later during the present year. There remains still some detailed research to be made for completeness of the early history. The one day which I spent in the courthouse at Greensburg was for me a first experiment in that kind of archival research, and naturally the time was largely used in getting acquainted with record books, their organization and the technique of using them for good results. The plan therefore is to go there for at least another day's search in old land deeds and wills for more detailed information of the earliest Mennonite settlers in East Huntingdon Township. For the material covering the past fifty years the volumes of the Herald of Truth, Gospel Witness, and Gospel Herald will need to be scanned. Extended interviews with the older leaders, specially Loucks and Kauffman, records of the church and Sunday school locally, and perhaps other sources of information will be helpful.

In November one Saturday afternoon Miss Ruth Ressler kindly carried Aaron Loucks and myself around in her motor car, just driving over the local communities, having Mr. Loucks point out as many of the old landmarks and old family homesteads as he knew. This was very instructive. On our schedule of further investigation for this spring, as soon as weather permits, is that of inviting an elderly lady, Mrs. Ridenour from the local congregation, to go on a drive and point out to us some old abandoned family burying grounds she happens to know of. In late November one afternoon I walked to Connellsville. Halfway up the long hill from Broadford, Aaron Loucks had once told me, there is an old burying ground right beside the road, at a point where the road makes a sharp bend. Once before, last June, I had stopped there but was driven away by an approaching rain storm before I was able to discover the exact spot. This time I came upon it. Found an old plot, with the original stones all lying over and partly covered from view by accumulated debris. One group of markers has been replaced by more modern stones, but the whole plot is evidently now entirely neglected. It is located partly on a steep slope, and the improvement of the highway below has encroached further on the hillside, so that erosion has made deep gullies reaching up into the plot. Most of the markers noted had the name Rist on them, perhaps indicating a family burial plot. One of the Mennonite ministers, Conrad Rist, is buried there. Also it is clear that this spring we must get together a group and go to the several old Mennonite burial plots hereabouts and make a systematic survey, copying all the old inscriptions which can still be recovered. These are a great aid for recovering family connections and church connections in many cases.

I plume myself a bit for having presented in my public paper at least a few facts which I had never read in the little write-ups of the local Mennonite congregation which had been made before. One is, that the first minister to settle along the south side of Jacob's Creek, Abraham Stauffer, was in fact a bishop. Another is the exact years when the first Mennonites bought land along Jacob's Creek, in 1789, 1790, 1791, and that the Shallenberger, Shank, and Strickler families were almost certainly Mennonites coming from Lancaster County, along with the Stauffer and Sherrick families. Another point I feel confident in advancing is that previous to 1852 the deacon in the Stonerville congregation was one Christian Stauffer. The evidence is twofold: On his gravestone he is entitled "Elder"; and in the Herald of Truth I found the obituary of a Nancy, widow of deacon Christian Stauffer. Also his family is recorded in the Oberholzer history, giving dates and so forth. This seems to be a new discovery, if correct.

January 20, Dies Luni, 1941   The winter has been mildish in general so far, with some real warm days. Several light snows have fallen, which in a number of days usually disappeared. Judging from reports, there has been less severe weather here than in the western prairie states. Just now a cold snap following a light snow is making us shiver, mostly from the change. Christmas Day, and that whole week in fact, was warm. There was no particular celebration this year at our house on Christmas Day. We ate turkey and the rest at a neighbor's, Ben Gamber's. The usual round of presents were on hand to be opened on Christmas Eve. Virgil received among other things a Tru-Vue outfit with twelve little films, an Erector Set, a big pocket knife, several books. One major purchase we made for his benefit was from the National Geographic Society, viz., the two-volume work on Hunting Wild Life by Camera and Flashlight, at a cost of five dollars. A year earlier we had invested in the Book of Birds from the same place, two large heavy volumes for five dollars. Much of the material in these two works is simple reproduction of things that appeared in the National Geographic Magazine in the course of many years. Among my gifts received was a Rand Electric Shaver from Estie. She had worked and earned some pin money, and got me this implement, partly because she was tired of seeing and hearing the process of stropping my safety razor blades. Now for two weeks I have used this instrument and must say that I shall probably become a one hundred per cent enthusiast for the dry-shaving program. In ten or twelve minutes I can remove a day's growth of stubble from my face with no messing around with soap and water and bay rum and talcum powder. At the end the skin is intact and all the time feels firm and healed up instead of half-sore as though it had been nearly butchered and slaughtered to pieces. Depending on how long this implement will function without additional expense, it may prove to be about as economical as my previous low-cost shaving program. Some men speak of a ten or twelve dollar a year expense for shaving, but it had never cost me that much to carry on the Sisyphean labor of removing my beard. I have always bought the higher priced, heavier and better quality blades and then sharpened them on a leather strop. The Gem blades were the ones used. I owned three different Gem safety razors. The first was purchased when a mere boy who thought he had to begin shaving at perhaps fourteen years of age. This one was stolen out of a suitcase, along with other articles, on our wedding trip in 1920. The second Gem lasted until 1936 or thereabouts. With these two razors came a simple handle in two parts, by means of which one could sharpen the blades on a straight razor strop. When I bought the third Gem it came without a stropping handle. Fortunately the one from the previous set was not worn out entirely, so it was kept and used with the new outfit. Thinking I had very cleverly gotten around this manufacturer's purpose to make me buy more blades, because they would not be sharpened for use after the first edge was worn off, I was rather elated. But alas, the makers had another way to get ahead of my plans to use blades a long time each: they made the blades of poorer quality so they could not be resharpened so well or so many times as formerly. All this already inclined my mind to the possibility of abandoning entirely the use of blades for shaving. Yet the first cost always kept me from venturing to make the change. Now that I have begun to use one, I will probably be a permanent convert to this more humane method of destroying this God-given mark of dignity bestowed on the male sex.

Estie worked in the order department of the bookstore of the House off and on, mostly on, for six weeks in November and December. Every year before, since we live here, she had been called upon to help out with the extra rush of Christmas orders, and therefore she was partly looking for a call to help out again this year. But several weeks before she was really ready to do outside work they called on her to help, the reason being that Anna Mumaw, the regular worker in the department, was out because of illness. Estie received about forty-six dollars in wages, working at the rate of thirty-five cents an hour. It was a strain, and in this case was continued to just about the limit of her endurance. The men folks at home tried to help out what they could in cleaning and washing dishes, but even at that it was too heavy a load for any long time. Most of her income thus received she spent for things she wanted to get but which she had not the courage to impose as yet on the family budget. One item was a Flex-Seal cooker, four-quart size of stainless steel. It is one of these new cooking devices, a simple implement whereby you cook things quickly under fifteen pounds pressure, so saving gas and time in cooking and processing foods more scientifically to preserve natural flavors and vitamins. Mrs. Yoder is specially interested in cookery and foods, and is alert to all newest developments in that line, particularly from a health standpoint. For years she has been doing much of her regular cooking in a large, heavy pressure cooker, which has disadvantages for regular meal preparation.

January 23, Dies Jovis, 1941   Just at this time I find myself partly incapacitated with a wrenched or injured knee. Doctor speaks of the ailment as bursitis, an inflammation of the bursae in the knee joint. The trouble was caused by a severe twist of the joint when out tramping on last Monday afternoon. Walking to Connellsville along the B & O tracks between Broadford and that place, I had to get out of the way of an approaching passenger train. Not satisfied with being in the gutter beside the rail bed I attempted quickly to step up toward the fence on a low bank. In heavy boots I failed to make the grade and to avoid losing balance swung quickly when weight of body was resting on right foot. Result was something in the knee was wrenched with almost an audible snap, and I was lame from then on. Could still walk without serious inconvenience. About fifteen minutes more brought me into town, from where, after a little business and an hour in the public library, I came home by trolley. The knee began to swell and grew more stiff. Now I hobble along with a walking stick and keep as quiet as possible and apply remedial measures between times, such as applications of Absorbine Jr. full strength. Hope the matter will be remedied completely before any long time passes by. With the approach of spring, it would be a calamity if hiking in fields and by-roads were impossible.

On October 1 I went on an overnight trip to Mahoning County, Ohio. The occasion for the trip was the request from the S. S. teachers' meeting for a lecture on Luke, since at that time the lessons in the Sunday school started on a course in the Gospel of Luke and in Acts. It was a pleasant experience to spend a few hours in a community where I had never been before. W. E. Oswald, superintendent of Sunday school who is a high school teacher in Youngstown, met me at the train at Salem. We ate supper in that town and from there went to Midway Church. Unbeknown to either of us but discovered as soon as we reached the church was the fact that another meeting had been called for that time and place. Bishop A. J. Steiner, the pastor in charge, explained that some considerable time before that he had received a letter from missionary-on-furlough Amos Swartzendruber asking for an appointment in that community for that evening. Steiner had then completely forgotten all about the matter and had made no appointment, and was reminded of his lapse of memory only by the appearance of Swartzendruber and his wife at his home that afternoon, several hours before time for an evening service. Hastily he had called as many people as he could by phone and made the forgotten appointment. So it turned out that they had a double service that evening. I took about fifty minutes to give my ninety-minute lecture, leaving out nearly half of what I had written. Happily I had a larger audience for my discourse through that misunderstanding than would have been the case otherwise. Thereafter the missionaries gave their talks, and everybody seemed pleased. Out of the collection taken at the service they gave me enough to cover railroad fare plus two dollars bonus. The night I spent at the home of Mr. and Mrs. Stephen Yoder, old acquaintances from Kansas days. Before eleven o'clock next day I was safely at home again. But the recollection still sends shivers up my back of how I came within a few seconds of missing my train at Greensburg on the way out in the afternoon. Taking A. J. Metzler's word for the trolley connections, I started from home too late. The car I planned to take went only to Hecla, and the bus which I then did take had only two minutes time if it was on time itself. Well, it was

on time luckily and I made about three blocks of distance and a long
flight of stairs in the two minutes, managing through the colored por-
ter's kindness and interest to get onto the steps of the dining car without benefit of ticket before the train started to move. I had not run
fast, and did not injure myself. That was one time when my physical
ability resulting from walking and hiking habitually stood me in good
stead. But believe me I'll never allow myself such close train connections again, if it can possibly be avoided. The nervous and mental
strain which I experienced in that ride to Greensburg was terrible.
Metzler, of course, is used to making train connections by a hair or
less and it does not affect his nerves at all. Maybe too, my period of
travelling to make speeches is about at its end again, so I need not
trouble myself much about train schedules. And that suits me just as
well, for there are more interesting things to do than go places to give
lectures.

Dies Lunae, January 27, 1941 The injured knee is still not quite normal
in performance, but its progress in that direction has been satisfactory
and gratifying. Three trips to Dr. Stamm's office have been made mostly for keeping a close check on its condition.

Snow, soft and wet, has been falling during the night. It is turning
into rain now. Wind, the little there is, comes from the east. All in
all our winter weather has been agreeable, very little of the severe
cold snaps with wind roaring in from southwest for days on end. One
can calculate that winter is at least one-half done by now, the Sun is
again moving northward in the sky, and the welcome springtime will be
with us again, even though that event may be still six months in the
future.

We have been making some extra purchases of a capital nature
during the past months, partly because it is to be expected that as the
war economy comes into operation prices will rise making such purchases more difficult for us who are on a fixed allowance schedule
for income. In September I sent an order to Montgomery Ward for
eight-power binoculars of French make. Another investment made last
July and August was some twenty dollars for orthophonic records at
a very low price.

I sent for and received eight symphonies by such composers as Bach,
Haydn, DeBussy, Mozart, Tschaikovsky and others. The reproduction of
these are very fine and we like them. One condition that made the low
priced recordings possible was the fact that the rendering orchestras
performed in each case without special previous practice, and did not
therefore permit their names to appear on the records. Therefore no
one knows who rendered the performance, but so far as my ear for
music is concerned they sound quite as good as if the musicians had
rehearsed to perfection before making recordings.

Dies Saturni, Kalends of February, 1941 As last winter, so again this
winter we are attending some of the lectures sponsored by the Academy
of Science and Art of Pittsburgh. Upon paying five dollars one receives
an annual membership card which admits the holder and one other person to every one of the eighteen or twenty lectures given during the season. The lectures are held on Thursday evenings, and many of them are

very good; nearly all are illustrated with pictures, slides or films. This year so far I have heard four of these lectures. November 7 Thomas C. Poulty lectured on the famous Snow Cruiser which was built in Chicago and taken to the Antarctic snow fields for expeditions of study and exploration. November 21 the lecture was by H. H. Nininger on the subject of Meteors and Meteorites. Mr. Nininger started the study of this subject while a professor at McPherson College in Kansas, and is today giving all his time to this pursuit, being perhaps the world's greatest authority on the subject. December 12 Vincent Palmer lectured on "Threshold of a New World," the new world being the deep-sea world for this man is a deep-sea diver and explorer. January 16 the lecture was on Color in the Arctic, films revealing the wonderful colors in Greenland and points north as seen on a summer's expedition. Mother and Virgil went on January 2 to see a lecture on Travel in U.S.A., which they reported as very good. We have a kind of standing arrangement to ride in Miss Ruth Ressler's motor car when she makes the trip. Last year we had a ticket for ourselves which we would loan out on the occasions when we did not choose to go ourselves. This winter we are saving half the expense by letting David Alderfer pay for half of the ticket which is in my name, so that he gets the chance to be the second party whenever he wants to go.

The lecture scheduled for January 30 was by Mr. Stotz on Early Architecture of Western Pennsylvania. For weeks and months I had looked forward to the opportunity of hearing this particular number. And then what should happen but that the roads were a sheet of treacherous ice and snow, the worst of the season just on that evening, too dangerous to venture out on such a drive. In preparation for hearing this lecture I looked through Mr. Stotz's fine book on the same subject as his scheduled lecture. He is an architect, and this large beautiful book is mostly photographs of surviving architecture of the time before 1860. There are also detailed architectural drawings and specifications of most of the buildings which are given in photographs. Some of his photographs are of particular interest because they are from this immediate vicinity. Among them are the Newmeyer Barn near Pennsville, built in 1796, and the Stoner Barn near Hawkeye. The latter is of brick, the former largely of stone. One is of the old spring house at West Overton on the old Overholt homestead, and unless my recollection errs from what I have heard say this was the building in which H. C. Fricke was born. It was built in 1838. Then there is a picture of the Mt. Vernon furnace near Wooddale, which I have not myself seen as yet. Also of particular interest is the fact that this book has several photographs of and pertaining to the Mennonite Church near Harmony in Butler County of this state. This is located north of Pittsburgh some distance and was built in 1825. It is a rather beautiful and well-preserved specimen of early architecture, made of brick, although the roof looks to be modern. It is no longer in use by Mennonites, and I did not grasp from what I read whether it is in use at all or is merely a shrine or relic kept up for historical reasons, or by whom. Naturally I cannot rest at ease now until I get to make a trip and see the place for myself. The place has an interesting history. The Rappists, a communistic group, first settled that community. In 1814 they sold everything to one named Ziegler, evidently a Mennonite, and there was a

Mennonite settlement there until the end of the century or longer. The history of that settlement from a Mennonite viewpoint has never been recorded. H. S. Bender once mentioned to me the need for such a study of that settlement, and I am ambitious enough to imagine it would be a nice project for me to take up after the Westmoreland-Fayette settlement has been duly studied and written up.

February 8, 1941 For several weeks weather has been wintry with snow, ice, and steady cold. For a few days we had hopes that more mildish weather was at hand, but yesterday and last night the mercury has been dropping, a strong west wind carried snow flurries, now thick now thin, and today we are shivering again more than before. In many ways solid footing beneath is more pleasant than slush and mud, yet people generally look forward with eager anticipation to spring and warm weather by the time February is here. The mythical ground hog did not see his shadow in these parts last Sunday, but he probably overslept and so our winter weather keeps up as before.

Among purchases made in recent months have been the following. In September eight-power binoculars acquired for the sum of about twenty-four dollars. The retail value of this glass is said to be about thirty-five dollars. For years, and especially since coming here among the hills, I have wished for good all-purpose binoculars. Calculating that the supply of these might be snatched up for military use and the manufacture be interrupted, and that prices would almost certainly rise before long, I stretched the family budget enough to invest the money. It is a fine glass, and barring accident will last me indefinitely. In the way of clothing equipment too we have invested some money. For outdoor wear and hiking I am well equipped. The Hi-cut boots and corduroy breeches purchased over three years ago are good and will last for many years to come, wearing them several times every winter. Bought recently another flannel shirt, and best of all a heavy mackinaw coat, blue color, heavy lined, and in every way a beauty, all for about five dollars from the Sears Roebuck sale price list. The old suede lined jacket is still very good except for outward appearance. For woodsing and rural road tramping it will be useful for years to come; only for street wear to Connellsville or locally, it seems too dingy and soiled for use. Estie has been making some capital purchases for household purposes. Several important items for cooking use have been acquired and some extra blankets for bedroom use have been ordered lately.

We need several small articles of furniture, specially a record cabinet and a small cabinet for the kitchen. It seems almost impossible to purchase exactly what we need, and it may be necessary to build what we want if we are to have them. I am such an unskilled workman and have such very crude tools and facilities for working that I hesitate to undertake trying to make these articles myself. If I had tools and facilities, it would be a pleasure to experiment and see what I could get done toward that end.

February 20, 1941 Following several weeks of moderately cold weather, steady and entirely bearable, last week gave us about four days of mildish temperature with real honest-to-goodness sunshine that was worth talking about. The days were so nice and they served to make one think and feel that now at last springtime is no longer far away. Perhaps, perhaps there would be no more severe or prolonged cold weather this season. It was a cruel and tantalizing hope, for now we are in the midst of our longest and severest storm period of the whole winter so far. The wind from west southwest comes roaring in upon us in unwearied and pitiless procession. Up here on the summit of Walnut Street it has its chance to strike most directly and with full force. It seems to take delight in making fullest use of its unhindered opportunity to drive the cold in at every crack and crevice. It comes tumbling, and rolling, and roaring and whistling round the windows on our side of the house, and with great glee rattles and shakes the window sash and sometimes pounds and beats and pummels and moans and groans and sighs and whines as it tries to get in even more than the loose-fitting windows will allow.

No long tramps have been part of my schedule for a month past, due to my injured knee. There are many points and places to visit as soon as ever the weather is mild and the ground solid, places for gathering further information and data pertaining to the local history. Miss Ruth Ressler is interested and she is volunteering to drive around some in the interest of the same cause. Meanwhile it will be possible to get inside tasks and duties done out of the way so as to be more free to spend time out-of-doors when the season for that comes.

The public mind in United States is in utmost confusion. Many are already hysterically warminded and urging that this nation help Britain with all possible aid. It looks as though this will be the real World War, of which the hostilities of twenty-five years ago were merely the opening skirmish. The issue of Christianity versus war is being sharply drawn in the thinking and discussion of many thoughtful persons. Many believe that democracy, righteousness, culture, and even Christianity itself can in this crisis be preserved only through force and power politics. Others believe as firmly that the use of such methods results only in destruction of the very things which their users mean to save. It is an interesting though trying time to live.

June 9, 1941 It is a sore shame that I have been so extremely dilatory in writing on these casual notes. The three and one-half months have been quite busy and yet I have no written record of what occupied my time during these months and weeks. April was a remarkable month, because it was mild and sunny much of the time. Fruit trees bloomed in full glory before the middle of the month. We have a piece of a lot to use for garden this year. May was not so favorable. Considerable clear weather, but numerous frosty mornings, sufficient freezing to ruin strawberries, grapes, some cherries, and perhaps other fruits. Lately there have been heavy rains and considerable warm weather.

Outdoor hikes have so far mostly taken me only moderate distances from home. In April Saturday forenoons were spent in copying tombstone inscriptions in the oldest sector of the Alverton Cemetery, and in the old Pennsville Cemetery. The work on the local history has made some progress. One day I spent in the courthouse at Uniontown and another at Greensburg. Occasionally some very interesting items of history come to light. Yet the detailed search for data has evidently only begun. Much of the work from this time forward will be that of leisurely and deliberately making personal contacts with older people in the communities around, piecing together bits and scraps of information, and so building up more complete data.

June 10, 1941   The principal work on hand this week is to complete for publication in the Mennonite Quarterly Review the article on the local Mennonite history of this section around Scottdale. My intermittent researches during past months have increased my personal interest in this project. While a score more or less of very tantalizing problems still remain to be solved, yet for this article to serve as a gesture of the one hundred fiftieth historical anniversary of this settlement, it should be published this year, even though it may be premature to try to publish anything final and authoritative on the subject. As my first venture in historical research and historical writing this project is very interesting. In case my efforts prove successful, I can see visions of spending the rest of my years in pursuing this hobby and the Mennonite settlements of western Pennsylvania offer a large and promising field of operations for someone. If no one takes it up as a trained historian, I may be directing such amateur abilities as I have toward that work. If only someone had devoted some systematic effort to the local history in this part fifty years sooner, much could have been recovered which is now perhaps irretrievably lost. Today I begin typing the revised manuscript on the early history here, the first one hundred years, which I prepared last November for the local sesquicentennial celebration. The manuscript for the period of the past fifty years is already practically in final form. Editor H. S. Bender is pushing to have these manuscripts appear in the July and October issues of the Review.

June 14, 1941   There has been rain and rain in recent weeks. It is good that there is moisture in the ground, for we have a garden again, first time since 1937. Mrs. Yoder would not be satisfied this year without a garden. On the other side of our alley Walter Loucks has a vacant lot, part of which he has been using in recent years. Upon application we secured the use of half of the lot and we have planted all kinds of things. But working the soil here is quite a different matter from the same process in Iowa, Kansas, or Indiana, the other states where we have done gardening before, or I at any rate. Here there are stones, stones, and stones. The hoe strikes them at every stroke and they are a general nuisance and inconvenience. Doubtful if I shall ever get used to farming where the soil is full of stones, but Estie is ambitious and will do all she can to make our gardening a success.

    The house in Kansas needs painting again, and the tenant and myself are trying to make plans to get it done during the coming summer or fall. The house is now over twenty years old and will depreciate in value steadily. Wish heartily that there would be some providential windfall in the form of a buyer for the place. With the prospect of general inflation in prices, it would be an advantage to own our home where we are living instead of over a thousand miles away. But to get something here that will suit our taste and ideals may be just as hard a task as to dispose of the property in Kansas. I always feel very timid and helpless in matters of finance and business transactions.

September 5, 1941   These occasional notes have been too "occasional" to be successful this year so far. With the occupation I have, where writing is a major part of my work, it is rather unnatural to take one's leisure in writing some more. Perhaps a brief day by day diary would be more successful now for me as a method of personal record. Past months have been very busy, so it seemed at the time at least. Second quarter 1942 lessons were done intermittently from June to August 15. Two weeks in mid-July were given to teaching a class of high school students in summer Bible school at the Pittsburgh Street school building.

On August 19 we all left for annual vacation, going to Iowa in Ira Miller's motor car. They had a total of seven passengers for the trip from here and return. We enjoyed a pleasant visit with home folks, and attended many sessions of General Conference, held by the site of the meetinghouse where as a boy and youth I attended Sunday school thirty and forty years ago. There would be many things to note down from past weeks; perhaps they would be as well forgotten as recorded. If possible some reminiscences of their events will be recorded in future notes.

September 6, 1941   Our little trip to Iowa was very interesting. Since it was conference time, we did not visit as much and as thoroughly with relatives as we might have liked, except with Father and Howard Gnageys, with whom he stays. Father continues about as he has been, slightly better perhaps than he was in 1938 when we visited him last before. Iowa still looks good to my eyes, all quite natural except for the people, very few of whom below the age of twenty-five or thirty I know any more. The climate and atmosphere are rather different from here. The stars in the night sky, as I looked at them again, seemed to sparkle and glisten and twinkle many times more brilliantly than they do in Pennsylvania. The air feels different, and the aspect of clouds is different.

With Father I discussed some matters of family and community history. Spent also an hour or so in the recorder's files at Iowa City, finding the dates when my great-grandfather, Henry Hochstetler, bought land in Iowa, and when grandfather, Tobias Yoder, bought his farm from Hochstetler. The former, I find, purchased various tracts of land in 1855 and 1856, and grandfather in March 1864 bought 160 acres from his father-in-law for $3500. Visited with Henry Gingerich, who told of much early history from memory. He has an unusually clear memory for detailed events in his own experience. For one thing he related some things about the early Sunday schools conducted in the settlement by the Amish. Among other matters too, Gingerich summarized for me the evidence that the earliest Sunday school in that community was conducted in 1866, earlier than the date given by Melvin Gingerich in his recent book on the Mennonites in Iowa. Henry Gingerich is an uncle of this author. The early date would place the Sunday school in Iowa among the earliest Amish and Mennonite Sunday schools. Whether it was a permanent and continuous affair after that is uncertain. There were then no meetinghouses, and Sunday schools were conducted in various district schoolhouses, some contemporaneously evidently.

Our attendance at the sessions of the General Conference was rather "faithful," as the saying is. That is, we took in the public sessions almost one hundred per cent. I myself missed the last one in order to be at home with Father yet during the last half day of our stay. Some persons more important than I sat in on the numerous delegate sessions, where the real discussions and debates were put on. But personally I have no taste at all for ecclesiastical politics and the heat of battle and debate over controversial matters. Several friends reported to me privately some of the things that were debated and battled over. The public meetings as programmed were good, though in general one might characterize them perhaps as spouting off words and phrases that have been rehearsed many times before. If necessary, this attendance at General Conference will suffice me for a good many years. Such great crowds still rather terrify and frighten me.

September 8, 1941   There has been much rain in this area in recent weeks. The last shower was on last Friday evening, when a real rain storm swept over this section. Saturday was a fair day, clear and sunny in the morning, with just the suggestion of possible clouds later in the day, and so it turned out. Thinking to take advantage of the sunshine while there was opportunity, I devoured some hasty sandwiches about eleven o'clock and then set out. I tramped in Bullskin Township. Made a line for the farm home of S. A. Detwiler, whom I had never seen before but had heard of as an elderly man. Found the man at home, a genial, interesting gentleman, seventy-two years old, broken in health, but still managing part of his farm. His grandfather, Henry Detwiler, and his father, John S. Detwiler, operated the well-known Detwiler Mills for many years. This man's wife was a Kaegy, whose ancestors were Dunkard, some of them very active as preachers and evangelists in early days. He spoke of an old German Bible which is stored away in their attic, and perhaps other old German books. I expressed the wish to see these some time, and if they would get them out I would stop again some later time and look at them. It is more and more evident that the only practical way to get trace of the old books used by Mennonites and Dunkards is to go to the old farmsteads and get people to search in their attics for whatever may be stored away there. Mr. Detwiler also informed me of the old Rice burial ground located about three-quarter mile north from his house. This was my first knowledge of this cemetery. Although apparently no Mennonites were buried there, I was glad to learn of it and to make a visit to the place. It is located on a small hill on the borderline between two farms. A fence of wooden boards once enclosed the plot, which was of considerable size, I would guess at least seventy-five or eighty feet square. The fence has fallen down for the most part. But the thick growth of saplings and young trees serves to keep the farmer's live stock from trespassing and destroying the spot completely. There are several dozen marble markers still in good condition, and as many more crude stone markers can be discerned. Many more graves are no longer marked, if they ever were, as one may judge from the numerous sunken places. Evidently for fifty years past no burials have been made in this plot.

There must be a score or more of these old family plots within a few miles from Scottdale, if one can discover them. The only way to learn of these is by talking with the older people, for they are usually back in the fields and unkempt so that from walking along roads, even though one walked within sight of one such, he would not know of it.

September 16, 1941 The fourth successive day of clear sunshine is here today. Could not get away yesterday to absorb any of the generous sun's rays, due to the fact that the July number of the Mennonite Quarterly Review was going through the press, and they were sending press proofs to my office all day long. Today I hope to get some outdoor air and sunshine. On Saturday we enjoyed a trip and picnic near Springs, about sixty miles away. Ruth Bender is having a cabin of logs built in Olen Bender's woods about one mile from Springs. It is not altogether completed as yet, but has walls, roof, floor, fireplace, bunks, table, drawers and some shelves. Miss Anna Mumaw taxied us all over from here. Left Scottdale at 11:15 in the forenoon and were happy for the privilege of inspecting the cabin and deciding on its merits and prospective value. Toasted "hot dogs" in the fireplace, and had a fine picnic lunch. The woods are thick and very pleasant to be in on a shiny, bright day. A few small open spots admit sunshine on and around the cabin during midday. Already we are contemplating to ask for the use of the place for a two-week vacation sometime next summer, if we have such a vacation then.

Just now tent meetings are being held in East Scottdale by the local Mennonite Congregation. A. J. Metzler is preaching nightly from the Epistle to the Romans. The effort is a typical evangelistic campaign with the accepted psychological attitudes and customs. The effort does some good no doubt. Yet it all seems a little distant from New Testament evangelism and historic Mennonite practice.

September 25, 1941 Today there are clouds in the sky, drab unfriendly-looking clouds sailing under a rather uncertain wind that blows. For nearly two weeks cloudless days were here, extraordinarily pleasant days. Sun shone rather warm, nights were cool. Over the equinox for one night there was a display of the aurora borealis, otherwise no atmospheric disturbance at all. The peaceful and gentle advent of autumn was very welcome, inspiring the hope and wish that this autumn may be characterized by the rare days which ushered it in.

Writing lessons for third quarter of next year; plan to go as rapidly as possible in finishing up the 1942 lessons. The third quarter is a series which I have not covered at any time in my writing – the book of Genesis. This is not the easiest part of the Bible to write Sunday school lessons on, as there are so many varied and radical opinions as to the interpretation of the earlier chapters of the book especially.

Estie has been canning fruit, such as she can get hold of, although comparatively little is being peddled from door to door this year. Virgil is in fourth grade and seems not to take the work this year so seriously; last year he had much written homework to do but this year none so far yet. Ordered four volumes of de Luxe Records at the low price, from same headquarters in Pittsburgh as last year, one symphony by Franck, and a condensed Opera by Wagner. Have decided that some money must be invested in pictures for walls of my office and also at home. Hard to know where to get them.

November 25, 1941 It seems to be impossible to write on these notes with any regularity for some reason. Many interesting activities and experiences have filled the months since the last "note" was penned in these pages. During October the S. S. lesson material for third quarter of 1942 was written out in manuscript form.

Early in October a meeting of the Curriculum Committee necessitated a trip to Goshen, Indiana. Returning from that place I stopped off overnight in Wooster, Ohio, for an interview with Mr. John D. Overholt regarding data on the history of his ancestors who once lived in Westmoreland County, Pennsylvania. Had an interesting and profitable visit. The man, who was a total stranger, entertained me at the best hotel in town, that is, paid the cost of my room and meals. The hours from eight to eleven o'clock in the evening I was at his large and finely furnished home near the campus of Wooster College.

One weekend in the last of October I spent at Lansdale, Pennsylvania, in Montgomery County. Had a pleasant and enjoyable trip, having been called there to make some speeches on a S. S. meeting program. Both going and coming I spent a half day in Philadelphia, one at the headquarters and library of the Pennsylvania Historical Society, and another mostly at Leary's Book Store. This month has been spent mostly at odds and ends: editing quarterly copy, trying to get the Horsch History manuscript moving on into a book, getting the remainder of our library materials from Horsch's house into the House library. Horsch died early in October; now all our library things can be collected at one place, instead of having them scattered around in two places. Hope to spend most of the time in January and part of February in further organizing the library books and materials so that I can find things when they are wanted. Then there has been some time given in recent weeks to the important hobby of collecting data on the local Mennonite history. Much remains to be done of detailed work, gathering information on the early families and their activities, from which one may partly construct the picture of the early Mennonite congregation and community in this place. The investigation is interesting and at times even exciting. Much of it will have to be done in the records at Greensburg and Uniontown, some in surveying old cemeteries, some by making personal contacts with people living on the old homesteads around and finding ways to search old attics for forgotten books or other materials. Am starting to write letters to local and more distant people as a means for opening contacts that might lead to some results. From now on one must expect to run up many a blind alley, but then one knows at least it is a blind one, and not one that leads to a "find." Then once in a while one will run into a real discovery too.

For the immediate future, six weeks or so, a writing assignment from the Mennonite Central Committee must be carried through, fourth quarter 1942 lessons must be written, and as a preface to this, a weekend trip to Goshen, Indiana, for a meeting of Mennonite General Conference Historical Committee.

November 27, 1941 This is Thanksgiving Day, not Mr. Roosevelt's Thanksgiving however, which was observed in some states last week. According to some reports this was to be the last year in which the President would proclaim a New Deal Thanksgiving, different from long-established tradition and practice. Today promises to be clear and beautiful, which will make a fine opportunity for an outdoor tramp and hike after the Thanksgiving dinner is put away under our belts. This dinner at our house will be relatively simple; some predictive hints suggested sausage and pumpkin pie as being the specials. Three years ago, the first Thanksgiving we spent in Pennsylvania, there was a blizzard and snowstorm, very cold and unpleasant. Two years ago there was a little snow on the ground at least in the mountains. I made a trip to the Stahl meetinghouse near Johnstown, going in the morning and returning late at night, travelling with David Alderfer. My reason for going on this trip was to make a speech, or read a paper, on the program of a peace and nonresistance conference. Of last year I have no hard and fast recollection, excepting that we were at the appointed morning service in the home church.

The year 1941 has been a year blessed with an unusual amount of sunshiny days and pleasant weather, or else the several previous years we lived here were exceptional in the amount of cloudiness. For we have appreciated the sunshine wonderfully much. Certain weeks in April, June, July, September stand out specially in memory in this respect.

December 1, 1941   First day of the first winter month, and it is cloudy, murky, yet mild and not unpleasant on the whole.

Today I started writing on an 18,000 word assignment from the Mennonite Central Committee, a pamphlet or textbook for use among the men in the Civilian Public Service Camps, as a part of the educational program. Title of mine is "Our Mennonite Heritage"; what they want is a kind of mutual back slapping effort perhaps, though it will be as nearly factual and objective as I can make it.

Last Saturday was a hike of sixteen to eighteen miles, a good, long, exploratory walk. Frost was heavy on grass in the morning, reminding me of mornings we used to go out in November in Iowa to husk corn from the stalk in the field. Left the house at 8:30 and headed southwest for Dawson. Stopped briefly at the Bethel and the Cochran cemeteries and reached Dawson about eleven o'clock. After exploring various points, a Catholic cemetery and a lofty hilltop, it was about twelve o'clock when I reached the cemetery near Vanderbilt, a rather extensive one. An hour and more was taken up with exploring this and copying inscriptions which interested me. Some lost generations of Mennonites are buried there, Shallenbergers, Stoners, Stricklers, Snyders. From Vanderbilt I tramped eastward and finally over picturesque roads reached Broadford, there crossed the Youghiogheny on an old abandoned railroad trestle. And so reached home at five-thirty o'clock, after a pleasant absence of nine hours. On Sunday Emanuel Hertzler, a former friend at Goshen College, now teaching near Pittsburgh, was guest at our house for dinner and the afternoon, also Ruth Bender and Ralph Bender.

December 13, 1941   Today rain is falling, skies are heavy and at three-thirty o'clock it appears to be already growing dark, so gloomy is the weather. A few films of snow lay on the ground during the past week, and the temperature dropped to sixteen degrees one morning.

Am coming near the end of one phase of my special writing assign-

ment from the Mennonite Central Committee. Have the typed manuscript of two parts complete, the rough first pencil draft of nine more
parts written out. There is one more to write out. Then it will all
be laid aside for two or three weeks and other work will be pushed.
Later about one week's work will see it all finished, provided it will
pass editorial inspection. Sunday school lessons manuscript for fourth
quarter of 1942 are on the list for immediate attention as soon as this
is possible. If nothing serious intervenes, January 10 should see both
projects carried through. I would now have the rough draft of the
Central Committee's booklet complete, had it not been that I took off
yesterday for a day of research in the archives at Uniontown. A letter
of inquiry received from a stranger in Eastern Pennsylvania pertaining
to information about a Jacob Eshleman who settled in this locality over
a century ago, gave the pretext for this excursion. Found a little information to relay to the inquirer, and so making a contact that may
bring me further information in course of time that bears on the local
Mennonite history. In recent trips to Connellsville and Uniontown I have
tried to concentrate attention on the local Reist families of early date.
They were Mennonites, at least at first, and it seems that about two
strains of them came in here, but what relation they were and what
family connection they had with other Reists in eastern counties I have
been unable to discover. Such are the problems and difficulties one
meets in pursuing what is otherwise a most enjoyable hobby and diversion.

The World War has at last gotten under way. Last Sunday the Japanese naval and air forces made surprise attacks on American possessions in the Pacific Ocean. Americans are generally very angry and
all called for war against Japan and the President has committed himself to the proposition that victory and nothing but complete victory
will be the goal. It all looks very clear and simple to the man in the
street, the average citizen. Yet one wonders if the provocation given
to the little brown man of the Orient was not perhaps equal to the
guilt of the sudden unprovoked attack. Many things can happen quickly
in this day and age of the world, yet it will take a miracle or its
equivalent to make this a short war. My guess will be a war of five
to ten years rather than less. The so-called gangster nations are of
course organized and prepared to the limit of their resources, while
the countries of the western hemisphere have scarcely begun to make
preparations. If the issue is not to be decided some way before the
U. S. has organized itself to something like its limit, then it will be
many years before peace will return to the world. Meanwhile the insane, murderous, stupid business must be carried on, so we are told,
regardless of the destruction of moral and spiritual values on an unprecedented scale. The whole affair is bound to be a victory for Mr.
Hitler and his philosophy, for every large nation on the globe will be
ruled by an iron dictator before complete victory will result for anyone. Hitler's world revolution is now certain to become a reality; all
are going insane.

December 27, 1941 The year again is drawing toward its close.
The past week has been a kind of vacation week. Last Monday morning I chanced to ride into Pittsburgh with Dick Cutrell. From there I

rode the Pennsylvania Railroad train to Warsaw, thence by bus to Goshen, where I arrived by 7:00 in the evening. After the night at Harold Benders', the Historical Committee of General Conference was in session for the day. Came back to Pittsburgh that same night. Spent from 9:30 to 3:00 nosing around in the old records at Greensburg, and reached home at 5:00 in the evening. Thursday of course was Christmas.

Yesterday was a mild, sunny day for the most part – the kind of day that calls one to tramp out-of-doors. Hoping that by chance there might be another such today, I did other things yesterday and neglected the opportunity for getting out. Today, alas, the clouds are heavy and a touch of rain or snow is in the air. So one is impressed with the folly of putting off a fine opportunity on the strength of the hope that another will come tomorrow.

It so turns out that since the meeting on Tuesday at Goshen, I have many added responsibilities, among them those of being treasurer of the committee and of the Historical Association which it sponsors, co-editor of the Historical Bulletin, and circulation manager and general promotor of the same Bulletin. The only consolation is that this work at least is in line with an interest of mine, more so than is true of some other things thrust upon me.

February 7, 1942   More than a month of the new year has flown by. Best of all the winter is more than half gone by, and it will not be many months before warm sunshine and balmy days will be here again. Along about this time of the year one begins to long for and definitely look forward to the return of warm weather; I get hungry and feel starved for sunshine.

The past weeks have been busy with routine schedule, although the slate has been getting cleaned off in right smart fashion of late. This week was devoted to editing and preparing copy for the second quarter German Quarterly copy. Last week was similarly taken up with the copy for third quarter teachers' and advanced quarterly copy. Two weeks ago I finished off the copy for the booklet assigned to me from the Mennonite Central Committee. The next pressing matter will be finishing up matters pertaining to the Horsch history, especially making the index to be printed at the end. This book is now being put through the press. So there is hope that after eighteen or nineteen months of work and worry this task will before long be completed and gotten off my hands. Have learned many things through this experience, even though it was hard at times.

Between scheduled events and agenda on my program, some other matters have been sandwiched and crowded in. The reprint of the article on the Mennonites of Westmoreland County, Pennsylvania is now under way. It is being reprinted from the Mennonite Quarterly Review type by the local congregation, according to decision at its January business meeting. Because in the necessary number of leaves according to multiples of eight, several pages were not taken up by the reprint proper, we prepared several features to fill up the space. One is a map of the local community which indicates the location of the early meeting houses and of the early land purchases in the settlement by Mennonites. Due to crowded schedule in the production departments it may be several weeks before the final product is finished.

Meanwhile as there has been opportunity during the winter months, I have continued tramping abroad for more historical data. Not so long ago a Strickler family history manuscript was brought to the House for printing. Through advance peeks at the manuscript more information about some early Mennonite settlers has come to hand. Also some problems were raised which were not visible in the darkness of ignorance. From the manuscript, I discovered the location of an early Strickler burial ground near Owensdale of which I had no knowledge, though I had practically decided by inference on the necessity of the existence of just such an one. Strangely enough, I had many times walked within a stone's throw of this plot in going along the road nearby. Two weeks ago today I visited the place, copied some of the data from the stones, but the wind was too damp and chilly to permit me to stand still long enough to copy them all. The same day I also stopped at the little plot just east of Owensdale, copied the inscriptions, mostly Boyd and Hurst. From there I followed on eastward the outline of the old public road that once ran from Owensdale almost in a straight line east to the old Pennsville meeting house and on eastward to Pennsville. It was not possible to tramp on the old bed all the way, due to the recent activities of a steam shovel in search of coal by the process known as strip mining. Yet it was interesting and almost romantic to trace the old road bed, part of the way still used as farmers' lane and elsewhere totally abandoned. At some points it was deeply worn and washed out. After a brief pause at the old Pennsville cemetery, I tramped home. Just the Saturday before that, I rode to Connellsville, read in the library for four hours or more, and when ready to take up my walking stick from its customary parking place it was not there. Hope the thief needs it as much as I do. Tramped home without a stick.

Dies Saturni, February 14, 1942 This month is one-half gone into history, and no regrets, since another six or eight weeks will bring us to the threshold of springtime, and more sunshine, walking out without hat and overcoat. Am always glad when spring comes in sight. This year one does not know whether to welcome the season as usual or not. For the warmakers in Europe will probably be looking forward to spring as an opportunity for new drives, pushes, and campaigns. In this country the confusion and hysteria is being worse confounded every day. Huge headlines in the dailies tell of smashing successes over the Japs every day, and in the smaller print they tell of the steady and rapid progress of the Japanese forces day by day. Some in this country are beginning to shout that we are being defeated or on the verge of being defeated. Months ago some, or other experts, were telling the world that Japan would not last more than a few weeks in a war against the almighty U. S. A.; their paper and tinder-built cities would be blown to bits and burned up in a hurry by air raids. Now the officials and columnists are ranting over their disappointment that the inhabitants of the U. S. A. are not getting angry and indignant and hysterical one-tenth fast enough, as though emotions would lick the Axis powers overnight. It is all a funny show for one who looks on and as a matter of principle tries not to be angry and hate other people. It may easily prove true yet that the U. S. A. should have confined its defense activities strictly to the western hemisphere, and held itself in readiness to serve as a minister of peace and reconstruction instead of assuming responsibility, or trying to do so, for the state of affairs all over the globe. Personally I believe Roosevelt's whole foreign and global policy has been a colossal and tragic mistake, and will be content to write that much down in this private way.

This week, on Tuesday, we bargained to purchase the Gilnett property at 714 Walnut Avenue. It so happened that we had about nine hundred dollars in the local bank, being surplus income over about three years. Question was what to do with it. The bank does not care for savings accounts, pays barely two per cent interest on such. Should I have paid off indebtedness of my own with this surplus on hand, for we have thirteen hundred of that to pay some time? In view of the possibility of inflation through rapidly rising prices, and the low price, $2000, at which this property was obtainable, we decided to make the jump now. Debts will not be affected much by inflation, in fact might even be more easily paid with inflated dollars. Besides we have uncollected salary outstanding to an amount that would nearly cover the old debts we have, except that we get no interest on what is owed to us, whiles we pay five per cent interest on what we owe. That is our way of financing. The house in Kansas is being well cared for, a new roof put on two years ago and now lately painted and repaired. For a number of years the annual monies for taxes and interest on the Hesston property has been drawn from the old salary account at Goshen. As long as that continues, I can use all the rent income from the house for my own purposes. So that is not a bad load to carry for the time being. Collection on the notes which I took over in lieu of most of the old unpaid salary account has been very slow so far. Am hoping for more rapid payments in the future. But with all the existing uncertainty there may easily be none at all for a long time – who knows.

We much wanted a place of our own, aside from the investment angle. A little more room outside, garden and a place for chickens, as occasion for a little more work for a growing boy, an opportunity for him to learn to do a few things and assume some degree of responsibility according to his ability. Estie as always is ambitious to raise lots and all kinds of things to eat, which is a good idea now that living costs are going up. The property we bought was signed over by Mr. Gilnett to a local bank about two years ago, and the bank was getting anxious to unload it, hence the low price at which the place was offered. The price asked for it was $2100; I made an offer to pay $2000 and they promptly accepted my bid. One does not stand to lose much in buying at that price unless a completely unseen social revolution sweeps the country; and we have made ourselves a nice little reservoir for all our surplus income for a number of years to come.

February 21, 1942 Winter has been off again on again this month, mostly on again. This is the third day of cold, raw, very chilling temperature. There are spells of snow flurries and some wind blowing, though not of gale proportions, fortunately.

This week has been devoted in my office to the making of an index to the Horsch history, with prospects of finishing up the job on that book within the next week. It is a fond hope just now, that March may be quite free of assigned routine duties and can mostly be devoted to creative reading, browsing and rearranging in the historical library and working on local Mennonite history matters. There will be some interruptions this coming week in connection with our new venture into the owning of real estate, house and lot. It is not yet clear where the money for the mortgage will be coming from, may have to fall back on the bank, though had hoped to get the necessary amount at a lower rate of interest than the bank would charge. It seems odd to go into such financial arrangements again, when past financial experiences have not been so excellent with us. The main consoling feature is the fact that in this case we are starting in on our venture at a rather different point in the economic cycle than the other time, with the hope we will fare better than before, at least not any worse.

We decided that a few alterations in household equipment would be desirable in the new quarters which we hope to occupy before long. The plan is that no longer will we devote a room exclusively for study and den, but will have desk and books in one end of the main living room. That makes necessary a smaller desk and one that more nearly matches the furnishings of a living room. The office desk, which I bought at Anderson's Book Store in Newton, Kansas in 1928, second-hand for twenty-five dollars, is now for sale at the same price or less perhaps. A living room desk will likely be purchased to take its place. Then instead of the old daybed, also purchased in 1928 or 1929, at Montgomery Ward in Newton, we must purchase a more comfortable studio couch. This morning all of us, including our weekend guest, Ruth Bender, went shopping at the furniture stores in Scottdale, it being still the time of their February sale. At Murphy's the ladies found a couch which they decided was just exactly what we needed. So we bought it subject to later delivery, and also a small bedroom rocker. So it appears that we are letting ourselves in for some changes and ventures in living. If the bottom falls out of everything – well, we shall wait and see.

January 21, 1943 Well, well, here we are, eleven months of time gone by without any notes of record made. It is a sad fact. The months in question have been filled with busy and many unusual and interesting happenings. Must try to set down in brief form from memory the principal events that will be worth remembering. Such is the state of affairs; when there are many interesting things that deserve to be recorded, then there is no time for doing the recording. Just now there is a lull and the idea of scribbling notes again occurred to me. It is not that all routine work is fully up to schedule, but am taking a few good deep breaths of leisure.

The special assignments are drawing on toward their completion. The Horsch volume on which I began doing editorial work about July, 1940, finally came out all finished about July of the past year. So far as my little part in its publication is concerned, I do not have any reason to feel ashamed. The choice of illustrations seems to meet with a favorable reception all around. All in all this editorial job served me as the occasion for a considerably wider acquaintance with Mennonite history and its pertinent literature. For this opportunity I am thankful, and hope to be able to follow it up as time goes on.

Now to survey in outline some of the high points in our activities since last February. The deal for the purchase of the old Gilnett property was closed the first days of March. I was able to arrange for a loan of $1400 from Mrs. Homer Kauffman of this place. We moved into the house on April 14, George and Dorothy Smoker having moved out. To close that phase of the story, the Smokers sailed for Africa, via Chile and Argentina in October or November. The most of their baggage was shipped from New York to Argentina, and was sunk to the bottom of the ocean by an Axis submarine.

Well, we moved, mostly by wheelbarrow, Anna Mumaw's passenger automobile, and the heavy pieces by Millers' transfer. Did I ever work hard and long days for a week or ten days getting moved and slowly settled! And garden planting had to be done too along the way. The matter of getting things arranged about the house required months.

January 22, 1943 As to work we did and had done to the house since we moved into it: late in May and early June we rearranged the kitchen. Austin Gilnett did the carpenter work, but there was also plumbing work done. Wife thinks it is very well arranged. The cupboards above the work table and sink were mere open shelves. We moved them of course, extended them up to the ceiling and also some in length. With Austin's help in Brilhart's mill I made nine doors, finished, fitted, painted and hung them. They do not yet have handles and catches. That job is on the slate for the near future. The worktable on one side of the sink is an open-shelf affair too. That is to be closed up yet and inlaid linoleum to be put on top and the whole painted. Then the kitchen will at last be finished.

In the living room I built book shelves from floor to ceiling, with the lower three shelves closed by means of doors. We papered the entire downstairs, working hard several days to remove numerous layers of old wallpaper.

On the outside of the house we placed a covering of Buff Brickside shingles, the thick kind that are insulated and help to keep the cold and wind out in some measure. Brilhart Lumber Company furnished the materials and Walter Shaulis did the work of putting it on. The total amount of the cost of this project was around three hundred dollars. At the same time while the carpenter was on the job we had him repair the corner of the back porch, and also remove the little dog-house style front porch and put a small projecting roof across the front of the house, and a neat entrance portal around the front door. The redesigning and rebuilding of the front porch platform and steps is still ahead, if war conditions do not prevent it for the duration. Last week Mr. Shaulis fitted six storm sash for the south and west windows. On last Saturday I put a priming coat of paint on these. They are to be hung up now, and regularly painted when spring comes. We were fortunate in getting a painter in November. He got most of his work done but not all around porches. His long ladders are nicely laid out on the grass waiting for spring to open up. Mr. Lewellyn did the painting. The house has taken on a rather changed appearance from what it had a year ago. The roof sprang a leak recently, so that will require some repairs as soon as warm weather comes along. Maintaining a building is a rather different proposition in this climate and surroundings than in Kansas where we owned property before. The soft coal somehow brings sulphur and fumes into the atmosphere which eat up paint and materials in a hurry.

June 11, 1943   It seems just impossible for me to write with any regularity on these notes. Life is becoming too complex and complicated for one's leisure and peace of mind. One hardly seems to live in the full sense when there are so many distractions that it is quite impossible to find leisure time for living. Upon coming here five years ago and having few routine duties aside from the work I was directly engaged to do, there was leisure time and freedom to take recreation and do creative reading and study. The leisure time for the first three or four years which was thus at my disposal I was able to spend with rich and satisfying returns. I began the intensive exploration of the local area, a hobby that has by no means yet been exhausted. Also I was able to browse in Mennonite history and literature, exploring the file of the Herald of Truth from beginning to end, a project that is not at all exhausted as yet. At that time I was watching for certain particular items on which I made notes and observations. Since then other lines of interest have opened up and I should scan over the volumes of the old Herald and other literature again for further notes and information. I was also during those early years able to spend more regular time in personal religious devotion and prayer than has been true since. One large invasion on leisure time is the fact that we have house, grounds and garden plots to care for. The routine duties about the House where I am employed have multiplied many times. Bringing the mail from the Post Office every morning takes out quite a lot of time in a year. Began this in January, 1942.

Among other routine work is the supervision of the German editing and proofreading. Mrs. Horsch does most of the regular proofreading in German, but there is always some to do at the House. Every week brings one or more German letters, orders, or what not which I translate for the benefit of the un-German officers of the House. There is occasional work in answering letters of inquiry regarding some historical things in connection with the library, and other details need attention almost constantly.

Beginning Monday morning and for ten days I will be giving most of my time to teaching in the local Summer Bible School. This is the third season I have been roped into the more or less silly procedure. On the whole I am developing the conviction that for the high school level it is not an effective place to do Bible teaching on the plan and program that the S. B. S. is organized and conducted. It appeals to me too much like a bit of foolish mummery, going through certain motions but not getting results accordingly. Other years for this teaching I took it very seriously and worked out somewhat more or less elaborate plans in advance. Felt it was only of very mediocre results. So this time I intend to "trust the Lord" for plans and aims and try the method of muddling through instead. It is most difficult for me to adapt my teaching method and aims to pupils of the early years of high school.

Since April first of this year we have been working hard on planting garden plots. Things are pretty well all planted now; not all things are "up" yet, though we hope beans, corn and late planted potatoes, and what else there may be, will appear shortly.

September 11, 1943   I feel quite thoroughly disgraced over my attempts to jot down some occasional notes. Once in three months is quite too seldom for any decent record of events. The summer weeks and months have been busy and in fact, quite intense. The work is beginning to ease off now more or less and will continue to do so. Estie worked and worked canning and canning. Filled all her jars and bought dozens more and will still buy some more. On the lot along Pittsburgh Street, which I rent from Abe Loucks, we planted twelve rows the full length of the lot. On June 3, a hot Thursday afternoon, Virgil and I put the seed in, six rows of early yellow hybrid corn, and six rows of Aunt Mary's white. The second and third weeks of August we harvested the hybrid corn and around the end of the month the other. The garden lot at home has been quite productive too. Over a third of it has its second crops coming on. String beans following peas, peas following early potatoes, spinach following string beans are some of the second crops we have. Tomatoes have done well and will produce heavily until frost comes. Staked up most of them and take off several bushels every week. Grapes are still to be taken off and put up. Fruit is generally scarce this season. We secured three bushels of peaches. A new venture this year for us has been the gathering of wild berries. Last fall I went out once for elderberries. This summer we really went into the business. It was a real success because I regularly combined sun bathing and berry picking. South and southeast of Everson, between one and two miles from our house, there are abandoned fields where berries grew in profusion this season. Virgil went with me a number of times, but I went in all perhaps seven or eight times, usually a full afternoon. First it was wild blackberries. Estie canned twenty-five or more quarts of these and we ate what we could at the time. That was in late July and early August. Recently it has been elderberries. We have nearly thirty quarts of pure rich elderberry juice put away, and is it good. Oh boy! This last Thursday was the last time I was out probably for this season. They are mostly past. Bushels and bushels of them have rotted or dried up and fallen off.

It has been a busy but interesting summer. We all hope frost and cold will stay away for another month. The summer is always too short in Pennsylvania to suit my taste. Our rainfall has been fine, whereas other places had floods early and drought later.

September 17, 1943 Am enjoying a kind of lull in activities this week. Getting up steam for doing the third quarter, 1944, Sunday School Lessons, which I want to start on next week. My ambition is to get the lessons copy done up in advance of schedule, so as to feel more free to do leisure time work such as working on library materials, browsing in Mennonite literature, and digging further into the local history. The past year I spent the major part of local research effort on the Fayette County part. Last March spent a day at Uniontown, and early in July spent three days in succession there again. On the last occasion I "discovered" for the first time the old tax assessors' lists, and found them very profitable sources of information, that is, so far as I was able to go in perusing them. I went systematically through the lists up to 1815 of Bullskin and of German Townships. To my sorrow I failed to find the parallel volume for Tyrone Township, which is as important as any for my purpose. Must enlist the help of the office there in trying to locate this volume. Another interesting line of work in this research has been that of finding records of the earliest land deeds pertaining to Mennonites and copying these, then platting the surveys at my leisure and so reconstructing the actual community of the early Mennonites and their farms. Have already platted quite a block of farms reaching from Jacob's Creek south to the Youghiogheny River. It is a fascinating pastime and helps much in reconstructing a picture of the settlement of 1800 and after. The time in Uniontown Courthouse is always too short to get everything done that I have planned. Yet one will sometime get pretty well to the end, and that end for northern Fayette County seems to be in sight. Then there will be the community in southwestern Fayette County to be worked over in a similar way, and likewise the community on the north side of Jacob's Creek in Westmoreland County. All this will afford spare time recreation and diversion for some time to come. This type of study and research opens up quite a number of vistas of further work that should be done. All the early Mennonite and Amish settlements in western Pennsylvania should be studied and data preserved for historians and posterity. Then furthermore there is the lure to do research in family history, especially of the Yoders of my own ancestry. The latter would require cooperative and personnel work of a type I am not gifted to do, except as an underling under some other's direction.

January 28, 1944 Alas and alack, here another number of months have sped by without any writing of notes! Life is simply too busy and too full for leisure to do things. Nearly one month of the new year is already in the past. Though busy and occupied with many things we have at our house many reasons for gratitude and thanksgiving to Providence. Life is enjoyable, if one can shut from his mind and consciousness the existence of the vast suffering on other parts of this mundane sphere.

Many things have transpired since last I found time to write. In many respects the year that lately closed was eventful and interesting. Time moves on and brings continual changes. Among the most important changes for us was the passing away of Father on December 15. He suffered a third stroke on the tenth, five days before he died. Brother-in-law Howard Gnagey sent us a message on a card at once after the final stroke occurred, and the next word that came was a telephone call from sister Ida at Wadsworth, Ohio, stating that Herman had called to announce Father's death. I told her I would go out for the funeral. She said she would not be able to go, but would call back to Herman and announce our plans. I left from Connellsville at a little before midnight and had a very pleasant train trip all the way, reaching Iowa City about 6:00 the next evening. By rare good luck I was able to get a reserved seat on the Rock Island Rocket train from Chicago, almost at the last minute. Usually all reservations on that train are made days and even weeks ahead of the time. Apparently some one had cancelled a reservation and I applied for it at the right moment to get a seat. From Iowa City I called Herman and he got me and soon I was at his place for supper.

The funeral was held on Friday afternoon at the home church. The service was neat and simple, in charge of the home ministers, and the burial was made in the cemetery about a mile from the church, where

Father's parents are buried, and Mother too. I remained with the folks over Saturday following and most of Sunday. Took the return train from Iowa City at 3:30 in the afternoon and after a less comfortable ride than going out, I reached home about 11:30 on Monday morning.

The old home surroundings and the people I saw brought back to memory long and vivid trains of thought and reverie, and the more so as one's heart was touched with the thought of Father's life work done and passing on to rest and reward. Things change, people grow older and grayer and feebler, all of which reminds one that time moves on and the time will come for all to lay aside the work of life and pass on to rest.

Dies Lunae, January 29, 1944 Besides the trip to Iowa for Father's funeral, I was called upon to make a number of train trips this past fall. Near the end of October I spent one day at Fort Wayne, Indiana, sitting in Curriculum Committee meeting at the Mennonite mission church. Rode the train at night going out and returning. Arriving at Greensburg in the morning on the way back, I took the opportunity to spend the day at the courthouse searching old tax records of East Huntingdon Township for historical data of interest.

The next trip was to Lancaster City for a three day session of the same Curriculum Committee, together with others. Committee met at Weaver's Book Store, on second floor at front by windows facing the street. Committee as a body visited Lancaster School one afternoon. Next trip was again to Lancaster, mainly and chiefly to appear on program of annual S. S. Officers' and workers' meeting held at Chestnut Street Church on last Saturday of November. Left home on Thanksgiving noon and was entertained by Ira Landis and family until Saturday morning. On Friday Ira introduced me to the archives and records of Lancaster County, where we looked up some data on Yoders in early Lancaster County. Found some clues which must be followed up farther elsewhere, one especially at Lewistown, Pennsylvania, Mifflin County. Ira also took me for a several hour visit to the Landis Museum, a place which is greatly improved over what it was in 1939 when I stopped there. They have a fine library building now, quite a worthy collection of books and materials.

Being down that way, I made the trip the occasion for a further visit of historical interest. On Saturday evening I rode with several men out to near Morgantown, where I was entertained over Sunday at the home of C. Z. Mast. On Sunday morning attended the Conestoga Amish Mennonite Church, and in evening someone took me to a newly organized congregation at Oley. From there Elam Hartz took me to his home for the night. Next morning he took me to an old Yoder homestead near Pleasantville. There Mast got me again and we went to Reading where I spent a little time in the courthouse records. In the afternoon we were disappointed to learn that the headquarters of the Berks County Historical Society were regularly closed on Mondays. Called at a lady's house in Reading where we saw an old, old Bible, said to have been brought to America by the Widow Yoder before 1712. On Tuesday morning left Mast's place by bus. Spent several hours in Lancaster Courthouse. Stopped off at Harrisburg between trains, visited the State House. Reached home by bedtime.

February 8, 1944 The year past brought to us many pleasant and interesting experiences. To many persons who are only interested in excitement and public activity, perhaps our pleasures and interests seem tame and prosaic, even dull. But such matters depend on one's taste. In actual historical field work I did not get so much done, but a good deal of archives work. Field work items have now piled up so that about a dozen trips long and short are clamoring and my feet soles are itching to get on the road with warmer weather and solid ground under foot. Anticipating the coming of suitable tramping conditions by March and April, I am now writing Sunday school lessons for first quarter, 1945. March 1 may see this project completed, which would put me several months ahead of schedule. Depending on weather conditions I plan to tramp a good deal this spring and do gardening too.

A new adventure of last summer was when Virgil and I took an extended hike on a camping trip. We left before light on a Monday morning near the end of June. We had our plans made for a three-day tramp. But as it worked out, we were back home by the second night, in some respects wiser, and yet well pleased with the adventure. We explored new territory, new to us at least, and discovered that the assumption tourist rooms or overnight lodging would be available almost anywhere along paved highways was a bad guess. We left Scottdale by trolley, and from Murphy's Siding, halfway between here and Connellsville, we took the hard road eastward and were presently climbing toward the top of the first ridge. By eight o'clock, the time the sun was up enough to make some heat, we were at the top. We continued on in the general direction of Indian Head, a town along Indian Creek. Stopped for noonday meal and rest along a fine mountain brook, built a fire to heat some food and had a pleasant refreshing rest. At about two o'clock we packed and loaded up again. I had a commodious knapsack borrowed from the Resslers. Virgil carried a black lunch box, a field glass, and walking stick. It was hot tramping under the midday sun. Had in mind that at or near Indian Head we would find ourselves a room to put up for the night. It was only five o'clock when we arrived at the place, a straggling one-street village with not a single room available for transient travellers. We bought a little food for the next day and started up the road along Indian Creek, northeastward, toward a place marked on the map as Champion. We watched and looked for signs indicating rooms for rent, but not one did we see. We kept going and going. Ate ice cream and cookies for evening lunch. Asked and inquired repeatedly along the way about getting a room for the night. The walking fortunately was pleasant in the cooler part of the day and weariness did not bother us much. We passed Melcroft and other small clusters of houses along the road. We were told of a kind of recreation park within a mile of Champion where various people were sure we could get a room for the night. About seven o'clock a rain cloud came up and rain began to fall. We had no protection excepting light sweaters. As rain actually began to fall no house or building was at hand for shelter, excepting a small place twice the size of a good doghouse, used evidently as a place to deposit milk cans for a truck to gather up. It had a good roof and we could both get inside and that was all. Virgil could sit with comfort; I had to hunch down and double up. The rain was blown in a little at the opening, otherwise we were kept dry. A half hour passed and the rain left off. After a little we reached this park place, to be informed that they have no beds for transients, only cottages for summer residents. Some rain was falling again and it was growing dusk now. After waiting a little for the rain to stop we went on again, back along the road we had come, to ask at the farmhouses for a bed to sleep in. After a number of refusals we did find a farm tenant's place, named Brown, where they reluctantly agreed to give us a bed to sleep in. It was dark by this time, and if our plea at this place had failed, we would have had no recourse but to go back to our doghouse shelter for the night and make the best of it. Had a good night of sleep. Next morning it was raining by showers and the prospect was rather dismal. We ate a little food we had with us, and by nine o'clock a few small patches of blue sky were visible through the clouds in the northwestern part of the sky, so we loaded up our packs and started out. Soon reached Champion, not more than a collection of houses. But there we got on what is called the county-line road, a road which runs along the boundary of Fayette and Westmoreland Counties. Saw the County Line Church of the Brethren, a place I had heard and read about. From that point we turned in the direction of home. It was pleasant going, the skies cleared, and a cool wind blew from the north. At noon we stopped several hours to roast wieners and fill our stomachs and rest. By three o'clock we were at White's Post Office, of which we had often heard. A mile west of there we came upon a cemetery which I examined and found of some interest. We kept moving leisurely up hill and down and by seven o'clock reached Mt. Vernon Park, where we were no longer strangers. Had thought originally to spend the night near there, but after eating and resting, I suggested that instead of searching again for a place to sleep, we could still walk to the trolley line at Iron Bridge by the time it would be dark. This tramp was longer than I had calculated and we were getting very weary and sore. But we made it and were at home by 10:30.

February 12, 1944 Today has brought us a change of weather with snow, a stiff west wind, and much lower temperature. January was almost unseasonably mild. Much moisture needs to fall in the next several months to make spring farming possible. I was ambitious last November, when abetted and encouraged by my wife I spaded up one-fourth of our house garden plot. I was able to get one truck load of manure, some of which was placed on the asparagus bed, while the rest I did not care to see lie in a heap and rot over the winter, so I dug it into the ground. Was also fortunate in getting a truck load of leaves, which the street cleaning department of the borough was glad to dump on our lot for the asking. Used these to cover up strawberries for the winter, as also some few other things. These all told will supply some humus and fertilizer for the plants on our lot. We had a plentiful crop of carrots and were casting about for ways to preserve them for winter and spring use. For some of these I carefully followed directions found in some gardening book, that is, dug a trench over a foot deep, lined it bottom and sides with cardboard paper, poured carrots in, covered with cardboard, and then heaped a pile of ground on top. They will doubtless stay till April or May. With another bed of carrots I decided to experiment, so I left them nicely planted in the soil just as they grew, and covered them

with four or five inches depth of wet leaf mulch. In January I dug out
about two rows of these and found them in perfect condition; no frost
was in the ground about them under the leaves. If by spring they still
are in good condition, I shall adopt that as my way to keep carrots
over winter. I have a hunch that beets and turnips could be kept in
the same way, unless the winter were extremely hard. We have parsnips and salsify still in the ground, and the frost makes them better
for use by spring than they would have been last fall.

Our extra lot of garden was really quite successful. The total cash
outlay for rent, plowing, fertilizer, and seed was between nine and ten
dollars. We sold sweet corn for canning at twenty cents a dozen ears,
and some single dozens besides for twenty-five cents, enough altogether
to just cover the cash outlay on the lot. We ate all the corn we could,
canned over eighty pints and dried several pounds. Then we got nearly
two bushels of potatoes, nearly a bushel of sweet potatoes, a scattering
of cucumbers, rutabagas, cabbage and radishes. Mr. Abe Loucks, who
owns the lot, could scarcely find expression for his astonishment at the
corn we produced on the lot. He said he never could get so very much
from that lot.

February 16, 1944 When in April, 1942, we bought from Abe Loucks
the lot of ground lying beside the house and lot we bought of the local
bank, we acquired with it an old two-room shack, sitting on the rear
up against the alley. Living in the shack is an old woman past eighty
years old, as independent and stubborn an old soul as I have ever seen.
She is a widow, having had a number of husbands, but never any children, so far as I have learned. At one time years ago she became a
member of the Mennonite congregation here but has since then belonged
to the Catholic Church, and perhaps others. Well, she is practically
married to the shack in which she lives, and the shack has outlived its
usefulness as a place of human habitation, in fact was originally built
as a temporary cook or bunk house for the convenience of construction
workers when the present building of the Mennonite Publishing House
was erected in 1921. The first year we had this shack in our possession, I did make necessary repairs on it, but the past year have refused to try to keep it up. The woman is old and forgetful and getting
feeble besides, and should not longer attempt to live by herself. As it
is someone must do most of her work for her. But she will not agree
to leave and enter the county home where she would have good care
and comfort. That to her mind would be an awful disgrace. But the
situation with her living quarters is moving toward a climax. She was
cut off in November from her pension, and now has only the little income from a property she still holds. In December a spell of zero
weather burst the water pipes in the shack, so she has no water except what is carried in for her cooking. Last summer already the
local health officers warned me that the place would hardly pass for
minimum health requirements. Since July I have accepted no rent
money from the lady, intimating she should find some other place to
live before winter. But she still sits in her stubbornness. A welfare
worker in town has been investigating and working to see if she could
be admitted to an aged veterans' home in Swissvale. If that fails to
develop, the sole recourse will be to ask the local health officials to

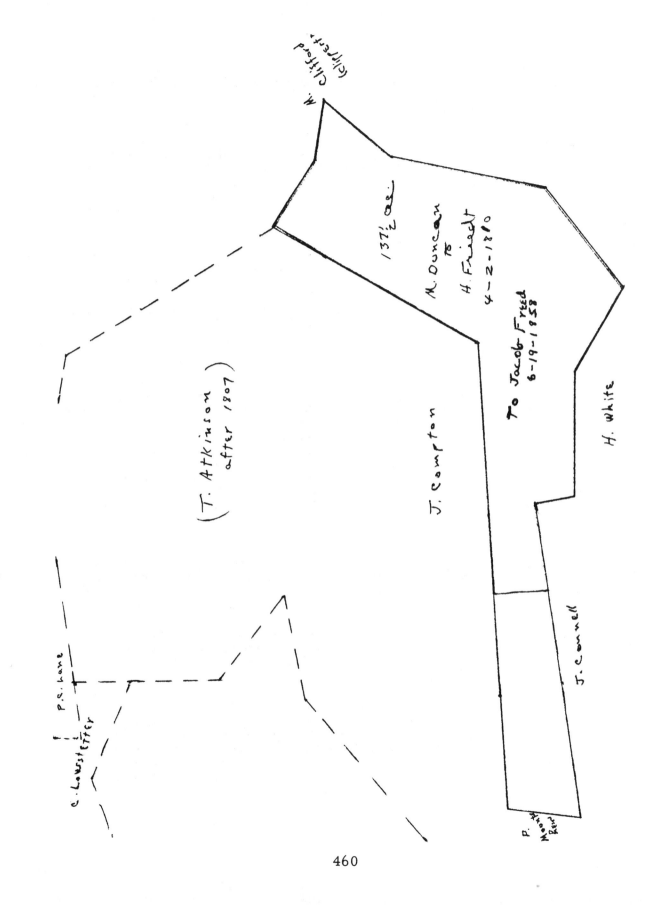

W. Clifford (Killbride?)

137½ Ac.

M. Duncan to H. Friacht 4-2-1810

To Jacob Freed 6-19-1858

H. White

J. Compton

(T. Atkinson after 1807)

J. Connell

P. Mountz Reim

P.S. Lane

C. Lowstetter

460

DB H-466

DB V-456

Facsimile of farm plat
(See pages 455, 462)

remove her to some other place, probably to the county welfare home. It is a rather pitiful case. The woman talks as if she were a Christian, but lacks the resources of a Christian character. Such roots as she has are in the spot where she lives, and she is helpless to face changes and adjustments for her own well-being. She is of such character and disposition that hardly anyone can bear to take her into their own home and care for her.

Woden's Day, February 23, 1944   A subject of tantalizing interest for several years is the old historic landmark and cemetery, known as the old Pennsville Mennonite (or Menist) Cemetery about two miles from Scottdale. A Mennonite meeting house stood on the site for a full century according to traditions and reports. Ever since coming to Scottdale and becoming interested in the local history of this section this old site and its history have fascinated me. A few folks are concerned to do something toward preserving the place and giving it some measure of care in keeping with its value as a landmark.

Several years ago I began in earnest to trace out the history of the land and the farms in the vicinity of the old place. I copied numerous surveys from the old deed books at Uniontown, learned by experiment the trick of platting these by means of sharp-pointed lead pencil, metric ruler and protractor. I searched out everything I could find pertaining to the surveys in that vicinity down to about 1860. Some gaps are left in the records, but am conceited enough to think I have found everything; but only the testimony of an expert could verify or expose my conceit. [See page 455. A facsimile of one of these plats appears on pages 460 and 461. Many more similar ones are in the Archives at Goshen College, Goshen, Indiana. — Ed.]

The question as to whether the present trustees of the Scottdale Mennonite Congregation may consider themselves the legal and rightful heirs and owners of this plot of ground is one to which we are seeking the answer. For we have in mind to make persistent efforts to clear and level off and seed to grass the whole plot and raise some endowment money for its perpetual care. I also like to envision making it a historical shrine, putting up a neat and suitable marker on the site of the old meeting house, giving the place a bit of publicity as a spot worth seeing.

Personally I would like to pledge myself to a kind of three- or five-year plan for putting the ground into shape. I would enjoy using it as my sun-parlor during the summer months, for getting some muscular exercise and doing a bit of community service all at the same time. There is no obstacle in the way of my starting on such a program at once this summer, except that I have no way to get tools back and forth, and as yet there is no tool house on the ground there. So we are expecting to keep on planning and working and hoping that something may open up and we can get the job accomplished. If my old shack on the alley should become vacant soon, I would at once offer material from it for the erection of a tool house. It is an interesting hobby, and I shall continue to work on it as I can.

Saturday, February 26, 1944   Today is a disappointment to me. Yesterday morning was one perfectly ideal morning for February, a heavy frost, clear skies, no wind, brilliant sunshine. In the afternoon a haze began to fill the sky, but nevertheless I strongly hoped this would still be a day for an outdoor hike. Instead of spending the afternoon on such a tramp, I worked in the office and triumphantly finished writing quarterly lessons for the first quarter, 1945. Spent twelve days doing the twelve lessons, at the rate of four days a week for three weeks, one of the first times in several years that I have actually been able to carry through such a working plan as desired and without interruption. In order to achieve that goal which was so nearly in sight, I successfully resisted the temptation to spend the afternoon out-of-doors. And today it is raining, raining, rain driven by an east wind. Therefore I must put off my outing to look for the early signs of spring. In order that my day would be comparatively free today for just such an outing, I spent from seven to eleven o'clock last evening painting in the bathroom at home. Today I am more or less at leisure for doing some odds and ends in a leisurely way.

In the weeks and several months to come I hope to do a great deal of leisure time work — reading, historical field work, creative writing, and the like. I have in mind a considerable scope of historical investigation that could be done this spring. Some of it is tramping over the country and will be conditioned by the weather and the state of the terra firma. This work I anticipate with fondness, only one must not expect to find answers to all the questions that he has in mind. That is too much to expect, but there is compensation in knowing that one has done his best to find the answers, and too one hits upon new lines of investigation, new leads and clues which open out upon new areas and vistas of information. There is always in the back of one's mind the faint hope or dream that sometime, somewhere one will run upon new and unknown records, data, or information, which will shed light upon the past history of this area. My thoughts are more and more beginning to be turned toward more distant communities as places to investigate Mennonite history in this section of the country. This is certainly a wide and unoccupied, unworked field of much needed investigation. It is work that should have been done fifty years ago, when people were still living whose recollection of things went back much nearer to the beginnings of things in these parts. As a hobby I enjoy this activity very much.

April 20, 1944 Since last scribbling in these notes varied experiences have come in my way. Around March 1 I worked hard for several days putting linoleum on the lower part of the bathroom walls; it was tedious and difficult work, fitting and pasting it on, and by the veriest tyro at that. Did manage to get out-of-doors on several afternoons. There were successive spells of cold, rain, snow, etc., all of which kept my neuritis and my nasal catarrh on the rampage and kept me pretty well down in the dumps.

Then I had a big week's vacation, which, after recuperating from this, left me feeling much better. Already in January Harry Diener wrote to invite me to come to Yoder, Kansas, early in April to participate in their 25th anniversary observance, commemorating the first organization of the Yoder Mennonite Church. My first reply was that I could not make the trip but would send a paper for their program.

Yet I felt an increasing wish I could be present for that special occasion. About the middle of March my good friend, D. J. Yoder, wrote a letter begging me to come, please, please, and hinting that enough persons of that place were wanting me to come so that they would make up some money for the cost of the trip. Well, after that plea it did not take long for me to decide to make the trip. I left on the evening of April 4, reached Hutchinson early morning of the sixth. Spent four delightful days among old friends and acquaintances there. Kansas looked good to me for a change, in spite of many changes from twenty-five years ago. On Sunday afternoon I was able to ride with friends to Hesston in time for the evening service at the college. Was entertained most kindly by my old friend and neighbor, Chris Hertzler. Spent Monday calling at the college and on perhaps a dozen old time neighbors. On Tuesday morning Chris took me to Newton. After a brief stop at Bethel College, I took the train for home at eleven o'clock. Made poor time and connections coming back, for it was Thursday morning, the 13th, before I reached home. After three or four days of recuperating I began to feel better than I had any time for a month. The friends at Yoder and Hesston expressed great appreciation for my coming; at Yoder they generously made up a purse of money, something more than enough to cover the entire cost of my trip.

October 18, 1944   Today was third in a succession of beautiful October days, clear sunshine, moderate temperature. Went out after noon for a midweek sunning and airing. Worked nearly three hours shirtless in the delicious sunshine. It was grand! The work was swinging a scythe in the old cemetery near Pennsville, where I have been putting in some spare time licks, so as to get the briers, sprouts and weeds cleared off. We now have a neat little tool shanty on the grounds there, so that one need not carry tools back and forth in order to do some work there at random, provided one walks to and back again. A busy, busy summer has passed, and no record has been written of its many interesting experiences and activities. Maybe some can be woven into these notes retrospectively. The plan now is to write a few lines at home every evening. Let's see if a record can be made that is more regular and systematic by this new procedure.

First killing frost this season came on Monday morning, October 16. Until then everything was still growing more or less, due to the abundance of moisture of the past months. We had a long and fruitful season this year. Warm weather came early in May and continued until recently. Everything in the garden grew lushly all summer, and we harvested many good things from ours.

October 19, 1944   Another fair day. But I was indoors most all day. This evening right after sunset the western horizon was a deep blood red color with pink-tinged clouds higher up in the sky. Rain is what it portends according to my idea, and I today feel dull and groggy at times, indicating some change in barometric pressure, according to my past experience. Wrote and typed a lesson for S. S. quarterly for next September on Joseph in prison in Egypt. Had it finished by soon after three o'clock. This evening at home I put away in the garage the garden stakes used with tomatoes and beans. Our garage is a delight since we have a cement floor in it, put in about a month ago. We try to organize everything in it neatly and orderly. I did the excavating for the floor and then C. A. Brilhart sent material and a couple of men to put down the floor. It altogether cost in cash outlay about forty dollars. The garage floor was a third major project of improvement on our premises this present year. In March we improved the bathroom with linoleum and paint. Did all work myself except for laying the floor linoleum. In June we rebuilt the front porch to the house, making it of brick and tile. Had to lay the brick walk myself, which took a lot of time and energy. I have vowed that for three years now we'll not take on any major improvement project!!

October 23, 1944 It has been a beautiful day. White frost on everything this morning, clear sunshine, no wind, genial temperature. Spent the day indoors, but did not get so much accomplished. For last two Sunday afternoons I have been unable to put in my full quota of time in sleeping, hence I suffer from an accumulated drowsiness and weariness; had to sleep an hour and a half after dinner, but failed to get altogether caught up at that. Ruth Bender was guest at our house over last weekend. For Sunday noon meal we were all guests at Frank Brilharts', and a good time was had by all, as the saying goes. Friday noon to Saturday noon we had a twenty-four hour rain, steady, slow, continuous. A walk in the vicinity of Jacob's Creek on Saturday showed the stream flowing full and swift. We had in mind all last week that Saturday would be a fine time to tramp and climb to the top of Chestnut Ridge. But the great rain put a damper on those plans. Am hopeful that the coming Saturday may make up for that disappointment. We could well do for six weeks without any falling moisture, six weeks of dry under foot before the first snow falls. That would be fine for some outdoor tramping and investigating. Mr. George Kelley, retired citizen of Scottdale, who occasionally comes around to preach Georgism as an economic doctrine for curing the world's ills, sat and talked in my office for more than an hour this afternoon. He is interesting to listen to, at least for a time. He wants me to read a book.

October 24, 1944 This morning it rained for no special reason, except that yesterday evening's clear sky had by morning been veiled in clouds. By afternoon and evening skies were clearing again. Temperature is mildish. Fire in the house heater adds comfort to the indoors.

Our garage, for such it was by origin, is slowly being organized. It is an interesting diversion, to arrange things and place them in some orderly and tidily arranged plan. Made a fourteen-inch wide shelf along most of one side for use as a work bench and general place for keeping things off the floor. In the northwest corner I built first a low platform for holding bags of garden fertilizer, trash barrel and suchlike things. Above this I suspended two shelves, one for holding empty bushel baskets, and the other for the one hundred twenty-five or more garden stakes stored away for the winter. The smooth fresh floor in the place is a pleasure to see and to walk on, and particularly after the old earth and cinder bottom which had been dug up by chickens. Perhaps, if someone wants to store a car, we might rent the space in the center for that purpose. But we shall use the space around the outside fully for our own needs. Am beginning to toy with the idea that we might have an automobile ourselves before too long. The possibilities of using it to get around for historical investigation makes the idea increasingly attractive.

October 26, 1944 This day started off beautifully, a spell of fog after daylight, then sunshine, balmy air. After noon dark heavy clouds came rolling in from the west, cooler air, and some threat of rain. It will be colder tonight and may clear off again in a day or two. Yesterday afternoon I walked out to the old Menist cemetery and spent three hours chopping down tall weeds, briars, and suchlike growths. For the last two months I have been putting in a few hours each week on this job and find I have just about cleared off the graveyard part which cannot be mowed by the power mower. It was a clear afternoon but with some haze in the air. Had my shirt off to get what is perhaps the last bit of sunshine for this year. It was comfortable enough while working, though the bit of wind was quite coolish.

Many of the chief dignitaries from about the House have left the country for a three- or four-day jamboree in Ontario, it being a special pow-wow in connection with a regular meeting of the Commission for Christian Education, etc., etc. There will be much speech-making and promotion and suchlike dust-raising stir. Am pleased to be able to stay at home and do a little work in quietness and "in secret." "Lord, deliver me from the necessity of going to conventions!"

November 7, 1944 National Election Day. Last week I eased up after a rather strenuous and sustained period of work, writing the lesson material for third quarter of 1945. I spent most of several days clearing away accumulated materials from my table and desk top at the office — organizing and filing away as space permitted. One day I spent at the courthouse in Uniontown, searching out data from old records. The situation at the Fayette County courthouse is very favorable for making one's time and travel count for the most possible. The superintendent of the building makes it his practice to reach the courthouse early, possibly at six o'clock or so. He has personal charge of the basement rooms where the old tax records are kept. Therefore one can make his day of research there as long as one cares for. Start in at 7:30 or before in the tax records, several hours before the Recorder of Deeds office opens at all. The Recorder of Wills office opens early too, at eight or before. Then the Deeds office stays open, at least so one can still get out, as late as five o'clock or past. By the end of nine hours of sustained work in the various types of records, I am usually weary enough to quit for the day, having a harvest of notes sufficient for several days' work in digesting and organizing.

November 16, 1944 A rainy, dreary day. The weatherman promises snow to follow. I have rather bungled my calendar for outdoor tramps this past while. The last Saturday in October I should have gone out in the country to lend a hand with the corn husking on D. Brilhart's farm; instead Boy and I tramped out to Green Lick Reservoir and up over the mountain side. A week later it rained in the afternoon. Last Saturday was cloudy but not wet, so I walked out and helped husk corn for a number of hours. Some thirty young boys had been working most of the day. They quit about five o'clock and ate supper. I kept on working till dark but had to quit because of growing darkness when there were still parts of two corn shocks left unhusked in the field. I had earlier rather definitely promised Dave I would help him husk just for the fun of it, and so felt obliged to do so.

For some weeks it has been in my plans to make an exploratory trip on foot down west into Lower Tyrone Township. Last Saturday would have been a fairly good day for that. This past Tuesday was a perfect day for it, but I kept myself on hand for checking German press proof, which then did not come until the day following. From data harvested in the courthouse records at Uniontown, I have approximately located on paper some early farms down that way, which I want to visit, also the site of a Dunkard meeting house in existence a century ago, and wish too to look for possible burial grounds of early Dunkard families. Am hoping for a good day Saturday.

January 4, 1945   I should make, and keep, a New Year's resolution to the effect that I will write diary notes more regularly in 1945 than I did in 1944. The New Year came in on Monday with a resounding blizzard, snow and strong wind, followed by zero temperature the next morning. The winter weather has been pronounced in nature and character. December 11 snow began to fall, and fell steadily for about twenty-four hours. Over Christmas it was milder and rainy, but snow and ice did not all go away before more came and colder weather. Have been recovering from a severe set-to of nasal congestion and indisposition. For a year past these occasional set-tos have somehow affected my stomach. Must be partly a nervous affliction, as appears.

I bought George Cutrell's share and interest in the tractor mower and plow outfit owned by a local tractor association. Paid fifteen dollars for it. Hope we can get some mowing done with it on the old cemetery this coming summer; d.v., as the saying is. I had kept in touch with things at the cemetery as best I could, after we no longer worked there. About Thanksgiving I was down and found everything O.K. On December 9, when I was next there, I found the door open, with gasoline tin can stolen. Padlock and hasp staple had been shot away by shotgun. Next Monday, barely ahead of the great storm, Brilhart's truck and a few of us went down and got the tractor home and parked it in our garage.

John Mosemann of Lancaster gave special lectures at the church over New Year's time.

January 10, 1945   My office is disrupted at present. Yesterday and the day before I was forced completely out of it, for a plasterer was working at repairing places on the walls. In the course of the weeks to come, they expect to scrub walls and clean everything thoroughly, an operation that is badly needed, and I suppose will paint the walls too. If I had more bookcase space, I could have more orderly arrangements about my office.

Have been handicapped the past weeks and still this week for getting fourth quarter of 1945 S.S. Lessons worked out as I had hoped and planned. My siege of indisposition is getting out of the way now, and

I hope to work more rapidly. Some of the lessons of this new S. S. course are difficult in the development and writing of them.

My hobby of investigating local Mennonite history becomes increasingly absorbing and interesting. Had expected that I would get to a period at some point and could let it rest for a while. No prospect in sight for that as yet! Have worked considerably on German Township, Fayette County, this past year, and am getting along in that area right well. More needs to be done there and in this area in the way of actually canvassing old farms and old buildings for possible books and papers which would give more information. That part is most difficult for me to do, lacking the time and opportunity and the "knack" for doing it readily. Sometimes this hobby threatens to become the main "horse," overtaking my real work.

January 12, 1945 Today it is rain and gloom. Yesterday it was cold and brilliant; the sun almost hurt one's eyes when one was out in it, so brightly did it shine, which was also so unusual for the past several months that one is quite unaccustomed to seeing the face of Old Sol displayed.

Have been pushing along in writing this week in spite of difficulties and obstacles. Nothing preventing, I hope to finish lesson eleven of fourth quarter, my fourth one for this week, by tomorrow noon. Many of them have been "repeaters" so far as the lesson text is concerned, and in such cases I unashamedly copy my explanatory notes from old quarterlies. If I did a good job before, why should I make them different just in order to have them different. Of course, I polish them a bit, or give them a slightly different slant to fit the viewpoint of the lesson in hand. That saves some hard thinking and study and work and enables one to make faster progress than when working in virgin Scripture ground.

Had hoped to get through this winter without being called upon by the Mennonite Central Committee to do any special assignment of work for them. But sure enough they are calling for my assistance in getting out a pamphlet dealing with the subject of conscription from the Mennonite standpoint. Some other planned matters will therefore have to be put off into the more distant future. Nevertheless I do hope to get all my "must" work done up by April 1, so as to be free for several months of hobby riding and side line efforts.

January 16, 1945 Colder weather today, not too cold, but quite pleasant in fact. Very heavy clouds, so that it seems dark all day long. Snow flurries flying makes it a very wintry day. Did not get my remaining two lessons of fourth quarter finished in the first two days of this week. Editorial chores and press proof hindered progress somewhat, and the mood did not fit with the occasion. Tomorrow I shall make a train trip to Cleveland for a meeting with H. S. Bender and several other men, apropos of another projected booklet by the MCC. The final lesson of the quarter will have to be for Friday.

Last evening all the families connected with the Publishing House met for a banquet dinner consisting of mashed potatoes, sauerkraut, wieners, pork, etc. Tables were spread in the pressroom and bindery, and a good time was had by all. The occasion was in honor of George

Cutrell and family who are pulling up by the roots and moving shortly to Denver, Colorado, where he has purchased a printing business of his own. George has been with the institution here for twenty-five years and more, and it makes a very considerable hole where he and his boys are pulling out. I hope incidentally that by the time I have been here twenty-five years I will be able to leave too, not to start a business of my own, but to retire, at least in part. The climate and atmosphere here are only tolerable and not specially desirable, especially for one who has lived on the western plains.

January 24, 1945   A week ago today I spent at Cleveland, Ohio. I left home at 5:30 in the morning and after missing one train I got to Cleveland at noon. Purpose was to meet with H. S. Bender, Jesse Hoover, and Don Smucker for planning a special booklet on the subject of conscription, to be gotten out at once. Smucker and I are assigned to the job of doing the writing, with three others to help, and then some others to check up on the results. For my part, am planning to spend February pretty solidly on this project. It is a keen disappointment to me not to be able to devote February to writing lessons for first quarter, 1946. I fear spring will come along before I get these written and then some other things will be calling for time and attention. There are so many matters of historical investigation that call for my attention, I dislike these interrupting projects. Yet these too present an opportunity for doing something useful. Personally I am not so sure of myself, nor feel so keen an inward urge to write on conscription as I did for previous MCC projects, like on nonresistance and on Mennonite heritage.

Last Saturday was a fine day for tramping, but I did not go far. Am waiting for a moderate day to make a trip to Uniontown for another day's work at the courthouse.

Pridie Kal. February, 1945   With this day one whole month of the new year is gone into history. The winter keeps on with rigor and determination. More snow has fallen this week, today sun is shining brightly, but with strong wind blowing, and it was about zero this morning.

Last Friday I spent delving into old records at Uniontown, but some results were altogether negative. Have now about covered the history of early Mennonite families in German Township. Gaps there are still to fill in, and for a long time I will be on the lookout for more data. Several days of leisurely tramping in German and Springhill and Nicholson Townships would be a great help. Then too I want very much to make investigations in Butler and Mercer Counties this spring and summer. It is a fascinating hobby and I become quite absorbed in its pursuit.

My old friend and neighbor, D. H. Bender, late of Oregon, was buried at Hesston, Kansas, yesterday. Ralph of this place went out for the funeral. Ruth spent Saturday and Sunday with us. George Cutrell and the remainder of his family left for Colorado on Monday.

My office has been uninhabitable for about two weeks, until today it has some semblance of order. They scrubbed the grime off the walls and the painter decorated with several coats of paint. If now I had fifteen or twenty feet more of book shelving space, I would be happily situated for a while.

Groundhog Day! 1945

Snow is flying today. The sun shines through faintly at times. The cold continues, only a bit moderated. And my own general indisposition continues too, on and off. Whether it is my reaction to the cold and sunless weather, or whether I have some incipient ailment, this is what I would like to know. Hope to see a doctor soon and ask him. I find myself wishing it were possible to regularly go South to the land of sunshine for the winter months. Maybe a sun-ray lamp would be a helpful piece of equipment to have.

The daily newspaper is rather more tense reading at present than usual. The Russians after months of inactivity did on January 12 launch their winter offensive with a vengeance. They were over three hundred miles away from Berlin at the start, and yesterday's paper gave the distance now left of their road to Berlin as less than fifty miles. To me the thing looks suspicious to say the least. Are the Germans purposely letting the Russians into their land, in order to bring about the "planned chaos" of Europe? Will the Americans be presently left "holding the sack" and returning home with their tails between their legs, so to speak? Well, one hopes not, yet all this is well within the range of possibilities, as it looks to me. The European politicians may all this while have been making an even bigger fool of Roosevelt than they did of Wilson a generation ago. Of course one ought to be an optimist, so they say, yet even many an optimist wakes up to sad disillusionment in time.

February 27, 1945   Since last making notes several weeks have passed by. Spent most of the time in a concentrated attempt to write up in crude form the substance of my reading and thinking on the subject of conscription, at least on the part assigned to me. The one consideration that specially urged me to get on with this as far as possible is the fact that Dr. Stamm told me over two weeks ago that I have a real, sure-enough hernia on my right side. It was not over a week before, that I first noticed anything at all to indicate something of the kind. He manipulated around on it some, and since then it is definitely uncomfortable much of the time. I reported to the doctor two weeks ago today my decision to have the repair work done at once, and had hoped it would be over with before this time. Only yesterday did I get the call to report at the hospital at Mt. Pleasant this evening in preparation for surgical attention inside the next few days. So that is my plan, to go to Mt. Pleasant after supper this evening and come back when I can. Things needing immediate attention are pretty well out of the way for the moment, and I hope by April I can begin to do some things, and meanwhile get rested up and recuperated for a good summer's work.

[Edward Yoder died March 28, 1945]

Edward's Parents
1920

His birthplace and boyhood home
Johnson County, Iowa

J. E. Yoder home
Reno County, Kansas
"This was as home to me from
1918-1920."

Apollo Quartet 1917-1918
S. Brubacher, W. Smith, E. Yoder, C. Graber

Apollo Quartet 1916-1917
M. Snyder, E. Yoder, K. Zook, D. Stoltzfus

Schoolhouses used for S.S. and Church Service
Yoder, Kansas

Harmony School - March to August, 1918

Laurel School - August 1918 to January 1919
Amish board secured court order to
evict group from this school.

Mennonite S.S. and Church Service, 1919
Yoder, Kansas

Store Building
Taught first singing school at this place, 1919

Yoder Mennonite Church built 1919

Edward with Chester Lehman
Hesston 1918-1919

Kansas Thresher 1919

Edward Yoder and Estie Miller
August 4, 1920

Edward and Boy
Communication without conversation

Graduation
M. A., SUI, August 1924

Edward Yoder: A Tribute

By Irvin B. Horst

(Given at the memorial service conducted October 12, 1957, by the
Pennsylvania German Society at the Scottdale, Pennsylvania, Cemetery)

We have met this morning to pay a tribute to one who was not only
an accomplished scholar, an astute historian, and a gifted writer among
us, but also a preacher of peace and a committed disciple of the lowly
Christ. Rare in history are the men to whom both scholars and saints
pay tributes. Rare also are the men who become peers in the halls of
Athens and who do not forsake the courts of Jerusalem. Edward Yoder
knew, no doubt, as few know in modern times, ". . . the glory that was
Greece, and the grandeur that was Rome," but there is evidence to
show that he also knew of truth beyond our empirical world of time and
space, the truth which comes through a childlike faith in Christ. Both
worlds for him, it appears, had some common borders; he saw them
whole.

It is no small attainment to move from the well-established cultural
patterns and the simple piety of a rural community in Iowa into the
complex academic life of our higher institutions of learning and to
emerge with a unified view of life and with one's faith intact. Edward
Yoder did not sever himself from his ancestral heritage. Providence
had placed him in the German Mennonite culture and faith, and this,
for all his wide education, he embraced more dearly. He was a devoted
servant of the church, and his intellectual abilities were dedicated to a
transmission of the best traditions in the Mennonite heritage. This attainment was due, one suspects, to a humbleness of mind, to a willingness
to dedicate a highly gifted intellect to the cause of the Christian Church.

In the academic world Edward Yoder was known as a Latin scholar. At
the Universities of Iowa and Pennsylvania he received recognition for his
studies of Cato, Varro, and Aulus Gellius. His major work in the field,
a book published in 1928 by the Linguistic Society of America, was a study
of certain syntactical relations in Aulus Gellius. To some it may appear
to be an anomaly that a German Mennonite farm boy became an accomplished Latinist – but this is to misjudge the mind of Edward Yoder.
There was nothing parochial about his interests. His intellectual pursuits
were broad and versatile. I remember examining his copy of an Anglo-
Saxon grammar, and I am told that he had ventured into both Hebrew
and Sanskrit.

If Edward Yoder made a contribution in the field of Latin studies chiefly
as a grammarian, let no one imagine that he gave his life to the minu-
tiae of classical scholarship. Nothing could be farther from the truth.
One relevant task to which he turned was the transcription and translation of the Latin poetry and letters of Conrad Grebel. Grebel, scion of
a proud Swiss family, brother-in-law of the Swiss humanist Vadian, was
the founder in 1525 of the Anabaptist movement. Looking back on this

scholarly work, now that thirty years have elapsed, one sees that Edward Yoder helped to fill out an important chapter in American Anabaptist historiography. His work was an impressive piece of scholarship in the beginning volumes of The Mennonite Quarterly Review. It made a substantial contribution toward the recognized biography of Conrad Grebel completed in 1950 by Harold S. Bender. His Epistolae Grebelianae, 1517-1525, it is hoped, will one day see the light of publication in book form.

During the twenties and thirties he made various scholarly contributions in the pages of the M.Q.R. Some members of this Society may recall that in 1932 he published a research note about "The Study of the Pennsylvania-German Dialect." His articles on state-church relationships and nonconformity also appeared during the thirties in the M.Q.R. During the same period he taught, chiefly in the fields of Bible and the classical languages, at Hesston College, Hesston, Kansas, 1928-32, and at Goshen College, Goshen, Indiana, 1926-28 and again 1933-38. It was typical of his scholarly bent that when he came to Scottdale in 1938 he began almost immediately a study of Mennonite settlements in Western Pennsylvania. The Mennonites of Westmoreland County, Pennsylvania appeared first in the M.Q.R. in 1941 and came out as a separate monograph in 1942. It was a pioneering work and a major contribution to the history of German life and influence in Western Pennsylvania.

It was chiefly as a writer in the broad field of religious literature, however, that Edward Yoder was engaged at the Mennonite Publishing House at Scottdale from 1938 until the time of his death in 1945. His advanced academic training proved to be an asset rather than a hindrance in his task of preparing commentaries on Old and New Testament texts for use in Mennonite Sunday schools. They were accepted by the rank and file of the membership in the church. The same can be said about his study manuals on Christian doctrine and the various pamphlets and tracts which he wrote. He turned a lucid phrase and cultivated a simple style. The quiet dignity of his writing, along with the clarity of expression, which doubtless owed much to his familiarity with the Latin classics, well became his subject material. These qualities facilitated the translation of his writings into foreign languages. Some of them have appeared in German and Dutch.

Among the better-known pamphlets from the pen of Edward Yoder are those on peace. Throughout the years of World War II, and before, he wrote courageously against the destruction of human lives and the flouting of moral values. He edited the peace pages of the Gospel Herald. Christians, he said, "by word and life must proclaim the truth that only unselfishness and sacrifice in obedience to God can bring about peace and security for men" (Gospel Herald, December 15, 1944, p. 758). Ordinarily he was not given to strong feelings or emotion, but his articles on peace and the nonresistant way of life were often eloquent. "The four apocalyptic horsemen," he once declared, referring to attempts to suppress hate with hate, "will not be unhorsed but merely supplied with fresh mounts, soon to ride harder than ever"(Ibid.). Edward Yoder was a convinced but not a dogmatic pacifist, and his calm, reasoned approach to the peace question was of inestimable value to many young people struggling with the issue, especially to those in Civilian Public Service camps.

Death took Edward Yoder prematurely at the age of fifty-one, when the church and his colleagues anticipated further work from his hand. He has been sorely missed in the historical, peace, and other enterprises of the Mennonite Church, as well as in the world of scholarship. But we are not here to lament his death. We are not of those who mourn with elegiac orations of Greece and Rome, and those who have no hope. We are here rather to give thanks to God for His abundant grace which was shed abroad so richly in the life of our brother. Before us is his example of unselfish devotion: a scholar who extended the horizons of knowledge, a writer and teacher who magnified his ancestral heritage, a disciple who was not offended at the "foolishness" of the Gospel. Let us emulate his example.

(Reprinted from Gospel Herald, November 26, 1957, by permission of the author and Mennonite Publishing House.)

INDEX

Fronto, 298, 301

Gaebelein, Frank E.
    An Evangelical's Defence, 57
Galileo, 417-18
garb, 6, 8-11
    (see also dress)
Gardner, Ernest A.
    Six Greek Sculptors, 69
Garrison, William Lloyd, 144
Gellius, Aulus, 77, 250, 263, 266
genealogy
    Frick, Henry Clay, 406
    Hochstetler, 380-81, 426, 428, 442
    Overholt, 406
    Yoder, 381-82, 426-31
General Conference, 6-7, 8, 29,
    260-63, 264, 266, 442
    Church Problems Committee of, 6
    Peace Problems Committee of, 28,
        94, 118
    Historical Committee of, 448
Germany, 39-40
Gibbon, Edward
    The Decline and Fall of the Roman
        Empire, 407
Gingerich, Fred, 105
Gingerich, Melvin, 243, 323, 442
    The Mennonites of Iowa, 390
Glotta, 24
Glover, T. R.
    Christ in the Ancient World, 315
    Jesus in the Experience of Men, 383
    The Jesus of History, 342
    Progress in Religion to the Christian
        Era, 386
    The World of the New Testament, 54, 298
Gnagey, Barbara (Yoder), sister, 43, 309
Gnagey, Howard, 179, 317, 410
Good Friday, 152
Goodspeed, Edgar J., 116
    The Curse in the Colophon, 274
    The New Barbarism, 160
Gordon, Ernest, 45
Goshen College, 12, 16, 18, 55, 61,
    70-71, 74, 126, 129, 131, 217, 304;
    (see also occupation)
Gospel Herald, 104, 187, 323
Graber, C. L., 237-38, 270, 313
Gray, Harold Studley
    Character: "Bad", 255
Grebel, Conrad, letters, 12-14, 25,
    39, 375, 397
Gregg, Richard B., 420
    The Power of Non-Violence, 244
Gunther, John
    Inside Europe, 384, 386

Hackett, Francis
    Henry the Eighth, 39, 63

Hall, James Norman, 109-10
Harper's Magazine, 24, 33, 43, 75, 209,
    232
Hartzler, Rev. J. S., 105
    Mennonites in the World War, 139
Hatch, Edwin
    Essays in Biblical Greek, 315
Haury, Dr., 87, 92, 127
Heering, Gerrit Jan
    The Fall of Christianity, 138
Henry the Eighth, 39, 63
Henry Thoreau, 398
Hershberger, Dr. Guy F., 43, 305, 344
Hertzler, Arthur E.
    The Horse and Buggy Doctor, 396-98, 401
Hertzler, Chris, 37, 40, 117, 119, 121-22,
    172
Hertzler, Ellen, 161
Hertzler, Dr. Silas, 203, 218
Hesston Audubon Society, 34
Hesston College and Academy, 5, 6, 18,
    22, 23, 32, 33, 46-47, 53, 62, 65,
    66, 68, 70-71, 79-80, 82, 85, 89,
    113-14, 139, 206, 256, 391; (see also
    occupation)
Highland Park College, 65
Historical Commentary on the Galatians, 92
Historical Grammar of the Greek New
    Testament, 262, 266, 315
history, author's philosophy of, 186,
    280-82
History of European Morals from Augustus
    to Charlemagne, 156, 158-60
Hitler, Adolf, and Nazism, 146, 203,
    380, 397, 403
Hobhouse, Walter
    The Church and the World in Idea
        and in History, 314
holidays
    Christmas, 63, 242, 274, 276-77,
        317-18, 379, 408, 434
    Easter, 208, 329, 387
    Independence Day, 38, 259
    New Year's Day, 67, 409
    Thanksgiving, 56, 241, 445-46
home improvements, Hesston, 1, 25, 28,
    72, 83, 170; Scottdale, 452, 464-65
Hoover, President, 7, 39, 62, 76, 135
Horace, 254-55, 302, 355
    Satires, 136, 157-58, 275-76
Horace and His Influence, 254
Hornack, A.
    Bible Reading in the Early Church, 231
Horsch, John, 196, 247, 320, 340-41, 362
    his collection of Mennonite history and
        literature, 410, 445, 450, 451
Horse and Buggy Doctor, 396-98, 401
Horst, John L., 249, 413
House of Exile, 385
Human Nature in the Bible, 395